£5

GENERAL AND
INORGANIC CHEMISTRY

GENERAL AND INORGANIC CHEMISTRY

BY

J. G. WILSON

B.Sc., A.R.C.S.T.

Formerly Senior Chemistry Master,
The Glyn County Grammar School, Ewell

AND

A. B. NEWALL

M.Sc., A.R.I.C.

Headmaster, Chesterton School, Cambridge

SECOND EDITION

CAMBRIDGE UNIVERSITY PRESS

Published by the Syndics of the Cambridge University Press
Bentley House, 200 Euston Road, London NW1 2DB
American Branch: 32 East 57th Street, New York, N.Y.10022

© Cambridge University Press 1966
This edition © Cambridge University Press 1970

ISBN: 0 521 07073 2

First published 1966
Reprinted 1968
Second edition 1970
Reprinted 1972 1974

Printed in Great Britain
at the University Printing House, Cambridge
(Euan Phillips, University Printer)

CONTENTS

v

CONTENTS

PREFACE TO THE FIRST EDITION

One of the foundations of modern chemistry is Dalton's Atomic Theory developed between 1801 and 1808. When the atomic hypothesis was put forward there was no *direct* evidence of the existence of atoms. But as time passed, the assumption of their existence and other assumptions concerning their properties and behaviour were found to explain more and more of the accumulating, experimentally determined facts of chemistry, and also to predict others successfully. The hypothesis was therefore raised to the status of a theory.

In the past fifty years chemistry has undergone revolutionary changes. It has been discovered that atoms are not indivisible particles, as Dalton thought, but are themselves made up of much smaller particles. The structures of atoms have been established in minute detail. Their sizes, weights and the arrangement of their parts are now known with high accuracy; so also are the sizes and shapes of molecules and the internal structure of crystals. As a result, atoms and molecules have become as real as test-tubes. Chemistry has achieved not merely a new look, but a major break-through to a deeper level of understanding. It is now possible to explain most of the properties of elements and their compounds in terms of their electronic, atomic and molecular structures. It is possible also to predict new properties successfully. Chemistry is no longer a vast collection of more or less unrelated facts many of which have to be learned by heart, but is now a mature science founded on clear, powerful principles which bind the facts together in an orderly system and make them intelligible and memorable. The object of this book is to present inorganic chemistry in this way to students beginning their advanced study of the subject in schools and universities.

J.G.W.
A.B.N.

PREFACE TO THE SECOND EDITION

We have complied with the IUPAC recommendations on nomenclature and the International System of Units (S.I.) as far as seems helpful and realistic at this stage. New sections on Vanadium, the Heat of Fusion and the Heat of Vaporisation of the elements have been added. Sections on the nucleus, electron cloud, double and complex salts as well as a number of the industrial processes have been extensively rewritten. We have also increased the number of questions at the end of each chapter.

J.G.W.

A.B.N.

ACKNOWLEDGEMENTS

We are much indebted to the staff of the Cambridge University Press and in particular Mr W. E. Slater for their valuable assistance and encouragement throughout the writing of this book. We wish also to express our thanks to Professor R. S. Nyholm, Dr A. G. Sharpe, Dr P. Sykes, Imperial Chemical Industries, Ltd, British Iron and Steel Federation, and to numerous colleagues and pupils whose comments, criticism, and advice helped us to solve many difficulties. Our acknowledgements are also due to Messrs Longmans Green and Co. for allowing us to reproduce diagrams from *An Introduction to Crystallography* by F. C. Phillips; and to Dr I. G. Wilson who helped with chapters 8 and 11. Finally to Mrs J. G. Wilson and Miss N. L. Smith, grateful appreciation for the help they gave in preparing and correcting the manuscript and proofs.

We are grateful to the examining boards listed below for their permission to publish questions from past examination papers.

The University of Cambridge Local Examinations Syndicate (C)
London University Entrance and School Examination Council (L)
Oxford Delegacy of Local Examinations (O)
The Oxford and Cambridge Schools Examination Board (O & C)
Joint Matriculation Board (J M B)
Welsh Joint Education Committee (W)
The letter S is used to indicate questions from an S-level paper.

We are also grateful to all those who have offered helpful suggestions since the book was published. Especially to Mr I. N. Mallinson whose thorough and thoughtful reading of the book unearthed many imperfections, and to Mr H. G. A. Anderson for a valuable list of comments.

PART I
GENERAL

I

THE PERIODIC CLASSIFICATION OF THE ELEMENTS

Since the collection and classification of facts is an almost spontaneous human activity it is at first sight surprising that the Periodic Classification of the Elements was not produced until 1869. Two reasons for this were (1) that a clear definition of an element as a substance which cannot be split up into two or more different substances was not developed and accepted till 1661 when Boyle's book *The Sceptical Chymist* was published, and (2) that elements do not normally occur free in nature and so only a small number of elements was in fact known at the time of Boyle, and for a hundred years later.

The first step forward was made by Lavoisier in 1789 when he classified the twenty-five or thirty elements known to him into metals and non-metals. This classification has proved to be a very fruitful one; it is still of fundamental importance, and always will be.

During the next eighty years many other elements were discovered, Dalton's atomic theory was developed (see ch. 2, p. 18), the vital concept of valency was given a clear numerical definition, and atomic weights were accurately determined. On these firm foundations more powerful ways of classifying the elements were developed, culminating in Mendeléeff's Periodic Classification (1869–71). This classification which places the elements in order of increasing atomic weight has remained unchanged in essentials to the present day. The following account of it includes the elements discovered since Mendeléeff's time, making a total of 105. The treatment assumes no knowledge of atomic structure. It should be emphasised that all classification is a process of grouping by similarities.

The Periodic Table

It is convenient in drawing up the Periodic Table to use the symbols of the elements instead of their names. A complete list of the elements in order of increasing atomic weights, with their symbols, is given below. When the

3

Table of Atomic Weights, 1971 (*Based on the assigned relative atomic mass of $^{12}C = 12.000$*) (Reproduced from *Chemistry in Britain*)

Atomic no.	Name	Symbol	Atomic weight	Atomic no.	Name	Symbol	Atomic weight
1	Hydrogen	H	$1.0079^{b, d}$	54	Xenon	Xe	131.30
2	Helium	He	$4.00260^{b, c}$	55	Caesium	Cs	132.9054^a
3	Lithium	Li	$6.941^{c, d, e}$	56	Barium	Ba	137.34
4	Beryllium	Be	9.01218^a	57	Lanthanum	La	138.9055^b
5	Boron	B	$10.81^{c, d, e}$	58	Cerium	Ce	140.12
6	Carbon	C	$12.011^{b, d}$	59	Praseodymium	Pr	140.9077^a
7	Nitrogen	N	$14.0067^{b, c}$	60	Neodymium	Nd	144.24
8	Oxygen	O	$15.9994^{b, c, d}$	61	Promethium	Pm	(147)
9	Fluorine	F	18.99840^a	62	Samarium	Sm	150.4
10	Neon	Ne	20.179^c	63	Europium	Eu	151.96
11	Sodium	Na	22.98977^a	64	Gadolinium	Gd	157.25
12	Magnesium	Mg	24.305^c	65	Terbium	Tb	158.9254^a
13	Aluminium	Al	26.98154^a	66	Dysprosium	Dy	162.50
14	Silicon	Si	28.086^d	67	Holmium	Ho	164.9304^a
15	Phosphorus	P	30.97376^a	68	Erbium	Er	167.26
16	Sulphur	S	32.06^d	69	Thulium	Tm	168.9342^a
17	Chlorine	Cl	35.453^c	70	Ytterbium	Yb	173.04
18	Argon	Ar	$39.948^{b, c, d, g}$	71	Lutetium	Lu	174.97
19	Potassium	K	39.098	72	Hafnium	Hf	178.49
20	Calcium	Ca	40.08	73	Tantalum	Ta	180.9479^b
21	Scandium	Sc	44.9559^a	74	Tungsten	W	183.85
22	Titanium	Ti	47.90	75	Rhenium	Re	186.2
23	Vanadium	V	$50.9414^{b, c}$	76	Osmium	Os	190.2
24	Chromium	Cr	51.996^c	77	Iridium	Ir	192.22
25	Manganese	Mn	54.9380^a	78	Platinum	Pt	195.09
26	Iron	Fe	55.847	79	Gold	Au	196.9665^a
27	Cobalt	Co	58.9332^a	80	Mercury	Hg	200.59
28	Nickel	Ni	58.71	81	Thallium	Tl	204.37
29	Copper	Cu	$63.546^{c, d}$	82	Lead	Pb	$207.2^{d, g}$
30	Zinc	Zn	65.38	83	Bismuth	Bi	208.9804^a
31	Gallium	Ga	69.72	84	Polonium	Po	(209)
32	Germanium	Ge	72.59	85	Astatine	At	(210)
33	Arsenic	As	74.9216^a	86	Radon	Rn	(222)
34	Selenium	Se	78.96	87	Francium	Fr	(223)
35	Bromine	Br	79.904^c	88	Radium	Ra	$226.0254^{a, f, g}$
36	Krypton	Kr	83.80	89	Actinium	Ac	(227)
37	Rubidium	Rb	85.4678^c	90	Thorium	Th	$232.0381^{a, f}$
38	Strontium	Sr	87.62^g	91	Protactinium	Pa	$231.0359^{a, f}$
39	Yttrium	Y	88.9059^a	92	Uranium	U	$238.029^{b, c, e}$
40	Zirconium	Zr	91.22	93	Neptunium	Np	$237.0482^{b, f}$
41	Niobium	Nb	92.9064^a	94	Plutonium	Pu	(244)
42	Molybdenum	Mo	95.94	95	Americium	Am	(243)
43	Technetium	Tc	98.9062^f	96	Curium	Cm	(247)
44	Ruthenium	Ru	101.07	97	Berkelium	Bk	(247)
45	Rhodium	Rh	102.9055^a	98	Californium	Cf	(251)
46	Palladium	Pd	106.4	99	Einsteinium	Es	(254)
47	Silver	Ag	107.868^c	100	Fermium	Fm	(257)
48	Cadmium	Cd	112.40	101	Mendelevium	Md	(256)
49	Indium	In	114.82	102	Nobelium	No	(256)
50	Tin	Sn	118.69	103	Lawrencium	Lr	(257)
51	Antimony	Sb	121.75	104	unnamed		
52	Tellurium	Te	127.60	105	Hahnium	Ha	
53	Iodine	I	126.9045^a				

^{a} Mononuclidic element.
^{b} Element with one predominant isotope (about 99–100 % abundance).
^{c} Element for which the atomic weight is based on calibrated measurements.
^{d} Element for which variation in isotopic abundance in terrestrial samples limits the precision of the atomic weight given.

^{e} Element for which users are cautioned against the possibility of large variations in atomic weight due to inadvertent or undisclosed separation in commercially available materials.
^{f} Most commonly available long-lived isotope.
^{g} In some geological specimens this element has a highly anomalous isotopic composition corresponding to an atomic weight significantly different from that given.

The values in brackets are those of the most stable isotope.

symbols of the first twenty elements *in order of increasing atomic weight* beginning with hydrogen are written in a horizontal row we get:

H He Li Be B C N O F Ne Na Mg Al Si P S Cl K Ar Ca.

Omitting hydrogen and helium meantime, and filling in the valencies and class (metal or non-metal) of the next eight elements the following table is obtained:

	Li	Be	B	C	N	O	F	Ne
Class	Metal	Metal	Non-metal	Non-metal	Non-metal	Non-metal	Non-metal	Non-metal
Valency	1	2	3	4	3	2	1	0

The valency given for nitrogen is its valency in ammonia, NH_3. Neon, one of the noble (inert) gases, forms no common compounds, and is therefore given a valency of zero. Before going any further, it will be seen that the trend of the valency figures suggests that the next element might well have a valency of one. The next element sodium has in fact a valency of one, and is a metal. It is known further that sodium has a strong physical resemblance to lithium and also forms very similar corresponding compounds: e.g. lithium chloride, like sodium chloride, is a white solid of high melting point, soluble in water, having a salty taste, and forming cubic crystals. It appears then that lithium and sodium must be classified together because of their great similarity. Instead therefore of separating lithium and sodium by seven other elements, sodium is put below lithium at the beginning of another row thus:

Li Be B C N O F Ne
Na

This placing of sodium immediately below lithium symbolises similarity by nearness, especially in the vertical direction.

If now the next elements are written along this new row, it is found that similar elements come below each other. The approximate atomic weight has been written below each element to emphasise the principle on which the sequence of elements is based. The lower valencies are also included.

	Li	Be	B	C	N	O	F	Ne
	6.9	9.0	10.8	12.0	14.0	16.0	19.0	20.2
	Na	Mg	Al	Si	P	S	Cl	Ar
	23.0	24.3	27.0	28.1	31.0	32.1	35.5	39.9
Valency	1	2	3	4	3	2	1	0

The valency figures, which apply to both rows, are very striking, and so also are the obvious resemblances between, for example, the halogens fluorine and chlorine, and the noble gases neon and argon. The more the chemistry of the above elements is studied the more striking are the physical and chemical resemblances between the elements in each of the vertical pairs. It begins to be clear that this method of classification is valid, simple, and powerful. It will be seen that one change in the atomic weight order has had to be made: the element next in order of atomic weight after chlorine is not argon, atomic weight 39.9, but potassium 39.1. It would be ridiculous to put potassium, a highly reactive metal of valency one in the same class as neon, a noble gas of zero valency; whereas potassium takes its place below sodium with great aptness.

Continuing in the same way with another row:

Valency	1	2	3	4	3	2	1	0
	Li	Be	B	C	N	O	F	Ne
	6.9	9.0	10.8	12.0	14.0	16.0	19.0	20.2
	Na	Mg	Al	Si	P	S	Cl	Ar
	23.0	24.3	27.0	28.1	31.0	32.1	35.5	39.9
	K	Ca	Sc	Ti	V	Cr	Mn	Fe
	39.1	40.1	45.0	47.9	50.9	52.0	54.9	55.9

Potassium, as already said, fits in well below sodium, and so does calcium below magnesium; but the next six elements are very much out of place. For example manganese, a metal whose most stable valency is two, has no obvious resemblance to chlorine, and iron, a metal with valencies of 2 and 3, has even less resemblance to the noble gas argon.

This serious difficulty is dealt with simply and boldly by omitting the disturbing elements meantime. Having lost the scent, the thing to do is to search around and try to pick it up again. The elements immediately after iron are cobalt, nickel, copper, zinc, gallium, germanium, arsenic, selenium, bromine (a halogen) and krypton (a noble gas). Krypton must be put below argon, and bromine below chlorine. Working back from krypton and bromine and allowing the elements to fall naturally into place, the table becomes:

Valency	1	2	3	4	3	2	1	0
	Li	Be	B	C	N	O	F	Ne
	6.9	9.0	10.8	12.0	14.0	16.0	19.0	20.2
	Na	Mg	Al	Si	P	S	Cl	Ar
	23.0	24.3	27.0	28.1	31.0	32.1	35.5	39.9
	K	Ca	* Ga	Ge	As	Se	Br	Kr
	39.1	40.1	69.7	72.6	74.9	79.0	79.9	83.8

* Ten elements have been omitted here.

The elements in the last row are found to fit very well into the scheme. In particular they display valencies which exactly match those of the elements vertically above them.

Groups and Periods

Continuing in the same way, and again omitting ten elements corresponding to the ten omitted before, another very satisfactory row is obtained. The same procedure with some modifications, continued to the eighty-eighth element radium, works consistently well and gives the following table.

The Main Group elements of the Periodic Classification

		Group numbers								
		I	II	III	IV	V	VI	VII	0	or VIII
	Period 1 |	← – – – – – – – – –H– – – – – – – – →							He⟍	
	Period 2	Li	Be |	B	C	N	O	F	Ne |	
	Period 3	Na	Mg	Al	Si	P	S	Cl	Ar |	Non-metals
Metals	Period 4	K	Ca *	Ga	Ge	As	Se	Br	Kr⟨	(23)
(21)	Period 5	Rb	Sr *	In	Sn	Sb	Te |	I	Xe |	
	Period 6	Cs	Ba †	Tl	Pb	Bi	Po	At	Rn⟋	
	Period 7	Fr	Ra †							

The stepped diagonal line divides the metals from the non-metals. Helium takes its place naturally above neon. Hydrogen is unique (p. 282). The vertical columns each of which contains a family of elements of great similarity are called Groups, and are numbered using Roman numerals. The horizontal rows are called Periods and are numbered as shown above using ordinary numerals. Note that hydrogen and helium together make up the first Period. The elements shown are called Main Group elements to distinguish them from the elements which have been left out of the table at the places shown by the asterisks and other symbols (†).

Extended form of complete Periodic Table

The Table is completed by splitting the Main Group Table vertically between Groups II and III, moving the sections ten spaces apart and inserting the omitted elements as shown in the table on p. 8. *All the elements brought back are called transition elements and all are metals.*

A comparison of the first three rows of transition elements (in Periods 4, 5 and 6) shows that the three elements in each vertical column have a

7

The Periodic Table (extended form)

	Main Groups		Transition elements										Main Groups					
Group	IA	IIA	IIIA	IVA	VA	VIA	VIIA	VIII			IB	IIB	IIIB	IVB	VB	VIB	VIIB	VIIIB
Period 1	1 H																	2 He
Period 2	3 Li	4 Be											5 B	6 C	7 N	8 O	9 F	10 Ne
Period 3	11 Na	12 Mg											13 Al	14 Si	15 P	16 S	17 Cl	18 Ar
Period 4	19 K	20 Ca	21 Sc	22 Ti	23 V	24 Cr	25 Mn	26 Fe	27 Co	28 Ni	29 Cu	30 Zn	31 Ga	32 Ge	33 As	34 Se	35 Br	36 Kr
Period 5	37 Rb	38 Sr	39 Y	40 Zr	41 Nb	42 Mo	43 Tc	44 Ru	45 Rh	46 Pd	47 Ag	48 Cd	49 In	50 Sn	51 Sb	52 Te	53 I	54 Xe
Period 6	55 Cs	56 Ba	57 La*	72 Hf	73 Ta	74 W	75 Re	76 Os	77 Ir	78 Pt	79 Au	80 Hg	81 Tl	82 Pb	83 Bi	84 Po	85 At	86 Rn
Period 7	87 Fr	88 Ra	89 Ac†															

Non-metals

Metals

* Lanthanides	58 Ce	59 Pr	60 Nd	61 Pm	62 Sm	63 Eu	64 Gd	65 Tb	66 Dy	67 Ho	68 Er	69 Tm	70 Yb	71 Lu
† Actinides	90 Th	91 Pa	92 U	93 Np	94 Pu	95 Am	96 Cm	97 Bk	98 Cf	99 Es	100 Fm	101 Md	102 No	103 Lr

104 (unnamed).   105 Ha = hahnium (in honour of the late Otto Hahn.)

family resemblance, similar to that found in the Main Group elements but less strong. For example, copper, silver, and gold (Au) all have low chemical activities and all come below hydrogen in the electrochemical series: they do not liberate hydrogen from water, steam, or acids, and they are resistant to atmospheric corrosion, a fact which makes them suitable for making coins and jewellery. Chromium, molybdenum (Mo) and tungsten (W) have considerable physical and chemical similarities, and so also with the other Groups.

In Period 6 immediately after lanthanum (La), a difficulty arises similar to the one first met with after calcium in Period 4: a group of elements, this time fourteen in number, interrupts the sequence of the transition elements lanthanum, hafnium, tantalum, etc. This difficulty is dealt with in the same way as before: the fourteen intruding elements are simply left out. Instead of putting them back now and thus extending the table still further, it is more convenient to list them separately at the foot of the main table. The fourteen elements, all metals, were originally called the rare-earth metals. They are now more usually called *lanthanides*. They are referred to by the general term of *inner-transition elements* since they are a transition series within a transition series. A second set of inner-transition elements, the *actinides*, occurring in Period 7 after actinium (Ac) is treated in the same way, since recent work has shown that the actinides are in fact analogous to the lanthanides. Like them they are all metals. The lanthanides and actinides are included in the table for the sake of completeness, but little more will be said about them in this book.

It must be made clear that the gaps now appearing in the first three periods exist only on paper, and have no significance.

A few new features appear in this final form of the Periodic Table. The numbers immediately above the elements are the serial (or ordinal) numbers of the elements in the table, starting with hydrogen, No. 1, and ending with hahnium, No. 105. These numbers are called the *atomic numbers* of the elements, thus hydrogen has atomic number 1, etc. Their significance will be discussed later.

In the table on p. 7 the Main Groups were given numbers I to VII with the noble gases 0. The question arises: how are the transition element Groups to be numbered? The most obvious scheme to try is to continue the sequence of Group numbers already used for the Main Group elements right along to cover the transition Groups also. Starting at the left-hand end of the third line of the table on p. 8 at Group I and continuing the numbers without a break, Group VII occurs at the top of the vertical column containing Mn, Tc, and Re. Switching now to the right-hand side of the table at Group III (ignore the letters attached to the Group numbers) and counting back, Group I occurs at the top of the vertical column containing Cu, Ag, and Au. Three columns of transition elements are at this stage left without any numbers. These three columns are then all included under a single new Group Number VIII as shown. To distinguish between the two different sets of seven Group Numbers I–VII, the letter A is attached to each member of the left-hand set, and the letter B to each member of the right-hand set thus giving the complete Group numbers shown. This notation can be justified only if the elements in Group IA, for example, show sufficient resemblance to those in Group IB to warrant using the same *number* for each Group. Such a resemblance is in fact found, although it varies in closeness from Group to Group. The relationship between the A and B families will be discussed later.

Numbers of elements in the Periods

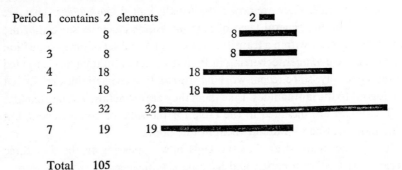

Period 1	contains	2	elements
2		8	
3		8	
4		18	
5		18	
6		32	
7		19	
	Total	105	

Note that there are 61 transition metals altogether, and a total of 82 metals in the 105 elements. There is good reason to believe that as yet unknown elements, of atomic numbers 106 and beyond, will in time be produced artificially.

Periodicity in the Periodic Classification

The most fundamental relationship in the classification, and the one from which it takes its name is that, when all the elements are arranged in horizontal rows in order of increasing atomic weights as described, similar elements occur at regular but not always equal intervals. Thus the eighth element from helium is neon, and the eighth element from neon is argon; again, the eighteenth element from argon is krypton and the eighteenth element from krypton is xenon. This recurrence of similar elements at regular intervals is an example of a general phenomenon called periodicity, and is described by the term *periodic*, a term which is therefore applied to the whole system and also the horizontal sets (periods) into which all the elements are divided. Other examples of periodic phenomena are the cycle of the seasons, and the motion of a pendulum. Periodicity can be shown most instructively by graphs. These will be used freely from now on. See, for example, graphs of density against atomic number, p. 196, and electrode potential against atomic number, p. 154.

If periods of equal lengths are made by omitting the transition elements, the table of Main Group elements is formed. The two categories—(1) the Main Group elements (44 in all) and (2) the transition elements (61 in all) —are sufficiently different to allow of separate treatment for much of their chemistry, and this method will often be adopted.

Relationships in the table of Main Group elements

A broad preliminary treatment based on this table (see p. 7) is given here.

1. Valency relationships

(a) Valency within the periods. Consider for example Period 3.

	IA	IIA	IIIB	IVB	VB	VIB	VIIB	0*
Period 3	Na	Mg	Al	Si	P	S	Cl	Ar
Hydrides	NaH	MgH_2	$(AlH_3)_n$	SiH_4	PH_3	H_2S	HCl	None
Valency with hydrogen	1	2	3	4	3	2	1	0
Oxides (highest valency)	Na_2O	MgO	Al_2O_3	SiO_2	$(P_2O_5)_2$	SO_3	Cl_2O_7	None
Valency with oxygen	1	2	3	4	5	6	7	0
Summary	1	2	3	4	$\begin{cases}3\\5\end{cases}$	$\begin{cases}2\\6\end{cases}$	$\begin{cases}1\\7\end{cases}$	$\begin{cases}0\\8\end{cases}$

* May also be termed VIIIB.

The two valency series, 1, 2, 3, 4, 3, 2, 1, 0 and 1, 2, 3, 4, 5, 6, 7, 0 are found in all Periods of the Main Group elements after Period 1 (except for N, O, and F in Period 2 which do not show the higher valencies 5, 6 and 7 respectively). If the valencies of all the Main Group elements (with the exceptions noted) are written in a row we have:

1, 2, 3, 4, 3, 2, 1, 0, 1, 2, 3, 4, 3, 2, 1, 0, 1, 2, 3, ..., etc.

and   1, 2, 3, 4, 5, 6, 7, 0, 1, 2, 3, 4, 5, 6, 7, 0, 1, 2, 3, ..., etc.

Each of these series is a striking example of a periodic relationship. It will be found that most trends within a Period are periodic.

(b) Valency within the Groups. All members of Group I for example have a positive valency of 1. This fact is indeed the most fundamental similarity between the members of the Group, and enables the formulae of all the compounds of each element in the Group to be written down in terms of general formulae, e.g. if the symbol for each element in Group I is represented by M then we have the general formulae MH, M_2O, MOH, MCl, MNO_3, M_2SO_4, etc. From what has been said, it is clear that it is possible to speak of a Group valency, i.e. a valency which is common to all (or most) members of the Group. The following rules are of great importance:

For Groups I, II, III, IV and 0 the group valency is the same as the Group number.

For Groups V, VI and VII there are two group valencies, one being the same as the Group number, the other (8—the Group number).

2. Trends in electropositivity and electronegativity

Metals are electropositive because they form positively charged ions (cations); non-metals are electronegative because they form negatively charged ions (anions). The strength of the tendency of metals and non-metals to form cations and anions respectively can be measured and is found to vary within wide limits. The more strongly electropositive or electronegative an element is the more chemically active it is, and the more stable its compounds are. Strongly electropositive metals form strongly basic oxides which react readily with water to give caustic alkalis of high solubility. Strongly electronegative elements, e.g. the halogens, form strongly acidic oxides which react with water to give strong oxo-acids.

(a) Period Relationship. In passing from left to right across the table there is a gradual change from a strongly electropositive metal, an alkali metal, in Group I, to a strongly electronegative non-metal, a halogen, in Group VII; that is, there is a steady increase in electronegativity. At some point in the Period, an element is reached which has some of the properties of a metal and some of the properties of a non-metal; it is said to be amphoteric or semi-metallic. Sometimes the element at this stage in the Period is in a sense neither electropositive nor electronegative: it does not form ions, therefore it does not form electrovalent bonds, but covalent bonds (see later, for example, carbon).

(b) Group Relationships. In passing down any (Main) Group there is a fairly steady increase in electropositivity. The result is that in Group I, for example, caesium is a considerably more electropositive metal than lithium.

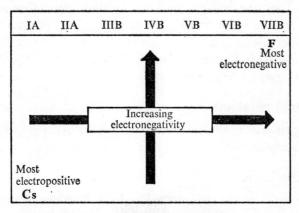

Fig. 1. Trends in electronegativity in Main Group elements.

The result of the same trend in Group VII is that iodine is more electropositive than fluorine, i.e. it is more metallic than fluorine. Iodine begins to show some slight resemblances to a metal in being a lustrous solid at ordinary temperatures. The Group trend can also be expressed by the statement that in passing up any Group there is a fairly steady increase in electronegativity.

These two trends are summarised in Fig. 1.

(c) Diagonal Relationship. There is a marked resemblance between lithium and magnesium, beryllium and aluminium, and boron and silicon.

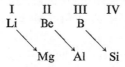

This relationship is also seen in other parts of the table. The reason is that as we move from left to right across the table there is an increase in electronegativity, while in moving down the table there is a decrease in electronegativity. Thus in moving diagonally from top left to bottom right the electronegativity will remain much the same; therefore, although the valencies of the diagonally related elements differ by 1, the elements and their corresponding compounds have similar properties wherever electronegativity is a major factor.

The diagonal relationship is also seen well in the elements situated along or near the diagonal stepped line separating the metals from the non-metals in the table on p. 7. These elements include beryllium, aluminium, gallium, germanium, arsenic, tin, antimony, lead, bismuth and polonium. They are similar in that they all show amphoteric properties. Physically they resemble metals, but in many chemical properties they resemble non-metals.

Electronegativity will be treated in greater detail in ch. 5. The statements that follow apply to the complete Periodic Table.

3. General relationship

The properties of an element are a rough average of the properties of the elements immediately surrounding it in the Periodic Table.

4. The Periodic Law

The properties of the elements are periodic functions of their atomic numbers, i.e. of the nuclear charges on their atoms (see p. 30).

Medeléeff's predictions on undiscovered elements

Mendeléeff was obliged to leave a number of vacant spaces in his Periodic Table in order to keep closely related elements in the same vertical columns. Six of those spaces are now filled by Sc, Ga, Ge, Tc, Rh and Po. Mendeléeff in 1871 stated boldly that the vacant spaces were reserved for undiscovered elements. Then, using the general relationship and Periodic Law summarised in (3) and (4) above, he went on to predict in great detail the properties of these yet undiscovered elements, and of their compounds. He also predicted that the elements would be found in nature associated with the ores of other stated elements. All his predictions were fulfilled, some very quickly: scandium was isolated in 1879 by the Swedish chemist Nilson; gallium in 1875 by the French chemist Boisbaudran; and germanium in 1886 by the German chemist Winkler, all with the predicted properties. The remarkable accuracy of Mendeléeff's predictions, which helped more than any other factor to establish the Periodic Classification, is illustrated in the following table for germanium.

Eka-silicon, Es (predicted in 1871)	Germanium, Ge (discovered in 1886)
Valency 4	Valency 4
Atomic weight, 72	Atomic weight, 72.6
Density, 5.5 g cm^{-3}	Density, 5.36 g cm^{-3}
Melting point high	Melting point, 958 °C
Atomic volume (atomic wt./density) 13	Atomic volume, 13.2
Es will be a dirty-grey metal	Ge is a greyish-white non-metal
Es will be obtained by reduction of EsO$_2$ or K$_2$EsF$_6$ with metallic sodium	Ge obtained by reduction of K$_2$GeF$_6$ with metallic sodium
The oxide EsO$_2$ will be obtained by heating the element in air. EsO$_2$ will be a white solid of high m.p. and density 4.7 g cm^{-3}. It will be amphoteric	Ge on heating in air gives GeO$_2$, a white solid m.p. 1100 °C and density 4.70 g cm^{-3}. It is amphoteric
The chloride EsCl$_4$ will be a volatile liquid b.p. < 100°C and density 1.9 g cm^{-3}	GeCl$_4$ is a volatile liquid, b.p. 83 °C and density 1.88 g cm^{-3}

Anomalies in the Periodic Table

With four pairs of elements, the order of atomic weights has had to be reversed. These are: argon and potassium; cobalt and nickel; tellurium and iodine; thorium and protactinium. The figures are:

	Ar	K	Co	Ni	Te	I	Th	Pa
Atomic no.	18	19	27	28	52	53	90	91
Atomic weight	39.9	39.1	58.9	58.7	127.6	126.9	232.0	(231)

The reasons for these anomalies are given in ch. 3, p. 32.

The significance of the Periodic System

The Periodic Classification of the elements is one of the greatest achievements of nineteenth-century science. By 1871 it had included all previous work in its field, broadening, deepening, and clarifying it; it rapidly became and has remained the foundation of the learning and teaching of the science of chemistry; and it thrust forward into the future with profound insights into the next great problem of physical and chemical science—the elucidation of the structure of the atom.

Exercises

1. Reproduce from memory as much as you can of (*a*) the Main Group Table, (*b*) the complete Periodic Table.
2. Give the meaning of the terms, atomic number, metal, metalloid, Period, Group, Main Group, transition element, lanthanide, actinide, A and B families, giving examples in each case.
3. Write notes on trends in the Periodic Table with illustrative examples.
4. Discuss the suggestion that, with advances in chemistry and physics, the Periodic Classification of the elements will be superseded.
5. Describe what is meant by (*a*) *a period*, (*b*) *a group* in the Periodic Classification. How does the type of bond formed by the elements of the second short period (sodium to argon) change with increasing atomic weight?

   Explain these changes from your knowledge of the atomic structures of the elements. (C)
6. What is meant by the terms *group, short period, long period, transition element* in the description of the periodic classification of the elements? Write out the Periodic Table of the elements from hydrogen to argon. Which of these elements form chlorides and what differences would you expect to find in the properties of these chlorides?

   How can the position of an element in the Periodic Table be used, together with its equivalent, to estimate its atomic weight? (CS)

2

ATOMIC STRUCTURE I:
THE DEVELOPMENT OF THE
ATOMIC THEORY

The atomic hypothesis

Speculations as to whether matter was either continuous, or discontinuous, i.e. all of one piece or composed of discrete particles, are known to have been made by philosophers in Greece and Rome over two thousand years ago. Even though famous English scientists such as Robert Boyle (1627–91) and Isaac Newton (1642–1726) were among many who believed that matter is composed of particles, they could produce no quantitative or qualitative experimental evidence to support their belief.

Evidence in support of the atomic hypothesis was provided by the experimentally based laws of chemical combination by weight.

(1) *Law of Conservation of Mass.* Matter cannot be created or destroyed in a chemical reaction, i.e. total mass before reaction = total mass after reaction.

(2) *Law of Constant Proportions.* A pure compound always contains the same elements chemically combined in the same proportion by weight.

(3) *Law of Multiple Proportions.* When two elements combine to form more than one compound the different weights of one element which combine with a fixed weight of the other are in a simple ratio.

(4) *Law of Reciprocal Proportions.* The relative proportions by weight in which two elements combine with a third element are in a simple ratio to those in which they combine (*a*) with one another or (*b*) with a fourth element.

Experiments have shown that these laws are not strictly applicable in all cases. For instance, it is now known that mass and energy are interconvertible and strictly it is necessary to add or subtract the mass equivalent of the energy taken in or given out during a chemical action before equating the mass of the products and of the reactants. As the energy changes in chemical reactions correspond to such minute masses they go undetected by conventional methods of chemical analysis. In atomic

17

reactions, however, the differences are extremely important. Similarly, the discovery of isotopes showed that if a combining element had a variable isotopic composition (see p. 34) the laws of Constant Proportions and Multiple Proportions would not be true. Furthermore, the composition of certain compounds found by chemical analysis does not always agree exactly with that calculated from the chemical formula based on the classical laws of chemical combination. Chemical analysis of iron(II) sulphide often reveals a smaller percentage of iron than that calculated from the formula FeS. The composition of iron(II) sulphide may be anywhere in the range $FeS-FeS_{1.14}$ and this is quite unaccounted for by the simple laws of combination.

Dalton's atomic theory

Although many eminent scientists believed in the atomic hypothesis, John Dalton did more to establish it than any other man, for he was able to show (1801–8) how it could be used to explain the laws of Combination by Weight. Dalton took the view that the measurable combination of materials in bulk was the result of the combination of their ultimate particles and that the mass relationships in bulk followed the same pattern as the mass relationship between the ultimate particles. For a given element the ultimate particles were assumed to be alike in size, shape and mass, homogeneous, unchanged by chemical action, and different in mass from the ultimate particles of every other element. Dalton assumed that combination always occurs by the union of atoms in simple whole number ratios. Because no evidence was available to establish what the numbers were, he assumed one atom of hydrogen combined with one atom of oxygen to give a molecule of water, HO. Similarly, ammonia was given the formula NH. We should not find fault with Dalton because of this: he was using the simplest numerical ratio, i.e. 1:1, the most valid method in the light of his knowledge. When there is no evidence to decide between a number of possibilities, investigation can only proceed by the method of trial and error: assume the simplest possibility to be true just because it is simplest, until it has been tried and failed, then try the next simplest and so on.

If atoms remain unchanged during chemical reactions and are neither created nor destroyed mass must be conserved. Dalton's atomic theory also accounts for the Law of Constant Composition, since if the atoms of a particular element are all identical in mass and a compound AB is formed by the combination of one atom of element A for every atom of element B, it follows that AB contains the atomic proportions by mass of element A and of element B. Any pure sample of AB will as a consequence have the same composition. Similar reasoning leads to the Law of Multiple Proportions. For if two elements A and B combine to form more than one compound it follows from the atomic theory these will have the formula AB, AB_2, A_2B, ..., etc. As the different weights of one element combining with a fixed weight of another correspond to different combining ratios of the atoms involved, these ratios will be $(B/A):(2B/A):(B/2A)$, i.e. $2:4:1$, a simple whole number ratio.

Atomic weights

Dalton found (inaccurately) that seven parts of oxygen and five parts of nitrogen combined separately with one part by weight of hydrogen. Therefore Dalton put the atomic weight of oxygen at seven times and nitrogen at five times that of hydrogen, which had arbitrarily been made the unit of atomic weight. In all this Dalton fully realised that his experiments determined combining weights (equivalent weights) which were not necessarily the same as the atomic weight. But since he lacked the evidence to decide on the correct numerical ratio in which the atoms combined he was forced to guess at it.

Gay-Lussac's law

A step towards finding the evidence Dalton lacked was made as the result of an important generalisation on the volumes of combining gases made by Gay-Lussac (1808): *when gases combine they do so in volumes that bear a simple ratio to one another and to the volume of the products if gaseous*, temperature and pressure remaining constant. The simple whole-number ratio existing between the volumes of reacting gases was taken to represent the ratio in which the *atoms* of the elemental gases combine. Thus if one volume of element A combined exactly with an equal volume of element B it was concluded that the two volumes contained an equal number of *atoms*. On this assumption Berzelius argued that as two volumes of hydrogen combined with one volume of oxygen to give water, then two atoms of hydrogen combine with one atom of oxygen to give a molecule of water. This gives the correct formula for water, H_2O, but it is based on the assumption, which will shortly be shown to be incorrect, that gaseous elements are composed of atoms. The assumption was known to be unsound for, as Dalton himself pointed out, if one reasons from the fact that

2 volumes of hydrogen + 1 volume of oxygen → 2 volumes of steam,

then 2 atoms of hydrogen + 1 atom of oxygen → 2 'compound atoms' of steam, and in order to produce one *compound atom* of steam it is necessary to split the atom of oxygen in half, which is forbidden by one of the fundamental postulates of the atomic theory.

The Avogadro–Cannizzaro contribution

The problem of establishing the correct molecular formula of the compounds produced by the combining elements, which was being hampered by the imprecise distinction scientists of the day were making between atoms and molecules, was finally resolved by Avogadro (1776–1856). He recognised that atoms of an element might *combine with themselves* and that the ultimate particles of an elemental gas could be molecules; and put forward (1811) the hypothesis that *equal volumes of all gases under the same conditions of temperature and pressure contain the same number of molecules.* If the smallest particle of oxygen capable of free existence is composed of two atoms at least, then in the reaction with hydrogen to form steam, which is now written

2 molecules of hydrogen + 1 molecule of oxygen →
2 molecules of steam,

each particle of oxygen can furnish two atoms and so the formation of two molecules of steam can be accounted for without contravening the postulates of the atomic theory. As the significance of Avogadro's hypothesis was not fully appreciated at the time, it was ignored. Confusion over atomic weights continued for some forty years until Cannizzaro (1858) published a convincing application of the views of his former teacher. He recognised that by Avogadro's hypothesis *the weight of equal volumes of gases or vapours at the same temperature and pressure are in the ratio of their molecular weight* and used this deduction to establish the molecular weight of volatile compounds relative to the weight of an atom of hydrogen which was chosen to be unity. Then, taking a large number of compounds of a particular element he worked on the principle that the atomic weight of the element would be the smallest weight of it occurring in the molecular weight of any of the compounds. The larger the number of compounds whose molecular weight can be found and whose percentage composition can be determined the greater the probability that one of them will have a molecule which contains only one atom of the element. The application of Cannizzaro's method to carbon is illustrated in the following table.

Atomic weight of carbon by Cannizzaro's method

Compound	Relative density (H = 1)	Molecular weight (M.W. = 2 × R.D.)	Percentage of carbon	Parts of carbon per M.W.
Methane	8	16	75.0	12
Ethane	15	30	80.0	24
Acetylene	13	26	92.3	24
Benzene	39	78	92.3	72
Carbon monoxide	14	28	42.9	12
Carbon dioxide	22	44	27.3	12

Further refinements in the determination of atomic weights continue to be made even to the present day, and the way in which accurate atomic weights have helped in establishing the constitution of atoms is outlined in the following sections.

The structure of atoms

During the time that the atomic and molecular theories of matter were developing, other experimental facts were being discovered which were to lead to the discovery of the structure of atoms. The more important of these findings will now be discussed briefly.

The Periodic Law

This law states that *the properties of the elements are a periodic function of their atomic weights* (1869). This discovery provided a method of systematising the known facts by means of a fundamental property of matter. Moreover, it provoked a new line of inquiry which arose from the many questions which the Periodic Table stimulated, e.g. why does the order of the elements follow the order of the atomic weights? What is the reason for the reversal of the order amongst the three pairs, argon and potassium, tellurium and iodine, cobalt and nickel? Why short Periods and long Periods? Why noble gases, transitional metal, and rare-earth elements? How is it that elements of very different atomic weight can have close chemical similarities, e.g. the alkali metals? Since the atomic weights themselves offered no explanation, it had to be sought elsewhere and *it appeared most likely* that although the weights might be different there existed similarities *inside* the various atoms. In this way a new hypothesis began to develop—*the internal structure of atoms.*

Faraday's laws of electrolysis

The ability of a solution or a fused salt to conduct electricity was investigated quantitatively by Michael Faraday (1831–4). He made two important discoveries:

(1) When a given quantity of current is passed through a solution of a salt or a fused salt it causes the decomposition of the fused salt; and decomposition of either the solvent or the salt of the solution. Moreover, the weights of the decomposition products which appear at the electrodes are directly proportional to the quantity of electricity used.

(2) The weights of the different substances liberated at the electrodes by the same quantity of electricity are in the same ratio as their chemical equivalents (combining weights).

It was already known that the combining weight of an element comprised a definite number of particles and since the same quantity of electricity (the Faraday constant, F, $96\,500$ C mol^{-1}) set free the combining weight of an element it was argued that the Faraday constant must also comprise a definite number of particles of electricity. Stoney (1874) calculated the charge on these particles of electricity by dividing the value of the Faraday constant by his estimate of the Avogadro number. As the decomposition products appeared in the proportions of their combining weights, which were known to be simply related to the atomic weights, it seemed that electricity and atoms were related. This conviction was strengthened as the result of accumulating evidence from discharge-tube experiments.

Cathode rays

Ordinarily air is a good insulator, but using a discharge tube it was found that at pressures below 10 mmHg, under a potential difference of about 10 000 V, the insulating properties break down and the air becomes conducting. A simple discharge tube is shown in Fig. 2.

At 10 mmHg pressure the air in the discharge tube glows like the familiar neon-tube signs, but as the pressure is reduced a number of other luminous effects are produced until at about 0.01 mmHg the air does not glow at all and only the glass of the tube itself fluoresces with a faint greenish light. Experiments showed that this was caused by bombardment of the glass by rays originating at the cathode. Goldstein (1876) named them cathode rays. W. Crookes (1879) and others investigated these rays and found they were able to cast a shadow of obstacles placed in their path; this showed that the rays travelled in straight lines. Furthermore, they possess *electromagnetic properties* since they could be deflected by a

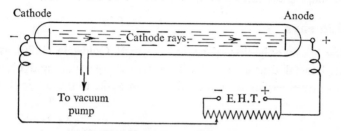

Fig. 2. A simple discharge tube.

magnet and by an electric field. Also a Faraday cylinder—a device for collecting electrical charge—became negatively charged when placed in their path.

The famous English physicist J. J. Thomson (1897) showed conclusively that the negatively charged cathode rays travelled in straight lines from the cathode to the anode and that in magnetic and electric fields the direction in which they were deflected corresponded to that for a stream of negatively charged particles. By means of quantitative experiments he was able to determine the ratio of the charge Q to that of the mass m of the cathode ray particles, and found that irrespective of the material of the cathode or the gas in the discharge tube the particles produced always had the same value for Q/m. It had already been reasoned that electricity probably existed in discrete units, and the particles characterised by J. J. Thomson were recognised to be these fundamental units of electricity and were called *electrons*. As it was not possible to arrive at the mass of the electron from the ratio Q/m without knowing Q, various attempts to determine the electronic charge were made. R. A. Millikan (1909) in his famous oil-drop experiment made an accurate assessment of the charge on the electron; and its mass is now known to be 1840 times smaller than that of a hydrogen atom.

As electrons are a universal constituent of all forms of matter Dalton's simple picture of a solid spherical atom was no longer adequate. To account for his findings Thomson (1895) proposed that an atom was a positive sphere of electrification inside which there was a regular array of a large number of electrons such that the structure was neutral as a whole. Like other theories of atomic structure developed at about the same time, this proved inadequate in accounting for facts uncovered in the growing volume of new phenomena discovered in the next fifteen years. Amongst these the discovery of positive rays, X-rays and radioactivity helped most of all in shaping the ideas about atoms which we hold today.

Positive rays

During his investigation of cathode rays, E. Goldstein (1886) used a perforated metal disc as a cathode in a discharge tube, and observed luminous rays emerging from it on the side opposite to the anode (Fig. 3).

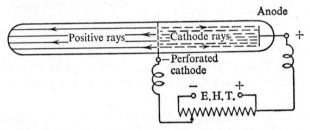

Fig. 3. A simple discharge tube showing the production of positive rays.

The rays were shown to be a stream of positively charged particles. The ratio of charge/mass was measured for them in the same way as for cathode rays and it was found that they were very much more massive particles than electrons and that the mass varied with the different gases that were placed in the tube. Electrons emitted from the cathode travel with high velocity towards the anode and inevitably collide with the gas molecules in the tube. If the collision is sufficiently energetic other electrons may be knocked out of the neutral molecule and so leave a positive particle. These are instantly accelerated towards the cathode; most of them collide with it and acquire additional electrons to regain neutrality. Others shoot through the holes in the cathode and their momentum carries them on to produce the positive rays.

X-rays

Another phenomenon associated with cathode rays was discovered by W. C. Röntgen in 1895. He noticed that at very low pressures the luminous area produced where the cathode rays struck the glass of the discharge tube emitted a new kind of radiation which he called X-rays. These rays are unaffected by magnets and penetrate materials ordinarily impervious to light. In certain respects they are similar to ordinary light waves, but they have a much shorter wavelength. Nowadays a tungsten filament is used to generate the electrons at the cathode and a tungsten target is used as the anode (Fig. 4).

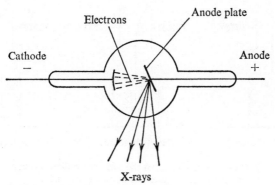

Fig. 4. Discharge tube modified to produce X-rays.

Natural radioactivity

As it had been shown that X-rays were connected in some way with that part of the discharge tube that exhibited fluorescence under the impact of cathode rays, Henri Becquerel decided to investigate some of the fluorescent materials at the Museum of Natural History in Paris where he was Professor of Physics. He found (1896) that even without the stimulus of sunlight to excite the fluorescence, crystals of a uranium salt (potassium uranyl sulphate) spontaneously emitted penetrating radiations which blackened photographic plates even when they were wrapped in light-proof paper. It was soon discovered that the radiations came from the uranium in the salt and a number of other elements, namely, thorium, polonium, radium and actinium were also found to be spontaneously emitting radiations. The French scientists Marie and Pierre Curie played a prominent rôle in all these investigations and Marie Curie (1898) gave the name *radioactivity* to this remarkable phenomenon.

Further experiments revealed that the radiations are not all identical but can be classed into three types called *alpha-rays*, *beta-rays* and *gamma-rays*.

Alpha-rays consist of positively charged particles which have a very weak penetrating power but produce marked ionisation in the gases through which they pass. Each particle was shown to have a mass four times as great as a hydrogen atom and to be equivalent to atoms of helium carrying a positive charge equal in magnitude to that of two electrons. When an alpha-particle gains two electrons it becomes a neutral helium atom.

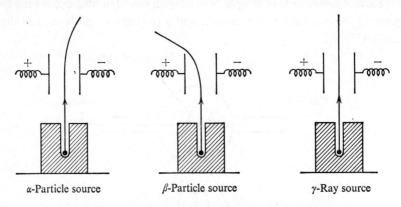

| α-Particle source | β-Particle source | γ-Ray source |

Fig. 5. The behaviour of the different radiations from radioactive materials in an electric field.

Beta-rays are composed of high-speed electrons. They cause much less ionisation in the gases through which they travel than alpha-particles but are much more penetrating and will pass through thin sheets of aluminium.

Gamma-rays have been shown to be similar to X-rays but with even shorter wavelengths. Their penetrating power is so great that several centimetres of lead may not completely stop them.

The differences in their electrical properties may be summarised by Fig. 5. All three types of radiation affect a photographic plate. Moreover, the emission of the particles takes place at a rate which varies only with the element and the size of the sample being studied and is totally independent of physical conditions or chemical reagents. Whilst it is emitting an α- or a β-particle, the element concerned changes into another element. To account for the facts of radioactivity Rutherford and Soddy (1903) proposed the *theory of spontaneous disintegration*. Atoms of the radioactive elements are thought to be unstable and capable of spontaneous disintegration (experiments were soon to show it was the nuclei of the atoms that were unstable), which continued at a rate characteristic of the particular element. The atom disintegrates by expelling an α-particle or a β-particle and simultaneously changes into another atom. This added to the growing conviction that atoms are more complex than Dalton's simple picture implied.

Radioactivity is exhibited by all the elements which follow bismuth (atomic number 83) in the Periodic Classification, and to a feebler extent, by at least nine of the lighter elements, for example, potassium (19) and rubidium (37). Since this radioactivity is a property of the elements as they are found in nature, it is called 'natural' radioactivity. In this way it is distinguished from the very common (and often useful) radioactivity that can be produced in elements by nuclear transformations and which is called 'artificial' radioactivity.

Rutherford's nuclear atom

In common with many scientists of his day Rutherford took an active interest in these newly discovered phenomena, and this led him to his famous nuclear theory of atomic structure. The theory was suggested as the result of observations on a fine beam of α-particles directed at a gold foil (see Fig. 6). Most of the particles passed straight through the foil, but a few were slightly deflected and occasionally one even underwent a deflection of 90° or more and literally bounced back off the foil. About one in 20 000 bounced back off a gold foil 6×10^{-5} cm thick, which consists of

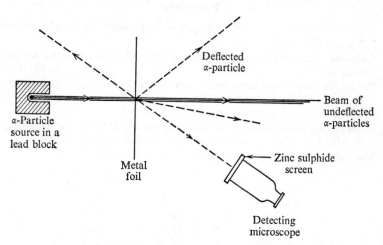

Fig. 6. The apparatus is enclosed in an evacuated vessel and the particles are detected as flashes on the zinc sulphide screen which is movable.

about 3000 layers of atoms close-packed togeher. With thicker foils a greater number of particles were deflected through large angles.

In no way could the existing theories about the nature of atoms account for the large angles through which some of the α-particles were turned. Accordingly Rutherford (1911) postulated that atoms each had a centre, or nucleus, which was minute compared with the volume of the rest of the atom but at the same time constituted almost all the mass of the atom and all the positive electricity, overall electrical neutrality being maintained by a number of electrons whose total charge was equal but opposite to that on the nucleus. On this *nuclear atomic theory* the heavy, positively charged α-particles were pictured as brushing straight through the relatively vast, diffuse electronic regions of the atom except in the unlikely event of the very small α-particle colliding with the equally small nucleus, then the large concentration of positive charge on the nucleus would exert such a powerful repulsive force on the similarly charged α-particle that it would be forced off its original course and possibly even recoil.

Experiments have shown that the nucleus of an atom is approximately 10^{-13} cm in diameter, which is about 100 000 times smaller than the diameter of the atom. Rutherford's basic postulate has therefore been thoroughly justified and the nuclear atom is an accepted fact. It was not, however, the final word in the development of the atomic theory, and the following chapters indicate how the understanding of the nature of atoms has continued to evolve.

Exercises

1. What evidence do you consider gives the most convincing proof that matter is made of atoms?
2. Given that the charge on the electron is 1.6×10^{-19} C, calculate the Avogadro number. (Answer $= 6.031 \times 10^{23}$.)
3. Define the terms *molecular weight and vapour density*. Using Avogadro's hypothesis deduce that the molecular weight is twice the vapour density. Mention any assumptions you may make.
4. What do you understand by the following terms: (*a*) Cannizzaro's principle, (*b*) atomic weight, (*c*) cathode rays, (*d*) positive rays, (*e*) X-rays?
5. The following data refer to some compounds of an element X:

Compound	Vapour density	% X in compound
Chloride	90.75	41.3
Oxide	198	75.8
Hydride	39	96.1
Fluoride	85	44.1

What value for the atomic weight of X is indicated by these data?

Calculate the molecular formula for each of the four compounds.

Given that the atomic number of X is 33, suggest a position for it in the Periodic Table, giving reasons for your answer. (C)

6. State what you understand by (a) the atomic weight, (b) the atomic number of an element and explain the significance of these terms in connection with atomic structure.

An element X has a specific heat of 0.106. When a solution of the sulphate of X is electrolysed 4.85 g of X is deposited at the cathode and one litre of oxygen, measured at 16 °C and 743 mmHg pressure, is evolved at the anode. Calculate the atomic weight of X. (C)

7. State (a) Gay Lussac's Law of gaseous volumes, and (b) Avogadro's Hypothesis. Illustrate by an example the importance of Avogadro's Hypothesis in the determination of the formulae of gaseous compounds. 20 cm³ of a mixture of ammonia and nitrogen were sparked in a eudiometer until the volume (measured at the original volume) had increased to 28 cm³. It was then brought into contact with sulphuric acid, when the volume decreased to 25 cm³. A volume of 30 cm³ of oxygen was added and the mixture sparked. After cooling, the volume of the residual gas was 37 cm³. Explain the changes observed, and calculate the volumes of ammonia and nitrogen in the original mixture. (J.M.B.)

8. Outline how Avogadro's Number can be accurately determined using X-ray diffraction.

Two different samples of iron(II) sulphide were found on analysis to contain 60.9 and 61.7 % of iron respectively. Both samples conducted electricity in the solid state. Account for these observations. (C)

3

ATOMIC STRUCTURE II:
THE NUCLEUS

Nuclear charge

From measurements on the scattering of α-particles by thin metal foils Rutherford attempted to assess the number of positive charges on the nucleus, but owing to the experimental difficulties involved achieved only partial success. He found that the number of elementary positive charges on the nucleus was approximately half the atomic weight.

A. van den Broek observed that a radioactive element which lost one α-particle per atom is transmuted into an element *two* positions nearer the beginning of the Periodic Table. As a loss of an α-particle meant the loss of *two* positive charges from an atom he suggested (1913) that successive positions in the Periodic Classification correspond to successive unit increases in the value of the nuclear charge. At about the same time H. J. G. Moseley was investigating the effect of X-rays on materials. He found that an incident beam of X-rays caused materials to emit radiations termed *characteristic X-rays*. Moreover, the characteristic X-rays from a particular element were essentially two radiations of differing frequencies, and these are called the K- and the L-series. The K-rays have higher frequencies than the L-rays and are thus much more penetrating. Moseley was able to establish a relationship between the frequency of the rays in a particular series emitted by an element and its ordinal position in the Periodic Table, i.e. its atomic number. From this he provisionally concluded that the atomic number was a fundamental property of each atom and probably represented the magnitude of the positive charge on the nucleus. A further and more accurate series of experiments on α-particle scattering was then made to establish the nuclear charge; the values obtained were in excellent agreement with the atomic numbers of the elements investigated, thus confirming Moseley's conclusion. It is now well established that the number of positive charges carried by the nucleus of an atom is the same as the atomic number of the atom, and in fact atomic number is frequently defined in this way.

Since an atom is neutral overall, the number of electrons it contains must equal the number of positive charges on the nucleus, and so the atomic number is also the same as the number of electrons in the atom. Therefore the atomic number of an element may be defined as:

(1) the ordinal position of the element in the Periodic Classification;

(2) the number of unit positive charges on the nucleus of an atom of the element;

(3) the number of extranuclear electrons in an atom of the element.

Nuclear mass

Discovery of the electron in the discharge-tube experiments described on p. 23 stimulated a search for the corresponding particle which carried a positive instead of a negative charge; but thorough investigations failed to discover any such particle. The smallest positively charged particle proved to have a charge equal in magnitude to that of the electron, but it had a mass equal to that of a hydrogen atom. These particles were produced in discharge-tube experiments in which hydrogen was the residual gas, and were presumed to be positively charged hydrogen ions H^+ produced by the loss of an electron from a hydrogen atom disrupted in the stream of cathode rays (i.e. high-speed electrons). The positively charged hydrogen ion was also identified as a product of nuclear transmutations brought about by bombarding certain light elements with α-particles. This suggested that it was an important constituent of other atoms and the name *proton* was formally assigned to it in 1920.

As electrons are so very much lighter than protons the mass of an atom is essentially the mass of its nucleus. In the hydrogen atom, where the electron contributes a greater percentage to the mass of the atom than in any other case, it only amounts to 0.055 % and in the uranium atom the electrons constitute only 0.002 % of the mass of the atom. Reasoning from the fact that the atomic number equals the number of unit positive charges on the nucleus, and that a proton carried a unit positive charge and was probably a fundamental particle, Rutherford suggested (1920) that the atomic number also represented the number of protons contained in the nucleus of the atom. But as protons had a mass of about 1 a.m.u. (the atomic mass unit is defined as one-twelfth of the mass of a ^{12}C atom, see p. 33) and the atomic number was about half the atomic weight of an element, the protons did not constitute all the nucleus and other particles must also be present; moreover they must be neutral overall. Chadwick confirmed Rutherford's prediction in 1932 when he discovered the *neutron*.

In the same year the positively charged electron or *positron* as it is called was also discovered. The neutron proved to be a neutral particle with a mass almost identical to that of a proton.

Isotopes

The discovery that some elements were composed of atoms of different mass but identical chemical properties was first made by J. J. Thomson (1913) who showed that the element neon (atomic weight 20.2) consisted of a mixture of two types of atoms of mass 20 and 22. The principle of the method, which was refined and extended by Aston with his mass spectrograph, was to ionise the atoms and then lead a narrow beam through

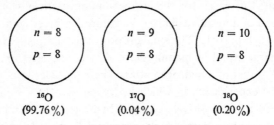

Fig. 7. Isotopes of oxygen (relative abundances shown in parentheses).

a magnetic and then an electric field. This had the effect of deflecting ions of different mass or carrying a different charge on to different trajectories. The ions finally struck a photographic plate. Consequently each atomic species was represented by an individual mark on the photographic plate and furthermore the intensity of the mark was used to deduce the relative abundance of the species. For example, the proportion of neon atoms with an atomic mass of 20 (^{20}Ne) was found to be about ten times that of the neon atoms with a mass of 22 (^{22}Ne). This gives a mean atomic weight of 20.2, in excellent agreement with the accepted value determined by chemical means.

The reason for the differing masses amongst the atoms of the same element is the differences in the number of neutrons in each *nucleus*. The number of protons, and therefore the number of electrons, must remain unchanged in the different atoms if the chemical properties are to remain unchanged, but the number of neutrons may vary and this will affect only the mass of the atom. Figure 7 shows the nuclei of the three different atoms found in naturally occurring oxygen (n, neutrons; p, protons). The mass of a nucleus is essentially the mass of the protons and neutrons (known collectively as *nucleons*) of which it is comprised.

32

As the different species of the same element occupy the same position in the Periodic Table they are termed *isotopes*.

Isotopes and the atomic weight scale

The standard for the chemical atomic weight scale has undergone a number of changes since the scale was first compiled. Until 1962 the oxygen standard O = 16.0000 was accepted as the most convenient. However, with the knowledge that ordinary atmospheric oxygen exhibited isotopy, two oxygen standards evolved: the *chemical* scale on which naturally occurring oxygen O = 16.0000, and the *physical* scale on which the most abundant isotope ^{16}O = 16.0000. Because the standard for atomic weights on the physical scale neglects the heavier isotopes of oxygen the atomic weights are all slightly greater than they are on the chemical scale. By choosing a new atomic weight scale based on the carbon isotope ^{12}C = 12.0000 the inconvenience of a dual scale is avoided and a standard better suited to modern methods of determining atomic weights is established. Only a few atomic weights have been appreciably altered by the change.

The whole number rule

Isotopy is not shown by all elements: there are nineteen which are composed of only one type of atom (and all of these have an odd atomic number). It is significant that the chemically determined atomic masses of these elements are all very close to whole numbers, the maximum divergence being only 0.2 a.m.u. Similarly, for the remaining elements the isotopic masses are all very close to whole numbers. The integer nearest to the atomic mass is called the *mass number* and it is normally used as a method of identifying isotopes. For instance, the two isotopes of copper have atomic masses of 62.96 and 64.95, i.e. mass numbers of 63 and 65 respectively. These are represented by the symbols ^{63}Cu and ^{65}Cu.

Substantial departures of chemically determined atomic masses from whole numbers are found only with those elements exhibiting isotopy; this

Isotope	Isotopic mass	Relative abundance (%)
^{35}Cl	34.97	75.53
^{37}Cl	36.97	24.47

Calculated atomic mass Cl = 35.46. Chemically determined value = 35.453.

is because the chemical methods used in determining atomic masses do not distinguish between different isotopes of the same element.

Values for the atomic weights of the majority of naturally occurring elements appear to be independent of the source of the element and the method of determination. In the majority of cases, therefore, the constituent isotopes of those elements composed of more than one nuclear species must always be present in the same proportion, as far as it is possible to measure. However, it has been found that in a few cases samples of an element from different sources show slight variations in the relative abundance of the isotopes. Combined oxygen in sea water contains a smaller percentage of oxygen-18 than atmospheric oxygen. The ratio of ^{10}B to ^{11}B atoms in boron derived from various sources has been found to differ up to as much as 3.8 %. Lead derived from various radioactive minerals also shows small differences in the relative abundance of its constituent isotopes and this leads to a slight variation in the chemically determined atomic weight.

Nuclear stability

Elements with atomic numbers 43 (technetium), 61 (promethium) and above 92 cannot be detected in nature. Amongst the remaining 90 naturally occurring elements there is a total of about 310 different atomic species (*nuclide* is an alternative term to atomic specie) of which about 50 are radioactive, i.e. unstable. A full understanding of why some nuclides are radioactive and others are stable has yet to be achieved.

Magic numbers. Nuclides in which there are 2, 8, 20, 28, 50, 82 or 126 of one kind of nucleon (neutron or proton) are noticeably stable. These numbers are termed *magic numbers*. A nucleus with a magic number of both neutrons and protons is particularly stable, e.g. $^{4}_{2}He$, $^{16}_{8}O$, $^{40}_{20}Ca$, $^{208}_{82}Pb$. This suggests a form of shell structure similar to that in the electron cloud.

Another significant feature about the number of neutrons and of protons in the nuclei of the 261 *stable* naturally occurring nuclides is shown in the following table.

Number of neutrons	Number of protons	Number of stable nuclides
Even	Even	157
Odd	Even	52
Even	Odd	48
Odd	Odd	4

Neutron to proton ratio. If the number of neutrons is plotted against the number of protons for each of the stable naturally occurring nuclides they all lie in a narrow curved band (see Fig. 8).

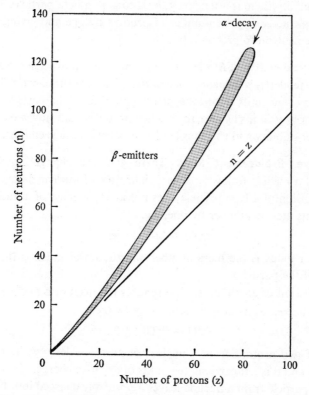

Fig. 8 The shaded area encloses the neutron–proton composition of all stable naturally occurring nuclides.

Those nuclides with relatively few protons have a tendency to contain an equal number of neutrons, i.e. the neutron to proton ratio is about 1. Nuclides with many protons have a neutron to proton ratio which rises to a maximum of about 1.5 for the heavier stable atoms.

As like charges repel each other the greater the number of protons packed into the minutely small nucleus the greater will be the tendency for it to fly apart. The progessive increase in the neutron to proton ratio with increasing atomic number reflects the tendency to reduce the effect of protons in a nucleus in order to maintain its stability. On the other hand equal numbers of neutrons and protons is a stabilising factor. Thus if the

35

proportion of protons falls below a certain minimum value the nucleus again becomes unstable.

Beta particle emitters. If a nuclide has too few protons to maintain nuclear stability there is a tendency for it to emit a beta particle. This has the effect of increasing the number of protons by one and giving a more favourable neutron to proton ratio.

Alpha particle emitters. Atoms with mass numbers above 209 are unstable and have a tendency to emit an alpha particle. This has the effect of lowering the mass by four units. However, as the loss of an alpha particle reduces the number of protons by two, the nuclide produced may now have too few protons for stability and will thus tend to be a beta particle emitter.

Radioactive displacement laws. These give the change in chemical identity of a nuclide following a particular type of nuclear decay.

(1) Emission of a beta particle does not alter the mass of a nuclide but increases its atomic number by one, e.g.

$$^{231}_{90}\text{Th} \rightarrow \,^{231}_{91}\text{Pa} + \,^{0}_{-1}e.$$

(The upper index is the mass number and the lower index is the atomic number of the particle).

(2) Emission of an alpha particle reduces the mass of a nuclide by four units and decreases its atomic number by two, e.g.

$$^{238}_{92}\text{U} \rightarrow \,^{234}_{90}\text{Th} + \,^{4}_{2}\text{He}.$$

Loss of two protons from a nucleus of an atom destroys its electrical neutrality and it is left carrying two units of negative charge. Similarly loss of a beta particle from a nuclide leaves a positively charged ion. Electrons are quickly absorbed or released by the surroundings to restore the balance.

(3) Emission of a gamma ray has no effect on the mass number or atomic number of a nuclide. In fact the emission of a gamma ray is always a subsequent event to the emission of an alpha or a beta particle. It may occur that the emission of one of these latter particles from a nuclide leaves it in an excited state, and in passing to the ground state it emits the surplus energy as a gamma ray.

Radioactive decay series. The heavy naturally occurring nuclides can be arranged into three decay series. In each series a nuclide of long half-life (see later) decays into a nuclide which is still unstable, and so on until a stable end product is reached. This is an isotope of lead in each case. The decay series commencing with $^{235}_{92}\text{U}$ is charted in Fig. 9.

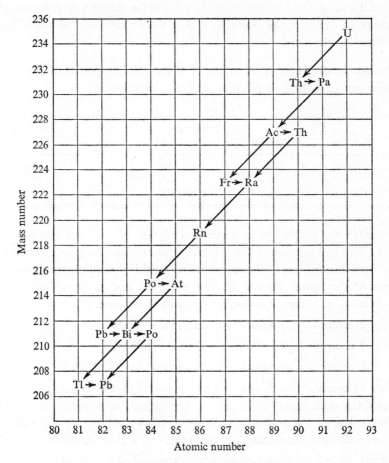

Fig. 9. A radioactive decay series.

Half-life of a radioelement. The reason why an unstable nuclide suddenly disintegrates is quite unknown. Moreover there is no known way of initiating or preventing nuclear disintegrations. They occur in an apparently random manner. However, although the activity of a particular radio-element has short-lived bursts and lulls there is an underlying steady rate of disintegrations. This rate varies only with the element and the size of the sample, i.e. the bigger the sample the greater the number of disintegrations which will be detected. A convenient way of expressing this rate of disintegration is based on the time taken for half the number of atoms in a sample of the element to decay. This value is the same no matter how large the sample and it is called the *half-life* of the element. As it is a simple matter to measure the half-life it is a convenient way of identifying radioactive elements.

Nuclear binding energy. A summary of the chief properties of the three main atomic particles is given in the following table:

Particle	Symbol	Relative mass $^{12}C = 12$	Mass no.	Electronic charge
Proton	^1_1H	1.007276	1	$+1$
Neutron	^1_0n	1.008665	1	0
Electron	$_{-1}^{0}e$	0.0005486	0	-1

Although the nucleus of an atom is composed of neutrons and protons it is a fact that the sum of the masses of these constituent particles *is never the same as the mass of the composite particle.* For example the measured mass of the helium nucleus is 4.002764 a.m.u. and as shown below the total mass of its constituent parts is significantly more, i.e.

2 protons $= 2 \times 1.007276 = 2.014552$ a.m.u.,

2 neutrons $= 2 \times 1.008665 = 2.017330$ a.m.u.,

2 neutrons $+ 2$ protons $= 1$ helium nucleus $= 4.030375$ a.m.u.

This difference between the observed and calculated values, sometimes called the *mass defect*, represents matter changed into energy; i.e. energy liberated when the protons and neutrons bind together into the nucleus. Interconversion of mass and energy in this way was predicted in Einstein's special theory of relativity, and he expressed the relationship by the equation $E = mc^2$. E is the energy in ergs equivalent to a mass m expressed in grams where c is the velocity of light in cm s^{-1}.

As like charges repel, some additional factor is required to account for the ability of protons to pack closely together in the nucleus. It is suggested that superimposed on the normal coulombic repulsion there is also a very much stronger attractive force which is only effective over very short distances, i.e. nuclear distances. These forces are responsible for nuclear stability. Using Einstein's equation given above, it is possible to calculate the energy equivalent of the mass defect. This energy, divided by the number of nucleons present in the nucleus, gives what is termed the *binding energy per nucleon* and this is taken as a measure of the magnitude of the force binding the nucleons. A unit of energy commonly used in nuclear studies is the *electron-volt* (eV) or *million electron-volt* (MeV). It is not an S.I. unit but will probably be around for some time yet; $1 \text{ eV} = 1.60 \times 10^{-19}$ J. One atomic mass unit has an energy equivalent of 931 MeV. Thus, the total binding energy of an alpha particle is 28.3 MeV. This is the amount of energy needed to disrupt an α-particle into its separate parts. It is interesting to compare this with the 3–4 eV needed to disrupt ordinary chemical bonds; i.e. energy changes in bond breaking are insignificant when compared to energy changes in nuclear reactions.

Nuclear energy

Apart from the values for ⁴He, ⁸Be, ¹²C and ¹⁶O it can be seen from the curve shown in Fig. 10 that the binding energy per nucleon changes

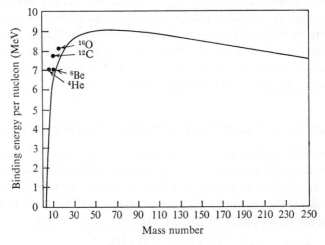

Fig. 10. Variation of binding energy per nucleon with mass number.

regularly with the mass number. It is instructive to note that the higher values for the four exceptions are associated with atoms having mass numbers which are multiples of four: this can be correlated with a whole number of α-particles which are known to be very stable.

The binding energy per nucleon is small for the lighter elements but rises rapidly to a broad maximum amongst the atoms of intermediate mass, after which it steadily decreases towards the heavier atoms. Thus less energy has been released per nucleon amongst the heavy and light elements than amongst the elements of intermediate mass.

Fission and fusion

The maximum in the curve represents maximum binding energy, maximum stability, and minimum energy of the nucleus. Therefore the transmutations of all lighter and heavier nuclei into those at the graph maximum will result in liberation of great quantities of energy.

When the nucleus of a heavy atom is split, the fragments constitute atoms in the intermediate mass range. For instance, an atom of uranium undergoes *nuclear fission* in a number of ways but the principal fragments are the nuclei of molybdenum and lanthanum atoms which have mass numbers of 95 and 139 respectively. During the fission the difference in binding energy which the nucleons exhibit in the uranium atom and in the fission products is released as energy. In the same way the nucleons in light atoms have released less energy per nucleon than they would if they had comprised the nuclei of heavier atoms, so that when light atoms fuse together to form heavier atoms more matter is converted into energy and this constitutes a further release of binding energy. In the hydrogen bomb atoms of hydrogen fuse to give atoms of helium, whereas in the ordinary atomic bomb heavy atoms split into smaller fragments.

Nuclear transmutations and artificial radioactivity

While studying the effect of bombarding nitrogen gas with α-particles Rutherford (1919) discovered the first non-spontaneous nuclear transformation. A collision between an α-particle and the nucleus of a nitrogen atom causes the ejection of a high-speed proton, and the residual particle is an isotope of oxygen. This may be summarised as follows

$$^{14}_{7}\text{N} + ^{4}_{2}\text{He} \rightarrow ^{17}_{8}\text{O} + ^{1}_{1}\text{H}.$$

An alternative notation expresses the same reaction thus

$$^{14}_{7}\text{N}(\alpha, p)^{17}_{8}\text{O}.$$

Here the symbol α represents the colliding α-particle and p the emitted proton. Further investigation revealed that nearly all the light elements before potassium in the Periodic Table could be made to undergo nuclear transmutation with the emission of protons by bombardment with α-particles from naturally occurring radioactive materials, e.g.

$$^{27}_{13}\text{Al} + ^{4}_{2}\text{He} \rightarrow ^{30}_{14}\text{Si} + ^{1}_{1}\text{H}.$$

Nuclear transmutations of this type are termed (α, p) reactions.

During their investigations of the effect of bombarding an aluminium foil with α-particles from the radioactive element polonium, I. Joliot-Curie and her husband F. Joliot noticed that neutrons and positrons (positive electrons) were emitted in addition to the protons expected for the reaction given above. The Joliots accounted for the production of the neutrons by the (α, n) reaction

$$^{27}_{13}\text{Al} + ^{4}_{2}\text{He} \rightarrow ^{30}_{15}\text{P} + ^{1}_{0}n$$

and suggested that the ^{30}P isotope of phosphorus was radioactive and decayed with the emission of a positron. This was confirmed and so constitutes the first recorded example of the production of an unstable isotope which cannot be found in nature. As the number of naturally occurring radioactive elements is limited, the possibility of producing further radioactive materials stimulated a search for ways of producing other instances of *artificial radioactivity* and nowadays radioactive isotopes of all elements are known. (*Note* not all isotopes are radioactive.)

Enormous progress in the production of artificial radioisotopes followed when the bombarding particles in the nuclear reaction were extended to include artificially accelerated particles. Complex electrical machines (cyclotrons, synchrotons, bevatrons, etc.) have been designed which are able to accelerate charged atomic particles (e.g. protons, electrons, etc.) to very high velocities. These projectiles are then used to bombard suitable targets, e.g. fast deuterons bring about the following (d, n) reaction

$$^{53}_{24}\text{Cr} + ^{2}_{1}\text{H} \rightarrow ^{54}_{25}\text{Mn} + ^{1}_{0}n.$$

Neutrons are very effective particles for producing nuclear transformations as they are electrically neutral and therefore suffer no repulsion when they approach a target atom. Slow neutrons are particularly suitable for producing artificial radioactivity. Thus fast neutrons emitted from a neutron source are passed through materials such as wax or water which are termed *moderators* and these reduce the speed of the neutrons without absorbing too many. As a consequence of their reduced speed *slow* neutrons spend a relatively longer time in the vicinity of a nucleus than *fast* neutrons and thus stand a better chance of being absorbed. For example, deuterium absorbs neutrons and is converted into another isotope of hydrogen called tritium

$$^{2}_{1}\text{H} + ^{1}_{0}n \rightarrow ^{3}_{1}\text{H}.$$

Nuclear fission and nuclear reactors

When the nucleus of an atom of uranium 235 absorbs a slow neutron it splits into two fragments which are not greatly different in mass (typical mass ratio 2:3) and a considerable amount of energy is liberated—even on nuclear standards (see p. 39). Furthermore, two or three neutrons are also ejected as the uranium atom undergoes fission. If precautions are taken to prevent too many of these neutrons being lost in side reactions, they lead to the fission of further uranium atoms and so produce a self-sustaining *chain reaction* (Fig. 11).

The core of a nuclear reactor is basically a matrix of uranium rods or plates arranged in a medium for moderating the speed of the neutrons (e.g. graphite, heavy water). A material which absorbs neutrons (e.g. boron, cadmium) can be introduced into the core to regulate the intensity of the

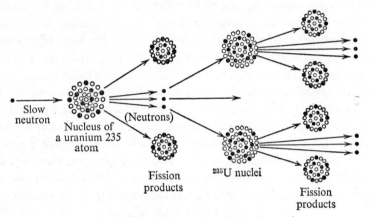

Fig. 11. Schematic representation of a chain reaction.

neutron flux and so control the chain reaction. Nuclear power stations utilise the heat developed by a nuclear reactor to produce steam for driving electric generators. Another important application of nuclear reactors is in the production of artificially radioactive materials. This is a consequence of the efficiency with which the slow neutrons produced in the core of the reactor are able to initiate nuclear transmutations.

Radiochemistry

Isotopes may often be used to ascertain the course of a chemical reaction. A convenient atom in one of the reactants in the reaction to be investigated is replaced by one of its isotopes which by virtue of its radioactivity (or different mass) is easily detectable and so acts as a label and allows the part it takes in the chemical (or physical) change to be traced. This is known as the *tracer technique* and elements utilised in this way are called *tracer elements*. The feature of radioactive materials which make them invaluable aids to analysis and experimental investigation is the fact that the radio-activity of minute quantities of material can be detected and measured quite simply even when ordinary methods of chemical analysis are impracticable.

Phosphorus-32. Isotopes, in particular phosphorus-32, have found important application in agriculture. Phosphorus-32 is produced in a nuclear reactor by subjecting a sulphur target to neutron irradiation when the reaction $^{32}S(n, p)^{32}P$ occurs. The way in which a growing plant can absorb phosphate fertiliser from the soil can be studied by labelling the phosphate with ^{32}P. Its progress through the plant can be detected with a Geiger counter, or photographically since the β-particles emitted by the ^{32}P tracer blacken a photographic plate; the amount of blackening is proportional to the concentration of the tracer. By placing a leaf, for example, against a photographic plate it is possible to obtain an autoradiograph which shows the distribution of the absorbed phosphate.

The ^{32}P isotope is also used in the treatment of certain kinds of cancer of the blood and skin cancer. Basically the role of radioactive isotopes in the treatment of malignant growth depends on their accumulation in the tissue of the growth which they will then destroy by the action of the emitted radiations.

Carbon-14. The problem of the mechanism of photosynthesis has been studied by using carbon-14 labelled carbon dioxide. By growing plants in air containing this gas the rate at which they absorb carbon dioxide from the air can be followed as ^{14}C is a β-particle emitter.

As a result of photosynthesis ^{14}C can be used to date events within the range 600–10,000 years ago.

Cosmic radiations bombarding the upper atmosphere cause the following nuclear raction to occur

$$^{14}_{7}N + ^{1}_{0}n \rightarrow ^{14}_{6}C + ^{1}_{1}H.$$

The ^{14}C isotope produced becomes uniformly distributed throughout the atmosphere as carbon dioxide gas. The proportion of these ^{14}C-labelled molecules is slight. But it is assumed to be maintained at a constant level. The ratio of ^{14}C to ^{12}C in growing plants is the same as that in the air. When the plant dies, however, and the ^{14}C is not replenished the proportion falls. So that after 5600 years only half as much ^{14}C remains. By comparing the radioactivity due to ^{14}C in the article under investigation (i.e. piece of wood, papyrus, cloth, etc.) and in the air, it is therefore possible to estimate its age.

Exercises

1. Explain what is meant by *radioactivity*. If an atom of radium successively loses three α-particles into what element will it have been transformed? Into what element would this atom be transformed by successively losing two β-particles, and what would be its mass number if the original radium atom had a mass number of 226?

2. (a) What are α, β and γ-rays and how may they be detected?

   (b) Radio-carbon $^{14}_{6}C$ is a β-emitter with a half-life of 5568 years; what does the half-life mean? What is the atomic number, atomic mass and name of the new atom that is formed as a result of this charge?

   (c) *EITHER*: new wood gives 15.3 counts per minute per gram of carbon whilst the wood from a very old tomb was found to give 10.1 counts per minute per gram of carbon. What is the approximate age of the wood?

   OR: Describe carefully *three* useful applications of radioisotopes other than dating by radio-carbon. (O)

3. (a) List the three main fundamental particles which are constituents of atoms. Give their relative charges and masses.

   (b) Similarly name and differentiate between the radiations emitted by naturally-occurring radioactive elements.

   For the particle which is common to lists (a) and (b) name *two* methods by which it can be obtained from non-radioactive metals.

   Complete the following equations for nuclear reactions by using the Periodic Table provided to identify the elements X, Y, Z, A and B and add the atomic and mass numbers where these are missing.

   $$^{207}_{82}Pb \rightarrow {}_{83}X + {}_{-1}^{0}e$$
   $$^{27}_{13}Al + {}_{0}^{1}n \rightarrow {}^{24}Y + {}_{2}^{4}Z$$
   $$^{14}_{7}N + {}_{2}^{4}Z \rightarrow {}^{17}_{8}A + {}_{1}B$$

   (J.M.B.)

4. Outline the preparation and one use of the radioisotope ^{32}P. Complete the following equations (α = alpha particle).

   $$^{9}Be + \alpha = {}_{0}^{1}n +$$
   $$^{27}Al + {}^{1}H = \alpha +$$

   Comment on the following:

   When a stream of low-energy α-particles (6 MeV) is directed at a thin foil of aluminium, most of the α-particles pass straight through and the remainder are either deflected or emerge from the same side as they originally entered. If the energy of the α-particles is increased to 10 MeV some α-particles are absorbed by the aluminium. (C)

5. Outline the use of the mass-spectrometer in the determination of atomic weights. Why is $^{12}C = 12$ now used as the standard in these determinations?

   The mass spectrum of an element X contained three peaks or lines at m/e 24, 25, and 26 of relative intensities 7.88 : 1.01 : 1.11. Explain these data and calculate the atomic weight of X. (C)

4

ATOMIC STRUCTURE III:
ELECTRONIC CONFIGURATION

All diagrams which attempt to show electron orbits are attempting to picture something which is not yet fully understood. However, it is helpful to consider electrons as particles speeding around the nucleus of an atom on circular or elliptical paths. The volume occupied by these orbits is loosely called the *electron cloud*. This is essentially spherical in shape and has fairly well defined boundaries.

Atomic spectra

It is possible to cause a material to emit radiant energy by subjecting it to an electric discharge, arc, or spark, or by heating it. If these radiations are analysed in a way similar to the resolving of white light into its component colours, a pattern of lines is obtained. Each line represents a radiation of a definite wavelength. The pattern of the lines is extremely important since it is different for each element. Since line spectra of this type originate in the atom they are called *atomic spectra*. The wavelength of the radiation corresponding to each line of the hydrogen spectrum has been determined with considerable accuracy, radiations beyond the visible region being detected with special instruments. After many years of detailed analysis it was found that the wavelengths could be classified into a number of series which could all be expressed by a simple formula

$$\frac{1}{\lambda} = R\left(\frac{1}{n^2} - \frac{1}{m^2}\right),$$

where λ is the wavelength of the line, R is a constant called *Rydberg's Constant* and equals 109 677.76 cm^{-1}, n and m are given integral values which determine the particular spectral series. These series, which are named after their discoverers, are calculated with the values m and n given on p. 46.

It is this striking pattern and orderliness of the lines in the spectrum of hydrogen which stimulated enquiry and furnished the information out of which modern ideas of the electronic structure of atoms evolved.

The atomic spectrum of hydrogen

Series	n	m
Lyman (1916)	1	2, 3, 4, ...
Balmer (1885)	2	3, 4, 5, ...
Paschen (1908)	3	4, 5, 6, ...
Brackett (1922)	4	5, 6, 7, ...
Pfund (1924)	5	6

Quantisation of energy

In order to account for the facts of *black-body radiation* Planck (1900) introduced the idea of *quantisation of energy*. According to this hypothesis radiant energy is emitted (or absorbed) in bursts rather than as a continuous flow. Each burst corresponds to a definite amount of energy which is a whole number multiple of a unit of energy called a *quantum*. The value of the quantum is related to the frequency of the radiation:

$$E \quad = \quad h \quad \times \quad v$$

(value of a quantum)   (Planck's constant)   (frequency of the radiation)

Bohr's interpretation of atomic spectra

Rutherford's suggestion, that the opposing effects of the inward attraction of the positively charged nucleus and the centrifugal force developed by the electron speeding round the nucleus keep it on a definite orbit where they just balance, had several serious objections. First, according to electromagnetic theory a negative electron orbiting in a positive field should continuously radiate energy. As a consequence it would lose energy, travel slower and spiral into the nucleus. Secondly, such a spiral path would produce a continuous range of wavelengths instead of the characteristic line pattern that is observed. Bohr applied Planck's quantum theory to the orbits of electrons in the hydrogen atom and assumed that:

(1) Electrons may only move on defined paths called *stationary states*.

(2) Energy of radiation is emitted or absorbed only when an electron moves from one stationary state to another.

(3) In any electron transition the energy difference between the initial and final stationary states equals one quantum of energy. The energy content of the quantum being equal to the frequency of the associated

46

radiation v multiplied by Planck's constant h. (*Note.* The reciprocal of the wavelength of a radiation equals the frequency.)

This immediately gives rise to the picture of an atom as a positive nucleus around which electrons circle on paths that are separated from each other since they must be at least one quantum of energy apart.

As the transition of an electron between two particular stationary states is always associated with the same difference in quantity of energy, radiation of a definite wavelength is emitted and a line in the atomic spectra is produced. Electrons which absorb energy from an electric discharge, arc, spark or heat jump into stationary states at higher energy levels but then they spontaneously resume their original stable levels and the energy absorbed is set free as radiant energy. Several electrons in an atom may be *excited* in this way, and a variety of stationary states are available for them to move up into; consequently a complex mixture of radiations of different wavelengths as shown will be produced, giving the charactersitic line spectrum of the atom as shown in Fig. 12.

The significance of the integral values of n and m quoted earlier is illustrated in figure 12. They designate the energy levels between which an electronic transition occurs to give the spectral line of corresponding frequency. If an electron is excited beyond the convergence limit of a spectral series ($n = \infty$) it is lost to the atom which is left as the ion H^+. Thus in the Lyman series the electronic transition from the ground state ($n = 1$) to the stationary state related to the convergence limit of the spectral lines corresponds to the ionisation energy of hydrogen.

By assuming that electrons move in circular orbits Bohr was able to construct a theoretical model of the hydrogen atom and calculate the wavelengths of the lines in its atomic spectra. The remarkable agreement between these values and those determined experimentally was a triumphant success for Bohr's theory. It was only possible to make calculations of this sort for the simplest atoms, as intractable complications developed as the atom became more complex.

Distribution of orbits

Whereas Bohr was able to account for the observed atomic spectrum of hydrogen on the basis of seven stationary states, many more such states, which can be taken to represent electron orbits, are needed in order to account for the whole range of spectral lines produced by the known elements. However, detailed analysis of spectra showed that the energy

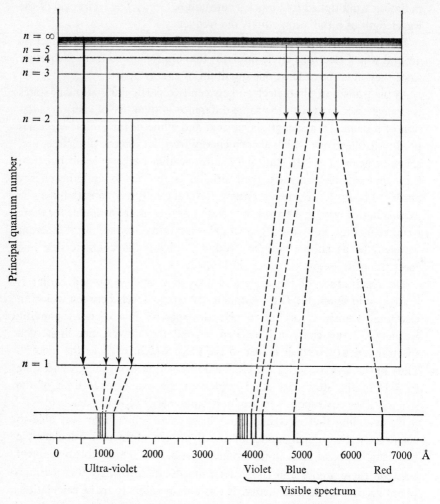

Fig. 12. Energy levels of the hydrogen atom, illustrating the origin of the Lyman and Balmer series in the hydrogen spectrum.

levels of the different electron orbits could be grouped into seven distinguishable bands, or *shells*, as they are termed.

Orbits are referred to in terms of *quantum numbers*. The principal quantum number, n which may have integral values from 1 to 7, and the subsidiary quantum number, l, which can have the values 0, 1, 2, ..., $(n-1)$. Electrons in the orbits with the subsidiary quantum number $l = 0, 1, 2$ or 3 are commonly termed s, p, d and f electrons respectively. It is also a practice to use the same notation for the particular electron orbit instead of the numerical value of *l*. The letters *s*, *p*, *d* and *f* (*s*, sharp; *p*, principal; *d*, diffuse; *f*, fundamental) were adopted by the pioneer spectroscopists to denote spectral lines associated with electronic transitions involving these orbits.

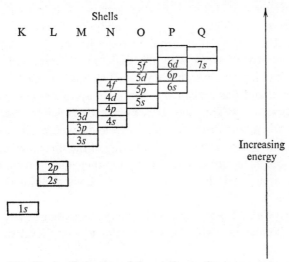

Fig. 13. An illustration of the overlap in the energy ranges
of the various shells.

Orbits with the same principal quantum number constitute a *shell*. Thus the electrons in the 4*s*, 4*p*, 4*d* and 4*f* orbits form the fourth shell. The letters K, L, M, N, O, P and Q are frequently used to designate the various shells instead of the principal quantum number.

Electrons in the same orbit are at the same level of energy. Orbits with the same subsidiary quantum number (i.e. *s*, *p*, *d*, and *f* electrons) are also at the same level of energy. But orbits with different subsidiary quantum numbers in the same shell differ in energies, even so, it is only over a relatively limited range. Shells of low principal quantum number cover energy ranges which differ fairly considerably from one another. After the first few shells however, the energy ranges of succeeding shells begin to overlap (Fig. 13).

Arrangement of electrons in orbits

Experimental evidence has suggested the following rules for describing the distribution of electrons amongst the various orbits outlined in the previous section.

(1) Each shell can accommodate up to $2n^2$ electrons, where n is the principal quantum number of the shell.

(2) Electrons always fill orbits of lowest energy first.

(3) Each orbit can accommodate only two electrons. Moreover, it is a condition that these two electrons differ in an important respect termed *spin*. This property of electrons may be pictured as their ability to spin in a clockwise or anticlockwise direction about some axis through their centre. Repulsion between electrons of opposite spin is not as strong as that between two electrons with the same spin. Thus pairing between oppositely spinning electrons has a marked stabilising effect on the orbit.

(4) The p, d and f levels can accommodate up to six, ten and fourteen electrons respectively. Thus they are in effect *shells* within *shells* (i.e. subshells) and are subdivided into three, five and seven orbits respectively. There is no difference in energy between any of the three p orbits until the atom is placed in a strong magnetic field; then these latent differences become apparent and the atom is able to emit additional radiations (Zeeman effect).

(5) *Hund's Rule* of maximum multiplicity states that in any free atom electrons will enter the orbits of a particular p, d or f level singly before pairing will occur.

The order of the elements in the Periodic Classification follows the stepwise increase in the number of electrons contained in the orbits, so that hydrogen, the first element, has its single electron in the $1s$ orbit, and so on (Fig. 14).

As a consequence of spin, and the splitting of the p, d and f levels, two quantum numbers are insufficient to characterise each electron in an atom and it is necessary to invoke both a spin quantum number and a magnetic quantum number. The *Pauli Exclusion Principle* states that no two electrons in any one atom may be described by the same set of four quantum numbers.

By applying the foregoing rules the electronic configuration of most elements can be accurately described and these are set out in full on pp. 612–13.

The Uncertainty Principle

We see objects by virtue of the light rays that strike them. If the object is a sub-atomic particle like an electron the radiation striking it may have sufficient force to move it. Gamma rays can be used to detect the position of an electron, but it is such a highly energetic type of radiation that it strikes the electron and accelerates it, making its velocity indeterminable. Less energetic forms of radiation like infra-red rays may not appreciably affect the motion of the electron, so that they could be used to determine its velocity. However, low energy radiations of this type have relatively long wavelengths, longer in fact than the diameter of the particle. The situation is now analogous to measuring the diameter of a hair with a ruler graduated in centimetres. Thus the boundaries of the particle cannot be

Element	Electron configuration	Pictorial representation of electron arrangement		
		1s	2s	2p
H	$1s^1$	↑		
He	$1s^2$	↑↓		
Li	$1s^2\,2s^1$	↑↓	↑	
Be	$1s^2\,2s^2$	↑↓	↑↓	
B	$1s^2\,2s^2\,p^1$	↑↓	↑↓	↑
C	$1s^2\,2s^2\,p^2$	↑↓	↑↓	↑ ↑
N	$1s^2\,2s^2\,p^3$	↑↓	↑↓	↑ ↑ ↑
O	$1s^2\,2s^2\,p^4$	↑↓	↑↓	↑↓ ↑ ↑
F	$1s^2\,2s^2\,p^5$	↑↓	↑↓	↑↓ ↑↓ ↑
Ne	$1s^2\,2s^2\,p^6$	↑↓	↑↓	↑↓ ↑↓ ↑↓

Fig. 14. Electronic configuration of the elements in Periods I and II (the up and down arrows signify electrons of opposite spin).

located and its position is uncertain. Therefore when dealing with sub-atomic particles like electrons it becomes impossible to define both the position and velocity simultaneously. This important characteristic of nature was first enunciated by Heisenberg in 1927 and is called the *Uncertainty Principle*. He showed that if Δx was the uncertainty in determining the position and Δp that in determining the momentum (momentum = mass of particle × velocity) then:

$$\Delta x . \Delta p \geqslant h.$$

(Plank's constant $h = 6.6252 \times 10^{-27}$ ergs.)

The wave-mechanical approach

Schrödinger (1926) developed a mathematical treatment for dealing with moving electrons which avoided the difficulties presented by the Uncertainty Principle. This was done by defining the position of an electron as a statistical probability of being somewhere within the space occupied by the atom rather than at a definite point as in the Bohr theory. The equations so derived are similar to those used to describe the propagation of waves. Since the wave-like properties of electrons are well established it was not inappropriate to describe the method as the mechanics of electron waves or *wave-mechanics*. The difference between the wave-mechanical approach and the Bohr method can best be visualised in the case of the hydrogen atom. On the Bohr theory the single electron follows a circular orbit which has a radius of 0.53 Å. According to wave-mechanics the electron has

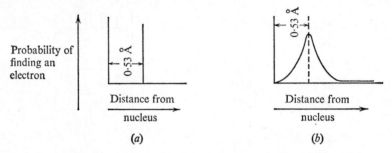

Fig. 15. Diagrammatic comparison of an electron orbit and an orbital.

a spherically symmetrical statistical distribution in the space occupied by the atom which rises to a maximum at the same distance from the nucleus as the Bohr orbit (Fig. 15).

The term *orbital* is used to describe the region in which an electron is most probably to be found and is clearly closely related to the well-defined orbit of the Bohr theory. Solving the wave equation for all but the very simplest atoms presents insuperable problems and this limits the effectiveness of the wave-mechanical approach. However, the wave equation for the hydrogen atom has been solved and effectively accounts for the hydrogen spectrum. More than one set of values satisfy the wave equation. Each set is characterised by four numbers—quantum numbers—which correspond to the quantum numbers of the Bohr theory. When the hydrogen atom is in the ground state (i.e principal quantum number $n = 1$) there is only one set of values which satisfy the wave equation and the electron orbital ($1s$) is spherically symmetrical as described above. In the first 'excited' state (i.e. $n = 2$) there are four possible solutions to the wave equation. These constitute the second shell and correspond to a $2s$ orbital and three $2p$ orbitals. In general all s orbitals are spherically symmetrical but have a greater radius with increasing values of n. The shape of p, d

and *f* orbitals are increasingly complex and strongly dependent on direction. Thus the three *p* orbitals are mutually perpendicular dumb-bell shaped lobes. The shaded figures shown in Fig. 16 represent *s* and *p* orbitals; the intensity of the shading in the *s* orbital corresponds to the relative probability of locating an electron, i.e. the electron density.

The range of orbitals and their energy state follows exactly the pattern described for the orbits of the Bohr atom. They are, however, derived in a more rigorous manner consistent with modern physical ideas.

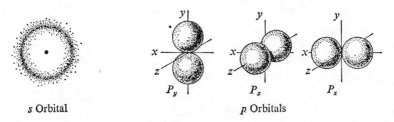

s Orbital   *p* Orbitals

Fig. 16. Shapes of *s* and *p* orbitals

Ionisation energies

Ionisation energies provide another method of investigating the arrangement of the electrons in an atom, which is particularly useful for studying multi-electron atoms. A certain amount of energy is required to withdraw completely the most loosely held electron from a gaseous atom (i.e. a single atom of the element). This is the *first ionisation energy* of the atom and is expressed in kilojoules per mole (kJ mol^{-1}) or kilocalories per mole (kcal mol^{-1}), N.B. the latter is not an S.I. unit, but 1 kcal = 4.184 kJ. To remove the next most loosely bound electron requires a further quantity of energy and this is the *second ionisation energy* of the atom...and so on with the third, fourth...and *n*th ionisation energies until all the electrons have been withdrawn. A plot of the logarithm of successive ionisation energies of the potassium atom is shown in Fig. 17. This clearly shows the relative energy states of the different electrons in an atom and how they adopt the *shell* pattern previously described.

Energy levels in multi-electron atoms

The variation in the energy of orbitals with atomic number in the first four shells only is illustrated in Fig. 18. Whereas the orbitals in each shell have the same energy in the hydrogen atom, with more complex atoms the orbitals not only have different energy levels but also move to lower energies. Of special importance is the fact that the energies of the orbitals do not always decrease in step, but irregularities occur owing to variations in the *screening effect* (see p. 67) of the different orbitals. Such a case occurs

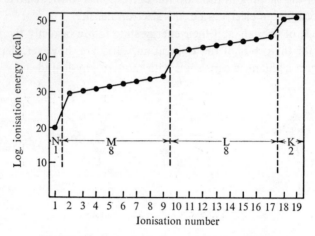

Fig. 17. Successive ionisation energies for potassium.

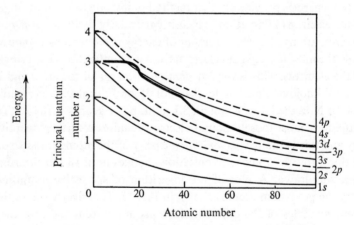

Fig. 18. Variation in the energy level of some orbitals with atomic number.

with potassium and calcium atoms; for the outer electrons enter the 4s level which, for these elements at least, has a lower energy than the 3d level. This has a profound effect on the chemistry of the subsequent elements as will be described later in the text (p. 523).

Exercises

1. Give an account of the changing concept of the atom from Dalton's time to the present.

2. Write notes on the following: (*a*) quantisation of energy, (*b*) electron shells, (*c*) orbitals, (*d*) ionisation energies.

3. Write down the electronic configuration of the elements in Period 4 from potassium to krypton inclusively.

4. Explain the formation of the line spectra of hydrogen and show how the line spectra are related to the electronic structure and ionisation energy of the atom. What evidence concerning atomic structure is provided by X-ray spectra? (C)

5. Explain what you understand by the terms (*a*) electron cloud, (*b*) outermost electron, (*c*) orbital.

6. Account for the trends in ionisation energy in (*a*) a Group, (*b*) a short Period, of the Periodic Classification of the elements.

7. Describe the important features in the electronic structure of atoms, taking examples up to atomic number 36 (Kr). Describe briefly the supporting experimental evidence. (CS)

5

ATOMIC PROPERTIES AND
THE PERIODIC TABLE

Relation between atomic structure and bulk properties of substances

The Periodic Table (1870) was produced by consideration of two fundamental properties of elements in bulk: (1) *atomic weight*, based on determination of vapour density leading to molecular weight, leading in turn to atomic weight; and (2) *valency*. The substances handled in the laboratory were known to consist of enormous numbers of particles—atoms or molecules or ions—but the origin of the charges on ions was not yet known. The properties of the atoms and molecules were assumed to be similar to the properties of the substances in bulk. At this stage any speculation about the properties of individual atoms, molecules or ions was based on knowledge of the bulk properties of substances.

With the elucidation of atomic structure, another set of properties depending on the structure of the atom is now available. These may be called *atomic properties*, and include among others (1) atomic number, (2) electronic configuration, (3) atomic radius, (4) ionic radius, (5) ionisation energy, and (6) electronegativity. It is essential to make a clear distinction between bulk properties and atomic properties. With the wealth of precise information now available it is possible to understand and explain many bulk properties in terms of atomic properties. This approach marks the greatest advance in the systematisation of chemistry since the formulation of the Periodic Classification. It is found that the study of atomic properties confirms classification based on bulk properties and explains the fundamental reasons underlying this classification. It forms also the basis for a detailed account of the behaviour and properties of elements and their compounds.

Relation between atomic number, nuclear charge, and total number of electrons in a neutral atom

The atomic number of an element is its serial (or ordinal) number in the Periodic Table starting with hydrogen (atomic number 1) and going up to hahnium (atomic number 105). As already described (p. 30), Moseley (1914) showed that the atomic number of an element is equal to the number of protons in the nucleus of its atom, and therefore also equal to the total number of electrons in its neutral atom, e.g. sodium is the eleventh element in the Periodic Table, and by definition its atomic number is 11. Also, each sodium atom has 11 protons in its atomic nucleus (i.e. its nuclear charge is $11+$), and a total of 11 extranuclear electrons.

Relation between the arrangement of electrons in an atom and the position of the element in the Periodic Table

Total no. of elements in each period		Maximum no. of electrons $(2 \times n^2)$ in each main quantum shell	
Period 1	2	1st or K shell	2
Period 2	8	2nd or L shell	8
Period 3	8 ⎫	3rd or M shell	18
Period 4	18 ⎭		
Period 5	18 ⎫	4th or N shell	32
Period 6	32 ⎭		

The correspondence between these numbers is striking. But the fact that Period 3 has the same number of elements as Period 2 (eight) and Period 5 the same number of elements as Period 4 (eighteen) is unexpected and needs explanation.

Beginning with hydrogen and following the order of atomic number, carry out an imaginary process of building up the electronic structure of the atom of each element by adding 1 electron to the atom of the preceding element (and 1 proton to its nucleus). The totals of electrons and protons thus arrived at are those found by Moseley to be correct. The following table shows the results of this operation for the first three periods and the beginning of the fourth. Hydrogen has one electron in the K shell; helium has two electrons in the K shell; lithium has two electrons in the K shell, and since the K shell is now complete, the third electron enters the L shell; and so on. This information is usually given in compact form by saying that the electronic configuration of hydrogen is K 1, of helium K 2, of lithium K 2, L 1 or simply H 1; He 2; Li 2, 1 and so on.

Period no.	Elements and their electronic configuration							
1	H 1	—	—	—	—	—	—	He 2
2	Li 2, 1	Be 2, 2	B 2, 3	C 2, 4	N 2, 5	O 2, 6	F 2, 7	Ne 2, 8
3	Na 2, 8, 1	Mg 2, 8, 2	Al 2, 8, 3	Si 2, 8, 4	P 2, 8, 5	S 2, 8, 6	Cl 2, 8, 7	Ar 2, 8, 8
4	K 2, 8, 8, 1	Ca 2, 8, 8, 2	Sc 2, 8, 9, 2	—	—	—	—	—

Period 1. Start of first or K shell; finish of first shell: 2 elements.
Hydrogen starts the first shell, which can hold two electrons only, and so both the first shell and the first period are completed at helium which has the stable noble gas configuration K 2.

Period 2. Start of second or L shell; finish of second shell: 8 elements.
With the first element, lithium, a new shell starts, and the building up of this shell continues to the end of the period, where at neon 2, 8 both the second shell and the second period are completed. Again, a noble gas ends the shell, indicating the great stability of an octet of electrons in an external shell.

Period 3. Start of third or M shell; stable octet in third shell: 8 elements.
With the first element, a new shell is started, and the building up of this shell continues to the end of this period at argon, a noble gas with the electron configuration 2, 8, 8. But although the period is complete the M shell is *not*, since it can hold up to 18 electrons. Eight electrons in the outermost shell is always an extremely stable configuration. The M shell is said to be *temporarily complete* with eight electrons.

Period 4. Start of fourth or N shell; first two elements, K and Ca. Reference to Fig. 18, p. 54, gives an understanding of the electronic configuration of elements of Period 4, and subsequent periods. At argon the 3s and 3p orbitals are completed giving a stable octet. Fig. 18 shows an overlapping of the third and fourth electron shells, with a consequent reversal of the order of the energy levels of the 4s and 3d orbitals, the 4s energy level being lower than the 3d. Since electrons enter the available orbital of lowest energy, it follows that, in the next element, potassium, atomic number 19, the additional electron (the 19th) enters the 4s orbital, not a 3d, giving potassium the electronic configuration 2, 8, 8, 1. This explains the interruption at argon of the expected build-up of the M shell to its maximum of 18 electrons. In the next element calcium the additional electron enters and completes the 4s orbital, giving calcium the electronic configuration 2, 8, 8, 2.

Period 4 (continued). Third element starts the First Transition Series (10 elements.) Fig. 18 also shows that at scandium, atomic number 21, the available orbital of lowest energy is again a 3d; the additional electron therefore enters a 3d orbital giving scandium the configuration 2, 8, (8, 1), 2; that is, the building up of the 3rd (M) shell continues with scandium after its interruption with potassium. Since the 3d sub-shell can accommodate ten electrons (two in each of its five orbitals) the process of building up the 3d sub-shell proceeds to completion at zinc. The electronic configurations of the first twelve elements in Period 4 are as follows:

K	Ca	Sc	Ti
2, 8, 8, 1	2, 8, 8, 2	2, 8, (8, 1), 2	2, 8, (8, 2), 2
V	Cr	Mn	Fe
2, 8, (8, 3), 2	2, 8, (8, 5), 1	2, 8, (8, 5), 2	2, 8, (8, 6), 2
Co	Ni	Cu	Zn
2, 8, (8, 7), 2	2, 8, (8, 8), 2	2, 8, (8, 10), 1	2, 8, (8, 10), 2

These figures are based on the spectra and ionisation energies of the elements. Note that chromium and copper (like potassium) have only one electron in the N shell, while all the others have two. Note also that the atoms of the elements of the first transition series all have *two* outer shells incomplete except copper and zinc, whose M shells are complete.

The ten elements scandium to zinc which account for the filling of the five 3d orbitals, form the *first transition series*. Because of the similarity in the number of electrons in their external shell, these elements all have a marked similarity: they are all metals; all except scandium show a valency of two; because of the nearness in energy levels of the 3d and 4s electrons, all except zinc and scandium can make use of 3d electrons as well as 4s electrons in forming chemical bonds, i.e. all except zinc and scandium show variable valency. Their chemistry therefore depends on the fact that they have two outer electron shells incomplete (with the exceptions noted), i.e. they can draw on two shells for valency electrons. They are the first horizontal series of elements to show a marked similarity throughout the series. They will be discussed more fully later.

Period 4 (concluded). Last six elements see the completion of the M shell. From Fig. 18 it is seen that after the completion of the $3d$ orbitals, the next ones to be filled are the $4p$ orbitals. The electronic configurations of the remaining six elements of the period are therefore:

Ga	Ge	As	Se	Br	Kr
2, 8, 18, 3	2, 8, 18, 4	2, 8, 18, 5	2, 8, 18, 6	2, 8, 18, 7	2, 8, 18, 8

In each of these elements the M shell has its full complement of 18 electrons, and the electrons in the outermost N shell are therefore the only valency electrons of these elements. The N shell is now temporarily completed with the stable octet at the noble gas krypton. These six elements, along with potassium and calcium at the beginning of Period 4, are therefore Main Group elements. They show the expected periodicity of properties from potassium to krypton, and also the expected strong family resemblances to elements above and below them in the same Group.

The energy level diagram required for the remaining periods becomes somewhat crowded, so it is easier at this stage to use a list of the orbitals in the order in which they are filled, that is in the order of increasing energy levels. The order is

$1s$,	$2s, 2p$,	$3s, 3p$,	$4s, 3d, 4p$,	$5s, 4d, 5p$,	$6s, 5d, 4f, 5d, 6p$,	$7s, 6d, 5f$
Period 1	Period 2	Period 3	Period 4	Period 5	Period 6	Period 7

Note that each period begins with two elements in which electrons enter the s orbital with the same number as the period. The order in which orbitals are filled can be indicated compactly for all the elements in the outline Periodic Table (on p. 61).

Period 5. Start of new shell, the fifth or O shell; second transition series; temporary completion of new shell. The building-up process in this period is almost the same as that in Period 4, but some slight differences occur in the transition series (see table on pp. 612–13).

It is seen that the table on p. 61 can be divided vertically into three blocks: the *s-block*, Groups IA and IIA; the *d-block*, Groups IIIA to IIB (transition metals); and the *p-block*, Groups IIIB to 0. The lanthanides and actinides (inner-transition metals) may be called the *f-block*.

Order in which sub-shells in atoms are filled

Period		IA	IIA		IIIA	IVA	VA	VIA	VIIA	VIII	IB	IIB		IIIB	IVB	VB	VIB	VIIB	0
		Main Group elements — s orbitals filling			Transition elements — d orbitals filling									Main Group elements — p orbitals filling					
1	1s	1 H																	2 He
2	2s	3 Li	4 Be										2p	5 B	6 C	7 N	8 O	9 F	10 Ne
3	3s	11 Na	12 Mg										3p	13 Al	14 Si	15 P	16 S	17 Cl	18 Ar
4	4s			3d	Sc	Ti						Zn	4p						
5	5s			4d	Y	Zr						Cd	5p						
6	6s			5d	57 La*	72 Hf						Hg	6p						
7	7s			6d	89 Ac†														

s-block d-block p-block

* Lanthanides, 4f orbitals filling Ce → Lu.
† Actinides, 5f orbitals filling Th → 105.

Period 6. Start of sixth or P shell. In this period the building-up process is similar to that in Periods 4 and 5, in that there is a transition series of ten elements starting in a similar place with the element lanthanum and finishing with mercury. But the building-up of this series is interrupted immediately after lanthanum by a transition series within a transition series, that is, an inner transition series. This inner series consists of the fourteen rare-earth metals or lanthanides. These elements account for the building up of the seven orbitals of the $4f$ sub-group, a process which starts with cerium and finishes with lutetium. Note that all the rare-earth metals have *three* incomplete electron shells, except ytterbium (atomic number 70) and lutetium (atomic number 71) which have two (see table, p. 613). The chemistry of the lanthanides is largely determined by the fact that they all have atoms with two electrons in the outermost shell (the sixth), and one other readily detachable $4f$ or $5d$ electron. In consequence these elements are remarkably similar: their most stable and common valency is a positive electrovalency of three. They are all highly electropositive metals with chemical properties resembling calcium, and, for those of higher atomic number, aluminium.

Period 7. Start of seventh or Q shell. The building-up of electron shells in this period follows closely that in Period 6. Here again a transition series begins with the third element in the period actinium. Again, there is an interruption of this series by an inner transition series, the actinides, in which the $5f$ orbitals are being filled. This inner transition series is completed after sixteen elements at hahnium, the last element to be discovered so far.

It is clear from the foregoing account that the number of electrons in the valency shells of the elements changes periodically with increase in atomic number.

Relation between electronic configuration and valency of the elements

General. (1) The chemical properties of the elements depend on the number and arrangement of the electrons used in the formation of chemical bonds. These electrons are called *valency electrons*.

(2) Valency electrons are usually found in electron shells which are incomplete.

(3) For Main Group elements, the valency electrons are found only in the external electron shell. The inner shells are either completely filled,

e.g. the K shell with 2 electrons, the L shell with 8; or temporarily complete with 8, e.g. the M shell in potassium, which has the configuration 2, 8, 8, 1.

(4) For most transition elements, the valency electrons are found in *two* shells: the external shell, and the penultimate shell whose *d*-electrons are often used in chemical reactions. But the *s* and *p* electrons in the penultimate shell are not used since together they form a stable octet.

(5) For inner transition elements (the lanthanides and the actinides) three incomplete shells are usually present. Some of their electronic configurations are, however, provisional. Actinides are able to use more *f* electrons in bonding than lanthanides.

(6) No uncombined atom ever has more than 8 electrons in its external shell.

Relation between electronic configuration and valency in the Periods (Main Group elements). Take for example Period 3, considering here only the lower valencies of phosphorus, sulphur, and chlorine:

Period 3	Element	Na	Mg	Al	Si	P	S	Cl	Ar
	Valency	1+	2+	3+	4	3	2−	1−	0
	Electronic configuration	2, 8, 1	2, 8, 2	2, 8, 3	2, 8, 4	2, 8, 5	2, 8, 6	2, 8, 7	2, 8, 8

The stable configuration for each of these atoms is an outermost shell of 8 electrons. The least energy change to achieve this configuration with sodium is the removal of one electron, leaving a sodium ion Na^+. Thus sodium has a positive valency of 1. Similarly magnesium has a valency of $2+$, and aluminium $3+$. With silicon the least energy change is the formation of four covalencies resulting in a stable octet. With phosphorus the octet is formed by making three covalent bonds. Sulphur can form two electrovalencies by gaining two electrons to form the octet, and by so doing the sulphur atom is converted into a sulphur ion S^{2-}. Sulphur may also form two covalencies. Chlorine gains 1 electron and therefore shows a negative electrovalency of 1: $Cl + e \rightarrow Cl^-$. Argon already possesses an octet, and therefore shows little or no tendency to chemical combination. Its valency is 0.

The same types of behaviour with modifications are found in the other Periods of the Main Group elements.

The Main Group elements (except H, N, O, F and the noble gases) also show a valency sequence 1, 2, 3, 4, 5, 6, 7, the same as the Group numbers.

Relation between electronic configuration and valency in the Main Groups. In every element in Group IA, for example, the external (valency) shell has only 1 electron, therefore all these elements show a positive electrovalency of 1.

Group IA	Electronic configuration
Li	2, 1
Na	2, 8, 1
K	2, 8, 8, 1
Rb	2, 8, 18, 8, 1
Cs	2, 8, 18, 18, 8, 1

This indeed is the fundamental fact which determines their great chemical similarity. The differences between them are accounted for by other atomic properties. The same broad considerations apply to the other Main Groups.

Atomic radii

The atomic radius of an uncombined atom cannot be defined strictly because of the uncertain boundary of electron clouds. But the distance between the nuclei of chemically combined atoms can be measured accurately. The (non-polar covalent) atomic radius of an element is defined as half the internuclear distance in the element when the bonds between atoms are single. A related but not identical quantity, confined to metals, is the metallic radius, which is defined as half the internuclear distance between atoms which are nearest neighbours in a metallic crystal.

Metallic radius is always greater than covalent atomic radius by an average of about $\frac{1}{8}$.

When the experimentally determined values of the atomic radii of the elements are plotted against their atomic numbers the graph shown in Fig. 19 is obtained. It is immediately clear that the graph rises and falls in a periodic manner, that is it has well-defined maxima and minima at regular though not necessarily equal intervals. But this in itself is not enough. In order that a periodic graph shall fit the Periodic Table it is essential that the periods in the graph should coincide at least broadly with the periods in the table. It is seen from the labelling at the top of the figure that this requirement also is fully met. It may therefore be concluded that this graph is another example of the truth of the Periodic Law which states that the properties of the elements are periodic functions of their atomic numbers.

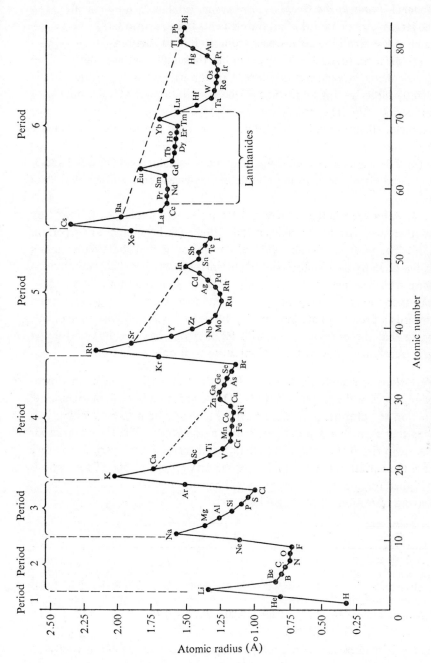

Fig. 19. Atomic radius in periods.

General trends in the Graph. (1) *Maxima.* (*a*) The alkali metal atom has the largest atomic radius of all the elements in each period. (*b*) The atomic radii of the alkali metals increase from lithium to caesium.

(2) *Minima.* (*a*) The halogen atom has the smallest atomic radius of all the elements in each period, except in the case of iodine which has a slightly larger radius than some of the transition metals in the middle of its period. (*b*) The transition metals are grouped round their own characteristic minima in the graph. (*c*) The radii of the halogens increase from fluorine to iodine.

(3) There is a curved fall from alkali metal to halogen in Periods 2 and 3, and from alkali metal to the middle of the transition metals in Periods 4 and 5.

(4) After each halogen there is a steep rise to a noble gas, followed by another steep rise to the alkali metal at the peak beginning a new period.

(5) The most remarkable general conclusion is that the largest atomic radius (2.35 Å for caesium) is only eight times the smallest (0.32 Å for hydrogen), while the largest atomic number is more than 100 times the smallest, and therefore, with increasing atomic number, there is no general trend towards a proportionate increase in atomic radius, a good example of this being that the uranium atom with 92 electrons has a radius of 1.42 Å; very nearly the same as the lithium atom with only 3 electrons.

Variations of atomic radii in the Periods. Comparing the main downward slopes of the graph in Periods 2, 3, 4 and 5, that is, lithium to fluorine, sodium to chlorine, potassium to iron, and rubidium to ruthenium, it is seen that there is a marked parallelism among them. The same is true for the steep rise from halogen to alkali metal seen in every period. In every case the variation is periodic in nature. An account of one of the periods will therefore be sufficient here. It will be convenient to consider Period 2, leaving transition elements till later.

Period 2	Li	Be	B	C	N	O	F	Ne
Atomic no.	3	4	5	6	7	8	9	10
Nuclear charge	3+	4+	5+	6+	7+	8+	9+	10+
Electronic configuration	2, 1	2, 2	2, 3	2, 4	2, 5	2, 6	2, 7	2, 8
Atomic radius (Å)	1.33	0.89	0.80	0.77	0.74	0.74	0.72	1.1

There is a decrease in radius from lithium to fluorine followed by an increase to neon (see Fig. 19, p. 65). A rough explanation of these facts may be outlined using Fig. 20 (*a*). The nuclear charge of the lithium atom is 3+. Consider the attraction of this nuclear charge on each of the two electrons in the K shell, and the repulsion of each electron on the other.

If the radius of the K shell is 1 unit, the attractive force is $(3 \times 1)/1^2 = 3$ force-units. Since the distance between the two electrons is 2 units, the force of repulsion between them is $(1 \times 1)/2^2 = \frac{1}{4}$ force-unit. The resultant attractive force is therefore roughly $2\frac{3}{4}$ units. This is equivalent to saying that the *effective nuclear charge* acting on the two K electrons is roughly $2\frac{3}{4}+$. In passing along the Period, each element has a nuclear charge of one more than its predecessor, so the electrons in the K shell are pulled closer and closer to the nucleus.

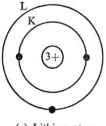

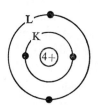

(*a*) Lithium atom. (*b*) Beryllium atom.

Fig. 20

Consider now the force acting on the single electron in the L shell of the lithium atom. This electron does not experience the full attraction of the nuclear charge because between the L shell and the nucleus there is a screen of the two *s* electrons in the completed K shell. These electrons have a spherically symmetrical field with the nucleus as centre, and therefore act as if they were situated at the centre. The nuclear charge is therefore reduced by two, giving an effective nuclear charge acting on the L electron of about 1+, almost two less than that on the electrons in the K shell. The result is that the L electron takes up a position in an orbit much further from the nucleus than the K shell, as shown in Fig. 20 (*a*). The effect of the two intervening electrons may be called a primary *screening effect*, to distinguish it from the reduction in effective nuclear charge caused by repulsion between electrons in the same shell, which is a secondary screening effect.

In the beryllium atom (Fig. 20 (*b*)) the nuclear charge is increased by one unit to 4+. The primary screening effect causes a reduction in nuclear charge of two as before. But there are now 2 electrons in the valency shell, and their mutual repulsion causes a secondary screening effect which, as in the K shell, reduces the nuclear charge by about $\frac{1}{4}$. The effective nuclear charge is therefore roughly $(4-2\frac{1}{4}) = 1\frac{3}{4}+$. The 2 electrons in the L shell are therefore pulled closer to the nucleus than the 1 electron in the L shell of the lithium atom. The beryllium atom is therefore smaller than the lithium atom.

In passing along the Period the primary screening effect remains unchanged, the nuclear charge increases by increments of $1+$, but the secondary screening effect increases steadily with increasing numbers of electrons in the valency shell. The overall result is that the effective nuclear charge continues to increase, but by a smaller amount with each new element. The atomic radius therefore continues to decrease in passing along the Period, but by a smaller and smaller amount, until the decrease in radius is almost halted, as the figures for nitrogen, oxygen, and fluorine show; and indeed with the last element neon the trend is reversed, and the radius increases substantially, because the noble gases are monatomic, and the internuclear distance between their atoms is the distance between non-bonded atoms held together by weak van der Waals' forces.

The same trends are found in Period 3 for similar reasons.

Variation of atomic radii in the Groups (non-periodic). In Fig. 21 the atomic radii of the elements arranged in Groups (omitting transition elements) have been plotted against atomic number. These graphs show clearly that in all these Groups the atomic radii increase with atomic number. The parallelism between the Groups is striking. It will therefore be sufficient at this stage to consider only one Group in detail, Group IA.

Atomic no.	Nuclear charge	Electronic configuration	Atomic radius (Å)	For comparison atomic radii of the noble gases	
Li 3	$3+$	2, 1	1.33	He	0.8
Na 11	$11+$	2, 8, 1	1.57	Ne	1.1
K 19	$19+$	2, 8, 8, 1	2.03	Ar	1.5
Rb 37	$37+$	2, 8, 18, 8, 1	2.16	Kr	1.7
Cs 55	$55+$	2, 8, 18, 18, 8, 1	2.35	Xe	1.9

There is a significant and fairly regular increase in radius from lithium to caesium. The essential point in the explanation of this trend is that a new electron shell starts with each element in the group, and this new shell must be at a greater distance from the nucleus than the outside shell of the preceding element, a noble gas. In lithium for example the atomic radius of 1.33 Å is about 0.5 Å larger than the helium atom of 0.8 Å; and with the other members of the Group the increase is almost the same. Because the radii of the noble gases increase from helium to xenon there must be an increase in the radii of the alkali metal atoms from lithium to caesium.

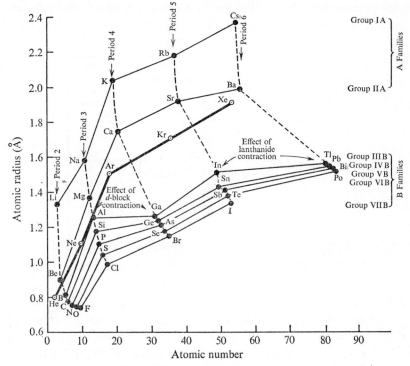

Fig. 21. Atomic radii in Main Groups.

The great increase in nuclear charge in passing down the Group is more than offset by the primary and secondary screening effects of the correspondingly increased number of electrons; i.e. the effective nuclear charge acting on the single valency electron decreases down the Group. A similar explanation holds for the other Groups.

The broad relationship so far discussed may be summarised as in Fig. 22. When Fig. 22 is compared with Fig. 1 (ch. 1, p. 13) an inverse relationship between atomic radius and electronegativity is seen. *Note*: A rough quantitative measure of electronegativity is got from the relationship

$$\text{electronegativity} = \frac{\text{effective nuclear charge}}{\text{covalent atomic radius}}.$$

69

Referring again to Fig. 21, p. 69, it is seen that the graphs fall into two classes, those of the A families and those of the B. In the B families it is seen that there is a much greater difference between the first and second elements than between any succeeding pair. The first element in each B Group is therefore anomalous, that is, unique in its Group in some respects since atomic radius is found to be closely related to chemical and physical properties. Taking Group IIIB as an example, the reason is that

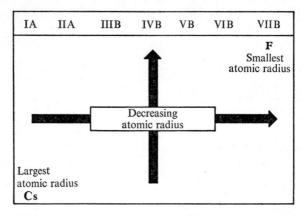

Fig. 22. Trends in atomic radius in Main Group elements.

aluminium follows immediately after magnesium in Period 3 whereas gallium in Period 4 comes after a transition series, so that ten transition metals intervene between gallium and calcium. In passing along these ten elements there is, as usual, a net *decrease* in atomic radius which reduces the atomic radius of Ga to that of Al. This effect is therefore the result of the *d-block contraction* in atomic radius. Further along the Group IIIB graph there is another significant flattening between indium and thallium, which is accounted for in the same way as before: in Period 6 there appears a series of fourteen inner transition metals, the lanthanides, which have no parallel in Period 5. These cause a *lanthanide contraction* similar in origin to the *d*-block contraction.

In the A familes the case is different. In Group IIA, for example, the increase from Be to Mg is not much more than from Mg to Ca, but the increase from Ca to Sr is much less. The reason is the same as for B families: Sr follows the first transition series, and so the *d*-block contraction reduces its atomic radius also.

Electronegativity

So far, the terms electropositive and electronegative have been used qualitatively to describe metallic elements and non-metal elements respectively. Although both terms are useful, it is desirable for the purpose of formulating a roughly quantitative scale to use only one. The term chosen is electronegativity, which is defined by Pauling *as the power of an atom in a molecule to attract electrons to itself.* In sodium chloride, for example, the chlorine atom has a much stronger attraction for electrons than the sodium atom, with the result that the valency electron of the sodium atom is pulled almost completely into the valency shell of the chlorine atom against the attraction of the sodium atom. Chlorine is therefore strongly electronegative, sodium wealky electronegative. The most electronegative element is fluorine. It is given an arbitrary value of about 4 on the electronegativity scale. Caesium, the least electronegative element, is given a low value of about 0.8. All the values are positive. There are several ways of calculating electronegativities one of the simplest being from the formula:

$$\text{electronegativity} = \frac{\text{effective nuclear charge}}{\text{covalent atomic radius}},$$

i.e. electronegativity is directly proportional to effective nuclear charge and inversely proportional to atomic radius. All methods give results which agree fairly well with each other, but all are somewhat arbitrary, for example electronegativities must vary somewhat with the valency being exerted. Nevertheless, the values obtained are of great use. At the very least the electronegativity scale may be regarded as a good working hypothesis and used as such.

Using the values calculated by Allred and Rochow, the graph of electronegativity against atomic number for all elements up to astatine has been drawn in Fig. 23. Periodicity is clear, and follows the same general pattern as with standard electrode potentials (p. 154).

In Fig. 24 graphs have been drawn showing the variation of electronegativity in the Main Groups. A comparison with Fig. 21, p. 69 (atomic radius), shows a remarkable similarity. (But note that the scale of electronegativity is drawn increasing downwards to make comparison easier.) The electronegativity graphs give a much more detailed picture of Group trends than has been given so far, although the broad conclusions already reached need little alteration.

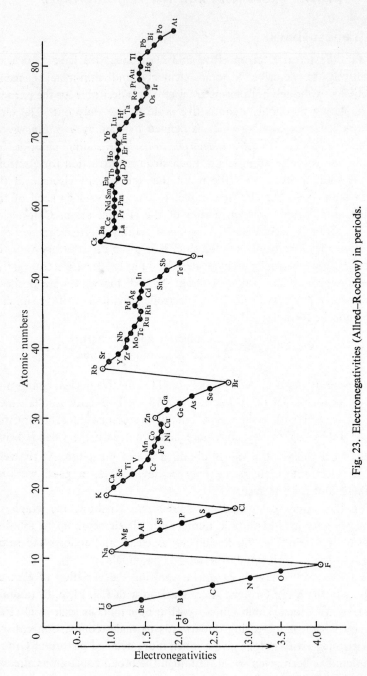

Fig. 23. Electronegativities (Allred–Rochow) in periods.

The most significant features are:

(1) The first element in each of the B families stands apart from all other members of its Group, because it is much more electronegative. This important fact accounts for much of the difference between its chemistry and the other members of its Group.

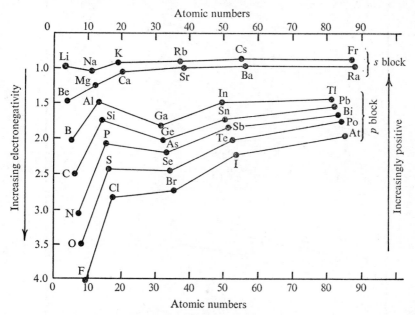

Fig. 24. Electronegativity plotted against atomic number (Main Group elements).

(2) A curious reversal of the Group trends of decreasing electronegativity with increasing atomic number is shown by the third member in each B family up to VIB. This is a result of the *d*-block contraction.

(3) There is little decrease in electronegativity from potassium to francium, or from calcium to radium.

Ionic radii

Most inorganic solids consist of ions. It is therefore important to know their sizes. X-ray analysis of ionic crystals gives an accurate value of the distances between the centres of ions (which are assumed to be spherical and in contact). From these internuclear distances tables of ionic radii have been drawn up. They have proved most valuable but not infallible. Three cautions are necessary:

73

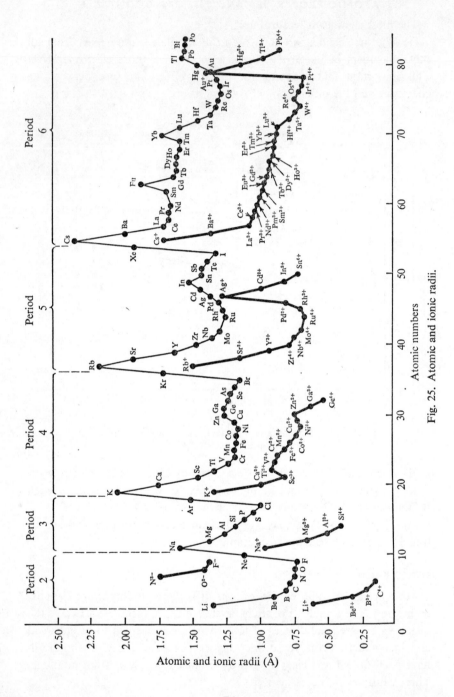

Fig. 25. Atomic and ionic radii.

(1) The size of an ion increases a little with its co-ordination number.

(2) When anions tend to be in contact with each other (as well as with cations) their mutual repulsions cause some distortion.

(3) The ionic radius of a metal gives inaccurate results when used in compounds having considerable covalent character, e.g. silver iodide.

Figure 25, p. 74, shows ionic radii plotted against atomic numbers for all the elements up to lead. Atomic radii are reproduced on the same sheet for comparison. Radii for some hypothetical ions, e.g. C^{4+} and Si^{4+}, have been included.

Trends in ionic radii in the periods. Ionic radii, like atomic radii, vary periodically with atomic number. There is a well-marked parallelism between the two sets of radii, which extends to the anions with this difference: the anions are much larger than the corresponding atoms, while the cations are usually much smaller. The explanation of the trends in atomic radii applies also to the very similar trends in ionic radii.

In Period 4 the bivalent cations from Ti^{2+} to Zn^{2+} show a d-block contraction similar to but larger than the corresponding contraction in atomic radius. The same is true of the lanthanide contraction for the trivalent cations La^{3+} to Lu^{3+} in Period 6.

Trends in ionic radii in the Main Groups. These are shown in Fig. 26. The graphs of ionic radii are similar to those of atomic radii (p. 69). In both, the graphs fall into two classes, A families and B families. In A families the first two members of each Group stand apart from the rest of the Group, while in B families only the first member stands apart. The reasons for the trends are the same in both sets (p. 70).

Relation between ionic and atomic radii. All cations are smaller than the neutral atoms from which they are formed (the only exception is Au^+), e.g. Na 1.57 Å, Na^+ 0.97 Å. The reason is that in the formation of cations, electrons in the external shells of atoms have been stripped off, while the nuclear charge remains the same, and so the effective nuclear charge has increased. All anions are larger than the corresponding neutral atoms because electrons have been added to complete the external shell, and although the nuclear charge remains unchanged the effective nuclear charge has decreased, e.g. Cl 0.99 Å, Cl^- 1.81 Å. Anions are always larger than cations except in RbF and CsF (AuF does not exist).

For a metal, the size of the cation decreases with increasing ionic charge, e.g. Mn, 1.17; Mn^{2+}, 0.80; Mn^{3+}, 0.66; Mn^{4+}, 0.52; Mn^{7+}, 0.46 Å.

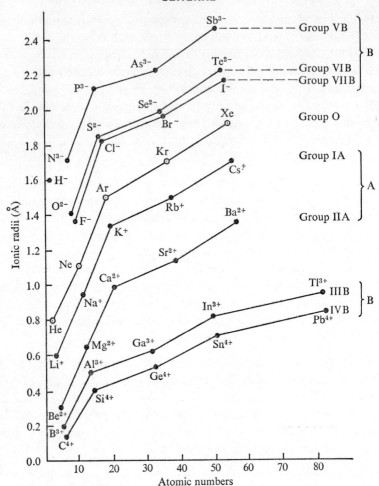

Fig. 26. Ionic radii (co-ordination no. 6) in the Main Groups.

Summary of trends in Main Groups

See Figs. 21, 24, and 26; also diagram on p. 77.

s-Block elements (1 A, II A). The *first two* elements stand apart from the rest of the Group because of their much lower atomic radii, higher electronegativities, and much lower ionic radii. The last three (or four) show a marked resemblance to each other and a steady trend.

p-Block elements (III B, IV B, V B, VI B, VII B). The *first* element stands apart from the others for the same reasons. But note that electronegativities show a significant reversal of trend with the third element in all B Groups (except VIIB).

All breaks in trend in the graphs are caused by the *d*-block and lanthanide contractions in atomic and ionic radii.

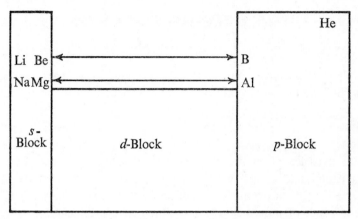

Note. There is no gap between Be and B, or Mg and Al.

Exercises

1. From memory, write in a vertical column the symbols of the Main Group elements: neon, silicon, boron, selenium, calcium, phosphorus, potassium, bromine. Alongside give their Group, Period, electronic configuration, atomic number, Group valencies and class (metal or non-metal).

2. From memory, complete the following table for Main Group elements of atomic number 3, 50, 33, 7, 38, 9, 13.

Atomic no.	Electronic configuration	Group	Period	Name	Class

3. Most of the common and economically important metals are transition elements. Explain the origin of the first transition series in terms of energy levels of electrons.

4. Give the meaning of the terms *s*-, *d*-, and *p*-blocks; *d*-block contraction, lanthanide contraction, covalent atomic radius, metallic radius. Give examples of each.

5. Discuss the relationship between the electronic structures of atoms and the modern form of the Periodic Table. In particular show how (i) families of elements, (ii) the short periods and (iii) the first long period, including the transition elements, are accounted for. Mendeléeff arranged the elements in ascending order of atomic weight; mention one pair of elements whose order had to be inverted to avoid a break in periodicity when this basis was used for classification. The helium family is now usually described as the **noble gases** rather than **inert gases**. Why has this change been made? (O)

6

THE DRIVING FORCE OF
CHEMICAL REACTIONS

The physical universe consists of matter and energy. These are interconvertible and indestructible; the total energy content of the universe is
constant.

Matter and energy are not continuous, but consist of discrete particles
separated by empty space. For the chemist the most important fundamental particles of matter are electrons, protons and neutrons. The
fundamental particles of energy are called *quanta*. All change in the
universe consists of the movement of particles in space. Chemical changes
are the result of movements and resulting rearrangements of electrons,
protons, and energy quanta.

Orderly movement of particles in fields of force

Space is permeated by fields of force: gravitational, electrostatic and
magnetic. This discussion of the causes of chemical change starts from the
statement that the universe in one of its aspects consists of particles or
collections of particles moving mechanically in fields of force. All masses
attract each other gravitationally; opposite magnetic poles attract; so do
particles carrying opposite electrostatic charges. Since matter is electrically
neutral overall, the total of positive charges equals the total of negative.
Consider a mixture of equal numbers of sodium ions, Na^+, and chloride
ions, Cl^-, separated from each other and mixed in random fashion. Each
positive ion attracts round itself as many negative ions as possible; each
negative ion attracts as many positive ions. The result is the formation
of a crystal of sodium chloride, held compactly together by powerful
electrostatic forces. It follows that there is a universal tendency for all
particles to move as close to each other as possible under the influence of
attractive fields of force, and thereby to achieve positions of minimum
potential energy; potential energy being energy of position in a field of
force. The potential energy lost when particles move towards each other
is converted into an equivalent amount of kinetic energy or radiant energy.

All particles in a field of force move in the same direction, i.e. in an orderly collective movement, and for this reason can be harnessed for the performance of mechanical work. Energy available for doing work is called *free energy*. A well-known large scale example of this process is the conversion of the potential energy of water in a high level reservoir into mechanical work either directly or by way of the generation of electricity.

Figure 27 shows the same kind of process in a simpler case.

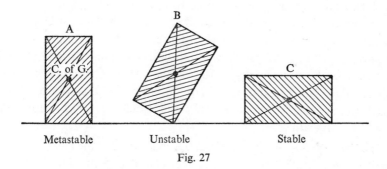

Fig. 27

If sufficient activation energy is supplied to the body in position A, it will move through position B to position C in which its centre of gravity is in the lowest possible position, a position of minimum potential energy, i.e. maximum stability.

The same principle applies to electrons in atoms: an electron tends to take up a position as close to the positively charged nucleus as possible, and in moving from an outer orbital to an inner one of lower potential energy (in an electrostatic field), the potential energy lost is transformed into a quantum of radiant energy which is emitted. Another example is the formation of an ion-pair, Na^+Cl^-, by reaction between an atom of sodium and an atom of chlorine, during which an electron is pulled out of the sodium atom into the chlorine by the greater attractive force of the nucleus of the chlorine, and the resulting ions are held together by electrostatic attraction. Again the resulting system is one of minimum potential energy, and again the loss in potential energy is converted into another form, this time heat, i.e. the reaction is exothermic.

Chemical reactions usually occur at constant pressure, often atmospheric, and may be accompanied by volume changes. The *heat content* of a system is represented by the symbol H. Changes in heat content, ΔH, (enthalpy) resulting from chemical reactions at constant pressure are measured by the quantity of heat liberated or absorbed in the reaction.

ΔH = (sum of the heat contents of the products) – (sum of the heat contents of the reactants).

If heat is liberated, the products have a *lower* heat content than the reactants. ΔH is therefore negative for exothermic reactions, positive for endothermic. In other words, a negative value for ΔH means that the *system* has lost heat to its surroundings. An important type of reaction is the heat of formation of a compound from its elements.

The standard heat of formation $\Delta H_f^\ominus$ is the quantity of heat liberated or absorbed when one mole of a chemical compound is formed from its elements; reactants and products all being in the standard state of 25 °C and 1 atmosphere pressure. The heat contents of the chemical elements in this standard state are taken as zero. In chemistry, quantity of heat is usually measured in kilocalories (kcal), or kilojoules (kJ) (1 kJ = 10^3 J, and 4.184 kJ = 1 kcal).

The small circle $\ominus$ in the symbol $\Delta H_f^\ominus$ indicates that the measurement is made under standard conditions. H_f means heat of formation.

Rule 1. Particles or bodies in fields of force tend to move as close together as possible, and thereby take up positions of minimum potential energy. The energy liberated in the process is available for doing mechanical work.

This tendency does not account for all chemical reactions. If it did all would be exothermic. One other fundamental tendency is required. It is of an opposite kind.

It was stated earlier that all particles are in a state of motion. This motion is perpetual, universal, rapid and in gases random. The kinetic theory of gases starts from this statement. In solids the motion consists of vibrations about a mean position in the crystal lattice, but the energy is still kinetic.

The inherent spontaneous random motion of particles (independent of fields of force)

A represents a box divided into two equal compartments. The gas in the left compartment is at greater pressure than that in the right. Now let the partition be removed. The number of molecules of gas moving from L to R will be greater than the number moving from R to L because of the greater number of molecules initially present in L. This will remain true until the molecules are uniformly distributed throughout the whole box as in B, when a state of dynamic equilibrium is reached.

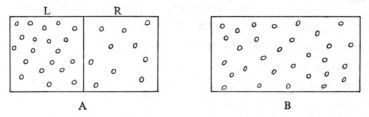

A   B

There is a fundamental difference between A and B. During the transition from A to B an overall movement of molecules from A to B takes place. This movement can be made to do work in the same way as the movement of particles in a field of force. In fact if the partition in A was gas-tight, movable, and frictionless it would behave like the piston in the cylinder of an engine. In B the case is entirely different: the movement of molecules continues, but has no overall component in any direction; there is no pressure difference on the sides of a partition placed across the box at any point, so no work can be done. The molecules in B are more mixed up or disordered than in A. This spontaneous increase in disorder in passing from system A to system B is an example of the second universal tendency needed to explain chemical and physical changes. The first tendency produces order, e.g. crystals of sodium chloride from crystals of sodium and chlorine gas, the second disorder; but the systems produced by both tendencies have lost some or all of their capacity for doing work, in the first case because the system is at a minimum of potential energy, in the second because it is at a maximum of kinetic disorder.

An obvious example of order is a pack of cards separated into suits each arranged in order of value. Shuffling produces disorder; the longer the shuffling the greater the disorder, as a rule. It is possible that continued shuffling would produce the original ordered state, but so improbable that the possibility can be ignored. If this is so with fifty-two cards, the probability that the spontaneous mixing of millions of molecules of say four different kinds will result in their orderly arrangement is so remote as to be negligible. It is clear that there is no natural tendency for un-mixing to take place. The statement that molecules mix spontaneously because of their random kinetic motion is therefore intelligible.

The disorder of a system is called its *entropy*, denoted by S. ΔS denotes change in entropy. Entropy is not a vague subjective concept, but an accurately measurable physical quantity as objective as length, specific heat or specific latent heat. Indeed it is measured in units involving some of the factors used in the last two of these: Joules per Kelvin or JK^{-1}.

Rule 2. Because of their inherent kinetic energies, particles tend spontaneously towards a state of maximum disorder. This movement can be harnessed to perform work, as is done in heat engines.

The tendencies stated in the two rules given above both produce systems in which available energy is lost by the system, therefore in both, the unavailable energy tends to a minimum. They are, however, opposite in nature since the first produces order among the particles, a decrease of entropy; the second produces disorder, an increase of entropy.

Entropy is a large subject. All that can be done here is to assume the truth of the equation now to be stated in terms of symbols, two of which have been given.

$$\Delta G \quad = \quad \Delta H \quad - \quad T\Delta S. \tag{1}$$

| change in free or available energy | change in total energy | change in unavailable energy |

Assuming the truth of the statement already given that the unit in which entropy is measured is JK^{-1} it is clear that the energy involved in a change of entropy ΔS at a temperature T is $T\Delta S$, the third term in the equation. The negative sign connecting the terms on the right-hand side indicates that the quantities symbolised are opposite in nature. G is the *free energy* of the system.

In equation (1), when ΔS is zero, $\Delta G = \Delta H$. If a reaction in which there is no entropy change is to take place spontaneously there must be a reduction in potential energy, in which case the action is exothermic, ΔH is negative and so therefore is ΔG.

When ΔH is zero, $\Delta G = -T\Delta S$. If a reaction in which there is no change in potential energy is to take place spontaneously, there must be an increase in entropy, that is ΔS must be positive and ΔG must therefore be negative as before.

An endothermic reaction, ΔH positive, can take place only if there is an increase in entropy such that the value of $T\Delta S$ is greater than that of ΔH, when again ΔG is negative.

The driving force of chemical reactions

Conclusion. *Chemical reactions at constant pressure take place only if they result in a decrease in the free energy of the system, that is in a negative value for ΔG.*

Melting of a solid involves the breaking up of an orderly arrangement of particles in a crystal lattice, and a consequent increase in entropy. An even greater increase in entropy results during evaporation or sublimation because of the great increase in volume and resulting disorder of particles in the vapour phase. This explains why the evaporation of water is a spontaneous process even though an endothermic one.

An example of a chemical reaction which is driven by increase in entropy (ΔH is virtually zero) is the isotopic exchange reaction between water and heavy water (deuterium oxide)

$$H_2O + D_2O \rightleftharpoons 2HOD.$$

HOD molecules are less symmetrical than H_2O or D_2O molecules. The forward reaction takes place because it results in an increase in entropy and therefore in a negative value for ΔG.

Equation (1) shows also that at low temperatures the effect of the term $T\Delta S$ will diminish, and at absolute zero it will be zero. All substances at or near absolute zero will have little or no disorder, in other words they will be crystalline solids. It is found that at ordinary temperatures the entropy term is often of little importance. As the temperature increases its influence becomes increasingly important because of the increasing kinetic energy of the molecules. Vigorous collisions between molecules of compounds will result in the breaking of bonds, and so increase in temperature results in decomposition of compounds into molecules of their elements, of molecules into atoms and eventually of atoms into electrons and atomic nuclei at very high temperatures.

Tables of free energies of formation for large numbers of substances over a wide range of temperature have been compiled. They are of great use in explaining and systematising chemical reactions, in predicting their probable course, and in stating that in certain cases reaction is impossible under certain conditions. Considerable use will be made of free energies in the chapter on the extraction of the metals (pp. 181–6).

Activation energy

Figure 27 shows a mechanical example of the need for activation energy in initiating a change from a metastable state to a stable one. The same need is found in most chemical reactions, which, although energetically possible and even favoured, often do not take place at all at ordinary temperatures. They have to be 'sparked off' by addition of a relatively small amount of energy. A mixture of two volumes hydrogen and one volume oxygen shows no sign of combination until a flame or spark is applied to it. Spontaneous combustion of any substance is fortunately rare.

Consider, for example, the formation of hydrogen iodide from its elements:

$$H_2 + I_2 \rightarrow 2HI.$$

When a hydrogen molecule and an iodine molecule approach each other closely, forces of repulsion between their electron clouds come into play and tend to force the molecules apart. If the kinetic energies of approach of the molecules are sufficient, the energy barrier may be overcome sufficiently for an intermediate unstable complex structure to be formed. This structure is called an *activated complex*. During this process there is a gradual increase of potential energy of the system and an equivalent decrease in its kinetic energy; this decrease is the activation energy of the reaction. Rearrangements of the electrons in the activated complex then take place bringing about a progressive loosening of the original bonds in the hydrogen and iodine molecules and formation of new ones between hydrogen and iodine atoms, the two processes taking place simultaneously. The net result is a release of energy greater than the activation energy, and a breaking up of the complex into two molecules of hydrogen iodide, which move off with renewed kinetic energies. These reactions are indicated thus:

$$
\begin{array}{ccc}
\text{H} \quad \text{I} & \text{H}\cdots\text{I} & \text{H—I} \\
| \quad | \;\rightarrow\; & \vdots \quad \vdots \;\rightarrow\; & \\
\text{H} \quad \text{I} & \text{H}\cdots\text{I} & \text{H—I} \\
& \text{activated} & \\
& \text{complex} &
\end{array}
$$

The energy-level diagram in Fig. 28 shows the general case. The reaction co-ordinate shows the state of the reaction at each of its stages.

A catalyst speeds up a reaction because it forms with the reactants an activated complex by a process in which less activation energy is absorbed. The complex breaks up liberating the catalyst and the reaction products.

84

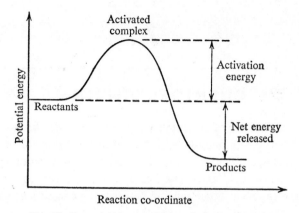

Fig. 28. Potential energy changes during a reaction.

Exercises

1. Write notes on heat content, entropy, free energy, activation energy.

2. Give equations for a few endothermic reactions and state the conditions necessary. How is it possible for such reactions to take place?

3. Summarise this chapter.

4. What do you understand by the terms *free energy*, *enthalpy* and *entropy*? What is the relationship between the standard free energy change, the standard enthalpy change and the standard entropy change in a chemical reaction?

In the reaction $$C_2H_4 + H_2 \rightleftharpoons C_2H_6$$

the activation energies of the forward and reverse reactions are 41 kcal mole^{-1} and 73 kcal mole^{-1} respectively. Explain how these two quantities are related to the enthalpy change of the reaction. (O & CS)

7

CHEMICAL BINDING

A most useful method of systematising chemistry is the broad classification of elements and compounds according to the nature of the bonding into *electrovalent, covalent* and *metallic* types. All substances of a particular type show certain distinctive features which are a consequence of the nature of the chemical bond existing between the constituent particles of the element or compound.

Why atoms combine

Inanimate objects tend to change to the state in which they are most stable. At its simplest, this is a state of minimum potential and kinetic energies. As energy must be conserved, a system can move to an energy minimum only by losing energy to its surroundings. The heat or light which is usually evolved during a chemical change is energy lost by the reactants in changing into products which are more stable.

Atoms with 8 electrons in the outermost shell and all the available orbitals filled are characteristic of the noble gas elements, and as these are also the most unreactive elements, this special arrangement of electrons is assumed to be the most stable. It is called the *noble gas structure*. Helium is an exception as it has only two electrons per atom, but these are sufficient to fill the occupied orbital, and also to complete the first shell.

The electronic arrangement in the noble gas atoms

Shell ...	K	L		M			N				O	
Orbital ...	*s*	*s*	*p*	*s*	*p*	*d*	*s*	*p*	*d*	*f*	*s*	*p*
He	2											
Ne	2	2	6									
Ar	2	2	6	2	6							
Kr	2	2	6	2	6	10	2	6				
Xe	2	2	6	2	6	10	2	6	10	.	2	6

By treating reactions as opportunities for the participants to redistribute their electrons into more stable arrangements, and by accepting the very great stability of the noble gas structure as a basic principle, it is possible to explain a great deal about the nature of chemical binding.

Electrovalent compounds

Alkali metal atoms have one more electron than the preceding noble gas in the Periodic Table, and if this electron is removed they are left with the noble gas structure. Loss of an electron destroys the electrical neutrality of the alkali metal atom and it becomes a positive ion (Fig. 29).

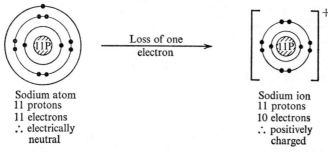

Loss of one electron

Sodium atom
11 protons
11 electrons
∴ electrically
neutral

Sodium ion
11 protons
10 electrons
∴ positively
charged

Fig. 29. Diagram showing the change of a sodium atom to a sodium ion.

A halogen element atom has one electron less than the noble gas which immediately follows it in the Periodic Table, so the capture of an electron by a halogen atom will give the eight electrons of the noble gas structure. As before, however, the electrical neutrality is destroyed, and the atom becomes a negative ion (Fig. 30).

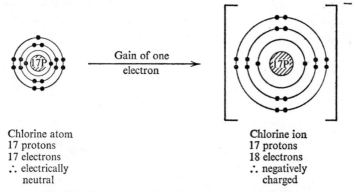

Gain of one electron

Chlorine atom
17 protons
17 electrons
∴ electrically
neutral

Chlorine ion
17 protons
18 electrons
∴ negatively
charged

Fig. 30. Diagram showing the change of a chlorine atom
to a chloride ion.

87

Sodium reacts energetically with chlorine to form the very stable salt sodium chloride. The essential chemical action is the capture of an electron from each sodium atom by each chlorine atom. For this transfer to be possible the two atoms must be in contact, for example as the result of a chlorine molecule colliding with a piece of sodium. After they have reacted the atoms are now oppositely charged ions in close association, and powerful electrostatic forces of attraction hold them in contact. Ions held together in this way are said to be linked by an *ionic bond* (Kossel, 1916), and compounds formed from this type of binding are called *electrovalent* or *ionic*.

The *electrovalency* of an element is the *number* of electrons its atom must gain or lose to attain a stable electron structure. Elements like the alkali metals or the halogens, whose atoms lose or gain only one electron, have an electrovalency of 1. As it is only the electrons in the outermost shell which are affected, only these need be shown in electronic equations representing the electron transfer, e.g.

$$Na^{\bullet} \ + \ {\underset{\times\times}{\overset{\times}{\times}} Cl \ {\overset{}{\times}}} \longrightarrow Na^+ \left[{\underset{\times\times}{\overset{\bullet\times}{\times}} Cl \ {\overset{}{\times}}} \right]^-$$

The alkaline-earth elements have an electrovalency of 2 since two electrons must be removed to expose the noble gas structure in the under-lying shell, e.g.

$$\bullet Mg \bullet \ + \ 2 \, {\underset{\times\times}{\overset{\times}{\times}} Cl \ {\overset{}{\times}}} \longrightarrow \left[{\underset{\times\times}{\overset{\times\bullet}{\times}} Cl \ {\overset{}{\times}}} \right]^- \ \overset{2+}{Mg} \ \left[{\underset{\times\times}{\overset{\times\bullet}{\times}} Cl \ {\overset{}{\times}}} \right]^-$$

In order to maintain overall electrical neutrality, doubly charged ions are always associated with two singly charged ions of opposite sign or another doubly charged ion of opposite sign, e.g.

$$\overset{\bullet\bullet}{\underset{\bullet\bullet}{\vdots O \, {\overset{\times}{\times}}}}^{2-} \qquad \overset{\bullet\bullet}{\underset{\bullet\bullet}{\vdots S \, {\overset{\times}{\times}}}}^{2-}$$

Covalent compounds

G. N. Lewis (1916) made an important suggestion which successfully accounted for the formation of compounds which were not of the electro-valent type. He stated that atoms might gain the noble gas structure with-out becoming ions, by a process of electron sharing. Hydrogen needs one

88

electron to form the helium electron structure and carbon needs four more electrons to form the neon electron structure; by sharing the electrons of four hydrogen atoms and, in turn, sharing with each of them one of its own electrons, all the atoms gain the noble gas electron structure. In this way it

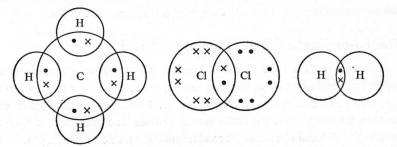

Fig. 31. Electronic formulae of methane, chlorine and hydrogen molecules.

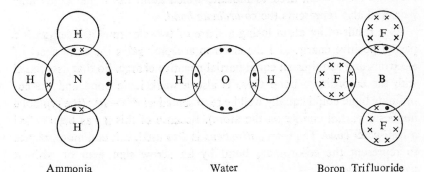

Ammonia   Water   Boron Trifluoride

Fig. 32. Electronic formulae of ammonia, water and boron trifluoride molecules.

$$\underset{H}{\overset{H}{H-C-H}} \; ; \quad \underset{H}{\overset{H}{H-N\!:}} \; ; \quad H-\overset{\cdot\cdot}{\underset{\cdot\cdot}{O}}-H \; ; \quad \underset{F}{\overset{F}{B-F}}$$

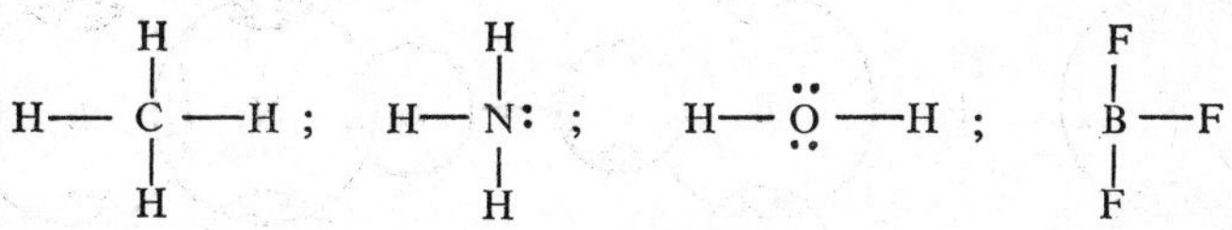

Fig. 33. Structural formulae of methane, ammonia, water and boron trifluoride molecules.

is even possible to account for the combination of like atoms (Fig. 31). A pair of electrons shared in this way constitutes a *covalent bond*. For simplicity, the two electrons of the covalent bond between two atoms can be replaced by a joining line. Compare Fig. 32 and Fig. 33.

The nitrogen atom of the ammonia molecule has its outermost shell built up from five to eight electrons by sharing three of them with the electrons from three hydrogen atoms, and two unshared electrons remain as a *lone pair*. The water molecule has two such lone pairs. Since the outermost shell of the boron atom contains only 3 electrons this process of electron sharing cannot increase this number beyond 6 electrons thus leaving an incomplete octet as in the boron trifluoride molecule.

The co-ordinate (dative) covalent bond

Molecules with a lone pair of electrons, like those of ammonia and water, frequently behave as electron donors and use the lone pair to form a covalent bond with an electron acceptor. Molecules which behave as electron acceptors have available vacant orbitals and gain extra stability from the additional electrons. Boron trifluoride is an electron acceptor and forms a stable addition compound with ammonia (Fig. 34).

An arrow is often used to indicate which atom has donated the lone pair, and also represents the *co-ordinate bond*.

As a result of an atom losing a share of two electrons it is left with a partial positive charge and the electron acceptor gains the extra share of electrons and acquires an equal partial negative charge. So that associated with the co-ordinate bond there is also a weak ionic bond and the co-ordinate bond could equally well be represented as $A^{\delta+} - B^{\delta-}$ (the symbol δ implies a partial charge on the atom). Because of this it has been called a *semi-polar bond*. The term *dative bond* is also used. It is common practice to represent the co-ordinate bond by an arrow sign with or without partial charges.

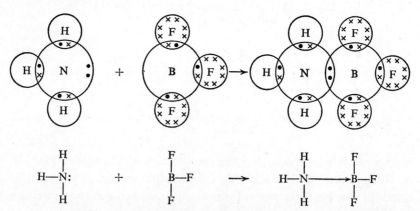

Fig. 34. Diagrammatic representation of the formation of a co-ordinate bond between an ammonia and a boron trifluoride molecule.

A further example is found in ammonium chloride which has additional interest as it contains an electrovalent and simple covalent linkages as well (Fig. 35). Covalently bound to the N atom in the NH_4^+ ion in this way, the hydrogen ion from the hydrogen chloride is indistinguishable from the other hydrogen atoms, and the positive charge is spread symmetrically over the whole structure giving it the characteristics of a unipositive ion. This then combines ionically with negative chloride ions in the usual way, ultimately producing an ionic solid.

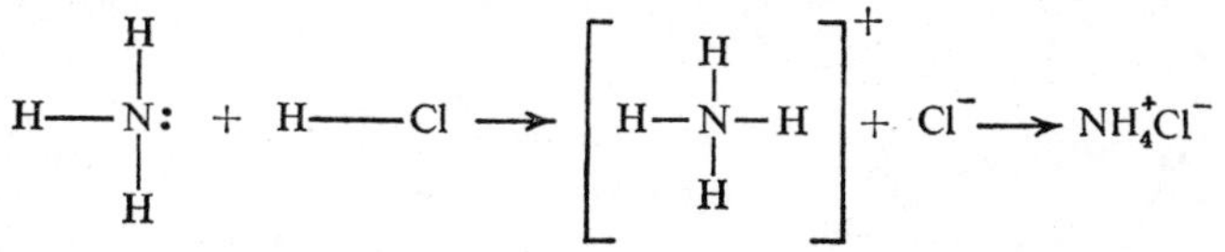

$$
\begin{array}{c}
\overset{\displaystyle H}{\underset{\displaystyle H}{H\!-\!\!N\!:}} \;+\; H\!-\!\!-\!\!Cl \;\longrightarrow\;
\left[\; \overset{\displaystyle H}{\underset{\displaystyle H}{H\!-\!\!N\!-\!H}} \;\right]^{+} +\; Cl^- \longrightarrow NH_4^+Cl^-
\end{array}
$$

Fig. 35. The combination of an ammonia and a hydrogen
chloride molecule.

The properties of a particular salt are conditioned by the size and charge of the cation. The alkali metals form unipositive ions which have large ionic radii. The ammonium radical has a single positive charge and a large radius; this explains why there are similarities between ammonium salts and the salts of the alkali metals.

Multiple bonds

Each of the two atoms in the molecule of nitrogen completes its octet by sharing three of the five electrons belonging to the other atom. Two electrons with opposed spins (see p. 50) constitute the ordinary covalent bond, and as the six shared electrons in the nitrogen molecule form three such pairs the result is three covalent bonds joining two atoms (Fig. 36). The two carbon atoms in the acetylene molecule are also joined by a triple bond.

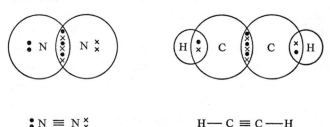

Fig. 36. Electronic formulae of nitrogen and acetylene molecules
showing the triple bonds.

Double bonds are formed in a similar way, as, for instance, in the ethylene and carbon dioxide molecules (Fig. 37). Double bonds are more common than triple bonds; bonds of higher order are unknown.

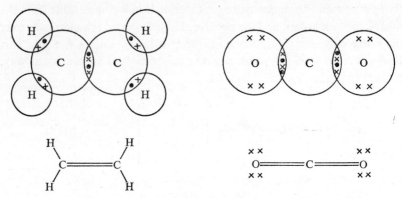

Fig. 37. Electronic formulae of ethylene and carbon dioxide molecules showing the double bonds.

Factors limiting electrovalency

1. Atomic radius. The attraction of a nucleus for an electron varies inversely as the square of the distance separating them. Thus the electrons on the periphery of a large atom are less firmly held than those in an atom of small radius. Because of this, small atoms do not form ions by electron loss as readily as the large atoms. However, small atoms capture additional electrons to form negative ions more readily than the large ones. This is because the electron can approach closer to the nucleus where the attraction is stronger and this increases the chance of its being drawn into the electron cloud.

2. Noble gas structure. Atoms whose electronic arrangement is only one electron different from the noble gas structure form ions more readily than those which differ by two electrons. It is even more difficult to form trivalent ions and the highest electrovalency is four, which is rarely shown, and then only by the cations of large atoms like those of tin and lead. The successive ionisation energies of an atom clearly illustrate the increasing difficulty with which the more highly charged cations are formed. The first four ionisation energies of aluminium are given below.

The first ionisation energy measures the work that must be done to separate the most loosely held electron from a neutral atom. This leaves a unipositive ion in which the remaining electrons are held more firmly,

Electron	1st	2nd	3rd	4th
Ionisation energy (kJ mol^{-1})	577	1816	2745	11573
Ion produced	Al^+	Al^{2+}	Al^{3+}	Al^{4+}

(1 kcal = 4.184 kJ)

owing to the increase in the effective nuclear charge (see p. 67). A higher ionisation energy is therefore needed to remove an electron from an Al^+ ion in order to produce an Al^{2+} ion than was needed to withdraw an electron from a neutral aluminium atom. This latter ion has an even greater effective nuclear charge and will lose an electron with even greater reluctance. The Al^{3+} ion has the noble gas electronic structure, and is the most stable ion. The fourth ionisation energy is very much greater than the first three. It is impossible to account for such an enormous increase in terms of effective nuclear charge, and it is attributed to the great stability of the noble gas structure and the difficulty experienced in disrupting it. Removal of electrons from an atom takes in energy. This is compensated for by exothermic factors shortly to be considered. Hence the endothermic ionisation process is limited by the amount of energy made available in the energy-releasing processes. As the energy needed to disrupt the noble gas structure lies far beyond that normally made available during compound formation, it restricts further ionisation, and this arrangement corresponds to the upper limit of positive electrovalency.

Non-metal atoms gain additional electrons and become negatively charged as a result. But as the charge on the anion builds up so does the repulsion towards a further electron. The positive charge on the nucleus of the atom is capable of holding up to two extra electrons, especially if it is a small atom. There is also evidence for an N^{3-} ion. Once the noble gas structure has been reached it has such an efficient screening effect (see p. 67) that it effectively shields the positive nucleus and prevents it from attracting further electrons into the ion. Consequently the noble gas structure also corresponds to the upper limit of negative electrovalency.

Atoms whose electron arrangement is only 1 electron different from the noble gas structure form ions more readily than those which have to lose or gain several electrons. Ions are formed more easily by atoms in those Groups adjacent to the noble gas Group, and then with steadily increasing difficulty in Groups which are further away. Also, because atomic radius increases as a Group is descended, positive ions are formed more readily by atoms at the bottom of the Group than by those at the top (and vice versa for negative ions).

3. 18-electron shell structure. Stable electron arrangements other than the noble gas structure are also known. For instance, among the B families of the Periodic Table, stable cations are formed by the metallic elements in Period 4 and subsequent Periods. When all the outermost electrons have been lost these elements form cations whose outer electron shell contains 18 electrons and not 8 as in the noble gas electron structure. For example, zinc has the electronic structure 2, 8, 18, 2. The stable ion of zinc is Zn^{2+} and its electron structure is 2, 8, 18.

However, although the 18-electron arrangement has a degree of stability it is not as great as the noble gas electron arrangement.

4. Inert pair effect. Among those elements which might be expected to form stable cations with the 18-electron shell structure a number form ions in which there is an incomplete loss of valence electrons. For example, lead has the electron configuration 2, 8, 18, 32, 18, 4. The detailed arrangement of electrons in the valency shell being

$$\begin{array}{c} s \qquad\qquad p \\ \boxed{\uparrow\downarrow}\quad\boxed{\uparrow\,|\,\uparrow\,|\,} \end{array}$$

. Lead forms well known stable ionic salts, e.g. $PbCl_2$, $PbSO_4$, in which the stable ion Pb^{2+} is present. Formation of this ion results from the removal of only two electrons from the lead atom, the two p electrons. The two s electrons have remained as part of the core of the ion; they are described as an *inert pair*. Hence the lead ion has the electronic configuration 2, 8, 18, 32, 18, 2. There is some resemblance between an inert pair and the pair of electrons in the helium atom.

Elements in the B families are the only ones which show the inert pair effect, and their tendency to behave in this way increases markedly as atomic number increases. Thus Pb^{2+} is much more stable than Sn^{2+}. A complete list of the elements which show the effect is given below.

II B	III B	IV B	V B	VI B
	Ga	Ge		
	In	Sn	Sb	Te
Hg	Tl	Pb	Bi	

As a result of inert pair formation an element displays an ionic valency two less than its normal Group valency, e.g. the following cations are known: In^+, Tl^+, Sn^{2+}, Sb^{3+}, Te^{4+}.

A partial explanation of the inert pair effect is given by the fact that the outer s electrons penetrate to some extent the 18-electron shell immediately below them. They are therefore less effectively screened from the attractive power of the nucleus and so are bound more tightly to the atom.

Covalency maxima

The stability of the noble gas structure is successful in accounting for the formation of a wide variety of compounds, but the idea has to be made more general and include other stable electron arrangements to account for the formulation of such compounds as phosphorus pentachloride, sulphur hexafluoride, iodine heptafluoride, and osmium octafluoride. Representing these compounds by conventional formulae shows clearly how the 'octet' of the central atom expands to include 10, 12, 14 and even 16 electrons in its outermost shell.

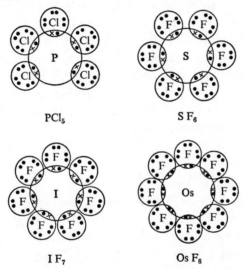

PCl₅   S F₆

I F₇   Os F₈

Fig. 38. Electronic formulae of phosphorus pentachloride, sulphur hexafluoride, iodine heptafluoride and osmium octafluoride molecules.

The maximum covalency an element can attain is given in the table on p. 96, which also illustrates the relationship that exists between covalency maxima and atomic structure.

The maximum covalency is by no means always reached, and is displayed by only a small number of elements. Fluorine has a marked tendency to produce the highest covalency in an element, and it is usually the fluorides which give most examples of *octet expansion*.

Elements in the second period have one s orbital, and three p orbitals in the outer valency shell. This enables them to accommodate four pairs of electrons, giving them a covalency maximum of 4. Elements in subsequent Periods can all make available the five d orbitals, thus providing space for a total of nine electron pairs in the outermost shell. Clearly these are not all utilised; otherwise the element would exhibit a covalency maximum of 9.

Period	Element	Maximum covalency	Maximum no. of shared electrons
1	H	1	2
2	Li to F	4	8
3 and 4	Na to Br	6	12
5, 6 and 7	Rb to U	8	16

Compounds in which the covalency maximum has been reached are unable to accept further electrons, and are therefore inert towards attacking reagents. For example, tetrachloromethane, CCl_4, is a very stable inert compound, but in silicon tetrachloride, $SiCl_4$, silicon has a covalency 2 lower than its maximum of 6, and it is very easily hydrolysed (see p. 376). Sulphur, another element in the same Period as silicon, reaches the maximum covalency in its hexafluoride, and this compound like tetrachloromethane is chemically inert.

Resonance

Not all covalent molecules can be satisfactorily represented by the simple electronic formulae just described. For example, the carbon dioxide molecule is generally represented as $O=C=O$. Now the interatomic distances in carbon–oxygen bonds are as follows:

$$C—O, 1.43 \text{ Å}; \quad C=O, 1.22 \text{ Å}; \quad C\equiv O, 1.10 \text{ Å}.$$

In carbon dioxide the carbon–oxygen bonds are both 1.15 Å in length. Also from the formula above the heat of formation of carbon dioxide is calculated to be 1447 kJ (346 kcal). The experimentally determined value is 1602 kJ (383 kcal).

To explain these differences between the behaviour expected for carbon dioxide with the formulae shown above and actual behaviour, it is suggested that the molecule can better be represented by taking other reasonable electronic formulae into account, e.g.

$$O \leftarrow C \equiv O; \quad O \equiv C \rightarrow O.$$

The actual molecule is now considered to be a *resonance hybrid* of all three possible structures. Thus to represent the molecule adequately it is necessary to mentally superimpose the characteristics of several separate formulae. A resonance hybrid of this kind is more stable than any of the possible contributing structures. This additional stabilising effect is termed *resonance energy*.

Other examples of resonating structures include CO, CO_3^{2-}, NO, N_2O, HNO_3, NO_3^-, SO_4^{2-}. These and others are mentioned at appropriate places in part III.

Ionic aggregates and lattice energy

If ions are assumed to be spherically symmetrical, then the charges on them give rise to spherically symmetrical electrostatic fields similar to the magnetic field surrounding a single magnetic pole, and when the ions come into contact the electrostatic field is similar to that of a short bar magnet:

Cation   Anion   Ion-pair

The arrows show the direction in which a positively charged particle will move if placed in the field. Since the ion-pair shown above still has a powerful electrostatic field permeating the space around it, other ions are attracted and cluster around in such a way that ions with unlike charges are in contact and ions with like charges are as far away from each other as possible. The clustering continues in all directions, with negative ions surrounded by positive ions, and these, in turn, surrounded by more negative ions building up into a three-dimensional ionic aggregate. The ions pack together in a definite pattern depending on their size, the charge they carry and the conditions under which they are combining. This pattern extends uniformly throughout the whole of the aggregate producing a *crystal lattice*.

A considerable amount of work has to be done to separate two oppositely charged ions in contact, and it is stored by the separated ions as potential energy. When they recombine, the potential energy of the system is lowered; and as energy must be conserved there is an equal increase in kinetic energy, and this usually appears as heat. All free ions possess this potential energy, and it is set free as they combine into a crystal lattice. Energy liberated in this way is called *lattice energy*, and it plays an important role in chemical binding.

A measure of the energy needed to convert an atom into a cation is given by the ionisation energy (see p. 53). In some cases a neutral atom is converted into a negative ion with an accompanying evolution of energy, but the doubly charged anions of the Group VIB non-metals take in energy during their formation and like all the cations are less stable than their corresponding atoms.

Energy must be transferred to the surroundings if the elements are to be more stable in combination than when they were separate. The energy set free in this way is called *heat of formation*. A comparison of the ionisation energy of sodium ($+494$ kJ mol^{-1}) and the electron affinity of chlorine (-356 kJ mol^{-1}) shows that both ions are formed with an overall energy deficit.

Yet sodium and chlorine combine with considerable evolution of heat. This apparent paradox is resolved if the lattice energy is taken into account. For example:

$$\text{The ionisation energy for } Na \rightarrow Na^+ + e = +494 \text{ kJ mol}^{-1}$$
$$\text{The electron affinity for } Cl + e \rightarrow Cl^- = -356 \text{ kJ mol}^{-1}$$
$$\text{The lattice energy of the } Na^+Cl^- \text{ crystal} = -510 \text{ kJ mol}^{-1}$$
$$\text{Energy surplus} = -372 \text{ kJ mol}^{-1}$$

Therefore, although the formation of an equal number of Na^+ and Cl^- ions results in an energy deficit these ions build up into an ionic crystal with the release of sufficient energy to leave an overall excess. Not all of this energy is released to the surroundings however, for it is necessary to take into account two other factors. First, energy is absorbed in breaking the metallic bond in sodium to produce free sodium atoms. Secondly, energy is also absorbed in breaking the covalent bond in molecules of chlorine to obtain separate atoms of chlorine. The Born–Haber cycle (Fig. 39) summarises all the steps involved in the formation of an ionic crystal. When the algebraic sum of all the energy factors is taken a final negative value for the heat of formation shows that the constituents contain less energy and are therefore more stable as an ionic crystal than as free elements.

Lattice energies determined experimentally from the Born–Haber cycle agree very well with the values calculated theoretically for compounds which are typically electrovalent. In a later section a fuller discussion of the different extent to which many compounds display ionic properties will be given, but it is sufficient at this stage to note that with the less extreme types of electrovalent compound there are wide discrepancies between theoretical and experimental lattice energies.

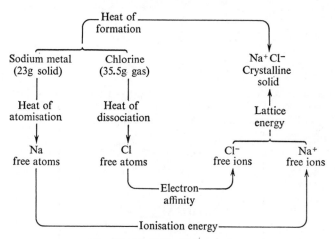

Fig. 39. The Born–Haber cycle.

The cohesive force between covalent molecules

Covalent molecules have no powerful attraction for each other like the ions in an ionic solid, as they have no strong external electrostatic field. For this reason, covalent molecules tend to remain as discrete particles and covalent materials are often gases or liquids at ordinary temperatures. Sodium chloride and hydrogen chloride clearly illustrate this difference (Figs. 40, 41).

It requires 510 kJ mol^{-1} to separate the ions of a Na$^+$Cl$^-$ crystal and 431 kJ mol^{-1} to separate the *atoms* of a hydrogen chloride molecule. Thus, the strength of the bond joining a sodium ion to a chloride ion is of the same order of magnitude as that joining an atom of hydrogen to an atom of chlorine in a molecule of hydrogen chloride. Forces of attraction between covalent *molecules* are very much weaker than normal covalent and electrovalent bonds, and in most cases are relatively easily overcome by thermal agitation. Weak intermolecular forces of this type are called van der Waals' forces, and they originate from three main mechanisms:

99

(1) attraction between permanent dipoles;

(2) attraction between permanent dipoles and induced dipoles;

(3) dispersion effect.

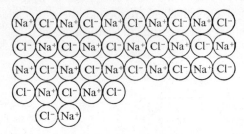

Fig. 40. Sodium and chloride ions binding firmly into a crystal lattice.

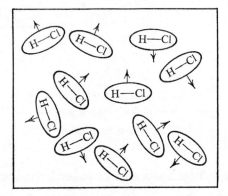

Fig. 41. Molecules of hydrogen chloride moving randomly in the gaseous state.

1. Attraction between permanent dipoles. Owing to the different electron attracting powers of chlorine and hydrogen atoms (see p. 71) the concentration of electrons around the chlorine atom is greater than the concentration around the hydrogen atom and an uneven charge distribution is produced (Fig. 42). The chlorine end of the molecule acquires a partial negative charge and the hydrogen end a partial positive charge. Molecules

(a)   (b)

Fig. 42. The shaded area represents the extent of the molecular orbital. The uneven electron distribution is equivalent to a separation of charge.

like that of hydrogen in which the negative charge is distributed equally, are said to be *non-polar*, and those like hydrogen chloride are said to be *polar*. When a positive and equal negative charge are separated in this way, the molecule is said to possess a *dipole*.

The attraction between unlike charges and repulsions of like charges causes the dipoles to arrange themselves so that unlike charges face each other. In this position, the molecules have an attraction for one another (Fig. 43).

(a)   (b)

Fig. 43. (a) Dipoles orientated in the opposite direction repel each other.
(b) Dipoles orientated in the same direction attract each other.

2. Attraction between permanent dipoles and induced dipoles. In some cases the electron cloud of a particle is large, diffuse, and easily distorted so that when close to the positive end of a permanent dipole the electron cloud will be drawn towards it. This disturbs the electron cloud in the particle, and induces a temporary dipole. Electron cloud distortion is called *polarisation* (Fig. 44). The positive end of the permanent dipole attracts the electrons of the polarisable atom or molecule, and so builds up a negative charge directly facing it. Therefore, the dipole and the induced dipole are favourably orientated to attract each other. Generally the induced dipole is superimposed on the permanent dipole present in a molecule of the compound.

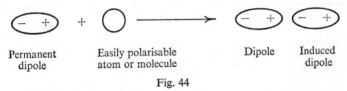

Permanent   Easily polarisable   Dipole   Induced
dipole   atom or molecule   dipole

Fig. 44

3. Dispersion effect. Although the physical significance of the dispersion effect cannot be exactly defined, it can be imagined as an *induced dipole-induced dipole* attraction. It is applicable to all types of molecule whether they be polar or non-polar, easily polarisable or non-deformable, but, in general, it increases with increases in the number of electrons per atom or molecule, especially if they are only loosely held. The attraction is strong where particles are close together, but rapidly weakens when they move apart. A comparison of the relative magnitudes of molecular interaction effects shows that for most simple molecules the attractive forces, or van der Waals' forces as they are frequently called, are almost exclusively determined by the dispersion effect. The mechanism of the effect is illustrated in Fig. 45.

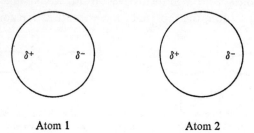

Atom 1   Atom 2

Fig. 45. Atom 1 is an instantaneous dipole, Atom 2 an induced dipole (δ^+, i.e. delta plus, equals a small positive charge; δ^-, i.e. delta minus, equals a small negative charge).

The dispersion of the rapidly moving electrons in a particle is unlikely to be uniform at any instant. This corresponds to an instantaneous accumulation of electrons in a particular region of the electron cloud and is equivalent to the formation of a temporary dipole. It will induce dipoles in adjoining atoms, and so a force of attraction will be set up between them.

Relative magnitudes of molecular interaction effects

Molecule	Dipole-dipole attraction	Dipole-induced dipole attraction	Dispersion effect
H_2	—	—	11.3
N_2	—	—	62
CH_4	—	—	117
Cl_2	—	—	461
CO	⌈0.0034	0.057	67
HCl	18.6	5.4	105
NH_3	84	10	93
H_2O	190	10	47

The dispersion effect provides an interesting correlation between molecular weights and boiling points. Heavy molecules in general contain more electrons than light ones, and so the attraction due to the dispersion effect is greatest in the heavy molecules. Heat of vaporisation (p. 203) is a measure of the energy needed to overcome the forces of attraction between molecules so that they become completely separated. As the boiling point is proportional to the heat of vaporisation, it is a convenient assessment of these attractive forces. Hence, normal molecular substances with large molecular weights have high boiling points, and those with small molecular weight have low boiling points. A good example of this trend is in the homologous series of paraffin hydrocarbons in which the lower members are gases, then as the series is ascended, liquids; higher members are waxy solids, which produce crystal lattices in much the same way as ions, except that they are molecular crystals and there are no powerful electrostatic forces binding the crystal together.

Distinctive properties of electrovalent and covalent compounds

Compounds may easily be classified as electrovalent or covalent as a result of some obvious differences in their properties.

1. Volatility. The boiling point is a convenient assessment of the attractive forces between the particles of a liquid (pp. 203–5). The boiling points given in the following table illustrate the big difference between the

Boiling point of some Main Group element chlorides (°C)

I		II		III		IV	
LiCl	1337	$BeCl_2$	500	BCl_3	12.6	CCl_4	76
NaCl	1442	$MgCl_2$	1000	$AlCl_3$	183	$SiCl_4$	57
KCl	1415	$CaCl_2$	1100	$GaCl_3$	205	$GeCl_4$	86.5
RbCl	1388	$SrCl_2$	1250	$InCl_3$	550	$SnCl_4$	114
CsCl	1289	$BaCl_2$	1350	$TlCl_3$	100	$PbCl_4$	Decomp

strength of an ionic bond and the relatively weak van der Waals' forces of attraction between covalent molecules. Rise of temperature increases the thermal agitation of covalent molecules, and a proportion acquire sufficient kinetic energy to break away from the attraction of surrounding molecules in the bulk of the material and become vaporised particles. Not all the particles in a liquid have the same energy. Some have greater energy, others less, but they tend to be close to the average value and only occasionally do the particles have energies which differ widely from the average. This is shown qualitatively in Fig. 46. Curves T_1 and T_2 represent the distribution of energies at a temperature T_1, and a higher temperature T_2 respectively. If P is the energy of escape, it can be seen that the area beneath the curve T_2 above this minimum of energy is greater than the area beneath the curve T_1. The increase in area represents the increase in the number of particles with sufficient energy to pass into the vapour state.

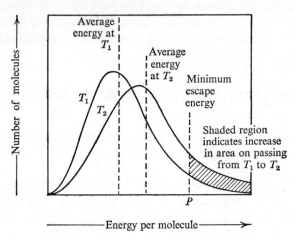

Fig. 46. Energy distribution curves.

The fragmentary particles of an electrovalent compound are all *giant structures* built according to an orderly crystal structure even though the particles themselves may show no external symmetry to the eye. When fused the crystal lattice is destroyed but the attraction between the ions still exists, and in order to vaporise such a system these forces have to be overcome. The strength of these forces is clearly demonstrated by the very high boiling points. Melting points of ionic solids are also very high, as the crystal lattice is very stable and difficult to disrupt. The weak van der Waals' forces of attraction in *molecular crystals* formed from covalent molecules are relatively easily disrupted and so covalent compounds can easily be distinguished from the high-melting crystalline ionic solids by the fact that they are gases, volatile liquids or solids of low melting point and boiling point.

Even though the binding is covalent in materials such as diamond, graphite, silica, etc., since these are *giant molecules* the melting point and boiling point are very high as disruption of the lattice necessitates the breaking of strong chemical bonds.

2. Solubility. When two liquids are miscible with one another, the particles of one intermingle with the particles of the other until they are uniformly distributed. Similarly, when a solid dissolves in a liquid its constituent particles spread uniformly throughout the solvent. With immiscible liquids or an insoluble solid no such intermingling occurs (Fig. 47).

Although a variety of factors affect the solubility of a solute in a solvent, broadly it may be stated that *like dissolves like*. Thus solids are more likely to dissolve in liquids if they are chemically similar, e.g. benzene C_6H_6 is a good solvent for other hydrocarbons.

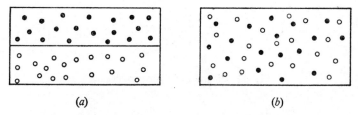

(a)   (b)

Fig. 47. (a) Immiscible liquids; two layers, no intermingling;
(b) solution: homogeneous mixing.

Before solute particles can freely intermingle with the solvent particles the solute–solute attractive forces must be overcome. Thus the lattice energy of the solute is an important factor in the dissolving process. Just as the breaking down of solute–solute attraction takes in energy so also does the breaking down of the attractive forces between the solvent particles as they intermingle with the solute particles. Because energy must be conserved the solute will not dissolve unless there is an available source of energy capable of supplying the energy needed by these endothermic processes. Interaction between the solute and solvent particles is an important energy-releasing process. This energy, called *solvation energy*, may not entirely compensate for the energy taken in, and in this case the difference is absorbed from the surroundings and the solute dissolves with a cooling effect. On the other hand if the solvation energy exceeds the amount of energy taken in, the solute dissolves with a release of energy and the solution heats up.

Water is one of the best solvents. This is the result of two important features: (1) it is a polar molecule, (2) it has a high dielectric constant ($k = 80$ for water; $k = 1$ for air). The polar nature of the water molecule is a consequence of it being V-shaped and of oxygen being very much more electron attracting than hydrogen (Fig. 48). The hydrogen end of the water molecule is attracted to negative ions, and the oxygen to positive ions, so that water molecules adhere to and cluster around both types of ion (Fig. 49).

Water held to ions in this way is called *water of hydration* (see p. 237), and is fairly easily removed in most cases by gentle heating, when the anhydrous salt will be obtained. Water of hydration facilitates the removal of ions from the crystal lattice; as water has such a high dielectric constant

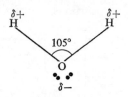

Fig. 48. Diagram of a water molecule.

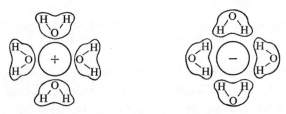

Fig. 49. Diagram showing the orientation of water molecules around ions.

this weakens the electrostatic attraction between the ions so that they are no longer as strongly bound together; and normal thermal agitation causes them to intermingle with the solvent and a solution is formed. The reverse process, in which hydrated ions collide with the crystal, lose their water of hydration and re-enter a vacant space in the crystal lattice, also takes place. When the number of ions leaving the crystal in a given time is equal to the number returning to it a state of dynamic equilibrium is reached, and the solution is now *saturated*.

Other solvents which are made up of polar molecules and have a high dielectric constant include hydrocyanic acid, liquid ammonia, and liquid hydrogen fluoride, but none of them is as widely applicable in its solvent action as water. They are also very much more difficult to handle. These solvents are all covalent compounds. As they are polar liquids their molecules attract each other quite strongly and non-polar compounds are unable to force the solvent molecules apart. This prevents intermingling and the formation of a solution. Therefore, most covalent compounds are insoluble in this type of solvent. When a covalent compound does dissolve in water it is because its molecules have a fairly high polarity, e.g. ethanol, acetic acid, and hydrogen chloride. In general, however, covalent compounds will dissolve in covalent liquids, i.e. 'like dissolves like'.

3. Conductivity. Covalent compounds are not themselves conductors of electricity since they contain no free ions or electrons. For the same reason, their solutions in covalent liquids (including water) do not conduct electricity. This is only correct if a careful distinction is made between those cases which are purely physical and in which no other change than that of simple dissolving is involved, and other cases in which the solvent reacts with the solute. For instance, the brown gas nitrogen dioxide dissolves readily in water. Clearly a chemical change takes place, because the brown colour of the nitrogen dioxide is discharged as the gas is taken up by the water. The nitric and nitrous acids produced in this reaction furnish ions and the solution becomes conducting.

Since solutions of ionic compounds contain hydrated ions able to move about fairly freely, these solutions are very good conductors of electricity. Molten ionic compounds consist entirely of ions which are free to move and therefore these melts are also good conductors of electricity. Ionic crystals are non-conductors of electricity because their ions are held rigidly in place in the crystal lattice, and are not forced to move under the influence of an applied e.m.f.

The hydrogen bond

There is good evidence for believing that a hydrogen atom bound to an atom of a highly electronegative element such as fluorine, oxygen or nitrogen has a simultaneous attraction for another highly electronegative atom. For instance, in the salt potassium hydrogen fluoride, KHF_2, the anion is HF_2^- and the hydrogen atom is thought to act as a bridge between the two fluorine atoms. The simplest interpretation of this structure is that the hydrogen atom bound to a very electronegative element like fluorine has such a small share of the electron pair that it is left with a partial positive charge. Because this positive charge is concentrated on such a minute particle the hydrogen atom is surrounded by an electrostatic field of enormous intensity, and attracts centres of high electron density. Since it is so small, a hydrogen atom is entirely surrounded by two atoms, and this is the maximum number of atoms with which it can form a bond.

Thus, the picture of the hydrogen difluoride anion is of a hydrogen fluoride molecule linked to a fluoride ion (Figs. 50, 51).

Although the hydrogen difluoride anion is an example of hydrogen bonding, it is not a typical example, as the hydrogen atom is symmetrically situated between the two fluorine atoms; in the majority of cases of hydrogen bonding the hydrogen atom is unsymmetrically placed between the two atoms it is linking together. A hydrogen atom linked to a highly

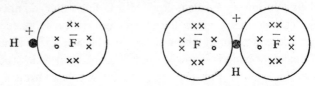

Fig. 50. The hydrogen fluoride molecule.   Fig. 51. The hydrogen difluoride anion.

electronegative element X (i.e. usually N, O or F) is usually shown hydrogen-bonded to an atom Y by a dotted line, i.e.

$$\overset{\delta-}{X}\!-\!\overset{\delta+}{H}\cdots\overset{\delta-}{Y}$$

The hydrogen bond is essentially an electrostatic bond. It is weaker than simple ionic or covalent bonds, but is stronger than ordinary van der Waals' forces of intermolecular attraction. An approximate measure of the order of magnitude of the strength of these bonds is given in the following table:

Bond type	kJ mol^{-1}	kcal mol^{-1}
Ionic Covalent	800–40	200–10
Hydrogen	40–4	10–1
van der Waals	< 2	< 0.5

Metallic binding

A pure metal is made up of atoms, all of the same kind. The part of the atom other than the outer electron shell is called the *core*. Metals are known to be close-packed arrangements of atoms and it is believed that the outer electron shells merge into each other. The structure of metals is thus represented as a lattice of atomic cores surrounded by a *flux*, or *sea* of electrons (Fig. 52).

No particular electron is associated with any particular atom. Each atomic core, however, has still on the average its valence electrons in its sphere of influence, even though they are not the same ones all the time. The negatively charged electronic flux is distributed uniformly throughout the lattice and attracts the positively charged cores; this binds them together equally strongly. Similarly, the cores attract the cloud and prevent it from dispersing. The electrons in this type of structure are said to be *delocalised* and the resulting bonding is called *metallic bonding*.

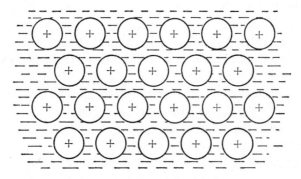

Fig. 52. Metallic binding. Positively charged *cores* in a continuous electron flux.

Each potassium atom, for example, has only one valency electron and this enters the electron flux. The resulting bonding is weak because of the single electron from each atom, and so potassium is a soft metal of low density and low melting point (64 °C). In metallic calcium there are two valency electrons per atom; the bonding force is therefore roughly twice as strong as with potassium and so calcium is harder, denser and of higher melting point (850 °C) than potassium. The process continues through scandium to chromium, which, because of its six valency electrons, is very hard, very dense and with a very high melting point (1900 °C). It is clear that the melting points (p. 202) are periodic.

Metallic bonding differs from ionic bonding in that there are no ions present, but it resembles it in that the bonding forces are non-rigid and non-directional. Metallic bonding differs from covalency in that metal atoms do not form separate molecules, but resembles it in that the atomic cores are bound together by being attracted to the electron cloud between them. An essential feature of metallic bonding is that the number of valency electrons possessed by each atom is much less than the number of atoms bonded to it. For example, aluminium has three valency electrons and a co-ordination number of 12.

Fajans' rules

In 1923 Fajans pointed out that if two oppositely charged ions were in contact, for instance in a crystal lattice, there was a *polarising effect* in addition to the coulombic attraction they exerted upon each other.

Anions are relatively larger than cations and their electrons are less rigidly held. A small highly charged cation may therefore be able to distort the electron cloud of a large anion and so increase the electron density between the nuclei. Fajans considered that covalent binding was an extreme case of polarisation in which there was an appreciable electron density between the nuclei of combining atoms. He therefore proposed that the tendency of a bond to show covalent character was most marked:

(1) the higher the charge on the cation or anion;

(2) the smaller the radius of the cation;

(3) the larger the radius of the anion.

However, although the idea of the polarisation of anions by cations is an important concept it is an oversimplification to regard this as the cause of covalent binding.

The nature of covalent binding

Combination between atoms may be represented as the result of overlap of their electron clouds (Fig. 53). In the same way as electrons in atoms occupy orbitals, so the electron cloud which surrounds a molecule

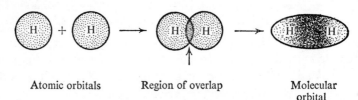

| Atomic orbitals | Region of overlap | Molecular orbital |

Fig. 53. Overlap of atomic orbitals.

can be described in terms of *molecular orbitals*. The statistical probability of locating an electron varies throughout the molecule but reaches a maximum in the region where the atomic orbitals overlap.

The region of overlap corresponds to a volume of greatest negative charge, and as both the positively charged nuclei experience a resultant attraction towards the centre of this region of maximum charge–density they are attracted towards each other and a covalent bond is formed. A positive nucleus is attracted only up to a certain minimum distance from the region of maximum electron density, since forces of repulsion which probably arise from interaction between the nuclei of the two atoms tend to keep them apart, and therefore both nuclei stay at a distance from one another where the attractive and repulsive forces just balance.

The length of the covalent bond joining the two nuclei has different magnitudes depending on the combining atoms. The internuclear distance in the hydrogen molecule is 0.74 Å. However, as thermal effects cause the molecules to vibrate, the bond lengthens and shortens rapidly like an oscillating spring and the measured bond length is the average distance between the nuclei of the two atoms.

In general, single bonds between two atoms are longer than double bonds between similar atoms, and triple bonds are shortest of all, e.g.

$$\text{C—C, 1.54 Å;} \quad \text{C=C, 1.35 Å;} \quad \text{C≡C, 1.20 Å.}$$

The formation of multiple bonds is accompanied by an increase in the overlap between the electron clouds of the combining atoms. It is probable that this increases the electron density between the atoms, thus strengthening the electrostatic attraction for the two nuclei, and so draws them closer together, i.e. multiple bonds are shorter and stronger than single bonds.

Electronegativity

Hitherto descriptions of the three principal types of chemical bond— ionic, covalent and metallic—have related to extreme examples. But as briefly mentioned on p. 71 atoms possess different electron-attracting powers (electronegativities) and this leads to an uneven electron distribution in the bond joining them. Thus, besides the two extremes of covalent and ionic bonds, there are bonds possessing *partial ionic character*, i.e.

$$\text{A—B} \longleftarrow \overset{\delta+ \ \delta-}{\text{A—B}} \longrightarrow \text{A}^+\text{B}^-$$
$$\text{covalent} \qquad \underset{\text{molecule}}{\text{polar}} \qquad \text{ionic}$$

A bond between atoms with little or no difference in electronegativity may be assumed to involve almost equal electron sharing and will be non-polar. Very large differences in electronegativity may be taken to imply *complete charge separation* in the bond, e.g. when the electronegativity difference is about 1.8 as in Na^+Cl^-.

To summarise:

(1) *Metals* tend to have a large atomic radius. Therefore outer electrons experience a relatively weak attraction towards the nucleus, as shown by the relatively low ionisation energies and electronegativities of metals.

(2) *Non-metals* tend to have a small atomic radius and a correspondingly stronger attraction for the outer electrons as shown by their relatively large ionisation energies and electronegativities.

(3) *Ionic binding* is found when there is a large difference in electronegativity between the combining atoms.

(4) *Covalent binding* is found in those bonds which link atoms that differ only slightly in electronegativity and have a relatively strong attraction for their outer electrons.

(5) *Metallic binding* is found between atoms which are identical or differ only slightly in electronegativity, but in this case the atoms have a relatively weak attraction for their outer electrons.

Intermediate bond types

Just as there is a continuous range of bond types between ionic and covalent, so there is also a continuous range between covalent and metallic, i.e.

$$\text{ionic} \xleftrightarrow{\quad\text{merging}\quad} \text{covalent} \xleftrightarrow{\quad\text{merging}\quad} \text{metallic.}$$

The transition of bond type from covalent to metallic is essentially the merging of molecular crystals through layer lattices and giant molecules into structures which become increasingly close-packed and in which the bonding loses its directional properties. Whereas covalent bonds are strongly directional in character and the valence electrons are localised in the direction of the bond, metallic binding is non-directional and the valence electrons are delocalised (see p. 109). More will be said about these various structural types in the next chapter.

Exercises

1. Give the electronic formulae of magnesium oxide, ethane, nitrogen, carbon tetrachloride, phosphorus trichloride, sodium fluoride.
2. Distinguish clearly between electrovalency and covalency illustrating your answer by reference to hydrogen chloride, sodium chloride, water, and carbon tetrachloride.

3. Account for the differences in (*a*) solubility, (*b*) conductivity, and (*c*) volatility between sodium chloride and tetrachloromethane in terms of the type of bonding they exhibit.

Point out why there is such a great difference in their chemical properties.

4. What physical properties do you regard as typical of metals? As far as possible account for these properties in terms of atomic structure.

5. Write explanatory notes on the following terms: (*a*) dative bond, (*b*) inert pair effect, (*c*) covalency maxima, (*d*) crystal lattice energy, (*e*) van der Waals' forces, (*f*) Fajans' rules.

6. Discuss the bonding that occurs in (*a*) metals, (*b*) ice, (*c*) ammonium chloride, (*d*) carbon dioxide, (*e*) silicon dioxide.

A compound, which can be recrystallised from water, is thought to be ionic in character. What two experiments would you carry out to indicate whether this is correct? (OS)

7. The following compounds have formulas which do not appear to be consistent with the normal valencies of the constituent elements. Discuss possible electronic or structural formulae for *four* of these compounds.

$$H_2O_2; KHF_2; KI_3; I_2O_5; CO; NO; NO_2; Fe_3O_4. \quad \text{(O \& C)}$$

8. What are covalency and electrovalency? Illustrate your answer with reference to chlorine and potassium chloride.

Give the shapes of *s* and *p* orbitals and, in terms of orbitals, account for the shape of the carbon tetrachloride molecule.

Explain why hydrogen chloride, which is covalent in the gaseous state, is ionic in water. (C)

9. Describe the electronic structures (main shells only) of the atoms of the elements of atomic numbers 3, 9, 12 and 15, and indicate the types of chemical bonds you would expect these elements to form.

Taking your examples from the short period which includes the elements of atomic numbers 11 to 18, write electronic formulae (valence electrons only) for the following: (*a*) the hydride of *one* metal, (*b*) the simplest chlorides of two non-metals. (W)

10. Comment on the following:

(*a*) Despite the thermochemical data contained in the following equations, sodium metal reacts vigorously and exothermically with chlorine gas.

$$\text{Na (c)} \rightarrow \text{Na}^+(\text{g}); \Delta H = 144 \text{ kcal},$$
$$\tfrac{1}{2}\text{Cl}_2(\text{g}) \rightarrow \text{Cl}^-(\text{g}); \Delta H = -61.8 \text{ kcal}.$$

In view of your comments, discuss why sodium chloride is soluble in water.

(*b*) The ionisation energies (expressed in electron volts, eV), of the elements in the first short period are:

Li, 5.4; Be, 9.3; B, 8.3; C, 11.3;
N, 14.5; O, 13.6; F, 17.4; Ne, 21.6. (C)

8

CRYSTALS AND MOLECULES

I. Crystals

Unit cells

Nearly all homogeneous solids are crystalline, that is to say their constituent ions, atoms or molecules are bound together in a regular manner to form some sort of framework. The geometrical properties of this framework are summed up in the *unit cell*—the smallest portion of the crystal which contains all the fundamentals without repetition. Since crystal lattices are made by stacking unit cells, like bricks, they show on a larger scale the same symmetry. There are only a few simple geometric solids which will stack together in such a way as to leave no spaces in between; the seven basic solids each have eight corners, twelve edges and six faces (Fig. 54).

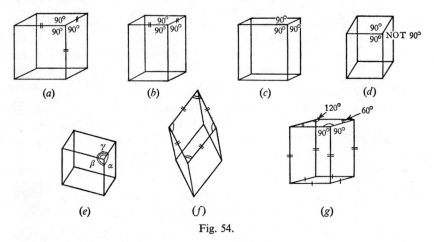

Fig. 54.

(a) **Isometric**: a cube.

(b) **Tetragonal**: a rectangular parallelepiped with one square cross-section.

(c) **Orthorhombic**: an irregular rectangular parallelepiped.

(d) **Monoclinic**: a parallelepiped with two rectangular cross-sections.

(e) **Triclinic**: an irregular parallelepiped.

(f) **Rhombohedral**: a rhombohedron.

(g) **Hexagonal**: a third segment of a hexagonal prism.

Symmetry elements

The best way to understand the symmetry of the cube (or any other unit cell) is to handle a model (Fig. 55).

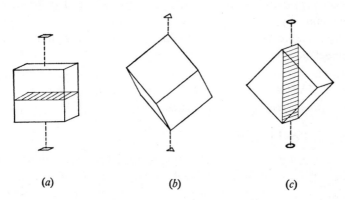

(a)   (b)   (c)

Fig. 55. The symmetry of the cube.

(1) The first thing to notice is that wherever there is a face, there is always an identical one opposite it through the centre. The cube has a *centre of symmetry*.

(2) When a solid can be divided by a plane into two mirror images, the plane is called a *plane of symmetry*. The cube has nine such planes. Three are parallel to the three pairs of faces (Fig. 55(a)); and six are diagonal planes joining the six pairs of opposite edges (Fig. 55(c)).

(3) When a solid can be rotated about an axis in such a way that it presents the same features more than once in a revolution, the axis is called an *axis of symmetry*. (Rotation about an axis of symmetry is said to generate congruency.) If a cube is rotated about an axis passing through the centres of opposite faces (Fig. 55(a)) it presents the same aspect four times every revolution. Such an axis is called a *tetrad*, in notation A_4 or □. The cube has three tetrads mutually at right angles. The axes which pass through opposite corners of the cube (Fig. 55(b))—there are four of them—generate congruency three times per revolution and are called *triads*, in notation A_3 or △. There are six axes which join the mid-points of opposite edges (Fig. 55(c)); these generate congruency twice every revolution and are called *diads*, in notation A_2 or ○ . The axis of sixfold symmetry, which occurs only in the hexagonal system, is called the *hexad*, in notation A_6 or ⬡.

The seven systems

Crystals are classified by their symmetry axes into seven systems, corresponding to the seven kinds of unit cell:

1. Isometric system (cubic): *four triads* arranged as the diagonals of a cube.

2. Tetragonal system: *one tetrad axis,* no triads.

3. Orthorhombic system: *three diad axes,* mutually at right angles.

4. Monoclinic system: *one diad axis* only.

5. Triclinic system: *no symmetry axes.*

6. Rhombohedral system (trigonal): *one triad axis*; no tetrads.

7. Hexagonal system: *one hexad axis.*

Form and orientation

A single uncompound crystal shape is called a *form*. Familiar examples are the cube, octahedron, tetrahedron and rhombohedron. This word 'form' must be treated cautiously; it is one of those innocent words used by scientists with a special significance. In crystallography it is never used in the sense of general shape and appearance. A particular form has the following characters:

(1) it has a constant number of faces, corners, and edges;

(2) *each face has exactly the same shape as the others*;

(3) the faces are arranged in a regular manner with constant angular relations.

Fundamentally a form is produced by the intersection of a constant number of infinite planes in space at particular angles. The shapes of faces are a corollary of the conditions of intersection, and absolute size has no place in the concept.

When building a structure of bricks, it is necessary for all of them to be in the same orientation, otherwise they will not fit together. The same is true of unit cells and consequently the relative orientation of crystal forms is very important. In order to have a standard of reference, three axes—x, y, z—are chosen which have a fixed relation to any unit cell and consequently to any particular crystal form. In Fig. 56 these are shown as dotted lines which would intersect at the centre of the forms. The three axes are mutually perpendicular in the cubic, tetragonal and orthorhombic systems, but not in the others. All the crystal drawings in this chapter are drawn strictly in the same orientation and projection. *Crystal forms can be combined only when they are in the same orientation*—and it is essential to think of them in this way.

The isometric or cubic system

There are four very important forms in this system (Fig. 56) and eleven others which are less frequently met with:

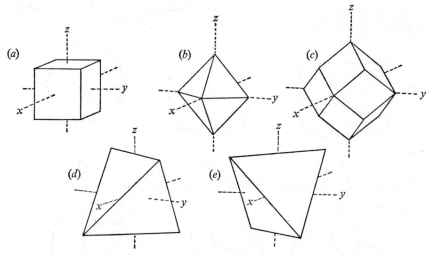

Fig. 56. Forms of the isometric system. (a) Cube, (b) octahedron, (c) rhombo-dodecahedron, (d) α-tetrahedron, (e) β-tetrahedron.

(1) *The cube* has eight corners, twelve edges and six faces which are square.

(2) *The octahedron* has six corners, twelve edges and eight faces which are equilateral triangles.

(3) *The rhombo-dodecahedron* has fourteen corners, twenty-four edges and twelve rhombic faces.

(4) *The tetrahedron* has four corners, six edges and four faces which are equilateral triangles.

Two tetrahedra are shown in α and β orientations. In these orientations both have their four triad axes in exactly the same orientation so that they are consequently distinct. If the two are combined to form a single crystal, the faces of one coincide with and flatten the corners of the other to produce a shape identical to that of the octahedron.

Suppose that these forms are like balloons which can be inflated or deflated at will without distortion. Imagine that you are looking at a black cube centred inside an invisible octahedron—both correctly orientated. Now imagine that the octahedron is deflated and shrinks slowly on to the cube. Contact is first made between the eight corners of the cube and the centres of the eight faces of the octahedron simultaneously. The effect is that the corners of the cube seem to be flattened, so that eight facets appear which are equilateral triangles (Fig. 57(*a*)). Further shrinking of the octahedron produces the shapes shown in Figs. 57(*b*), (*c*). The final stage is when the octahedron has shrunk so much that the cube has been squeezed completely into the shape of an octahedron (Fig. 56(*b*)).

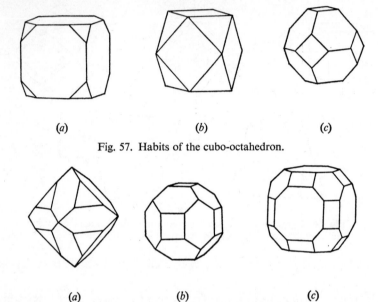

(*a*) (*b*) (*c*)

Fig. 57. Habits of the cubo-octahedron.

(*a*) (*b*) (*c*)

Fig. 58. Isometric multiple forms. (*a*) Octahedron and rhombo-dodecahedron, (*b*) cube and rhombo-dodecahedron, (*c*) cube, octahedron and rhombo-dodecahedron.

This process is called combining forms, and the product is a multiple form. In this case the multiple form is called a cubo-octahedron. When one form is developed much more than the other, the crystal is said to have the *habit* of that form; Fig. 57(*a*) shows a crystal with a cubic habit, and Fig. 57(*c*) a crystal with octahedral habit. *Habit is the dominant form.* Two forms can be combined only when:

(1) *they are in the same system and the unit cells are identical*;

(2) *they are in the same orientation.*

These conditions are necessary to stack unit cells without leaving any spaces.

It can be seen from Fig. 57 that the shapes of the faces are not in themselves fundamental, the cube faces are sometimes square and sometimes eight-sided; the octahedral faces may be triangular or six-sided. However, in any particular combination, for a given habit, all the faces of a particular form are still identical.

The tetragonal system

In this system there are three important forms:

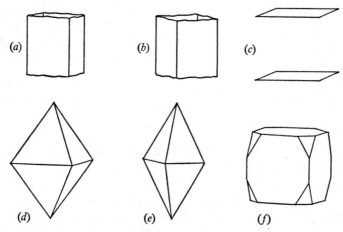

Fig. 59. Forms of the tetragonal system. (a) α-prism, (b) β-prism, (c) basal pinacoid, (d) α-bipyramid, (e) β-bipyramid, (f) a multiple form—α-prism, β-bipyramid and basal pinacoid.

(1) *The tetragonal prism* has four faces, four edges and no corners. It is an infinite tube with a square cross-section. Because the ends of the tube are not closed it is called an *open form*. There are two prisms, α and β, identical in shape but different in orientation. If they are combined, a prism with octagonal cross-section is formed.

(2) *The tetragonal bipyramid* is like an octahedron but its triangular faces, although *isosceles*, are not equilateral. It occurs like the prism in α and β orientations (Fig. 59(d), (e)). It also varies in its proportions along the z-axis.

(3) *The basal pinacoid* consists of two parallel and infinite planes which occur only at right angles to the z-axis (Fig. 59(c)). Because it is an open form it must be combined with another form before it can produce a crystal.

The multiple form (Fig. 59(f)), which looks rather like a cubo-octahedron, is composed of an α-tetragonal prism, a β-tetragonal bipyramid and a basal pinacoid. The facets are isosceles triangles.

The orthorhombic system

This has three forms only:

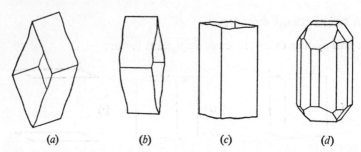

Fig. 60. Forms of the orthorhombic system. (*a*) *x*-prism, (*b*) *y*-prism, (*c*) *z*-prism, (*d*) a multiple form—*x*-, *y*-, *z*-pinacoids; *x*-, *y*- and two *z*-prisms; an orthorhombic bipyramid.

(1) *The orthorhombic prism* is an open tube with rhombic cross-section. The angles of the rhombus may vary any amount. The prisms may occur parallel to the *x*-, *y*- or *z*-axes and are termed *x*-, *y*- and *z*-prisms respectively.

(2) *The orthorhombic bipyramid* has a rhombic cross-section normal to *any* of the axes. The faces are in the shape of scalene triangles. It is similar to the tetragonal bipyramid but occurs only in the *β* orientation. It may vary both in proportion along the axes and in angular proportions of the cross-section.

(3) *The pinacoids* are exactly the same as in the tetragonal system but may occur normal to the *x*-, *y*- or *z*-axes, i.e. the *x*-, *y*- and *z*-pinacoids.

Fig. 60(*d*) shows a fairly complex multiple form; it is a crystal of $PbSO_4$.

The monoclinic system

There are only two forms: the pinacoid and the prism.

In the monoclinic system the *y*-axis is a diad which is perpendicular to a plane of symmetry (Fig. 61(*a*)). The crystals have a very characteristic squashed look about them.

(1) *The monoclinic prism* is rhombic in cross-section and identical to the orthorhombic prism in shape. It may occur in any position in which the prism axis is contained within the plane of symmetry (Fig. 61).

(2) *The pinacoid* is identical in shape to other pinacoids. It may occur *either* normal to the *y*-axis—the *y*-pinacoid—*or* in any position normal to the plane of symmetry—the symmetry-plane pinacoids.

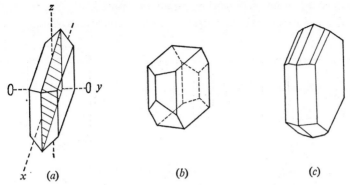

Fig. 61. Monoclinic multiple forms. (a) y-pinacoid, two prisms; (b) y-pinacoid, two symmetry-plane pinacoids, one prism; (c) y-pinacoid, four prisms.

The triclinic system

This system has only two forms. There are no symmetry axes or planes and the forms may occur in any orientation. A crystal is made up entirely of one type of form or the other—but not both.

(1) *The pedion or single face.* At least four are necessary to close the crystal.

(2) *The pinacoid.* At least three are required to close the crystals. Such crystals have a *centre of symmetry.*

The hexagonal and rhombohedral (trigonal) systems

These two systems are very similar. The hexagonal system has a hexad axis parallel to the z-axis, and the rhombohedral system a triad axis in the same position. Each system has three important forms but two of these are shared by the other system, so that it is only possible to classify the crystal when one of the unique forms is present.

(1) *The hexagonal prism* is an open tube with hexagonal cross-section. It occurs with axis parallel to the z-axis in α and β orientations. It is common to both systems.

(2) *The hexagonal bipyramid* is a bipyramid with hexagonal cross-section confined to the hexagonal system. It varies in proportion along the z-axis, and has α and β orientations.

(3) *The rhombohedron* has six faces all of which are rhombuses. It can vary in its proportions and occurs in α and β orientations. It is unique to the rhombohedral system.

(4) *The basal pinacoid* which is always orientated normal to z-axis.

Figure 62(c) shows a crystal of calcite composed of a rhombohedron and a hexagonal prism. It belongs to the rhombohedral system.

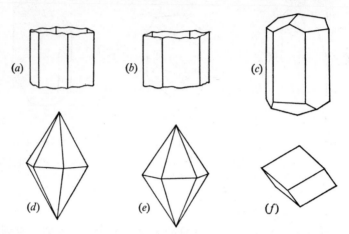

Fig. 62. Forms of hexagonal and rhombohedral systems. (a) α-hexagonal prism, (b) β-hexagonal prism, (c) α-hexagonal prism and β-rhombohedron, (d) α-hexagonal bipyramid, (e) β-hexagonal bipyramid, (f) α-rhombohedron.

Crystal analysis

To determine the system to which a crystal belongs and to establish what forms are present, apply the following rules:

1. Determine the system. *Count and specify all the symmetry axes present and correlate with the correct system.* See list on p. 116.

2. Count the number of forms. The faces of a single form are *all of the same size and shape*, and they are *regularly related to each other*.

3. Identify each form separately. Given—*the system, the number of faces,* and their *angular relationships*— the form can be identified immediately. If the form does not correspond to any described here, it can easily be found in any textbook of crystallography.

II. Internal structure of solids

Crystals can be classified according to the type of force holding the constituent particles together. There are five main types of bonding: ionic, covalent, metallic, van der Waals', and hydrogen bonding. They give rise to the following types of crystal:

    (1) ionic crystals;

    (2) giant molecular crystals (mainly covalent);

(3) layer structures (mainly covalent plus van der Waals');

(4) molecular crystals (covalent plus van der Waals'; covalent plus hydrogen bonding);

(5) metallic crystals.

Structure of elements: metals

Most metals crystallise in one of three main types of structure, all of which are held together by metallic bonding only. Since the forces holding the atoms of metals together are non-directional and all the atoms are of the same size and kind, the principle governing the crystal structures of metals is simply that all the atoms pack together as closely as possible in order to attain a position of minimum potential energy. Atoms are treated as spheres in the following discussion.

Closest packing of spheres. Figure 63 shows the closest possible packing of uniform spheres in one layer. Note that the central atom marked 1 is surrounded by six spheres touching it, the lines joining the centres of these six spheres forming a regular hexagon. Note also that the atoms may be considered in groups of three, with a rather small space between each group, the lines joining the centres of the three spheres forming an equilaterial triangle; these spaces form hollows on the surface layer. If a sphere is put on top of the first layer so that it rests in the hollow between any group of three spheres the space enclosed between the four spheres is called a *tetrahedral hole or site* because it is enclosed by four spheres whose centres lie at the apices of a regular tetrahedron. This site is of great importance in understanding crystal structures.

A second layer of spheres, resting in the hollows of the first layer, is shown in Fig. 64. The central sphere of the first layer, which is in contact

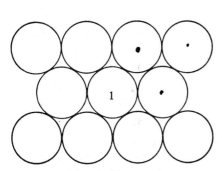

Fig. 63. Plan: one layer.

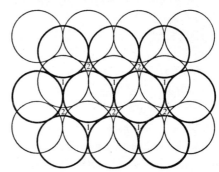

Fig. 64. Plan: two layers.

with six spheres in its own layer, is now shown also in contact with three more spheres in the second layer. Imagine now another layer similar to the second but situated *below* the first. The central sphere in the first layer is now in contact with six in its own layer, three in the second, and three more in this imaginary layer: a total of twelve. Its *co-ordination number* is therefore 12. This co-ordination number in the closest packed layer is characteristic of all metallic structures with closest packing, and is the maximum co-ordination number possible with spheres of equal radius.

Consider now a third layer on top of the two shown in Fig. 64. There are two different arrangements possible for this.

First arrangement. The spheres may be placed in the hollows marked 1, so that each sphere will be directly above one in the first layer. The third layer will then be exactly similar in position to the first. If *A* is used to represent

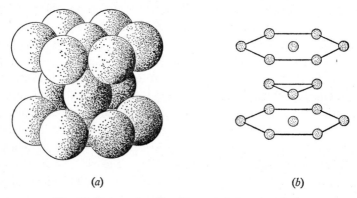

(a)   (b)

Fig. 65. Picture elevation. Hexagonal closest packed.

the arrangement in the first layer, and *B* that in the second, then the building-order described is *ABABAB*... and so on. This structure is called *hexagonal closest packed* because it has an axis of sixfold symmetry at right angles *to the layers of closest packing,* i.e. at right angles to the plane of the paper in Fig. 64. A unit cell for this arrangement is shown in Fig. 65; Fig. 65(*a*) showing full-sized spheres in contact, Fig. 65(*b*) the corresponding space lattice. Note that the spheres in the top and bottom faces are close packed but those in the side faces are not.

Second arrangement. The spheres may be placed in the hollows marked 2 in Fig. 64. In this position they lie directly above holes between the first layer spheres and therefore have different positions from the spheres in the first layer. Using *C* to represent the arrangement of the third layer, this building order is *ABCABC...* and so on. This structure is called *cubic closest packed* since it has the symmetry of the cube. A unit cell and space lattice for it are shown in Fig. 66.

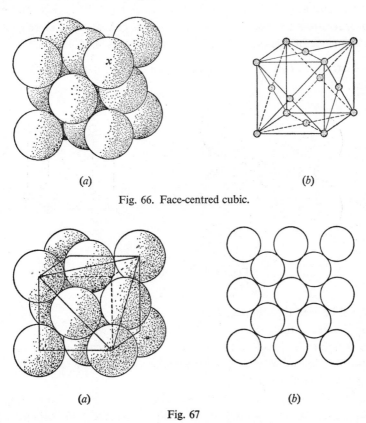

(a)   (b)

Fig. 66. Face-centred cubic.

(a)   (b)

Fig. 67

Inspection of Fig. 66 shows that there is a sphere at the centre of each face of the cube. This arrangement is therefore called the *face-centred cubic structure*. It is obvious that the spheres forming the faces of the unit cell in Fig. 66(a) are not close packed. If the building up of the front layer of this cell is continued (Fig. 67(b)), the holes are seen to be bounded by four spheres and have a squarish appearance. If a similar-sized sphere is pressed into one of these holes from the front, and another from the back the space enclosed is called an *octahedral hole or site* since it is bounded by six touching spheres with their centres at the corners of a regular octahedron. Octahedral sites, like tetrahedral sites, are of great importance in understanding crystal structures. If the sphere marked x in Fig. 66(a) is removed, the exposed layer has six spheres Fig. 67 (*a*), which can be grouped in threes with a roughly triangular hole between them, i.e. a close-packed arrangement. All the close-packed layers in the face-centred cubic structure are in planes at right angles to the body-diagonals of the cube and show a co-ordination number of twelve, the same as in hexagonal close packing. The sequence of layers along the body-diagonal is *ABCABC*....

Third arrangement. A unit cell and space lattice for this type are shown in Fig. 68.

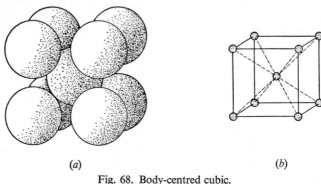

(*a*)   (*b*)

Fig. 68. Body-centred cubic.

It will be seen that there is a sphere at the centre of the cube, with eight other spheres at the corners of the cube in contact with the central sphere. This structure is therefore called the *body-centred cubic* structure. It has a co-ordination number of 8 and the packing is not quite so close as in the other two metallic structures.

About fifty metals have either (or both) face-centred cubic or hexagonal close-packed structures, and about twenty have the body-centred cubic structure. Some common metals in each type are:

Face-centred cubic: copper, silver, gold, platinum, calcium, lead, iron, nickel.

Hexagonal close-packed: magnesium, zinc, chromium, nickel.

Body-centred cubic: the alkali metals, iron, chromium.

In the first two types there is 26 % *of empty space between the atoms*, in the third 32 %.

There are no broad general trends in metallic structure in passing along the Periods.

Structure of elements: non-metals

These form three main types of crystals: (1) giant molecules, (2) layer structures, (3) molecular crystals.

As with metals, all the atoms are of the same kind, but the covalent bonding forces in non-metal elements are very different from those in the metals, and give rise to molecules (molecules are never found in typical metallic crystals). Because each non-metal atom can form only a limited number of covalent bonds (four or less are usual) and because these are arranged each in its own specific direction in space relative to the others (see p. 143) the shapes of their molecules (and hence the shapes of their crystals) are determined by the number of covalent bonds which their atoms can form, i.e. by the valencies of the elements, which also determine their position in the Periods. When a non-metal has more than one valency, the lower valency is used in forming its molecule (and crystal), the valency being given by the $(8-N)$ rule, where N is the Group number.

The noble gases are a special case. Being very inactive they do not form molecules. However, when they are cooled sufficiently they form crystalline solids because the very weak van der Waals' forces of attraction between their atoms are still strong enough to bind the atoms into crystal lattices when the kinetic energy of the atoms is sufficiently reduced. The forces of attraction acting in all directions cause the atoms (assumed to be spherical) to pack as closely as possible just as in the case of metals. The solids all have face-centred cubic structures.

Returning to the other non-metals, consider for example, those of Periods 2 and 3, omitting boron in Period 2 which is a semi-metal.

Period 2. Carbon (diamond and graphite structure). The two allotropes of carbon, diamond and graphite, have quite different structures, both of which are important.

(1) *The diamond structure (cubic system).* This structure is determined by the fact that the valency of carbon is 4. Each carbon atom forms with its neighbours four covalent bonds (sp^3 hybridised) disposed tetrahedrally; i.e. each carbon atom is surrounded by four others whose centres are at the corners of a regular tetrahedron with the carbon atom at its centre, the central atom being in contact with the other four. The centres of all the carbon atoms are the same distance apart (1.54 Å). Representing the position (but not the size) of the atoms by a small circle, Fig. 69(*a*) is obtained. Extending the structure to include more carbon atoms Fig. 69(*b*)

is obtained. In this, not all of the carbon atoms have been given their full complement of bonds. The whole figure is tetrahedral, the area of the triangular base increasing as the diagram is extended downwards.

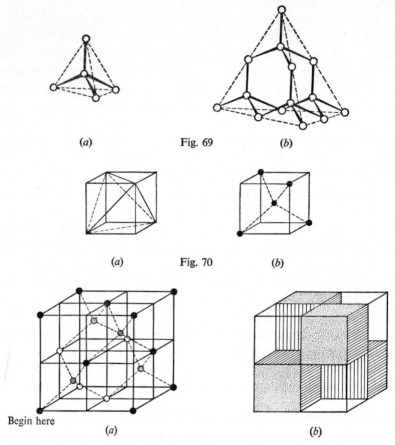

(a)   Fig. 69   (b)

(a)   Fig. 70   (b)

Begin here

(a)   (b)

Fig. 71. Unit cell of diamond (cubic).

If now a single tetrahedron with its carbon atoms is inserted into a cube, the result is as in Fig. 70(b). The orientation of the tetrahedron is of course not as in Fig. 69(a) where it is standing on a face, but as in Fig. 70(a) where it is balancing on an edge. It is seen that only four of the corners of the cube are furnished with carbon atoms. This structure is therefore far from close-packed.

The next figure is drawn by making the small cube of Fig. 70, the bottom left-hand cube of a large cube containing eight small cubes Fig. 71(a).

The internal bonds of this small cube are continued till the large cube is furnished with carbon atoms. Four extra carbon atoms, with no bonds shown, are added to complete the pattern. These are bonded to other carbon atoms outside the structure shown.

The unit cell of diamond is important in its own right, and also because it is found in other elements and many compounds. In it, only four of the eight little cubes have atoms at their *centres*. These four are shown shaded in Fig. 71(*b*). This emphasises that the structure is far from close-packed. Indeed two-thirds of the structure is empty space, as against one-third in the body-centred structure of some metals (p. 126), where all the small cubes have an atom at their centres. Diamond is described as a three-dimensional *giant molecule* (or macromolecule). Its C.N. is 4.

(2) *The graphite structure: a layer structure (hexagonal system)*. This structure (Fig. 72) consists of layers of carbon atoms in each of which the atoms are arranged in a regular hexagonal network. Each mesh contains six carbon atoms (as in the benzene molecule), the whole layer forming a two-dimensional giant molecule with indeterminate boundaries (Fig. 73). The distances between the centres of the carbon atoms in the layers are all equal (1.42 Å). Each carbon atom is surrounded by three

carbon atoms thus ⌃•, i.e. C.N. 3. The sigma bonds between the

carbon atoms are sp^2 hybrid bonds with bond angles 120°. Each carbon atom uses three electrons for these bonds. The fourth electron is in an

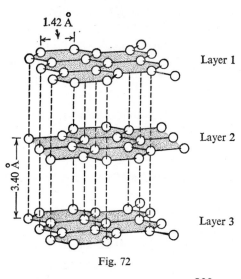

Layer 1

Layer 2

Layer 3

1.42 Å

3.40 Å

Fig. 72

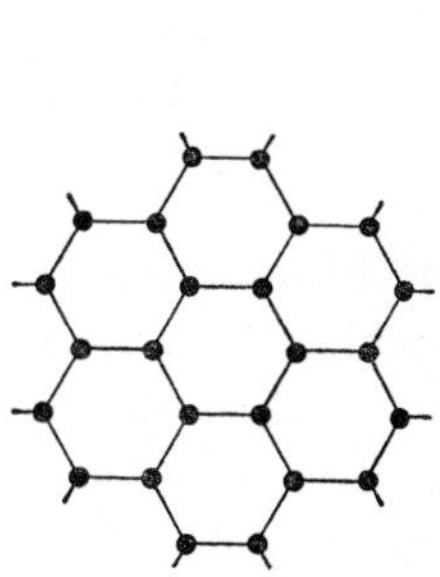

Fig. 73

unhybridised p orbital. These electrons are delocalised and form a cloud above and below the sigma bonds, thus giving π-bonding in addition to sigma bonding, hence the shorter internuclear distance (1.42 Å) in graphite, compared with diamond (1.54 Å). The electrons should be thought of as able to move throughout all the branches of the network, resembling in this respect the electrons in a metallic structure, but in two dimensions. The layers are 3.40 Å apart, held together by weak van der Waals' forces. Note that each atom in layer 1 is directly above a corresponding atom in layer 3.

Period 2. Nitrogen, oxygen and fluorine. The atomic radii graphs (p. 69) show that, apart from H and He, the elements, B, C, N, O, F in Period 2 have much smaller radii than any of the other elements. Because of this C, N and O more readily form stable multiple covalent bonds than any other element, the closer approach of the atoms permitting the necessary sideways overlap of p orbitals for double and triple bonds.

Nitrogen. Each nitrogen atom, valency three, uses its three unpaired electrons to link up with another nitrogen atom to form the nitrogen molecule $:N\equiv N:$ or N_2 containing a triple covalent bond. Since there are no unpaired electrons left over to form covalent bonds with other nitrogen atoms or molecules, the nitrogen molecules are attracted to each other only by weak van der Waals' forces and nitrogen is therefore a gas under ordinary conditions, although it can be solidified at low temperatures forming *molecular crystals.*

Oxygen has two unpaired electrons in its valency shell, and so it is usually divalent. As with nitrogen, the bonding electrons are used to link two oxygen atoms together giving the diatomic molecule O_2. This is often represented as $O{=}O$, but, as will be seen later (p. 468), the bonding is not as simple as this. Oxygen at low temperatures solidifies forming molecular crystals.

Fluorine like nitrogen and oxygen forms a diatomic molecule

$$:\overset{\cdot\cdot}{\underset{\cdot\cdot}{F}}\overset{xx}{\underset{xx}{\times}}F^{\times}_{\times} \quad \text{or} \quad :\overset{\cdot\cdot}{\underset{\cdot\cdot}{F}}{-}\overset{\cdot\cdot}{\underset{\cdot\cdot}{F}}: \quad \text{or} \quad F_2.$$

In this case the single unpaired electron in one atom along with that in another form a single covalent bond.

The three elements, nitrogen, oxygen and fluorine resemble each other in forming diatomic molecules (with C.N. therefore 1), in being gases under ordinary conditions, and in forming molecular crystals at low temperatures.

Period 3. Non-metals: silicon, phosphorus, sulphur and chlorine.

Silicon forms a giant molecule with the diamond structure.

White phosphorus, covalency $(8-N) = 3$, differs from nitrogen (in the same group) in forming a tetratomic molecule P_4 (Fig. 74) in which only single covalent bonds are present. Its shape is tetrahedral (but there is no atom at the centre of the tetrahedron) C.N. 3. Because of its considerable molecular weight of 124, white phosphorus is a crystalline solid but has a low melting point of 44 °C. The molecules in the crystal lattice are bound together by weak van der Waals' forces forming a molecular crystal.

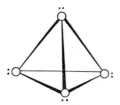

Fig. 74. P_4 molecule.

Fig. 75. S_8 molecule.

Rhombic sulphur, a solid of melting point 114 °C, differs from oxygen (in same group) in forming an octatomic molecule S_8 whose shape is a puckered ring (Fig. 75). Each sulphur atom displays a covalency of two $(8-N)$. Sulphur, like phosphorus forms molecular crystals.

Chlorine resembles fluorine in forming a diatomic molecule Cl_2 in which the atoms are linked by a single covalent bond. Solid chlorine forms molecular crystals.

Note that in all the non-metallic structures the elements have a valency of $(8-N)$. The allotropy of oxygen, phosphorus, and sulphur will be considered later in their respective Groups.

Broad trends in structure of elements

Interesting transitions between the main crystal types can be found in both Periods and Groups (see later). Period 5 is a good example.

	C.N.
Ag: true metal, face-centred cubic	12
Cd and In: distorted close-packed	
Sn (white): distorted close-packed	6
Sn (grey): giant molecule (diamond structure)	4
Sb (metallic): layers—covalent bonding within layers, metallic bonding between them	
Sb (yellow): molecular crystal Sb_4 (as P_4)	3
Te: chains—covalent bonding within chains, metallic bonding between them	2
I: molecular crystal I_2	1

Summary of trends in structure and bonding in elements across the Periods

	Mainly close-packed metallic structures: F.C.C., H.C.P. and B.C.C.		Giant molecules, layers or chains (stable allotropes)		Molecular crystals		
	IA---IB	IIB	IIIB	IVB	VB	VIB	VIIB
2	Li		B	C	N	O	F
3	Na		Al	Si	P	S	Cl
4	K----Cu	Zn	Ga	Ge	As	Se	Br
5	Rb---Ag	Cd	In	Sn Grey	Sb	Te	I
				Sn White			
6	Cs ---Au	Hg	Tl	Pb	Bi		

P (white), As (white), Sb (yellow) and Se (red) are unstable allotropes not shown in the table. They all form molecular crystals.

Each of the major sub-divisions of the Periodic Table into structural types as shown above also corresponds to the change in the predominant type of bonding shown by the elements. The type of bonding shown in each sub-division is outlined in the following table.

	Metallic crystals	Giant molecules	Molecular crystals
Structure	Close-packed metallic structure	(a) Three-dimensional, e.g. diamond (b) Two-dimensional (layers), e.g. graphite (c) One-dimensional (chains) e.g. tellurium	Molecular crystals consisting of discrete molecules
Bonding	Metallic	(a) Covalent (b) Covalent in the layers, van der Waals' between layers (c) Covalent in the chains, metallic bonding between chains	Covalent within the molecules. Van der Waals' between the molecules

Structure of compounds

There are three main types: ionic crystals, giant-molecular crystals (including layer lattices) and molecular crystals. The division is not clear-cut; pure ionic or pure covalent bonds are unknown.

Ionic crystals

1. The sodium chloride structure (cubic system). The number of chloride ions that can pack round a single sodium atom is limited by the relative size of the ions (p. 76: Na^+, 0.95 Å; Cl^-, 1.81 Å). In Fig. 76 the

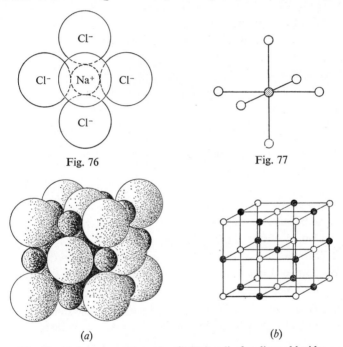

Fig. 76   Fig. 77

(a)   (b)

Fig. 78. (a) Ions drawn to scale. (b) Unit cell of sodium chloride: ●, sodium ion; ○, chloride ion.

four Cl^- ions in the plane of the paper each touch the Na^+ ion but do not touch each other (because of mutual repulsion). An additional Cl^- ion can be packed in front of the central sodium ion, and another behind making six in all. The sodium ion is said to have a *co-ordination number* of 6.

The diagram can be made clearer by representing the position of the *centre* of each ion by a *small* circle and by giving a perspective view (Fig. 77). The three axes of symmetry are mutually at right angles. The Cl^- ions are as far as possible from each other, the angular distance between any two being 90°; i.e. they are equally spaced. To satisfy the empirical formula NaCl, each Cl^- ion must have six Na^+ ions in contact with it (but the Na^+ ions are widely separated). The Cl^- ion also has C.N. 6. There is still an electrostatic field permeating the space outside the structure, so it continues to attract other ions or ion pairs, and the structure shown in Fig. 78 is built up, the process continuing indefinitely.

A framework on which the constituents of a crystal can be shown arranged in a symmetrical way is called a *space lattice*. The sodium chloride structure may be described as a face-centred cubic arrangement of chloride ions with sodium ions in the octahedral holes.

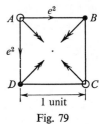

Fig. 79

It may be asked why an ionic crystal holds together, since it contains equal numbers of equally charged cations and anions, and while unlike charges attract each other, like charges repel. Consider a small square, length of side 1 unit, from the lattice (Fig. 79). The forces acting between charged particles are given by the formula

$$\text{Force} = \frac{Q_1 Q_2}{kd^2},$$

where k is the dielectric constant and d the distance between the centres of the particles. $k = 1$ if the charges are separated by air or a vacuum. Ion B attracts ion A with force $= (e^2/1^2) = e^2$, where e is the size of the charge on an electron or proton. Ion D attracts ion A with the same force e^2. The resultant of these two forces (represented by the diagonal) is equal to $\sqrt{2} \cdot e^2 = 1.414e^2$. There are similar forces of $1.4e^2$ pulling ions B, C and D towards the centre of the square. The force of mutual repulsion between ions A and $C = e^2/(\sqrt{2} \times \sqrt{2}) = 0.5e^2$. The resultant of the forces of attraction and repulsion acting on ion A along AC is therefore

$$1.4e^2 - 0.5e^2 = 0.9e^2.$$

Thus each ion is attracted to the centre of the square.

Note. (1) Since the crystal is composed of ions, not atoms, it must not be said that the substance ionises when dissolved in water (or melted): it is already ionised. It *dissociates*, i.e. the particles leave the crystal lattice and are scattered through the solution (or melt).

(2) It is incorrect to talk about a *molecule* of sodium chloride. There are no Na^+Cl^- groups separated from each other in the crystal. NaCl is an empirical formula, not a molecular formula.

Contents of a unit cell. See Fig. 78(*b*).

An ion at a corner of the cell is shared by 8 cells, i.e. $\frac{1}{8}$ each
An ion on an edge of the cell is shared by 4 cells, i.e. $\frac{1}{4}$ each
An ion on a face of the cell is shared by 2 cells, i.e. $\frac{1}{2}$ each
An ion whose centre lies inside the cell is not shared and counts as 1
Therefore the contents of the sodium chloride unit cell Fig. 78(*b*) are:

	Na^+	Cl^-
8 chloride ions at the corners at $\frac{1}{8}$ each	—	1
6 chloride ions on the faces at $\frac{1}{2}$ each	—	3
12 sodium ions on the edges at $\frac{1}{4}$ each	3	
1 sodium ion inside the cell	1	
Total	4	4

This total corresponds to an empirical formula of NaCl, as it must.

Many compounds with empirical formula *AB* crystallise with the sodium chloride structure (see pp. 138–9).

Before going on to consider the three other most common structures of ionic crystals (binary compounds) some principles underlying all ionic structures will be stated.

At least two elements are needed to form an ionic crystal, one for the cation, the other for the anion. All ionic crystals are therefore compounds. Conversely crystals of elements are never ionic.

Since anions are larger than cations (except F^- in Rb^+F^- and Cs^+F^-, which is smaller), it is necessary to start by considering the packing of anions around cations.

The ratio of the co-ordination numbers of the cation and the anion must be the same as the ratio shown in the empirical formula, so that overall electrostatic neutrality is achieved. Thus for Na^+Cl^- the ratio of the C.N.'s is 6:6, the same as in the formula.

The principle underlying the structure of ionic crystals is that each cation attracts round itself and makes contact with as many anions as possible, while each anion repels other anions to as great a distance as possible. In this way, minimum potential energy and maximum stability of the system is achieved. When anions are in contact with each other, the structure tends to be unstable.

The number of anions able to pack round a cation depends on the relative sizes of the cation and anion, i.e. on the radius ratio

$$\frac{\text{radius of cation}}{\text{radius of anion}} = \frac{r_C}{r_A};$$

a ratio almost always less than 1.

Radius ratio rule. The three most important geometrical figures in structural chemistry are the cube (regular hexahedron), the regular octahedron, and the regular tetrahedron; all are forms of the cubic system of crystals (p. 117). Figure 80 shows spheres in contact with each other, with their centres at the corners of these figures.

At the centre of each figure is a space enclosed by the surrounding spheres. These spaces are called cubic, octahedral and tetrahedral holes respectively. If the spheres represent anions, and cations are put into the central spaces so that they fit neatly and touch each of the surrounding spheres, the C.N. of the cation in Fig. 80(*a*) is 8, in (*b*) 6 and in (*c*) 4.

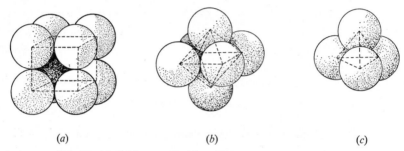

(*a*)	(*b*)	(*c*)

Fig. 80. (*a*) Cubic co-ordination, (*b*) octahedral co-ordination,
(*c*) tetrahedral co-ordination.

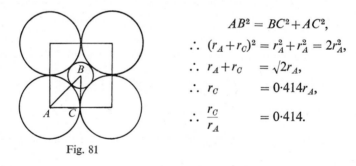

$$AB^2 = BC^2 + AC^2,$$
$$\therefore \; (r_A + r_C)^2 = r_A^2 + r_A^2 = 2r_A^2,$$
$$\therefore \; r_A + r_C = \sqrt{2}\,r_A,$$
$$\therefore \; r_C = 0.414\,r_A,$$
$$\therefore \; \frac{r_C}{r_A} = 0.414.$$

Fig. 81

The radius ratio is calculated for each structure as shown for (*b*). Figure 81 is a horizontal cross-section through Fig. 80(*b*).

Since the anions are touching each other, this ratio is critical. If the anions are larger, the cation loses contact with them, the structure becomes unstable and tends to change to tetrahedral co-ordination in which only four anions contact the cation and the anions are no longer in contact with each other. If the anions are smaller, the structure is stable up to the point when there is enough room to pack 8 anions around the cation; the structure then changes to cubic co-ordination. The radius ratio for cubic co-ordination is 0.73 and for tetrahedral co-ordination 0.23.

The discussion may be summed up in the following table:

Radius ratio rule

Type of co-ordination	C.N. of cation	Radius ratio range within which structure stable
Cubic	8	0.73 and above
Octahedral	6	0.41–0.73
Tetrahedral	4	0.23–0.41

The radius ratio rule is found to agree well with the observed structures of most ionic crystals. It is a good example of a use of ionic radii.

For the sodium chloride structure:

$$\frac{r_C}{r_A} = \frac{0.95}{1.81} = 0.53$$

$$\therefore \text{ C.N.} = 6:6, \text{ bonding ionic.}$$

The radius ratio rule is true only for ionic crystals not for covalent.

2. The caesium chloride structure, CsCl (cubic system). This is very similar to the body-centred cubic structure in metals (p. 126), except that there is a Cs^+ ion at the centre of the cube and Cl^- ions at its corners, C.N. 8:8. It is incorrect to describe the CsCl structure as body-centred cubic because this term implies that the atom or ion at the centre is the same as those at the corners. The bonding is essentially ionic, as indicated by the high C.N. of the cation.

3. The fluorite structure, CaF_2 (cubic system). Each Ca^{2+} ion is surrounded by eight F^- ions at the corners of a cube (Fig. 82). (The Ca^{2+} ion at the top marked A is joined by dotted lines to four F^- ions below it

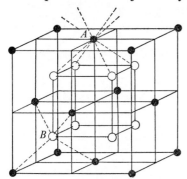

$$\frac{r_C}{r_A} = \frac{0.99}{1.36} = 0.73,$$

C.N. = 8:4, bonding ionic.

Fig. 82. Fluorite structure: ●, Ca^{2+}; ○, F^-.

and to four others above, not shown.) Each F⁻ ion is surrounded by four Ca^{2+} ions arranged tetrahedrally (see B in figure). The C.N. of the fluorite structure is 8:4 (same ratio as CaF_2). The high C.N. of the cation indicates ionic bonding. Another way of regarding the structure is as a face-centred cubic arrangement of Ca^{2+} ions, with F⁻ ions filling all the tetrahedral holes, which are situated two on each body-diagonal of the cube.

The structure shows some resemblance to the cristobalite structure (p. 382), in the tetrahedral arrangement of ions in the small cubes; the essential difference is that in CaF_2, which is ionic, there is an F⁻ ion at the centre of each little cube, whereas in cristobalite (SiO_2, C.N. 4:2), which is covalent, there is a silicon atom at the centre of every second cube. The CaF_2 structure is therefore much more closely packed. The eight F⁻ ions, each at the centre of a small cube, are themselves at the corners of a cube as shown in Fig. 82.

The anti-fluorite structure is identical in pattern with the fluorite structure but differs in that the anions and cations have changed places. An example is Na_2O, C.N. 4:8.

4. The rutile structure, TiO₂ (tetragonal system).

The unit cell is tetragonal (Fig. 83), i.e. one axis (horizontal in diagram) is longer than the two others which are equal. In rutile, each Ti^{4+} ion is surrounded by six O^{2-} ions arranged octahedrally (see A at cell centre), and each O^{2-} ion by three Ti^{4+} ions at the corners of a nearly equilateral triangle (see B), C.N. 6:3 (same ratio as in TiO_2). The structure may also be regarded as a distorted body-centred cubic arrangement of Ti^{4+} ions, with O^{2-} ions in positions of threefold co-ordination.

High co-ordination numbers (8 or 6) are evidence of ionic binding.

Other compounds with the same structures as those considered are:
Caesium chloride. CsBr, CsI, TlCl, NH_4Cl, NH_4Br.
Sodium chloride. All Group IA halides (except CsCl, CsBr, CsI);

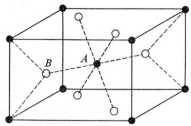

$$\frac{r_C}{r_A} = \frac{0.68}{1.40} = 0.49,$$

C.N. 6:3, bonding ionic.

Fig. 83. Rutile structure: ●, Ti^{4+}; ○, O^{2-}.

hydrides of Group IA; oxides and sulphides of Group IIA (except BeO, BeS); AgF, AgCl, AgBr, MnO, FeO, NiO, CoO, MnS.

Fluorite. Fluorides of Ca, Sr, Ba; Cd, Hg, Pb; $SrCl_2$.

Rutile. MgF_2, $CaCl_2$, $CaBr_2$, MnF_2, FeF_2, CoF_2, NiF_2, ZnF_2, MnO_2, SnO_2, PbO_2.

Three-dimensional giant molecules

1. The zinc blende structure, ZnS (cubic system). This is very similar to the diamond structure (p. 128). The unit cell is cubic (like diamond) and the arrangement of atoms is the same in both; the difference is that in zinc blende, zinc and sulphur atoms alternate with each other. Each zinc atom is surrounded tetrahedrally by four sulphur atoms, and each sulphur atom tetrahedrally by four zinc atoms, C.N. 4:4. Each atom is linked by predominantly covalent bonds to its four neighbours. Of the eight electrons needed for four bonds six are provided by each sulphur atom and two by each zinc atom. All the valency electrons of the sulphur and zinc atoms are used in the structure.

In diamond the total number of valency electrons shared by each atom is eight; the same is true of zinc blende. Many binary compounds of elements whose valency electrons total eight have the zinc blende structure. It follows that the pair of elements must be either from Group IVB, e.g. silicon carbide, SiC, or from Groups symmetrically placed on each side of Group IVB, e.g. AlP, BeS, CdS, HgS, CuCl, CuBr, CuI, AgI.

All the above compounds are semi-conductors (p. 192); so are the elements silicon and germanium which also have the diamond structure.

2. The β-cristobalite structure, SiO_2 (cubic system). See pp. 381, 382.

Two-dimensional giant molecules: layer structures

The cadmium iodide structure, CdI_2 (hexagonal system). This is an example of a number of predominantly covalent structures. The essential feature of these is that each layer is a kind of sandwich and the whole structure is made by stacking layers on top of each other with a space between. In CdI_2, each sandwich consists of a filling of Cd^{2+} ions enclosed on each side by I^- ions (Fig. 84). Each Cd^{2+} ion is surrounded by six I^- ions arranged octahedrally. Each I^- is at the apex of a triangular pyramid with three Cd^{2+} ions at the corners of the base, C.N. 6:3. The Cd^{2+} ions are thus all on one side of the I^- ions, so the environment of the I^- ions is not symmetrical. This lack of symmetry is characteristic of layer structures and is caused by a considerable polarisation of large ions by small doubly charged cations. The layers consist of close-packed I^- ions with Cd^{2+} ions in the octahedral holes. The octahedra are not standing on their apices but lying on their faces. Each octahedron is surrounded by six others with which it shares six edges. (The pattern can be shown clearly by making seven thin-cardboard octahedra and packing them to form a roughly hexagonal layer.) The bonding within the layers is partly ionic, partly covalent because of polarisation. Between the layers the bonding is by van der Waals' forces. The crystals are therefore soft and cleave easily between the layers, forming flakes.

Other compounds with the CdI_2 structure are: CaI_2, $MgBr_2$, MgI_2; $FeBr_2$, FeI_2, $CoBr_2$; SnS_2, TiS_2; PbI_2.

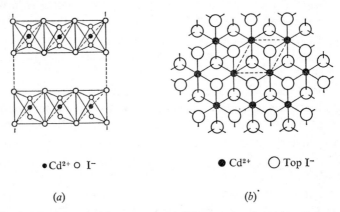

$\bullet Cd^{2+}$ $\circ$ I^- $\bullet$ Cd^{2+} $\bigcirc$ Top I^-

(a)   (b)

Fig. 84. Cadmium iodide structure. (a) Side view showing a row from each of two layers; (b) plan view, one layer.

Molecular crystals

Molecular crystals consist of discrete molecules held together by van der Waals' forces. The shapes of molecules and the bonding within them are considered in the next section.

It is not possible to give simple general trends on structure of compounds in relation to the Periodic Table as was done for elements, because the number of compounds is enormous. Much can be done to systematise the subject by considering variation in structure of large classes of binary compounds, oxides, chlorides, hydrides, sulphides and carbides across the Periods and down the Groups. This has been done to a considerable extent in other parts of the book (see index).

III. Covalent molecules

Pasteur (1848) suggested that those substances in the liquid state or in solution which affect polarised light (i.e. a beam of light whose waves all lie in one plane) have an asymmetrical arrangement of the atoms in their molecules and exhibit optical isomerism (see any good textbook of organic chemistry). Le Bel and van't Hoff independently pointed out (1874) that the asymmetrical arrangement of atoms in the molecules of optically active organic compounds corresponds to a carbon atom with four different radicals attached to it. Van't Hoff suggested that if the four valency bonds of a carbon atom are directed towards the corners of a regular tetrahedron and each is attached to a different radical then, because no plane or axis of symmetry can be drawn through the structure, another structure which is a non-superposable mirror-image of the first could also exist (Fig. 85). This provided a simple explanation of the occurrence of optical isomerism and gave real meaning to the geometry of molecules.

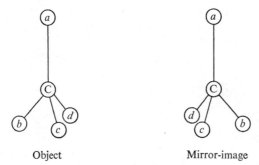

Object   Mirror-image

Fig. 85. An asymmetric carbon atom and its mirror-image.

Hybridisation

The spatial characteristics of atomic orbitals provide an important approach to the structure of covalent molecules. Thus s orbitals are spherically arranged around the nucleus of the atom, whereas the three orbitals in a given p sub-shell extend outwards along three axes at right angles to each other (see p. 53). Because of this it may be anticipated that atoms which use these orbitals for bond formation have bonds at right angles to each other. Usually, however, the geometry of molecules does not correspond to that predicted from a consideration of the orientation of the simple s, p, d and f orbitals which may be used in the bonding. This is because the process of bond formation leads to a certain amount of rearrangement. Thus, it can be shown that an atom with one s and three p orbitals can form four equivalent bonds directed towards the corners of a regular tetrahedron. Each of these four new orbitals is called an sp^3 *hybrid orbital*, i.e. an orbital which is derived by mixing one s orbital and three p orbitals. Carbon provides one of the more important examples of sp^3 hybridisation (see p. 360). However, if instead of using all three p orbitals in the process of hybridisation only two are included, it can be shown that this will result in three equivalent sp^2 orbitals lying in a plane at angles

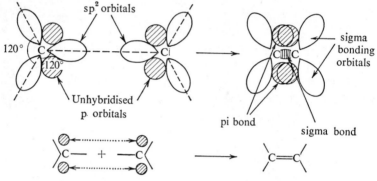

Fig. 86. Double bond formation through orbital overlap.

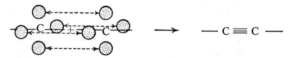

Fig. 87. Triple bond formation through orbital overlap. Each carbon atom has two unhybridised p orbitals.

of 120° to each other. Such an arrangement can be used to account for carbon to carbon double bonds (Fig. 86). Overlap of an sp^2 orbital of one carbon atom with that of another produces a σ-bond; simultaneously the unhybridised p orbital in each of these atoms also overlap and this produces a π-bond which is rather weaker than a σ-bond in the case of carbon. The strength of a covalent bond is roughly related to the extent to which the orbitals forming the bond overlap. As a result the carbon atoms are joined by two bonds of unequal strength.

Besides the two cases of hybridisation already mentioned, carbon also shows sp hybridisation. In this case there are two co-linear sp orbitals and two unhybridised p orbitals. Overlap of sp orbitals from two carbon atoms joins them by a σ-bond. Also formed are two π-bonds formed by the overlap of the two p orbitals in each uncombined atom. This gives three bonds and is the arrangement in acetylene (C_2H_2) which is a linear molecule with a carbon to carbon triple bond (Fig. 87).

The electron pair repulsion theory

The shapes of simple molecules can also be deduced by applying the following concepts:

(1) *Electron pairs in the outer shell of the central atom in a covalent molecule largely determine the geometry of the molecule.*

(2) *Electron pairs repel one another and arrange themselves in space so as to be as far apart as possible and thus tend to reduce the forces of repulsion to a minimum.*

Fig. 88. A molecule of mercury(II) chloride.

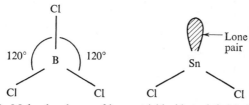

Fig. 89. Molecular shapes of boron trichloride and tin(II) chloride.

In a simple covalent molecule like mercury(II) chloride the mercury atom shares an electron pair with each of the two chlorine atoms and these are farthest apart when they lie on opposite sides of the mercury atom and the bonds are directed along the straight line joining them (Fig. 88).

With three pairs of electrons around the central atom two possibilities arise: (1) all three are employed in bonding, e.g. BCl_3; (2) one pair is not used in bond formation and exists as a lone pair, e.g. $SnCl_2$. Three electron pairs are at their greatest distance apart when they lie at the corners of an equilateral triangle. Hence, molecules in which there are three pairs of electrons will have bonds which lie in the same plane and radiate from the centre making angles of 120° with each other (Fig. 89). The tin(II) chloride molecule is V-shaped and the angle between the bonds is less than 120°. In order to take this and similar examples into account a third assumption must be made.

(3) *Electron pairs exert greater repulsion if they are uncombined, i.e. repulsion between electron pairs diminishes in the order lone pair/lone pair, long pair/bonding pair, bonding pair/bonding pair.*

The lone pair, not being pulled out by the nucleus of an attached atom is therefore closer to and repels more strongly other electron pairs in the atom.

Molecules in which the central atom has four electron pairs in its outer shell may adopt either of three shapes (Fig. 90), depending whether:

(*a*) all the electron pairs are being used for bonding, as in methane, CH_4, when the molecule will be tetrahedral;

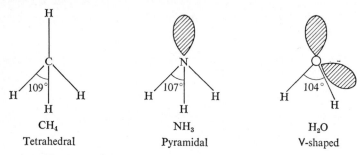

Fig. 90. Molecular shapes of methane, ammonia and water.

(*b*) only three pairs are being used for bonding as in ammonia, when the molecule will be pyramidal;

or (*c*) only two pairs are being used for bonding as in water, when the molecule will be V-shaped.

As the number of lone pairs increases so does the repulsion on the remaining bonding pairs and so they are pushed further together and the bond angle decreases from the tetrahedral angle (109°) in CH_4, to 107° in NH_3, and 104° in H_2O. It is interesting to note that amongst the hydrides of Group V the bond angle diminishes with decreasing electronegativity of the central atom. A similar effect occurs in Group VI,

NH_3	PH_3	AsH_3	SbH_3
107°	94°	92°	91°

	H_2O	H_2S	
	104°	92°	

$\longrightarrow$

Central atom becomes less electronegative

As the attraction of the central atom for electrons falls, the bonding pairs are less closely held. Thus in the N—H bonds the electron pairs are nearer the nitrogen atom than they are to the phosphorus atom in the P—H

144

bonds. The electron pairs in NH_3 are therefore nearer each other than in PH_3 and hence repel each other more strongly.

A summary of some of the shapes shown by molecules in which there are up to seven electron pairs in the outer, or valency shell, is given below:

Total number of electron pairs in valency shell	Arrangement of electron pairs in space	Number of bonding pairs	Number of lone pairs	Shape of molecule	Example
2	Linear	2	0	Linear	$HgCl_2$
3	Equilateral triangle	3	0	Triangular	BCl_3
		2	1	V-shaped	$SnCl_2$
4	Regular tetrahedron	4	0	Tetrahedral	CH_4
		3	1	Pyramidal	NH_3
		2	2	V-shaped	H_2O
5	Trigonal bipyramid	5	0	Trigonal bipyramid	PCl_5
		4	1	Irregular tetrahedron	SF_4
		3	2	T-shaped	ClF_3
6	Octahedron	6	0	Regular octahedron	SF_6
		5	1	Square pyramid	IF_5
7	Pentagonal bipyramid	7	0	Pentagonal bipyramid	IF_7

Exercises

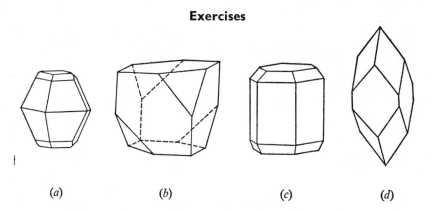

(a)　　　　　(b)　　　　　(c)　　　　　(d)

1. For each of the crystals shown above: (a) identify the system; (b) count the number of forms present; (c) identify each form separately.

2. Collect and tabulate information from part II of this book on trends in structures of oxides, chlorides and hydrides across the Periods. Are any general trends shown? If so state them.

3. From values of ionic radii obtained from the graph on p. 76, calculate the radius ratio for sodium chloride, potassium iodide, calcium oxide, calcium sulphide, barium fluoride, tin(IV) oxide, silver chloride. From these results estimate their probable structures and compare with the actual structures given on pp. 138–9.

4. Comment on the structure or bonding in **four** of the following substances:
   (a) plastic sulphur;
   (b) hydrogen fluoride;
   (c) ice;
   (d) nitrogen oxide (NO);
   (e) iron pentacarbonyl ($Fe(CO)_5$);
   (f) copper(II) sulphate pentahydrate;
   (g) lithium aluminium hydride.   (O & C)

9

ELECTROCHEMICAL SERIES OF
THE ELEMENTS

In this chapter notes on the electrochemical series, electrode potentials, and related topics (cells, electrolysis) will be given. For a fuller account reference should be made to a textbook of physical chemistry.

Solubility of the elements in water

A striking fact is that the great majority of elements are insoluble in water. Some exceptions are the alkali metals and the more electropositive alkaline earth metals. These dissolve in water, if the term 'dissolve' is extended to include cases where an obvious chemical action takes place. Iodine is slightly soluble, and the other halogens are all soluble, but here also the action is partly chemical. Other gaseous non-metallic elements including the noble gases have some slight solubility.

Metal crystals (p. 108) consist of lattices of atomic cores surrounded by a sea or cloud of non-localised valency electrons; there are no negative ions. Consider a metal plate partly immersed in water. Owing to thermal agitation the atomic cores of the metal are in a constant state of vibration about their mean position in the metallic lattice. Some of the atomic cores at the surface will at a given instant be moving outward with a kinetic energy of the same order as that needed to enable them to escape from the attraction of the electrons in the metal (cf. evaporation at a liquid surface, or sublimation at a solid), and become ions. When an ion tends to leave the surface of the metal, it is surrounded by water molecules with their oxygen atoms towards the ion. By electrostatic attraction the $\delta-$ charges on the oxygen atoms assist the positively charged ion to leave the metal to become an independent hydrated ion. The overall action in three stages is:

(1) Formation of separate individual atoms from the metal crystal lattice,

$$\underset{\text{lattice}}{M \text{ (solid)}} \rightarrow \underset{\text{atom}}{M \text{ (gas)}}; \Delta H \text{ positive.}$$

The energy absorbed is the *sublimation energy* of the metal. (The vapours of all metals consist mainly of free atoms.)

(2) Formation of metal ions from metal atoms,

$$\underset{\text{atom}}{\text{M (gas)}} \rightarrow \underset{\text{ion}}{\text{M}^{n+}} + ne; \quad \Delta H \text{ positive.}$$

The energy absorbed in this is the *ionisation energy* of the metal.

(3) Hydration of ions,

$$\text{M}^{n+} + \text{aq.} \rightarrow \text{M}^{n+} \text{ aq.}; \quad \Delta H \text{ negative.}$$

The energy evolved in this reaction is the *hydration energy* of the cation.

When the hydration energy is of about the same magnitude as the sum of the sublimation and ionisation energies, some of the metal will dissolve, forming ions in solution. It is essential to note that only the positively charged particles in the metal pass into solution; the electrons are left behind on the surface of the metal. These electrons and the cations in solution form two layers known as the *Helmholtz double layer*, as shown in Fig. 91. The layers remain close together because of the great electrostatic attraction between the opposite charges. This separation of charges means that a potential difference exists between the solution and the metal. Movement of metal ions from the metal into the solution is opposed by the potential difference because the positive ion has to move against the attraction of additional electrons left behind in the metal and also against the repulsion of the layer of positive ions already formed in the solution. There is also a movement of ions in the opposite direction as metal ions from the solution are re-deposited on the metal. When the number of ions moving in each direction is the same a dynamic equilibrium results and the potential difference remains unchanged under the given conditions

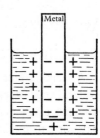

Fig. 91. Helmholtz double layer.

$$\text{ions leaving metal} \rightleftharpoons \text{metal ions leaving solution.}$$

The constant value for the given conditions is called the *electrode potential* for the couple metal ion/metal atom.

Before outlining how electrode potentials are measured under standard conditions it must be made clear that the action between a metal and water does not stop at the stage described above. This is very obvious in the cases of sodium and calcium where the reactions proceed till all the metal has 'dissolved'

$$2\text{Na} + 2\text{H}^+ + 2\text{OH}^- \rightarrow 2\text{Na}^+ + 2\text{OH}^- + \text{H}_2.$$

Here hydrogen ions from the water, attracted by the negative charge on parts of the metal surface (acting as a cathode) have been discharged by excess electrons from the metal, thus enabling more sodium ions to enter the solution. The same kind of action takes place with most metals, but is stopped in most cases by the formation of a film of insoluble hydroxide on the surface of the metal (see p. 210).

Measurement of standard electrode potentials

In spite of dissolution of the metal, formation of hydroxides, and evolution of hydrogen, the constant value of electrode potentials can be measured. Consider connecting one lead from a voltmeter or potentiometer to the metal plate in Fig. 91, and putting the other lead into the liquid as near to the metal as possible without causing a short circuit. If the wire from the voltmeter is made of the same metal as the plate there will be no potential difference between the two because each will have the same potential difference with respect to the liquid. If the wire is made of some other metal, there will be a potential difference between the surface of the wire and the water, characteristic of this metal, so the potential difference recorded by the voltmeter will be the e.m.f. of a cell whose electrodes are made of two different metals. This is not what is required. In these circumstances a suitable reference electrode is chosen, and its electrode potential is arbitrarily given the value zero. Since electrode potentials *vary with temperature, pressure of any gases concerned, and concentration of ions in solution*, these factors must be fixed for standard measurements. The reference electrode is the standard hydrogen electrode at 25 °C. It consists of a platinum plate coated with platinum black (finely divided platinum deposited on the plate by electrolysis), partially immersed in dilute sulphuric or hydrochloric acid containing 1 mole of hydrogen ions per litre. Pure hydrogen at a pressure of one atmosphere is passed continuously through the acid round the platinum so that the platinum is in contact with both the gas and the solution (see p. 150). A dynamic equilibrium between the gaseous hydrogen and hydrogen ions in solution is established, both forward and backward reactions being catalysed by the platinum black.

$$H_2 \rightleftharpoons 2H^+ + 2e.$$

The metal electrode in every case is partly immersed in a solution containing ions of the same metal at a concentration of 1 mole per litre. The two electrodes are connected as shown in Fig. 92 and the potential difference between them is measured by a voltmeter or, for more accurate work, a potentiometer. Since the potential of the standard hydrogen electrode is given the value zero on the scale of electrode potentials, the potential difference as measured below, is called the standard electrode potential for the reaction

$$Zn^{2+}+2e \rightarrow Zn.$$

N.B. The sign given to the standard electrode potential is by convention, that of the charge on the metal.

If $E^{\ominus}$ represents the standard electrode potential, then the above statements may be summarised as:

$E^{\ominus}$ for Zn^{2+}/Zn is -0.76 V (minus because the zinc becomes negatively charged by loss of Zn^{2+} ions). The apparatus is a voltaic cell of e.m.f. 0.76 V. The reaction concerned must always be indicated as above.

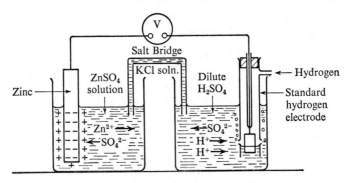

Fig. 92. Measurement of standard electrode potential.

Electrons in this zinc/hydrogen cell flow from the zinc to the hydrogen electrode in the external circuit. The actions in the cell are therefore:

at zinc electrode $Zn \rightarrow Zn^{2+}+2e$, oxidation of Zn (p. 161). (1)

As electrons are drawn away from the zinc by the hydrogen electrode, the equilibrium at the zinc electrode is disturbed and more zinc ions pass into solution to restore the equilibrium potential difference. Zinc ions at the zinc plate therefore increase in concentration, with the result that zinc ions are repelled through the solution towards the salt-bridge and thence eventually into the right-hand compartment.

Electrons arriving at the hydrogen electrode from the wire, discharge hydrogen ions from the acid in contact with the platinum plate thus:

at hydrogen electrode $2H^++2e \rightarrow H_2$, reduction of H^+. (2)

The concentration of hydrogen ions at the platinum plate is therefore reduced, and more move in to replace them, thus causing a steady stream of hydrogen ions towards the platinum. Unpaired sulphate ions at the hydrogen electrode cause an excess negative charge in the solution, with the result that sulphate ions are repelled towards the left-hand compartment. Transport of charges through the electrolyte is brought about by one-way submarine ionic ferries migrating through the solution.

The overall reaction in the cell is

$$\text{(1) and (2)} \quad Zn + 2H^+ \rightarrow Zn^{2+} + H_2.$$

To say that the standard electrode potential for the couple Zn^{2+}/Zn is -0.76 V is roughly equivalent to saying that the e.m.f. driving the displacement of hydrogen from dilute sulphuric acid by zinc is 0.76 V. A more accurate statement is that the e.m.f. of the standard zinc hydrogen cell is 0.76 V. A similar type of statement may be made about the displacement of hydrogen from water or any aqueous solution by any element.

The processes taking place in voltaic cells are similar in nature, though opposite in direction, to those during electrolysis, the essential difference being that cell processes are spontaneous, while in electrolysis the e.m.f. must be supplied from outside the system. It is therefore convenient to use the same terminology for both. Electrode and electrolyte are terms already commonly used, but anode and cathode must be defined so that they also may apply. The *anode* is the electrode at which electrons are produced. The *cathode* is the electrode at which electrons are consumed (*cathode, consumed*). Reaction (1) in the zinc/hydrogen cell is electron producing, therefore in this case zinc is the anode. Reaction (2) is electron consuming, therefore the hydrogen electrode is the cathode. As always, the anions present (SO_4^{2-}) move to the anode and the cations (H^+ and Zn^{2+}) to the cathode.

The question of *polarity* of the electrodes is confusing, but polarity can be deduced for each case. In our example the electrons flow from zinc to hydrogen, hence the hydrogen cathode is the positive pole of the cell, and the zinc anode the negative pole. *This is a reversal of the polarity during electrolysis.* The flow of free electrons in any cell or electrolysis is always through the metallic conductor, never through the electrolyte.

When a copper rod, partly immersed in a molar solution of copper(II) sulphate (1 mole of Cu^{2+} per litre) is combined with the standard hydrogen electrode, the standard electrode potential is $+0.34$ V (positive because Cu^{2+} ions discharged at the copper neutralise electrons); but in this case the flow of electrons is from the hydrogen electrode to the copper. The hydrogen is therefore the anode (electron producing) and the copper the cathode (electron consuming). At the anode, hydrogen molecules are split into atoms which are then forced (by the copper) to release their electrons to form hydrogen ions thus:

at anode $\qquad H_2 \to 2H^+ + 2e.$

The electrons flow to the copper cathode where they discharge copper(II) ions, the copper formed being deposited on the electrode:

at cathode $\qquad Cu^{2+} + 2e \to Cu \downarrow;$

overall reaction $\qquad Cu^{2+} + H_2 \to 2H^+ + Cu \downarrow.$

It is clear that the standard electrode potentials for the couples Zn^{2+}/Zn and Cu^{2+}/Cu must have opposite signs. Standard electrode potential for the couple (Cu^{2+}/Cu) is 0.34 V.

The electrochemical series

When the electrode potential reactions are arranged in the order of their standard electrode potentials, the result is the electrochemical series. The table on p. 153 gives this series for almost fifty of the most important reactions. Only those elements which form ions in solution have electrode potentials; therefore non-metals form a tiny part of the complete series. Of the forty-seven elements listed here, only four, the halogens, are non-metals, (hydrogen and arsenic behave as metals).

The sign given to the standard electrode potential is that of the charge on the metal. For all metals above hydrogen in the series it is negative; this means that the Helmholtz layer in the solution is positive, consisting as it does of cations.

It must be emphasised that all the data in the table refer to *aqueous media*.

A fact of great importance is that the electrochemical series is also the *redox* (*reduction–oxidation*) *series*, because reduction is gain of electrons, and oxidation is loss of electrons (p. 161). The metals at the top of the series release electrons most easily under standard conditions forming ions which pass into solution. That is why the metals acquire the highest negative potentials. They are therefore the most powerful reducing agents. The atoms of a given metal will reduce the ions of any metal below it in the series, thus displacing the second metal from aqueous solution:

$$Zn + Cu^{2+} \to Zn^{2+} + Cu \downarrow.$$

Non-metal atoms do not release electrons, but non-metal ions do. A non-metal ion will reduce the atom of any non-metal below it in the series; e.g. bromide ion reduces chlorine:

$$Br^- + \tfrac{1}{2}Cl_2 \to \tfrac{1}{2}Br_2 + Cl^-.$$

Electrochemical Series for the reactions between elements and their ions X^{n+}/X (aqueous media at 25 °C)

Half-reaction

Oxidising agent		Reducing agent	Standard electrode potential $E^{\ominus}$ V
$Cs^{+}+e$	⇌	Cs	−3.04
$Li^{+}+e$	⇌	Li	−3.04
$Rb^{+}+e$	⇌	Rb	−2.99
$K^{+}+e$	⇌	K	−2.92
$Ba^{2+}+2e$	⇌	Ba	−2.90
$Sr^{2+}+2e$	⇌	Sr	−2.89
$Ca^{2+}+2e$	⇌	Ca	−2.87
$Na^{+}+e$	⇌	Na	−2.71
$La^{3+}+3e$	⇌	La	−2.52
$Mg^{2+}+2e$	⇌	Mg	−2.37
$Y^{3+}+3e$	⇌	Y	−2.37
$Sc^{3+}+3e$	⇌	Sc	−2.10
$Be^{2+}+2e$	⇌	Be	−1.70
$*HfO^{2+}+2e$	⇌	Hf	−1.68
$Al^{3+}+3e$	⇌	Al	−1.66
$Ti^{2+}+2e$	⇌	Ti	−1.63
$*ZrO^{2+}+2e$	⇌	Zr	−1.53
$V^{2+}+2e$	⇌	V	−1.18
$Mn^{2+}+2e$	⇌	Mn	−1.18
$Zn^{2+}+2e$	⇌	Zn	−0.76
$Cr^{3+}+3e$	⇌	Cr	−0.74
$Ga^{3+}+3e$	⇌	Ga	−0.52
$Fe^{2+}+2e$	⇌	Fe	−0.44
$Cd^{2+}+2e$	⇌	Cd	−0.41

Stronger reducing agents ← Increasing ease of oxidation

Stronger oxidising agents — Increasing ease of reduction →

Half-reaction

Oxidising agent		Reducing agent	Standard electrode potential $E^{\ominus}$ V
$In^{3+}+3e$	⇌	In	−0.34
$Tl^{+}+e$	⇌	Tl	−0.34
$Co^{2+}+2e$	⇌	Co	−0.28
$Ni^{2+}+2e$	⇌	Ni	−0.25
$Sn^{2+}+2e$	⇌	Sn	−0.14
$Pb^{2+}+2e$	⇌	Pb	−0.13
$H^{+}+e$	⇌	$\frac{1}{2}H_2$	0.00
$Sb^{3+}+3e$	⇌	Sb	+0.21
$Bi^{3+}+3e$	⇌	Bi	+0.23
$As^{3+}+3e$	⇌	As	+0.25
$ReO_2+4H^{+}+4e$	⇌	$Re+2H_2O$	+0.25
$Cu^{2+}+2e$	⇌	Cu	+0.34
$\{\frac{1}{4}O_2+H_2O+2e$ (In alkaline solution 1 M)	⇌	$2OH^{-}\}$	+0.40
$\frac{1}{2}I_2+e$	⇌	I^{-}	+0.54
$Hg_2^{2+}+2e$	⇌	2Hg	+0.80
$Ag^{+}+e$	⇌	Ag	+0.80
$Os^{2+}+2e$	⇌	Os	+0.85
$Pd^{2+}+2e$	⇌	Pd	+0.85
$\frac{1}{2}Br_2+e$	⇌	Br^{-}	+1.07
$Pt^{2+}+2e$	⇌	Pt	+1.20
$\frac{1}{2}Cl_2+e$	⇌	Cl^{-}	+1.36
$Au^{3+}+3e$	⇌	Au	+1.50
$\frac{1}{2}F_2+e$	⇌	F^{-}	+2.80

Stronger reducing agents ← Increasing ease of oxidation

Stronger oxidising agents — Increasing ease of reduction →

* Equations should be: $HfO^{2+}+2H^{+}+4e \rightleftharpoons Hf+H_2O$; $ZrO^{2+}+2H^{+}+4e \rightleftharpoons Zr+H_2O$.

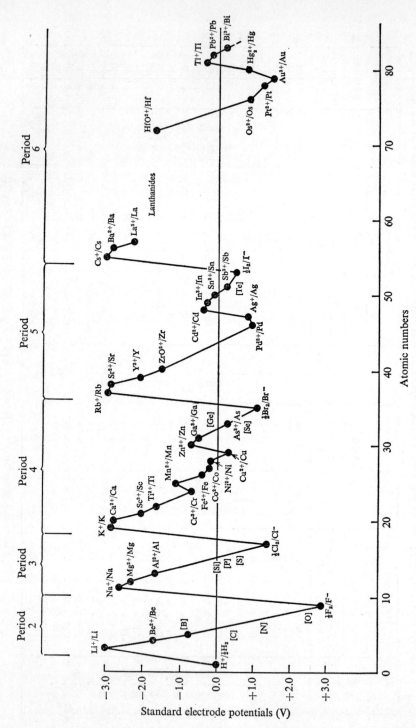

Fig. 93. Standard electrode potentials of the elements plotted against atomic numbers.

Thus fluoride ion is the weakest reducing agent. On the other hand fluorine is the strongest oxidising agent and lithium ion the weakest.

The displacing actions may be summarised thus:

(1) A metal will displace or tend to displace from aqueous solution any metal with a less negative standard electrode potential, i.e. lower in the series. Hydrogen is included with the metals.

(2) A non-metal will displace or tend to displace from aqueous solution any non-metal with a smaller *positive standard electrode potential*, i.e. higher in the series. This applies to the displacement of hydroxyl ion (see table on p. 153).

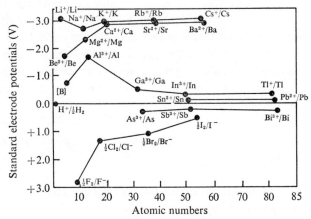

Fig. 94. Standard electrode potentials of Main Group elements plotted against atomic numbers.

Graphs of standard electrode potential against atomic number are given in Figs. 93 and 94. The first of these is a good example of periodicity. When considering particular examples of standard electrode potentials, it is necessary in every case to state the couple, e.g. Fe^{2+}/Fe, Zn^{2+}/Zn.

Relation between electrochemical series and position in Periodic Table

This is most easily brought out by comparing electrode potential graphs with those of electronegativity (p. 73). (The relationship between electronegativity and position in the table was considered fully on pp. 71–3.) Periodicity of the two quantities shows a broad similarity. Main Group trends are very similar in extreme Groups IA, IIA and VIIB, but significantly different in intermediate Groups including transition Groups, p. 614.

Uses and limitations of the electrochemical series

The complete series and all selections from it, are based on standard electrode potentials. Standard conditions are (1) temperature 25 °C, (2) molar concentration of ions in *aqueous* solution, (3) gaseous pressures of one atmosphere. The series is a redox series for these elements which form ions in solution. Important non-metals such as carbon, silicon, nitrogen and phosphorus which do not form ions in aqueous solution are *not* included. Statements based on the electrochemical series concerning reducing power, oxidising power and general chemical activity are completely valid only for reactions in aqueous solution under the specified standard conditions. The series is readily extended to cover reactions in aqueous solution under non-standard conditions, especially those involving changes in ionic concentration (see next section). A further very important extension is made to include all redox reactions in aqueous solution, especially those involving oxo-anions, e.g. permanganate, dichromate, p. 166.

Summary. The extended redox potential series covers the large and important part of chemistry which is concerned with ionic reactions in aqueous solution.

Electrode potentials in aqueous solution under non-standard conditions

One of the most important conditions laid down in measuring standard electrode potentials (p. 149), is that the elements forming the electrodes must dip into *solutions of their own ions at unit concentration*, i.e. 1 mole per litre. For other concentrations different values of electrode potentials are obtained. The following expressions enable potentials E, for any concentration of (1) metal ions and (2) non-metal ions, to be calculated.

$$E = E^{\ominus} + \frac{0.059}{n} \log_{10} [M^{n+}],$$

$$E = E^{\ominus} - \frac{0.059}{n} \log_{10} [\text{non-}M^{n-}],$$

where $E^{\ominus}$ is the standard electrode potential, n the valency and [ ] denotes concentration in mole per litre in each case.

These formulae show that, because of the logarithmic relation, *only very large changes in concentration have much effect on the values of electrode potentials.*

Crucial cases are the potentials of the *hydrogen electrode* in neutral water, $[H^+] = 10^{-7}$ or pH = 7 (pH is the logarithm of hydrogen ion concentration with sign reversed); and in molar alkali solution,

$$[H^+] = 10^{-10}, \quad pH = 14.$$

Neutral water $E = 0.00 + 0.059 \log_{10} [10^{-7}] = -0.41$ V,

        or $E = -0.059$ pH $= -0.41$ V;

molar alkali $E = -0.059 \times 14$ $= -0.83$ V;

see pp. 213, 223 for applications of these values.

Two other cases essential in considering discharge of *hydroxyl ions* by non-metals from aqueous solution, pp. 223, 215, are obtained from the half-reaction:

molar alkali $\frac{1}{2}O_2 + H_2O + 2e \rightleftharpoons 2OH^-, \quad E^\ominus = +0.40$ V;

neutral water $E = 0.40 - 0.059 \log_{10} [10^{-7}] = +0.81$ V.

Redox reactions in solid and gaseous states

These dry-way reactions take place over a wide range of temperature from normal up to 2000 °C and beyond. Surprisingly, the redox series serves as a rough guide here too. Thus the general activity of metals decreases in passing down the series and the activity of non-metals decreases up the series. Stability of corresponding compounds of the metals, e.g. oxides, carbonates, sulphates, nitrates, is greatest at the top. Examples of these trends are seen in occurrence of metals and ease of reduction of their compounds: sodium is never found free; gold always. Sodium oxidises very rapidly in air, gold not at all. Compounds of metals of Groups I A and II A near the top of the series are very difficult to reduce, while near the bottom, compounds are reduced easily, often by gentle heating even without a reducing agent.

However, in spite of the broad truth of the above statements it is highly dangerous to use redox potentials to make detailed predictions on the course of chemical reactions taking place under conditions so different from those in which redox potentials are measured. For all chemical reactions the best method is that outlined in ch. 6 using standard free energies. This is universally valid. The difference between the order in the free energy series for the oxides of some important metals, and their order in the redox potential series, both at 25 °C, is shown strikingly in the list on p. 158.

	Standard free energy of formation of oxide, $\Delta G^\ominus$ (kcal/8 g oxygen)		Standard electrode potential (V)			Standard free energy of formation of oxide, $\Delta G^\ominus$ (kcal/8 g oxygen)		Standard electrode potential (V)	
	Value	Order	Order	Value		Value	Order	Order	Value
Ca	−72	1	7	−2.87	Na	−45	8	8	−2.71
Be	−70	2	10	−1.70	Mn	−43 (MnO)	9	12	−1.18
Mg	−68	3	9	−2.37	Cr	−42 (Cr$_2$O$_3$)	10	14	−0.74
Sr	−67	4	6	−2.89	K	(−40)	11	4	−2.92
Li	(−67)	5	1	−3.04	Zn	−38	12	13	−0.76
Ba	−63	6	5	−2.90	Rb	(−36)	13	3	−2.99
Al	−63	7	11	−1.66	Cs	(−35)	14	2	−3.04

Note: (1) Hydrogen is seventeenth in $\Delta G^\ominus$ order but twenty-first in S.E.P. order.
(2) The order of other important metals is very similar in both series.
(3) Estimated values of $\Delta G^\ominus$ are enclosed in brackets.

Another factor of great importance is the effect of temperature on standard free energies of formation of oxides and other compounds: at high temperatures the order of reducing power of elements is often reversed (see p. 184).

Exercises

1. Describe and explain the energy changes taking place during the formation of a Helmholtz double layer when a metal plate is immersed in water.
2. Describe the standard hydrogen electrode, and explain how it is used in the measurement of standard electrode potentials, taking zinc and copper as examples. State the sign convention used for standard electrode potentials.
3. How is the electrochemical series set up? Explain in detail why the series is also called the redox series, giving illustrative examples from metallic and non-metallic elements.
4. Give an account of the uses and limitations of the electrochemical series.
5. Explain what is meant by the *electrochemical series* of elements. Arrange copper, sodium, hydrogen, iron, zinc and aluminium in the order in which they occur in this series.
   Comment on the following facts:
   (*a*) Aluminium pipes can be used to convey nitric acid but not sulphuric acid or sodium hydroxide solution;
   (*b*) sheet iron rusts in use less rapidly when galvanised than when tinned;
   (*c*) Copper will dissolve in dilute nitric acid but not in dilute sulphuric acid;
   (*d*) copper oxide but not zinc oxide can be reduced by hydrogen. (C)
6. Give, in tabular form, a comparative treatment of the action of hydrochloric, nitric and sulphuric acids on the metals copper, lead and mercury. Com-

ment on the way in which the results of the action of these acids are in accordance with the position of the metals in the electrochemical series. (L)

7. Outline the *chemical principles* involved in the extraction of aluminium, zinc and iron from their usual natural sources, discussing the relevance of the positions of these elements in the *electrochemical series* in choosing the method used. (L)

8. Discuss concisely the factors that determine the position of an element (*a*) in the periodic system and (*b*) in the electrochemical series.

Give **three** properties of an element that can be better predicted from a knowledge of its position in the periodic system and **three** properties that can be better predicted from its position in the electrochemical series. (CS)

10

OXIDATION AND REDUCTION

The term oxidation originally meant addition of oxygen to elements. It was soon extended to include compounds and then to include all reactions in which oxygen was used up. In this sense it is a very important process in its own right, including as it does, burning, rusting and the vital processes of internal respiration of animals and plants.

The term was further extended gradually over the years until suddenly with the development of the electronic theory of valency, it expanded greatly to include possibly half of all chemical reactions, as will now be shown.

All chemical reactions involve the transfer or rearrangement of electrons (or protons) among atoms. Consider the oxidation of magnesium:

$$2Mg + O_2 \rightarrow 2MgO \quad \text{or} \quad Mg + \tfrac{1}{2}O_2 \rightarrow MgO.$$

The reaction consists in the movement or transfer of two electrons from the magnesium atom to the oxygen atom:

$$Mg \rightarrow Mg^{2+} + 2e; \quad \tfrac{1}{2}O_2 + 2e \rightarrow O^{2-}.$$

Oxidation of magnesium involves loss of electrons, but these electrons have been captured by the oxygen atom. The oxygen atom has therefore undergone the reverse of oxidation, i.e. it has been reduced to oxide ion. Clearly the two processes of oxidation and reduction take place at the same time. The overall equation is therefore an oxidation–reduction or redox reaction. Consider next the reaction between sodium and chlorine:

$$2Na + Cl_2 \rightarrow 2Na^+Cl^-.$$

This can be split into two parts

$$2Na \rightarrow 2Na^+ + 2e \quad \text{(loss of electrons by sodium)},$$
$$Cl_2 + 2e \rightarrow 2Cl^- \quad \text{(gain of electrons by chlorine)}.$$

This reaction is very similar to the magnesium–oxygen reaction. For this reason *the term oxidation is expanded to include all reactions involving loss of electrons, and reduction to include those involving gain of electrons.*

In the two examples given so far the transfer of electrons is complete or almost complete because of the big difference in electronegativity between the weakly electronegative metals and the strongly electronegative non-metals. When there is a small difference in electronegativity between the combining elements the transfer of electrons is only partial, resulting in polar covalent bonds, not ionic bonds, e.g.

$$C + O_2 \rightarrow CO_2; \quad H_2 + Cl_2 \rightarrow 2HCl.$$

It is useful to make a final extension of the term oxidation–reduction to include these cases also:

Electronic definition of oxidation–reduction

(1) *Oxidation is the complete or partial removal of electrons from an atom, molecule or ion;* or *oxidation is loss of electrons.*

(2) *Reduction is the complete or partial addition of electrons to an atom, molecule or ion;* or *reduction is gain of electrons.*

(3) *The two processes of oxidation and reduction take place simultaneously.*

Note that the role of the more electronegative atom in a redox reaction is a very active one: it pulls the electrons away from the less electronegative atom against the attraction of its atomic nucleus. The electrons of the less electronegative atom are not 'lost'; they are forcibly removed.

It might be thought that the term oxidation–reduction now includes so many different reactions that it has lost its value. The reverse is true. It has resulted in the arrangement of all the elements in a series with the most powerful elementary reducing agent at the top, and the most powerful elementary oxidising agent at the bottom. This series, the electrochemical series or redox series of the elements, has been considered (p. 153). A similar series including compound ions will be considered later (p. 166).

Oxidising and reducing agents

(1) *An oxidising agent* (or *oxidant*) *is an atom, molecule, or ion which readily captures electrons.*

(2) *A reducing agent* (or *reductant*) *is an atom, molecule or ion which readily releases electrons.*

Common oxidising agents: oxygen, chlorine, bromine and other non-metals, nitric acid, potassium permanaganate, potassium dichromate.

Common reducing agents: hydrogen and most metals, carbon, carbon monoxide, sulphurous acid, hydrogen sulphide, tin(II) chloride, iodide ion (often from hydriodic acid). Further examples of redox reactions will be given later in this chapter and throughout the book.

Oxidation number (or state)

Oxidation numbers are related to valency. They represent the charge an atom in a compound would have if the electron-transfer tendency caused by electronegativity differences were carried to completion. The following rules result:

(1) The sign of an oxidation number is put before the number to distinguish it from valency.

(2) Atoms in the elementary state have zero oxidation number.

(3) The oxidation number of an ion is the same as its ionic charge number. Thus oxygen always has an oxidation number of -2, except when it occurs in a peroxide linkage, —O—O—, i.e. O_2^{2-}, when each oxygen atom has an oxidation number of -1; and in superoxides, e.g. KO_2 in which oxygen has an oxidation number of $-\frac{1}{2}$ (p. 249); and also in OF_2 oxygen difluoride, in which oxygen has an oxidation number of $+2$. Metals of Groups IA and IIA have oxidation number of $+1$ and $+2$ respectively.

(4) The oxidation number of hydrogen is $+1$ in most of its compounds; but -1 in the metallic hydrides, e.g.

$$H^{+1}Cl^{-1}, (H^{+1})_2O^{-2}, Na^{+1}H^{-1}.$$

(5) When two or more atoms of the same element occur in a compound the oxidation number of the element is an average of the oxidation number of the group.

(6) The algebraic sum of the oxidation numbers of the atoms in a compound is zero (for electrical neutrality).

(7) When the oxidation number of an element in a compound is not known, it is calculated from those of the others by using rule (6), e.g. to find the oxidation number of manganese in potassium permanganate fill in the known oxidation numbers thus $K^+Mn(O^{-2})_4$, hence Mn^{+7}. Similarly in $(K^+)_3Fe(CN^-)_6$, iron is Fe^{+3} and the compound is potassium hexacyanoferrate(III), while $(K^+)_4Fe^{+2}(CN^-)_6$ is potassium hexacyanoferrate(II).

Oxidation numbers are of great use in balancing redox equations, in fixing ionic charges, and in deciding whether or not a reaction is an oxidation–reduction. Oxidation numbers lead to another modification of the definitions of oxidation–reduction thus:

Oxidation is a reaction in which the oxidation number of an element is increased;

Reduction is a reaction in which it is decreased.

Examples of redox reactions

$$[O^0] + 2H^{+1}Cl^{-1} \rightarrow (H^{+1})_2O^{-2} + Cl_2^0.$$

The oxygen has been reduced (decrease in oxidation number from 0 to −2). The chlorine in HCl has been oxidised (increase in oxidation number from −1 to 0).

$$(H^{+1})_2S^{-2} + Cl_2^0 \rightarrow 2H^{+1}Cl^{-1} + S^0 \downarrow.$$

The sulphide ion has been oxidised (increase in oxidation number from −2 to 0). The chlorine has been reduced (decrease in oxidation number from 0 to −1).

$$Pb^{+2}S^{-2} + 4(H^{+1})_2(O^{-1})_2 \rightarrow Pb^{+2}S^{+6}(O^{-2})_4 + 4(H^{+1})_2O^{-2}.$$

The sulphide ion has been oxidised (increase in oxidation number from −2 to +6). The oxygen ion in hydrogen peroxide has been reduced (decrease in oxidation number from −1 to −2).

Balancing redox equations

When writing redox equations, it is useful to write the ion-electron half-reaction for the oxidation separate from that for the reduction; then, if necessary, multiply each by the number required to make the number of electrons the same in each; then add them. Two methods will be shown: (1) the ion-electron method, (2) the oxidation number method. The first is probably the better. The reaction in each case is the oxidation of iron(II) sulphate solution with potassium permanganate ($KMnO_4$) solution in the presence of dilute sulphuric acid. It is always essential to know the products of the reaction: in this case the manganese(II) ion Mn^{2+} and iron(III) ion.

1. Ion-electron method. Each oxygen atom in the MnO_4^- ion is covalently bonded to the central Mn atom. These bonds must be broken and the oxygen atoms removed in order to leave Mn^{2+} ion. This reaction therefore involves transfer of oxygen atoms as well as electrons. The oxygen appears in the products as water. Thus balancing by atoms and electrons we have

$$MnO_4^- + 8H^+ + 5e \rightarrow Mn^{2+} + 4H_2O \quad \text{(reduction of } MnO_4^-\text{)}. \quad (1)$$

The equation for oxidation of iron(II) ion to iron(III) ion is

$$Fe^{2+} \rightarrow Fe^{3+} + e \quad \text{(oxidation)}. \quad (2)$$

This equation must be multiplied by 5 to equalise the number of electrons in each half reaction, and the resulting half-reactions added thus

$$5Fe^{2+} \rightarrow 5Fe^{3+} + 5e$$

$$\frac{MnO_4^- + 8H^+ + 5e \rightarrow Mn^{2+} + 4H_2O}{MnO_4^- + 8H^+ + 5Fe^{2+} \rightarrow Mn^{2+} + 5Fe^{3+} + 4H_2O.}$$

2. *Oxidation number method.* The oxidation number of Mn in permanganate ion $[MnO_4]^-$ is $+7$, while that of Mn^{2+} ion is $+2$. Reduction of MnO_4^- therefore requires a decrease in the oxidation number from $+7$ to $+2$, thus requiring the addition of $5e$ giving as before:

$$MnO_4^- + 8H^+ + 5e \rightarrow Mn^{2+} + 4H_2O.$$

Calculation of equivalent weights of oxidising and reducing agents

The gram-equivalent weight of an oxidising agent is the weight which contains 8 g of available oxygen. For a reducing agent, it is the weight which combines with 8 g of oxygen. In terms of electron loss or gain: *the equivalent weight of an oxidising or reducing agent* is the atomic or formula weight divided by the number of electrons gained or lost by one atom, molecule or ion in the reaction in question. (This follows from the fact that $H \rightarrow H^+ + e$.)

The same reaction will be used as in the last section.

1. *Ion-electron method and oxidation number method.*

$$KMnO_4 \equiv MnO_4^- \equiv 5e \quad \text{(p. 163)}.$$

Therefore the equivalent weight of $KMnO_4$ is one-fifth of its formula weight. Also

$$Fe^{2+} \rightarrow Fe^{3+} + e.$$

Therefore the equivalent weight of Fe^{2+} is its ionic weight, and the equivalent weight of an iron(II) salt is its formula weight (including water of crystallisation).

2. *Available oxygen method.*

$$2KMnO_4 \equiv K_2O + 2MnO + 5[O],$$
$$2KMnO_4 \equiv 5[O].$$

Five atoms of oxygen is 80 parts by weight or 10 equivalent weights, therefore the equivalent weight of $KMnO_4$ is one-fifth of the formula weight.

Standard redox potentials for all redox reactions in aqueous solution

The electrochemical series is a redox potential series confined to the elements. In each case the half-reaction couple consists of a metal (reduced form) and its ion (oxidised form), e.g. the Fe^{2+}/Fe couple in the half-reaction $Fe^{2+} + 2e \rightleftharpoons Fe$. This series can easily be extended to include all other redox reactions, e.g. those in which the couple consists of two ions, Fe^{3+}/Fe^{2+}, instead of an element and one ion Fe^{2+}/Fe. The same apparatus is used (p. 150) one half always being the standard hydrogen electrode, the other the redox couple under consideration. The standard redox potential is the e.m.f. of the cell formed from the two half-cells.

Measurement of these additional redox potentials will be described by two examples:

1. Iron(III) and iron(II) ions as oxidising and reducing agents. The ion-electron half-reaction is

$$Fe^{3+} + e \overset{\text{reduction}}{\underset{\text{oxidation}}{\rightleftharpoons}} Fe^{2+}.$$

oxidised reduced

form   form

In the apparatus on p. 150 the right-hand side is unchanged; but the Zn electrode on the left-hand side is replaced by a platinum wire, and the molar $ZnSO_4$ solution by a solution of a mixture of iron(II) and iron(III) ions each of which is in molar concentration. The reactions are:

$$Fe^{3+} + e \xrightarrow{\text{reduction}} Fe^{2+} \qquad E^{\ominus} = +0.76 \text{ V}$$

$$\underline{\tfrac{1}{2}H_2 \xrightarrow{\text{oxidation}} H^+ + e \qquad E^{\ominus} = 0.00 \text{ V}}$$

$$Fe^{3+} + \tfrac{1}{2}H_2 \longrightarrow Fe^{2+} + H^+ \quad \text{e.m.f.} = 0.76 \text{ V.}$$

This result shows that hydrogen is a better reducing agent than iron(II) ion; in other words hydrogen reduces iron(III) ions. The mechanism in the cell is that hydrogen gas gives up electrons to the platinum plate of the hydrogen electrodes. These pass round to the Fe^{3+}/Fe^{2+} half-cell where they are taken up by the Fe^{3+} ions. If the current is allowed to flow all the Fe^{3+} ions are eventually reduced to Fe^{2+} ions.

2. Potassium permanganate as oxidising agent in acid solution. The half-reaction is

$$MnO_4^- + 8H^+ + 5e \overset{\text{reduction}}{\underset{\text{oxidation}}{\rightleftharpoons}} Mn^{2+} + 4H_2O, \quad E^{\ominus} = 1.52 \text{ V.}$$

In the left-hand cell of the apparatus (p. 150) the solution in this case is a mixture of MnO_4^- ions and Mn^{2+} ions each in molar concentration, with H^+, the other reactant, also present in unit concentration (1 mole per litre), the other half-cell being as always the standard hydrogen electrode. Note especially that one of the reactants in the reduction is H^+. As will be shown later (p. 168), increase in the H^+ ion concentration increases the value of the redox potential.

Some standard redox potentials and half-reactions

Couple			Half-reaction	Redox potentials $E^\ominus$ (V)		
			$\xleftarrow{\hspace{1cm}}$ Oxidation $\xrightarrow{\hspace{1cm}}$ Reduction $\xrightarrow{\hspace{1cm}}$			
Na^+/Na			$Na^+ + e \rightleftharpoons Na$	-2.71		
Fe^{2+}/Fe			$Fe^{2+} + 2e \rightleftharpoons Fe$	-0.44		
Cr^{3+}/Cr^{2+}			$Cr^{3+} + e \rightleftharpoons Cr^{2+}$	-0.41		
$H^+/\frac{1}{2}H_2$	Increasing ease of reduction,	i.e. stronger oxidising agents	$H^+ + e \rightleftharpoons \frac{1}{2}H_2$	0.00	Increasing ease of oxidation,	i.e. stronger reducing agents
$\frac{1}{2}I_2/I^-$			$\frac{1}{2}I_2 + e \rightleftharpoons I^-$	$+0.54$		
O_2/H_2O_2			$O_2 + 2H^+ + 2e \rightleftharpoons H_2O_2$	$+0.68$		
Fe^{3+}/Fe^{2+}			$Fe^{3+} + e \rightleftharpoons Fe^{2+}$	$+0.76$		
$\frac{1}{2}Br_2/Br^-$			$\frac{1}{2}Br_2 + e \rightleftharpoons Br^-$	$+1.07$		
$\frac{1}{2}Cr_2O_7{}^{2-}/Cr^{3+}$			$\frac{1}{2}Cr_2O_7{}^{2-} + 7H^+ + 3e \rightleftharpoons Cr^{3+} + \frac{7}{2}H_2O$	$+1.33$		
$\frac{1}{2}Cl_2/Cl^-$			$\frac{1}{2}Cl_2 + e \rightleftharpoons Cl^-$	$+1.36$		
MnO_4^-/Mn^{2+}			$MnO_4^- + 8H^+ + 5e \rightleftharpoons Mn^{2+} + 4H_2O$	$+1.52$		
MnO_4^-/MnO_2			$MnO_4^- + 4H^+ + 3e \rightleftharpoons MnO_2 + 2H_2O$	$+1.69$		
$\frac{1}{2}F_2/F^-$			$\frac{1}{2}F_2 + e \rightleftharpoons F^-$	$+2.80$		
			Oxidised form Reduced form			

In tables such as the above, oxidising and reducing agents are arranged in order of their oxidising and reducing powers. This enables the course of any redox reaction to be understood and in many cases predicted. The oxidised form in a given couple will oxidise the reduced form in any other couple above it in the table, i.e. having a smaller positive or greater negative redox potential. The reduced form in any couple will reduce the oxidised form in any couple below it, i.e. having a greater positive or less negative redox potential. Some examples will illustrate this:

(1) Chlorine will oxidise bromide ion to bromine, and iodide ion to iodine:

$$\tfrac{1}{2}Cl_2 + Br^- \rightarrow \tfrac{1}{2}Br_2 + Cl^-.$$

(2) Permanganate ion in acid solution ($E^\ominus = 1.52$ V) will oxidise iron(II) ion to iron(III) ($E^\ominus = 0.76$ V); so will dichromate ion in acid solution ($E^\ominus = 1.33$ V). The equation with dichromate is

$$\tfrac{1}{2}Cr_2O_7{}^{2-} + 7H^+ + 3e \xrightarrow{\text{reduction}} Cr^{3+} + 3\tfrac{1}{2}H_2O$$

$$3Fe^{2+} \xrightarrow{\text{oxidation}} 3Fe^{3+} + 3e$$

$$\rule{6cm}{0.4pt}$$

$$\tfrac{1}{2}Cr_2O_7{}^{2-} + 7H^+ + 3Fe^{2+} \xrightarrow{\text{redox}} 3Fe^{3+} + Cr^{3+} + 3\tfrac{1}{2}H_2O.$$

(3) Permanganate ion in acid solution ($E^\ominus = 1.52$ V) will oxidise chloride ion to chlorine ($E^\ominus = 1.36$ V) thus:

$$MnO_4^- + 8H^+ + 5e \longrightarrow Mn^{2+} + 4H_2O$$

$$\frac{5Cl^- \longrightarrow 2\tfrac{1}{2}Cl_2 + 5e}{MnO_4^- + 8H^+ + 5Cl^- \longrightarrow 2\tfrac{1}{2}Cl_2 + Mn^{2+} + 4H_2O.}$$

But dichromate ion in acid solution ($E^\ominus = 1.33$ V) will not oxidise chloride ion. This is why standard dichromate solution is used to titrate iron(II) ions in the presence of hydrochloric acid, while permanganate solution is unsuitable because it oxidises the chloride ion as well.

(4) MnO_4^- ion in acid solution will oxidise Cr^{3+} to $Cr_2O_7^{2-}$. The action takes place at an appreciable rate only at or near boiling point.

It should be noted that standard redox potentials tell us which reactions are energetically possible; they do not in themselves tell us anything directly about reaction rates, although, roughly speaking, it may be said that a reaction involving two half-reactions with widely different potentials is likely to go faster than one where the potential differences are small. For an accurate assessment, however, other factors must be considered. It should also be noted that standard redox potentials refer to standard conditions. Under different conditions the potentials are different.

Nitric acid as oxidising agent. The oxidising agent here is nitrate ion in presence of hydrogen ion. The commonest reduction products of nitric acid are NO_2 (with concentrated HNO_3) and NO (with dilute HNO_3). Reduction of NO_3^- to NO_2 or NO requires transfer of oxygen atoms as well as electrons. In this it resembles reduction of MnO_4^- ion, and the necessary equations are arrived at in a similar way.

With concentrated HNO_3:

$$NO_3^- + 2H^+ + e \rightarrow NO_2 + H_2O, \quad E^\ominus = 0.81 \text{ V.}$$

With dilute HNO_3:

$$NO_3^- + 4H^+ + 3e \rightarrow NO + 2H_2O, \quad E^\ominus = 0.96 \text{ V.}$$

It is seen from the values of $E^\ominus$ that nitric acid oxidises iron(II) ion to iron(III).

Sulphuric acid as oxidising agent. This takes place with hot concentrated H_2SO_4. The process is similar to that with nitric acid. The oxidising agent is sulphate ion in presence of hydrogen ion. The chief reduction product is SO_2. The half-reaction is:

$$SO_4^{2-} + 4H^+ + 2e \rightarrow SO_2 + 2H_2O.$$

Redox potentials under non-standard conditions

The oxidising or reducing power of a redox couple depends on the concentration of all species taking part in the reaction and used up during its course. The redox potential of a couple under any conditions is given by the following equation (for its derivation see textbooks of physical chemistry).

$$E = E^{\ominus} + \frac{0.059}{n} \log_{10} \frac{[\text{Ox.}]^p}{[\text{Red.}]^q}$$

where $E^{\ominus}$ is the standard redox potential, n the number of electrons transferred in the ion-electron equation for the half-reaction, $[\text{Ox.}]^p$ the concentration of the ions in the oxidised state (or the products of their concentrations if there are two or more reactants) raised to the appropriate power and $[\text{Red.}]^q$ has a similar meaning. For the MnO_4^-/Mn^{2+} couple the equation is:

$$MnO_4^- + 8H^+ + 5e \rightarrow Mn^{2+} + 4H_2O$$

and therefore the redox potential is

$$E = 1.52 + \frac{0.059}{5} \log_{10} \frac{[MnO_4^-][H^+]^8}{[Mn^{2+}]}.$$

The concentration of the water is taken as constant, assuming reaction takes place in dilute solution.

It is seen that the potential of the couple increases with increasing acidity, and increases rapidly because of the 8th power of the hydrogen ion concentration. Keeping the $[MnO_4^-]/[Mn^{2+}]$ ratio at the standard condition of 1:1, the redox potentials for varying hydrogen ion concentrations are calculated (and confirmed by experiment) to be:

	H^+ moles per litre	E (V)
	10	1.61
Standard	1	1.52
	0.1	1.43
	0.01	1.33
	10^{-6}	0.96
Neutral solution	10^{-7}	0.86

It is seen from these results and those on p. 166 that MnO_4^- ion in N H_2SO_4 will oxidise Cl^-, Br^-, and I^- to the corresponding halogen, while in extremely dilute H_2SO_4 (10^{-6} N) it will oxidise I^- to $\frac{1}{2}I_2$, but not Br^- nor Cl^-.

Anodic oxidation and cathodic reduction

Chemical reactions taking place spontaneously in galvanic cells, or under the influence of an external e.m.f. during electrolysis always take place at the electrodes and involve ions in the electrolyte. There is no chemical reaction during the transfer of electrons through the metallic conductor which completes the circuit. At the anode two types of reaction are possible: (1) the anode captures electrons from the arriving anions which are therefore discharged, or (2) cations pass from the metal of the anode into the electrolyte leaving electrons on the anode. Anodic reactions are therefore always oxidations, e.g. evolution of oxygen at the anode:

$$2OH^- \rightarrow H_2O + \tfrac{1}{2}O_2 + 2e.$$

Here the oxidation number of one oxygen atom in an OH^- group is increased from -2 to 0 (oxidation) while the oxidation numbers of the hydrogen atoms and the other oxygen atom remain unchanged. Another important example is the electrolysis of dilute H_2SO_4 or chromic acid solution with an aluminium anode. This results, not in the passage of Al^{3+} ions into solution as might be expected, but in the formation of oxygen which reacts with the metal producing a tenacious, durable, thickened film of Al_2O_3 on its surface. Aluminium so treated is said to be *anodised*. Its resistance to corrosion is greatly increased. Suitable dyes added to the bath are adsorbed by the Al_2O_3 giving attractively coloured films.

Cathodic reactions, on the other hand, are always reductions. Deposition of metals at the cathode during electrolysis is a very important example of this:

$$M^{n+} + ne \rightarrow M^0.$$

Summary

Chemical reactions taking place in galvanic cells or during electrolysis are simple electron-transfer reactions, the function of the metallic conductor ('external circuit') being merely to link the two electrodes.

Note. Redox reactions involve *electron transfer*. Acid-base reactions (p. 229) involve *proton transfer*. They differ in that redox reactions cause a change in oxidation number, acid-base reactions do not.

Exercises

1. Give oxidation numbers to the elements in the following compounds remembering that ions in ionic compounds are often best treated as individual entities. Name each compound.

    Molecules: SO_2, SO_3, CO, CO_2, NO_2, N_2O_3, N_2O_5, SiO_2, H_2SO_4, H_2CrO_4, CrO_2Cl_2, $SOCl_2$, $NOCl$.

    Ionic compounds: BaO_2, Cu_2O, Al_2O_3, $K_2Cr_2O_7$, $K_3Cu(CN)_4$, $Cu_2Fe(CN)_6$, $(NH_4)_2SO_4$, NH_4NO_3.

2. (a) Find the oxidation number of the central atom in the following ions, given the ionic charges and oxidation number of oxygen as -2. Name the ions: $(MnO_4)^-$, $(NO_2)^-$, $(NO_3)^-$, $(PO_4)^{3-}$.

    (b) Given the oxidation numbers of Si, Al and O as $+4$, $+3$ and -2 respectively, deduce the charge on the following ions:

    (SiO_4), (Si_2O_7), (SiO_3), $Si_2O_5)$, $(AlSi_3O_{10})$, $(AlSi_3O_8)$, $(AlSi_2O_6)$.

3. Using the ion-electron method give half-reactions and final equations for:

    (a) reduction of iron(III) ions by tin(II) ions; (b) oxidation of chromium ion to dichromate by permanganate ion in acid solution; (c) action of concentrated nitric acid on copper (main product NO_2); (d) action of $(1+1)$ nitric acid on copper (main product NO).

4. Give an account of the effect of hydrogen ion concentration on the oxidising power of potassium permanganate.

5. Discuss the development of the concepts of oxidation and reduction. Illustrate your answer by considering the changes of molecular or atomic structure (if any) which occur in the following changes:

    (a) SO_2 to SO_3 (b) CaO to CaO_2 (c) F_2 to F_2O

    (d) K_2CrO_4 to $K_2Cr_2O_7$ (e) CH_4 to CCl_4 (f) MnO_4^- to Mn^{++}.   (OS)

6. Define the terms 'oxidation' and 'reduction' in as many ways as you can.

    Identify the oxidising and reducing agents in each of the following processes, and discuss the application of your definitions to them.

    (a) the reaction of hydrogen peroxide with acidified potassium iodide;

    (b) the reaction of hydrogen peroxide with acidified potassium permanganate;

    (c) the passage of hydrogen over heated sodium;

    (d) the addition of metallic calcium to water;

    (e) the reaction of hydrogen sulphide with moist sulphur dioxide.   (L)

7. Give, with one example of each, **three** different ways other than by addition of oxygen, in which you could recognise that oxidation had taken place in a reaction.

    Sulphur dioxide, manganese dioxide and hydrogen peroxide can, in different reactions be oxidising or reducing agents. Explain why this is so and give one example of each type of reaction for each substance. (O & C)

8. Discuss the various types of chemical reactions which are described by the terms *oxidation* and *reduction*. Give what you consider is the most widely applicable definition of these terms.

    What do you understand by the term *standard oxidation potential*?

    Describe one use of a table of *standard oxidation potentials*.   (O & C)

PART II

ELEMENTS IN PERIODS

II

OCCURRENCE OF THE ELEMENTS

The occurrence, mode of extraction, and the properties of the elements (and also of their compounds) can be understood broadly from the Periodic Table, the electrochemical series, and free energies.

The parts of the earth accessible to man and from which substances can therefore be extracted are: (1) the atmosphere, (2) the seas and other waters—the hydrosphere—and (3) the earth's crust to a depth of a few miles. The earth's crust is about 20 miles thick and is called the lithosphere (Greek *lithos*, 'a stone').

Since most elements except oxygen, nitrogen and the noble gases are extracted from the earth's crust or from the waters on it, it is convenient to give the composition of the lithosphere and hydrosphere taken together.

Eighty-eight elements are found in nature either free or combined, but about 99 % of the weight of the combined lithosphere and hydrosphere is accounted for by only ten elements (three non-metals, seven metals). Oxygen alone accounts for almost half the total.

Percentage composition by weight of the lithosphere and hydrosphere taken together

Oxygen	49.2 ⎫		Chlorine	0.20
Silicon	25.7 ⎬ 82.4 %		Phosphorus	0.10
Aluminium	7.5 ⎭		Manganese	0.08
Iron	4.7 ⎫		Carbon	0.08
Calcium	3.4 ⎮		Sulphur	0.06
Sodium	2.6 ⎬ 15 %		Barium	0.04
Potassium	2.4 ⎮		Nitrogen	0.03
Magnesium	1.9 ⎭		Fluorine	0.03
Hydrogen	0.9		Strontium	0.02
Titanium	0.6		Bromine	0.01
	———		All others	0.45
	98.9			———
				1.10

The inclusion of the atmosphere makes practically no difference to these figures.

Origin of the elements

It has been estimated that the composition of the universe as a whole is 90 % by weight hydrogen and 9 % by weight helium. Much evidence got from the artificial synthesis of elements using cyclotrons has led to the development of various theories of the synthesis of the atomic nuclei of all the elements from hydrogen in the interior of the stars. Our sun consists mainly of hydrogen and helium, and this fact is taken to indicate that the earth was not formed from the sun, as was previously thought, but from a companion star.

Occurrence of elements wholly or partly in the uncombined state

Twenty-five elements are found uncombined in nature. It is clear that these elements must as a rule be very stable, indeed almost chemically inert, to have remained unaffected by other elements and compounds under varying conditions of temperature and pressure on or near the surface of the earth throughout geological time. As a rule the elements must therefore be weakly electropositive or weakly electronegative in the wide sense (p. 71).

No less than seven are present in the atmosphere, and indeed the atmosphere consists largely of these seven: oxygen, nitrogen, and the five noble gases helium, neon, argon, krypton and xenon. It is surprising to find oxygen in this group since it is one of the most electronegative and reactive of all the elements at moderately high temperatures and combines readily with most other elements. The reason is that, of the very large total amount of oxygen, almost all is present combined as oxo-salts or oxides, including water. Only a minute fraction of the whole remained uncombined because all the elements that could be oxidised in the prevailing conditions had been oxidised. Thus excess oxygen collected in the atmosphere. Nitrogen although strongly electronegative is a rather inert gas because it forms a very stable molecule.

Two other non-metal elements, carbon and sulphur, are found uncombined in relatively large quantities. The chief deposits of free or almost free carbon are the coals and anthracites: sedimentary rocks of vegetable origin laid down at a fairly late date in the evolution of the earth and therefore not subjected to the fairly high temperatures needed to oxidise the carbon. Graphite and diamonds are almost pure carbon. The deposits of native sulphur are often of volcanic origin, are highly localised, and have had little chance to mix with and then combine with other elements.

The next three are the metalloids arsenic, antimony and bismuth. Arsenic is weakly electronegative and the other two weakly electropositive.

The remaining thirteen elements are all transition metals which are weakly electropositive. Nine of them make up Group VIII of the Periodic Table; three others, the coinage metals copper, silver and gold belong to Group IB, which lies immediately to the right of Group VIII; while the last, mercury, is in Group IIB to the right of gold. These thirteen metals form a compact central block in the Periodic Table as shown:

Group VIII			Group IB	Group IIB
Iron	Cobalt	Nickel	Copper	—
Ruthenium	Rhodium	Palladium	Silver	—
Osmium	Iridium	Platinum	Gold	Mercury

In the transition metals, electrode potential and chemical activity usually decrease in descending the Groups. This is clearly seen above, the first triad in Group VIII, iron, cobalt and nickel, being more reactive than the two lower triads. It is surprising that iron should be found free in nature since it rusts so readily. It is found mainly in meteorites along with nickel and cobalt, the alloy formed being much more resistant to rusting than iron itself.

All the above facts agree well with the position of the elements in the Periodic Table and in the electrochemical series. Thus no elements in Groups IA, IIA, IIIB, or VIIB are found free in nature, nor is any element above hydrogen in the electrochemical series, with the already mentioned exceptions of iron, cobalt and nickel.

Occurrence of compounds of the elements

This type of occurrence is vastly more important than occurrence in the uncombined state. Here again consideration of stability is the key to understanding. The present existence of compounds in the earth's crust and seas is a proof of their stability. Any chemical changes which could take place have taken place or are now proceeding so slowly as to be negligible for most purposes.

Types of compounds and overall abundance

There are five factors of primary importance in accounting for the most common types of compound formed:

(1) the great abundance of the elements oxygen, silicon, and aluminium which together make up 82.4% by weight of the total;

(2) the great abundance of the metals iron, calcium, sodium, potassium, and magnesium which together make up 15% of the total;

(3) the great affinity of silicon and aluminium for oxygen;

(4) the great stability to heat, non-volatility, and insolubility of silicon dioxide (silica, SiO_2) and of aluminium oxide (alumina Al_2O_3);

(5) the weakly acidic nature of silica and alumina leading to the formation of highly stable, insoluble, silicates and alumino-silicates of the metals potassium, sodium, calcium, magnesium and iron.

Because of the above facts, the major chemical reactions which have taken place among the elements can be thought of, first, as the combination of oxygen with most of the other elements, metals and non-metals, forming basic and acidic oxides; and secondly as the combination of basic oxides and acidic oxides to form oxo-salts. As a result of these reactions most of the earth's crust consists of the minerals quartz (a form of silica); felspars, which are light coloured alumino-silicates of sodium, potassium and calcium; and the *mafic* minerals which are dark coloured silicates of calcium, magnesium and iron. (The adjective 'mafic' is formed from the first letters of the words magnesium and ferrum.)

So far only the most abundant compounds have been considered. Little has been said of the many compounds which, though occurring in very small amounts, are yet of major economic importance. Although the total weight of all these compounds is very small measured as a percentage of the weight of a shell of the earth 20 miles thick, yet from man's point of view they are of paramount importance. Indeed carbon which is 0.08% of the total would seem to be almost negligible, but where would we be without it? If the elements or compounds of the elements carbon, iron, chlorine, sulphur, tin, manganese, nickel and the rest had remained uniformly distributed in the crust, sea or air as they were to a large extent when these were formed in the first place, the task of extracting them in substantial quantities would have been impossible. How did it ever come about that the separation of these compounds from each other into economically workable deposits of ore took place? This is a complicated question, but some of the factors involved are indicated in the next section.

Origin of economic ores

Of the dense metals so important to man only iron (5% by weight) and titanium (0.6%) occur as an appreciable proportion of the whole crust. Chromium, zinc, lead, tin, copper and manganese amount to less than 0.3% only, although aluminium constitutes 8% of the whole. If it were not for the fortunate circumstances which produce ore concentrations an industrial society would be impossible. The natural processes take place in three stages.

The first parting

During the condensation of the earth from gaseous stellar material several separate fluid phases formed. These fluid phases were originally immiscible liquids and a gas phase. Further cooling solidified the liquids to form concentric zones in the earth, and the gas phase separated to give the hydrosphere and atmosphere. The core of the earth is thought to consist of a nickel-iron alloy and most of the remainder of the earth consists of silicates. It is very likely that thin layers of sulphide material occur at the base of the crust or lower in the mantle. There is a preferential but not exclusive concentration of certain elements in different layers, as follows:

Metallic core. Mainly transition metals: Mn, Fe, Co, Ni, Mo, Ru, Rh, Pd, Re, Os, Ir, Pt, Au.

Sulphide layers. Mainly B family elements: Cu, Ag, Zn, Cd, Hg, Ga, In, Tl, Ge, Sn, Pb, As, Sb, Bi, P, S, Se Te.

Silicate crust and hydrosphere. Mainly A family elements: Li, Na, K, Rb, Cs, Be, Mg, Ca, Sr, Ba, B, Al, Ti; the rare earths; and V, Cr, Zr, Nb, Mo, Hf, Ta, W, F, Cl, Br, I, C, Si, O, H.

Atmosphere. Uncombined oxygen, nitrogen and the noble gases.

A glance at the Periodic Table will show how close the correspondence is between these associations and the Groups and Periods of the former.

The second parting

The sulphide ores of important metals such as copper, zinc and lead occur as deposits in fissure systems called veins. In these veins the different metal sulphides occur in a definite zonal arrangement from the centre of the earth in this approximate order: copper, zinc, lead, silver, arsenic, antimony, mercury. This order of increasing distance from their origin corresponds to an increasing volatility of the sulphides. Under conditions of local heating the deep sulphide layers partially volatilise at temperatures below their melting point and the vapours are deposited in cool fissures in the upper crust. Where these veins cross limestones, the latter are often replaced by the ores and mining of these local concentrations is particularly profitable.

The crystallisation of the silicate magmas such as basaltic or granite lavas is completely different. The order of crystallisation from any complex melt is not simple but depends on the relative concentrations of the components. Certain minerals, however, tend to crystallise first, and if they are denser than the melt they sink to form gravity concentrations of one mineral. Some iron deposits of magnetite and the main sources of chromium, nickel and platinum are of this nature. This process of fractional crystallisation not only tends to concentrate the initial crystals, but also enriches the residual liquids in low melting point and volatile constituents. The main period of crystallisation involves the formation of silicate chains, sheets and lattices. The spaces in these for metal ions are restricted to certain size limits and if certain ions do not fit into these they are left in the residual liquids until the very end of crystallisation. In the last phase of solidification of a granite mass there is a liquid fraction very rich in volatiles—chlorides, fluorides, borates, steam, etc.—and in metallic ions which have the wrong size or charge to fit into the silicate frameworks of the main rock-forming minerals (felspars, micas, amphiboles and pyroxenes). These are expelled into veins about the granite to form important sources of fluorspar, tin, tungsten, molybdenum, beryllium, lithium, uranium, rubidium, caesium, tantalum, niobium, and the rare earths.

The third parting

The preceding processes of concentration are concerned with the crystallisation of minerals from hot primary vapours, solutions, and magmas. These deposits are further re-concentrated by the action of surface erosional and weathering agents which break up, decompose, dissolve and finally redeposit the material in a different form. Over 90 % of the worlds' mineral resources are secondary to the initial crystallisation. There are three products of the chemical weathering of an igneous or metamorphic rock: first the insoluble residual products of decomposition of rock minerals; secondly the solutions produced during this process; thirdly the fragmented remains of undecomposed resistant minerals.

In hot wet climates decomposition of micas, felspars and pyroxenes may be almost complete so that all that remains is an insoluble hydrated residue of iron and aluminium oxides called laterite. If this is very rich in either iron or aluminium it can be used as an economic ore for the metal. In fact nearly all the world's aluminium is produced from the aluminous laterite bauxite. Similar residual concentrations of manganese and nickel ores are also mined. In temperate climates the residual minerals are the clays which are important for their physical properties rather than their chemical content.

The most common resistant mineral which is never decomposed is quartz. Most metal ores, however, are resistant to weathering and are also much denser than quartz. Running water tends to concentrate these heavy minerals in pockets called *placers*, in the lee of sandbanks, and other places where the current suddenly drops. Particularly important deposits of gold, diamonds, and cassiterite (tin-stone) have formed in this way.

The carbonic and humic acids in the soil have a strong decomposing effect on silicate minerals giving rise to hydrogen carbonate and colloidal hydroxide solutions. The main ions carried away are Na^+, K^+, Ca^{2+}, Mg^{2+}, Fe^{2+} and Mn^{2+}. Of these Na^+, K^+ and Mg^{2+} stay in solution, unless they crystallise during the evaporation of inland seas or salt lakes in desert climates. In the evaporation of such a sea, the least soluble salts crystallise first and form a layer at the base of the basin. A stratigraphic section of evaporite deposits such as those at Stassfurt, shows increasing solubility upwards. The deposits are made on a foundation of magnesian limestone. The bulk of such deposits consists of gypsum, anhydrite, and rock salt, but the final liquids are rich in magnesium and potassium chlorides and sulphates which form a complex series of double salts. In desert lakes locally important deposits of sodium carbonate, sodium borate, sodium and potassium nitrates, sodium sulphates, and sodium iodate may form under special conditions.

Iron and manganese do not build up in the sea indefinitely; they are precipitated in a number of forms—hydrated oxides, carbonates or silicates. In a reducing environment both Fe^{2+} and Mn^{2+} are quite soluble. In an oxidising environment, however, the Fe^{2+} is oxidised and hydrolysed to produce a positive colloid and the Mn^{2+} by the same process produces a negative colloid. The two colloids precipitate each other by charge neutralisation.

Organisms in the sea are of great importance in precipitating Ca^{2+} in the form of $CaCO_3$. Oil and coal similarly are the remains of organic matter, the former marine, the latter terrestrial and vegetable. In this case the main mineral constituent is carbon, derived originally from CO_2 in the atmosphere.

In conclusion, the factors governing the mechanisms of mineral concentration and the associations produced are simple chemical and physical properties such as density, volatility, solubility, ionic radius, valency and charge. These properties are simply and directly related to the Periodic Table and thence to atomic structure.

Exercises

1. Summarise the general treatment of occurrence of the elements, given in the first part of this chapter.
2. Summarise the section on ore-genesis.
3. Compare the distribution of the elements with the separation of cations into groups in qualitative analysis.
4. Compare the separation of cations into groups in qualitative analysis with the grouping of metals in the Periodic Table.

12

EXTRACTION OF ELEMENTS
FROM ORES

Metals are much more numerous than non-metals and will be considered first and more fully.

General principles of extraction of metals

The chief ores in order of economic importance are (1) oxides, (2) sulphides, (3) chlorides, (4) carbonates.

It is usual to convert sulphides and carbonates into oxides before reduction, because oxides are more easily and efficiently reduced than sulphides. Most attention therefore will be given to oxide ores.

Because the metal is always the most electropositive part of an ore and so has a positive oxidation state, the formation of the free metal from its ore is always a reduction: $M^{n+} + ne \rightarrow M^0$.

In large-scale production of metals, economic considerations are of paramount importance: the cheapest possible method is chosen. Two main processes are used:

(1) *High temperature reduction (pyrometallurgy) with carbon,* the cheapest of reducing agents and one of the most powerful at high temperatures, partly because carbon monoxide exists and is stable at high temperature (see p. 183).

(2) *Electrolysis of molten compounds of the metal,* or of their aqueous solutions, involving cathodic reduction of metal ions. This method is especially useful where electric power is cheap.

The electrochemical series and the electronegativity series give some guidance as to the most suitable methods for winning metals from ores (p. 157). But the best approach to an understanding of the subject is by using free energies (ch. 6). The relationship between free energy G, heat of reaction H (heat evolved is negative), and entropy S at constant pressure is given by the equation (p. 82)

$$\Delta G = \Delta H - T\Delta S,$$

where the symbol Δ represents the change taking place in these quantities as a result of the chemical reaction. For example:

ΔS = (sum of entropies of products) − (sum of entropies of reactants).

As already stated (p. 83), the condition necessary for a reaction to take place is that ΔG must be negative, i.e. there must be a decrease in free energy. A negative value for ΔH (exothermic reaction) and a positive value for ΔS (increase of entropy during reaction) both contribute to a negative value for ΔG.

Increase in the volume of a system during a reaction means increase in entropy (p. 83) and therefore a positive value for ΔS. From equation (p. 181) it follows that for reactions where ΔS is positive, ΔG becomes more negative with rise in temperature and conversely, provided pressure remains constant. The relationships are approximately linear (p. 184). Note especially that an upward slope of a graph from left to right signifies that ΔG becomes *less negative* with rise in temperature, i.e. the reaction is less and less favoured as the temperature rises. The converse is also true. (See table below.)

There are three possible reactions of carbon with oxygen. Some of the changes in each, including the effect of rise in temperature on ΔG, are given in the following table.

Reaction	ΔH	Volume change	ΔS	$T\Delta S$	Effect of rise in T on ΔG	Conclusions
$C + O_2 \rightleftharpoons CO_2$ 1 vol. 1 vol.	Negative	None	Small or zero	Small or zero	Little or none	Forward reaction takes place, but is not much affected by rise in temperature
$2C + O_2 \rightleftharpoons 2CO$ 1 vol. 2 vol.	Negative	Increase	Positive	Large and positive	Becomes more negative	The forward reaction becomes more and more favoured as the temperature rises
$2CO + O_2 \rightleftharpoons 2CO_2$ 2 vol. 1 vol. 2 vol.	Negative	Decrease	Negative	Large and negative	Becomes less negative	Forward reaction becomes less and less favoured as the temperature rises

In any reduction of a metal oxide with carbon (or any other element) there is a competition between the metal and carbon for the oxygen. An element's power of combining with oxygen is measured by the decrease in free energy during formation of its oxide, the more negative the value of ΔG the greater is the combining power. Changes in free energy are measured under standard conditions. $\Delta G^\ominus$ is the standard free energy of formation of 1 mole of a compound from its elements; reactants and products all being in the standard state of 25 °C and 1 atmosphere pressure.

Free energies of *elements* are fixed arbitrarily as zero, therefore changes in free energies during reaction are called simply the free energies of the reaction. The values of $\Delta G^\ominus$ to be used for oxides are those obtained in reactions involving 1 mole of oxygen. *The element whose oxide has the most negative value of ΔG wins the competition and combines with the oxygen.*

The treatment so far has been qualitative. It can be made quantitative using values of the standard free energies of formations of many compounds over a wide range of temperature obtained by a large variety of experiments and calculations. These figures may be treated graphically in the way used by Ellingham in which graphs of standard free energies of compounds, $\Delta G^\ominus$, against temperature are drawn. Figure 95 (p. 184) shows one such set of graphs for oxide formation.

The element whose oxide has the most negative free energy of formation is the best reducing agent for oxides, and has the most stable oxide. Its graph is the lowest of all in Fig. 95. It is seen that this element is calcium (at least up to 2000 °C). The order of reducing power of the elements for oxides at room temperature is got from the vertical column on the left-hand side of the diagram. Comparison of this order with that of the electrochemical series shows some similarities but many differences. At moderate and high temperatures there are a considerable number of reversals of order shown by intersections of the graphs. At a given temperature an element will reduce the oxide of any element above it in Fig. 95 provided the temperature is high enough to supply the necessary activation energy.

A general inspection of Fig. 95 shows that all but two of the graphs slope up quite steeply from left to right, and are roughly parallel. An upward slope signifies a decrease in reducing power with rise in temperature. The graph for the oxidation of carbon to carbon monoxide is unique: it slopes down steeply from left to right throughout the whole of its length and cuts clean across almost all the other graphs, i.e. in this reaction, carbon's reducing power increases with rise in temperature, until at 2000 °C carbon is the third most powerful reducing agent after calcium and aluminium. The graph for oxidation of carbon to carbon dioxide is also unique in running

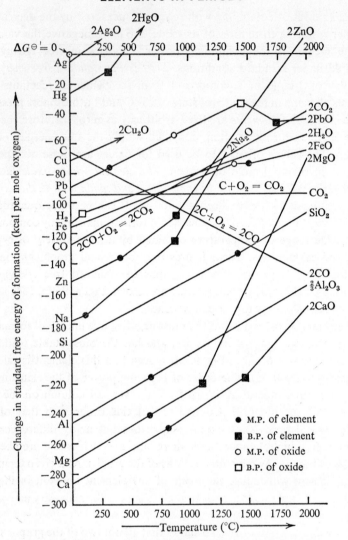

Fig. 95. Change of $\Delta G^\ominus$ with temperature, *for oxide formation.*

a level course, showing that temperature has no effect on this reducing action of carbon.

Volume changes with their consequent entropy changes are the decisive factors causing all other changes in trends in the graphs. Two kinds of volume change are found:

(1) Those arising from the chemical reaction, e.g. during the reaction $2Mg + O_2 \to 2MgO$ there is a loss of one volume of oxygen because the

metal is solid up to 650 °C and does not boil till 1100 °C; while magnesium oxide remains solid till 2800 °C.

(2) Those arising from changes of state of elements or oxides. The graphs show that the boiling points of metal oxides are reached in one case only, lead(II) oxide, which will therefore be omitted from the general remarks.

Melting of the metals produces a small volume change; but when the metals boil a large volume of vapour is produced and removed by combination with oxygen to form solid oxides. This decrease in volume (along with that caused by removal of oxygen in the reaction) causes a decrease in entropy (ΔS negative) and so ΔG becomes less negative ($\Delta G = \Delta H - T\Delta S$). This accounts for the fact that the gradients of the graphs increase considerably at and above the boiling points of the metals. It is concluded that increase in temperature causes a substantial decrease in the reducing power of the metals.

Examples of use of Fig. 95. (1) The great power of carbon as a reducing agent for oxides at high temperatures depends on the increase in volume and therefore entropy in the reaction $2C + O_2$ (1 vol.) $\rightarrow$ 2CO (2 vol.). This in turn depends (a) on the extremely low volatility of carbon even at very high temperatures, and (b) on the existence of a thermally stable monoxide of carbon. Consideration of the equation

$$C + O_2 \text{ (1 vol.)} \rightarrow CO_2 \text{ (1 vol.)}$$

during which there is no change in volume, makes the point clearer.

(2) Calcium and aluminium are clearly marked out for manufacture by electrolytic processes because of the very high temperatures (over 2000 °C) required for reduction of their oxides with carbon, and the technical difficulties entailed. Magnesium oxide, because of the low boiling point of the metal (see Fig. 95), can be reduced with carbon at any temperature above that of the intersection of their graphs, i.e. at about 1650 °C, but electrolysis is more commonly used.

(3) Magnesium will reduce aluminium oxide below about 1300 °C, at which temperature the graphs of $2Mg + O_2 \rightarrow 2MgO$, and

$$\tfrac{4}{3}Al + O_2 \rightarrow \tfrac{2}{3}Al_2O_3$$

intersect. Above 1300 °C aluminium will reduce magnesium oxide and the oxides of all other metals even calcium, which, however, needs an even higher temperature than 2000 °C. These facts are the basis of the *thermite process* for extraction of metals (p. 349).

(4) Magnesium will reduce carbon dioxide to carbon at temperatures below about 1800 °C, as in the well-known experiment in which burning magnesium is plunged into a jar of carbon dioxide. But carbon reduces magnesium oxide above 1650 °C as stated in (2), carbon monoxide being formed.

(5) Sodium is a much less powerful reducing agent in its action with oxygen than calcium, magnesium, aluminium, and silicon. Sodium reduces oxides of carbon at temperatures below about 1100 °C, but above this temperature carbon reduces sodium oxide to the metal. The speedy decline in sodium's reducing power with rise in temperature is hastened by entropy changes taking place when sodium melts and boils.

Accurate information about the reducing power of hydrogen with metal oxides, and that of metals on water and steam at any temperature below 2000 °C is quickly obtained from Fig. 95, or from similar sets of graphs containing a more complete set of metals. Indeed graphs like these, including also reduction of sulphides and chlorides, are of great value in discussing almost all pyrometallurgical reactions. It is found that sodium is one of the best reducing agents for chlorides.

Some exercises on this section are given at the end of the chapter.

Electrolysis of molten compounds of metals, usually the chloride, is commonly used in the manufacture of the alkali metals and alkaline earth metals. For details, see relevant chapter in part III.

General procedures for extraction of metals

The overall process usually involves three stages: concentration of the ore, reduction, and purification or refining of the metal.

Concentration of the ore

Ores vary greatly in quality, but most contain considerable quantities of worthless siliceous or other matter (gangue). Before concentration proper is carried out, the ore is broken up into lumps which are then ground down to a size, often a fine powder, suitable for the next operation.

Physical methods make use of differences in density or magnetic properties.

(1) *Washing*. Ores are usually denser than gangue, which can be washed away in a stream of water. Examples: galena, PbS, mixed with limestone; cassiterite, SnO_2, mixed with silicates.

(2) *Magnetic separation* is used in the separation of wolframite, the

principal ore of tungsten, from cassiterite with which it is found. The tungsten ore is attracted by a magnet, the cassiterite is not.

(3) *Froth flotation* is a widely used and important method for sulphide ores. The finely powdered ore is mixed with water to which has been added a suitable oil. The oil wets the sulphide particles, the water wets the gangue. Air is then blown through; small air bubbles attach themselves to the oiled particles which are buoyed up and carried to the surface, leaving the gangue at the bottom. The froth is skimmed off and the sulphide recovered. For example, galena and zinc blende, ZnS, often occur together mixed with gangue. Galena is first removed in the froth, then, by suitably altering the concentration of oil and other additives, zinc blende is similarly removed.

Chemical methods including heating, roasting, and leaching.

(1) *Heating and roasting.* Some moist hydrated iron ores are heated to drive off water. Roasting in air is sometimes used to remove water, carbonaceous matter, and to convert sulphides and carbonates to oxides, e.g. with zinc blende and zinc carbonate.

(2) *Leaching with aqueous solvents* (*hydrometallurgy*). One of the best known examples of this is the extraction of metallic gold from gangue by treating the finely powdered mixture with sodium cyanide solution with free access of air. Gold dissolves as a complex cyanide, and is precipitated thereafter by the addition of zinc.

Zinc ores may be leached with dilute sulphuric acid; so may oxide and carbonate ores of copper.

Leaching under pressure with aqueous ammonia solution is used in the concentration of nickel(II) sulphide ores.

Reduction

The principles of the two most important processes—(1) high temperature reduction with carbon or carbon monoxide (e.g. iron, zinc, tin) and (2) electrolysis of molten compounds of metals or their aqueous solution— have already been discussed. So also has the thermite process (p. 185) used for extraction of chromium and manganese.

Purification (refining)

(1) *Preferential oxidation of impurities* and their removal as slag or gas is suitable for removal of impurities which have a greater affinity for oxygen than the metal to be purified. Manufacture of steel from pig-iron is the

most important example of this (pp. 559–63). Another example is in the extraction of copper, during which iron(II) sulphide is separated from copper(I) sulphide by oxidation to iron(II) oxide followed by combination with silica to form a slag (pp. 583–4). In the purification of tin and lead, the molten metals are mixed with air. Oxides of the impurities rise to the surface and are removed.

(2) *Electrolysis* is used to produce a pure metal directly from its molten compounds, e.g. aluminium, and metals of Groups IA and IIA. Zinc, nickel, lead and copper are purified by electrolysis of aqueous solutions containing their ions.

(3) *Liquation* is carried out by melting the metal and allowing it to flow away from infusible impurities; used for metals of low melting point, e.g. tin and lead.

(4) *Distillation* forms an integral part in the extraction of zinc, cadmium, and mercury. A further distillation, usually in vacuum, gives a very pure product.

Vacuum distillation is also used to produce metals of Groups IA and IIA in a high degree of purity.

(5) *Formation of carbonyls* (p. 400). Very pure nickel and iron are made by forming their volatile carbonyls, which are then decomposed by heating.

(6) *Zone refining*. This recently developed method is used to produce silicon and germanium of extreme purity. A small high-frequency induction furnace is placed round one end of a long rod of the element, and a thin cross-section of the element is melted. The furnace is then moved slowly along the rod. Pure crystals of the element separate from the melt. but impurities remain in the liquid and are carried along to the other end, which is cut off.

Extraction of non-metallic elements

For this, see under the individual elements in part III.

Exercises

Use Fig. 95, p. 184, in answering these questions.

1. Explain the breaks in trend of the graph showing the effect of temperature on the free energy of formation of (*a*) magnesium oxide, (*b*) sodium oxide, and (*c*) lead(II) oxide.
2. Using Fig. 95 and also Le Chatelier's principle, explain how it is possible to prepare silicon by reduction of silica with magnesium, and to prepare magnesium by reduction of magnesium oxide with silicon,

$$SiO_2 + 2Mg \rightleftharpoons Si + 2MgO; \quad \Delta H \text{ negative.}$$

3. Collect and systematise information from Fig. 95 on (*a*) the effect of metals on water and steam, and (*b*) hydrogen as a reducing agent for metal oxides.
4. Summarise the methods used in refining metals.
5. Name **four types** of naturally occurring compounds from which metals are commonly extracted. Quote one specific example to illustrate each type and outline the essential chemical reactions by which the metal is extracted in each case.

    State **three** characteristic properties of transition elements, illustrating your answer by reference to the chemistry of iron and copper.   (J.M.B.)
6. Describe how any industrially important metal (*except iron*) is extracted from one of its common ores.

    Discuss the reasons why the process which you describe is used for this particular metal in preference to other methods of reducing metal ores.

    Suggest one method in each case which might be used to obtain (*a*) calcium from calcium carbonate, (*b*) mercury from mercury(II) oxide, giving reasons for your choice.   (O & C)
7. Pure metals are usually isolated from their ores by reduction. Describe the isolation of

    (*a*) zinc from zinc blende (ZnS),

    (*b*) iron from haematite (Fe_2O_3),

    (*c*) aluminium from bauxite ($Al_2O_3 . nH_2O$),

    (*d*) manganese from pyrolusite (MnO_2).

    Details of the purification of the metals and concentration of the ores are not required. Comment upon the methods of reduction used and suggest reasons for their choice.   (CS)

13

PHYSICAL PROPERTIES OF THE ELEMENTS

The emphasis in this chapter will be on trends across the Periods. Group trends will be referred to in part III.

One of the broadest and most useful generalisations in chemistry is the division of the elements into metals and non-metals. This classification is based on certain distinctive physical and chemical properties.

With the exception of hydrogen all the elements in Group IA are strongly electropositive metals, while all the elements in Group VIIB up to iodine are strongly electronegative non-metals. It follows that in passing along any Period from left to right there is a gradual but complete change of character from metal to non-metal. Somewhere in each Period therefore elements will be found poised between the two classes, and there will be some difficulty in deciding to which class they belong. These elements are called metalloids or semi-metals. Thus the classification is by no means rigid. The table of Main Group elements is reproduced below, showing the zig-zag line dividing metals from non-metals, and, on each side of this, broken lines are drawn indicating roughly the zone of metalloids. An interesting complication arises because of the allotropy of some of the elements in or near the metalloid zone. One of the allotropes is usually more metallic than the others. A good example of this is tin, one of whose allotropes, white tin, is a metal, while the other, grey tin, has some well marked non-metallic properties.

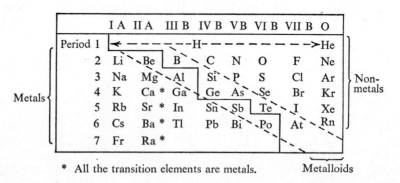

* All the transition elements are metals.   Metalloids

190

Metals

All metals have five important physical properties in common.

(1) They are good conductors of electricity.

(2) They are good conductors of heat.

(3) Their electrical conductivity *decreases* with rise in temperature.

(4) They are malleable and ductile, i.e. they can be hammered into sheets or drawn into wire without any loss of continuity in their structures, that is, without development of cracks, ruptures or any weaknesses.

(5) They have a characteristic metallic lustre.

In addition, most of the well-known metals have high densities, high melting points, high tensile strength and sonority (ring when struck). Mercury is exceptional in being a liquid at ordinary temperatures. Gallium (m.p. 29.8 °C) and caesium (m.p. 28.5 °C) melt on a hot day.

Non-metallic elements

These are quite clearly distinguishable from the metals. They are bad conductors of heat and electricity. Their (small) electrical conductivities *increase* with rise in temperature. They are brittle. Most of them have low densities, melting points, tensile strengths and sonorities. When non-metallic elements show metallic properties, they never show more than a few. Thus graphite is classed without difficulty as a non-metal because, even though it is lustrous, has a high melting point, and is a fairly good conductor of electricity, its conductivity increases with rise in temperature, and is very much greater in the direction along which it can be cleft than at right angles to this plane, a property not shown by metals. In addition graphite is neither malleable nor ductile.

Structure and bonding of the elements in Periods

Metals. A general account of this has already been given (pp. 123–26). All metals crystallise in one or another of the three main close-packed structures: face-centred cubic, hexagonal close-packed, and body-centred cubic. There is little or no relationship between the position of a metal in a Period and its structure type.

Non-metals. See pp. 127–32.

Explanation of physical properties of the elements in terms of atomic properties

1. *Electrical conductivity.* The high conductivity of the metals as a class is readily explained by the fact that the electrons responsible for metallic bonding (p. 108) are able to move freely throughout the whole metal. These electrons are moving from one singly occupied orbital to another throughout the metal and the movement is no greater in one direction than another; it is random. On applying even a very small potential difference to a piece of metal the random electron movements are transformed into an orderly unidirectional stream of electrons towards the higher potential; i.e. metals are good conductors of electricity.

If conductivities are calculated per mole instead of per centimetre-cube, it is found that the highest conductivities are shown by the alkali metals and the coinage metals (Groups IA and IB) while the conductivities of the transition metals of Group VIII are among the lowest. There is in fact a rough tendency for the conductivities of the metals to decrease in passing from left to right along a Period.

In non-metallic elements there is no free random movement of the electrons because there are no singly occupied orbitals of suitable energy for them to move into. The electrons are therefore localised in the covalent bonds, and are unaffected by the application of a potential difference unless it is very large, in which case the energy supplied is sufficient to remove electrons from the covalent bonds. Non-metals are therefore bad conductors (insulators). In the case of a few non-metals, germanium and silicon for example, the energy required to remove electrons from covalent bonds and start them streaming through the solid is much less than with others. These non-metals are said to be *semi-conductors.*

2. *Thermal conductivity.* Metals are good conductors of heat because the mobile electrons can transport thermal vibrations from one part of the structure to another. Non-metallic elements are bad conductors because they contain no mobile electrons.

3. *Effect of temperature on electrical conductivity.* When metals are heated their conductivities decrease. This is because the atomic cores vibrate with greater amplitude when heated and cause more obstruction to the smooth flow of the electrons between the rows of cores.

When non-metals are heated their extremely small conductivities increase only very slightly because of the difficulty of removing electrons from their very stable covalent bonds.

When metalloids (semi-metals) are heated their small conductivities increase very greatly because the electrons in their covalent bonds are less tightly held than in the case of the other non-metals. The added heat energy increases the kinetic energy of the atoms or molecules to such an extent that some of the loosely bound electrons are shaken free, and are then available to form an electric current when a potential difference is applied. The increased movement of the atoms in the metalloid increases the resistance offered to the flow of electrons, but this effect is much less than that of the increase in the number of mobile electrons.

Since the conductivities of metals increase with fall in temperature it is interesting to inquire how far this process goes. It is found that some metals when cooled to temperatures approaching absolute zero, suddenly lose all electrical resistance and are then said to be *super-conductors.* A current set up by induction in a ring of metal, which has been made superconducting, will continue to flow for days.

Some metals which become superconducting, and the temperature needed, are: tin (4 K), lead (7 K), cadmium (1 K). There are about twenty altogether. The phenomenon is not fully understood.

4. Malleability, ductility and elasticity. All substances when pulled, pushed, or subjected to shear stress, change their shape. Most substances return to their original shape when the force is removed, providing it is not too great; such substances are said to possess elasticity. When the force is applied, the atoms, ions or molecules of which the substance is composed are moved a little way out of their equilibrium positions, and when the force is removed they return to their original positions. Metals possess a high degree of elasticity.

If the force is increased steadily a stage is reached when the substance is strained beyond its elastic limit. The substance may then (1) splinter into fragments or (2) remain intact but fail to return to its original shape when the force is removed.

Non-metal elements belong to the first group; metals to the second. For example, when metals are hammered, rolled or drawn into wire their shapes are greatly altered by this extremely drastic treatment. At the end of it, however, they are still intact and substantially unaffected. They have given ground slowly but have not broken. They are said to have suffered *plastic deformation* and to be malleable and ductile. Non-metal elements, on the other hand, are brittle.

To explain this behaviour in terms of atomic structure, consider part of the lattice of a metal, and for comparison part of the lattice of an ionic crystal, e.g. sodium chloride, both subjected to shearing forces. Only the front faces of the crystals are shown. Consider also shearing forces being applied to a non-metal solid element, e.g. diamond or graphite.

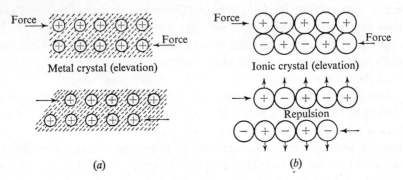

Metal crystal (elevation)   Ionic crystal (elevation)

Repulsion

(a)   (b)

Fig. 96. Effect of shearing forces on (a) metal crystals,
(b) ionic crystal (a compound).

In Fig. 96(a) it is clear that the structure of the metal has not been altered in any way. The forces of attraction between the mobile electrons and the two layers of positive atomic cores are the same as at the first, apart from the overlap. The metal is therefore still intact and unchanged. It has merely suffered plastic deformation. The plane mid-way between the two layers of atomic cores is called a *glide plane* or *slip plane*. Metals with face-centred cubic structures have many glide planes at different angles to each other, e.g. silver, copper, gold, lead, platinum, and are therefore highly malleable and ductile, showing plastic flow in all directions. Metals with body-centred cubic structure have fewer glide planes and are less malleable, e.g. iron, chromium. Metals with hexagonal closest-packed structures flow easily in one plane only, e.g. zinc, magnesium.

In (b) the case is different. Whereas at first the two layers were bound together strongly by the electrostatic attraction of vertical pairs of oppositely charged ions, after the movement they are repelled equally strongly by the electrostatic repulsion of vertical pairs of ions of like charge. The result is that the crystal splits or cleaves along the plane between the layers. Planes such as these are called *cleavage planes.*

Crystals of non-metallic elements may be cleft, but they do not undergo plastic deformation. They are always brittle because their covalent bonds are rigid and strongly directed. Under the influence of strong forces the covalent bonds between certain planes break and the crystal cleaves.

Solid non-metallic elements form crystals of two kinds: (1) giant molecules, e.g. diamond; (2) molecular crystals in which the units in the lattice are molecules, e.g. sulphur. Cleavage always takes place along planes between which the forces of attraction are weakest. Diamond crystals with their covalent bonding are extremely hard and rigid but can be cleft along well defined planes. This cleavage causes rupture of all the covalent bonds crossing the plane. In sulphur the forces binding the molecules to each other are weak. Sulphur is therefore very brittle and easily cleft and splintered.

One other point about metals needs mention. The forces required to cause plastic deformation in metals can be calculated. The calculated forces turn out to be approximately a thousand times as great as those found by experiment. The explanation is: atoms or rows of atoms may be missing from their place in the crystal lattice. The resulting holes or tunnels in the lattice are called dislocations. Deformation does not take place by the slipping of a whole layer of atoms bodily over another layer, but by the movement of one row of atoms into the dislocation, followed by the movement of the next row into the space left by the first and so on until the dislocation moves right across and out of the crystal in the opposite direction to the movement of the rows of atoms. Calculations show that the forces required to bring about this type of slip are in fact very nearly the same as the experimentally determined ones.

5. Lustre. The electrons in the surface of the metal are able to absorb radiation of all the wavelengths found in light. The absorbed energy causes the electrons to vibrate more vigorously and this in turn causes them to emit radiation. Thus almost all the light is reflected, giving the metals their characteristic lustre. The small amount of energy absorbed is converted into heat energy, so no light is transmitted through the metal and therefore metals are opaque.

Densities of the elements (in solid or liquid state)

Variation of density in the Periods. The graph of density against atomic number given in Fig. 97 shows clearly that density varies periodically. The alkali metals occupy the minima at the beginning of each Period, and the halogens or noble gases the minima at the end. The maxima are occupied by elements near the middle of each Period: carbon, aluminium, and the transition metals nickel and copper, ruthenium, and osmium, which is the densest of all the elements (22.5). One Period follows much the same pattern as another.

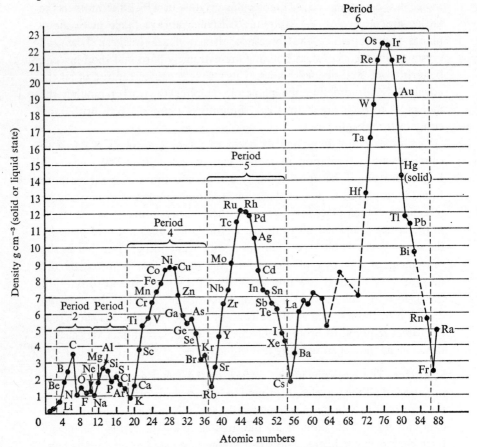

Fig. 97. Densities of the elements in Periods.

Consider Period 3 in more detail. A graph of this on an enlarged scale is shown in the lower part of Fig. 98. The graph rises almost in a straight line from sodium through magnesium to aluminium. This trend is then reversed, and there is a fairly steady fall to the end of the Period at argon. White phosphorus lies somewhat below the general trend, and rhombic sulphur a little above it.

The densities of the elements are determined mainly by four atomic properties: atomic weight; the volumes of individual atoms; the type of packing in the crystal; and the valency of the element.

(1) *Atomic weights*: these follow the same order as the atomic numbers.

(2) *The volumes of individual atoms*: these are proportional to the cube of the atomic radii. Note particularly that atomic radii are obtained by measurements on the elements in bulk and therefore include the effects of increased nuclear charge and increase in the number of valency electrons

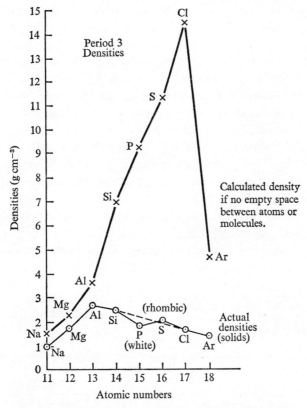

Fig. 98. Graphs of (i) actual densities, and (ii) atomic densities.
Note. The radius used for the metals is the metallic atomic radius, not the covalent radius.

found in moving across the Periods, i.e. the atomic radii as measured include the effect of increased bonding forces in the elements in moving across the Periods.

(3) *The type of packing* of the atoms or molecules in the crystals. This factor determines the closeness of the packing and hence the total volume of 'empty space' between the atoms or molecules in crystals.

From factors (1) and (2) taken together, a quantity which may be called 'atomic density' ($=$ (weight of one atom in grams)/(volume of one atom in cm^3)) can be calculated, given that $\frac{1}{16}$ of the weight of one oxygen atom (atomic weight 16) is 1.66×10^{-24} g. Now imagine a piece of sodium made by packing sodium atoms together with no empty spaces between them; the density of sodium would then be its 'atomic density'. A graph of atomic densities as defined above has been drawn above the graph of the actual densities in Fig. 98. The difference between the two densities for any element gives an indication of the total volume of empty space between the atoms or molecules in a crystal of that element and hence indicates also the type of packing. In the three metals, sodium, magnesium and aluminium, the proportion of empty space does not change much and corresponds to that actually found in metallic close-packing. At silicon the gap is very much wider, indicating a different type of packing (diamond structure), while with phosphorus, sulphur and chlorine the very wide gap indicates the much less close packing in molecular crystals. At argon, the gap narrows again indicating a return to a close-packed structure which is in fact face-centred cubic.

It is seen therefore that deductions made from atomic properties agree fairly well with the observed facts.

Note. In face-centred cubic and hexagonal close-packings a quarter of the total space is empty, the atoms occupying three-quarters. It follows that

$$\text{atomic density} = \tfrac{4}{3} \text{ actual density} \quad \text{or} \quad \frac{\text{atomic density}}{\text{actual density}} = 1.33.$$

Similarly with the others:

	Empty space	Atomic density / actual density
F.C.C. and H.C.P.	$\frac{1}{4}$	1.33
B.C.C.	$\frac{1}{3}$	1.50
Diamond structure	$\frac{2}{3}$	3.00

Calculations from atomic densities and actual densities may therefore be used to find the structures of elements.

(4) *Valency*: see p. 109.

Variation of density in the Groups. From Fig. 99 it is seen that, for all the elements including transition metals, there is an almost universal and substantial increase in density in passing down any Group. The increases

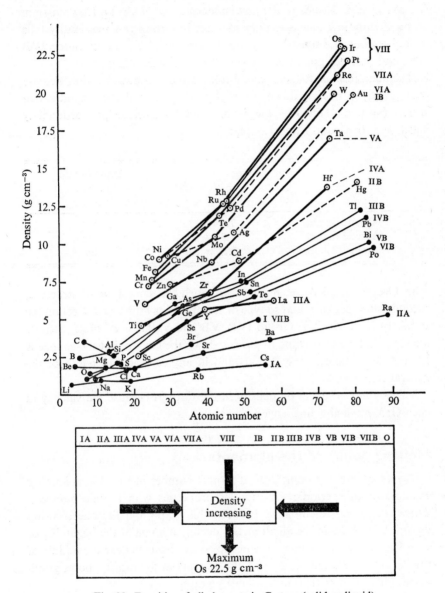

Fig. 99. Densities of all elements in Groups (solid or liquid).

with transition metals are much greater than with Main Group elements. Three slight exceptions to the first statement are: in Group IA potassium has a slightly lower density than sodium; in Group IIA the density falls from beryllium 1.8 to calcium 1.6 and rises thereafter; and in Group IVB diamond (but not graphite) has a higher density than silicon.

The main reasons for the general trend are that atomic weights increase very greatly in passing down any group, while the volumes of individual atoms ($= \frac{4}{3}\pi r^3$ where r is the atomic radius) increase proportionately much less. In Group I for example:

	Li Cs	Approximate rate of increase
Atomic weight	7.0 → 133	19 times
Atomic radius	1.5 → 2.6	$1\frac{3}{4}$ times
Atomic volume	$\propto 1.5^3 \propto 2.6^3$	5 times

In Group IA all the elements have much the same type of structure, metallic close-packing, and so type of structure has little or no effect on the trend. In some Groups, Group IVB, VB and VIB, for example, there is a change in type of packing in passing down the Group, but the change is more gradual than in the Periods and in any case acts to reinforce the general trend.

Valency has no effect on density in the Groups because the valency in each Group remains unchanged.

Melting points of the elements

The graph melting point against atomic number in Fig. 100 is another example of the periodic variation of properties with atomic numbers. There is a broad resemblance between this graph and the one showing densities. Here again the alkali metals occupy minima at the beginning of each Period and the maxima are occupied by elements near the middle of the Periods. In Periods 4, 5 and 6 the maxima in the melting-point graph occur a little earlier than in the density graph.

When the kinetic energy of the particles in a crystal is increased by heating, a stage is reached when it overcomes the lattice energy of the crystal. The particles then tear themselves out of the lattice far enough to be able to slip past each other, i.e. the solid melts. Furthermore, the stronger the bonding force the higher the melting point. The bonding force between the particles of giant structures (metals, giant molecules, ionic compounds) is generally several orders of magnitude greater than that between the particles of molecular crystals. The difference, in fact, between the strength of ionic, covalent and metallic bonds and the strength of the weak van der Waals' force of attraction (see p. 108). Increase in bonding force also tends to increase the density of metals by pulling the cores closer together.

Melting point trends in the Periods. These closely follow the trends in bonding force between the stable particles comprising the crystalline element. Thus the sharp drop in melting point in passing from carbon to nitrogen in Period 2 marks the change from giant structure to molecular crystal (see p. 122).

Across a Period the strength of the bonding force between the atoms of a giant structure varies progressively with the extent to which the valency electrons contribute to the bonding. Thus in passing along Period 2 the number of electrons participating in the bonding rises progessively from one per atom for lithium to a maximum of four per atom for carbon. The parallel increase in the melting points of these elements in quite striking, see Fig. 100.

Molecular crystals have low melting points as a consequence of the weak van der Waals' force of attraction between the molecules (or atoms if the element is a noble gas). Generally the higher the molecular weight of the molecules comprising the crystal the higher is its melting point. Since the molecular weight of both phosphorus (P_4) and sulphur (S_8) is substantially greater than that of other elements in Periods 2 and 3 which form molecular crystals, their melting points are correspondingly much higher (see Fig. 100). It is interesting to note that both sulphur (MW = 256) and iodine (MW = 254) melt at about 114 °C.

Variation of melting points in the Groups. No comprehensive statement is possible here, but there are rough trends as atomic number increases:

Main Group elements. In Group IA there is a fairly steady but slight fall. In Groups VIB, VIIB and 0, there is a fairly steady but slight rise. The other Groups have broken trends.

Transition metals. All the Groups show a considerable rise in melting point, except the Copper Group (little change), the Zinc Group (a considerable fall), and the Scandium Group (first a rise, then a substantial fall, partly accounted for by an exceptional rise in atomic radius from the second member yttrium to the third, lanthanum).

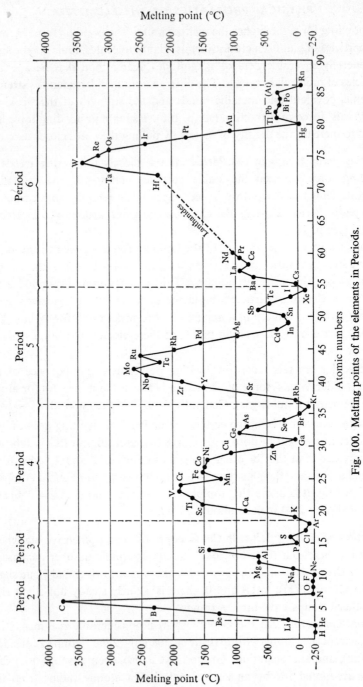

Fig. 100. Melting points of the elements in Periods.

Heats of fusion of the elements

Heat of fusion is defined as the quantity of heat energy measured in joules absorbed by 1 mole of a substance at its melting point and 1 atmosphere pressure in changing from a solid to a liquid. The *specific latent heat* of a substance is similarly defined except that it refers to 1 gramme of a substance and not 1 mole (i.e. formula weight in grammes). Thus heat of fusion gives a measure of the energy needed to break down the rigidity of the crystal lattice *at its melting point*.

Alternatively, since solids generally expand slightly on melting, heat of fusion may be taken as a measure of the work done in pulling the lattice slightly apart against the forces binding it together. Fusion is accompanied by a disordering of the particles and it is this which in general tends to produce the slight expansion. Nevertheless the particles still remain in contact as shown by the negligible effect of pressure on liquids.

Since melting points and heats of fusion are both directly related to the strength of the bonding force they closely follow the same periodic variation.

Boiling points and heats of vaporisation

At the boiling point thermal agitation has now increased to such a pitch that particles can tear themselves away from the bulk of the liquid and enter the vapour phase at such a rate they produce a vapour pressure equal to atmospheric pressure. Particles can evaporate directly from a solid but the rate of evaporation is slow.

Heat of vaporisation is defined similarly to heat of fusion except that it refers to the phase change liquid to vapour. Heat of vaporisation measures the work done in *completely* separating the particles of a liquid against the forces of attraction acting between them. It is therefore greater than the corresponding heat of fusion.

The phase change solid to liquid still leaves the particles in contact whereas vaporisation separates them. Fusion of a metal therefore, does not separate its atomic cores from the surrounding electron flux. Thus the metallic bond is not broken during fusion. Moreover, it is a very strong bond and considerable energy is needed to separate the atoms of a metal as can be seen from the high boiling points and heats of vaporisation of the metallic elements. The same effect is shown by other giant structures.

Since the weak van der Waals' force between the particles in a molecular crystal is substantially weakened during fusion little extra effort is then

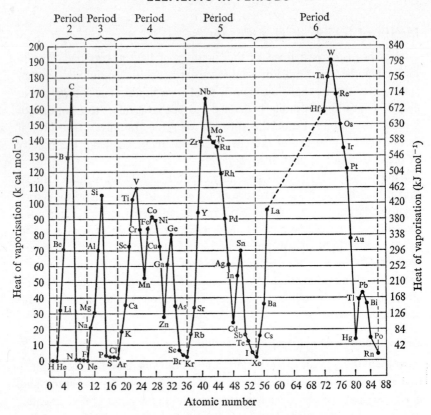

Fig. 101. Heats of vaporisation of the elements in Periods.

needed to completely separate the particles. This is shown by the low boiling points and heats of vaporisation of these elements.

The temperature interval between the melting point and boiling point of those substances which form molecular crystals is relatively short. On the other hand those substances which form giant structures (metals, giant molecules, ionic crystals) melt and still retain most of the strong bonding force that existed between the particles in the crystal. Therefore these structures have a relatively big difference between the melting point and the boiling point for it is only at this latter temperature that the particles are completely separated and the strong bonds broken. There is a similar distinction shown by the difference between heat of fusion and heat of vaporisation of a substance.

Variation of heats of vaporisation in the Periods

The first four elements in both Periods 2 and 3 are all giant structures, i.e. metals and giant molecules (B, C and Si). All these elements have relatively high heats of vaporisation. There is a progressive steep rise across the Period in step with the number of electrons per atom participating in the bonding force. This is essentially the same bonding force that existed in the crystal. As with melting points the dramatic drop from carbon to nitrogen in Period 2 and from silicon to phosphorus in Period 3 marks the change from giant structure to molecular crystal.

The trends in Period 4 can be interpreted in a similar manner. There is, however, an additional broad peak between scandium and zinc corresponding to a series of elements with characteristically strong metallic bonding. The breaks in the curve at manganese and zinc (see also cadmium and mercury in Period 5 and Period 6 respectively) are especially significant. They are evidence of much weaker metallic bonding in these elements compared with their neighbours in the Period. In these elements the electrons are entirely contained in filled or half-filled sub-shells. It is known that electrons in filled or half-filled sub-shells have additional stability and it is suggested that they do not participate fully in forming the metallic bond.

Summary: The structure of the element has the most profound effect on its physical properties. The atomic radius and the number of electrons per atom available for bonding are the properties which largely determine what structure an element will display. Since these are both periodic properties structure also shows broad periodic trends. Thus, in general, all physical properties show similar periodic trends.

Exercises

1. Calculate the *atomic* densities (p. 197) of some Period 4 elements from the metallic radii of the metals and the covalent atomic radii of the non-metals. From the ratio (atomic density/actual density), estimate the structure of each element (p. 198) and compare with their structures as indicated on pp. 126, 132.

	K	Ca	Ti	Cr	Fe	Cu	Zn	Ga	Ge	As	Se	Br
Radii (Å)	2.35	1.97	1.47	1.29	1.26	1.28	1.37	1.53	1.22	1.21	1.17	1.14
										Grey	Grey	
Actual density	0.86	1.55	4.50	7.10	7.86	8.92	7.14	5.91	5.35	5.70	4.80	3.12

2. On the same sheet draw graphs of atomic density and actual density against atomic number for the elements in question 1. Compare these with the graphs given for Period 3, p. 197.

3. Draw the graph of boiling points of the elements against atomic number, up to the end of Period 6, using data from a Handbook of Chemistry and Physics. Is boiling point a periodic function of atomic number? Compare the trends with those of the graph of melting points on p. 202 by drawing this graph also, on the same sheet.

4. Predict the relationship between the heat of fusion and the melting point of a substance that contracts on melting, and give your reasons.

14

CHEMICAL PROPERTIES OF THE ELEMENTS

In this chapter a comparative general account of the chemical properties of the elements including transition metals is given, with emphasis on trends within the Periods. A revision summary of the broad chemical differences follows in the table below.

Metals	Non-metals
(1) Electropositive, i.e. their atoms form cations by releasing electrons	(1) Electronegative, i.e. their atoms form anions by capturing electrons; or form covalent compounds by sharing electrons
(2) Deposited at the cathode during electrolysis	(2) Deposited at the anode during electrolysis (if they form ions)
(3) Displace the hydrogen of acids directly or indirectly to form salts	(3) Do not form salts with the element as cation
(4) Form basic or amphoteric oxides, except that higher oxides of transition metals are acidic	(4) Form acidic or neutral oxides
(5) Their hydroxides are basic or amphoteric	(5) Their hydroxides are oxo-acids
(6) Their halides are salts (with very few exceptions)	(6) Their halides are not salts
(7) Do not combine readily with hydrogen. Metal hydrides are either ionic solids or alloy-type solids	(7) Readily combine with hydrogen to give covalent hydrides, which are usually gaseous at room temperature

The chemical behaviour of the elements follows from the atomic properties given in section (1) of the table and may be broadly summarised thus:

(a) Metals, $M \rightarrow M^{n+} + ne$.

(b) Non-metals either (i) $X + ne \rightarrow X^{n-}$,

or (ii) $X \cdot + . Y \rightarrow X : Y$

(n is the electrovalency of the element and is a simple whole number).

Metals usually act as reducing agents because their valency electrons are easily captured. Strongly electronegative non-metals act as oxidising agents because their atoms readily capture electrons.

Action with air

The atmosphere always contains water vapour and carbon dioxide, together with small quantities of sulphur dioxide and hydrogen sulphide, especially in the vicinity of industrial areas. Water vapour and acidic gases greatly increase atmospheric corrosion. Unless otherwise stated, the reactions described here are those which take place using elements of the purity found in normal laboratory reagents and atmospheric air *at ordinary ('room') temperature*. The action of air on the elements is almost always the action of a gas on a solid. Most elements are attacked by the oxygen of the air. Further, all oxides of metals are solids at room temperature, and so are some non-metal oxides. It follows that in the great majority of cases the initial reaction of air on elements consists of an attack by oxygen on a solid surface, resulting in the formation of a new solid. These facts have a profound effect on the extent of the action.

Although oxygen is relatively inert at room temperature, it is the second most electronegative element and therefore has a strong tendency to capture electrons and form the oxide ion O^{2-}, so that with elements which readily release electrons, i.e. metals, oxide formation will occur at the surface. A useful rough rule here is that the greater the difference in electronegativity between an element and oxygen, the more vigorous will be the initial action. More vigorous means more rapid. Increase in the speed of the reaction results from heat evolved as the reaction proceeds. In general, the greater the electronegativity difference the more heat is evolved. From the electronegativity trends in the Periodic Table, it follows that the vigour of the initial reaction will diminish from left to right across the Periods and increase down the Main Groups.

Metals

With metals the action is

$$\text{oxygen} + \text{electrons from metals} \rightarrow O^{2-} + \text{cations.}$$

Nitrogen is very inert at room temperature, but is the third most electronegative element, and nitrides are formed slowly by some metals, e.g. calcium, strontium and barium, when exposed to air.

After the primary attack has taken place, a film of oxide is formed on the surface of the metal (and on some non-metals). Whether the reaction will continue depends on whether the oxide film protects the element from further oxidation. This, in turn, depends mainly on two factors: (1) the density of the oxide compared with that of the metal, and (2) its solubility in water (always present in air). If the volume of the oxide formed is less than the volume of the metal used up in forming it, the film will not be continuous, and so will be porous and non-protective. If the volume of the oxide is greater than the volume of the metal used in forming it, the film will be continuous, non-porous and protective.

On continued exposure to the atmosphere, the oxide will tend to form the hydroxide by adsorption of water molecules from the air or by reaction with liquid water condensing on the surface. The more electropositive the metal, the greater the tendency to form its hydroxide, and the more soluble the hydroxide formed. Very soluble hydroxides give saturated solutions of high concentration, which have vapour pressures lower than the pressure of water vapour in air of average temperature and humidity. These solutions will, in consequence, absorb more water molecules from the air, i.e. the hydroxides will be deliquescent. The layer of solution so formed will allow dissolved oxygen to pass through to the metal beneath, and in some cases the water itself will react with the metal forming hydrogen. In any case, the reaction will continue till all the metal has reacted.

Consideration of the densities of metals and their oxides shows that non-protective oxide films are formed from metals of exceptionally low density, and valencies not exceeding two, i.e. alkali metals and alkaline earth metals (except beryllium). All other metals, except iron, form protective films at ordinary temperatures. This approach is too simple but gives a rough guide. Often the films are so thin as to be invisible, e.g. with vanadium, chromium and nickel. Further, the alkali metals form hydroxides which are very soluble in water, and are therefore deliquescent; the alkaline earth metals form hydroxides which are either slightly soluble or fairly soluble, but are not usually deliquescent; all other metals form insoluble oxides or hydroxides.

With the strongly electropositive metals of Groups IA and IIA the action does not stop with hydroxide formation. Carbonates or even hydrogen carbonates are eventually formed.

Transition metals are all less electropositive and also less reactive than calcium. They show a very considerable similarity among themselves, seen strikingly in the fact that they constitute horizontal series of ten elements, all of which are metals. The transition metals fit quite well into the trends indicated for the Main Group elements. Consider Period 4. All (except iron) are stable in the atmosphere at ordinary temperatures, because of the formation of a thin film of oxide. Iron is exceptional in that it rusts steadily in moist air, especially when liquid water condenses on its surface. A non-protective layer of hydrated iron(III) oxide is formed. With copper and zinc, the last of the Period 4 transition metals, the protective layer of oxide undergoes a further change. Copper(II) oxide is gradually converted into a tough protective film of green basic copper(II) sulphate,

$$CuSO_4 . 3Cu(OH)_2,$$

by adsorption of water and oxides of sulphur from the air, while zinc oxide is converted into grey basic zinc carbonate, $ZnCO_3 . Zn(OH)_2$, by adsorption of water and carbon dioxide.

Non-metals

Non-metals do not react with air at room temperature, except phosphorus and arsenic. Phosphorus reacts slowly with moist air at room temperature forming a white smoke of phosphorus trioxide (P_4O_6), and burns vigorously and completely in air at about 50 °C, forming white clouds of phosphorus pentoxide (P_4O_{10}).

The discussion may be summarised, and the trends across the Periods shown in the following table.

Action of air on elements at ordinary temperature

	Group I A	Group II A	Transition metals Metals of Group III B		Non-metals
Primary re-action oxide formation	Very rapid →	Rapid	Formation of protective oxide film with →————→————→ diminishing vigour		No action except with P and As
Secondary reactions	Fairly quickly to carbonate or hydrogen carbonate	→ Slowly to carbonate	No action on the element but possible conversion of →————→————→ oxide film into hydroxide or basic carbonate		No action

Almost all solid elements, especially when finely divided, burn when heated in air.

Action with water, acids and alkalis

This account will be restricted to the reactions of the elements with (1) water, (2) the non-oxidising acids, hydrochloric acid and dilute sulphuric acid, and (3) aqueous solutions of sodium hydroxide or potassium hydroxide. These liquids have this in common: they contain hydrogen ions, hydroxyl ions and water molecules. The primary reaction in most cases is *displacement of ions*. Ionic reactions can be systematised in terms of standard electrode potentials of the elements because electrodes made of the elements are in contact with aqueous solutions during measurements of electrode potentials (see p. 149). The reactions of the elements (not all the elements react), especially metals, with these liquids are all *spontaneous processes*, and may be classed as corrosion processes in aqueous solution. So are the reactions taking place in the apparatus used in measuring standard electrode potentials. All are electrochemical in nature.

In Fig. 102 the graphs of the standard electrode potentials of the elements of Periods 3 and 4 against atomic numbers have been reproduced from Fig. 93, p. 154. The curves shown are typical of those obtained with any of the Periods.

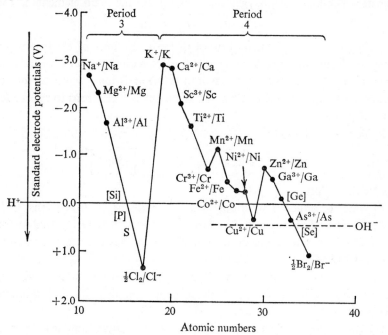

Fig. 102. Standard electrode potentials against atomic numbers (Periods 3 and 4).

Reactions involving displacement of ions

Cation formation. Metals and hydrogen, i.e. electropositive elements, displace one another from aqueous solution by transfer of electrons from an element higher in the electrochemical series to one lower, e.g.

$$Na + H^+ \rightarrow Na^+ + \tfrac{1}{2}H_2.$$

Because sodium has a greater negative standard electrode potential than hydrogen, it displaces hydrogen ions from solution, the one valency electron of the sodium atom being captured by the hydrogen ion. It is not possible for the atom of an electropositive element to displace the ion of an electronegative element. Reactions of the type

$$Na + \begin{bmatrix} {}^{\times\times}_{\times}Cl^{\times}_{\times} \\ {}_{\times\times} \end{bmatrix}^- \rightarrow Na^+ + \begin{bmatrix} {}^{\cdot\times\times}_{\times}Cl^{\times}_{\times} \\ {}_{\times\times} \end{bmatrix}^{2-}$$

do *not* take place, because an elementary anion has as many electrons as it can take for a stable noble-gas type configuration.

Anion formation. Strongly electronegative non-metallic elements can displace less strongly electronegative elements from solution by electron transfer. The halogens, oxygen and sulphur are the main elements in this class, e.g.

$$\tfrac{1}{2}Cl_2 + Br^- \rightarrow Cl^- + \tfrac{1}{2}Br_2.$$

But electronegative elements cannot displace the ions of electropositive elements from solution, because non-metals require to gain electrons in order to achieve stability and pass into solution as ions, while the ions of electropositive elements, e.g. Na^+, have no valency electrons to release for this purpose.

Reactions of the type

$$\begin{matrix} {}^{\times\times}_{\times}Cl^{\times}_{\times} \\ {}_{\times\times} \end{matrix} + \begin{bmatrix} {}^{\cdot\cdot}_{}Na{}^{\cdot\cdot}_{} \\ {}_{\cdot\cdot} \end{bmatrix}^+ \rightarrow \begin{bmatrix} {}^{\times\times}_{\times}Cl^{\times}_{\times} \\ {}_{\times\times} \end{bmatrix}^- + \begin{bmatrix} {}^{\cdot\cdot}_{}\cdot Na{}^{\cdot\cdot}_{} \\ {}_{\cdot\cdot} \end{bmatrix}^{2+}$$

do *not* take place.

In water or aqueous solutions of acids or alkalis, hydroxyl ions, OH^- are present. OH^- is the ion of an electronegative entity OH, a *free radical* corresponding to an atom of a non-metal. OH^- has the same relation to OH as Cl^- has to Cl.

Two important parallel rules follow from the above remarks, and from the previous discussion of the electrode potential series and standard electrode potentials. They are:

(1) *An electropositive element* with a greater negative standard electrode potential than hydrogen displaces or tends to displace hydrogen from

water or aqueous solutions of acids or alkalis; the greater the difference the more vigorous the reaction.

(2) *A strongly electronegative element* with a greater positive standard electrode potential than hydroxyl, displaces or tends to displace hydroxyl radicals or oxygen from water or aqueous solutions of acids or alkalis; the greater the difference in their electrode potentials, the more vigorous the reaction.

Figure 103 illustrates these rules as applied to the particular electro-chemical potential series for Periods 3 and 4 (with the addition of fluorine, iodine, and hydroxyl).

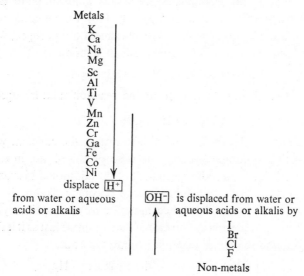

Fig. 103. Displacement of H^+ and OH^- from aqueous solutions.

Reactions involving formation of covalent bonds

With water and with sodium hydroxide solution a number of secondary reactions take place. These will be considered later.

Action of water on elements

Unless otherwise stated, the reactions with water described here are those which take place using elements of the purity found in normal laboratory reagents, and ordinary distilled water. This contains a small amount of dissolved oxygen which affects the action in some cases.

Note. The potential of the hydrogen electrode in neutral water is -0.41 V, therefore metals with a more negative standard electrode potential than this displace or tend to displace hydrogen from neutral water.

The ions present in water are (1) hydrogen ions in very low concentration, 10^{-7} mole per litre, and (2) hydroxyl ions OH^- in the same very low concentration, the dynamic equilibrium between these ions and water molecules being represented by the equation

$$H_2O \rightleftharpoons H^+ + OH^-, \quad K_w = [H^+] [OH^-] = 10^{-14}.$$

Metals

Consider sodium, for example. Since it has a much more negative standard electrode potential than hydrogen (-0.41 V), the initial reaction of sodium on water is a very vigorous displacement of hydrogen, with the formation of sodium ions and hydroxyl ions in solution

$$Na + H^+ + OH^- \rightarrow Na^+ + OH^- + \tfrac{1}{2}H_2.$$

The removal of hydrogen ions from the reaction mixture upsets the equilibrium
$$H_2O \rightleftharpoons H^+ + OH^-.$$

More water molecules therefore ionise to restore the constant value of K_w. Some of the additional hydrogen ions so produced are, in turn, removed by interaction with sodium atoms; but the additional hydroxyl ions accumulate in the solution, which becomes increasingly alkaline. The reaction proceeds quickly to completion because sodium hydroxide is very soluble in water, and is removed from the surface of the sodium as fast as it is formed.

With magnesium the *initial* reaction is quite vigorous,

$$Mg + 2H^+ + 2OH^- \rightarrow Mg^{2+} + 2OH^- + H_2.$$

Since magnesium hydroxide has a very low solubility, its solubility product is very quickly reached, i.e. the solution becomes a saturated solution of magnesium hydroxide. Immediately this stage is reached the reaction slows down almost to a halt because of the formation of a protective film of magnesium hydroxide on the surface of the metal (cf. action of air on the elements).

In passing along the Periods, the metals become less electropositive, and so their hydroxides become less and less soluble. The result is that after the initial quick displacement of hydrogen and formation of a protective hydroxide layer, the action (as a rule) stops. Metals having greater positive standard electrode potentials than hydrogen do not react with water (in absence of dissolved air), copper for example. The reaction of water on the metals in any Period is therefore similar to that of the action with air.

Non-metals

On the right-hand side of the Periodic Table, the rule is that non-metals with a greater positive electrode potential than hydroxyl ($+0.81$ in neutral water, p. 157) displace it from water, the greater the potential difference the more vigorous the reaction. The reactions are, however, not simple displacements. With chlorine the initial reaction is vigorous but reversible. but reversible.

$$HO^- + Cl-Cl \rightleftharpoons HOCl + Cl^-.$$

The reaction involves the splitting of the chlorine molecule into atoms, the displacement of the OH^- ion by a chlorine atom ($Cl + OH^- \rightarrow Cl^- + OH$) and the simultaneous formation of a covalent link between the other chlorine atom and the hydroxyl free radical OH, to form a molecule of hypochlorous acid, a very weak almost un-ionised acid. The final equation shows the formation of a mixture of hydrochloric acid and hypochlorous acid,

$$H^+ + OH^- + Cl_2 \rightleftharpoons H^+ + Cl^- + HOCl.$$

A similar reversible reaction takes place with bromine, but the forward reaction does not proceed so far as with chlorine,

$$H^+ + OH^- + Br_2 \rightleftharpoons H^+ + Br^- + HOBr.$$

Non-metals with a smaller positive electrode potential than hydroxyl do not react with water, e.g. carbon, phosphorus; also iodine, whose standard

Action of water on elements at ordinary temperature

	Group I A	Group II A	Transition metals	III B metals	Metal-loids	Other non-metals	Group VII B
Primary formation of hydr-oxide and hydrogen	Very vigorous →	Vigorous except Mg →	Diminishing vigour →		← No action ←		Rapid formation of HX and HOX, reversible reactions, except I_2, no reaction
Secondary	To com- pletion →	To com-pletion (except Mg)	Decreasing solu-bility of the hydroxide. Action stopped by hydroxide film →				

electrode potential is $+0.54$ V. The trends across Periods 3 and 4 may be summarised in the table on p. 215 (omitting scandium, vanadium, and gallium for lack of consistent information).

Exceptions

(1) Manganese is the only transition metal which liberates hydrogen steadily from water. Two reasons for this are (*a*) manganese has a distinctly greater negative standard electrode potential than chromium, which precedes it in Period 4 (see graph), and (*b*) although its hydroxide is very slightly soluble it has little protective action,

$$Mn + 2H^+ + 2OH^- \rightarrow Mn^{2+}(OH)_2^- + H_2 \uparrow.$$

(2) Iron reacts with water containing dissolved oxygen, but the action stops if and when the dissolved oxygen has been used up.

Action of acids on elements

This section is restricted to the non-oxidising acids, hydrochloric acid and dilute sulphuric acid. The action of concentrated sulphuric acid and of nitric acid will be considered later with the other properties of these acids. Magnesium and the elements in Period 4 will be discussed as fairly typical.

The chemical species present in the acids here considered are:

(1) hydrogen ions in high concentrations, e.g. 1 mole per litre in M HCl or 0.5 M H_2SO_4;

(2) hydroxyl ions in extremely low concentration, e.g. 10^{-14} mole per litre in M HCl or 0.5 M H_2SO_4;

(3) water molecules in very high concentration;

(4) chloride ions or sulphate ions in high concentration. In most cases these ions take no part in the reactions; but where insoluble chlorides or sulphates are formed their role is paramount.

Broadly speaking, the reactions are the same as with water, only much more vigorous and proceeding to completion. An understanding of these reactions follows naturally from the account of the reactions with water. The most significant differences between acids and water in this context are that the hydrogen ion concentration in acids is much higher than that in water, while the hydroxyl ion concentration is and *must remain* proportionately lower.

Metals

The effect of these differences is seen clearly with magnesium, e.g. *with water,*

primary action:

$$Mg + 2H^+ + 2OH^- \rightarrow Mg^{2+} + 2OH^- + H_2 \uparrow, \tag{1}$$

secondary action: $Mg^{2+} + 2OH^- \rightarrow Mg^{2+}(OH)_2^- \downarrow. \tag{2}$

The formation of slightly soluble magnesium hydroxide on the metal surface slows the action almost to a stop. When acids are present in the water, the additional hydrogen ions remove hydroxyl ions as fast as they are produced (as in equation (1)) forming molecules of water, and the concentration of hydroxyl ions in solution is prevented from becoming large enough to cause the solubility product of magnesium hydroxide to be exceeded. Solid magnesium hydroxide therefore does not form on the surface of the metal, so the primary action continues vigorously to completion. Furthermore, the speed of the primary reaction is increased because of the increased concentration of hydrogen ions. Since magnesium chloride and magnesium sulphate are very soluble in water there is no formation of an insoluble salt on the metal. What has been said about magnesium applies generally to all metals.

When a chloride or sulphate has a low solubility in water, the formation of an insoluble layer on the metal surface may slow down the reaction or stop it altogether. For example, with calcium and dilute sulphuric acid the reaction at first is very vigorous, but soon appears to have stopped, the metal having been covered with a layer of white calcium sulphate (slightly soluble in dilute sulphuric acid). Some time later, the layer is prised off, perhaps by pressure of hydrogen. This process of layer formation and removal is repeated regularly, and after a number of hours the calcium has reacted completely.

With exceptions similar to the above, the vigour of the reaction of metals with these acids therefore follows the order of the standard electrode potentials closely. Titanium is less reactive than iron. This is ascribed to its tendency to adopt a passive state.

Manganese, having the greatest negative electrode potential of the six remaining transition metals, reacts much more readily than any of them. With nickel and cobalt, whose electrode potentials are very little more negative than that of hydrogen, the action is very slow. In every case hydrogen is liberated and, under these reducing conditions, the cations formed in solution are always in their lowest valency states, except with titanium, thus: titanium Ti^{3+} (bivalent titanium compounds are known), chromium(II) Cr^{2+}, manganese(II) Mn^{2+}, iron(II) Fe^{2+}, cobalt(II) Co^{2+} and nickel(II) Ni^{2+}.

Copper, having a positive standard electrode potential, does not react with either dilute acid (in the absence of air), but boiling concentrated hydrochloric acid reacts with copper, liberating hydrogen (p. 586). Pure zinc in spite of a standard electrode potential of -0.76 V reacts very slowly with either acid. These and other anomalies will be considered later. Both zinc and gallium have greater negative standard electrode potentials than iron (see graph on p. 211) and both metals react quite vigorously with both acids, provided the metals are not too pure. (The same proviso applies to most other metals.)

Non-metals

Since the concentration of hydroxyl ions in acids is much smaller than in water, the primary action of non-metal elements with acids—i.e. the possible displacement of hydroxyl ions—is slower than it is with water, if it takes place at all. Thus, hydrochloric acid and dilute sulphuric acid have little or no action on any of the non-metal elements except in the case of fluorine, chlorine and bromine, where action is the same as with water, but less vigorous. With fluorine there is an additional reaction with hydrochloric acid, the displacement of chlorine from it, followed by the reaction of chlorine with water.

The broad trends across the Periods are illustrated in the following diagram for Period 4.

Action of non-oxidising acids on elements at ordinary temperature

	K Ca (Sc) <u>Ti</u> <u>V</u> Cr Mn Fe Co Ni Cu Zn Ga	Ge As Se	Br
Evolution of hydrogen and formation of metal ions in solution	Violent Very action →vigor-→ Diminishing vigour →→— ous	No action ←— Diminishing	Moderate action as with water ⎯ vigour
	Exceptions to the trend are underlined	No action except with boiling conc. HCl	

Extent and rate of reactions

The speed and extent of the reactions between metals and acids depend on other factors besides the standard electrode potentials, and the solubility of the salt produced. A number of these may be dealt with quickly.

(1) *Temperature.* Increase in temperature has the usual effect of increasing the speed.

(2) *State of division of the metal.* The finer this is the greater the surface exposed and the faster the reaction.

(3) *Concentration of the acid.* Up to a point the more concentrated the acid the quicker the action because the greater the concentration of hydrogen ions.

(4) *Purity of the acid.* Impurities may act as positive or negative catalysts.

(5) *Solubility in acid of the oxide film* which forms very quickly on the surface of all metals on standing in air. Aluminium is a case in point. Here the initial reaction with dilute sulphuric acid is very slow because the oxide film is almost insoluble in the acid. It is much more readily soluble in hot concentrated hydrochloric acid and the reaction in this case is very vigorous.

Three other factors of great importance are (1) the purity of the metal, (2) the concentration of hydrogen ions and metal ions in the solution, and (3) the hydrogen over-potential of the metal. The second of these has already been considered (pp. 156–7).

Purity of the metal. Impure metals usually react more quickly than pure onces because the particles of impurity set up tiny voltaic cells all over the metal surface, currents flow in these cells, and if the impurities have a less negative electrode potential than the metal, the metal (anode) passes into solution. The well-known effect of adding a little copper(II) sulphate solution to dilute sulphuric acid when acting on zinc illustrates this,

$$Cu^{2+} + Zn \rightarrow Cu \downarrow + Zn^{2+}.$$

Copper deposited on the surface of the zinc sets up voltaic cells in which zinc is consumed. Hydrogen is liberated easily at the copper surface because the hydrogen over-voltage of copper is considerably lower than that of zinc.

Zinc, standard electrode potential -0.76 V, would be expected to displace hydrogen from hydrochloric acid and dilute sulphuric acid. It does this vigorously when somewhat impure, but with pure zinc the action is very slow. The explanation is to be found in the phenomenon of over-voltage.

Over-voltage or over-potential. If two standard hydrogen electrodes (p. 149) are set up side by side in the form of a voltaic cell and connected externally by a conductor, Fig. 104(a), there is no potential difference between the electrodes since the interchange of hydrogen ions and hydrogen at each electrode is identical, and so no current flows in the circuit.

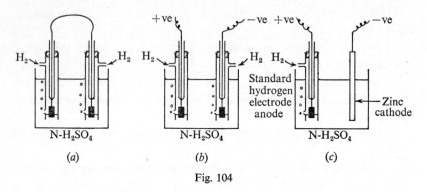

Fig. 104

If now *a very small e.m.f.* from an external source is applied to the electrodes so that the left-hand electrode is the anode (Fig. 104(b)) a small current flows and electrolysis takes place. At the cathode H$^+$ ions are discharged by gaining one electron each from the cathode to form hydrogen atoms. These then combine to form hydrogen molecules. The final result is that hydrogen is evolved,

$$H^+ + e \rightarrow H; \quad 2H \rightarrow H_2 \uparrow.$$

At the anode the reverse process takes place. Hydrogen molecules are split into atoms. The hydrogen atoms lose one electron each to the anode forming H$^+$ ions which pass into solution.

Now let one of the hydrogen electrodes be replaced by a rod of pure zinc as shown in Fig. 104(c), the electrolyte surrounding both electrodes being still normal sulphuric acid. When an external e.m.f. is applied, with the zinc as cathode, it is found that no current flows until a voltage of 0.70 is reached. Electrolysis then begins and hydrogen is evolved at the zinc cathode (hydrogen ionises and passes into solution at the anode). This *extra* voltage needed to bring about the evolution of hydrogen at the surface of a zinc cathode under the conditions shown is called the hydrogen over-voltage (over-potential) of zinc. Note (1) that the zinc is in an electrolyte whose hydrogen ion concentration is 1 mole per litre, (2) that the discharge of *zinc* ions is not in question, and (3) there are no zinc ions in solution.

The hydrogen over-potentials of some common metals are given in the table below. In measuring over-potentials the metal is made the cathode, the standard hydrogen electrode is the anode, and the electrolyte is normal sulphuric acid or hydrochloric acid, i.e. the hydrogen ion concentration is 1 mole per litre.

Hydrogen over-potentials (volts) of some metals in M HCl at current density of 1 mA cm^{-2}

Group VIII			Group IB	Group IIB	Group IIIB	Group IVB
Fe	Co	Ni	Cu	Zn	Ga	Ge
0.4		0.33	0.5	0.70		
		Pd	Ag	Cd	In	Sn
			0.46	0.99	0.80	0.85
		Pt	Au	Hg	Tl	Pb
		Black, 0.0	0.15	1.04	1.05	0.88
		Polished, 0.25				
		Low over-potentials	Low over-potentials	High over-potentials	High over-potentials	High over-potentials

Hydrogen over-potential increases slowly with rise in current density. The figures in the above table indicate a maximum in the O.P. curves at Group IIB (associated with a minimum in the M.P. curves).

Effect of dilute sulphuric acid (or hydrochloric acid) on zinc. This action is very slow because of the high over-potential of zinc. The e.m.f. of the standard zinc/hydrogen cell is 0.76 V. This is almost the same as the hydrogen over-potential of zinc, 0.70 V, therefore the evolution of hydrogen at the zinc is very slow and so also is the passage of zinc into solution as zinc ions.

With impure zinc, as already stated, hydrogen is evolved at the surface of the impurity provided the hydrogen over-potential of the impurity is lower than the e.m.f. of the zinc/impurity cell.

When impure zinc is amalgamated with mercury a surface of pure zinc and mercury is presented to the action of the acid. The concentration of zinc in solution in mercury is much less than with zinc in the solid state; this leads to a less negative value of the electrode potential of the zinc. The result is that the e.m.f. of the amalgamated zinc/mercury cell is less than the hydrogen over-voltage of mercury, which is very high (1.04 V), and so the action is much slower than with unamalgamated impure zinc.

Causes of hydrogen over-potential. It is of interest to note that metals with high hydrogen over-potentials have low melting points. This is at least a useful aid to memory.

There is a close relation between over-potentials and position in the Periodic Table as seen from the table on p. 221. The metals with high hydrogen over-potentials occur in Groups II B, III B, and IV B, immediately after those metals which display typical transitional properties, one of these properties being ability to act as catalysts. This suggests that there is a connection between catalytic power and hydrogen over-potential: the greater the catalytic power the lower the hydrogen over-potential. The reactions taking place during the evolution of hydrogen at the surface of an electrode are,
$$H^+ + e \rightarrow H,$$
and
$$H + H \rightarrow H_2.$$
Metals which are good catalysts for these reactions increase the velocity of the reactions, and so decrease the potential required for the evolution of hydrogen at their surfaces, i.e. they have low hydrogen over-potentials. Metals which are poor catalysts for these reactions have high hydrogen over-potentials. Catalytic effect is probably one factor in over-potential, but the subject is a complex one and not well understood.

Other gases show over-potentials. Since many electrolyses take place in aqueous solution, oxygen over-potentials are important. The oxygen over-potentials of some metals are at 1 mA cm^{-2}: gold 0.53, polished platinum 0.45, lead 0.31, iron 0.25, platinised platinum 0.25, nickel 0.10. A number of factors affect the size of over-potentials, the most important one being current-density.

Action of solutions of caustic alkalis on elements

In this section it is sufficient to deal with sodium hydroxide solution at ordinary temperature only, since the reactions of the other common caustic alkalis, the hydroxides of potassium, calcium, barium, and lithium, are essentially the same.

Sodium hydroxide solution contains:

(1) Sodium ions in high concentration (hydrated but written as Na$^+$ for simplicity). These remain unchanged throughout the reaction, but in the case of the element sodium they produce a concentration effect.

(2) Hydrogen ions H$^+$ (or H$_3$O$^+$) in extremely low concentration (10^{-14} moles per litre in M NaOH solution).

(3) Hydroxyl ions OH$^-$, in high concentration. It is the presence of this high concentration of hydroxyl ions which accounts for the differences

between the reactions of the elements with sodium hydroxide solution, and their reactions with water alone.

(4) Water molecules.

Note. The potential of a hydrogen electrode in molar aqueous alkali is -0.83 V (p. 157).

There are three primary types of reaction between elements and sodium hydroxide solution. The first two are ionic displacement reactions, the third involves the formation of covalent bonds between the element and oxygen.

(1) *Displacement of hydrogen (or sodium) from solution by a metal of greater negative standard electrode potential than hydrogen in aqueous alkali (-0.83 V).*

The only cations present are Na^+ and H^+. No metal can displace sodium permanently from sodium hydroxide solution, because any sodium atoms formed immediately react with hydrogen ions from dissociation of water liberating hydrogen and regenerating sodium hydroxide solution. The reactions of the metals (including sodium itself) are therefore usually of the same type as with water alone, but somewhat slower.

(2) *Displacement of hydroxyl or oxygen from solution by a non-metal of greater positive standard electrode potential than oxygen, O_2/OH^-, $E^\ominus = +0.40$ V (see table, p. 153).*

For example, fluorine, the element with the highest positive electrode potential, displaces oxygen from fairly concentrated sodium hydroxide solution in two stages thus,

$$2HO^- + F\text{-}F \rightarrow 2HO + 2F^-,$$

$$2HO \rightarrow H_2O + \tfrac{1}{2}O_2.$$

(3) *Reactions of hydroxyl ions and water molecules with weakly electro-negative non-metals.*

In every case complex oxo-anions or hydroxy-anions are produced in which the element has formed covalent bonds with oxygen, and hydrogen is produced. None of these reactions is a displacement of hydrogen by discharge of hydrogen ions.

Amphoteric metals

Amphoteric metals such as aluminium and zinc can react according to either scheme (1) or scheme (3).

The elements of Period 3 (Na, Mg, Al, Si, P, S, Cl) will now be considered in turn. Brief accounts of the experimental facts will be given first, followed immediately by some explanation of the reactions.

Period 3. Metals

Sodium. When a piece of sodium is put into sodium hydroxide solution a violent reaction takes place, the concentration of sodium hydroxide in the solution increases, and hydrogen is liberated,

$$Na + H^+ + OH^- \rightarrow Na^+ + OH^- + \tfrac{1}{2}H_2 \uparrow.$$

As more sodium is added, the increase in concentration of sodium ions in solution causes (1) a slight reduction in the tendency of sodium metal to pass into solution as ions, and (2) a proportionate decrease in hydrogen ion concentration, and a consequent slight decrease in the rate of discharge of hydrogen ions. There is therefore some decrease in the vigour of the reaction although the rise in temperature of the solution offsets this to some extent. The action continues until all or nearly all the water in the solution has been decomposed, i.e. until the solution becomes sodium hydroxide, which solidifies when the liquid is cooled to room temperature. (With *fused* sodium hydroxide: $2Na + 2NaOH \rightarrow 2Na_2O + H_2 \uparrow$.)

Magnesium. Water acts very slowly on magnesium because of the protective film of slightly soluble magnesium hydroxide formed on the surface of the metal. With sodium hydroxide solution, the action is even slower because the solubility of magnesium hydroxide is less in the presence of a high concentration of hydroxyl ions than in pure water. Magnesium is a strongly electropositive metal. Its hydroxide is therefore not amphoteric, and so there is no tendency for magnesium hydroxide to dissolve in excess of sodium hydroxide solution.

Thus for the first two metals of the Period, the reaction is essentially the same as with water.

Aluminium reacts vigorously (especially if the solution is warmed) and the reaction goes to completion (see p. 225). It is clear that the activity of aluminium in alkaline solution is caused by the removal of the protective film of hydroxide by interaction with the alkali,

$$Al(OH)_3 + OH^- \rightarrow [Al(OH)_4]^-,$$

and the resulting exposure of the metal to the action of the solution. The concentration of hydrogen ions in N-NaOH solution is extremely small: 10^{-14} mole per litre. The potential required for the discharge of hydrogen ions at a *hydrogen electrode* with this concentration of hydrogen ions is -0.83 V. The hydrogen over-voltage at an aluminium electrode is approximately 0.5 V; therefore the discharge potential of hydrogen at aluminium in alkaline solution is approximately $(-0.87-0.5) = -1.33$ V. In alkaline solution the concentration of Al^{3+} ions is reduced much below molar concentration by their conversion into aluminate ions, so the electrode potential at the alumium surface becomes much more negative than the standard electrode potential of aluminium $(-1.66$ V$)$. It is in fact -2.35 V. The electrode potential of aluminium in alkaline solution is therefore much more negative than that required for the discharge of hydrogen ions at its surface, and evolution of hydrogen at the aluminium takes place,

$$Al + 3H^+ \rightarrow Al^{3+} + 1\tfrac{1}{2}H_2, \tag{i}$$

$$Al^{3+} + 4OH^- \rightarrow [Al(OH)_4]^-, \tag{ii}$$

(i) and (ii) $\qquad Al + OH^- + 3H_2O \rightarrow [Al(OH)_4]^- + 1\tfrac{1}{2}H_2.$

Period 3. Non-metals

The non-metals in Period 3 are silicon, phosphorus, sulphur, and chlorine. It is convenient to begin with chlorine, the most reactive of these.

Chlorine differs from the other non-metals of Period 3 in being fairly soluble in water. It is the only one of these non-metals which reacts with *water*, the reaction being reversible (p. 215),

$$H^+ + OH^- + Cl\text{-}Cl \rightleftharpoons HOCl + Cl^- + H^+.$$

In sodium hydroxide solution, the forward reaction proceeds to completion because of the removal of hydrogen ions of both the hydrochloric acid and the hypochlorous acid by hydroxyl ions:

$$2NaOH + Cl_2 \rightarrow NaCl + NaOCl + H_2O$$

or $\qquad 2Na^+ + 2OH^- + Cl\text{-}Cl \rightarrow 2Na^+ + Cl^- + OCl^- + H_2O.$

Hypochlorite ions are fairly stable at room temperature, but in hot solution they disproportionate, giving chloride and chlorate ions.

$$3ClO^- \rightarrow ClO_3^- + 2Cl^-.$$

The reactions of the non-metals of Period 3 with sodium hydroxide solution are summarised below, with aluminium included for comparison, since it behaves here as a non-metal at least partly,

$$Al + OH^- + 3H_2O \rightarrow Al(OH)_4^- + 1\tfrac{1}{2}H_2\uparrow,$$

$$Si + 2OH^- + H_2O \rightarrow \quad SiO_3^{2-} \quad + 2H_2\uparrow,$$
$$\text{silicate ion}$$

$$P_4 + 3OH^- + 3H_2O \rightarrow PH_3 \quad + 3(H_2PO_2)^-,$$
$$\text{white} \qquad\qquad\qquad \text{hydrogen phosphite ion}$$

$$3S + 6OH^- \rightarrow 2S^{2-} + SO_3^{2-} + 3H_2O,$$
$$Cl_2 + 2OH^- \rightarrow Cl^- + ClO^- + H_2O.$$

In every case, one of the products is an oxo-anion or hydroxy-anion containing the element. Where the element is able to form more than one type of anion, the one actually formed is that with the lowest oxygen content: hypophosphite, sulphite, and hypochlorite.

The reactions may be explained by supposing that in all cases (except chlorine) hydrogen is first formed by the reaction between the element, hydroxyl ions and water molecules. The possibility of combination between the element and hydrogen must now be considered. Hydrides of aluminium and silicon are not formed in aqueous solution; hydrogen is therefore evolved.

Phosphorus and hydrogen have approximately the same electronegativity and combine readily to form phosphine, PH_3, which is stable in aqueous solution and does not react with sodium hydroxide solution because it is basic. Phosphine (mixed with some hydrogen) is therefore evolved. The equation for the overall reaction may be built up from the equations for the two steps described above.

$$P + OH^- + H_2O \rightarrow (H_2PO_2)^- + H, \qquad \text{(i)}$$

$$3 \times \text{(i)} \qquad 3P + 3OH^- + 3H_2O \rightarrow 3(H_2PO_2)^- + 3H, \qquad \text{(ii)}$$

$$P + 3H \rightarrow PH_3; \qquad \text{(iii)}$$

overall (ii) and (iii),

$$P_4 + 3OH^- + 3H_2O \rightarrow PH_3 + 3(H_2PO_2)^-.$$

Red phosphorus does not react with sodium hydroxide solution.

Sulphur is considerably more electronegative than hydrogen. Its hydride H_2S is therefore stable in water and weakly acidic in nature. It therefore reacts with sodium hydroxide forming sodium sulphide in solution. Neither hydrogen nor hydrogen sulphide is evolved in the overall reaction.

$$S + 2OH^- + H_2O \rightarrow SO_3^{2-} + 4H, \qquad \text{(i)}$$

$$2S + 4H \rightarrow 2H_2S, \qquad \text{(ii)}$$

$$2H_2S + 4OH^- \rightarrow 2S^{2-} + 4H_2O; \qquad \text{(iii)}$$

overall (i) + (ii) + (iii)

$$3S + 6OH^- \rightarrow 2S^{2-} + SO_3^{2-} + 3H_2O.$$

The reaction is slow but does not stop at the formation of sulphite and sulphide. Polysulphides and thiosulphates are also formed.

Exercises

1. Write an essay on the action of air on the elements.
2. Give an account of the displacing reactions of non-metal elements on water, and aqueous acids and alkalis.
3. Write an essay on over-potential, and its effect on the action of metals on water, and aqueous acids and alkalis.
4. Summarise the effect of solutions of caustic alkalis on the elements of Period 3.
5. The elements listed below constitute the second and third periods of the Periodic Table.

$$\text{Li} \quad \text{Be} \quad \text{B} \quad \text{C} \quad \text{N} \quad \text{O} \quad \text{F} \quad \text{Ne}$$
$$\text{Na} \quad \text{Mg} \quad \text{Al} \quad \text{Si} \quad \text{P} \quad \text{S} \quad \text{Cl} \quad \text{Ar}$$

   (a) Describe the variation in properties of the chlorides of the elements in the third period, selecting **three** illustrative examples.
   (b) Describe, with examples, **two** differences in properties between elements of the second period and the corresponding elements of the third period.
   (c) Some elements of the second period have similar chemical properties to an element in the third period but in an adjacent group. Choose any such pair of elements and point out **two** similarities between them. (O & C)
6. Describe the physical and chemical properties which distinguish a *metal* from a *non-metal* and explain how these properties are related to the electronic structures of the elements. Name any element which is classed as a metal but has some of the chemical characteristics of a non-metal.
   Give examples of its metallic and non-metallic properties. (O & CS)

15

ACIDS, BASES AND SALTS

Empirical distinctions between acids and bases

Acids which only contain hydrogen combined to a non-metallic element other than oxygen are known as *hydracids*. Most acids also contain oxygen; these are known as *oxo-acids*. Some of the more important experimental generalisations about acids and bases are given below.

Acids

(1) All acids contain hydrogen which may be replaced by a metal or electropositive radical (e.g. NH_4^+).

(2) Acids in aqueous solution (*a*) turn blue litmus red; (*b*) taste sour; (*c*) evolve hydrogen with *active* metals; (*d*) neutralise bases; (*e*) decompose carbonates.

Bases

(1) Bases are the oxides and hydroxides of metals.

(2) Bases dissolve in acids to form a salt and water only.

(3) Bases in aqueous solution; (*a*) turn red litmus blue; (*b*) have a soapy feel.

An attempt to rationalise acidic and basic properties

To account for the characteristic properties of acids and bases Arrhenius suggested in 1887 that all aqueous solutions of acids contained an excess of H^+ ions and all aqueous solutions of bases (alkalis) contained an excess of hydroxyl ions OH^-. He proposed, in effect, that acid properties are the properties of the H^+ ion and basic properties are the properties of the OH^- ion. He also believed that the H^+ ions or OH^- ions were formed by the dissociation of the acid or base as it dissolved in the water.

Up to a point these ideas are correct and helpful but we now know that an H^+ ion cannot exist independently in aqueous solution but is always chemically combined with a molecule of water.

$$\underset{H}{\overset{H}{\diagdown}}\ddot{O} + H^+ \rightarrow \left[\underset{H}{\overset{H}{\diagdown}}\overset{H}{\underset{}{\diagup}}O\cdot\right]^+ \quad \text{hydroxonium ion.}$$

In aqueous solution therefore, it is the hydroxonium ion H_3O^+ rather than the H^+ ion which is responsible for acidic properties. Furthermore, as will be seen later, without some mechanism of this kind it is not clear why an acid should produce H^+ ions on addition to water, and it also prepares the way for a more widely applicable and precise definition of the nature of acid–base properties.

The Brönsted–Lowry concept of acids and bases

Brönsted and Lowry proposed independently in 1923 the following definition:

An acid is a proton donor.

A base is a proton acceptor, and always has a lone pair of electrons to donate.

Consequently in the ionisation of hydrogen chloride in water:

$$\underset{H}{\overset{H}{\diagdown}}\ddot{O} + H-Cl \rightleftharpoons \left[\underset{H}{\overset{H}{\diagdown}}\overset{H}{\underset{}{\diagup}}O\cdot\right]^+ + Cl^-.$$

A molecule of water accepts a proton from a molecule of hydrogen chloride and is therefore a base. However, the ionisation is reversible and in the back reaction as shown above the hydroxonium ion H_3O^+ donates a proton to a chloride ion and is therefore an acid. As the chloride ion accepts a proton it behaves as a base. Thus, in this equilibrium HCl and H_3O^+ are acids and H_2O and Cl^- are bases. Moreover they comprise two acid–base pairs:

$$\underset{\text{acid}}{HCl} \underset{+H^+}{\overset{-H^+}{\rightleftharpoons}} \underset{\text{base}}{Cl^-} \; ; \; \underset{\text{base}}{H_2O} \underset{-H^+}{\overset{+H^+}{\rightleftharpoons}} \underset{\text{acid}}{H_3O^+}.$$

When an acid and a base may be interconverted in this way simply by the gain or loss of a proton they form what is termed a *conjugate acid–base pair*.

In general:

$$\underset{\substack{\text{conjugate}\\\text{acid}}}{HA} \underset{+H^+}{\overset{-H^+}{\rightleftharpoons}} \underset{\substack{\text{conjugate}\\\text{base}}}{A^-} \; ; \; \underset{\substack{\text{conjugate}\\\text{base}}}{B:} \underset{-H^+}{\overset{+H^+}{\rightleftharpoons}} \underset{\substack{\text{conjugate}\\\text{acid}}}{HB^+}.$$

By identifying the members of each conjugate acid–base pair with the same numerical subscript and combining them the reaction scheme obtained is generally applicable to all acid–base combination, i.e.

$$HA + B: \rightleftharpoons A^- + HB^+.$$
$$\text{acid}_1 + \text{base}_2 \qquad \text{base}_1 + \text{acid}_2$$

Examples:

Sulphuric acid	$H_2SO_4 + H_2O \rightleftharpoons HSO_4^- + H_3O^+$
Nitric acid	$HNO_3 + H_2O \rightleftharpoons NO_3^- + H_3O^+$
Acetic acid	$CH_3COOH + H_2O \rightleftharpoons CH_3COO^- + H_3O^+$
Ammonium ion	$NH_4^+ + H_2O \rightleftharpoons NH_3 + H_3O^+$
Water	$H_2O + H_2O \rightleftharpoons OH^- + H_3O^+$

In the last example above it will be seen that water acts both as an acid and as a base. Many substances act in this way, e.g. HSO_4^-, $Al(OH)_3$, HCO_3^-. Thus in addition to the ionisation given above sulphuric acid ionises a stage further, $\qquad HSO_4^- + H_2O \rightleftharpoons SO_4^{2-} + H_3O^+,$

and in this case the HSO_4^- ion behaves as an acid.

Relative strengths of acids and bases

Although acid–base combination can be represented by a general reaction scheme as shown above it is important to realise that the process is reversible and that the proportion of reactants to products varies between wide limits for different systems. Aqueous solutions of hydrogen chloride, sulphuric acid and nitric acid exhibit the characteristic properties of acids to a marked degree and have about the same facility for conducting electricity as known ionic compounds at the same concentration. This evidence suggests complete ionisation of these acids in solution. Proton donation is therefore virtually complete. In other words these acids have a relatively strong tendency to donate a proton and are termed *strong acids*. Acetic acid, hydrogen sulphide and even ammonium ions in aqueous solution show the characteristic properties of acids, but only feebly. Acetic acid solutions are much poorer conductors than those of ionic compounds, indicating only slight ionisation. Since these acids have weak proton-donating tendencies they are called *weak acids*. Between these two extremes are moderately strong acids such as sulphurous, nitrous and phosphoric, in which a fair proportion of the molecules are ionised in aqueous solution. *Strength* and *concentration* of an acid and an alkali are different properties and the terms must be distinguished. Whereas the one relates to proton-donating ability the other is a measure of the ratio of acid or alkali to water in the solution, so that it is possible to have a dilute strong acid, e.g. dilute sulphuric acid, and also a concentrated weak acid, e.g. glacial acetic acid.

Just as the strength of an acid is defined as its tendency to donate a proton to a base, e.g. water, so the strength of a base is defined as its ability to accept a proton from an acid, e.g. water. To be meaningful, proton donating or accepting ability must be related to a common standard; in this case it is water.

Again, as the ionisation of an acid is affected both by temperature and dilution, comparisons of acid–base strengths must be made under standard conditions. A weak acid like acetic acid ionises more completely with increasing dilution, and theoretically all *acids* are strong acids at infinite dilution at which point complete ionisation will have occurred. The following table lists a number of acids in order of decreasing acid *strengths* in aqueous solution together with their conjugate base.

Acid–base chart

	Conjugate acid		Conjugate base	
	Name	Formula	Formula	Name
↑ Decreasing acid strength ↓	Sulphuric acid	H_2SO_4	HSO_4^-	Hydrogen sulphate ion ↑
	Hydrogen chloride	HCl	Cl^-	Chloride ion
	Nitric acid	HNO_3	NO_3^-	Nitrate ion
	Hydroxonium ion	H_3O^+	H_2O	Water
	Phosphoric acid	H_3PO_4	$H_2PO_4^-$	Dihydrogen ortho-phosphate ion
	Acetic acid	CH_3COOH	CH_3COO^-	Acetate ion
	Hydrogen sulphide	H_2S	HS^-	Hydrogen sulphide ion
	Hydrogen cyanide	HCN	CN^-	Cyanide ion
	Ammonium ion	NH_4^+	NH_3	Ammonia
	Hydrogen carbonate ion	HCO_3^-	CO_3^{2-}	Carbonate ion
	Water	H_2O	OH^-	Hydroxide ion
	Ethanol	C_2H_5OH	$C_2H_5O^-$	Ethoxide ion
	Hydrogen	H_2	H^-	Hydride ion ↓ Decreasing base strength

Acid strength in effect refers to the extent to which the acid ionises in aqueous solution in the range of concentrations normally met with in the laboratory (i.e. 0.1 molar to 1.0 molar). In the complete absence of water no ionisation is possible and the acids are neutral covalent materials. Pure sulphuric acid, hydrogen chloride, acetic acid, etc., are poor conductors of electricity and show none of the characteristic acid properties if water is rigorously excluded.

The trends in acid strength and basic strength shown in the table above illustrate an important principle: *the stronger the acid the weaker the conjugate base.* For example, in dilute aqueous solution there will be no undissociated (unionised) molecules of sulphuric acid, and so the tendency of a hydrogen sulphate ion to combine with a proton is essentially nil. On the other hand, an aqueous solution of acetic acid will contain a high proportion of acetic acid molecules but relatively few acetate ions. Here the acetate ions have a stronger tendency to combine with a proton than water molecules and the equilibrium,

$$CH_3COOH + H_2O \rightleftharpoons CH_3COO^- + H_3O^+,$$

is displaced strongly in favour of CH_3COOH.

Levelling effect of the solvent

In aqueous solution all strong acids are extensively ionised into hydroxonium ions and their conjugate base. Because of this their solutions all show equal acid strength, for the same acid—hydroxonium ion—is common to them all. No matter how strong the acid, it will be reduced to the strength of the hydroxonium ion in aqueous solution.

Both the hydride ion and the ethoxide ion are stronger bases than the hydroxide ion but in aqueous solution they all show the same alkalinity. This is because ethoxide ions and hydride ions are stronger bases than the hydroxide ion and react completely with water to produce OH^- ions, i.e.

$$H_2O + C_2H_5O^- \rightleftharpoons C_2H_5OH + OH^-.$$

Basicity of an acid

Acids may be defined as monobasic, dibasic or tribasic depending on whether they contain one, two or three hydrogen atoms per molecule of acid, which may be replaced by a metal or electropositive radical. Alternatively, the basicity of an acid is the number of hydroxonium ions which one molecule of the acid is capable of producing in aqueous solution:

Monobasic acids	HCl, HBr, HI, HNO_3, CH_3COOH
Dibasic acids	H_2SO_4, H_2SO_3, H_2CO_3, $(COOH)_2$
Tribasic acids	H_3PO_4, H_3AsO_3

Care must be taken to define basicity only in terms of replaceable (ionisable) hydrogen, i.e. CH_3COOH is not tetrabasic.

Oxo-salts

As well as being practically 50% by weight of the earth's crust, oxygen is the second most electronegative element and it is small wonder that the greater part of inorganic chemistry is concerned with compounds containing this element. Salts in which the acid radical contains oxygen, e.g. SO_4^{2-}, CO_3^{2-}, NO_3^-, PO_4^{3-}, etc., are termed oxo-salts, as distinct from the simple binary salts such as chlorides and sulphides.

Normal and acid salts

A normal salt is formed if all the hydrogen of an acid is replaced by a metal or electropositive radical. However, if only part of the replaceable hydrogen per molecule of the acid is replaced, an acid salt is produced. Since monobasic acids contain only one atom of replaceable hydrogen per molecule they do not form acid salts. Dibasic acids form a normal and an acid salt, tribasic acids form a normal and two acid salts, e.g.

Acid	Acid salts	Normal salts
H_2SO_4	$NaHSO_4$	Na_2SO_4
H_3PO_4	NaH_2PO_4	Na_3PO_4
	Na_2HPO_4	

The aqueous solution of an acid salt of a strong acid is strongly acidic owing to the concentration of hydroxonium ions, H_3O^+, produced, i.e.

$$Na^+ + HSO_4^- + H_2O \rightleftharpoons Na^+ + SO_4^{2-} + H_3O^+.$$

In contrast, the aqueous solution of an acid salt of a weak acid is often alkaline (see p. 243), i.e.

$$Na^+ + HCO_3^- + H_2O \rightleftharpoons Na^+ + OH^- + H_2CO_3.$$

Basic salts

A basic salt may be regarded as a compound of the normal salt and the base from which it is derived, e.g.

Basic zinc chloride $ZnCl_2 + Zn(OH)_2 \rightarrow 2Zn(OH)Cl$

Basic lead(II) acetate $(CH_3COO)_2Pb + Pb(OH)_2 \rightarrow 2Pb(OH)(CH_3COO)$

Bismuth oxide chloride $BiCl_3 + Bi_2O_3 \rightarrow 3BiOCl$

A basic salt may be considered as a metallic hydroxide in which only some of the hydroxyl groups are replaced by acid radicals, e.g.

$$Mg(OH)_2 \qquad\qquad\qquad Mg(OH)Cl$$

Magnesium hydroxide   Basic magnesium chloride

$$Bi(OH)_3 \qquad\qquad Cl\!-\!Bi\!-\!\boxed{OH}\!-\!^{H_2O}\longrightarrow BiOCl$$

Bismuth(III) hydroxide   Bismuth oxide chloride

Double salts

It sometimes occurs that crystals obtained from a mixed solution of two simple salts are quite distinguishable from crystals of the original salts and that their composition may be represented by a chemical formula. Compounds formed in this way are called *double salts*. For example, if equimolar proportions of iron(II) sulphate and of ammonium sulphate are dissolved in the minimum quantity of hot water, and the solution cooled, pale green crystals of ammonium iron(II) sulphate,

$$(NH_4^+)_2SO_4^{2-}\ Fe^{2+}SO_4^{2-}.6H_2O,$$

are deposited. Double salts can generally be expressed as the combination of two simple salts, e.g.

Potash alum $K_2SO_4.Al_2(SO_4)_3.24H_2O$

$$\text{or}\quad K^+Al^{3+}(SO_4^{2-})_2.12H_2O$$

Potassium $KCl.MgCl_2.6H_2O$
magnesium chloride $\qquad\text{or}\quad K^+Mg^{2+}3Cl^-.6H_2O$

In most respects double salts are similar to normal salts. Double salts form ionic crystals and conduct electricity when fused or in aqueous solution. The solution of a double salt gives the characteristic reactions of the ions of which it is composed. Generally a double salt is comprised of one acid radical and two cations—it is this feature which distinguishes a double salt from a normal salt.

For simplicity the framework of the crystal lattice of a normal or a double salt can be thought of as a close-packed arrangement of a particular anion. In a normal salt one kind of cation is distributed uniformly throughout the holes in this anion lattice. A double salt generally contains two kinds of cation and these too are distributed uniformly throughout the anion lattice. A close-packed lattice may contain two types of hole (pp. 123 and 125), e.g. tetrahedral and octahedral. Thus the smaller of the two cations will occupy the tetrahedral holes and the larger cation will occupy the octahedral holes.

This very simplified picture is modified by several factors. Many double salts contain water of crystallisation and it is molecules of water rather than simple anions that close-pack around the cations. In other cases the bonding between the smaller more highly charged cation and its neighbouring anions in the lattice departs considerably from simple ionic and displays some covalent character. These are the less extreme form of double salt and are beginning to show characteristics of a complex salt. (See later.)

Mixed crystals and isomorphism

It is not always possible to represent the composition of the crystals obtained from a mixed solution of two simple salts by a definite chemical formula. In these cases the proportions of the constituents may vary continuously over a wide range depending only upon the concentration of the individual salts, and these are called *mixed crystals*. Generally mixed crystal formation is restricted to substances which crystallise in the same crystal form and moreover the mixed crystal also exhibits the same form. Materials which crystallise in this way are therefore said to be *isomorphous*. They may be visualised as a solid solution of one salt in the other. The criterion for mixed crystal formation is that the constituent particles of the two substances are sufficiently identical in shape and size to replace one another within the crystal lattice without destroying its stability or altering its form. As a rule substances which form mixed crystals and are isomorphous are (*a*) of a similar chemical type, and (*b*) represented by similar formulae. For salts which are isomorphous each central atom of the interchangeable anions usually belongs to the same numerical Group of the Periodic Table although they are often in different families, i.e. A or B, e.g. S, Se; S, Cr; Cl, Mn. Salts shown in each of the columns below are isomorphous with each other:

$KClO_4$	$Al_2(SO_4)_3 . 12H_2O$	K_2SO_4	$FeSO_4 . 7H_2O$
$KMnO_4$	$Cr_2(SO_4)_3 . 12H_2O$	K_2SeO_4	$NiSO_4 . 7H_2O$
	$Fe_2(SO_4)_3 . 12H_2O$	K_2CrO_4	$ZnSO_4 . 7H_2O$

With very few exceptions isomorphous compounds form *overgrowth* crystals. For example, if an octahedral crystal of chrome alum

$$KCr(SO_4)_2 . 12H_2O$$

235

is suspended by a thread in a saturated solution of $KAl(SO_4)_2 . 12H_2O$ the crystal continues to grow and this is clearly shown by the colourless overgrowth of potash alum on the violet chrome alum crystal. Even though they form overgrowth crystals, not all isomorphous compounds are able to form mixed crystals, e.g. calcite $CaCO_3$ and sodium nitrate, $NaNO_3$.

Complexes (co-ordination compounds)

A mixed solution of two simple salts frequently yields a compound which is not a double salt. Instead of giving the characteristic reactions of the ions from which it must be composed it shows new distinctive features instead. For example, when a solution of iron(II) sulphate is treated with an excess of potassium cyanide solution and is then evaporated to crystallising point yellow crystals deposit. These crystals show the properties of K^+ ions but not those of Fe^{2+} and CN^- ions, instead the properties of a new ion, $[Fe(CN)_6]^{4-}$, are shown. This is an example of a type of compound known as a *complex* or more generally as a *co-ordination compound.*

Complexes contain a central atom or ion surrounded by a number of oppositely charged ions or neutral molecules, usually referred to as *ligands*. It is the type of bonding between the central atom or ion and the ligands which give complexes their distinctive features. Ligands attach to the central metal atom or ion by acting as electron pair donors (see p. 90). This is not to imply that the bonding is a simple co-ordinate (dative) covalency. The actual state of the bonding will merge somewhere between this extreme and that of a simple ionic or ion-dipole attraction. Complexes are readily formed by the *d*-block elements as they have the necessary vacant orbitals of appropriate energy to accommodate the donated electrons. The number of electron pairs so accommodated is called the *co-ordination number* of the central atom or ion.

Complexes may be positively or negatively charged and if so the complex ion is indicated by enclosing it in square brackets, e.g.

$$[Cu(NH_3)_4]^{2+} \qquad\qquad [AlF_6]^{3-}$$

Tetrammine copper(II) ion   Hexafluoroaluminate ion

$$[Zn(OH)_4]^{2-}$$

Tetrahydroxozincate ion

Complexes can also be neutral, for example, in tetracarbonyl nickel(o), $Ni(CO)_4$, each nickel atom is co-ordinated to four neutral carbon monoxide molecules.

Not all complex ions are as stable in solution as the hexacyanoferrate(II) ion, $[Fe(CN)_6]^{4-}$. Others may dissociate in solution and establish an equilibrium with the stable particles out of which it is composed, e.g.

$$Ag^+ + 2NH_3 \rightleftharpoons [Ag(NH_3)_2]^+.$$

Applying the equilibrium law:

$$K = \frac{[Ag(NH_3)_2]^+}{[Ag^+].[NH_3]^2}.$$

From which it follows that a very large value for K corresponds to a high concentration of the complex ion. In effect this measures the stability of the complex ion. Values of K, *stability constants*, extend over a continuous range from the extremely high values which correspond to the stablest complexes to low values which indicate that dissociation is practically complete and the substance is behaving as a double salt.

Logically OH^-, SO_4^{2-}, NO_3^-, NH_4^+, etc. are complex ions, but they are conventionally regarded as being simple ions.

Water of crystallisation

Many salts crystallise from aqueous solution with molecules of water bound into the crystal lattice in an orderly fashion so that they form an integral part of the framework. Such salts are said to be *hydrated* and to contain *water of crystallisation*. Moderate heating, either at atmospheric or reduced pressure, is generally sufficient to drive out the water of crystallisation from a hydrated crystal. During this process the crystal lattice is destroyed and the structure of the anhydrous material, which sometimes falls to a powder, is radically altered. Dehydration of coloured hydrates is generally accompanied by a change of colour and in many cases colour is lost entirely.

Colours of the hydrated and anhydrous forms
of some common hydrated sulphates

Salt	Hydrate	Anhydrous
$MnSO_4.5H_2O$	Pink	White
$FeSO_4.7H_2O$	Green	White
$CoSO_4.7H_2O$	Red	Pale red
$NiSO_4.7H_2O$	Green	Yellow
$CuSO_4.5H_2O$	Blue	White

Attention has already been drawn (p. 106) to the hydration of ions in aqueous solution arising out of the dipolar nature of water molecules. Hydrated ions are in fact complex ions and are formally referred to as *aquo* complexes, e.g. the hexaquo cobalt(III) ion $[Co(H_2O)_6]^{3+}$. All but the very largest monovalent cations (e.g. Rb^+, Cs^+, and NH_4^+) are hydrated in solution. It does not follow that the state of hydration of an ion in aqueous solution is the same as that in a crystal lattice. For example, in aqueous solution the copper(II) ion is surrounded by four strongly bound water molecules positioned at the corners of a square; undoubtedly the other two positions above and below the square will be occupied by less strongly bound water molecules at a slightly greater distance away, i.e. the ion is essentially $[Cu(H_2O)_6]^{2+}$; whereas the copper(II) ions in crystalline copper(II) sulphate are associated with only four molecules of water (see Fig. 105). However, many hydrated ions do maintain their identity in crystalline hydrates and in solution, e.g.

$$[Be(H_2O)_4]^{2+} \quad \text{and} \quad [Ni(H_2O)_6]^{2+}.$$

The attraction of a cation for a water molecule is essentially electrostatic and the more highly charged the cation the stronger will be the force of attraction. Furthermore, for ions of the same charge, the positive field at the surface of a large cation is less intense than that at the surface of a small cation, so that the surrounding water molecules are held more firmly by cations of small radius. For example, in a comparison of the number of solid hydrates formed by each alkali metal in a given series of salts, 76% of the lithium salts were hydrated, 74% of the sodium salts and 23% of the potassium salts. Scarcely any hydrates of caesium and rubidium are known, and those that do exist are thought to be instances in which it is the anion and not the cation that is hydrated. Thus, *the general increase in ionic radius down a Group is parallelled by a decrease in the extent of hydration of the ion.* Generally speaking the large univalent ions (K^+, Rb^+, Cs^+, NH_4^+, Ag^+, Au^+) crystallise anhydrous. On the other hand, the aluminium ion, Al^{3+}, for instance, is both small and trivalent, factors which promote the formation of hydrated crystals.

As the oxygen atom is much larger than the two hydrogen atoms it constitutes the bulk of the water molecule, and to a first approximation the extent to which a positive ion can be hydrated is restricted by the number of oxygen atoms that can be close-packed around it. Depending on its radius ratio with oxygen (see p. 136) the metal ion will have a certain co-ordination number (i.e. 2, 4, 6, 8 or 12) and this will be the maximum number of oxygen atoms with which it can be in contact in a close-packed structure. Co-ordination numbers of four and six are the most common. Structurally a co-ordination number of four suggests four molecules of water (i.e. oxygen atoms) arranged tetrahedrally round the metal cation, and a co-ordination number of six suggests that the metal cation will be surrounded by six molecules of water arranged octahedrally (see p. 136). In most cases the number of molecules of water of crystallisation is greater or less than the maximum co-ordination number of the cation. Briefly this is accounted for by two effects. First, oxygen atoms surrounding the cation can come partly from water molecules and partly from the oxygen of the oxo-anions. For instance, the co-ordination number of the Ca^{2+} ion in gypsum, $CaSO_4.2H_2O$, is 8 and besides the two water molecules, the Ca^{2+} ion is surrounded by six oxygen atoms from the sulphate groups. Thus, in a solid hydrate, the positive ion may be in any one of three conditions: (1) anhydrous, (2) fully hydrated, and (3) partly hydrated. In the first and last categories, the close-packing of oxygen atoms around the cation will be completed by the acid radicals. Remember that radicals are polyatomic non-spherical particles whose bonding orbitals have directional properties. The water molecule has a tetrahedral charge distribution (see p. 265) and the size, shape and directional co-ordinating properties of this and the acid radicals lead to more complicated structures than might be supposed from this simplified account. Secondly, in some cases the number of molecules of water of crystallisation exceeds the co-ordination number of the cation. The vitriols (i.e. $MSO_4.7H_2O$ where M represents Zn^{2+}, Mg^{2+}, Fe^{2+}, Co^{2+}, Ni^{2+} or Mn^{2+}) are examples of this type of hydrate. Many more sulphates are similar to the vitriols in that they crystallise with an odd number of molecules of water of crystallisation, e.g. $CuSO_4.5H_2O$. Dehydration of the heptahydrates and the pentahydrates is relatively easy as far as the monohydrate stage, but this last molecule of water is held tenaciously by the lattice, and is only driven off at temperatures of 200–300 °C. Although the structures of these monohydrates is as yet unknown, the *odd* molecules of water of crystallisation in the fully hydrated salts are known to be linked between the hydrogen atoms of the water of crystallisation attached to the cation and the oxygen atoms of the SO_4^{2-} ions. This type of linkage is illustrated in Fig. 105 for copper(II) sulphate, the dotted lines represent hydrogen bonds. The co-ordination of the copper(II) ion is 6. In crystalline hydrated copper(II) sulphate each copper(II) ion is surrounded by four molecules of water of crystallisation in a plane, and two oxygen atoms from different sulphate ions complete the octahedral environment of the cation. The fifth molecule of water is hydrogen-bonded between this hydrated cation and the sulphate ions.

Generally salts crystallise from aqueous solution with an even number

239

of molecules of water of crystallisation. Besides the exceptions to this rule amongst the sulphates, a few nitrates are known which crystallise with an odd number of molecules of water of crystallisation, e.g. $Cu(NO_3)_2.3H_2O$, and again water of crystallisation is thought to be hydrogen-bonded into the crystal lattice in a manner similar to that described for sulphates.

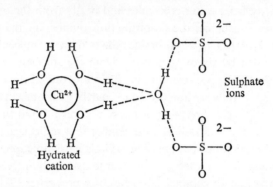

Fig. 105. An illustration of the positioning of the water molecules in crystalline copper(II) sulphate.

General methods of preparation of salts

These may be conveniently classified as follows:
(1) *Methods for soluble salts*
   Acid + carbonate = salt + CO_2 + H_2O;
   Acid + base = salt + H_2O;
   Acid + metal = salt + H_2;
   Direct combination.
(2) *Methods for insoluble salts*
   Precipitation reactions.
   Direct combination.

1. Preparation of soluble salts. Provided that it is stable and readily available, the parent acid is usually the best starting material for preparing a salt. Depending which is the most suitable, the free metal, the oxide, the hydroxide or the carbonate of the particular element, is dissolved in the acid and when the resulting solution is evaporated to crystallising point and allowed to cool, crystals of the required salt separate out. Dilute acids are preferable and a *slight* excess prevents the formation of basic compounds and facilitates good crystallisation.

*General summary of the solubility in water
of the salts of the commoner acids*

Salt	Solubility
Nitrates and nitrites	All soluble
Chlorides and bromides	All soluble except $AgCl$, Hg_2Cl_2, $CuCl$, $SbOCl$, $BiOCl$ which are insoluble. $PbCl_2$ is sparingly soluble (the solubility of bromides is similar to that of chloride)
Sulphates*	All soluble except $PbSO_4$, $BaSO_4$, $SrSO_4$, Hg_2SO_4 which are insoluble. $CaSO_4$ is slightly soluble
Carbonates* Sulphites* Sulphides Phosphates	Are insoluble except for those of Na^+, K^+ and NH_4^+ which are soluble

* Hydrogen sulphates, hydrogen carbonates and hydrogen sulphites are generally soluble in water.

Acid + carbonate. As carbonates are generally readily available, relatively cheap, and dissolve in strong acids without exception (unless the resulting salt is insoluble) they are widely used for preparing salts.

Acid + base. Oxides of the more electropositive elements and the lower oxides of multivalent metals (i.e. basic oxides), generally dissolve in acids to form a salt and water. Hydroxides often dissolve more readily than the corresponding oxide which in some cases dissolves only with difficulty. Hydroxides of the strongly electropositive elements are again preferable as the oxide reacts rather violently with the acid. As the hydroxides of the strongly electropositive elements are soluble in water, unless calculated quantities are used, it is necessary to use an indicator to determine when the acid has been neutralised completely (inability to dissolve more solid in the acid is usually an adequate indication of completed reaction). The indicator colour can be removed by shaking the solution with a little decolorising charcoal and then filtering.

As carbonic and sulphurous acids are unstable, the required carbonate or sulphite may sometimes be prepared by using carbon dioxide or sulphur dioxide instead. These instances will be referred to when appropriate in part III and similarly for the preparation of salts of acetic acid and boric acid.

Acid + metal. As nitric acid is an oxidising agent, it enters into secondary reactions either with the metal producing oxides of nitrogen, or with the nascent hydrogen produced in solution to form ammonium salts. Weakly electropositive metals (i.e. below hydrogen in the e.c.s.) do not dissolve in non-oxidising acids (e.g. HCl, dilute H_2SO_4), whereas at the other end of the scale the strongly electropositive metals react too violently to make the method of any practical value.

Direct combination. This method is limited to the preparation of binary compounds such as chlorides, bromides, iodides and sulphides. It is particularly useful for preparing anhydrous salts when dehydration of the hydrated form by heating would cause hydrolysis, e.g. $AlCl_3$. Hydrogen chloride may be substituted for chlorine in preparing chlorides, and as it gives reducing conditions it is used to prepare the lower chloride in cases of variable valency. For example, in the chlorides of iron:

$$2Fe + 3Cl_2 \rightarrow 2FeCl_3,$$

$$Fe + 2HCl \rightarrow FeCl_2 + H_2.$$

2. Preparation of insoluble salts. *Precipitation reactions.* An insoluble salt will separate from the solution obtained by mixing a solution containing its cation with one containing its anion, e.g.

$$Ag^+ + NO_3^- + Na^+ + Cl^- \rightarrow Ag^+Cl^- + Na^+ + NO_3^-.$$

Since precipitation is a reaction between ions, it is best represented by ionic equations. It will be noticed in the example above that neither the Na^+ nor the NO_3^- ions take part in the chemical change but serve only as 'spectator' ions. Concisely, the reaction is best represented thus:

$$Ag^+ + Cl^- \rightarrow Ag^+Cl^- \downarrow.$$

A pure, normal carbonate is not always precipitated by adding a solution containing a dissolved carbonate to a solution of a soluble salt of the metal. This is because the carbonate ion is hydrolysed in aqueous solution:

$$CO_3^{2-} + H_2O \rightleftharpoons OH^- + HCO_3^- \quad \text{(considerable)},$$

and $\qquad HCO_3^- + H_2O \rightleftharpoons OH^- + H_2CO_3 \quad \text{(very slight)}.$

As there is a fair concentration of hydroxyl ions present in the solution it tends to precipitate basic carbonates, e.g.

$$CuCO_3 . Cu(OH)_2; \quad 2PbCO_3 . Pb(OH)_2.$$

Basic precipitates may be avoided by using a solution of an alkali metal hydrogen carbonate, or by bubbling carbon dioxide into a solution of a salt of the metal whose carbonate is required, or by applying both procedures simultaneously. These techniques increase the concentration of hydrogen carbonate ions; this reduces the concentration of hydroxyl ions formed and the equilibrium is displaced in favour of the carbonate ions.

Hydrogen sulphide or ammonium sulphide solution are the best reagents for precipitating sulphides.

Direct combination. Halides and sulphides may be prepared by this method, e.g. FeS.

Properties of salts

Action of water on salts. The behaviour of water towards salts may be classified as follows:

(1) no effect (insoluble salts);

(2) dissolves the salt to give a neutral solution;

(3) dissolves the salt and reacts with the anion to give an alkaline solution;

(4) dissolves the salt and reacts with the cation to give an acid solution.

Although it is common practice to talk of the hydrolysis of salts, it is strictly the anion or the cation that is hydrolysed.

Hydrolysis of anions. Any anion in aqueous solution may be considered to be in an acid–base equilibrium with the water. If the anion is a weak base, i.e. the anion of a strong acid, it will have almost no tendency to accept a proton from a water molecule to form an undissociated molecule of the acid. For example, in dilute solution the equilibrium

$$NO_3^- + H_2O \rightleftharpoons HNO_3 + OH^-$$

is displaced completely in favour of NO_3^- which is the expected result for a neutralisation reaction of this type. However, if the anion is a strong base, i.e. the anion of a weak acid, it may tend to accept a proton from a water molecule and lead to the accumulation of undissociated acid molecules in solution, e.g.:

$$CH_3COO^- + H_2O \rightleftharpoons CH_3COOH + OH^-,$$
$$S^{2-} + H_2O \rightleftharpoons HS^- + OH^-,$$
$$CN^- + H_2O \rightleftharpoons HCN + OH^-.$$

Although the anions given above are all weaker bases than the hydroxide ion, partial hydrolysis must occur because solutions of such salts as sodium acetate, sodium sulphide and potassium cyanide turn red litmus blue. The hydrolysis of acetate ions as shown above proceeds to the right to only a few per cent. By boiling sodium sulphide or potassium cyanide solution complete hydrolysis may be effected. This is because in the first instance the HS^- ion hydrolyses a stage further.

$$HS^- + H_2O \rightleftharpoons H_2S + OH^-$$

and the H_2S, like the HCN, being volatile, is driven from the solution and the equilibrium adjusts to compensate for this loss, and eventually only sodium or potassium hydroxide solution remains. Other salts which give alkaline solutions include alkali metal carbonates, sulphites, hypochlorites and the salts of monobasic organic acids.

Hydrolysis of cations. As a simple test with litmus will show, ammonium salts, such as the chloride and sulphate, dissolve in water to give a feebly acidic solution. Just as an acid–base equilibrium is established between the water and the anions dissolved in it, a similar equilibrium is established between water and hydrogen-containing cations, e.g.

$$NH_4^+ + H_2O \rightleftharpoons NH_3 + H_3O^+.$$

Ammonia molecules may be considered to be in competition with the water molecules for protons, and as ammonia is the stronger base it captures the greater proportion. However, as the solution reacts acid, some water molecules must gain a proton at the expense of an ammonium ion for the necessary concentration of hydroxonium ions to be established.

In addition to ammonium salts, many others dissolve in water to give acid solutions, e.g. aluminium chloride, iron(III) chloride, copper(II) sulphate, zinc chloride, etc. At first sight the cations of these salts would not seem able to act as proton donors as they contain no hydrogen. However, this is only partially true for in aqueous solution all but the large univalent cations are hydrated, e.g.

$$[Fe(H_2O)_6]^{3+}, \quad [Al(H_2O)_6]^{3+}, \quad \text{etc.}$$

In order to account for the acidity of these solutions, it is suggested that proton-donating power of a water molecule is greatly enhanced when attached to cations as water of hydration. The electron-attracting power of the oxygen atom in such a water molecule is increased by the presence of the positively charged ion, and this assists the withdrawal of electrons from the hydrogen atoms giving them an even greater partial positive charge and increased protonic character. On this basis, the hydrolysis of iron(III) ions could be formulated as follows:

$$[Fe(H_2O)_6]^{3+} + H_2O \rightleftharpoons [Fe(H_2O)_5OH]^{2+} + H_3O^+,$$
$$[Fe(H_2O)_5OH]^{2+} + H_2O \rightleftharpoons [Fe(H_2O)_4(OH)_2]^+ + H_3O^+,$$
$$[Fe(H_2O)_4(OH)_2]^+ + H_2O \rightleftharpoons Fe(OH)_3 . 3H_2O + H_3O^+.$$

The successive stages in the hydrolysis of a hydrated iron(III) ion shown here leading to the formation of a neutral molecule of hydrated iron(III) hydroxide, are necessary in order to account for the *small amount* of this material deposited whenever iron(III) chloride is dissolved in water. Each step in the hydrolysis becomes increasingly more difficult as the charge on the cation falls and its electron-attracting power weakens. Consequently it is reasonable to suppose that the hydrolysis lies well to the left in the first equilibrium shown above.

The extent to which hydrolysis of this type proceeds varies from cation to cation but is most marked with quadrivalent and trivalent ions. An acidic solution is also formed by a salt of a strong acid with zinc, cadmium, mercury(II), lead(II) or copper(II) ions.

Action of acids on salts. Apart from their ability to precipitate insoluble salts and to counteract the hydrolysis of cations described in the previous section, dilute mineral acids have no noticeable action on the salts of strong acids, e.g. chlorides, sulphates and nitrates. However, the salts of weak acids such as carbonates, sulphites, sulphides and cyanides are decomposed by dilute mineral acids. In all these examples, it is the anion of the salt and the hydroxonium ion of the acid which interact, i.e.

$$CO_3{}^{2-} + 2H_3O^+ \rightleftharpoons H_2CO_3 + 2H_2O \rightleftharpoons CO_2\uparrow + 3H_2O,$$
$$SO_3{}^{2-} + 2H_3O^+ \rightleftharpoons H_2SO_3 + 2H_2O \rightleftharpoons SO_2\uparrow + 3H_2O,$$
$$S^{2-} + 2H_3O^+ \rightleftharpoons H_2S\uparrow + 2H_2O,$$
$$CN^- + H_3O^+ \rightleftharpoons HCN\uparrow + H_2O.$$

As the products of the acid–base equilibrium, which is established in each of these examples, includes a volatile acid or an unstable acid which decomposes to give a volatile product, the equilibrium adjusts to compensate for the loss of this product from the reaction mixture, and the reaction proceeds to completion. In general whenever an acid is volatile (or is unstable and decomposes to give volatile products) it can be displaced by one that is less volatile. Thus concentrated sulphuric acid will react with any salt-like halide (i.e. fluoride, chloride, bromide or iodide) liberating the gaseous hydrogen halide (see p. 511). Also whenever a nitrate is heated with concentrated sulphuric acid (b.p. 338 °C) vapours of the more volatile nitric acid (78 °C) are evolved, e.g.

$$Cl^- + H_2SO_4 \rightarrow HSO_4{}^- + HCl\uparrow,$$
$$NO_3{}^- + H_2SO_4 \rightarrow HSO_4{}^- + HNO_3\uparrow.$$

Action of alkalis on salts. Common alkalis such as the hydroxides of sodium, potassium and ammonium are used in precipitation reactions to prepare insoluble hydroxides. Ammonium hydroxide is a weak alkali and will not precipitate the hydroxide if it is slightly soluble, e.g. $Ca(OH)_2$. Also an excess of ammonium hydroxide will frequently redissolve the precipitate owing to complex ion formation, e.g. copper(II) and zinc hydroxides redissolve in excess reagent.

Just as a stronger acid will displace a weaker or more volatile acid from its salts, so a stronger base will displace a weaker or more volatile base from its salts. Thus, sodium, potassium and calcium hydroxide all displace ammonia from ammonium salts. They also displace other weak bases such as amines from their salts, e.g. methylamine from methylamine hydrochloride,

$$CH_3NH_3{}^+Cl^- + OH^- \rightarrow Cl^- + H_2O + CH_3NH_2\uparrow.$$

Action of heat on salts. In general, simple binary compounds, particularly the halides, are stable to heat. Oxo-salts, however, are more frequently decomposed on heating, carbonates and nitrates in particular.

Carbonates. All decompose on heating, save those of sodium and potassium. Carbon dioxide is evolved and the corresponding oxide remains, except in the case of ammonium carbonate when ammonia and steam are also evolved,

$$MgCO_3 \rightarrow MgO + CO_2,$$

$$(NH_4)_2CO_3 \rightarrow 2NH_3 + CO_2 + H_2O.$$

Nitrates. All decompose on moderate heating and four types of behaviour may be distinguished.

(1) Very strongly electropositive metal nitrates (i.e. Group IA, except Li) decompose into the nitrite with the evolution of oxygen (see p. 316).

(2) Very weakly electropositive metal nitrates (i.e. below copper in the electrochemical series) decompose into the free metal, nitrogen dioxide and oxygen (see p. 609).

(3) All other nitrates (except ammonium nitrate) decompose to give the oxide of the metal, nitrogen dioxide and oxygen, e.g.

$$2M(NO_3)_2 \rightarrow 2MO + 4NO_2 + O_2.$$

(4) Ammonium nitrate decomposes into dinitrogen oxide, N_2O, and steam.

Sulphates are generally more stable to heat than either carbonates or nitrates. Strong heating, however, will drive sulphur trioxide vapour out of some sulphates, e.g. iron(III) sulphate, $Fe_2(SO_4)_3$, leaving the oxide of the metal. If this oxide is a powerful enough reducing agent it will reduce some of the sulphur trioxide to sulphur dioxide, e.g. with iron(II) sulphate:

$$2FeSO_4 \rightarrow 2FeO + 2SO_3$$
$$2FeO + SO_3 \rightarrow Fe_2O_3 + SO_2$$
$$\overline{2FeSO_4 \rightarrow Fe_2O_3 + SO_2 + SO_3}$$

A complete explanation of oxo-salt stability cannot be made but a number of important factors are apparent. The most stable salts are formed by the metals of Groups IA and IIA, and the stability of the salt increases down the Group. Thus, the larger the cation, the more stable the oxo-salt. Furthermore, the more ionic the salt, i.e. the more completely the anion controls its electrons, the more stable the salt. Alkali metal sulphates are amongst the most ionic of oxo-salts and also the most stable. Generally anions have a relatively large and easily deformable electron cloud. Consequently they will be more easily polarised by small cations of high charge than by large cations of low charge. Stability is therefore thought to be associated with the polarising effect of the cation and the ease of deformability of the anion. Hydrated salts are more numerous than anhydrous ones. Water of hydration generally surrounds the cation; not only does this increase its size and so reduce its polarising ability but it also implies complete electron transfer from cation to anion, making the salt fully ionic. When the water of hydration is driven off, these stabilising factors are destroyed and this frequently results in simultaneous decomposition of the salt.

Exercises

1. Give an account of the Brönsted–Lowry theory of acids and bases.
2. Explain the following terms: (a) complex salt, (b) double salt, (c) weak acid, (d) water of crystallisation.
3. Show by means of equations how each of the following salts may be prepared: (a) potassium nitrate, (b) lead(II) sulphate, (c) zinc carbonate, (d) iron(II) sulphate, (e) aluminium chloride, (f) calcium sulphate from calcium carbonate, (g) lead(II) chloride from lead.
4. Explain what is meant by *salt hydrolysis.*
   Make a list of the anions and cations you would expect to undergo hydrolysis in aqueous solutions.
5. Show how the effect of water on the chloride of the element illustrates the trend from metal to non-metal across Period 3 (Na–Cl).
   As far as you can, interpret the trend in terms of the type of bonding exhibited by the different chlorides.
6. Compare and contrast (i) the structure, and (ii) the reactions of complex and double salts using ammonium iron(II) sulphate and potassium hexacyanoferrate(II) as examples.

7. Explain what you understand by (*a*) the concentration, (*b*) the strength, (*c*) the basicity, and (*d*) the dissociation constant of an acid. Describe in detail one experiment to demonstrate that sulphuric acid is dibasic and another experiment to show that hydrochloric acid is a stronger acid than acetic acid. (L)

8. Describe how you would obtain in the laboratory pure specimens of:
(*a*) lead chloride from metallic lead;
(*b*) anhydrous iron(III) chloride from metallic iron;
(*c*) phosphorus trichloride from phosphorus.

How do iron(III) chloride and phosphorus trichloride behave when treated with water? (J.M.B.)

9. By means of equations and brief notes on reaction conditions, indicate the methods by which the following may be prepared:
(*a*) iron(III) sulphate from metallic iron;
(*b*) lead(II) sulphate from metallic lead;
(*c*) anhydrous aluminium chloride.

Write equations showing the effect of heat on (*d*) hydrated iron(II) sulphate; (*e*) red lead (trilead tetroxide); (*f*) silver nitrate. (J.M.B.)

10. Give *one* example, with formula, of each of the following: (*a*) acid salt, (*b*) double salt, (*c*) complex salt. Describe briefly how you would prepare an acid salt in the laboratory. Point out the essential differences between a double salt and a complex salt.

Give, with explanations, *two* examples illustrating the use of complex salt formation in qualitative analysis. (J.M.B.)

16

OXIDES, HYDROXIDES AND OXO-ACIDS

Classification of oxides

A broad classification based on the internal geometrical structure of oxides is first made into normal oxides, suboxides, peroxides and super-oxides. In the following notes E stands for any element other than oxygen.

Normal oxides. Contain E—O bonds, but no E—E or O—O bonds. These bonds may be ionic or covalent, e.g. $Ca^{2+}O^{2-}$, $O=C=O$. Normal oxides are by far the most important and numerous class. In them oxygen has an oxidation number of -2, and E an oxidation number normal for its Group.

Suboxides. Contain E—E bonds as well as E—O bonds, but no O—O bonds, e.g. carbon suboxide (a gas), C_3O_2, i.e. $O=C=C=C=O$. The oxidation number of carbon in this oxide is $+1\frac{1}{3}$, because most of its valencies are used in bonds with itself. Suboxides are of little importance.

Peroxides. Contain O—O bonds as well as E—O bonds, but no E—E bonds, e.g. H_2O_2 (H—O—O—H), Na_2O_2, K_2O_2. The oxidation number of oxygen in peroxide is -1. All peroxides give hydrogen peroxide when treated with water, or dilute acids. They are therefore 'salts' of hydrogen peroxide. Peroxides are formed by all the metals of Groups I A and II A except beryllium. They contain the ion $[O_2]^{2-}$, i.e. $\left[:\overset{..}{\underset{..}{O}}—\overset{..}{\underset{..}{O}}: \right]^{2-}$.

Superoxides. Are related to peroxides, but contain the ion $[O_2]^-$ in which oxygen has the oxidation number $-\frac{1}{2}$. Its structure is $\left[:\overset{.}{\underset{..}{O}}—\overset{..}{\underset{..}{O}}: \right]^-$.

All the metals of Group I A (except lithium) form superoxides, e.g. KO_2. Attention will now be concentrated on normal oxides.

Normal oxides

This most important class is divided into subclasses: *basic*, *acidic*, *amphoteric*, and *neutral* oxides, depending on their behaviour with water, aqueous acid, and alkalis. These oxides can be arranged in a series beginning with the strongly basic and ending with the strongly acidic. In passing along the series there is a gradual transition through weakly basic, amphoteric, and weakly acidic.

Basic oxides (anhydrides of bases) are always oxides of metals (in oxidation state $+4$ or less) e.g. thorium oxide ThO_2. Strongly basic oxides are soluble in water and react with it forming alkalis in solution. The others are insoluble. All react with acids to give a salt and water only e.g. using molecular equations meantime:

$$Na_2O + H_2O \rightarrow 2NaOH; \quad MgO + 2HCl \rightarrow MgCl_2 + H_2O.$$

Acidic oxides (acid anydrides) are oxides of non-metals. Most acidic oxides, e.g. CO_2, SO_2, P_4O_{10}, are soluble in water and react with it giving acids in solution. All react with alkali (e.g. NaOH) to give a salt and water only, the non-metal being present in an oxo-anion, e.g.

$$SO_2 + H_2O \rightarrow H_2SO_3;$$
$$SiO_2 + 2NaOH \rightarrow Na_2SiO_3 + H_2O \quad \text{(sodium silicate)}.$$

Amphoteric oxides are oxides of weakly electropositive metal, e.g. Al, Zn, Sn. They show basic or acidic character depending on conditions: they react as basic oxides with acids, and as acidic oxides with bases, e.g.

$$ZnO + 2HCl \rightarrow ZnCl_2 + H_2O; \quad ZnO + 2NaOH + H_2O \rightarrow Na_2[Zn(OH)_4]$$
$$\text{sodium zincate.}$$

All amphoteric oxides are insoluble in water.

Neutral oxides show neither acidic nor basic character. They are insoluble in water. Well-known examples of this class, which is a small one, are carbon monoxide, dinitrogen monoxide, and nitrogen monoxide. Water may be regarded as a neutral oxide, but is more correctly classed as an amphoteric hydroxide H(OH).

Explanation of behaviour of normal oxides. This is most conveniently done in terms of electronegativity differences. All elements, except fluorine, are less electronegative than oxygen. The E—O bonds in oxides are therefore always polar or ionic. In the water molecule they are polar because of the moderate electronegativity difference between H(2.1) and O(3.5). The $H^{\delta+}$ can be removed as a proton, the molecule thus acting as an acid. The oxygen atom, with its lone pair and partial negative charge, can accept a proton, the molecule then acting as a base. Water is therefore amphoteric.

In most metal oxides the bonds are ionic. Consider calcium oxide. Calcium has a low electronegativity of 1.04. The oxygen atom in the oxide has therefore captured two electrons from the calcium atom, so that the

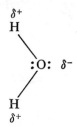

calcium oxide lattice is ionic (with sodium chloride structure, p. 133). When $Ca^{2+}O^{2-}$ is added to excess water both Ca^{2+} and O^{2-} ions are attacked by water molecules which approach in attitudes governed by the attraction of opposite charges. The oxide ion is very strongly basic, having four lone pairs of electrons and carrying a double negative charge. It captures a proton from the water molecule thus:

$$\left[:\ddot{O}:\right]^{2-} + \begin{array}{c}{}^{\delta+}H\\ :\ddot{O}:\delta-\\ {}_{\delta+}H\end{array} \longrightarrow 2\left[:\ddot{O}:H\right]^{-}$$

Water molecules attack Ca^{2+} ions forming hydrated ions Ca^{2+} (aq.).

Electronegativities of some common non-metals are P 2.06, S 2.44, C 2.5, N 3.07.

E—O bonds in non-metal oxides are polar-covalent because of the relatively small differences in electronegativity between the non-metals and oxygen. The reactions between water and CO_2 and SO_3 are on p. 252.

Oxides of transition metals with oxidation states of more than +4, e.g. CrO_3 and Mn_2O_7, are covalent and acidic because the energy required for the formation of Cr^{6+} or Mn^{7+} ions is so great that it is not available in ordinary chemical reactions.

The acidic behaviour of amphoteric oxides is caused by the removal of OH^- ions from solution rather than the donation of protons,

$$ZnO + 2OH^- + H_2O \rightarrow [Zn(OH)_4]^{2-} \text{ (zincate ion).}$$

$$
\begin{array}{c}
\overset{\delta+}{H} \\
\diagdown \\
\quad O\,\delta- \\
\diagup \\
\overset{\delta+}{H}
\end{array}
\;+\;
\begin{array}{c}
\overset{\delta-}{O} \\
\parallel \\
\overset{\delta+}{C} \\
\parallel \\
\underset{\delta-}{O}
\end{array}
\;\longrightarrow\;
\begin{array}{c}
H{-}O \\
\diagdown \\
\qquad C{=}O \\
\diagup \\
H{-}O
\end{array}
$$

$$
\begin{array}{c}
H \\
\diagdown \\
\quad O\,\delta- + {}^{\delta+}H{-}\colon O \\
\diagup \\
H
\end{array}
\quad
\begin{array}{c}
H{-}O \\
\diagdown \\
\qquad C{=}O \\
\end{array}
\;\rightleftharpoons\; H_3O^+ \;+\; HCO_3^-
$$

$$
\begin{array}{c}
\overset{\delta+}{H} \\
\diagdown \\
\quad O\,\delta- \\
\diagup \\
\underset{\delta+}{H}
\end{array}
\;+\;
\begin{array}{c}
\overset{\delta-}{O} \\
\parallel \\
{}^{\delta+}S{=}O\,\delta- \\
\parallel \\
\underset{\delta-}{O}
\end{array}
\;\longrightarrow\;
\begin{array}{c}
H{-}O \quad O \\
\diagdown \diagup \\
S \\
\diagup \diagdown \\
H{-}O \quad O
\end{array}
\;\xrightarrow{+\,H_2O}\; H_3O^+ \;+\; HSO_4^-
$$

Preparation

(1) *Direct combination* by heating or burning the element in air or oxygen. This is effective with most elements. With some oxides, e.g. Na_2O, the metal is heated in a limited supply of oxygen, otherwise the peroxide is formed.

(2) *Decomposition with steam.* Heat element in steam, e.g. preparation of CO and Fe_3O_4.

(3) *Thermal decomposition of* OH^-, CO_3^{2-}, NO_3^-. This method is suitable for all but the least electronegative metals, those of Group IA and some in Group IIA.

(4) *Oxidation of element with concentrated* HNO_3, e.g. SnO_2, GeO_2.

(5) *For acidic oxides, dehydration of the acid* sometimes gives the oxide, e.g. CO_2, SO_3, SiO_2 (p. 384), N_2O_5, CrO_3 (p. 545), Mn_2O_7 (p. 554).

(6) *Some acidic oxides are made by reduction of oxidising acids by metals,* e.g. SO_2 from H_2SO_4; NO and NO_2 from HNO_3.

Properties

Some of these have already been given (p. 250). In addition, basic oxides, being essentially ionic, are solids of high melting point and boiling point. So also are most amphoteric oxides, e.g. Al_2O_3, SnO_2 and ZnO, either because they have very high lattice energies because of high charges on the metal ion (Al^{3+}, Sn^{4+}), or because they form a giant molecular structure (ZnO). Acidic oxides are covalent, usually gases (CO_2, SO_2, NO_2, N_2O_3), volatile liquids (N_2O_5), or volatile solids of low melting point (SO_3, P_4O_6, P_4O_{10}, CrO_3). SiO_2 is exceptional in being a solid of high melting point; this is because of its giant molecular structure (p. 382).

Trend in properties of the oxides in Periods. It is already fairly clear that the change from strongly basic to strongly acidic oxide takes place because of the increasing electronegativity of the element and the consequent decreasing difference in electronegativity between oxygen (3.50) and the element. This is the same trend as is found in passing along any Period, e.g. Period 3.

	Na	Mg	Al	Si	P	S	Cl
Electronegativity (E.N.)	1.0	1.2	1.5	1.7	2.1	2.4	2.8
E.N. (oxygen)– E.N. (element)	2.5	2.3	2.0	1.8	1.4	1.1	0.7
Oxide	Na_2O	MgO	Al_2O_3	SiO_2	P_4O_{10}	SO_3	Cl_2O_7
Acid–base character	Strongly basic	Basic	Amphoteric	Weakly acidic	Acidic	Strongly acidic	Very strongly acidic
Structure	Antifluorite	Sodium chloride	Corundum	β Cristobalite	Molecular crystals (p. 140)	Molecular crystals (p. 140)	Liquid
Bonding	Ionic	Ionic	Ionic	Covalent	Covalent	Covalent	Covalent

The table shows clearly that in a series of normal oxides of *different* elements the acidity of the oxide increases substantially with increase in proportion of oxygen, i.e. with increase in oxidation number of the element. This is an important general rule and applies also to different oxides of the *same* element, e.g. SO_3 is much more acidic than SO_2; Cl_2O_7 than the other oxides of chlorine (p. 259). Many important examples are found with transition metals: CrO basic, Cr_2O_3 amphoteric, CrO_3 strongly acidic (p. 544).

Hydroxides and oxo-acids

Since basic oxides plus water form basic hydroxides, acidic oxides plus water form oxo-acids (acidic hydroxides), and amphoteric oxides plus water form amphoteric hydroxides (hypothetically), it follows that the classification of hydroxides is essentially the same as that of oxides, and the relationship between the classes is also the same. Oxo-acids may be regarded in the first instance as hydroxides of the non-metals. The replaceable hydrogen atoms in oxo-acids are always found in hydroxyl groups.

Hydroxides of the metals

These are of two quite distinct kinds:

(1) *Hydroxides of metals of low electronegativity, mainly those of Groups IA and IIA*, e.g. $NaOH$, KOH, $Mg(OH)_2$, $Ca(OH)_2$, $Ba(OH)_2$. These are crystalline ionic solids, those of Group IA being very soluble in water, those of Group IIA being soluble or slightly soluble, and all giving strongly alkaline solutions. They are *caustic alkalis* except for the very slightly soluble $Mg(OH)_2$ and the slightly soluble $Ca(OH)_2$.

(2) *Hydroxides of metals of moderate electronegativity*, e.g $Al(OH)_3$, $Fe(OH)_3$, $Cr(OH)_3$, $Pb(OH)_2$. These are insoluble compounds formed as gelatinous precipitates. They are usually represented by definite formulae as above, but in fact the precipitates contain variable and indefinite amounts of chemically combined water, which accounts for their jelly-like appearance. They are more accurately described as *hydrous oxides* and formulated as $M_xO_y.nH_2O$. The same may be said of a number of very weak acids which also form gelatinous precipitates, e.g. silicic acid, $SiO_2.nH_2O$, and stannic acid $SnO_2.nH_2O$.

Preparation

Soluble hydroxides. (1) Action of the metal on water, e.g. $NaOH$, KOH, $Ca(OH)_2$, pp. 307, 325.

(2) Action of water on the oxide, e.g. $Ca(OH)_2$, $Ba(OH)_2$, p. 329.

(3) Action of milk of lime on a solution of the carbonate, e.g. $NaOH$, KOH, pp. 308, 307. Milk of lime is a suspension of calcium hydroxide in lime-water.

(4) Electrolysis of a solution of the chloride, e.g. $NaOH$, p. 308.

Insoluble hydroxides. Precipitation by adding NH_3 solution to a solution of a salt of the metal.

Hydroxides of Group IA are not decomposed by heating; the others lose water, leaving the oxide. Other properties of hydroxides have been indicated above. See also under individual names.

Oxo-acids (hydroxides of non-metals)

Note on naming oxo-acids. Where there is only one oxo-acid of an element there is no difficulty: the suffix *-ic* is added to the name of the element (sometimes suitably shortened), e.g. carbonic acid.

When an element forms more than one oxo-acid having the central atom in different oxidation states, the most common, important or stable one, or the one with the highest proportion of oxygen, is named as above, e.g. sulphuric acid, nitric acid, phosphoric acid, chloric acid ($HClO_3$). An acid with less oxygen is given the suffix *-ous*, e.g. sulphurous acid, H_2SO_3, chlorous acid, $HClO_2$. An acid with less oxygen than the *-ous* acid is named by prefixing *hypo-* (Greek 'under') to the *-ous* acid. An acid with more oxygen than the *-ic* acid is named by prefixing *per-* (Latin 'through'), e.g.

HOCl	$HClO_2$	$HClO_3$	$HClO_4$
Hypochlorous	Chlorous	Chloric	Perchloric
acid	acid	acid	acid

Some oxo-acids are known which are also hydroxides of non-metals, e.g. boric acid, $B(OH)_3$; orthosilicic acid, $Si(OH)_4$; and telluric acid, $Te(OH)_6$. In most cases, however, when there are four or more hydroxyl groups attached to the central atom, two (or even four) of these groups react, water being eliminated and the remaining oxygen atom attached by a double bond thus:

The oxo-acid containing the highest proportion of water combined with the acidic oxide is in these cases called the *ortho*-acid, the next *pyro*- and the next *meta*-. Thus $H_3PO_4(P_2O_5.3H_2O)$ is orthophosphoric acid; $H_4P_2O_7(P_2O_5.2H_2O)$ is pyrophosphoric acid; and $HPO_3(P_2O_5.H_2O)$ is metaphosphoric acid.

Oxo-acids having the central atoms in their highest oxidation states (same number as the Group) are shown in the table on p. 256 for each of the Main Groups.

It is seen that, starting at Group IV, the basicities of the acids decrease steadily from 4 to 1; also that the number of oxygen atoms round the central atom in oxo-anions (its co-ordination number) is 4 in each case, i.e. the oxo-anions have the same tetrahedral structure.

	III	IV	V	VI	VII
Period 2	B^{+3}	—	—	—	—
Period 3	—	Si^{+4}	P^{+5}	S^{+6}	Cl^{+7}
Formula of acid	H_3BO_3	H_4SiO_4	H_3PO_4	H_2SO_4	$HClO_4$
Name of acid	Boric acid	Orthosilicic acid	Ortho-phosphoric acid	(Ortho)- sulphuric acid	Perchloric acid
Formula of anion	BO_3^{3-}	SiO_4^{4-}	PO_4^{3-}	SO_4^{2-}	ClO_4^{-}

The chief factor governing the co-ordination number of the central atom in oxo-anions is the size of the central atom: the small Period 2 boron atom (atomic radius 0.80 Å) has room for only three oxygen atoms round it, hence BO_3^{3-}; whereas the larger atoms of Period 3 (and 4) Si (1.17 Å), P (1.10 Å), S (1.04 Å) and Cl (0.99 Å) can accommodate four oxygen atoms; and the still larger atoms of Period 5 can accommodate six, e.g. TeO_6^{6-}, the oxo-anion of telluric acid $Te(OH)_6$. It is shown on p. 258 that the strengths of oxo-acids depend on their formulae: in particular, hydroxy acids (those with hydroxyl groups only) are always very weak, e.g. $Te(OH)_6$ is very weak, while sulphuric acid $SO_2(OH)_2$ is strong.

Explanation of the chemical behaviour of hydroxides of metals and non-metals in aqueous solution. Electronegativity differences account for differences in chemical behaviour here, just as with oxides. As before, water plays a cardinal part. Oxo-acids and hydracids in the absence of water are covalent liquids (H_2SO_4, HNO_3) or gases (HCl). They ionise only under the influence of the solvent. Two different ionic dissociations in water are possible for any hydroxide, e.g. E—O—H,

$$(1) \quad E{\vdots}O—H \rightarrow E^+ + OH^- \left.\vphantom{\begin{array}{c}a\\b\end{array}}\right\} \text{ basic behaviour,}$$
$$E^+ + aq. \rightarrow E^+(aq.)$$

$$(2) \quad E—O{\vdots}H \rightarrow H^+ + EO^- \left.\vphantom{\begin{array}{c}a\\b\end{array}}\right\} \text{ acidic behaviour.}$$
$$H^+ + H_2O \rightarrow (H_3O)^+$$

Ionisation takes place between the atoms where the electronegativity difference is greatest, because the bond between them is the more polar, and therefore the process of ionisation is already more advanced. Consider, for example, NaOH and HOCl (the small figures below are the electronegativities or their differences).

(1)

Na————O————H

1.0   3.5   2.1

(2.5)   (1.4)

(2)

Cl————O————H

2.8   3.5   2.1

(0.7)   (1.4)

In (1)   aq   +   Na⫶O—H   ⟶ $Na^+(aq)$ + OH^-,   basic behaviour

In (2)   Cl—O⫶H   +   O⟨H,H⟩   ⟶ H_3O^+ + ClO^-,   acidic behaviour

As an example of an amphoteric hydroxide take zinc hydroxide, omitting the reaction with water for simplicity:

Acidic dis-
sociation $2H^+ + ZnO_2^{2-} \rightleftharpoons$ H—O—Zn—O—H $\rightleftharpoons Zn^{2+} + 2OH^-$ sociation.

2.1 3.5 1.7

(1.4)(1.8)

basic dis-

The differences in electronegativity are sufficiently similar for both dissociations to be possible, depending on the conditions in solution. In acid solution the reaction goes to the right because H^+ ions from the acid remove OH^- ions and so encourage further basic dissociation of $Zn(OH)_2$. In alkaline solution the reaction goes to the left because OH^- ions from the alkali remove H^+ ions thus favouring the acidic dissociation, and OH^- ions also suppress the basic dissociation by a concentration effect. Actually the acidic dissociation is not quite that given above. Instead the $Zn(OH)_2$ adds two hydroxyl groups to form a new complex ion,

HO—Zn—OH + $2OH^- \rightarrow [Zn(OH)_4]^{2-}$ zincate ion.

This is an acidic dissociation because removal of OH^- ions increases the proportion of H^+ ions in solution.

Strengths of oxo-acids

Pauling has stated two empirical rules giving important general relationships.

257

Relation between successive dissociation constants of the same oxo-acid

Rule 1. *The successive dissociation constants K_1, K_2, K_3 for a polybasic acid are in the approximate ratio,* $1:10^{-5}:10^{-10}$, e.g. application of the law of mass action (see textbook of physical chemistry) to the dissociation of phosphoric acid gives:

$$H_3PO_4 \rightleftharpoons H^+ + H_2PO_4^- \quad (1), \qquad K_1 = \frac{[H^+][H_2PO_4^-]}{[H_3PO_4]} = 0.75 \times 10^{-2}$$

(by experiment);

$$H_2PO_4^- \rightleftharpoons H^+ + HPO_4^{2-} \quad (2), \qquad K_2 = \frac{[H^+][HPO_4^{2-}]}{[H_2PO_4^-]} = 0.62 \times 10^{-7}$$

(by experiment);

$$HPO_4^{2-} \rightleftharpoons H^+ + PO_4^{3-} \quad (3), \qquad K_3 = \frac{[H^+][PO_4^{3-}]}{[HPO_4^{2-}]} = 1.0 \times 10^{-12}$$

(by experiment).

It is seen that H_3PO_4 is a fairly strong acid with respect to its first dissociation; $H_2PO_4^-$ ion is a weak acid; HPO_4^{2-} ion a very weak acid. The great differences between the values of these constants are explained roughly as follows. Because of the electrostatic attraction of opposite charges, it is more difficult to remove H^+ ion from $(H_2PO_4)^-$ ion than to remove it from the uncharged (H_3PO_4). Similar reasoning applies to the third dissociation. Compare the fact that the second ionisation energy of a metal is approximately twice the first and so on (for valency electrons) e.g. Ca 590 (1st), 1059 (2nd) kJ mol^{-1}.

Note. Rule 1 should be used only with oxo-acids in which all the oxygen atoms are attached to *one* central non-metal atom. Even then the rule is only roughly true, the ratios given being average values.

Value of the first dissociation constants of different oxo-acids

Rule 2. *The first dissociation constant of any oxo-acid* $XO_m(OH)_n$ *is determined by* m: *the greater the value of* m, *the stronger the acid.*

Note. m is the number of oxygen atoms *not* present in hydroxyl groups. When $m = 0$ the acid is very weak with $K_1 = 10^{-7}$ or less, e.g.

Boric acid $B(OH)_3$ or H_3BO_3	$K_1 \simeq 10^{-9}$
Hypochlorous acid $Cl(OH)$	$K_1 \simeq 10^{-8}$
Telluric acid $Te(OH)_6$ or H_6TeO_6	$K_1 \simeq 1.6 \times 10^{-9}$

When $m = 1$ the acid is fairly weak with $K_1 \simeq 10^{-2}$, e.g.

Sulphurous acid $SO(OH)_2$ or H_2SO_3	$K_1 \simeq 10^{-2}$
Phosphoric acid $PO(OH)_3$ or H_3PO_4	$K_1 \simeq 10^{-2}$
Nitrous acid $NO(OH)$ or HNO_2	$K_1 \simeq 0.5 \times 10^{-3}$

When $m = 2$ the acid is strong with $K_1 \simeq 10^2$, e.g.

Sulphuric acid $SO_2(OH)_2$ or H_2SO_4	$K_1 \simeq 10^3$
Nitric acid $NO_2(OH)$ or HNO_3	$K_1 \simeq 10^1$

When $m = 3$ the acid is very strong with $K_1 \simeq 10^8$, e.g.

Perchloric acid $ClO_3(OH)$ or $HClO_4$	$K_1 \simeq 10^8$

The second rule is a roughly quantitative expression of the well-known qualitative rule that the strength of an oxo-acid increases with the increase in the proportion of oxygen in the acid-anhydride (see table and text on p. 253). The oxo-acids of chlorine are a good example.

Acid	$\begin{cases} HClO \text{ or} \\ Cl(OH) \end{cases}$	$HClO_2$ or $ClO(OH)$	$HClO_3$ or $ClO_2(OH)$	$HClO_4$ or $ClO_3(OH)$	
m	0	1	2	3	
Acid strength	Very weak	Fairy weak	Strong	Very strong	$\begin{cases} \text{See values} \\ \text{of } K_1 \\ \text{above} \end{cases}$
Oxo-anion	$(ClO)^-$	$(ClO_2)^-$	$(ClO_3)^-$	$(ClO_4)^-$	

A simple explanation of these facts is that co-ordination of additional strongly electronegative oxygen atoms to the chlorine atom of the HOCl molecule pulls electrons away from the chlorine atom, and this pull is communicated through the chlorine atom to the H—O bond, causing an increase in the partial positive charge of the H atom. Representing electron movement by arrows this can be shown thus:

Another way of looking at the question is to consider the backward reaction in $HA \rightleftharpoons H^+ + A^-$. In passing from $(ClO)^-$ to $(ClO_4)^-$ there is a great increase in size of the anion. In $(ClO)^-$ the single negative charge is distributed over a small anion: the charge intensity at the surface is therefore much greater than with the large ion $(ClO_4)^-$ and so there is a much greater tendency for the backward reaction to take place in the case of $(ClO)^-$.

Acid chlorides

Inorganic oxo-acids, like organic carboxylic acids, form acid chlorides when one or more of the hydroxyl groups in the oxo-acid is replaced by chlorine. Thus acetic acid $CH_3 . C {\overset{O}{\underset{OH}{\Big<}}}$ forms acetyl chloride $CH_3 . C {\overset{O}{\underset{Cl}{\Big<}}}$.

The name of the acid chloride is got by changing *-ic* in the acid to *-yl*. Similarly sulphuric acid $SO_2(OH)_2$ forms sulphuryl chloride SO_2Cl_2; carbonic acid $CO(OH)_2$ forms carbonyl chloride $COCl_2$; nitric acid $NO_2(OH)$ forms nitryl chloride NO_2Cl; nitrous acid $NO(OH)$ forms nitrosyl chloride $NOCl$; chromic acid $CrO_2(OH)_2$ forms chromyl chloride CrO_2Cl_2.

Preparation. Acid chlorides are often obtained by the action of phosphorus pentachloride on oxo-acids. Other methods are given under the particular acid chloride.

Properties. Most acid chlorides are covalent volatile liquids or gases, readily hydrolysed by water, a reaction which regenerates the oxo-acid and forms hydrochloric acid,

$$SO_2Cl_2 + 2H_2O \rightleftharpoons H_2SO_4 + 2HCl.$$

An interesting exception is uranyl chloride UO_2Cl_2, the acid chloride of uranic acid $UO_2(OH)_2$ or H_2UO_4. Uranyl chloride is a soluble yellow solid and is a salt (ionic) containing the complex uranyl cation $(UO_2)^{2+}$.

Exercises

1. Write notes on (*a*) the classification of oxides, and (*b*) the further classification of normal oxides.

2. The most instructive, yet concise, formula for an oxo-acid is in the form $XO_m(OH)_n$, e.g. sulphuric acid $SO_2(OH)_2$. Write similar formulae for chlorous, orthosilicic, carbonic, permanganic, acetic, selenic and arsenious acids. Classify these acids as very weak, weak, strong, or very strong by means of Pauling's second rule, p. 258.

3. Give brief statements, with illustrative equations, of methods for preparing (*a*) oxides, (*b*) hydroxides of the metals, and (*c*) oxo-acids.

4. Repeat question 2 above, for the oxo-acids of Period 3 given in the table on p. 256. What conclusion may be drawn as to the trend across this Period?

5. Name any six of the classes into which oxides are usually placed, and give **two** examples of oxides of each class you have quoted. How do oxides of the type XO_2 react with (a) water, (b) hydrochloric acid? Name **one** oxide of the type XO_2 which would not react with either.

20 cc. of a gaseous oxide of chlorine decomposed on heating yielding 30 cc. of gaseous decomposition products. This volume was reduced by 20 cc. on shaking in the cold with sodium hydroxide solution. All volumes were corrected to s.t.p. Determine the formula of the oxide and write equations for the reactions taking place. (J.M.B.)

6. Comment on and, where you are able, suggest reasons for the following observations.

(a) Na_2O dissolves in water to give an alkaline solution: Cl_2O dissolves in water to give an acidic solution.

(b) Cl_2O is a gaseous oxide, its molecule being V-shaped: Na_2O is an ionic compound which has an infinite 3-dimensional lattice structure.

(c) Al_2O_3 forms a hydrated oxide which is basic, but the addition of alkali produces a solution containing the aluminate anion, AlO_2^-.

(d) SiO_2 and CO_2 are both acidic oxides. SiO_2 is a solid of high melting-point, whereas CO_2 is a gas.

(e) N_2O is a gaseous, neutral oxide, its molecule being linear. (CS)

17

HYDRIDES

Hydrides are a family of binary compounds of hydrogen. While precise distinctions cannot be made in every case, it is possible to recognise three types of hydride.

Ionic hydrides. These are compounds of hydrogen and an alkali metal or an alkaline earth metal; they have ionic lattices, high melting points and behave as electrolytes when fused.

Covalent hydrides. The rest of the Main Group elements form hydrides of this type. All the simple ones except water are gaseous at room temperature.

Metallic hydrides. Some transition metals have the ability to absorb and retain hydrogen. The most striking example is that of palladium which can absorb 800 times its volume of hydrogen. This is termed *occlusion* and it can usually be reversed by heating in a vacuum. Usually the composition of these substances cannot be expressed by conventional formulae based on the laws of chemical combination and their formulae are *non-stoichiometric* (e.g. $TiH_{1.73}$). The properties of these substances (termed *interstitial* hydrides), which may be solid solutions of hydrogen in the metal, rather than true compounds, are not very different from the parent metal.

The simplest hydrides of the elements in the Main Groups are listed in the following table.

Some binary compounds of hydrogen

I	II	III	IV	V	VI	VII
LiH	BeH_2	B_2H_6	CH_4	NH_3	H_2O	HF
NaH	MgH_2	$(AlH_3)_x$	SiH_4	PH_3	H_2S	HCl
KH	CaH_2	Ga_2H_6	GeH_4	AsH_3	H_2Se	HBr
RbH	SrH_2	InH_3	SnH_4	SbH_3	H_2Te	HI
CsH	BaH_2	TlH_3	PbH_4	BiH_3	H_2Po	—

Ionic hydrides $\qquad\qquad$ Covalent hydrides

$\rightarrow$ Change from basic character to acidic character $\rightarrow$

Preparation

1. By direct combination. Moving from left to right across a Period there is a progressively greater readiness of elements to form covalent hydrides by direct combination with hydrogen. The reaction of hydrogen with the elements of the second Period is summarised below.

Lithium. Ionic hydride.

Beryllium. No action.

Boron. No action.

Carbon. Small amounts of methane are formed by striking an electric arc between carbon electrodes in an atmosphere of hydrogen.

Nitrogen. A reversible combination occurs when the two gases are heated in the presence of a catalyst,

$$N_2 + 3H_2 \rightleftharpoons 2NH_3.$$

Oxygen. Hydrogen readily burns in oxygen to form water. The combination is explosive when the hydrogen and oxygen are in the proportions required by the formula: $2H_2 + O_2 \rightarrow 2H_2O.$

Fluorine. The combination with hydrogen is explosive even at $-250\ °C$,

$$H_2 + F_2 \rightarrow 2HF.$$

With the exception of beryllium and magnesium, the first two elements in a Period combine with hydrogen quite readily. As these are the most electropositive of the elements the reaction is essentially an electron transfer to the non-metal with simultaneous formation of an ionic crystal lattice, e.g. $2Na + H—H \rightarrow 2Na^+H^-.$

The hydrogen molecule is broken up; both atoms gain the electronic structure of helium, that is, they become negatively charged hydrogen ions.

Magnesium, which is rather less powerfully electropositive, can be made to combine directly with hydrogen but it is better to prepare the hydride indirectly by the use of lithium aluminium hydride.

Beryllium hydride is also made indirectly from lithium aluminium hydride, e.g. $2BeCl_2 + LiAlH_4 \rightarrow 2BeH_2 + LiCl + AlCl_3.$

It is probable that magnesium hydride is ionic but the structure of beryllium hydride is uncertain.

Both ammonia and hydrogen chloride are prepared industrially by direct combination but it is not a widely used method of preparing covalent hydrides.

2. *By decomposition of a binary compound with an acid or water.* This is the best general method of preparing covalent hydrides. In this method the hydrogen used to form the hydride comes from either the acid or the water. All the non-metals (not the noble gases) form compounds with one or other of the metals. A representative few are shown here:

Aluminium carbide Al_4C_3	Magnesium nitride Mg_3N_2	Calcium oxide CaO	Calcium fluoride CaF_2
Magnesium silicide Mg_2Si	Calcium phosphide Ca_3P_2	Iron(II) sulphide FeS	Sodium chloride $NaCl$

In naming these compounds the non-metal is always given the ending *-ide*.

Aluminium carbide, magnesium nitride and calcium phosphide are decomposed by water, evolving methane, ammonia and phosphine respectively:

$$Al_4C_3 + 12H_2O \rightarrow 4Al(OH)_3 + 3CH_4 \uparrow,$$
$$Mg_3N_2 + 3H_2O \rightarrow 3MgO + 2NH_3 \uparrow,$$
$$Ca_3P_2 + 6H_2O \rightarrow 3Ca(OH)_2 + 2PH_3 \uparrow.$$

Hydrogen fluoride and hydrogen chloride are liberated by the action of concentrated sulphuric acid on any fluoride or chloride. Many of the other binary compounds are decomposed by dilute hydrochloric acid, e.g.

$$CaF_2 + H_2SO_4 \rightarrow CaSO_4 + 2HF \uparrow,$$
$$FeS + 2HCl \rightarrow FeCl_2 + H_2S \uparrow.$$

Aluminium hydride is known only as a non-volatile solid polymer; it also exists in an ethereal solution of lithium hydride and aluminium chloride,

$$3Li^+H^- + AlCl_3 \rightarrow AlH_3 + 3Li^+Cl^-.$$

Lithium hydride and aluminium chloride in ether solution lead to the formation of lithium aluminium hydride. This is fairly soluble in ether whereas lithium chloride is not. Since the lithium chloride precipitates the equilibrium is shifted to favour the formation of the hydride complex ion,

$$4Li^+H^- + AlCl_3 \rightleftharpoons Li^+AlH_4^- + 3Li^+Cl^- \downarrow.$$

It is a good reagent for preparing diborane, B_2H_6,

$$4BCl_3 + 3Li^+AlH_4^- \rightarrow 2B_2H_6 + 3Li^+Cl^- + 3AlCl_3.$$

Structure

1. Ionic hydrides. These are all ionic structures containing M^+ and H^- ions. The H^- ion has an ionic radius of 2.1 Å, rather bigger than the chloride ion, 1.81 Å. The ions in the hydrides of the alkali metals all pack in the same way producing a lattice identical to that of sodium chloride which belongs to the cubic system (see p. 133). The alkaline earth-metal hydrides all have the same crystalline lattice but the packing is less orderly than that in the alkali metal hydrides.

Evidence for a negative ion of hydrogen was first obtained by the electrolysis of fused lithium hydride and confirmed by the electrolysis of calcium hydride. Hydrogen appears at the *anode* in both cases and with calcium hydride quantitative measurements showed it was liberated in accordance with Faraday's Laws.

2. Covalent hydrides. Hydride formation of the elements of Group IV, V, VI and VII leads to the completion of the electron octet of the central atom in every case. The eight electrons in the outer shell of the central atom separate into four pairs and as the electrostatic repulsion between them is a minimum when they adopt a tetrahedral configuration (see p. 144) this is the basic structure of these hydrides. In Group IV each electron pair is used for binding and a hydrogen atom is located at each of the four corners of a regular tetrahedron. In passing across a Period from Group IV to Group VII the number of additional electrons needed to complete the octet falls accordingly and the number of hydrogen atoms in a molecule of the hydrides of a particular Group falls stepwise from four to one, so that the number of non-bonding or lone pairs steadily increases until it reaches three in the hydrogen halides. This is illustrated in the diagrams for the hydrides of the elements in the second Period (Fig. 106). The lone pairs are represented by shaded lobes.

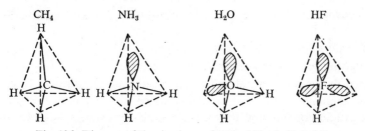

Fig. 106. Diagram of the simple covalent hydrides in Period 2.

All the simple hydrides in the Carbon Group have the tetrahedral structure. The simple hydrides of the Nitrogen Group all have one lone pair and the nuclei of the atoms give the molecule a pyramidal structure. Again, the molecules of the simple hydrides of the Oxygen Group are all V-shaped and the other positions of the basic tetrahedral structure are occupied by the lone pairs. The hydrogen halide molecules are linear.

Boron forms a series of hydrides most of which are volatile. Boron hydrides are very sensitive to air and moisture, often inflaming spontaneously. The structure of the hydrides of boron is unusual in that they are all electron-deficient compounds, that is, without sufficient valency electrons to form the requisite number of single covalent bands.

The polar nature of covalent hydrides

There are two effects to consider: (1) the polar nature of the bonds within a particular hydride molecule; and (2) the polar nature of the molecule as a whole. As the elements become more electronegative from left to right across a Period the attraction for electrons increases. The electronegativities of carbon and hydrogen are 2.5 and 2.1, respectively. This small difference in electron-attracting ability prevents the electrons from being drawn appreciably towards the carbon atom and so the bonds in methane are only feebly polar. With successive elements in the same Period, however, the difference in electronegativities becomes considerable (N, 3.0; O, 3.5; F, 4.10) and bonds of a highly polar nature are produced. The withdrawal of electrons from the hydrogen towards the fluorine atom causes such a separation of the positive and negative centres in the molecule (see p. 100) that it has about a 50% ionic character.

When the molecule is symmetrical like that of methane the polarities of the individual bonds exactly cancel each other and the overall molecule is non-polar. All the hydrides of Groups V, VI and VII are unsymmetrical and the electrical centre of the electrons does not coincide with the electrical centre of the positive nuclei and the molecules are all polar. Ammonia, water and hydrogen fluoride are much the most polar of the covalent hydrides.

Physical properties

1. *Melting points and boiling points.* The three-dimensional ionic lattice formed by the alkali metal and alkaline earth-metal hydrides confers on these compounds those properties associated with strong non-directional electrostatic bonding and they are all white crystalline solids with fairly high melting and boiling points.

The gaseous nature of the covalent hydrides is consistent with the weak van der Waals' forces of intermolecular attraction between neutral molecules of low molecular weight. Water is an exception and the melting point and boiling point of ammonia and hydrogen fluoride are also anomalous. This is shown in Fig. 107, where the boiling points of the various hydrides are plotted and those in the same Group joined by tie

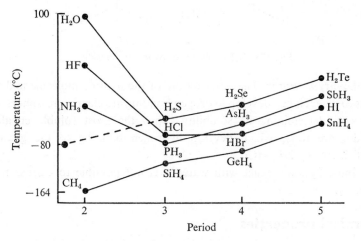

Fig. 107. Boiling points of the simple covalent hydrides.

lines. With the exception of methane the boiling points of simple covalent hydrides in the second Period are considerably greater than their homologues in the third Period. As an example, if the boiling points of the hydrides of the oxygen group are extrapolated back the boiling point of water would be about -80 °C. It was evidence of this kind which added support to the idea of hydrogen bonding (see p. 107) since this would lead to molecular association in both solid and liquid states of hydrogen fluoride, water and ammonia. In these states the molecules are thus more complex than their simple formula would suggest. The homologues of these hydrides in the third Period—hydrogen chloride, hydrogen sulphide and phosphine—show hydrogen bond formation to a negligible extent owing to the decreased electronegativity and larger size of the chlorine, sulphur and phosphorus atoms. Hydrogen bonding is strongest in hydrogen fluoride and association persists into the vapour state. Solid hydrogen fluoride consists of long zig-zag chains and fragments of these chains are present just above the boiling point (Fig. 108). The broken line represents the hydrogen bond. The hydrogen bond is of electrostatic origin and is limited to the most electronegative atoms (fluorine, oxygen and nitrogen) and the anomalous properties of these elements in combination with hydrogen can usually be traced to the influence of hydrogen bonding. Generally the hydrogen bond is longer than the covalent molecular bond. Thus although the hydrogen bond is symmetrical in hydrogen fluoride and HF_2^- this is not so for water, ammonia, etc.

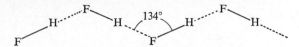

Fig. 108. H_4F_4 polymer of hydrogen fluoride.

2. Solubility in water. The polar nature of the hydride molecule and the extent to which it can develop hydrogen bonding are clearly predominating factors in determining its solubility. Thus the most soluble covalent hydrides are those which develop hydrogen bonding to the greatest extent, i.e. NH_3, HF, HCl.

As ionic hydrides react with water it is not possible to discuss their solubility.

Chemical properties

The chemical reactions of hydrides can be broadly classified into:

(a) the reactions of the hydride ion;

(b) the reactions of covalently bound hydrogen.

These may be correlated with the position in the Periodic Table and the structure of the hydride. The periodic variation in properties of the hydrides may be illustrated by the elements in Period 2, as the trends in the other Periods are analogous.

1. Basic character. The hydride ion is one of the most powerful proton acceptors. It is a much stronger base than the hydroxyl ion and has no difficulty in withdrawing a proton from a water molecule,

$$H^- + H—OH \rightarrow H—H + OH^-.$$

Thus ionic hydrides are easily hydrolysed by water with the evolution of hydrogen and the formation of an alkaline solution. As the second metal in a Period forms a less soluble hydroxide, than the first, the alkaline earth-metal hydrides are not able to furnish such a high concentration of hydroxyl ions in solution when they are hydrolysed as are the alkali metal hydrides. These latter hydrides can therefore produce a more strongly alkaline solution.

Boron and hydrogen have almost the same electronegativity and the hydridic character of the hydrogen in diborane is very feeble. In subsequent Groups there is no tendency for the hydrogen of the hydride to behave as a proton acceptor.

However, owing to the lone pair of electrons in the nitrogen atom of ammonia it has quite a strong tendency to accept protons and behaves as a strong base. The water molecule has two lone pairs of electrons and can also accept protons but it is a feebler base than ammonia. Hydrogen fluoride has no basic properties.

2. Acidic character. It is found that in passing from Group IV to Group VII along a period the hydrides become increasingly acidic. This can be correlated with the increasingly powerful electron attracting property (i.e. electronegativity) of the elements towards the end of the Periods. Withdrawal of electrons from the hydrogen atoms in a molecule leaves them as *incipient* protons and so assists in the dissociation of the hydride. Thus the forward reaction in the following equilibrium proceeds more readily across Period 2.

$$XH_n + H_2O \rightleftharpoons XH^-_{(n-1)} + H_3O^+.$$

$XH^-_{(n-1)}$ represents the following anions:

$$CH_3^- < NH_2^- < OH^- < F^-.$$

$$\xrightarrow{\hspace{6cm}}$$
order of increasing stability

Of these only the hydroxyl ion, OH^-, and fluoride ion, F^-, are formed in aqueous solution. The methide ion, CH_3^-, and amide ion NH_2^-, are both more strongly proton accepting (i.e. basic) than a water molecule and therefore unstable in aqueous solution.

In passing up a Group the hydrides become less acidic. This is contrary to the trend in electronegativity and appears to contradict the correlation that was made across the Periods between trends in acid strength and trends in electronegativity. This is because electronegativity was related directly to acid strength and this is an oversimplification. Increasing electronegativity of the central atom:

(*a*) increases the partial positive charge on an attached hydrogen atom;

(*b*) increases the stability of the anion of the acid produced by loss of a proton;

(*c*) strengthens the bonds to the hydrogen atoms with which it is combined.

The first two factors favour dissociation of the hydride and account for the increase in acid character across the Periods. The third factor stabilises the molecule and makes dissociation more difficult. In ascending a Group, electronegativity increases so that factors (*a*) and (*b*) tend to make the hydride at the top of the Group the strongest acid. Acting in the opposite sense is factor (*c*). In contrast to the trend across the Periods this is now the predominating influence and the weakest acid is at the top of the Group and the strongest is at the bottom. Thus in Group VII the order of increasing acid strength is HF < HCl < HBr < HI.

3. Reducing action. Proton acceptors are defined as bases, and reducing agents are commonly described as electron donors. The hydride ion is unique in that there are many reactions in which it serves simultaneously as both a base and a reducing agent as they are defined above. In the reaction with water the hydride ion accepts a proton from the water molecule and thus shows basic character. But the hydride ion donates (shares) its electron pair to each participating proton, and a molecule of hydrogen is formed. The hydride ion is oxidised (oxidation number increases from -1 to 0) and the proton from the participating water molecule is reduced (oxidation number decreasing from $+1$ to 0). Thus the ionic hydrides are powerful reducing agents.

A very useful commercial source of hydride ions is lithium aluminium hydride and it is an extremely powerful reducing agent much used in organic chemistry, e.g.

$$CH_3-\overset{\underset{|}{H}}{C}{=}\overset{\cdot\cdot}{\underset{\cdot\cdot}{O}} \; + \; H\overset{\cdot\cdot}{.}^- \xrightarrow[\substack{\text{from} \\ AlH_4^-}]{\substack{\text{Dry} \\ \text{ether}}} \left[CH_3-\overset{\underset{|}{H}}{\underset{H}{C}}-\overset{\cdot\cdot}{\underset{\cdot\cdot}{O}}{.} \right]^- \xrightarrow{H_2O} CH_3-\overset{\underset{|}{H}}{\underset{H}{C}}-O-H + OH^-$$

Acetaldehyde   Ethanol

Many covalent hydrides also act as reducing agents as they dissociate to produce hydrogen. As mentioned in the previous section the electronegativity of the central atom is an important factor in determining the stability of the molecule. In general the trends in reducing power of the hydrides can be equated with the trends in electronegativity. Thus, reducing action amongst the hydrides diminishes across the Periods and up the Groups, e.g.

Period 2:

$$NaH \quad MgH_2 \quad (AlH_3)_x \quad SiH_4 \quad PH_3 \quad H_2S \quad HCl$$

diminishing reducing action

$$\longrightarrow$$

Group VII:

$$HI \quad HBr \quad HCl \quad HF$$

diminishing reducing action

$$\longrightarrow$$

Formation of higher hydrides

So far the discussion has been on the simple hydrides formed by the elements, but there are a few elements, notably carbon, silicon, germanium, nitrogen, phosphorus and boron, which are able to form higher hydrides. Carbon is unique in this respect and the carbon hydrides or *hydrocarbons* as they are more usually called are sufficiently numerous and diverse to form an important section of organic chemistry. Silicon shares with carbon the ability to combine with itself, but to a very much reduced degree. Even so silicon forms a series of volatile hydrides known as *silanes* which are comparable to the paraffins. They have the general formula $Si_nH_{(2n+2)}$ and the first six members are known. Germanium resembles silicon closely in its capacity for hydride formation. Monogermane GeH_4, digermane Ge_2H_6 and trigermane Ge_3H_8 have been prepared. Hydrazine, N_2H_4 and disphosphine, P_2H_4 are higher hydrides of nitrogen and phosphorus respectively.

Exercises

1. Discuss the differences shown by the members of the series methane, ammonia, water, hydrogen fluoride. (L)
2. What Group trends can be distinguished among the ionic and covalent hydrides? Attempt to correlate these trends with changes in atomic structure.
3. Discuss the effect of hydrogen bonding on the following properties: (*a*) boiling point, (*b*) solubility, (*c*) acid strength.
4. Give an account of the properties of the hydrides of nitrogen, oxygen and fluorine. In what ways and for what reasons, do these compounds differ from one another and from the corresponding compounds of phosphorus sulphur and chlorine? (CS)
5. Give a *comparative* account of the properties of the hydrides of the common non-metallic elements. (C)

PART III

ELEMENTS IN MAIN GROUPS

Summary of the procedure that will be adopted in dealing with Groups

Similarities within a Group

All members have a number (N) in common

N is $\begin{cases} \text{(1) The Group number.} \\ \text{(2) The number of electrons in the external (valency) shell. Inert} \\ \quad\ \text{ gases may be numbered VIII B.} \\ \text{(3) The maximum Group valency (except that N, O, F, Br do not} \\ \quad\ \text{ have this valency).} \end{cases}$

In addition, all members of Groups VB, VIB, and VIIB have Group valencies of $(8 - N)$. Valencies other than the Group valencies are common in Groups IIIB to VIIB.

Differences within a Group—Group trends

Differences must exit. What has to be made clear is that the differences are orderly and graded, i.e. there are predictable general trends in passing down the Groups.

Atomic number. It follows immediately from the number of elements in each Period that the successive differences in atomic number in passing down each Group are (omitting H and He):

> For s-block Groups: 8, 8, 18, 18, 32;
> For p-block Groups: 8, 18, 18, 32.

Atomic weight. Successive differences (omitting H and He) are approximately as follows (average values):

For s-block Groups: 16, 16, 46, 46, 88; e.g. Li = 7, Na = 23, K = 39, Rb = 85, Cs = 133, Fr = [223].

For p-block Groups: 16, 46, 46, 88; e.g. C = 12, Si = 28, Ge = 73, Sn = 120, Pb = 207.

Atomic radius, electronegativity, ionic radius. See p. 76.

Maximum covalency. See p. 95.

Inert pair effect. See p. 94.

18

GROUP 0: THE NOBLE GASES

Helium, neon, argon, krypton, xenon, and radon are known collectively as the *noble gases*. Alternative terms include the *rare gases* and the *inert gases*. Radon is radioactive.

Atomic properties of Group 0 *elements*

Element	Symbol	Atomic number	Atomic weight	Covalent radius (Å)	Ionisation energy kcal mol^{-1}
Helium	He	2	4.003	0.93	566.8
Neon	Ne	10	20.179	1.31	497.2
Argon	Ar	18	39.948	1.74	363.4
Krypton	Kr	36	83.80	1.89	322.8
Xenon	Xe	54	131.3	2.09	279.7
Radon	Rn	86	222	2.14	247.9

Relationship of Group 0 to the Periodic Table

Each noble gas is placed at the end of a completed period in the Periodic Table and therefore they occupy the last column of the *p*-block elements. However, the regular horizontal relationships which exist between the elements in any Period alter abruptly after the halogens, and they show no similarities to the noble gases—except that both the halogens and the noble gases are non-metallic elements. Furthermore, following the natural order of atomic numbers each noble gas element precedes an alkali metal and in this case there is the acute change in chemical type from a non-reactive non-metal to a highly reactive metal. Group 0, therefore bears no relationship to its neighbouring Groups (i.e. Group VIIB and Group IA) in the Periodic Table. However, Group trends in the noble gases run roughly parallel to those of Groups IA and IIA.

General Group features

It will already be realised from ch. 7 that the remarkable unreactivity of the noble gases is attributed to the fact that they have an electronic structure in which there are no incomplete sub-shells. A table showing the electronic arrangement of the noble gases is given on p. 86. As each noble gas atom has a stable electron structure and no tendency to gain or lose electrons (but see p. 278) they are given a formal valency of zero. No other Group of elements is more closely similar than the noble gases. Prior to 1962 their chemistry was essentially a recital of their physical properties, which vary down the Group from lightest to heaviest in a regular manner similar to the trends shown in the other Main Groups. Since then, however, it has been found that compounds of krypton, xenon, and radon can be prepared and it is no longer true to regard these elements as completely inert. If the ionisation energies of the noble gases are compared with those of other elements it will be seen that although those of helium and neon are much greater than all others, the first ionisation energy of xenon is nearly the same as that of bromine and appreciably less than that of chlorine. Because of this the possibility of compound formation with highly electronegative elements is not so surprising.

Occurrence

All the noble gases with the exception of radon are constituents of the air. A summary of their relative abundance in per cent by volume of the atmosphere is shown below:

$$
\begin{array}{lll}
& \text{Neon} -1.8 \times 10^{-3} & \\
\text{Argon} -0.9 & \text{Krypton} -1.1 \times 10^{-4} & \text{Xenon} -8.7 \times 10^{-6} \\
& \text{Helium} -5.2 \times 10^{-4} &
\end{array}
$$

$\longrightarrow$

decreasing abundance

Argon is therefore about thirty times more abundant than the carbon dioxide in the air, but the other noble gases are relatively scarce. Whenever a radioactive element decays by emitting α-particles helium is formed. It therefore tends to accumulate in minerals and rocks containing radioactive elements and is released when they are heated. Enormous quantities of natural gas containing up to and sometimes exceeding 1% of helium escape from gas wells in North America.

All isotopes of radon are radioactive and as the longest lived (^{222}Rn) has a half-life (see p. 37) of only 3.825 days, no appreciable amounts accumulate and they tend to exist in equilibrium with the radioelement from which they originate, i.e. radon (^{222}Rn) from radium, thoron (^{220}Rn) from thorium and actinon (^{219}Rn) from actinium.

Isolation

Neon, argon, krypton and xenon can be isolated during the fractional distillation of liquid air. Quantities of helium are separated from North American natural gas by condensing out the accompanying gases and then effecting further purification by passing the residue over charcoal at the temperature of liquid air. Helium, unlike most other gases is not adsorbed and therefore escapes, whereas the impurities are retained. Annual production of argon in the U.K. is about 10 000 tons.

Uses

A helium–oxygen mixture is inhaled by deep-sea divers in preference to air as the helium dissolves in the blood to a lesser extent than nitrogen. So when the pressure is released, as the diver resurfaces, less gas bubbles form in the blood and a dangerous condition is avoided. Although helium is twice as dense as hydrogen it is still very light compared with air and has the advantage over hydrogen for filling balloons and airships in that it is non-inflammable. Liquid helium is used as a coolant in low-temperature research and in nuclear reactors. It is also used in gas thermometers for low temperature work.

Argon, or an argon–nitrogen mixture, is placed in gas-filled electric light bulbs and radio tubes to prevent excessive volatilisation of the incandescent filament. It is also used in Geiger counters and in welding when an inert atmosphere is required to prevent the formation of oxide films. This latter application consumes most of the 10 000 tons of argon used annually.

Neon is widely used in illuminated signs either alone or mixed with other gases to give a variety of colours.

Noble gases are used in some metallurgical processes, e.g. production of titanium.

Physical properties

These elements are all colourless, odourless gases which are relatively difficult to liquify as testified by their low boiling points (see p. 278). Moreover, the very short temperature interval between melting point and boiling point indicates the ease with which the solid vaporises.

Physical properties of the noble gases

Element	m.p. (°C)	b.p. (°C)	Solubility in water (cm³ l⁻¹ at 20 °C)
Helium	-272	-269	13.8
Neon	-249	-246	14.7
Argon	-189	-186	37.9
Krypton	-157	-153	73.0
Xenon	-112	-107	110.9
Radon	-71	-65	—

Very weak interatomic attractive forces, i.e. van der Waals' forces, exist between the atoms of these elements and this accounts for their ease of vaporisation. As the Group is descended the strength of the van der Waals' forces increases, since the atoms get larger and more polarisable (see p. 101). This is a factor in explaining the rise in boiling point down the Group.

Argon is rather more soluble in water than oxygen and in general the noble gases have a relatively high solubility which increases down the Group.

Chemical properties

Claims to have prepared compounds of the noble gases have been made ever since their discovery by Sir William Ramsay in 1892. Among these have been the formation of *enclosure* compounds or *clathrate* compounds (from the Latin word *clathratus*, 'enclosed or protected by cross bars or grating'), as they are called. If quinol crystals (p-$C_6H_4(OH)_2$) are allowed to grow from an aqueous or alcoholic solution under a noble gas pressure of 10–40 atmospheres, atoms of the gas are trapped in cavities in the crystal lattice. The crystals are quite stable but on heating or dissolving in water the gas is released. A number of hydrates have also been reported but again these are in reality clathrate compounds in which noble gas atoms are trapped in a lattice formed by the water molecules. However, in none of these compounds is a noble gas atom chemically bonded to another atom and it was only in 1962 that such a compound was conclusively established. N. Bartlett found that a molecule of the powerfully oxidising gas platinum hexafluoride PtF_6, combined with a molecule of oxygen to give a salt, dioxygenyl-hexafluoroplatinate(v), by a process of electron transfer.

$$PtF_6 + O_2 \rightarrow (O_2)^+(PtF_6)^-.$$

As the first ionisation energy of molecular oxygen (1176 kJ) is almost the same as that of xenon (1167 kJ) it was realised this element appeared to be within the oxidising range of platinum hexafluoride. When the deep red platinum hexafluoride vapour was mixed with an excess of xenon gas at room temperature an immediate yellow precipitate of xenon hexafluoroplatinate(v), $Xe^+(PtF_6)^-$, was formed. Further research into the action of hexafluorides on xenon suggested that it formed a fluoride or fluorides. The first of these compounds was formed by heating five volumes of fluorine with one of xenon to 400 °C in a nickel can, followed by rapid cooling in water, when white crystals of xenon tetrafluoride, XeF_4, were deposited. Samples of this compound were also produced by passing fluorine and xenon into a nickel tube at dull red heat. Xenon hexafluoride XeF_6 was prepared by heating xenon to 300 °C with a large excess of fluorine under 60 atmosphere pressure. A difluoride has also been prepared.

At room temperature all three xenon fluorides are white crystalline solids. The hexafluoride is the most volatile and melts at 46 °C to a yellow liquid. Unlike the tetrafluoride the hexafluoride cannot be stored in silica vessels as it rapidly reacts to produce xenon oxide tetrafluoride—a compound prepared more effectively by simply mixing the hexafluoride with an equimolar quantity of water,

$$2XeF_6 + SiO_2 \rightarrow SiF_4 + 2XeOF_4,$$
$$XeF_6 + H_2O \rightarrow 2HF + XeOF_4.$$

Complete hydrolysis of the hexafluoride or tetrafluoride leads to the formation of xenon trioxide, a colourless non-volatile violently explosive crystalline solid with the molecular formula XeO_3,

$$6XeF_4 + 12H_2O \rightarrow 4Xe + 2XeO_3 + 3O_2 + 24HF,$$
$$XeF_6 + 3H_2O \rightarrow XeO_3 + 6HF.$$

A tetrachloride and a dichloride of krypton have also been prepared, the former by passing an electric discharge through a mixture of krypton and fluorine at the temperature of liquid nitrogen. It is a colourless solid but is much less stable than XeF_4 and rapidly decomposes into its elements at 60 °C. Radon also appears to form compounds with fluorine.

The compound $Na_4XeO_6 . 8H_2O$ has been reported from xenon.

Structure

The low melting point and easy volatility of the noble-gas fluorine compounds is indicative of covalent binding. Moreover, information about the shapes of the different molecules accumulated so far, is consistent with

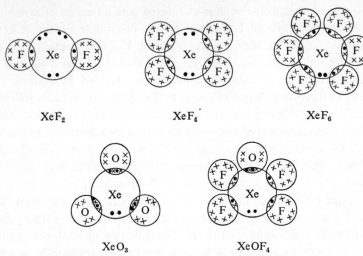

XeF_2 XeF_4 XeF_6

XeO_3 $XeOF_4$

Fig. 109. Electronic formulae of some noble gas compounds.

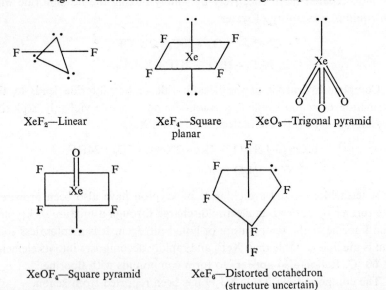

XeF_2—Linear XeF_4—Square planar XeO_3—Trigonal pyramid

$XeOF_4$—Square pyramid XeF_6—Distorted octahedron (structure uncertain)

Fig. 110. Molecular structure of some noble gas compounds.

the shapes predicted by the simple electron-pair repulsion theory (p. 143). Thus, Fig. 109 shows the structures electronically. According to the electron-pair repulsion theory these molecules will adopt the shapes shown in Fig. 110.

Exercises

1. The elements of Group 0 have been termed *rare*, *inert* and *noble*. What are the merits and demerits of each of these names?
2. How far do the properties of the noble gases correspond to their position in the Periodic Table?
3. Write an account of the isolations, properties, and uses of the noble gases.
4. Give an account of the experimental observations which led to the discovery of the noble gases, and describe a chemical method of preparing crude argon from air. Comment on the importance of the noble gas group in the study of the periodic classification of the elements and the understanding of atomic structures. The atomic numbers of the inert gases are He, 2; Ne, 10; Ar, 18; Kr, 36; Xe, 54. (W)
5. Give an account of the way in which a knowledge of the properties and electronic structures of the rare gases has been of use in advancing our understanding of valency and the periodic system of the elements. (O & C)

19

HYDROGEN, WATER AND HYDROGEN PEROXIDE

Hydrogen

According to some theories hydrogen is the starting material from which all the matter in the universe is composed. Elements of higher atomic weight are believed to have been formed by nuclear transformations occurring in stars. About 90% of the matter in the known universe is hydrogen and at the temperatures prevailing in stars (about 10^8 °C) thermonuclear reactions are certainly feasible, and indeed they can readily be used to account for a source of stellar energy, e.g. the sun. Hydrogen is widely distributed on earth but almost entirely in combination with other elements. It is, however, far less abundant in the earth's crust than it is in the universe as a whole.

Position in the Periodic Table

Hydrogen is unique. There is no compelling reason for placing it in any particular Group of the Periodic Table. Like the elements of Group IA (alkali metals) the hydrogen atom has only one valence electron. On the other hand, like the elements of Group VIIB (halogens) the hydrogen atom is only one electron short of gaining the electronic configuration of a noble gas, i.e. helium. It is interesting to note that the electronegativity of hydrogen (2.1) lies between that of boron and of carbon and is appreciably different from that of lithium (0.97) and also of fluorine (4.1).

Hydrogen shows little tendency to form simple ions. The H^+ ion is formed only in discharge tubes, and the H^- ion is formed only when hydrogen is combined with one of the highly electropositive elements of Group IA or Group IIA. The hydrated proton, H_3O^+, is, however, a commonly occurring complex ion of hydrogen.

In the main, hydrogen tends to combine covalently with other elements. This is in contrast to the behaviour of the Group IA metals whose compounds are largely ionic in character. But it shows similarity to the Group VIIB elements as they form covalent compounds with non-metals and the less electropositive metals. Also, with the more electropositive metals the Group VII B element is present as the halide ion, i.e. F^-, Cl^-, Br^-, I^- (cf. H^-).

Furthermore, like the halogens, hydrogen is a non-metal and occurs in the elementary state as a diatomic molecule containing a single bond.

General features

Under ordinary conditions hydrogen is not particularly reactive owing to the stability of the hydrogen molecule which must be dissociated before reaction will occur (for dissociation energy, see p. 499). Combinations involving hydrogen may be broadly classified as follows, depending on the fate of the hydrogen atom:

(1) electron loss producing the hydroxonium ion H_3O^+ (see below);

(2) electron gain producing the negative hydrogen ion H^-;

(3) electron pairing and covalent bond formation.

Loss of an electron by a hydrogen atom uncovers the atomic nucleus, which in this case is a single proton H^+. Such a particle with no electron cloud and a radius about 100 000 times smaller than an alkali metal atom is incapable of independent existence in ordinary chemical reactions and is usually present as the hydroxonium ion H_3O^+. A considerable amount of energy is required to separate the single electron from a hydrogen atom, and even in combination with the most powerfully electronegative elements (i.e. F, O and N) hydrogen is covalently bound. However, hydrogen combined to a strongly electron attracting atom or group of atoms, has an appreciable partial positive charge so that in aqueous solution it may separate as a hydrated proton, H_3O^+; normally the molecule of water of hydration is omitted, and the hydroxonium ion is abbreviated to H^+, it being understood that in solution this particle is always hydrated, just as Na^+, Ca^{2+} and Al^{3+} are hydrated.

Process (2) above is exothermic, but the energy released is not as great as the energy required to dissociate the hydrogen molecule and withdraw an electron from an atom of a different element. However, when hydrogen reacts with one of the metals of Group I A or II A there is an overall excess of energy (evolved as heat) owing to the formation of an ionic crystal lattice. Consequently only when hydrogen combines with the very strongly electropositive elements does it form the hydride ion H^-.

As two electrons are sufficient to complete the K shell the covalency of hydrogen is limited to one.

Hydrogen covalently bound to an atom of a strongly electronegative element (F, O or N) is able to form a weaker bond (a hydrogen bond, see p. 107) with another atom on which there is a region of high electron density, e.g. a fluorine, oxygen or nitrogen atom. The hydrogen difluoride anion $(F—H \cdots F)^-$ illustrates this phenomenon. Under these circumstances, hydrogen shows an apparent valency of two.

Occurrence

Water is the best known and most widely distributed compound of hydrogen. Living matter generally contains some combined hydrogen and it also occurs in natural petroleum and coal. On heating coal in the absence of air the gas evolved contains about 50% hydrogen.

Industrial preparation

1. From Hydrocarbons. In countries like the U.K. which have ample supplies of natural gas (methane) this is the most economical starting material.

Steam reacts with methane at high temperatures:

$$CH_4 + H_2O \rightleftharpoons CO + 3H_2; \quad \Delta H = +206 \text{ kJ mol}^{-1}.$$

An excess of steam, a nickel catalyst and high temperature (750 °C) are used to favour a high equilibrium yield of hydrogen. Then by leading the gaseous mixture at about 500 °C over a suitable catalyst (e.g. a mixture of iron, chromium and cobalt oxides) the carbon monoxide will reduce steam to hydrogen and become oxidised to carbon dioxide in the process,

$$CO + H_2O \rightleftharpoons CO_2 + H_2; \quad \Delta H \text{ negative.}$$

Carbon dioxide can be removed by absorbing it in hot potassium carbonate solution under pressure. Remaining traces of carbon dioxide and any unreacted carbon monoxide can be eliminated by washing the gas with an ammoniacal solution of copper(I) acetate, the hydrogen remaining being sufficiently pure for most purposes. There is a similar process starting with naptha.

2. From water gas (Bosch Process). Steam is reduced to hydrogen by passing it through a stack of coke at 1000 °C. At the same time this oxidises the coke to carbon monoxide which escapes from the converter together with the hydrogen as a gaseous mixture called *water gas*

$$C + H_2O \rightarrow CO + H_2; \quad \Delta H \text{ positive.}$$

The procedure for isolating the hydrogen is then similar to that described above.

Laboratory preparation

1. *Displacement by metals.* As explained on p. 212, metallic elements with a more negative standard electrode potential than hydrogen will displace it from water, acids and aqueous alkalis provided that their hydrogen overpotential is not too high (e.g. Pb) and that the surface of the metal does not become coated with a protective film. In all these cases the metal reduces the H^+ ions present in solution, e.g.

$$2H^+ + 2Na \rightarrow H_2 \uparrow + 2Na^+.$$

Generally hydrogen is displaced from water by sodium amalgam (p. 305) as the pure metal reacts too violently. Alternatively sodium may be added to methanol or ethanol in preference to water as they give a steadier and less hazardous reaction,

$$2C_2H_5OH + 2Na \rightarrow 2C_2H_5O^- + 2Na^+ + H_2 \uparrow$$

Ethanol   Ethoxide
ion

(this is a convenient way of disposing of sodium residues).

Hydrogen is usually prepared in the laboratory from granulated zinc and dilute sulphuric acid. If required pure, the gas is bubbled through concentrated potassium permanganate solution to remove any reducing gases, e.g. H_2S, SO_2, then through silver nitrate solution which reacts with any arsine, AsH_3, or phosphine, PH_3, produced from the impurities in the zinc. Water vapour and any remaining traces of acidic gases are removed by passing the gas over solid potassium hydroxide. Iron filings, tin and magnesium are other metals which are commonly used. Hydrochloric acid is equally effective, but as nitric acid is an oxidising agent, it tends to react with the displaced hydrogen and so little is evolved except in the action of very dilute nitric acid on magnesium or manganese.

2. *Thermal decomposition of steam.* On strong heating steam decomposes to a slight but measurable extent,

$$2H_2O \rightleftharpoons 2H_2 + O_2.$$

However, in accordance with Le Chatelier's principle, if the oxygen is removed from the equilibrium the reaction proceeds so as to produce more oxygen and correspondingly increases the percentage of hydrogen. Therefore, steam decomposes appreciably when in contact with a strongly heated element capable of oxide formation under the prevailing conditions. In practice steam is led over red hot iron or white hot coke (p. 284),

$$3Fe + 4H_2O \rightleftharpoons Fe_3O_4 + 4H_2.$$

This process has also been used on the large scale.

3. Hydrolysis of hydrides. The salt-like hydrides of the alkali and alkaline earth-metals all contain the hydride ion H^- which is rapidly hydrolysed by cold water:

$$H^- + H-OH \rightarrow H-H + OH^-.$$

Physical properties

Hydrogen is the lightest known gas. It is colourless, odourless and almost insoluble in water (about as soluble as nitrogen, see p. 420). The hydrogen molecule is non-polar and as is to be expected for such a simple molecule, the intermolecular forces of attraction are very weak, and the melting and boiling points are correspondingly low. Hydrogen has the highest diffusion rate of all gases.

Physical properties of hydrogen

Melting point	$-257.3\ ^{\circ}C$
Boiling point	$-252.8\ ^{\circ}C$
Solubility ($cm^3/100\ cm^3$ at 20 °C)	1.8
Density (at s.t.p.)	$0.08987\ g\ l^{-1}$
Critical temperature	$-239.9\ ^{\circ}C$

Chemical properties

1. Combustion. Hydrogen burns in air with an almost invisible pale blue flame to form water. It does not support combustion.

2. Combustion with non-metals. Under ordinary conditions only fluorine combines spontaneously with hydrogen. Sunlight catalyses the combination with chlorine. Oxygen combines with hydrogen only after ignition. Bromine, sulphur and iodine react with hydrogen only on heating and there is no appreciable combination with nitrogen without the presence of a catalyst (more details on p. 427).

3. Combination with metals. All the metals in Groups IA and IIA, with the exception of beryllium, combine directly with hydrogen on heating to form an ionic hydride. In general there is no direct combination between hydrogen and any of the remaining metals. Interactions do occur, however, owing to the formation of *interstitial hydrides* (p. 262).

4. Reducing action. Oxides of the less strongly electropositive metals are reduced by heating in a current of hydrogen, e.g.

$$CuO + H_2 \rightarrow H_2O + Cu.$$

As the oxide ions are converted to molecules of steam by the hydrogen, the electrons transferred reduce the metal ions,

$$O^{2-} + H—H \rightarrow H—O—H + 2e,$$
$$Cu^{2+} + 2e \rightarrow Cu.$$

The oxides of sodium, potassium, calcium, magnesium, aluminium and zinc are unaffected by heating in hydrogen below 1000 °C (see p. 185).

Whereas a reduction is not usually effected by a stream of ordinary gaseous hydrogen, if the hydrogen is generated in the solution to be reduced (i.e. nascent hydrogen) it produces strongly reducing conditions. For instance, a solution of iron(III) sulphate is reduced to iron(II) sulphate by adding iron filings and dilute sulphuric acid. As hydrogen gas bubbles off at the same time *two* electron absorbing processes are proceeding simultaneously, i.e.

$$Fe^{3+} + e \rightarrow Fe^{2+},$$
$$2H^+ + 2e \rightarrow H_2.$$

In the acid the metal furnishes an electron-releasing process,

$$Fe \rightarrow Fe^{2+} + 2e.$$

Although the reducing action of nascent hydrogen is not yet fully understood it seems certain that the metal used to displace the hydrogen is of primary importance. A solution of a chromium(III) salt in dilute acid is reduced to chromium(II) ($Cr^{3+} \rightarrow Cr^{2+}$) by the addition of zinc whereas the addition of iron or tin will not effect the reduction; facts wholly consistent with the standard electrode potential of these metals in acid solution. Thus it is suggested that reductions of this type are determined by the ease with which the dissolving metal can transfer electrons to the ions to be reduced, i.e. on the electropositivity of the metal, and not on the state of the hydrogen. The role of the hydrogen is obscure and it appears to take no part in the reaction.

Atomic hydrogen

Molecules of hydrogen are dissociated into atoms by striking an electric arc between tungsten electrodes in hydrogen gas at atmospheric pressure. Atomic hydrogen is an active reducing agent and rapidly converts many elements to the hydride, e.g.

$$S \rightarrow H_2S, \quad I \rightarrow HI, \quad Sb \rightarrow SbH_3.$$

It also reduces many metallic oxides, chlorides and sulphides to the metal.

As the atoms of hydrogen recombine (iron as well as other metals catalyse the recombination) the energy required to dissociate the molecules 432 kJ mole^{-1} (103 kcal mole^{-1}) is released. In the atomic hydrogen torch a jet of hydrogen is blown through the electric arc on to the metal to be welded, so great is the evolution of heat as the atoms recombine at the surface of the metal that it fuses. As the hydrogen produces an inert atmosphere and strongly reducing conditions, it prevents the hot metal oxidising.

Uses

About half a million tons of hydrogen are consumed annually:

(1) *Ammonia (p. 427) and nitric acid (p. 447)* account for over half the hydrogen used.

(2) *Methanol* is produced on the very large scale by passing a mixture of carbon monoxide and hydrogen, obtained from the steam reforming of natural gas or naptha, over a copper catalyst at 200–300 °C and 50 atmospheres pressure,

$$CO + 2H_2 \rightarrow CH_3OH.$$

(3) *Margarine* and certain cooking fats are obtained from animal and vegetable oils such as whale oil and olive oil. The oil is heated in the presence of finely divided nickel and hydrogen is blown through the oil under pressure. Under these conditions hydrogen adds to the double bonds in the carbon chain of the oil molecules. This has the effect of raising the melting point of the oil so that on cooling it becomes solid.

Part of the carbon chain
in the oil molecule
showing the double bond

Addition of hydrogen
converts the double bond
into an ordinary single bond

(4) *Organic chemicals* such as cyclohexanol, aniline, alcohols, cyclo-hexylamine and nylon 66 are produced on the large scale by processes using hydrogen.

(5) *Airships and balloons* are sometimes filled with hydrogen. However, although it is the lightest gas, its inflammability is a dangerous shortcoming.

(6) *Welding* is frequently carried out with an oxy-hydrogen flame or an atomic hydrogen torch.

Deuterium and tritium

Hydrogen exhibits isotopy. Besides ordinary hydrogen which is called *protium* in this context, there are two other isotopes called *deuterium*, symbol D and *tritium*, symbol T, respectively. In no other case are the isotopes of an element distinguished by individual names. This emphasises the special circumstances relating to the isotopy of hydrogen. The nuclear constitution of the three isotopes is illustrated below:

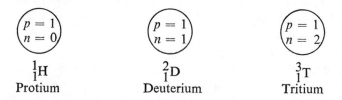

$$\begin{array}{ccc} p=1 & p=1 & p=1 \\ n=0 & n=1 & n=2 \end{array}$$

| $_1^1\text{H}$ | $_1^2\text{D}$ | $_1^3\text{T}$ |
| Protium | Deuterium | Tritium |

Thus the deuterium and tritium atoms respectively have nearly two and three times the mass of a protium atom. It is because their masses are so exceptionally different from one another, more so than in any other example of isotopy, that the isotopes of hydrogen are so specially significant. Deuterium occupies one part in 6400 of naturally occurring hydrogen. Tritium atoms are radioactive (half-life 12.5 years) and therefore do not occur in any appreciable amount in naturally occurring hydrogen compounds or the hydrogen generated from them.

Properties of hydrogen determined by the nature of the electron cloud are the same for protium and deuterium. Besides the simple diatomic molecules H_2 and D_2 natural hydrogen also contains the *mixed* molecule HD. These differ only in those properties which depend on mass, e.g. the boiling point of deuterium is 3.3 °C higher than that of hydrogen, its rate of diffusion is slower and its rate of reaction is also slower than that of hydrogen.

Deuterium oxide, D_2O, better known as *heavy water*, is obtained as a residue after the prolonged electrolysis of ordinary water, as under suitable conditions protium is discharged roughly six times more readily than deuterium. Large quantities of almost pure deuterium oxide are produced in Norway where the enormous quantities of electricity required are supplied cheaply owing to the abundance of hydro-electric power. Heavy water has a greater density than ordinary water, and in general there are small but significant differences in all their physical properties.

Physical properties of H_2O *and* D_2O

	H_2O	D_2O
Boiling point (°C)	100	101.42
Melting point (°C)	0	3.82
Density at 20 °C (g cm⁻³)	0.998	1.105
Temperature of maximum density (°C)	4	11.6

The chemical behaviour of deuterium oxide is qualitatively identical to that of ordinary water but the increased mass leads to slower rates of reaction. Generally deuterium compounds have a lower reactivity than their corresponding hydrogen compound.

When hydrochloric acid is added to heavy water there is an instantaneous *exchange reaction* between the deuterium and protium,

$$H^+ + D—O—D \rightleftharpoons D^+ + H—O—D.$$

Any hydrogen atom capable of ionising in aqueous solution will enter into exchange reactions of this type with heavy water, e.g. when ammonium chloride is dissolved in heavy water:

$$\begin{bmatrix} H \\ | \\ H—N—H \\ | \\ H \end{bmatrix}^+ + D—\overset{..}{O}: \rightleftharpoons H—\overset{H}{\underset{H}{N}}: + \begin{bmatrix} D—\overset{..}{O}—D \\ | \\ H \end{bmatrix}^+$$

$$\rightleftharpoons \begin{bmatrix} D \\ | \\ H—N—H \\ | \\ H \end{bmatrix}^+ + D—\overset{..}{O}:, \text{ etc.}$$

$NH_2D_2^+$, NHD_3^+ and ND_4^+ ions are formed similarly, showing that all four hydrogens of the ammonium ion are identical.

Uses

(1) *Nuclear reactors.* Fast neutrons emitted during the fission of ^{235}U are too highly energetic to sustain a *chain reaction*, but on passing through deuterium oxide they are slowed down to energies at which they are capable of causing the disintegration of other ^{235}U nuclei. Furthermore, deuterium diminishes the number of effective neutrons to a smaller extent than does protium. Because of these properties deuterium oxide is used as a *moderator* in nuclear reactors.

(2) *Reaction mechanisms* have been followed successfully by using deuterium as an *isotopic tracer* (p. 42) and also by exchange reactions involving deuterium atoms.

(3) *Formation of other deutero-compounds* is easily accomplished with heavy water, e.g. deutero-sulphuric acid and deutero-acetylene,

$$D_2O + SO_3 \to D_2SO_4,$$
$$CaC_2 + 2D_2O \to Ca^{2+}(OD^-)_2 + C_2D_2 \uparrow.$$

Water

Much of the chemistry of water has been dealt with in chs. 14 and 17 as well as in other places in the text.

Physical properties

A comparison of the physical properties of water and the other hydrides of Group VIB is given on p. 266. Unusual properties of water include:

(1) A remarkably high melting point and boiling point for a covalent compound of such low molecular weight (p. 267).

(2) A maximum density at 4 °C.

(3) High specific heat and heats of fusion and vaporisation.

(4) High dielectric constant (p. 105).

All these properties are a consequence of the dipolar nature of the V-shaped H_2O molecule (p. 105).

Chemical properties

Water shows a wide variety of reactions. The term *hydrolysis* is frequently used to describe reactions in which it is a principal reagent. For convenience a brief summary of the more important reactions of water described elsewhere in the text is given below.

1. Dissociation. Although water is extremely stable slight ionic dissociation does occur at ordinary temperatures (see p. 214),

$$2H_2O \rightleftharpoons H_3O^+ + OH^-.$$

At temperatures above 1000 °C steam dissociates slightly into hydrogen and oxygen and this is an important factor in accounting for the reaction of steam with hot metals (see p. 285).

2. Action with elements (see p. 211).

3. Hydrolysis of salts (see p. 243).

4. Decomposition of binary compounds (see p. 264).

Hardness of water

When water is agitated with soap a lather is produced. Sodium stearate, $C_{17}H_{35}COO^-Na^+$, is a typical soap. Water derived from natural sources such as springs, rivers and wells usually contains dissolved solids. Principally these dissolved solids are the hydrogen carbonates and sulphates of calcium and magnesium. Calcium and magnesium stearate are both insoluble in water so that when soap is agitated with water containing Ca^{2+} or Mg^{2+} ions they precipitate out as a curdy scum,

$$Ca^{2+} + 2C_{17}H_{35}COO^- \rightarrow (C_{17}H_{35}COO^-)_2Ca^{2+} \downarrow.$$

The total hardness of water is made up of two types: *temporary* and *permanent*. Temporary hardness can be removed by boiling. This is because it is caused by the hydrogen carbonates of calcium and magnesium which decompose in boiling water, precipitating Ca^{2+} and Mg^{2+} ions from solution as the corresponding carbonate,

$$Ca^{2+} + 2HCO_3^- \rightarrow CaCO_3 \downarrow + H_2O + CO_2 \uparrow.$$

Permanent hardness is that hardness which is not removed by boiling and is due to the presence of soluble salts (other than hydrogen carbonates) of calcium and magnesium, usually the sulphates.

The use of a hard water in the domestic supply increases the quantity of soap used in washing. It also forms a *scale* or *fur* on the inside surface of kettles, hot-water pipes, boilers, etc. This is because the hydrogen carbonates in solution are decomposed on boiling to give the corresponding carbonate, which being insoluble precipitates out and accumulates as an adhering deposit on the walls of the container. Besides the possibility of restricting the inside diameter of pipes and eventually blocking them, because the scale is a poor conductor of heat it reduces the heat conducting properties of the metal.

Enormous quantities of water are used as a raw material in industry. Here the degree of softening and purification depends on circumstances. Clearly water supplied to steam boilers needs to have the temporary hardness removed to prevent scaling; whereas cooling water would need no purification.

Several methods exist for removing hardness:

1. Boiling the water. This removes only temporary hardness and is uneconomical.

2. Addition of slaked lime. Calcium hydroxide reacts with calcium hydrogen carbonate precipitating calcium carbonate,

$$Ca(HCO_3)_2 + Ca(OH)_2 \rightarrow 2CaCO_3 \downarrow + 2H_2O.$$

This is known as *Clark's method* of softening. A quantity of calcium hydroxide calculated to react exactly with the calcium in solution is added to the water to be softened. Excess calcium hydroxide is to be avoided as it introduces Ca^{2+} ions into the water and thus makes it hard again. Calcium hydroxide also removes magnesium hydrogen carbonate from solution. This method does not remove permanent hardness.

3. Addition of sodium carbonate (washing soda). The carbonates of the Ca^{2+} and Mg^{2+} ions in solution precipitate out on addition of sodium carbonate. Sodium ions left in solution have no effect on soap and so the method removes both temporary and permanent hardness.

4. Calgon softening. Water used for industrial processes is sometimes softened with a salt called sodium hexametaphosphate which is usually marketed under the name Calgon. This material ionises in water to give a complex anion which contains sodium,

$$(NaPO_3)_6 \rightleftharpoons 2Na^+ + Na_4P_6O_{18}{}^{2-}.$$

This complex anion has the ability to absorb a Ca^{2+} ion in place of two Na^+ ions which are released into the water:

$$Ca^{2+} + Na_4P_6O_{18} \rightleftharpoons 2Na^+ + CaNa_2P_6O_{18}{}^{2-}.$$

As this process absorbs the Ca^{2+} ions and no scum is formed it is particularly useful for water softening in laundries.

5. Ion-exchange resins. Just as it is possible for Ca^{2+} ions to displace Na^+ ions from the complex phosphate anions in Calgon, so other materials (known as ion-exchange resins) can also absorb Ca^{2+} ions with the release of Na^+ ions or H^+ ions (i.e. H_3O^+ ions in solution). The essential difference between these materials and Calgon is that they are giant organic molecules to which acidic groups, e.g. carboxyl, –COOH, are attached. Granules of the resin are packed into a column through which the hard water is passed. The Ca^{2+} ions are absorbed and H_3O^+ ions, for instance, are released in their place. Various resins may be produced. The type described so far are known as cation-exchangers but anion-exchangers are also known in which $SO_4{}^{2-}$ or Cl^- ions can be replaced by OH^- ions, for instance.

A hard water may not only be softened but completely demineralised and used instead of distilled water by first passing down a column of cation-exchanger, which will remove all the Ca^{2+}, Mg^{2+} and Na^+ ions from solution and replace them with an equivalent quantity of H_3O^+ ions. If this water is next led through an anion-exchanger OH^- ions are exchanged for the Cl^- and SO_4^{2-} ions left in solution. The OH^- and H_3O^+ ions combine to form water and thus foreign ions are completely eliminated.

After a time the resin becomes exhausted and is no longer able to exchange ions with the water. Cation-exchange resins can be regenerated with hydrogen ions by steeping in acid, or with Na^+ ions by steeping in sodium chloride solution. It is then washed free of these solutions before use. Similarly anion-exchange resins can be regenerated with sodium hydroxide solution.

Permutit, a naturally occurring zeolite is also an ion-exchanger. This consists of an interlocking three-dimensional lattice of aluminium, oxygen and silicon atoms which make up an alumino-silicate anion throughout which Na^+ ions are regularly dispersed. When a hard water is passed over granules of permutit (designated by Z) the Ca^{2+} and Mg^{2+} ions are replaced by Na^+ ions and the water is softened:

$$Ca^{2+} + Na_2Z \rightarrow CaZ + 2Na^+,$$

$$Mg^{2+} + Na_2Z \rightarrow MgZ + 2Na^+.$$

A concentrated solution of sodium chloride can be used to regenerate the permutit when it is exhausted:

$$2Na^+ \text{ (excess)} + CaZ \rightarrow Na_2Z + Ca^{2+}.$$

Composition

1. Volumetric composition of steam. It is found by experiment that hydrogen and oxygen combine together in the proportion of 2:1 by volume. By conducting the experiment above the boiling point of water so that the steam does not condense it is found to occupy two-thirds of the total volume of original gases under the same conditions of temperature and pressure.

2 volumes of hydrogen + 1 volume of oxygen → 2 volumes of steam.

It follows from Avogadro's hypothesis that

2 molecules of hydrogen + 1 molecule of oxygen → 2 molecules of steam.

Given that hydrogen and oxygen both have diatomic molecules, 1 molecule of steam will contain 2 atoms of hydrogen and 1 atom of oxygen. Thus, the molecular formula of steam is H_2O.

2. Gravimetric composition of water. The proportions by weight in which hydrogen and oxygen combine was established notably by Dumas in 1842 and then more accurately by Morley in the 1890's. From their results the empirical formula H_2O was obtained for water.

Hydrogen peroxide, H_2O_2

Hydrogen forms two oxides: water and the much less stable hydrogen peroxide.

Laboratory preparation

In general any true peroxide will yield hydrogen peroxide when treated with a mineral acid. Usually hydrated barium peroxide is stirred into ice-cold dilute sulphuric acid,

$$BaO_2 + H_2SO_4 \rightarrow BaSO_4 \downarrow + H_2O_2.$$

The residue of barium sulphate and unreacted barium peroxide is filtered off and a dilute solution of hydrogen peroxide remains. Dilute orthophosphoric acid may be used in place of the sulphuric acid.

Concentration up to about 60 % H_2O_2 can be achieved by evaporation from a smooth porcelain dish on a water bath. Provided the temperature does not rise much above 70 °C decomposition of the hydrogen peroxide is only slight. Distillation under reduced pressure can increase the concentration to about 90 % H_2O_2, when it is a colourless syrupy liquid.

Industrial preparation

Large quantities of hydrogen peroxide are made by the electrolysis of an acidified solution of ammonium sulphate, i.e. ammonium hydrogen sulphate. At the platinum anode the HSO_4^- ion is oxidised to peroxodisulphate, $S_2O_8^{2-}$,

$$2HSO_4^- \rightarrow S_2O_8^{2-} + 2H^+ + 2e.$$

At the lead cathode hydrogen is evolved,

$$2H^+ + 2e \rightarrow H_2 \uparrow.$$

When the peroxodisulphate solution is distilled under reduced pressure hydrolysis occurs,

$$S_2O_8^{2-} + 2H_2O \rightarrow 2HSO_4^- + H_2O_2,$$

and an aqueous solution containing about 30 % hydrogen peroxide distils over.

Physical properties

Pure hydrogen peroxide is a colourless, odourless syrupy liquid. It boils at 152 °C, melts at -1.7 °C and has a density of 1.4 g cm^{-3}.

Hydrogen peroxide has a covalent molecule and is dipolar. Its structure is shown in Fig. 111.

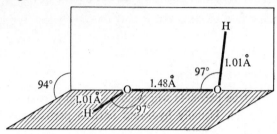

Fig. 111. Diagram of a hydrogen peroxide molecule.

Chemical properties

1. Decomposition. Pure hydrogen peroxide is unstable and the decomposition is catalysed by light and by a wide variety of materials which include dust, finely divided metals, manganese(IV) oxide, alkalis, etc.; sometimes the decomposition is explosive.

Aqueous solutions of hydrogen peroxide decompose slowly into water and oxygen, more rapidly in the presence of catalysts such as those indicated above, $$2H_2O_2 \rightarrow 2H_2O + O_2 \uparrow.$$

2. Oxidising action. Hydrogen peroxide can act as a powerful oxidising agent, in acid solution it will oxidise iodides to iodine, and iron(II) salts to iron(III):
$$2I^- + H_2O_2 + 2H^+ \rightarrow I_2 + 2H_2O,$$
$$2Fe^{2+} + H_2O_2 + 2H^+ \rightarrow 2Fe^{3+} + 2H_2O.$$

In aqueous solution sulphites and sulphides are oxidised to sulphates, e.g. black lead(II) sulphide is oxidised to lead(II) sulphate,
$$PbS + 4H_2O_2 \rightarrow PbSO_4 + 4H_2O,$$
$$SO_2 + H_2O_2 \rightarrow H_2SO_4.$$

3. Reducing action. Although hydrogen peroxide is an oxidising agent, in the presence of another powerful oxidising agent it sometimes shows reducing properties depending on the conditions. Thus in alkaline conditions iron(III) salts are reduced to iron(II), and silver oxide is reduced to the metal:
$$2Fe^{3+} + H_2O_2 + 2OH^- \rightarrow 2Fe^{2+} + 2H_2O + O_2 \uparrow,$$
$$Ag_2O + H_2O_2 \rightarrow 2Ag + H_2O + O_2 \uparrow.$$

An important reaction occurs in acid solution with potassium permanganate and is used for the estimation of hydrogen peroxide in volumetric analysis,

$$2KMnO_4 + 3H_2SO_4 + 5H_2O_2 \rightarrow K_2SO_4 + 2MnSO_4 + 8H_2O + 5O_2 \uparrow,$$

ionically:

$$2MnO_4^- + 6H^+ + 5H_2O_2 \rightarrow 2Mn^{2+} + 8H_2O + 5O_2 \uparrow.$$

A sensitive test for hydrogen peroxide is to shake it with acidified dilute potassium dichromate solution to which a little ether has been added. On settling out the upper ether layer is coloured blue with peroxochromic acid, $HCrO_5$.

Volume strength

The strength of a solution of hydrogen peroxide is frequently expressed as the number of cubic centimetres of oxygen that 1 cm³ of the solution can liberate at s.t.p. when it decomposes into water and oxygen. From the equation for its decomposition it follows that 68 g of hydrogen peroxide liberate 22.4 litres of oxygen at s.t.p.

Uses

Hydrogen peroxide is a useful household antiseptic and also finds application as a mild bleach, removing the colour from such materials as hair and textiles. Latterly it has found use as a fuel in rocketry.

Exercises

1. Discuss the difficulties encountered in allocating a position to hydrogen in the long form of the Periodic Table. What do you consider to be the best position? Give your reasons.

2. State one laboratory method for preparing hydrogen by displacement with a metal from each of the following: (a) water, (b) an acid, (c) an alkali. Explain why it would be impracticable to use either copper or lead.
    How and under what conditions does hydrogen react with (i) sodium, (ii) sulphur, and (iii) iron(III) sulphate?

3. Explain the term *hardness of water*. Indicate its cause and outline the methods used for its removal.
    Briefly, give the reasons for softening water on the industrial scale.

4. Describe a laboratory method for preparing a dilute solution of hydrogen peroxide. How does it react with the following: (a) sodium hydroxide solution, (b) silver oxide, (c) an acidified solution of potassium permanganate, (d) chromic acid.
    What is the *volume strength* of a normal solution of hydrogen peroxide?

5. Give a concise account of the different types of natural waters. What is meant by the hardness of water and how is it estimated.

   Describe *two* methods employed for the large-scale softening of hard water. (L)

6. Describe the preparation of very pure hydrogen. Discuss the reactions of hydrogen with (i) chlorine, (ii) iodine, (iii) acetylene, (iv) nitrogen. (L)

7. How may a concentrated aqueous solution of hydrogen peroxide be prepared?

   Describe *two* reactions in each case in which hydrogen peroxide reacts as (*a*) an oxidising agent, (*b*) a reducing agent.

   Calculate the concentration in grams per litre of a 10-volume solution of hydrogen peroxide. (C)

8. **Either:** How, and under what conditions, does water react with carbon, chlorine, fluorine and iron? What light is thrown on the chemical character of a metal by its reaction with water?

   Or: Describe, with examples, *three* general types of reaction in which water can take part. Compare the reactions of water with sulphuryl chloride, bismuth(III) chloride and sodium carbonate. (O & C)

9. Outline **one** method for the manufacture of hydrogen from **either** crude oil **or** natural gas. State **two** important uses of hydrogen.

   Give explanations and illustrative reactions for the following statements.
   (i) The hydrides of the elements Na, P, S, Cl, show increasing acidity with increasing atomic number.
   (ii) The hydrides of the elements F, Cl, Br, I, show increasing reducing power with increasing atomic number. (C)

20

GROUP IA: THE ALKALI METALS

Atomic properties of the alkali metals

Element	Symbol	Atomic no.	Atomic weight	Atomic radius (Å)	Ionic radius M⁺ (Å)
Lithium	Li	3	6.94	1.33	0.60
Sodium	Na	11	22.99	1.57	0.95
Potassium	K	19	39.10	2.03	1.33
Rubidium	Rb	37	85.47	2.16	1.48
Caesium	Cs	55	132.91	2.35	1.69
Francium	Fr	87	(223)	—	—

Francium is a short-lived radioactive element about which little more need be known as this stage.

Relationship of Group IA to the Periodic Table

Immediately preceding each alkali metal in atomic number in the Periodic Table there is a noble gas element. In passing from Group 0 to Group IA, i.e. from unreactive non-metal to highly reactive metal, there is the most abrupt change of chemical type in the whole of the Periodic Classification. Group IIA elements are also highly electropositive metals, and their close relationship to the alkali metals is outlined in the Period trends amongst the Main Group elements discussed in part II. The properties of lithium and its compounds are markedly different from those of the other alkali metals, and bear certain resemblances to magnesium. This is an example of the diagonal relationship.

General Group features

In the outermost shell of each alkali metal atom there is only one electron, and the loss of this electron converts the atom into a unipositive ion which has the same electronic configuration as the noble gas which immediately precedes it in the Periodic Classification. Owing to the pronounced screening effect of the noble gas electron structure the outermost electron in the alkali metal atom experiences a greatly reduced electrostatic attraction from the positively charged nucleus (see p. 67 for an account of *effective nuclear charge*). As a consequence, the alkali metal atom has an appreciably larger radius than any of the other atoms in the same Period and the first ionisation energies of the alkali metals are the lowest amongst the elements.

Within the Group there is a progressive increase in atomic radius with increasing atomic number; a factor which will tend to reduce ionisation energies. On the other hand, increasing nuclear charge will tend to increase them. The greater number of electrons between the outermost electron and the nucleus in the heavier atoms will also tend to reduce the ionisation energies by increasing the screening effect. As can be seen in the following table the resultant of these three effects is a progressive decrease in ionisation energies down the Group, at least, as far as caesium, which is therefore the easiest to ionise of all.

Electronic configurations and ionisation energies
($kcal\ mol^{-1}$) of the alkali metals

Element	Electronic configuration	First ionisation energy	Second ionisation energy	Third ionisation energy
Li	2.1	124	1743	2822
Na	2.8.1	118	1090	1652
K	2.8.8.1	100	733	1060
Rb	2.8.18.8.1	96	634	(1084)
Cs	2.8.18.18.8.1	90	548	(807)

(1 kcal = 4.184 kJ)

In order to withdraw an electron from the unipositive ion it would be necessary to disrupt the very stable noble gas electron structure. Consequently, the second ionisation energy is very much greater than the first and effectively prevents the alkali metals from ever showing a greater electrovalency than one. Because the alkali metals form stable ions more readily than any other element they are the most reactive of metals, and because the ease of electron loss increases down the Group so also do their reactivities. However, it is essential to remember that unipositive alkali metal ions are produced in reactions with other elements during which negative ions are also formed, and that the overall reaction is exothermic only because of the large release of energy that occurs when the ions form a crystal lattice or become solvated.

Chemically, the alkali metals are an example of extreme metallic behaviour. Thus their electrode potentials are among the highest of all, and they have a powerful affinity for oxygen and even displace hydrogen from cold water.

Electronegativities and electrode potentials
of the alkali metals

Element	Electro-negativity	Electrode potential M^+/M (V)
Lithium	0.97	-3.04
Sodium	1.01	-2.71
Potassium	0.91	-2.92
Rubidium	0.89	-2.99
Caesium	0.86	-3.04

It follows directly from their very low ionisation energy that the electro-negativities of the alkali metals will be amongst the very lowest. Thus, the compounds of the alkali metals are of an extreme ionic type, and show the characteristic properties associated with ionic binding, particularly so as the Group is descended. With few exceptions, they are all white crystalline solids of high melting point which dissolve in water to give conducting solutions. The highly ionic nature of the binding in the oxides, chlorides, and hydrides is clearly shown by their properties:

Oxides: these are extremely basic and dissolve violently in water to give strongly alkaline solutions.

Chlorides: dissolve in water to give a neutral solution of the simple hydrated ions which can be converted back into the anhydrous salt by evaporation, i.e. no hint of hydrolysis.

Hydrides: are crystalline solids containing the hydride ion, H^-.

The salts of the alkali metals are, as a rule, more soluble in water than those formed by the metals of any other Group in the Periodic Table. In general solubilities vary progressively down the Group. Broadly, the solubilities of the alkali metal salts of strong acids (HI, HNO_3, $HClO_3$) diminish down the Group whereas the salts of weak acids have solubilities which increase down the Group. Furthermore, the solubilities of chlorides, bromides, sulphates and nitrites decrease as far as potassium and then increase to caesium. Thus, apart from the hydroxide and carbonate, potassium salts are generally less soluble than sodium salts.

Lithium and sodium form appreciable numbers of solid hydrates. The hydrates of potassium are much fewer and with rubidium and caesium they are practically non-existent.

The elements
Occurrence

The alkali metals are far too reactive to occur native. Their compounds are widespread, however, generally occurring together, with those of sodium and potassium predominating. These latter two elements are quite abundant, each comprising about 2.5 % of the earth's crust.

Rock salt. Sodium chloride, NaCl, is the most important source of sodium. Extensive deposits, probably formed by evaporation of enclosed bodies of salt water, are found in the United States, France, Germany, and China. Industrially important salt fields in the United Kingdom are found in Cheshire and South Durham.

Chile saltpetre. Sodium nitrate, $NaNO_3$, from the Atacama desert, in northern Chile, is a valuable source of nitrate.

Trona. Sodium sesquicarbonate, $Na_2CO_3.NaHCO_3.2H_2O$ occurs in saline residues with other minerals such as *borax*, $Na_2B_4O_7.10H_2O$.

Carnallite. $KCl.MgCl_2.6H_2O$ is the principal source of potassium and is found in the Stassfurt salt deposits.

Isolation

Before isolating the free metal it is necessary to obtain a pure compound containing it. By crystallising a hot solution of the appropriate mineral it is possible to obtain a pure sodium or potassium compound, e.g. the chloride.

The great affinity of these elements for oxygen makes the reduction of the oxide with carbon impracticable as extremely high temperatures would be required. At present the metals are liberated from the fused chloride by electrolysis. The highly successful Downs process for isolating sodium is typical.

Downs process. Sodium chloride melts at about 800 °C which is close to the boiling point of sodium (883 °C), and sodium vapour ignites spontaneously in air. A more serious obstacle to the electrolysis of the fused chloride is that at the high temperature needed the liberated sodium dissolves in the fused electrolyte, making it a metallic type conductor, and thus brings electrolytic decomposition to an end. To overcome these difficulties, calcium chloride is added to the sodium chloride, and this lowers its melting point to such an extent that the cell can be worked at about 600 °C. Even though three parts of calcium chloride are added to every two parts of sodium chloride, since the minimum voltage needed to cause electrolytic decomposition of calcium chloride at 600 °C is appreciably higher than that for sodium chloride, only minor quantities of calcium are set free, and as it is almost immiscible in the molten sodium and much denser it is readily separated.

In a typical cell a cylindrical steel container about 8 ft high and 4–5 ft in diameter is fitted with a large vertical graphite rod which serves as the anode. Two semi-circular steel plates concentric with and surrounding the anode act as the cathode. A cylindrical steel gauze diaphragm is suspended between the electrodes to prevent the sodium discharged at the cathode coming in contact with the chlorine evolved at the anode and reforming sodium chloride,

process at the anode $\qquad Cl^- \rightarrow Cl + e,$

$$Cl + Cl \rightarrow Cl_2;$$

process at the cathode $\qquad Na^+ + e \rightarrow Na.$

Sodium is less dense than the electrolyte and rises to the surface from where it is led into an external reservoir. The chlorine is led off and collected as an important by-product. By feeding purified dry sodium chloride on to the electrolyte the cell may be kept running continuously.

Physical properties

Alkali metals show typical metallic character by their ability to conduct heat and electricity and their silver-white lustre when freshly cut. However, their hardness, melting point, boiling point and density are all very much lower than the average values for metals. As each alkali metal atom has only one electron in the outermost shell and an exceptionally large atomic radius weak metallic binding results and the elements are therefore soft, low melting and low boiling. Alkali metal atoms have volumes so much larger than the average value for metals that much less mass can be packed into a unit volume and low densities result.

There is a fairly uniform change in all the properties as the Group is descended. Lithium is the hardest; sodium is soft enough to be cut with a penknife and to be extruded as wire through a simple manual press; potassium is putty-like and can easily be moulded.

Physical properties of the alkali metals

Element	Density (g cm^{-3})	m.p. (°C)	b.p. (°C)
Li	0.53	180	1336
Na	0.97	98	883
K	0.86	63.5	759
Rb	1.53	39	700
Cs	1.90	28.5	670

At high temperatures the vapour of each of these elements is completely monatomic. However, just above the boiling point the vapour of each alkali metal contains about 1% of diatomic molecules (Li_2, Na_2, K_2, Rb_2 and Cs_2). This is the most obvious example of covalent binding shown by these elements. The strength of the covalent bond becomes progressively weaker down the Group. The elements all impart a characteristic colour to the bunsen flame, a property associated with the outermost s electron.

Chemical properties

1. Air. Lithium is the least active towards damp air and is tarnished slowly. Sodium and potassium tarnish rapidly; rubidium and caesium catch fire in air. It is usual to store the first three elements under paraffin and the rest *in vacuo*. The behaviour of sodium on exposure to air is typical; a film of the oxide forms and this combines with the moisture of the air to form first the hydroxide then its solution which then slowly absorbs atmospheric carbon dioxide and is converted to the carbonate, so that a white crust of changing composition is gradually built up.

The rapidity with which they are tarnished by air illustrates their great affinity for oxygen.

On combustion in air they all burn to form an oxide. Lithium imparts a carmine colour to the flame. Burning sodium has a characteristic bright yellow flame, and the potassium flame is lilac coloured.

2. Water. All these metals liberate hydrogen from cold water. On descending the Group the reaction becomes increasingly vigorous.

Lithium floats on water, causing a steady evolution of hydrogen, but does not fuse (melting point 180 °C).

Sodium fizzes about on the surface of the water from which it liberates hydrogen. The heat of the reaction causes the sodium to fuse, but it does not inflame unless its motion is restricted.

Potassium, *rubidium* and *caesium* react with increasing violence, the metals fuse and the heat liberated is even sufficient to ignite the evolved hydrogen, and the metal itself. In each case the hydroxide is also formed, and remains in solution,

$$2M + 2H—O—H \rightarrow 2M^+ + 2OH^- + H_2.$$

3. Combination with non-metals. Those non-metallic elements which have high or moderately high electronegativities, such as the halogens, oxygen, sulphur, phosphorus and hydrogen, combine most actively with the alkali metals. So great is the heat of reaction in some cases that the metal ignites. Lithium is the least active alkali metal. It combines directly with hydrogen only at red heat, whereas sodium will combine at temperatures about 360 °C. Lithium, however, is the only one to combine directly with nitrogen, lithium nitride being formed,

$$6Li + N_2 \rightarrow 2Li_3N \quad \text{(cf. magnesium)}.$$

In all its reactions, potassium is similar to sodium, but it reacts more vigorously. Rubidium and caesium are similar to potassium but even more violent in reaction.

Such is the affinity of these elements for non-metals, they are often used to reduce oxides and chlorides of less electropositive metals (see p. 535).

4. Amalgams. All the alkali metals dissolve in mercury with the evolution of heat to form amalgams. Sodium amalgam (Na/Hg) is a liquid when the proportion of sodium is low and solid when the proportion of sodium is high; it is a useful strong reducing agent.

Uses

Large quantities of sodium are converted into other chemicals, e.g. sodium cyanide, sodium peroxide. Titanium metal and lead tetraethyl (a common 'anti-knock' additive to petrol) are produced commercially by processes involving the use of sodium. Because of its high thermal conductivity and low melting point sodium is used as a coolant in nuclear reactors.

Compounds

Hydrides, MH

Alkali metal hydrides are white crystalline solids best prepared by direct combination of the metal with hydrogen (see p. 263). Each has the sodium chloride lattice structure in which the anion is the hydride ion, H^-. This ion reacts rapidly with any substance capable of furnishing a proton and forms hydrogen gas, e.g. water,

$$H^- + H—OH \rightarrow H—H + OH^-.$$

They all dissociate at high temperatures. Lithium hydride is far more stable than the others and resembles closely the alkaline earth-metal hydrides (see hydrides, p. 262).

Oxides

On heating in oxygen lithium, sodium and potassium burn to form a different oxide in each case:

Element	Monoxide	Peroxide	Superoxide
Lithium	Li_2O	—	—
Sodium	—	Na_2O_2	—
Potassium	—	—	KO_2

Excepting that of lithium, the monoxides of the elements are usually prepared by reducing the nitrate or nitrite with the metal, e.g.

$$2KNO_3 + 10K \rightarrow 6K_2O + N_2.$$

Sodium peroxide is produced commercially by first burning metallic sodium to sodium monoxide in a current of dry air at 200–250 °C, in a rotary tube; and then taking the oxidation a stage further in another rotary tube, by the use of oxygen.

All the oxides are crystalline solids, but the colour deepens down the Group and towards the higher oxides. Lithium and sodium monoxide are white and potassium monoxide like sodium peroxide is whitish yellow; potassium superoxide is yellow. A characteristic property of strongly electropositive metals is the highly ionic nature of their oxides. As a result, the alkali metal oxides are all completely and instantaneously hydrolysed by water. Lithium oxide is hydrolysed quietly in water, but as the Group is descended and the electropositivity of the metal increases the monoxide hydrolyses with increasing violence. The rubidium and caesium compounds inflame and almost explode. The corresponding hydroxide is produced in each case,

$$O^{2-} + H—OH \rightarrow OH^- + OH^-.$$

Sodium peroxide contains the peroxide anion $^-O—O^-$, and is hydrolysed by ice-cold water into a mixed solution of sodium hydroxide and hydrogen peroxide,

$$^-O\!-\!O^- + 2H_2O \rightarrow 2OH^- + H_2O_2.$$

Hydrogen peroxide is unstable in alkaline solution and at higher temperatures it begins to decompose with the evolution of oxygen. Sodium peroxide turns white on exposure to air owing to its conversion into hydroxide and carbonate by atmospheric moisture and carbon dioxide with which it reacts with evolution of oxygen,

$$2\,{}^-O\!-\!O^- + 2CO_2 \rightarrow 2CO_3{}^{2-} + O_2.$$

Potassium superoxide, KO_2, is a compound formed from potassium ions and superoxide ions, $^-O\!-\!O$. It dissolves in cold water with the evolution of oxygen,

$$2[O\!-\!O]^- + 2H_2O \rightarrow 2OH^- + H_2O_2 + O_2.$$

Hydroxides, MOH

The preparation of these compounds by the action of water on the metal or the monoxide is of academic interest only. Lithium, sodium, and potassium hydroxides are all manufactured on a very large scale and widely used as raw materials. The methods used can be divided into two main categories

(1) precipitation reactions;
(2) electrolytic methods.

The principle of the first method is to precipitate out unwanted ions and leave a solution of the alkali. For instance, if potassium carbonate and calcium hydroxide are slurried together, heated and then allowed to settle a solution of potassium hydroxide may be decanted,

$$Ca^{2+} + 2OH^- + 2K^+ + CO_3{}^{2-} \rightleftharpoons CaCO_3 \downarrow + 2K^+ + 2OH^-.$$
$$\text{least}$$
$$\text{soluble}$$

Alkali metal chlorides form conducting solutions, and as these metals are high in the electrochemical series, their ions remain in solution during electrolysis and hydrogen is evolved at the cathode. Preferential discharge of chloride ions enables hydroxyl ions formed by ionisation of the water to accumulate in the solution. Provided the concentration of hydroxyl ions around the anode is kept low not too many are discharged and a dilute solution of the hydroxide is produced. Electrolytic processes for producing these hydroxides are of two principal types:

(1) those using cells with a porous diaphragm between the electrodes so that the liberated chlorine is prevented from coming in contact with the alkaline solution formed at the cathode;

(2) those in which the cathode is a flowing stream of mercury.

The 'mercury cathode' cells serve the same purpose as the 'diaphragm' cells in that as the alkali metal ion discharges it amalgamates with the mercury which then removes it from the vicinity of the liberated chlorine. The amalgam is subsequently decomposed by water in a separate cell. Hydrogen is liberated and a solution of the alkali metal hydroxide is formed. The mercury is then recirculated. If the products from the anode and cathode are not kept separate they will react to form hypochlorites and chlorates in the following way,

$$Cl_2 + 2OH^- \rightarrow Cl^- + ClO^- + H_2O,$$
$$3Cl_2 + 6OH^- \rightarrow 5Cl^- + ClO_3^- + 3H_2O.$$

The more highly developed industrial countries have a much greater demand for chlorine than for sodium hydroxide, i.e. for such things as organic chlorinations (e.g. production of polyvinyl chloride). This puts the lime-soda process at an economic disadvantage and in the U.K. plants working this process have largely closed down. Even so, were it not for the fact that the surplus sodium hydroxide produced by meeting the current demand for chlorine can be exported, alternative methods of producing sodium hydroxide would be sought.

The lime-soda process. The reaction is reversible and as dilute solutions favour the conversion into sodium hydroxide, sufficient sodium carbonate (soda ash) to give a 10–12 % solution is dissolved in water and heated by passing in steam. Enough calcium oxide (lime) to give a saturated solution of calcium hydroxide and leave a 10 % excess is stirred into this solution. After about 2 hours the solid is allowed to settle, and a liquor containing about 10 % sodium hydroxide is decanted.

The electrolytic method using a mercury cathode cell. The essential part of the cell is a long steel trough. A shallow stream of mercury flows continually along the cell floor, which is inclined for this purpose. A deep layer of purified saturated sodium chlorine solution flows in the same direction. Chlorine is evolved at the graphite anodes which are supported parallel to and just above the mercury surface. Sodium liberated at the flowing cathode forms an amalgam with the mercury and is thus prevented from reacting with the aqueous electrolyte to form an alkaline solution of sodium chloride, or with dissolved chlorine diffusing from the anode. Because of the high hydrogen over-potential at a sodium amalgam surface the voltage required for the discharge of hydrogen ions exceeds that required for the discharge of sodium ions which are therefore discharged preferentially.

The amalgam is led into a separate elongated sloping trough and flows against a counter-current of water. Closely packed grids of iron or graphite float on the surface of the amalgam. Both these materials have a low hydrogen over-voltage and promote decomposition of the amalgam. Hydrogen is evolved and a solution of sodium hydroxide is formed. The sodium hydroxide liquor leaving this secondary cell usually contains about 50% of sodium hydroxide.

The electrolytic method using a diaphragm. Cells of various design are used, but they have a common function, and that is to cause the solution on the anode side of the porous diaphragm to percolate through to the cathode side. The diaphragm is usually a thin sheet of asbestos impregnated with barium sulphate and this prevents the chlorine evolved at the graphite anode passing into the cathode compartment. Chloride ions are discharged preferentially owing to their much greater concentration in the neighbourhood of the anode. Solution diffusing through the diaphragm meets the steel gauze cathode where hydrogen is discharged. This leaves an accumulation of hydroxyl ions in solution. By maintaining the level of electrolyte on the anode side of the cell higher than that on the cathode side this counteracts the migration of hydroxyl ions towards the anode and together with sodium ions they flow through into the cathode compartment and constitute a solution containing 10–12% of sodium hydroxide. Some chloride ions also diffuse through the diaphragm and sodium chloride is the chief impurity of sodium hydroxide (*caustic soda*) produced by this method.

Evaporation and purification of the sodium hydroxide solution. For most industrial purposes, 50% caustic liquor is satisfactory. Diaphragm and lime-soda liquors are evaporated to this concentration under reduced pressure. Impurities such as sodium chloride and sodium carbonate are less soluble in the 50% sodium hydroxide solution than in the 10–12% solution. After evaporation they crystallise out on cooling and can be filtered off. Solid sodium hydroxide is obtained by evaporating to about 70% strength and then driving off the rest of the water by heating to about 500 °C in cast-iron pots.

Properties. These hydroxides are white crystalline solids which melt at moderate temperatures (NaOH, 322 °C) without decomposition. The solids all deliquesce in air and are very soluble in water. The most important feature of these aqueous solutions is the fact that they are strongly alkaline. Moreover, dilute equimolar solutions of these hydroxides have the same alkalinity—there is no increase down the Group as might be expected. This is because such solutions have the same concentration of hydroxyl ions, OH⁻, as a consequence of these highly ionic compounds being completely dissociated under these conditions. The solubility increases down the Group. They dissolve to a lesser extent in organic solvents which are miscible with water, and an ethanolic solution of potassium hydroxide is a useful reagent in organic chemistry. Owing to their highly basic character alkali metal hydroxides are frequently used to absorb acidic gases, e.g. carbon dioxide.

Action of strong alkalis on the elements is fully described in ch. 14, p. 211. Alkali metal hydroxides are used in a great many neutralisation (p. 241) and precipitation reactions.

As a strong base liberates a weak base from its salts alkali metal hydroxides all liberate ammonia from ammonium salts on warming.

$$NH_4^+ + OH^- \rightleftharpoons H - \underset{\underset{H}{|}}{\overset{\overset{H}{|}}{N}} \cdots H - \underset{\underset{H}{|}}{O} \rightleftharpoons H_2O + NH_3.$$

Uses. The following table lists the principal uses of sodium hydroxide in the U.K.

	Approx. annual consumption (in 1000 tons)
Chemicals and dyes	250
Rayon and cellophane	200
Exports	160
Soap and detergents	75
Oil refining	60
Paper and pulp	25
Aluminium production	20
Textile finishing	20

Potassium hydroxide is also principally used in producing other chemicals, e.g. potassium cyanide and potassium permanganate. It is also used in the manufacture of soft soaps.

Chlorides, MCl

Sodium and potassium chlorides occur naturally and are important raw materials. General methods of preparation for soluble salts (p. 240) are all applicable except that the metal and the oxide react too violently with dilute hydrochloric acid for this method to be practicable.

They all form highly ionic transparent cubic crystals, which dissolve easily in water. Sodium chloride is unique, as its solubility increases only very slightly with increasing temperature. Lithium chloride is one of the most deliquescent substances known; the other chlorides in the Group are not deliquescent unless they contain deliquescent impurities such as magnesium chloride; the usual impurity in ordinary domestic salt. Although they all form crystals of similar shape the structure of the lattice of caesium chloride (p. 137) is different from that of the rest, as it is possible to close-pack eight chloride ions around the large Cs^+ ion whereas the smaller cations such as Na^+ can only accommodate six near neighbours. The chemistry of these compounds is essentially the chemistry of the chloride ion, Cl^-.

Uses. Electrolysis of sodium chloride, whether as the fused salt or its aqueous solution, is used to produce sodium, sodium hydroxide, chlorine, sodium hypochlorite and sodium chlorate.

Bromides, MBr

These are produced commercially by special methods. Laboratory methods include those described for chlorides and also the dissolving of bromine in a warm concentrated solution of the hydroxide, i.e.

$$3Br_2 + 6OH^- \rightarrow 5Br^- + BrO_3^- + 3H_2O.$$

This solution of bromide and bromate is evaporated to dryness and the residue is heated with charcoal to convert the bromate to bromide,

$$2BrO_3^- + 3C \rightarrow 2Br^- + 3CO_2.$$

After triturating with water, filtering and evaporating the colourless cubic crystals of the bromide are obtained. The structure of the bromide is the same as that of the chloride.

Iodides, MI

The same general methods used in the preparation of bromides can be applied to the preparation of iodides, which they resemble very closely.

Many polyhalides of alkali metals are known, the most important being the tri-iodides. Lithium and sodium do not form tri-iodides; but iodine dissolves reversibly in potassium iodide solution forming potassium tri-iodide, KI_3,
$$I^- + I—I \rightleftharpoons (I—I—I)^-.$$

Several iodides ordinarily insoluble in water dissolve in potassium iodide solution owing to the formation of complex anions. For example, mercury(II) iodide dissolves in potassium iodide solution,
$$HgI_2 + 2I^- \rightarrow [HgI_4]^-.$$
When made alkaline with potassium hydroxide solution this is *Nessler's reagent*. It gives a yellow colour with traces of ammonia and a brown precipitate with larger quantities.

Sulphides, M_2S

If an aqueous solution of the hydroxide is saturated with hydrogen sulphide the corresponding hydrogen sulphide, MHS, is obtained. Lithium hydrogen sulphide is not stable under ordinary conditions, but $NaHS.3H_2O$ and $2KHS.H_2O$ may be crystallised from solution. To obtain the sulphide, an equivalent amount of the alkali is added to the solution of the hydrogen sulphide and then evaporated. The monosulphides, $Na_2S.9H_2O, K_2S.5H_2O$ separate on crystallisation. The amount of water of crystallisation and the solubility decrease down the Group. They are all highly ionic and are extensively hydrolysed in aqueous solution, evolving hydrogen sulphide and reacting alkaline,
$$S^{2-} + 2H_2O \rightleftharpoons H_2S + 2OH^-.$$

Carbonates, M_2CO_3

The general procedure for preparing these carbonates in the laboratory is to halve a given solution of the hydroxide and saturate one half with carbon dioxide. This produces a solution of the hydrogen carbonate and if the rest of the hydroxide solution is added to this and the solution evaporated crystals of the carbonate will separate.
$$OH^- + CO_2 \rightarrow HCO_3^-,$$
$$HCO_3^- + OH^- \rightarrow CO_3^{2-} + H_2O.$$
Commercially, very large quantities of sodium carbonate are produced by the ammonia-soda process (Solvay process).

The ammonia-soda process. This may be summarised by the following hypothetical equation,
$$2NaCl + CaCO_3 \rightarrow Na_2CO_3 + CaCl_2.$$

As calcium carbonate does not react directly with sodium chloride solution the desired result cannot be obtained in one step. Saturated sodium chloride solution pumped up from flooded salt mines is freed from foreign ions (e.g. Mg^{2+}, Ca^{2+}, Fe^{3+}, Al^{3+}) by precipitating them as carbonates or hydroxides. Ammonia is dissolved in the sodium chloride solution and the ammoniacal liquor is cooled and pumped up to the top of a series of high towers (Solvay towers). Carbon dioxide obtained from the burning of calcium carbonate (limestone) to calcium oxide (lime) is blown under pressure ($2\frac{1}{2}$ atmospheres) into the bottom of some of these towers. The purpose of the ammonia is to displace the equilibrium,

$$CO_2 + H_2O \rightleftharpoons HCO_3^- + H^+,$$

to the right, and so produce a high concentration of HCO_3^- ions, by combining with the H^+ ions ($NH_3 + H^+ \rightarrow NH_4^+$). Carbonation is continued until the solution is saturated with hydrogen carbonate ions. At this stage Na^+, HCO_3^-, NH_4^+, and Cl^- ions all exist in solution together at about 20–40 °C and their different concentrations are such that 70–75% of the sodium ions crystallise out as the hydrogen carbonate. As this is accompanied by the evolution of a considerable amount of heat it is necessary to cool the towers,

$$Na^+ + Cl^- + NH_4^+ + HCO_3^- \rightleftharpoons NaHCO_3 \downarrow + NH_4^+ + Cl^-.$$

The hydrogen carbonate precipitate is separated from the mother liquor on rotary filters where it is washed reasonably free of ammonium chloride. It is then fed into large rotary driers, called calciners, where heat decomposes the sodium hydrogen carbonate to sodium carbonate (*soda ash*), steam and carbon dioxide. The carbon dioxide is cooled, washed and fed back into the Solvay towers for reabsorption

$$2NaHCO_3 \rightarrow Na_2CO_3 + H_2O + CO_2.$$

The residue of lime from the burning of the limestone is made into an aqueous suspension and added to the solution of ammonium chloride leaving the rotary filters. This reaction liberates ammonia which is distilled off by means of steam and reabsorbed in the incoming sodium chloride solution. Small amounts of ammonia are added to make up for the inevitable losses,

$$2NH_4^+Cl^- + Ca^{2+}(OH^-)_2 \rightarrow 2NH_3 + 2H_2O + Ca^{2+}Cl_2^-.$$

The calcium chloride solution formed in the ammonia recovery process is largely waste product. Some of the soda ash is recrystallised to give *washing soda*, $Na_2CO_3 \cdot 10H_2O$.

Potassium hydrogen carbonate is too soluble to be prepared by the Solvay process. It is obtained most conveniently by treating potassium hydroxide solution with carbon dioxide to give the hydrogen carbonate which is then heated to produce the carbonate.

Properties. The anhydrous carbonates are white powders; the potassium salt is deliquescent and the sodium salt absorbs water to form the monohydrate, $Na_2CO_3.H_2O$. With the exception of lithium carbonate, which is only sparingly soluble, they are all soluble in water and the solubility increases down the Group. On evaporation, sodium carbonate solution deposits crystals of the decahydrate, $Na_2CO_3.10H_2O$, which effloresce in dry air to give the monohydrate, $Na_2CO_3.H_2O$. Potassium carbonate forms $K_2CO_3.2H_2O$. Aqueous solutions are strongly alkaline owing to hydrolysis. Besides being a weak acid and therefore largely undissociated, carbonic acid is also unstable and solutions of carbonates, or hydrogen carbonates, evolve carbon dioxide slowly on boiling,

$$CO_3{}^{2-} + H_2O \rightleftharpoons OH^- + HCO_3{}^- \rightleftharpoons OH^- + H_2CO_3 \rightleftharpoons H_2O + CO_2 \uparrow.$$

The alkali metal carbonates are stable to heat, except lithium carbonate which, like magnesium carbonate, decomposes at high temperatures to the oxide and carbon dioxide,

$$Li_2CO_3 \rightarrow Li_2O + CO_2.$$

It is the small size of the Li^+ ion which causes the behaviour of the lithium compounds to show differences from the behaviour of the compounds of the other elements in the Group. Thus the stability of the crystal lattice of the oxide compared to the carbonate is greater in the case of lithium than any of the other alkali metals.

The hydrogen carbonates are all thermally unstable and easily decompose to the carbonate on heating. Alkali metal hydrogen carbonates are less soluble in water than the carbonates and can be precipitated by bubbling carbon dioxide into saturated solutions of the latter. Potassium hydrogen carbonate is much more soluble than sodium hydrogen carbonate. Solutions of alkali metal hydrogen carbonates are slightly alkaline owing to hydrolysis.

Uses. Large quantities of sodium and potassium carbonates are used in the manufacture of glass. Sodium carbonate is also used in the production of caustic soda and other sodium salts, in the manufacture of soap and detergent cleansers, and in papermaking.

Nitrates, MNO₃

Both the sodium and potassium compounds occur naturally as *Chile saltpetre* and *saltpetre*, respectively. Potassium nitrate is produced from the cheaper sodium nitrate by a process of fractional crystallisation. When hot saturated solutions of sodium nitrate and potassium chloride are mixed the resulting solution is more than saturated with respect to sodium chloride, and it crystallises out until its concentration reaches the normal solubility of sodium chloride in hot water. The salt is filtered off and the solution cooled. As the solubility of sodium chloride barely alters with change of temperature, no appreciable amounts of sodium chloride will be deposited; but nearly pure potassium nitrate crystals are deposited, as it is less soluble in the cold than any of the other salts. The solubility curves of the different salts in solution are shown in Fig. 112.

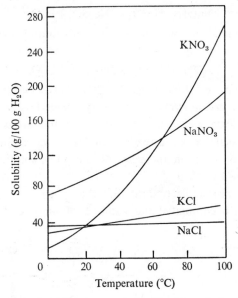

Fig. 112. Solubility curves of the chlorides and nitrates of sodium and potassium.

In contrast to the other nitrates in the Group those of lithium and sodium are deliquescent possibly as a result of their smaller ionic size (see p. 239).

Sodium and potassium nitrate both melt at moderate temperatures (NaNO₃, 316 °C; KNO₃, 336 °C), and evolve oxygen on further heating.

But the decomposition is exceptional as it leads to the formation of a nitrite, and not an oxide or the metal which is more generally the case, i.e.

$$2NO_3^- \rightarrow 2NO_2^- + O_2.$$

Lithium nitrate decomposes into lithium oxide, nitrogen dioxide and oxygen (cf. alkaline earth metal nitrates).

Sodium and potassium nitrites are crystalline solids with a slight yellow colour.

Uses. Sodium nitrate is used as a fertiliser and in the manufacture of other chemicals, but unlike potassium nitrate it cannot be used in gunpowder as it is deliquescent.

Sulphates, M_2SO_4 and hydrogen sulphates, $MHSO_4$

Sulphates are easily prepared by neutralising dilute sulphuric acid with an appropriate amount of the alkali and then crystallising, e.g.

$$2NaOH + H_2SO_4 \rightarrow Na_2SO_4 + H_2O.$$

By using two equivalents of acid to one of alkali and then evaporating, the acid salt crystallises out,

$$NaOH + H_2SO_4 \rightarrow NaHSO_4 + H_2O.$$

Sodium sulphate crystallises as $Na_2SO_4.10H_2O$, whereas potassium sulphate crystals are anhydrous and very much less soluble. Sodium sulphate decahydrate is efflorescent, leaving the anhydrous salt.

The hydrogen sulphates are readily soluble in water, and the solution has a strongly acid reaction and behaves as a dilute solution of sulphuric acid, $HSO_4^- + H_2O \rightleftharpoons H_3O^+ + SO_4^{2-}$.

The sulphates are stable to heat, but the hydrogen sulphates are decomposed; water is eliminated and a salt containing the pyrosulphate ion is produced:

At higher temperatures pyrosulphates evolve sulphur trioxide and the normal sulphate remains,

$$S_2O_7^{2-} \rightarrow SO_4^{2-} + SO_3 \uparrow.$$

The sulphates are isomorphous with each other, and form alums and double sulphates; lithium sulphate is an exception as it is not isomorphous with the others, neither does it form alums.

Orthophosphates, M_3PO_4

Alkali metal orthophosphates are white crystalline solids which readily dissolve in water, except lithium orthophosphate, Li_3PO_4; which is insoluble. Disodium hydrogen orthophosphate, $Na_2HPO_4.12H_2O$, is the commonest (often referred to simply as 'sodium phosphate') and may be prepared in the laboratory by neutralising phosphoric acid with caustic soda using phenolphthalein as an indicator since it changes from colourless to pink at the completion of the reaction,

$$H_3PO_4 + 2OH^- \rightarrow HPO_4^{2-} + 2H_2O.$$

If x cm³ of acid were used and y cm³ of alkali added then if $y/2$ cm³ of the alkali is added to x cm³ of acid and the resulting solution evaporated, crystals of sodium dihydrogen phosphate NaH_2PO_4 separate,

$$H_3PO_4 + OH^- \rightarrow H_2PO_4^- + H_2O.$$

With $3y/2$ cm³ of alkali and x cm³ of acid crystals of trisodium orthophosphate may be obtained on evaporation,

$$H_3PO_4 + 3OH^- \rightarrow PO_4^{3-} + 3H_2O.$$

Thus, solutions of this last salt are alkaline and solutions of the dihydrogen orthophosphate are slightly acidic whilst those of disodium hydrogen orthophosphate are neutral.

When heated, disodium hydrogen orthophosphate loses water and forms sodium pyrophosphate, $Na_4P_2O_7$.

Sodium dihydrogen orthophosphate behaves similarly,

$$2NaH_2PO_4 \xrightarrow{200\,°C} Na_2H_2P_2O_7 + H_2O.$$

Exercises

1. Account for the trends in (a) atomic radius, (b) ionisation energies, and (c) electronegativities amongst the alkali metals.
2. Explain why the boiling points of Group IA elements decrease down the Group whilst those of Group VIIB increase down the Group.
3. Account for the variation in the boiling points of Group IA chlorides.
4. 'The alkali metals are the most metallic elements.' Discuss this statement with particular regard to (a) physical properties, (b) chemical properties.

5. Give a brief account, without diagrams, of the manufacture of sodium carbonate, explaining carefully the reasons for the physical and chemical conditions under which the process is carried out.

Give two industrial uses of sodium carbonate.

How would you measure the proportions of the monohydrate, $Na_2CO_3.H_2O$, and the decahydrate in a mixture of the two hydrates if you had available a one tenth molar solution of hydrochloric acid? Explain briefly how you would calculate the answer from your measurements. (O)

6. (a) How are the existence of families and periods in the classification of the elements explained in terms of atomic structure?

(b) Rubidium is next to potassium in Group 1 of the Periodic Table.

From your knowledge of the chemistry of potassium and sodium and their compounds, discuss the properties you would expect to find in rubidium, and in its hydride, hydroxide, carbonate and chloride. (O)

7. Compare, with explanations, the reactions of sodium hydroxide and am-ammonium hydroxide (or ammonia) with each of the following substances: nickel(II) sulphate; aluminium sulphate; calcium chloride; hot diluted nitric acid; acetaldehyde. (O & C)

8. What is an atomic spectrum?

Explain how observations of atomic spectra lead to information on electronic energy levels and ionization energies.

Describe the electronic structures of atoms of lithium, sodium and potassium. How does a knowledge of these structures help in understanding the similar chemical properties of these elements? (O & CS)

21

GROUP IIA:
THE ALKALINE EARTH METALS

Group IIA consists of the elements beryllium, magnesium, calcium, strontium, barium, and radium. Radium is radioactive. Its chemistry is very similar to that of barium. Little more need be said about it in this chapter.

Relationship of Group IIA to the Periodic Table

Group IIA forms the second column of the *s*-block in the Periodic Table. Its members are more electronegative than the corresponding elements of Group IA but less electronegative than the corresponding elements in Group IIIA.

There is a marked diagonal relationship between beryllium and aluminium (p. 357), between lithium and magnesium (p. 338), and also between magnesium and scandium (Group IIIA). The relationship between the A and B families as illustrated by magnesium and zinc, is fairly close (p. 596).

There is no break in trend in passing along the Period from Group IIA to Group IIIA.

General Group characteristics

Atomic properties of Group IIA elements

	Symbol	Atomic no.	Atomic weight	Electronic configuration							Maximum Group valency	covalency shown
				K	L	M	N	O	P	Q		
Beryllium	Be	4	9.01	2	2	—	—	—	—	—	2	4
Magnesium	Mg	12	24.31	2	8	2	—	—	—	—	2	—
Calcium	Ca	20	40.08	2	8	8	2	—	—	—	2	—
Strontium	Sr	38	87.62	2	8	18	8	2	—	—	2	—
Barium	Ba	56	137.34	2	8	18	18	8	2	—	2	—
Radium	Ra	88	226.03	2	8	18	32	18	8	2	2	—

Similarities between members of the Group

The fundamental similarity is that, being in Group IIA, they all have two electrons in their external (valency) shell, and eight electrons in their penultimate shell except beryllium which has two. All therefore show a positive electrovalency of 2 and form stable bivalent cations M^{2+} with a noble gas electronic configuration. Because of the powerful screening effect of inner closed shells, effective nuclear charges of the elements are very small, the valency electrons are therefore weakly bound, and the elements exist as close-packed metals with 'pooled' electrons. All are true metals, shown by their structure.

The last four metals have large atomic radii and correspondingly small ionisation energies. The M^{2+} cations are large, moderately charged and have a noble gas electronic configuration. These factors all contribute to making them highly electropositive, second only to the alkali metals in this respect. All have low electronegativities, though distinctly higher than those of the corresponding elements in Group IA. The chemistry of the Group is the chemistry of M^{2+} ions, except for beryllium whose compounds always have considerable covalent character.

Differences within the Group

Further atomic properties of Group IIA elements

Element	Metallic radius (Å)	Atomic radius (Å)	Ionic radius of M^{2+} (Å)	Electro-negativity (Allred–Rochow)	Standard electrode potential (V) $M^{2+}+2e \rightleftharpoons M$
Beryllium	1.12	0.89	0.31	1.47	−1.70
Magnesium	1.60	1.36	0.65	1.23	−2.37
Calcium	1.97	1.74	0.99	1.04	−2.87
Strontium	2.15	1.91	1.13	0.99	−2.89
Barium	2.24	1.98	1.35	0.97	−2.90

Graphs incorporating the data in the last four columns are given in chs 5, 9. Beryllium, and to a less extent magnesium, stand apart from the rest of the Group, as seen by the break in trend in each graph at calcium; the trends being very similar to those in Group IA. Calcium, strontium and barium are very similar elements with almost straight line trends, so that the properties of strontium are nearly the average of those of the other two. The same relation holds for beryllium, magnesium and calcium.

The atomic and ionic radii of beryllium are very much the smallest in the Group. Indeed the beryllium atom is by far the smallest of all metal atoms, just as the Be^{2+} ion is of all ions. Being doubly charged and very small it has a strong field-intensity, which explains beryllium's marked tendency to form covalencies, and the amphoteric nature of the metal, its oxide and hydroxide. The maximum covalency of beryllium is 4.

The compounds of beryllium and barium are poisonous.

The elements

Occurrence

These metals are much too electropositive to occur free in nature. Calcium (3.4% of lithosphere) and magnesium (1.9% of lithosphere) are major constituents of the earth's crust and are found widely dispersed as silicates in igneous rocks, and as other compounds in large localised deposits. Barium (0.04% of lithosphere) and strontium (0.02% of lithosphere) are still high in the list of order of abundance of all the elements, but beryllium (0.0006% of lithosphere) is about half-way down the list although still much more abundant than silver. The only commercial source of beryllium is *beryl*, $Be_3Al_2(SiO_3)_6$.

The oxides and hydroxides are not found free, except BeO and MgO, because they are strongly basic and so react with water and carbon dioxide. The sulphides are not found free, because they react with water, forming soluble hydrogen sulphides. Chief native compounds of the elements are the insoluble or slightly soluble oxo-salts (carbonates, sulphates, phosphates), and in the case of magnesium the *soluble* double chloride *carnallite* $KCl.MgCl_2.6H_2O$ deposited by evaporation from inland seas (p. 179).

All the elements occur as carbonates and sulphates. Calcium carbonate in the form of chalk and limestone and magnesium as the double carbonate *dolomite*, $CaCO_3.MgCO_3$, make up whole mountain ranges and countrysides. Calcium carbonate occurs also as *aragonite* and *calcite*. Other carbonates are *magnesite*, $MgCO_3$; *witherite*, $BaCO_3$; and *strontianite*, $SrCO_3$ (first discovered in the Argyllshire village of Strontian). The metal strontium was first isolated from this compound by Davy in 1808.

The sulphates occur as *kieserite*, $MgSO_4.H_2O$; *anhydrite*, $CaSO_4$, and *gypsum*, $CaSO_4.2H_2O$; *celestine*, $SrSO_4$; and *barytes*, $BaSO_4$. Large quantities of calcium are found as *phosphorite*, mainly $Ca_3(PO_4)_2$; *apatite* $3Ca_3(PO_4)_2.CaF_2$; and *fluorite* or *fluorspar*, CaF_2.

Magnesium and calcium compounds formed by the weathering of igneous rocks are found in all soils and in most fresh waters as hydrogen carbonates, sulphates, and chlorides, causing hardness. Epsom salt, $MgSO_4.7H_2O$, was got from spring water at Epsom in 1695. Sea water contains a fairly small but important quantity of magnesium ions (about one-eighth of the weight of sodium ions present).

Magnesium is present in the green compound chlorophyll found in green plants. Calcium is found in bones as the double salt

$$3Ca_3(PO_4)_2.CaCO_3.H_2O$$

and as $CaCO_3$ in egg shells and sea shells.

Isolation

Chief ores or other sources from which the metals are extracted are: for magnesium, carnallite, magnesite or dolomite and sea water; for calcium, $CaCO_3$; for strontium, $SrCO_3$; and for barium, $BaCO_3$ and $BaSO_4$.

All the metals may be prepared industrially by the electrolytic reduction of the fused chlorides. Electrolysis of aqueous solutions of the chlorides with a mercury cathode may also be used, the resulting amalgam being heated to drive off the mercury. (All Group IIA metals except beryllium were first isolated by Davy in 1808 in this way.) Thermal reduction of the oxide is also used in some cases. Technically magnesium is the most important of these metals.

Beryllium. By electrolysis of a fused mixture of beryllium chloride (made from beryl) and sodium chloride at 350 °C. Sodium chloride is added to increase conductivity of the melt, since $BeCl_2$, because of its considerable covalent character, is a poor conductor.

Magnesium. (1) The chief process is the electrolysis of fused magnesium chloride prepared from sea water. Quicklime (CaO) made by calcining oyster shells ($CaCO_3$), limestone, or dolomite is slaked and added in slight excess to sea water. Magnesium hydroxide is precipitated, allowed to settle, then filtered off:

$$Mg^{2+} + 2OH^- \rightarrow Mg(OH)_2.$$

The hydroxide is dissolved in hydrochloric acid and $MgCl_2.6H_2O$ crystallised by evaporation, removed and dehydrated by heating until the composition $MgCl_2.1\frac{1}{2}H_2O$ is reached (further heating causes hydrolysis). Final dehydration takes place in the electrolytic vessel. $MgCl_2.1\frac{1}{2}H_2O$ is then added to the molten electrolyte which consists of magnesium chloride with sodium chloride added to improve the conductivity and to lower the melting point to a temperature of about 700 °C. Electrolysis is carried out using a graphite anode, and, as cathode, the iron vessel containing the melt,

at cathode $\qquad$ $Mg^{2+} + 2e \rightarrow Mg$;

at anode $\qquad$ $2Cl^- - 2e \rightarrow Cl_2$.

Molten magnesium rises to the surface, where it is protected from reaction with oxygen or nitrogen of the air by a current of town gas. The magnesium is removed by ladles. The anode is surrounded by a porcelain tube up which the chlorine passes to be converted to hydrogen chloride for the first part of the process. The tube also prevents chlorine from reacting with the magnesium, and the magnesium from contacting the anode and causing a short circuit.

When carnallite is used as the source of magnesium, it is first dehydrated in the way described above for $MgCl_2 \cdot 6H_2O$.

(2) Magnesium is also manufactured by the thermal reduction of its oxide, using silicon as the reducing agent. This reaction is the reverse of the exothermic reaction used in the laboratory preparation of silicon (p. 364),

$$SiO_2 + 2Mg \rightleftharpoons Si + 2MgO; \ \Delta H \text{ negative.}$$

It follows from Le Chatelier's principle, that the reduction of MgO by silicon is favoured by high temperature and by the removal of magnesium vapour from the equilibrium mixture.

Dolomite is calcined to the oxides,

$$CaCO_3 \cdot MgCO_3 \rightarrow CaO + MgO + 2CO_2.$$

The oxides are then mixed with powdered ferrosilicon, an alloy of 75 % Si and 25 % Fe made by the high temperature reduction of silica with carbon in the presence of iron, and the mixture heated to 1200 °C under greatly reduced pressure:

$$2MgO + 2CaO + Si \rightarrow Ca_2SiO_4 + 2Mg.$$

The magnesium vapour formed passes out of the furnace and is condensed in air-cooled receivers.

Calcium. Calcium is manufactured by the electrolysis of fused anhydrous calcium chloride obtained as a by-product of the ammonia-soda process in which calcium carbonate is one of the raw materials.

A fused mixture of calcium chloride (melting point 770 °C, density 2.5 g cm^{-3}) with calcium fluoride added to lower the melting point to about 650 °C is electrolysed in an iron vessel lined with graphite, which acts as *anode*. The heating effect of the current keeps the electrolyte at a working temperature of about 700 °C. The *cathode* is a vertical retractable, hollow, water-cooled iron tube, which at the start has its foot touching the surface of the melt. The local temperature is just above the melting point of calcium (melting point 850 °C, density 1.55 g cm^{-3}). The molten calcium formed remains at the surface and solidifies on the end of the cooled iron cathode, which is gradually raised so that a rod of calcium forms and thereafter acts as a cathode. The metal is protected from oxidation by a layer of solid electrolyte sticking to it. The calcium must be solidified rapidly otherwise molten calcium would diffuse rapidly through the melt and be lost by re-oxidation. Chlorine is liberated at the anode, as in the manufacture of magnesium. The calcium is about 98 % pure. A metal of high purity may be made by distillation in vacuum.

Strontium and Barium. Such small quantities as are required of strontium and barium can be made, like calcium, by the electrolysis of the fused chloride. The chloride is made by the action of hydrochloric acid on the naturally occurring carbonate.

Physical properties of Group IIA elements

Element	Appearance	Density (g cm^{-3})	m.p. (°C)	b.p. (°C)
Be	Silvery grey metal	1.86	1280	2900
Mg	Silvery white metal	1.75	650	1105
Ca	Silvery white metal	1.55	850	1440
Sr	Silvery yellowish metal	2.60	770	1370
Ba	Silvery yellowish metal	3.60	720	1140
Ra	Silvery white metal	5.00	700	1140

General trends are similar to those of the alkali metals. Passing down both Groups the metals decrease in melting point, boiling point and hardness (Be, very hard; Ba, very soft). Decreases are explained by increases in atomic radii down the Group, which results in a corresponding decrease in bond strength. There is no clear reason why the melting point of magnesium does not fit into the trend. Densities decrease from Be to Ca then increase to Ba. Note that beryllium is the only metal with a low density and a high melting point. (See Uses, p. 326.)

Chemical properties

1. Air. All the metals tarnish in air forming a film of oxide, the speed of the reaction increasing from Be to Ba. The film is protective in the case of Be and Mg, but non-protective with the others so that the action continues till the metals have reacted completely, the final product being a mixture of carbonate MCO_3, with some nitride M_3N_2. Calcium is best stored under paraffin; with strontium and barium this is essential. Barium is so reactive that when finely divided it inflames spontaneously in air at ordinary temperatures.

All the metals burn brilliantly when heated in air, forming the oxide along with some nitride. The proportion of nitride increases as the Group is descended. Flame colorations are: Ca, brick red; Sr, crimson; Ba, pale green.

2. Water (p. 215). The rate of reaction increases from Be to Ba for two related reasons: (*a*) in passing from Be to Ba the metals show a progressively greater negative value of the standard electrode potential, see graph on p. 155, and (*b*) increased solubility of the hydroxides (p. 330). Thus beryllium does not react at all with water, cold or hot, because of the insolubility of its hydroxide; magnesium reacts very slowly with cold water, slowly with boiling water; amalgamated magnesium reacts more vigorously, because formation of a protective hydroxide layer is prevented. Calcium reacts moderately quickly with cold water, strontium more quickly and barium vigorously (but less so than sodium). The reaction goes to completion with the last three metals, hydrogen being evolved and a solution or suspension of the hydroxide formed.

Beryllium does not react with steam even at red heat, but burning magnesium burns brilliantly in steam forming the hydroxide and hydrogen.

3. Acids. *Hydrochloric and dilute sulphuric*

$$M + 2H^+ \rightarrow M^{2+} + H_2.$$

Reaction with beryllium takes place on warming. With the others actions are vigorous except with calcium, strontium, barium and dilute sulphuric acid, when the slight solubility of the sulphate MSO_4 retards the action.

H_2SO_4 concentrated. Cold concentrated acid has little or no action on Be or Mg, but when heated, sulphur dioxide is evolved and the sulphate of the metal formed.

HNO₃ dilute. No action with Be. Very dilute nitric acid (1 %) with Mg gives hydrogen, but more concentrated acid gives oxides of nitrogen.

HNO₃ concentrated. Be is rendered passive. With Mg the action is vigorous giving oxides of nitrogen.

4. Aqueous alkalis. Because the metals, except beryllium, are highly electropositive, there is no action with sodium hydroxide solution, other than the reaction with water. Beryllium shows its amphoteric nature by reacting in a way similar to aluminium, hydrogen being evolved and sodium beryllate formed in solution

$$Be + 2OH^- + 2H_2O \rightarrow [Be(OH)_4]^{2-} + H_2.$$

5. Combination with non-metals. The metals are powerful reducing agents combining directly and often vigorously at suitable temperatures with the highly electronegative non-metals oxygen, the halogens, nitrogen, sulphur and phosphorus; and with carbon. Calcium, strontium and barium combine with hydrogen. Almost all the compounds formed are essentially ionic, even beryllium carbide Be_2C; but surprisingly $BeCl_2$ is of intermediate bond type, perhaps more covalent than ionic.

6. Further reactions with compounds. Group IIA metals are all powerful reducing agents. Magnesium, the best known metal in the Group, may be used to reduce almost any oxide leaving the free element, e.g. burning magnesium continues to burn in steam, CO, CO_2, SO_2, NO, N_2O, reducing them to hydrogen, carbon, sulphur and nitrogen respectively. Magnesium reduces SiO_2 to Si on heating. It reduces the oxides of Na, K, Rb and Cs to the metals when heated. Calcium is an even more powerful reducing agent especially at high temperatures (p. 184).

Dry magnesium reacts vigorously with alkyl halides in ethereal solution producing Grignard reagents in solution, e.g.

$$Mg + CH_3I \longrightarrow Mg \overset{\displaystyle CH_3}{\underset{\displaystyle I}{\diagdown}} \quad \text{(methyl magnesium iodide).}$$

Uses

Magnesium is used in much greater quantities than other members of Group IIA. Beryllium and calcium come next. Strontium and barium have no economically important uses.

Low densities together with relatively high strengths, and the chemical activity of magnesium and calcium are the properties on which their uses depend.

1. Alloys. Magnesium alloys are used in large quantities in aircraft, motor and other industries. Two important alloys are:

(*a*) *magnalium* (Al + 10–30 % Mg) and (*b*) *magnesium–zirconium alloy* (Mg, 96.3 %; Zn, 3 %; Zr, 0–7 %). Beryllium is a hard, light, strong metal of high melting point and resistance to corrosion, an unusual combination of properties and an attractive one to engineers. Its use is likely to develop greatly. At present its chief alloy is *beryllium-bronze* (98 % Cu, 2 % Be) which, after suitable heat treatment, has remarkable properties: it is as hard and tough as the best steels; its power to withstand continual flexing without showing fatigue is greatly superior to that of steel; its resistance to corrosion is as good as that of stainless steel; it does not cause sparks when struck. Consequently it has replaced steel in making valve springs and other engine parts subject to continual vibration and for tools to be used near explosive gases or solids.

An alloy of lead with a small quantity of calcium to harden it is used in cable covers and bearings.

2. As reducing agents. Magnesium and calcium are used in the extraction of certain elements from their compounds, e.g. silicon, titanium, chromium, uranium, plutonium.

Beryllium, magnesium and calcium are also used as deoxidants in metallurgy. They are added in small quantities to the molten metal to reduce oxides and sulphides to the metal, the magnesium and calcium compounds separating as a slag. They are also added to molten metals during casting, to remove dissolved oxygen and nitrogen which cause blow-holes when the casting solidifies. Another use is to produce high vacua in radio valves by removal of residual oxygen and nitrogen as oxides and nitrides.

3. Miscellaneous. Beryllium is used in making windows for X-ray tubes, because X-rays readily penetrate metals of low atomic number. Magnesium is used to make cans to hold uranium in nuclear reactors, because of its low absorbing power for neutrons. Mixed with an oxidising agent it acts as flashlight powder in photography, star-shells and incendiary bombs. As a sacrificial anode to protect iron pipe lines: bars of magnesium electrically connected to the iron are buried in the earth and act as anodes in the electrolytic processes of corrosion. Magnesium having a higher electrode potential than iron and its impurities, goes into solution in the moist earth and the iron remains unaffected.

Calcium is used (*a*) as a dehydrating agent for ethanol, (*b*) in the manufacture of *hydrolith*, CaH_2 (p. 328).

Compounds

Hydrides, MH_2

All metals of Group IIA form hydrides with this formula. All except BeH_2 are made by heating the metals with hydrogen (under pressure for MgH_2). Their affinity towards hydrogen increases down the Group. For BeH_2, see p. 263.

The hydrides are colourless or grey crystalline solids. When heated they decompose into their elements. CaH_2 is the most stable to heat (up to $800\,°C$); BeH_2 the least stable, decomposing at $125\,°C$.

They all react with water with increasing readiness down the Group,

$$MH_2 + 2H\text{—}OH \to M^{2+} + 2OH^- + 2H_2\uparrow.$$

CaH_2 under the name *hydrolith* is used as an easily portable source of hydrogen.

See also Hydrides (p. 262). For structure, see p. 265.

Oxides, MO

The oxides, MO, are much too reactive to occur free except for very small quantities of the least reactive, MgO and BeO.

Preparation. They may be made by the general methods (p. 252). The first four oxides are conveniently made in the laboratory by heating the carbonate in open vessels, thus allowing the carbon dioxide to escape. $BaCO_3$ requires a temperature of about $1500\,°C$ before the pressure of its carbon dioxide reaches 1 atmosphere. The oxide is more easily made by heating the nitrate, $Ba(NO_3)_2$.

Oxides of Mg, Ca and Ba are made on a large scale by heating their naturally occurring carbonates, *magnesite*, *limestone* and *witherite* respectively,
$$MCO_3 \rightleftharpoons MO + CO_2.$$

$BaCO_3$ begins to melt at the high temperature required for reasonably quick conversion. To avoid this it is mixed with carbon, which removes the carbon dioxide (by combining with it to form carbon monoxide) and so allows the forward reaction to proceed at a much lower temperature,

$$BaCO_3 + C \to BaO + 2CO.$$

Calcium oxide, *quicklime*, is made industrially (lime-burning) in very large quantities, either in vertical shaft-kilns fired from the bottom by producer gas (made on the spot), or in rotary kilns inclined to the horizontal and fired as above by producer gas or oil. In both cases the carbon dioxide is swept away by the convection draught produced by the burners. The backward reaction is thus prevented from taking place and the reaction proceeds at a temperature of about 800 °C, well below that required to raise the CO_2 pressure of $CaCO_3$ to 1 atmosphere.

Physical properties. All the oxides are white crystalline solids, ionic and with sodium chloride structure (co-ordination number 6:6) except beryllium oxide which has the wurtzite structure (C.N. 4:4) and is partly covalent. Melting points are very high, increasing a little from beryllium oxide (2530 °C) to a maximum at magnesium oxide (2800 °C), then decreasing steadily to a minimum at barium oxide (1928 °C). The trend from magnesium to barium oxide indicates a decrease in bonding forces caused by a gradual increase in ionic radius from Mg^{2+} (0.65 Å) to Ba^{2+} (1.34 Å).

Perhaps the partial covalent character and different structure of beryllium oxide account for a much lower melting point than would be expected from its exceptionally low ionic radius (0.31 Å).

Chemical properties. All the oxides are strongly basic except beryllium oxide which is amphoteric.

Air. All the oxides except beryllium oxide absorb water vapour and carbon dioxide from the atmosphere, forming first hydroxides then basic carbonates or carbonates. Beryllium oxide being less chemically active does not react.

When barium oxide is heated in air or oxygen at about 400 °C barium peroxide BaO_2 is formed. Strontium oxide forms a peroxide in this way only under great pressure. Calcium and magnesium do not form peroxides in this way, and beryllium forms no peroxide.

Water. Beryllium oxide neither reacts with nor dissolves in water. The others react forming hydroxides, magnesium oxide slowly, calcium, strontium and barium oxides with great vigour and evolution of much heat, increasing down the Group. The process is called *slaking*, and calcium oxide may reach a temperature sufficient to boil any excess water; barium oxide may become incandescent,

$$O^{2-} + H_2O \rightarrow 2OH^-.$$

Reactions with acidic oxides. The oxides react with, for example, carbon dioxide, sulphur dioxide, silicon dioxide and phosphorus pentoxide at suitable temperatures forming the corresponding salts,

$$6CaO + P_4O_{10} \rightarrow 2Ca_3(PO_4)_2.$$

Beryllium oxide and magnesium oxide (when made at low temperature), although very slightly soluble in water, react readily with dilute acids.

Carbon. All the oxides when heated strongly with carbon form carbides. Beryllium carbide has the formula Be_2C, the others MC_2 (p. 393).

Uses. Beryllium oxide is used in making porcelain crucibles because of its refractory nature (high melting point) and low thermal expansion. For the same reason and also because it is an excellent electrical insulator it is used in sparking plugs. Magnesium oxide and calcium oxide are used to make refractory bricks for furnace linings. Calcium oxide is also used in very large quantities to make calcium hydroxide. Barium oxide is used to make the hydroxide and peroxide.

Hydroxides, $M(OH)_2$

These hydroxides do not occur free in nature, except $Mg(OH)_2$ as the mineral *brucite.*

Preparation. As beryllium hydroxide is insoluble in water and magnesium hydroxide very slightly soluble they are made by precipitation by hydroxyl ions from aqueous solutions containing the metal ions. The others are made by slaking the oxides.

Physical properties. All are white solids. Solubilities increase considerably down the Group from beryllium hydroxide (insoluble) to barium hydroxide (fairly soluble).

	$Be(OH)_2$	$Mg(OH)_2$	$Ca(OH)_2$	$Sr(OH)_2$	$Ba(OH)_2$
Solubility (g/100 g water at 20 °C)	Insoluble	0.002	0.15	0.9	4.0

Solubility of calcium hydroxide decreases with rise in temperature; the others increase, magnesium hydroxide slightly but strontium and barium hydroxide greatly. Calcium hydroxide solution is called *lime water* and barium hydroxide solution *baryta water.*

Increase in solubility of the hydroxides down the Group is explained partly by the following facts: (1) ease of ion formation increases; (2) lattice energy decreases with increase in internuclear distance $(r_1 + r_2)$ (p. 135); (3) $Be(OH)_2$ is essentially covalent because of the high polarising effect of the small Be^{2+} ion, $Ba(OH)_2$ is essentially ionic.

Group IIA hydroxides are much less soluble than the corresponding hydroxides of Group IA, for similar reasons.

Chemical properties. *With water, acids and alkalis.* Beryllium hydroxide is insoluble in water, but soluble in acids and also in excess sodium hydroxide solution forming a solution of sodium beryllate. It is therefore amphoteric. The other hydroxides react with dilute hydrochloric acid, for example, forming chlorides, but none reacts with sodium hydroxide solution; all are therefore basic. Their solutions are strongly alkaline to litmus. Conductivity experiments show characteristic increases in basic strength down the Group in this case from weak to very strong.

Heat. The temperature at which the hydroxides begin to decompose increases down the Group from about 300 °C for beryllium and magnesium hydroxides to about 700 °C for barium hydroxide,

$$M(OH)_2 \xrightarrow{\text{heat}} MO + H_2O,$$

or

$$(OH^-)_2 \longrightarrow O^{2-} + H_2O.$$

Air. In air, the hydroxides, except beryllium, absorb a certain amount of water vapour, but they are not deliquescent. Moist hydroxides absorb carbon dioxide from air forming carbonate or basic carbonate.

CO_2. Reactions of carbon dioxide with lime water, and the reactions of the final solution of calcium hydrogen carbonate, find exact parallels with solutions of strontium and barium hydroxides.

A suspension of a *little* magnesium hydroxide or magnesium carbonate in water when treated with carbon dioxide forms a solution of magnesium hydrogen carbonate. When this solution is boiled the white precipitate formed is a basic carbonate of magnesium, not a normal carbonate as with the others.

Chlorine. For formation of hypochlorites and chlorates, see bleaching powder, p. 516.

Ammonium salts. All the hydroxides except beryllium hydroxide react with ammonium salts, ammonia being liberated (as with alkali metal hydroxides),

$$OH^- + NH_4^+ \rightleftharpoons NH_3 + H_2O.$$

Uses A suspension of magnesium hydroxide in water, known as milk of magnesia, is used in medicine as an antacid.

Calcium hydroxide is by far the most useful of the hydroxides. Large quantities are used in making builders' mortar, a mixture of slaked lime, sand and water, which sets in air by loss of water and absorption of carbon dioxide, forming hard rock-like calcium carbonate. Plaster is similar to mortar, but other materials are added, e.g. hair, plaster of Paris. Whitewash is a thin paste of calcium hydroxide and water for coating walls and ceilings.

Calcium hydroxide is the cheapest of all alkalis and is used in this capacity in making (1) bleaching powder (p. 516); (2) sodium hydroxide

(p. 308); (3) in the ammonia-soda process (p. 312); (4) for neutralising acids in the soil; (5) in water softening; and (6) in sugar refining, where it combines with cane-sugar (sucrose) forming an insoluble saccharate which is removed from the mother-liquor (molasses), the sugar being recovered by decomposing the saccharate with CO_2.

Strontium hydroxide may be used instead of calcium hydroxide in sugar refining; it is more efficient. Barium hydroxide, being poisonous, cannot be used.

Barium hydroxide. An aqueous solution (baryta water) is used in laboratories in testing for carbon dioxide and as a standard alkali free from carbonate because of the insolubility of barium carbonate.

Chlorides, MCl_2

Preparation. For general methods, see p. 241. The chlorides crystallise from concentrated and cooled aqueous solutions as colourless hydrates with 4, 6, 6, 6 and 2 molecules of water respectively. When the hydrated chlorides of magnesium and calcium are heated, some hydrolysis takes place, basic chlorides being formed. To obtain the pure anhydrous chlorides their hydrates must be heated in a current of hydrogen chloride. For strontium and barium chlorides this is not necessary because of their greater ionic character and consequent resistance to hydrolysis.

Physical properties.

	Appearance	m.p. (°C)	Equivalent conductivity of fused chlorides	Structure and bonding	Solubility in water 20 °C (g/100 g)	Solubility in ethanol
$BeCl_2$	White solid fuming in moist air, deliquescent	405, sublimes at 490	0.1	Infinite chains covalent, C.N. 4:2	Very soluble	Very soluble
$MgCl_2$	White solid, deliquescent	714	29	Layer lattice	Very soluble, 54	Moderately soluble
$CaCl_2$	White solid, deliquescent	782	52	Rutile C.N. 6:3, ionic	Very soluble 82	Moderately soluble
$SrCl_2$	White solid, not deliquescent	875	56	Fluorite C.N. 8:4, ionic	Very soluble, 55	Slightly soluble
$BaCl_2$	White solid, not deliquescent	962	65	Irregular, C.N. of Ba = 9, ionic	Very soluble, 37	Almost soluble

Increase in ionic character of the anhydrous chlorides with increase in size of cation down the Group is seen clearly in the co-ordination numbers of the structures and is confirmed by their other properties, including conductivities of the fused chlorides. The range is from essentially covalent beryllium chloride to essentially ionic barium chloride. Increase in melting point is explained by the greatly increased ionic bonding forces from beryllium to barium.

General decrease in solubility down the Group is the reverse of the trend shown by hydroxides.

Chemical properties. With the exception of barium, all the chlorides form ammines, e.g. $BeCl_2.4NH_3$, $MgCl_2.6NH_3$, $CaCl_2.8NH_3$, $SrCl_2.8NH_3$. It is more instructive to write co-ordination compounds in the form $[Mg(NH_3)_6]Cl_2$. These ammines decompose when heated, with increasing ease from beryllium to strontium, and also when dissolved in water.

Anhydrous calcium chloride cannot be used to dry ammonia because it forms an ammine. Neither can it be used to dry ethanol because it forms a compound $CaCl_2.4C_2H_5OH$.

The bromides and iodides are similar to the chlorides but slightly less ionic because of the greater anionic radius.

Fluorides, MF₂

These are more ionic than the corresponding chlorides because of the smaller radius of the fluoride ion. Beryllium fluoride has the β cristobalite structure (p. 382), magnesium fluoride, the rutile structure, and the others the fluorite structure.

Uses of Group IIA halides. The chlorides are used for the manufacture of the metal. A mixture of magnesium chloride and magnesium oxide with water is used as a cement (Sorel cement). Mixed with sawdust this cement is used as a floor covering.

Calcium chloride is used in laboratories as a drying agent and barium chloride in the detection and determination of sulphate by precipitation of barium sulphate.

Carbonates, MCO₃

All except beryllium carbonate occur native (p. 321). All are white solids almost insoluble in water. Hydrates are known for the first three members of the group:

$$BeCO_3.4H_2O, \quad MgCO_3.5H_2O, \quad CaCO_3.6H_2O.$$

Preparation. For the carbonates of calcium, strontium and barium, sodium carbonate solution is added to a solution containing the required cation, the anhydrous carbonate being precipitated. With magnesium and beryllium, sodium carbonate, because of its partial hydrolysis to hydroxide, gives a precipitate of basic carbonate. The normal carbonates are made by using sodium hydrogen carbonate solution instead,

$$Mg^{2+} + 2HCO_3^- \rightarrow MgCO_3\downarrow + H_2O + CO_2.$$

Beryllium carbonate is so unstable that it must be made in the presence of excess CO_2.

Physical properties. Temperatures of complete decomposition to the oxide (pressure of $CO_2 = 1$ atmosphere) are, beginning with $BeCO_3$: 25 °C, 540 °C, 900 °C, 1290 °C and 1360 °C. Very marked increase in thermal stability is explained by the decrease in polarising power of the M^{2+} ion on the CO_3^{2-} ion with increase in size of the cation. All the carbonates are almost insoluble in water.

Chemical properties. The carbonates react with acids as usual, except where formation of an insoluble salt stops or slows down the action, e.g. dilute sulphuric with the carbonates of calcium, strontium and barium. For action of CO_2, see p. 331.

Hydrogen carbonates, $M(HCO_3)_2$

Known only in solution, these cannot be isolated because of their very unstable nature.

Uses. All the carbonates are used as the most important sources of other compounds of the metals, or of the metals themselves. Limestone is used in making quicklime, cement, glass and sodium carbonate; in neutralising soil acidity, and as a flux in smelting iron ore. After purification it is used in tooth pastes, metal polishes and putty (mixed with raw linseed oil). Limestone and dolomite are used as building stones. Barium carbonate is added in making the glass of television tubes to prevent exposure to X-rays. It is also used as a de-sulphating agent and as an ingredient in enamels.

Nitrates, $M(NO_3)_2$

All the metals of the Group form nitrates. Hydrates of these are known for the first four members, the commonest being $Be(NO_3)_2 . 4H_2O$, $Mg(NO_3)_2 . 6H_2O$, $Ca(NO_3)_2 . 4H_2O$, $Sr(NO_3)_2 . 4H_2O$. Barium nitrate does not form any hydrates stable at room temperature.

Preparation. The usual methods for soluble salts are used, e.g. action of dilute nitric acid on the oxide, hydroxide or carbonate. The nitrates crystallise from concentrated and cooled solutions as the hydrates listed above.

Properties. All are colourless or white crystalline solids readily soluble in water. Nitrates (hydrated or anhydrous) of the first three metals are readily soluble in alcohol, the others almost insoluble. Except for $Sr(NO_3)_2.4H_2O$ all the hydrates are deliquescent. Only calcium, strontium, and barium form anhydrous nitrates. Only calcium nitrate $Ca(NO_3)_2$ is hygroscopic.

Effect of heat. $Be(NO_3)_2.4H_2O$ melts on gentle heating. Hydrolysis takes place and is complete at 200 °C leaving a residue of BeO. $Mg(NO_3)_2.6H_2O$ is also hydrolysed and is completely decomposed to MgO at 400 °C. These results show the partial covalent character of the salts.

Calcium and strontium hydrates readily form anhydrous salts at about 100 °C. The barium salt is already anhydrous. These results show the decreasing affinity for water of Ca^{2+}, Sr^{2+} and Ba^{2+} ions with increase in ionic radius.

The anhydrous nitrates of calcium, strontium and barium require a progressively higher temperature for decomposition to the oxide and in each case the nitrite is formed as an intermediate product (cf. nitrates of alkali metals). Strong heating is needed to convert barium nitrate to barium oxide, $\quad 2M(NO_3)_2 \rightarrow 2MO + 4NO_2\uparrow + O_2\uparrow.$

The increase in stability of these nitrates down the Group is explained by the increase in ionic character with increase in ionic radius. Their melting points also increase from calcium to barium for the same reason.

Solubilities of the nitrates decrease from beryllium, very soluble, to barium, fairly soluble, although calcium nitrate is out of line being more soluble than magnesium nitrate.

Uses. Calcium nitrate with the addition of quicklime to make it almost non-hygroscopic is used as a fertiliser.

Strontium nitrate is used in fireworks to give a crimson flame, and barium nitrate to give a green one.

Beryllium nitrate is used as a hardener for incandescent gas-mantles.

Sulphates

All members of the Group form sulphates which, with the exception of beryllium sulphate occur native (p. 321). The common hydrates are, $BeSO_4.4H_2O$, $MgSO_4.7H_2O$ (Epsom salt) and $CaSO_4.2H_2O$ (gypsum).

Preparation. Beryllium and magnesium sulphates are very soluble, calcium sulphate slightly soluble, and the others almost insoluble. They are prepared by the usual methods. The precipitate formed from a fairly strong solution containing Ca^{2+} ions is the dihydrate $CaSO_4.2H_2O$.

Properties. All are white crystalline non-deliquescent solids. A point of interest about calcium sulphate is that its solubility increases with rising temperature to a maximum at 40 °C and then falls. This may cause deposits of calcium sulphate as a hard intractable scale in boilers, since many boiler feed-waters contain some dissolved calcium sulphate making them permanently hard.

Effect of heat. The common hydrates on gentle heating (300 °C for beryllium, 200 °C for magnesium and calcium) lose their water of crystallisation and form the anhydrous salts (little or no hydrolysis takes place, even with $BeSO_4.4H_2O$ because of the non-volatility of sulphuric acid). Further heating causes the anhydrous sulphates to decompose giving off oxides of sulphur and leaving oxides of the metals. Decomposition temperature increases from $BeSO_4$ (600 °C) to $BaSO_4$ (1500 °C). Melting points of the sulphates show a similar increase.

Stages in the dehydration of $CaSO_4.2H_2O$ are important. At 120 °C it loses three quarters of its water of crystallisation giving $2CaSO_4.H_2O$, plaster of Paris. A paste of this with water sets quickly because of the reformation of the dihydrate as a mass of interlocking crystals. If plaster of Paris is heated to 200 °C, it becomes anhydrous and is said to be *dead-burnt*, because a plaster made from it sets slowly.

Barium sulphate fused with sodium carbonate is largely converted into barium carbonate which may then be dissolved in dilute hydrochloric or nitric acids to give soluble salts. When heated strongly with carbon, barium sulphate is reduced to the sulphide which is soluble in dilute hydrochloric or nitric acid. Barium sulphate is fairly soluble in hot concentrated sulphuric acid due to the formation of the hydrogen sulphate $Ba(HSO_4)_2$. Because of the formation of a double or complex sulphate, calcium sulphate is soluble in saturated ammonium sulphate solution,

$$2NH_4^+ + SO_4^{2-} + Ca^{2+} + SO_4^{2-} \rightleftharpoons 2NH_4^+ + [Ca(SO_4)_2]^{2-}.$$

Sulphates of strontium and barium do not show this reaction. All the sulphates of the Group except barium sulphate form double sulphates of the type $M_2^{I}SO_4.M^{II}SO_4$ with alkali sulphates.

Uses. Magnesium sulphate ($MgSO_4.7H_2O$) is used as a purgative, as a filler in making glazed paper, and as a mordant in dyeing. Plaster of Paris is used in building and in making casts. It expands on setting and gives good detail.

Large quantities of anhydrite are used in the manufacture of sulphuric acid and ammonium sulphate. Barium sulphate is used in X-ray work. It is opaque and non-poisonous (because insoluble) and is fed to patients before X-ray tests of the alimentary canal. Barium sulphate is also used as a pigment in paint manufacture and as a filler for paper, rubber, etc.

Orthophosphates, $M_3(PO_4)_2$

Calcium orthophosphate is the only important phosphate in the Group. It occurs native (p. 321). Almost insoluble in water, soluble in dilute acids, its chief use is in making calcium superphosphate a valuable fertiliser (p. 453).

Magnesium ammonium orthophosphate, $MgNH_4PO_4.6H_2O$, is formed as a white precipitate when disodium hydrogen orthophosphate solution is added to a cold solution containing Mg^{2+} ions, NH_4^+ ions, and a considerable excess of ammonia,

$$Mg^{2+} + NH_4^+ + PO_4^{3-} + 6H_2O \rightarrow MgNH_4PO_4.6H_2O\downarrow.$$

This reaction serves as a test for the presence of Mg^{2+} ions. If a quantitative result is required the precipitate is filtered off, washed and heated strongly. This converts it into magnesium pyrophosphate which is weighed,

$$2MgNH_4PO_4.6H_2O \rightarrow Mg_2P_2O_7 + 2NH_3\uparrow + 13H_2O\uparrow.$$

Sulphides, MS

Preparation. (1) By the action of hydrogen sulphide on the heated oxides

$$MO + H_2S \rightleftharpoons MS + H_2O.$$

(2) Reduction of the sulphate by heating with carbon.

Properties. They are white or pale yellow phosphorescent solids, almost insoluble in water, but decomposed by it to form a mixture of the hydroxide and the hydrogen sulphide

$$2MS + 2H_2O \rightarrow M(OH)_2 + M(HS)_2.$$

Nitrides, M_3N_2

All members of the Group form nitrides when the metal is heated in nitrogen. The nitrides are white or pale yellow solids, decomposed by water to give ammonia,

$$M_3N_2 + 6H_2O \rightarrow 3M(OH)_2 + 2NH_3.$$

337

Solubility of compounds of Group IIA metals

Beryllium salts are usually very soluble. Calcium, strontium and barium form series of corresponding compounds which show very regular trends in solubility as in most of their properties. A simple rule covering all their salts is: hydroxides, oxalates and fluorides increase in solubility from calcium to barium; all other salts decrease.

Because of the very low solubility of its oxalate, calcium may be identified and determined quantitatively by precipitation as calcium oxalate.

Carbonates of calcium, strontium and barium are made use of in qualitative analysis, during which they are precipitated by addition of ammonium carbonate solution in presence of NH_4OH and NH_4Cl. Magnesium carbonate is more soluble than the other carbonates of the Group. It is not precipitated under these conditions, because (1) NH_4^+ ions react with and remove CO_3^{2-} ions to form hydrogen carbonate ions to such an extent that the solubility product of $MgCO_3$ is not exceeded,

$$NH_4^+ + CO_3^{2-} \rightleftharpoons NH_3 + HCO_3^-;$$

(2) some of the Mg^{2+} ions are locked up by combining with Cl^- ions to form complex $[MgCl_4]^{2-}$ ions.

Again because of small solubilities, barium sulphate is used in the detection and quantitative determination of barium; barium chromate in the separation of Ba^{2+} ions from Ca^{2+} and Sr^{2+} ions in qualitative analysis by dissolving the mixed carbonate precipitate in dilute acetic acid and precipitating barium chromate (pale yellow) with potassium chromate solution.

Complex compounds

Beryllium forms a large number of stable complexes, magnesium a fair number of less stable, and calcium, strontium and barium very few.

Beryllium shows its maximum covalency of four in $[Be(H_2O)_4]^{2+}$ and $[Be(NH_3)_4]^{2+}$.

The halides of the metals form complex compounds with sugars. Examples of complex anions are: $[BeO_2]^{2-}$ or $[Be(OH)_4]^{2-}$, $[BeF_4]^{2-}$ fluoroberyllate ion, and $[MgF_4]^{2-}$ (unstable).

Similarities between lithium and magnesium (diagonal)

Lithium resembles magnesium and both differ from the other members of Group IA in the following respects:

(i) small atomic and ionic radii;

338

(ii) formation of nitrides when heated in molecular nitrogen;

(iii) formation of normal oxides on burning;

(iv) hydroxides, carbonates, and nitrates decomposed much more easily on heating, forming oxides; hydrogen carbonates are known only in solution, being too unstable to exist in the solid state;

(v) hydroxides are not deliquescent, and are much less soluble in water;

(vi) fluorides, orthophosphates and carbonates are sparingly soluble in water;

(vii) hydrogen carbonates are more soluble than carbonates.

Exercises

1. Write a short general account of the chemistry of the elements of Group II A.
2. The atomic properties and bulk physical properties of strontium are very nearly the average of those of calcium and barium. Illustrate this from the data in this chapter.
3. A similar statement may be made about the compounds of strontium. Illustrate this for the oxides, hydroxides, chlorides, carbonates and sulphates.
4. Show the relationship between the properties, including atomic properties, and uses of the elements of Group II A.
5. Zinc, magnesium and calcium are in the same group in the Periodic Table. Give in tabular form for these elements:
   (a) the electronic structure of the elements,
   (b) the action of water on the elements,
   (c) the method of manufacture (in outline) of the elements,
   (d) the action of caustic alkali on the oxides of the elements,
   (e) the action of water on the sulphides.
   From the information given, comment on marked differences in properties between the elements and between their compounds.   (L)
6. Magnesium is prepared by either an electrolytic or a non-electrolytic method. Describe *one* of these methods starting from magnesium oxide and state *one* advantage or disadvantage of the method you have chosen.

   By what chemical test would you prove the presence of magnesium and calcium ions in a solution in which these (and H_3O^+) were the only cations present?

   A sample of magnesium contaminated with magnesium oxide was dissolved in 30 c.c. of 2N hydrochloric acid. 448 c.c. of hydrogen corrected to s.t.p. were evolved; and 16 c.c. of N sodium hydroxide were required to complete the neutralisation of the excess hydrochloric acid. Determine the percentage of magnesium metal in the given sample.   (J.M.B.)
7. Describe the preparation of *each* of the following from calcium carbonate:
   (a) bleaching powder, (b) calcium sulphate dihydrate, (c) calcium carbide, (d) calcium cyanamide.

   State and explain **one** use for **each** compound.

   Why is calcium oxide a common impurity in anhydrous calcium chloride?   (C)

339

8. Magnesium and iron are both manufactured by reduction of their oxides. Outline the physical and chemical principles involved in each industrial process. (L)

9. Explain the following statements:

(*a*) Barium sulphide is converted to barium hydroxide on the addition of water.

(*b*) Pure iron when placed in contact with concentrated nitric acid is rendered 'passive'.

(*c*) The addition of aqueous ammonia to zinc sulphate solution gives a white precipitate which dissolves in excess of aqueous ammonia.

(*d*) On addition of a solution of oxalic acid, calcium oxalate is completely precipitated from calcium acetate solution but only partially from calcium chloride solution. (C)

10. Name three magnesium minerals, and give an account of *one* method of extracting magnesium.

State exactly how you would analyse an alloy which you are told consists only of magnesium and zinc, in order to prove the presence of these two metals.

Compare the properties, physical and chemical, of (*a*) the oxides, (*b*) the sulphides, of magnesium and zinc. (O)

11. Give in outline the chemistry of the metal calcium and of *four* of its compounds which are of importance in nature or industry. (O & C)

22

GROUP IIIB: BORON AND ALUMINIUM
(GALLIUM, INDIUM, THALLIUM)

Boron is a non-metal, the others are metals, but lack the regular close-packed structure of true metals. Gallium, indium and thallium are quite rare and not of great practical importance. Enough will be said to justify their inclusion in the Group.

Relationship of Group IIIB to the Periodic Table

Group IIIB forms the first column of the p-block of the Periodic Table (p. 61). There is no gap (except paper) between beryllium and boron, or magnesium and aluminium. But gallium and indium are separated from calcium and strontium by ten transition metals; and thallium from barium by eighteen. This affects all their atomic properties (as has been shown) and in consequence all bulk properties. The elements of Group IIIB are more electronegative than the corresponding elements of Group IIA and less electronegative than those of Group IVB.

A strong diagonal relationship exists between boron and silicon (p. 409) and between beryllium and aluminium (p. 357). The relationship between A and B families is close, e.g. aluminium stands in a more normal Group relationship to scandium than it does to gallium. Indeed there is some justification for putting boron and aluminium at the top of Group IIIA instead of IIIB. There is no break in trend in passing along Periods 2 and 3 from Group IIA to IIIB.

Similarities between members of the Group

The fundamental similarity is that, being in Group IIIB, they all have three electrons in their external valency shell. They are the first elements with valency electrons in more than one orbital, thus s^2p^1; but they all show valency 3 because one s electron is readily promoted giving the configuration s^1p^2, i.e. $\boxed{\uparrow}\ \boxed{\uparrow\,|\,\uparrow\,|\ \ }$. The penultimate shells in the boron and aluminium atoms have the stable helium and neon number of electrons, 2 and 8 respectively. All except boron are metals, forming M^{3+} ions.

General Group characteristics

Atomic properties of Group III B elements

	Symbol	Atomic no.	Atomic weight	Electronic configuration						Group valency	Other valencies	Maximum covalency
				K	L	M	N	O	P			
Boron	B	5	10.81	2	3	—	—	—	—	3 Covalent	—	4
Aluminium	Al	13	26.98	2	8	3	—	—	—	3 Ionic and covalent	—	6
Gallium	Ga	31	69.72	2	8	18	3	—	—	3 Ionic	2, 1	6
Indium	In	49	114.82	2	8	18	18	3	—	3 Ionic	1	6
Thallium	Tl	81	204.37	2	8	18	32	18	3	3 Ionic	1	6

Differences within the Group

These follow the established trends for B families in the Main Groups (pp. 76–7).

Further atomic properties of Group III B elements

	Covalent atomic radius (Å)	Ionic radius of M^{3+} (Å)	Electro-negativity (Allred–Rochow)	Standard electrode potential (V) $M^{3+} + 3e \rightleftharpoons M$
B	0.80	0.20 (hypothetical)	2.01	—
Al	1.25	0.50	1.47	−1.66
Ga	1.25	0.62	1.82	−0.52
In	1.50	0.81	1.49	−0.34
Tl	1.55	0.95	1.44	+0.72
				Tl^+/Tl, $E^\ominus = -0.34$

See pp. 69, 76, 73 for graphs incorporating the data given in the first three columns of the table.

Boron. This stands apart from the other members of the Group. The main reasons are as follows:

(1) It has a very much lower atomic radius, higher electronegativity, and much lower ionic radius. The hypothetical B^{3+} ion has an extremely

small radius and high charge, therefore a very high field-intensity, so high that the ion is in fact never formed under ordinary circumstances, i.e. boron is a non-metal, the only one in the Group and the only member all of whose compounds are covalent.

(2) It is unique among non-metals in having less than four valency electrons. The great electron-accepting power of the boron atom in many of its complex compounds is the result of this electron deficiency (p. 349). Aluminium has this power but to a much less extent.

(3) The maximum covalency of boron is 4 (all the others show 6 or more).

(4) It does not show the inert pair effect (gallium, indium and thallium do, but not aluminium).

Aluminium. The small size and large charge of the Al^{3+} ion gives it a high field-intensity. This accounts for (1) the considerable tendency of the aluminium atom to form covalencies, (2) the high hydration energy of the ion, an example of the use of covalency in stabilising a cation in aqueous solution, and (3) the high lattice energies of the ionic compounds of aluminium, e.g. Al_2O_3. The chief factor in giving aluminium its relatively large negative electrode potential, by far the highest in the Group, is the high hydration energy of the Al^{3+} ion.

Aluminium has a maximum covalency of 6 in some of its complexes, e.g. $[AlF_6]^{3-}$ but does not show the inert pair effect. The electronegativity of aluminium is almost as low as that of thallium, the lowest in the Group.

Gallium, indium and thallium. As a result of the *d*-block contraction, gallium has the same atomic radius as aluminium and a *greater* electronegativity, a reversal of the usual trend. Electronegativities fall from gallium to thallium, as expected with increase in atomic radius. All three have a maximum covalency of 6.

Unlike boron and aluminium, gallium, indium and thallium show the inert pair effect, and therefore form monovalent compounds, whose stability increases down the Group. Ga^+ compounds are very unstable, In^+ compounds, e.g. InCl are not very stable, but compounds of Tl^+, e.g. thallium(I) hydroxide TlOH, are stable and indeed TlOH, because of the large ionic radius and small charge of the Tl^+ ion, is soluble in water giving a strongly alkaline solution (resemblance to NaOH).

Little more will be said on gallium, indium, and thallium.

The elements
Occurrence

Aluminium (7.45% of lithosphere) is the third most common element in the earth's crust, and the commonest of metals. Boron (0.005% of lithosphere) is uncommon. The others are rare and widely dispersed: Ga 0.001%, In and Tl each 0.00001% of the lithosphere.

Boron, because of its great affinity for oxygen is never found free, always combined with oxygen, e.g. in *borax*, sodium tetraborate decahydrate, $Na_2B_4O_7 . 10H_2O$, and *kernite*, the tetrahydrate $Na_2B_4O_7 . 4H_2O$; also as boric acid in hot springs in volcanic regions.

Aluminium, like boron and for the same reason, is not found free. In combination with oxygen it is found widely dispersed in enormous quantities in rocks as alumino-silicates (p. 388), in clays and *kaolin* (china clay) which are hydrated aluminium silicates; in large quantities as the hydrated oxide *bauxite* $Al_2O_3 . 2H_2O$, the chief source of the metal; and also as the anhydrous oxide, *corundum*. *Cryolite*, sodium hexafluoro-aluminate, Na_3AlF_6 is used in the manufacture of aluminium from bauxite.

Isolation

Boron. An impure amorphous form is got from borax, which gives boric acid when treated with hydrochloric acid. Dehydration of boric acid with heat gives the anhydride boric oxide, B_2O_3, which is reduced to boron by heating with magnesium.

A purer crystalline form is got by the reduction of boron tribromide vapour with hydrogen in an electric arc,

$$BBr_3 + 1\tfrac{1}{2}H_2 \rightarrow B + 3HBr \uparrow.$$

Aluminium. Aluminium is always manufactured from bauxite (processes starting with clays are much more costly). Electrolytic refining of aluminium is also costly, so the bauxite is purified to begin with. Aluminium, containing as impurity metals such as iron, which are more electronegative than aluminium, is very easily corroded by local action and is worthless for most purposes.

Purification of bauxite. The chief impurities are oxides of iron, silicon and titanium. Bauxite is roasted in air to convert iron(II) oxide to iron(III). The residue is finely powdered, then digested with strong NaOH solution under pressure. Al_2O_3 passes into solution as aluminate ion,

$$Al_2O_3 + 2OH^- \rightarrow 2AlO_2^- + H_2O.$$

Impurities remain undissolved as iron(III) oxide, titanium(IV) oxide, and sodium aluminium silicate. The solution is removed, diluted and seeded by adding crystals of pure $Al(OH)_3$, which precipitate pure $Al(OH)_3$ from solution. The precipitate is removed, washed, and dehydrated by heating strongly, leaving alumina, Al_2O_3.

Electrolysis. Electrode potentials in the molten state are roughly the same as those in aqueous solution.

Pure aluminium oxide is dissolved in molten cryolite in a carbon-lined iron tank acting as a cathode. The anodes used are of the continuous self-baking Söderberg type, formed by the action of the furnace heat on a mixture of pitch, anthracite and/or coke, fed into a steel casing and gradually lowered into the charge. The heating effect of the current melts the solid and maintains the required temperature of about 950 °C. Ions present in the melt are Na^+, Al^{3+}, O^{2-} and F^-, all in substantial amounts. Aluminium is discharged at the cathode since it has a smaller negative electrode potential than sodium. Oxygen is discharged at the anode since it has a smaller positive electrode potential than fluorine. At cathode: $Al^{3+}+3e \rightarrow Al\downarrow$; at anode: $2O^{2-} \rightarrow O_2+4e$.

Liquid aluminium at 950 °C is slightly more dense than the electrolyte and sinks to the bottom of the tank whence it is tapped at regular intervals. Liberated oxygen attacks the anodes forming oxides of carbon. The aluminium obtained is 99.9 % pure.

The process is carried on at Kinlochleven on the boundary between Argyllshire and Inverness-shire where 10 % of the total used in the U.K. is produced; and at Invergordon in Ross and Cromarty.

Physical properties

Density trends. The 'atomic' densities are approximately $B = 6$, $Al = 3.6$ and $Ga = 9.8$. From B to Al there is a change in structure, Al (C.N. 12) being much more closely packed than B (C.N. 6). This effect wipes out the fall in atomic density and leaves a slight rise in actual density. The great rise in atomic density from Al to Ga is reduced by the change in structure (Al, C.N. 12; Ga, C.N. 7), leaving a still considerable rise in actual density. The rises from Ga to In, and In to Tl are explained in a similar way.

Trends in hardness, melting point and boiling point. There is a great decrease in hardness, boron being almost as hard as diamond and thallium even softer than lead; and a fairly steady decrease in boiling point. Melting points decrease greatly from B to Ga, then increase moderately

Physical properties of Group III B elements

| Element | Appearance | Structure | | | Density $(g\ cm^{-3})$ | m.p. $(°C)$ | b.p. $(°C)$ | Electrical conductivity |
		Type	C.N.	Bonding				
B	Black lustrous solid	Unique	6	Mixed covalent and metallic	2.50	2300	2550	Very poor
Al	Silvery white metal	Slightly distorted F.C.C.	12	Metallic	2.70	660	2450	Very good
Ga	Silvery white metal	Irregular	7	Mixed covalent and metallic	5.91	29.8	2240	Moderate
In	Silvery white metal	Slightly distorted F.C.C.	12	Metallic	7.28	155	2050	Good
Tl	Silvery white metal	Slightly distorted H.C.P.	12	Metallic	11.85	304	1470	Moderate

to Tl. All these trends are explained in a rough general way by the overall increase in atomic radius, which results in corresponding decrease in bond strength. Irregularities are caused mainly by structural changes. The most striking feature in any of the trends is the plunge in melting point from boron (2300 °C) to gallium (30 °C) which has no parallel in the boiling points. The result is that Ga is liquid over the remakable range of more than 2000 °C. The low melting point of gallium is probably caused by the fact that its structure consists partly of Ga_2 molecules.

Chemical properties of boron and aluminium

As stated already (p. 343) boron is covalent in all its compounds; and aluminium shows a strong tendency to covalency, although the Al^{3+} cation is present in AlF_3, Al_2O_3, Al_4C_3 and as the hydrated ion $[Al(H_2O)_6]^{3+}$ in some of its salts.

Crystalline boron is almost inert chemically. The following reactions are those of amorphous boron (brown solid) and aluminium.

1. Air. Both boron and aluminium are stable in air at ordinary temperatures. In the case of aluminium this is because of the formation of a highly protective film of oxide which can be removed by rubbing with mercury or mercury(II) chloride solution. This forms an amalgam which reacts readily with moist air, and the surface of the metal soon becomes covered with a furry growth of oxide and hydroxide.

Both elements burn when heated in air, forming a mixture of oxide and nitride (B_2O_3, BN; Al_2O_3, AlN). When a piece of thick aluminium wire is held vertically in a bunsen flame it melts but no liquid drops off; the molten metal is held in a pear-shaped sack of oxide. This shows the remarkable strength (lattice energy) of aluminium oxide.

2. Water has no action on boron or aluminium. In the case of Al the oxide film protects it. Sea water corrodes Al readily. Boron reacts readily with steam at red heat forming boric acid and hydrogen,

$$2B + 6H_2O \rightarrow 2H_3BO_3 + 3H_2\uparrow.$$

Aluminium does not react with steam even at high temperature because of the protective film of oxide.

3. Acids. *HCl.* Boron being a non-metal does not react with HCl. Aluminium reacts slowly with cold dilute HCl, rapidly with hot concentrated because of the solubility of Al_2O_3 in HCl,

$$Al + 3H^+ \rightarrow Al^{3+} + 1\tfrac{1}{2}H_2\uparrow.$$

H_2SO_4. The dilute acid has little or no action on B or Al but for different reasons. Boron is a non-metal and cannot displace hydrogen ions from solution. The oxide film on the aluminium is not soluble in dilute sulphuric acid.

Hot concentrated sulphuric acid reacts vigorously as an oxidising agent with both elements, forming boric acid and aluminium sulphate respectively, and being itself reduced to SO_2,

$$2B + 3H_2SO_4 \rightarrow 2H_3BO_3 + 3SO_2\uparrow,$$
$$2Al + 6H_2SO_4 \rightarrow Al_2(SO_4)_3 + 6H_2O + 3SO_2\uparrow.$$

HNO_3. Boron and aluminium behave very differently with nitric acid. Boron reacts with dilute or concentrated nitric acid, which oxidises it to boric acid,

$$2B + 6HNO_3 \rightarrow 2H_3BO_3 + 6NO_2\uparrow.$$

Aluminium is unaffected by dilute nitric acid, cold or hot, and by cold concentrated nitric acid. The metal is rendered passive because of an unreactive oxide layer. The concentrated acid when heated to about 90 °C reacts quite vigorously with aluminium, oxides of nitrogen being evolved.

4. Alkalis. Boron dissolves in fused caustic soda or potash (but not in aqueous solutions) giving metaborate ion and hydrogen,

$$B + OH^- + H_2O \rightarrow BO_2^- + 1\tfrac{1}{2}H_2\uparrow.$$

Aluminium dissolves in aqueous caustic soda or potash giving aluminate ion and hydrogen,

$$Al + OH^- + 3H_2O \rightarrow [Al(OH)_4]^- + 1\tfrac{1}{2}H_2\uparrow.$$

The protective Al_2O_3 film has been removed by OH^- ions, because aluminium oxide is amphoteric.

5. Combination with non-metals. Boron and aluminium combine directly with halogens, oxygen, sulphur, nitrogen, and carbon forming binary compounds; the more electronegative the other elements are, the more readily does combination take place; e.g. with fluorine, the most electronegative, combination takes place in the cold; with carbon, the least electronegative, high temperatures are required. The compounds formed with boron are similar to those with aluminium except for carbides, thus: BF_3, AlF_3, etc.; B_2O_3, Al_2O_3; B_2S_3, Al_2S_3; BN, AlN; but B_4C, Al_4C_3 (see pp. 394–5).

6. Reducing action. Because of their great affinity for oxygen and other electronegative elements, boron and aluminium are powerful reducing agents. Examples are given below.

Uses

Boron is used both as a deoxidiser in the manufacture of some metals, in making hard alloy steels, as a neutron absorber in the production of nuclear energy and as an additive to the semi-conductors silicon and germanium.

Metal borides e.g. molybdenum boride and titanium diboride are hard and with high melting points up to 3000 °C. They are used in aircraft and space vessels where sudden changes of temperature may occur; also in high speed cutting tools for metals.

Aluminium, because of its cheapness, low density, resistance to atmospheric corrosion, good malleability, ductility, electrical and thermal conductivity, power of forming alloys, considerable strength and hardness, and great reducing powers, is used in very large quantities.

Domestic uses. In making pans, kettles, teapots. Alkaline solutions, e.g. washing soda, attack aluminium; prolonged contact should therefore be avoided.

Alloys. These are used in the aircraft, motor car and building industries for frames, sheeting, engine parts, etc. Two important alloys are *magnalium*, Al + 10 to 30 % Mg, *duralumin* 95 % Al, 4 % Cu, $\tfrac{1}{2}$ % Mg, $\tfrac{1}{2}$ % Mn.

Electrical industry. Aluminium is used to replace copper for conductors where lightness is of paramount importance, e.g. overhead cables in the grid system are made of aluminium wires twisted round reinforcing steel wires.

Aluminium powder is used in paints and explosives (ammonal).

As a reducing agent: (1) to remove oxygen and nitrogen from molten iron and steel thus preventing blow-holes in castings, (2) in the preparation of Cr from Cr_2O_3, Mn from MnO_2 and Ti from TiO_2. Aluminium powder is mixed with the oxides, and on ignition by a fuse, reduces the oxides to metals, the heat of the reaction melting the metal which collects on the floor of the vessel. Welding of steel rails *in situ* is carried out in a similar way by packing a mixture of Al powder and Fe_2O_3 round the joint and igniting the mixture with a fuse. Molten iron is formed and joins the rails. These are examples of thermite or Goldschmidt processes.

Miscellaneous. As foil for wrapping foods and confectionery, and for milk bottle tops; for surfacing mirrors of large telescopes.

Compounds of boron and aluminium

Boron is unique in being the only non-metal element with less than four electrons in its valency shell. The compound boron trichloride, in which boron forms three covalencies has the valency electrons of the elements arranged thus:

$$\overset{\displaystyle Cl}{\underset{\displaystyle Cl{\times} \quad {\cdot}Cl}{\underset{\times \, \cdot}{\overset{}{B}}}}$$

The boron atom has a *sextet* of electrons, not an octet. As a result in its tricovalent compounds it has a strong tendency to accept a lone pair of electrons from a donor molecule, thus achieving the stable octet, and its maximum covalency of four, e.g. boron trichloride reacts with ammonia to form a stable addition compound:

$$Cl-B{\overset{\displaystyle Cl}{\underset{\displaystyle Cl}{\Big\backslash}}} \quad + \quad \overset{\displaystyle H}{\underset{\displaystyle H}{:N-H}} \longrightarrow Cl-\overset{\displaystyle Cl}{\underset{\displaystyle Cl}{B}}-\overset{\displaystyle H}{\underset{\displaystyle H}{N}}-H$$

Acceptor Donor

Aluminium's tendency to form covalencies is considerable but much less than boron's. So also is its tendency to form addition compounds. Aluminium differs from boron in having a maximum covalency of 6.

349

Hydrides

Boron forms a series of hydrides, the simplest of which is diborane B_2H_6; aluminium forms one hydride $(AlH_3)_x$.

Diborane, B_2H_6, (so called because its formula is similar to that of ethane C_2H_6, and disilane, Si_2H_6) is prepared by the action of lithium aluminium hydride on boron trichloride in ethereal solution (p. 264),

$$4BCl_3 + 3LiAlH_4 \rightarrow 2B_2H_6\uparrow + 3LiCl + 3AlCl_3.$$

Diborane is a colourless gas, spontaneously inflammable in air at room temperature and immediately hydrolysed by water,

$$B_2H_6 + 6H_2O \rightarrow 2H_3BO_3 + 6H_2\uparrow .$$

Its structure cannot be shown as in (1) below, because the seven covalent bonds would require a total of 14 valency electrons, while the total number available is only 12. There is good evidence for structure (2). In this the two hydrogen atoms on the left and the two on the right are joined to the boron atoms by normal covalent bonds shown by solid lines, thus accounting for eight electrons. The remaining four, one from each hydrogen and boron atom, are delocalised and accommodated two in each of the dotted channels B--H--B. In each of these channels, the electron cloud formed by the two delocalised electrons embraces three atomic nuclei forming a *three-centre bond*. Covalent compounds which contain less than the number of electrons required for normal covalencies are said to be *electron deficient*.

(1) Incorrect   (2)

For the preparation of aluminium hydride $(AlH_3)_x$, see p. 264. It is a covalent polymer of unknown structure. On gentle heating it decomposes into its elements.

Chlorides

Preparation. These, like all the halides of boron and aluminium, can be prepared by direct synthesis. Both are usually made by the general reaction shown below for $AlCl_3$ (used in its manufacture),

$$Al_2O_3 + 3C + 3Cl_2 \xrightarrow[\text{temperature}]{\text{high}} 2AlCl_3 + 3CO.$$

Properties. BCl_3 is a covalent compound, gaseous at room temperature but condensing to a colourless fuming liquid at $12.5\,°C$. The gas consists of single planar molecules. As previously stated, it readily accepts a lone pair of electrons to form addition compounds, e.g. $H_3N^+\!\!-\!\!^-BCl_3$. Water hydrolyses it, the first step being probably the formation of an addition compound $H_2O^+\!\!-\!\!^-BCl_3$ which then decomposes, giving the final products boric acid and hydrochloric acid,

$$BCl_3 + 3H_2O \rightarrow H_3BO_3 + 3HCl.$$

Aluminium chloride may be made by dissolving aluminium in concentrated hydrochloric acid and allowing the solution to crystallise, when colourless, deliquescent ionic crystals of aluminium chloride hexahydrate are formed, $AlCl_3.6H_2O$ or $[Al(H_2O)_6]Cl_3$. When the salt is heated it is completely hydrolysed by its own water of crystallisation leaving a residue of Al_2O_3.

Anhydrous aluminium chloride cannot be made by heating the hydrate in air because of hydrolysis; it is made by passing dry chlorine over the heated metal. The anhydrous chloride is a white deliquescent volatile solid which fumes in moist air, is soluble in most organic solvents, and is

violently hydrolysed by water, properties which indicate a covalent character. It has a layer structure with some ionic character, but, on heating, it sublimes at $183\ °C$ giving a covalent vapour consisting of dimeric molecules Al_2Cl_6 with the structure shown above. Each aluminium atom achieves an octet by accepting a lone pair of electrons from a chlorine atom. The vapour dissociates on heating giving $AlCl_3$ molecules, the dissociation being complete at $800\ °C$.

Fluorides

Preparation. Boron trifluoride is conveniently made as shown in the equation,

$$B_2O_3 + 3CaF_2 + 3H_2SO_4\ \text{(conc.)} \xrightarrow{\text{heat}} 2BF_3 + 3CaSO_4 + 3H_2O.$$

Aluminium fluoride is usually made by the action of hydrofluoric acid on the metal at ordinary temperature, or by passing hydrogen fluoride gas over heated Al_2O_3.

Properties. BF_3 is a colourless highly reactive covalent gas fuming in moist air. Its molecule is a very strong electron acceptor (like BCl_3). It reacts violently with water, the first stages being as with BCl_3, but the hydrofluoric acid formed reacts with unhydrolysed BF_3 giving fluoroboric acid HBF_4 which contains the stable fluoroborate ion BF_4^-,

$$4BF_3 + 3H_2O \rightarrow H_3BO_3 + 3H^+ + 3BF_4^-.$$

AlF_3 is very different. An ionic solid of high melting point sparingly soluble in water, it is chemically very unreactive, e.g. it is decomposed only very slowly by fusion with KOH. Its structure is ionic, C.N. 6:2.

Uses of chlorides and fluorides. Boron trifluoride and aluminium tri-chloride have very important uses as catalysts in organic synthesis and in cracking and polymerisation of petroleum. Indeed the former is one of the most important of all catalysts. These reactions depend on their power of forming intermediate addition-compounds with electron-donor molecules. Thus BF_3 forms adducts with organic nitrogen and oxygen compounds, e.g. amines, ethers, aldehydes and ketones. $AlCl_3$ on the other hand, catalyses reactions involving organic halides, e.g. the Friedel-Crafts reaction for making toluene from benzene and chloromethane,

$$C_6H_6 + CH_3Cl \rightarrow C_6H_5CH_3 + HCl.$$

Oxides

Preparation. *Diboron trioxide*, B_2O_3, the anhydride of orthoboric acid, H_3BO_3, is made by heating the acid. The action has three stages:

$$H_3BO_3 \xrightarrow{100\ °C} HBO_2 + H_2O; \quad 4HBO_2 \xrightarrow{140\ °C} H_2B_4O_7 + H_2O;$$
Orthoboric acid $\qquad$ Metaboric acid

$$H_2B_4O_7 \xrightarrow[\text{heat}]{\text{red}} 2B_2O_3 + H_2O.$$
Tetraboric acid

Aluminium oxide, alumina Al_2O_3, is made by heating the hydrated oxides, the hydroxide, the nitrate or the sulphate.

Uses. Al_2O_3 is used in the manufacture of aluminium; as a furnace lining; a constituent of cements, an abrasive, an adsorbent in chromatography, and as a catalyst or catalyst-support in organic preparations.

Properties. B_2O_3 is a colourless or white glassy solid (covalent) which melts in a bunsen flame. Weakly acid, it dissolves in water to give boric acid H_3BO_3. It appears to act as a base by combining with phosphorus pentoxide but the product is a double oxide rather than a salt.

Al_2O_3 is a very refractory white solid (melting point 2300 °C), insoluble in water. When prepared by a method not requiring more than red heat, it is soluble in acids and aqueous alkalis, and is therefore amphoteric. When strongly heated its structure is modified and it becomes insoluble in acids or aqueous alkalis, but is soluble in fused alkali. Its structure (corundum) is ionic, C.N. 6:4.

Hydroxides

Boric acid or orthoboric acid, H_3BO_3, always acts as an acid. It is prepared by adding excess of concentrated hydrochloric acid to a hot strong solution of borax. On cooling, boric acid crystallises and is purified by recrystallisation,

$$Na_2B_4O_7 + 2HCl + 5H_2O \rightarrow 4H_3BO_3 + 2NaCl.$$

It forms white shining plates like soap flakes in appearance and to touch. It is appreciably volatile in steam; slightly soluble in cold water, and moderately soluble in hot. Like all compounds of boron it is covalent and is a very weak tribasic acid (weaker than carbonic acid). For action of heat, see p. 352.

Aluminium hydroxide $Al(OH)_3$ is formed as a colourless almost invisible gelatinous precipitate when a solution of ammonium hydroxide or sodium hydroxide is added to a solution of an aluminium salt. It is insoluble in excess ammonium hydroxide but soluble in excess sodium hydroxide solution forming hydroxy-aluminate ions by addition of one or more hydroxyl ions to each molecule of hydroxide. This is the equation for the acidic ionisation of $Al(OH)_3$,

$$Al(OH)_3 + OH^- \rightarrow [Al(OH)_4]^-; \quad Al(OH)_3 + 3OH^- \rightarrow [Al(OH)_6]^{3-}.$$

$Al(OH)_3$ has a very small solubility in water, but when freshly precipitated it is readily soluble in acids, and alkali hydroxides, thus showing its amphoteric nature. If left standing it changes in structure to a form which is insoluble in acids or alkalis. When heated it is decomposed into water and alumina Al_2O_3. During precipitation, the gelatinous $Al(OH)_3$ has a great power of adsorbing molecules and ions from solution. This can be shown with dyes and coloured ions, e.g. Co^{2+}, Ni^{2+}. Sometimes the $Al(OH)_3$ appears white and opaque because of adsorption of colourless ions from solution.

Some explanation of the relative acid and base-forming powers of $B(OH)_3$ and $Al(OH)_3$ may be given, using the ideas on p. 256. (1) The bonds between boron and oxygen in $B(OH)_3$ are less polar than the corresponding bonds in $Al(OH)_3$ because boron is much more electronegative than aluminium. There is therefore more tendency for OH^- and Al^{3+} ions to be formed with $Al(OH)_3$ since the process is further advanced. (2) The B—O bond lengths are much shorter than the Al—O bond lengths because boron has a much smaller atomic (and ionic) radius than aluminium. The energy required to separate OH^- ions (when formed) from Al^{3+} ions is proportionately less than would be required with $B(OH)_3$. Indeed with $B(OH)_3$, B^{3+} and OH^- ions are not formed at all. For these reasons $Al(OH)_3$ is weakly basic, $B(OH)_3$ is not basic. $Al(OH)_3$ is also weakly acidic and $B(OH)_3$ more acidic.

Uses. Boric acid is used as a mild antiseptic under the name boracic acid. For the uses of aluminium hydroxide see aluminium sulphate (p. 356).

Disodium tetraborate, borax, $Na_2B_4O_7.10H_2O$

This, the most important salt of boric acid, is made from the minerals *borax* and *kernite* by dissolving in water, filtering and crystallising at a temperature below 60 °C; above this temperature the pentahydrate is formed.

Borax forms colourless crystals, sparingly soluble in cold water, readily soluble in hot. Like sodium carbonate it is the salt of a strong base and a very weak acid, and so it is considerably hydrolysed in solution, which has an alkaline reaction. A standard solution of borax is therefore used in standardising hydrochloric and sulphuric acid solutions, the indicator being methyl orange or methyl red which are unaffected by boric acid.

Borax bead test. When borax on a loop of platinum wire is heated strongly in a bunsen flame, it froths as the water of crystallisation is driven off and, on cooling, leaves a glassy bead of anhydrous sodium tetraborate, which may be regarded as a compound of sodium metaborate and boric oxide, $2NaBO_2.B_2O_3$. When a coloured salt of a transition metal, e.g. $CoSO_4$, is heated with the bead until the mixture melts, the non-volatile acidic oxide, B_2O_3, drives out the volatile acidic oxide SO_3 leaving the borax bead coloured deep blue with cobalt metaborate in solid solution,

$$CoSO_4 + B_2O_3 \rightarrow Co(BO_2)_2 + SO_3\uparrow.$$

A number of transition metals give characteristic bead colours in this test in qualitative analysis.

Uses. Borax is used in the manufacture of heat-resisting glasses and enamels; as a flux in soldering and brazing since it cleans the metal surface by dissolving oxides; and in the laboratory as described.

Carbides

See pp. 392–6.

Sulphides

Al_2S_3 and B_2S_3 are made by heating the element with sulphur. They cannot be prepared in aqueous solution because they are immediately hydrolysed by water giving hydroxides and hydrogen sulphide.

Oxo-salts

The non-metal boron forms no oxo-salts because formation of these depends on the existence of cations to replace the hydrogen ions of the oxo-acids; B^{3+} does not exist.

Aluminium hydroxide is a very weak base and so its salts with strong acids are readily hydrolysed by water giving acidic solutions, and its salts with weak acids are unstable or do not exist at all, e.g. aluminium carbonate does not exist. When sodium carbonate or hydrogen carbonate solution is added to a solution containing Al^{3+} ions, the hydroxide is precipitated and carbon dioxide evolved,

$$2Al^{3+} + 3CO_3^{2-} + 3H_2O \rightarrow 2Al(OH)_3\downarrow + 3CO_2 \uparrow .$$

Aluminium sulphate, $Al_2(SO_4)_3 . 18H_2O$

Preparation. On the industrial scale it is made by (1) heating kaolin with concentrated sulphuric acid or (2) heating bauxite with dilute sulphuric acid. The product from bauxite contains iron(III) sulphate. It may be made in the laboratory, in the usual way, by the action of concentrated H_2SO_4 on the metal, oxide or hydroxide, followed by slight dilution. The resulting solution deposits crystals of $Al_2(SO_4)_3 . 18H_2O$.

Properties. Aluminium sulphate is a colourless, crystalline, ionic solid, readily soluble in water. The solution has an acid reaction because of partial hydrolysis, and contains $[Al(H_2O)_6]^{3+}$ ions. The anhydrous salt is obtained by careful heating of the hydrate. With further strong heating, $Al_2(SO_4)_3$ decomposes in the usual way with sulphates, sulphur trioxide being evolved, some sulphur dioxide and oxygen, and a residue of alumina remains.

Uses. (1) In paper manufacture it is added to the pulp to strengthen the product by binding the fibres. (2) It is also used as a mordant in dyeing cloth (Latin *mordere*, 'to bite'). The cloth is soaked in a solution of aluminium sulphate (or potash alum) and then in sodium carbonate solution which precipitates $Al(OH)_3$ in the fibres. When the treated cloth is put in solution of the dye, the $Al(OH)_3$ adsorbs the dye and binds it firmly to the cloth. (3) It is added to water to purify it for human consumption: the Al^{3+} ions cause coagulation and precipitation of suspended and colloidal particles, which, along with bacteria present, are then adsorbed and carried down by $Al(OH)_3$ precipitated by hydrolysis. A similar method is used for the purification of sewage. (4) Cloth may be water-proofed by precipitating $Al(OH)_3$ in its fibres. (5) A solution of $Al_2(SO_4)_3$ or potash alum is used in 'foam' fire extinguishers for use on petrol or oil fires.

Alums

These are series of isomorphous double salts with the general formula $M^IM^{III}(SO_4)_2.12H_2O$, where M^{III} is Al^{3+}, Cr^{3+}, Fe^{3+}, etc., (see pp. 234–5), and M^I is an alkali metal or ammonium.

Potassium chromium(III) sulphate. Chrome alum $K_2SO_4.Cr_2(SO_4)_3.24H_2O$

This is made by acidifying a solution of potassium dichromate with dilute sulphuric acid, reducing with sulphur dioxide, keeping the temperature below 50 °C, then allowing the solution to cool and crystallise. Deep purple octahedral crystals of chrome alum separate

$$K_2Cr_2O_7 + 3SO_2 + H_2SO_4 \rightarrow K_2SO_4 + Cr_2(SO_4)_3 + H_2O.$$

Chrome alum is used in the tanning of leather, which then becomes more hard-wearing; also in dyeing.

Aluminium nitrate, $Al(NO_3)_3.9H_2O$

This is conveniently made by adding equivalent quantities of lead nitrate solution to aluminium sulphate solution, filtering off the precipitated lead(II) sulphate and crystallising the filtrate. Its most common hydrate is $Al(NO_3)_3.9H_2O$. It decomposes as usual on heating leaving alumina.

Complexes of boron and aluminium

Both elements form many complexes, some of which have been mentioned. Examples are as follows.

Complex cations. Boron forms none. The hydrated aluminium ion $[Al(H_2O)_6]^{3+}$ is present in aqueous solutions of all aluminium salts and in some crystals. These solutions are acidic because of reactions such as,

$$[Al(H_2O)_6]^{3+} \to [Al(H_2O)_5OH]^{2+} + H^+.$$

Complex anions. Examples are fluoroborate ion $[BF_4]^-$; fluoro-aluminate ions $[AlF_4]^-$ and $[AlF_6]^{3-}$, the last being present in cryolite, Na_3AlF_6; hydroxy-aluminate ions $[Al(OH)_4]^-$ and $[Al(OH)_6]^{3-}$.

Molecular complexes. These include the addition compounds formed by BF_3, BCl_3 and $AlCl_3$.

Similarities between beryllium and aluminium (diagonal)

General. Although their cationic charges and radii are different, the ratios ionic charge/ionic radius are very similar—Be^{2+} 6.6, Al^{3+} 6.0—i.e. the field strengths of the cations are similar and very high, so that both metals are on the borderline between covalency and electrovalency. Their electro-negativities are the same (1.47), and their standard electrode potentials almost the same: Be^{2+}/Be, $E^{\ominus} = -1.7$ V.; Al^{3+}/Al, $E^{\ominus} = -1.66$ V.

Elements. Both metals form an oxide film at room temperature which protects them against further oxidation at moderate temperatures and against corrosion by water or attack by steam even at high temperatures. Both are rendered passive by nitric acid, and react moderately with HCl. Both dissolve in NaOH solution with evolution of hydrogen and formation in solution of beryllate and aluminate respectively, showing their amphoteric nature.

Compounds. Both form polymerised, covalent hydrides. Their oxides are refractory white solids insoluble in water but soluble in acids and alkali, therefore amphoteric. Their hydroxides are white, insoluble, amphoteric solids; chlorides are white deliquescent solids of low melting point, fuming in moist air, readily soluble in and hydrolysed by water, very soluble in ethanol, and therefore covalent. Their sulphates are readily soluble in water; carbides are ionic and are methanides, i.e. they react with water to give methane.

Exercises

1. Describe and explain the varied valency changes in passing down Group III B.

2. From a knowledge of trends in the Periodic Table and the chemistry of its neighbours, deduce in as great detail as possible the physical and chemical properties of gallium and its principle compounds.

3. The most immediately useful and important relationship in the Periodic Table is the Group relationship. Does the diagonal relationship as exemplified by the close similarity between beryllium and aluminium, boron and silicon, cast any doubt on the fundamental validity of arrangement of elements in Groups? Give reasons for your answer.

4. From a knowledge of boron and aluminium and the trends in Group III B and Period 6, deduce in as great detail as possible the physical and chemical properties of thallium. Give reasons for your answers, and check their accuracy.

5. What is meant by the term *alum*? Explain why alums are considered to be double salts.

Describe in outline how you would prepare pure samples of (*a*) potassium aluminium alum, starting from aluminium foil; (*b*) ferric ammonium alum from iron filings.

What is the effect of adding sodium hydroxide to an aqueous solution of **each** of these alums? (C)

6. Give an account of the method by which aluminium is manufactured. Starting from aluminium, how would you prepare (*a*) anhydrous aluminium chloride, (*b*) pure aluminium oxide, (*c*) aluminium sulphide? Give **two** uses of aluminium as a reducing agent. (C)

7. Explain how aluminium is obtained from its purified oxide. How and under what conditions does aluminium react with (*a*) sodium hydroxide, (*b*) ferric oxide.

Describe how you could prepare pure dry crystals of potassium aluminium alum starting from aluminium foil, potassium hydroxide and dilute sulphuric acid.

Explain the observation that the addition of sodium hydroxide to aqueous alum leads to the formation of an aluminium hydroxide precipitate which is dispersed by excess alkali. (J.M.B.)

8. From its position in the Periodic Table give a reasoned prediction of the chief chemical and physical properties of element 31 and of such of the following compounds of this element as you believe are likely to exist:

oxide, hydroxide, carbonate, sulphide, sulphate, chloride.

Suggest how the element is likely to occur in nature and how it would be extracted. (J.M.B.)

9. Give an account of the sources and extraction of aluminium and describe the principal chemical and physical features of its oxide, hydroxide, chloride and sulphate. (O & C)

23

GROUP IVB: THE CARBON GROUP

Group IVB consists of the elements carbon, silicon, germanium, tin, and
lead.

Relationship of Group IVB to the Periodic Table

Group IVB is in the p-block of the Periodic Table (p. 61), and the elements germanium, tin, and lead therefore follow the transition metals in
their Periods. In consequence they have eighteen electrons in their penultimate shell (see table), a fact which affects their properties. The elements
in the Group are more electronegative than the corresponding elements of
Group IIIB, less electronegative than those of Group VB.

There is a strong diagonal relationship between boron and silicon (see
p. 409). The relationship between the A and B families is close. Group
IVA consists of the metals titanium, zirconium and hafnium. A comparison
of titanium with tin is given on pp. 537–8.

General Group characteristics

Atomic properties of Group IVB elements

Element	Symbol	Atomic no.	Atomic weight	Electronic configuration K L M N O P						Group valency $= N$	Ionic valencies $= N$ and $(N-2)$	Maximum covalency shown
Carbon	C	6	12.01	2	4	—	—	—	—	4	4⁻	4
Silicon	Si	14	28.1	2	8	4	—	—	—	4	—	6
Germanium	Ge	32	72.6	2	8	18	4	—	—	4	4⁺	6
Tin	Sn	50	118.7	2	8	18	18	4	—	4	2⁺, 4⁺	6
Lead	Pb	82	207.2	2	8	18	32	18	4	4	2⁺, 4⁺	6

This is the only Group in the Periodic Table which contains both true metals
and non-metals. Carbon is a typical weakly electronegative non-metal, which
is almost always quadricovalent. Lead is a true metal whose most important
valency is a positive electrovalency of two. It is difficult at first sight to see
how the inclusion of carbon and lead in the same Group can be justified. It
should be a main purpose of any treatment of Group IVB to justify this.

Similarities between members of the Group

The fundamental similarity is that, being in Group IV B, they all have four electrons in their external (valency) shell. In the ground state their atoms have their valency electrons in the s^2p^2 configuration, i.e.

$$\begin{array}{cc} s & p \\ \boxed{1\downarrow} & \boxed{1\,|\,1\,|\,} \end{array},$$

but they all show the Group covalency of four because one s electron is readily promoted to the vacant p orbital thus:

$$\begin{array}{cc} s & p \\ \boxed{1} & \boxed{1\,|\,1\,|\,1} \end{array}.$$

By sp^3 hybridisation (p. 141) the atoms form four equivalent atomic orbitals directed towards the corners of a regular tetrahedron. The stable octet is then achieved by the formation of four covalencies. This is the chief type of bond formed by carbon and silicon (but not by the other members of the Group—see next section).

Differences within the Group

These follow the established trends in the B families of the Main Groups (pp. 76–7).

Further atomic properties of Group IV B elements

	Atomic radius (Å)	Ionic radius E^{4+} (Å)	Electro-negativity (Allred–Rochow)	Standard electrode potentials (V)
C	0.77 (diamond)	0.16	2.50	—
Si	1.17	0.42	1.74	—
Ge	1.22	0.53	2.02	—
Sn	1.41 (white)	0.71	1.72	$Sn^{2+}+2e = Sn$ -0.14
Pb	1.54	0.84	1.55	$\begin{cases} Pb^{2+}+2e = Pb \\ \quad -0.13 \end{cases}$
Pb^{2+}		1.20		

In passing down the Group there is a change in the nature of the element in conformity with the general decrease in electronegativity (Si is anomalous here). Carbon and silicon are non-metals, germanium is a semi-metal, tin and lead are metals.

Carbon stands apart from the other members of its Group; for example, the difference between the atomic radii of carbon and silicon is 0.40 Å, which is greater than that between silicon and the last member of the Group, lead, which is 0.37 Å. It shows sufficient family resemblance to be easily recognised as a fellow-member (see p. 374), but its differences are great enough to justify the statement that it is unique. Thus it differs not only from silicon, but from all other elements except hydrogen in the enormous number and variety of its compounds. There are about twenty times as many carbon compounds (usually containing hydrogen) as there are compounds of all the other elements together (excluding hydrogen). For this reason compounds of carbon are dealt with in detail in a separate branch of chemistry—organic chemistry.

Reasons for the uniqueness of carbon.

(1) *Carbon has a half-filled valency shell and a maximum covalency of* 4. By the promotion of one electron from the *s* orbital to a vacant *p* orbital, the carbon atom has one electron in each of its four available orbitals, one vacancy in each of them, and no lone pairs. By forming four co-valencies the carbon atom in its compounds acquires (*a*) an octet, (*b*) its maximum covalency of four and (*c*) a fully shared octet, i.e. one containing no lone pairs. It therefore cannot act as an electron donor (no lone pairs) or an electron acceptor (no available orbitals). Carbon compounds are therefore stable and even relatively inert in many cases (e.g. the paraffins).

(2) *Carbon forms very stable bonds with itself and with many other elements.* The stability of some of these bonds is shown in the following average single bond energies (N.B. 1 kcal = 4.184 kJ):

$$C-C, 83; \quad C-O, 84; \quad C-H, 99: \quad C-Cl, 80 \text{ kcal mol}^{-1}.$$

Further, carbon atoms are able to link covalently to form stable chains, which may contain from two up to very large numbers of carbon atoms.

In these chains only two valencies of carbon are used, leaving the other two free to link with other elements or with other carbon atoms (forming branched chains). The chains act as a backbone or skeleton on which an enormous number of compounds can be formed. Because of the uni-valency of hydrogen and the great strength of the C—H bond, hydrogen plays a conspicuous part in such compounds. In addition, rings and networks of rings can be formed, the most important being the benzene ring of six carbon atoms. (*Note*. The minimum valency needed by an element to form a chain is two. Oxygen and sulphur might therefore be expected to have this power. Oxygen has not (except in peroxides) but sulphur has, e.g. in its molecule S_8, in plastic sulphur, and in the thionic acids (p. 494). By forming two covalent links the covalencies of sulphur are satisfied, each atom having an octet, and so there is little tendency for other elements to combine with sulphur atoms along the chain (as they do so freely in the case of carbon).

(3) *Carbon forms reasonably stable multiple covalent bonds with itself and other elements* especially oxygen and nitrogen, e.g.

$$\diagup_\diagdown\!C=C\diagdown^\diagup \;, \quad -C\equiv C- \;, \quad \diagup_\diagdown\!C=O \;, \quad \text{and} \;\; -C\equiv N$$

(4) *Carbon has a much smaller atomic radius, and a much greater electronegativity than the other members of the Group.*

(5) *Carbon does not show the inert pair effect* (p. 94).

The other elements of the Group have maximum covalencies greater than 4. They can therefore act as electron acceptors.

Silicon. The average single bond energies for bonds containing Si are instructive (N.B. 1 kcal = 4.184 kJ),

Si—Si, 42;   Si—O, 89;   Si—H, 75 kcal mol^{-1}.

The chemistry of silicon is determined largely by two factors: (1) the great strength of the Si—O bond. Compounds of silicon containing other bonds show a strong tendency to be converted into compounds containing Si—O, (2) The maximum covalency of silicon is 6. The great stability of Si—O bonds is seen most clearly in the composition of the earth's crust, in which structures of the following type predominate,

$$
\begin{array}{ccccc}
-\overset{|}{\underset{|}{Si}}-O-\overset{|}{\underset{|}{Si}}-O-\overset{|}{\underset{|}{Si}}- \\
\overset{|}{\underset{|}{O}} & & \overset{|}{\underset{|}{O}} & & \overset{|}{\underset{|}{O}} \\
-\overset{|}{\underset{|}{Si}}-O-\overset{|}{\underset{|}{Si}}-O-\overset{|}{\underset{|}{Si}}- \\
\overset{|}{\underset{|}{O}} & & \overset{|}{\underset{|}{O}} & & \overset{|}{\underset{|}{O}} \\
-\overset{|}{\underset{|}{Si}}-O-\overset{|}{\underset{|}{Si}}-O-\overset{|}{\underset{|}{Si}}-
\end{array}
$$

Silicon differs from carbon in the fact that it does not form long stable chains of silicon atoms because the Si—Si bond is much less stable than the Si—O bond.

Tin and lead. Passing down the Group to tin and lead, the inert pair effect (p. 94) becomes a major factor. Quadricovalent compounds decrease in stability down the Group with increasing stability of the inert pair of s electrons in the valency shell. With lead the chief valency is an ionic valency of 2, i.e. Pb^{2+} is the more stable species. Thus lead(IV) chloride is very unstable and a powerful oxidising agent decomposing into the very stable ionic salt, $PbCl_2$, which is difficult to oxidise. Tin(IV) chloride, $SnCl_4$, on the other hand, is more stable than tin(II) chloride, $SnCl_2$, which is a powerful reducing agent in aqueous solution.

A few well-known ionic compounds containing Group IVB elements in the $+4$ oxidation state are: GeO_2 and SnO_2 (in their rutile modification), PbO_2, SnF_4 and $SnCl_4.5H_2O$. Carbon forms C^{4-} ions in some carbides, e.g. Al_4C_3 (p. 394).

Finally all the elements except carbon show a covalency of 6 in complex ions.

It is of interest to note that hydrogen, like carbon, is unique, and for somewhat similar reasons. It has a half-filled valency shell and a maximum covalency of one, equal to the number of electrons in its valency shell. By forming one covalency the hydrogen atom acquires (1) a stable duplet, (2) its maximum covalency, and (3) a fully shared electron shell, i.e. one containing no lone pairs. It therefore cannot act as an electron donor (no lone pairs) or an electron acceptor (no available orbitals). The stability of the paraffins and the enormous number of carbon–hydrogen compounds are partly due to those properties of hydrogen.

The elements
Occurrence

Carbon (0.08 % by weight of the earth's crust) is the only element in the Group to occur uncombined. It does so as diamonds, graphite and in coals and anthracites. Important compounds of carbon are the mineral oils (petroleum) which are mixtures of hydrocarbons; and the carbonates, chalk, limestone and marble (all $CaCO_3$), magnesite ($MgCO_3$) and dolomite ($CaCO_3.MgCO_3$). Carbon also occurs as carbon dioxide (1) in the atmosphere (0.03 % by volume, 0.04 % by weight), (2) dissolved in the ocean partly as carbon dioxide and partly as hydrogen carbonates of sodium, calcium and magnesium. Of great importance is the occurrence of carbon compounds in plants and animals.

Silicon, unlike carbon is not found free in nature. It is the second most abundant element in the earth's crust (25.7 % by weight) where it is a major constituent of most rocks, either as silica, silicates or aluminosilicates.

Germanium is a rare element. Some germanium is recovered from flue dusts and coal ashes.

Tin makes up only 0.004 % by weight of the earth's crust. Its chief ore is tin-stone or cassiterite SnO_2.

Lead (0.0002 % by weight of earth's crust) occurs chiefly as galena, PbS.

Isolation

Carbon. Naturally occurring diamonds, graphite, coals and anthracites are isolated by mining, followed by the sorting out of the products from the bulk mined materials.

Most graphite is now made by the Acheson process at Niagara, where electric power is very cheap. Coke mixed with silica is heated for about 20 hours in an electric furnace using a current of several thousand amperes. It is thought that the formation of the graphite is brought about by the growth of minute graphite crystals already present in the coke.

Diamonds are now manufactured from graphite. This was first done in 1955 by subjecting graphite to a pressure of about 1 million lb/in.² at a temperature of about 3000 °C in the presence of a catalyst. The diamonds obtained are very small but are of great use in industry.

Silicon is prepared in the laboratory by the reduction of dry powdered silver sand (silica, SiO_2) with magnesium powder, p. 184. The mixture is heated in a crucible or test-tube,

$$SiO_2 + 2Mg \rightleftharpoons Si + 2MgO; \ \Delta H \text{ negative.}$$

The cooled products are treated with hot dilute hydrochloric acid which dissolves the magnesium oxide leaving the silicon as a brown powder.

Silicon is manufactured by reducing silica with coke in an electric furnace,
$$SiO_2 + 2C \rightarrow Si + 2CO \uparrow.$$

Silicon made in this way is a grey crystalline solid with a metallic lustre.

An alloy of silicon and iron (about 25 %) called ferrosilicon is made in the same way except that the reaction mixture contains iron oxide also.

Germanium is manufactured by the reduction of the dioxide GeO_2 with carbon or hydrogen, $GeO_2 + 2H_2 \rightarrow Ge + 2H_2O$.

Tin. Cassiterite is pulverised, then washed free of earthy impurities by running water, the heavier tin(IV) oxide falling to the bottom. It is then roasted in air to remove arsenic and sulphur as oxides. The tin(IV) oxide is then reduced by heating with carbon,

$$SnO_2 + 2C \rightarrow Sn + 2CO \uparrow.$$

The tin is purified first by liquation, i.e. by melting it on a sloping hearth and allowing the easily melted tin to drain away from the solid impurities. Final purification is achieved by stirring the molten tin with poles of green wood. The gases formed (mainly steam) cause mixing of the liquid. Impurities are thereby oxidised by the air, the oxides rise to the surface as a scum and are removed.

Lead. Galena usually occurs along with zinc blende (ZnS). Lead(II) sulphide is first separated from the zinc sulphide and gangue by froth flotation (see p. 187).

The lead(II) sulphide is roasted to the oxide,

$$2PbS + 3O_2 \rightarrow 2PbO + 2SO_2 \uparrow.$$

The oxide is then reduced with coke in a blast furnace (in much the same way as in iron production),

$$PbO + CO \rightarrow CO_2 \uparrow + Pb.$$

Silver is removed from the lead by the Parkes process. Lead may be purified further by electrolysis using lead(II) fluorosilicate, $PbSiF_6$, as the electrolyte.

Physical properties

The most striking fact about the data is that there is a quite remarkable and fairly steady Group trend in *all* the properties.

All the elements are solid at room temperature.

Allotropy in Group IVB. Only two elements in the Group show allotropy: carbon and tin. One of the allotropes is more metallic in physical properties (lustre, conductivity, etc.).

Carbon exists in two allotropic forms, diamond and graphite. Diamond is found in the form of small usually colourless transparent crystals. It is the hardest substance known. Graphite shows an enormous contrast to diamond. It is a black shiny opaque very soft crystalline solid. Other

Physical properties of Group IV B elements

Element	Allotropes	Class of element	Appearance	Crystal		Hardness	Density (g cm⁻³)	m.p. (°C)	b.p. (°C)	Electrical conductivity
				Structure	Co-ordination number					
Carbon	Graphite	Non-metal	Black lustrous solid	Graphite	3	Very soft	2.22			Fairly good in direction parallel to planes
	Diamond	Non-metal	Colourless transparent crystal	Diamond	4	Hardest known substance	3.51	3750	4200	Non-conductor
Silicon	None	Metalloid	Brown or grey solid	Diamond	4	Very hard	2.49	1420	2300	Semi-conductor
Germanium	None	Metalloid	Silvery solid	Diamond	4	Very hard	5.35	950	2750	Semi-conductor
Tin	Grey	Metalloid	Grey solid	Diamond	4	Hard	5.75	—	—	Semi-conductor
	White	Metal	Silvery solid	Distorted close-packed	6	Soft	7.28	232	2360	Good
Lead	None	Metal	Silver solid	Cubic close-packed	12	Very soft	11.34	327	1750	Good

varieties of carbon, e.g. coke, charcoal, soot, are composed of minute crystals of graphite and are said to be microcrystalline. Graphite is the stable allotrope. Although diamond is meta-stable, it shows no spontaneous tendency to revert to graphite.

Tin exists in three allotropic forms: white tin, grey tin, and brittle tin. White tin is the well-known form. It is stable at temperatures between 13 and 160 °C. At low temperatures, during a severe winter for example, ordinary white tin slowly changes to grey tin. Grey tin is much less dense than white tin, so the change is accompanied by a considerable increase in volume, the result of which is first the formation of wart-like excrescences on the surface of the metal and finally the reduction of the whole mass to a grey powder. This phenomenon is called 'tin-pest'. At temperatures over 160 °C white tin is gradually converted into a much harder allotrope called brittle tin. These changes in tin are reversible by reversing the temperature. Tin therefore exhibits *enantiotropy* (see p. 470). The differences between allotropes of any solid substances are always caused by difference in structure. Because of this, allotropy of solids is called polymorphism.

Structure and bonding in the elements. The most common structure in the Group is the diamond structure (pp. 127–8), which is a typically covalent structure. It is shown by carbon, silicon, germanium, and grey tin. Lead does not show this structure, nor does any other element, but many compounds do.

Uncut diamonds are usually regular octahedra, occasionally tetrahedra, and therefore their crystals belong to the cubic system, the octahedron and tetrahedron being common forms of this system. When subjected to strong forces, diamond cleaves along planes parallel to the octahedral faces, because fewer covalent bonds pass through these faces per unit area than in any other direction.

It is a remarkable fact that (in one of their allotropes) the first four elements in the Group all have the diamond structure. In this structure the co-ordination number is four. The trend of the co-ordination numbers down the Group is also impressive: from three in graphite, through four for the diamond structures of the middle elements, to six in white tin and twelve (the maximum possible) in lead. These numbers show very clearly the steady transition from non-metal through metalloid to true metal as the Group is descended (and also the transition from covalent bonding to metallic bonding).

367

For the structure of graphite see p. 129. The delocalised electrons in the π-bonds of the layers account for the conductivity of graphite in directions parallel to the layers. The conductivity is negligible at right angles to the layers. Individual layers are 3.40 Å apart, held together by very weak van der Waals' forces. This accounts for the extremely easy cleavage of graphite in directions parallel to the layers, and for its use as a solid lubricant. The lubricating property is aided by layers of gases adsorbed from the air.

The physical properties of the elements can be explained to a considerable extent in terms of their structure and other atomic properties, as will now be shown.

Group trends in hardness. Graphite is the softest element in the Group. The extreme contrast between graphite and diamond is entirely due to difference in structure. In graphite the *atoms* in the layers are strongly covalently bound; but the distance between the centres of two corresponding atoms in adjacent layers is about two and a half times that between atoms within the layers. Further the forces binding one layer to the next are very weak. Hence the easy cleavage. In the diamond structure, rupture is very difficult in any direction because there is no direction along which rupture can take place without the breaking of very strong rigid covalent bonds. One factor responsible for this strength is the very low atomic radius of carbon (in diamond) 0.77 Å giving a bond length of 1.54 Å. Hardness and brittleness almost always go together.

In passing down the Group from diamond to lead there is a great but not uniform decrease in hardness. From diamond to grey tin the decrease is fairly uniform, although there is no change in structure, and is caused by an increase in the bond length thus: diamond, 1.54; silicon, 2.34; germanium, 2.44; grey tin, 2.80. But grey tin is very much harder than white tin. This indicates a change in structure. White tin has a fairly close-packed metallic structure in which there are no rigidly directed covalent bonds and therefore a typical metallic malleability is found. Lead is even softer than tin because of a more uniform metallic structure. Another factor is that in both these metals there probably exists an inert pair in the atomic core and so only two of the four electrons in the outer shell are available to join the electron pool which binds the cores together.

Group trends in density. The general rule for all Groups including transition metals is that there is an almost universal and substantial increase in density in passing down a Group (see p. 199). This is seen to

368

be so here except for diamond which is considerably denser than silicon. This reversal is entirely due to the *great* increase in atomic radius from carbon 0.77 Å to silicon 1.17 Å. The atomic weight of silicon is approximately twice that of carbon but the volume of the silicon atom ($\frac{4}{3}\pi r^3$) is more than three times as great as that of carbon, while the structures are the same.

There is a fivefold increase in density from graphite to lead.

Group trends in melting point. There is no general trend in melting points in passing down the Main Groups of elements, largely because of changes in structures in the Groups; but trends in each Group can be explained in terms of structure and bond-type. Figure 113 shows the

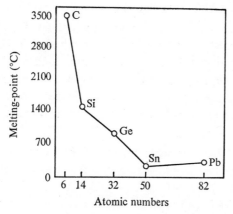

Fig. 113. Melting points of Group IV B elements plotted against atomic numbers.

data for the Group. The very high melting point of diamond is caused by the great energy needed to break the strong covalent C—C bonds. In passing from carbon to germanium the bond lengths increase and bond strengths decrease: C—C, 83; Si—Si, 42; Ge—Ge, 40 kcal mol⁻¹. These decreases explain the lower melting points of silicon and germanium. There is a further and bigger fall to tin and then a slight rise to lead. Tin and lead have metallic structures and with these there is no need to break strong rigid covalent bonds to bring about melting. What is required is a weakening of the forces of cohesion by a slight increase in the distance between the atomic cores. A contributory factor is the inert pair effect noted under hardness. The effect explains why tin and lead have unusually low melting points compared with many other metals.

Group trends in electrical conductivity. The table shows clearly the expected trend from a non-metal through semi-metals to metals.

The semi-conductors, graphite, silicon and germanium, are poorish conductors at room temperature, but their conductivity increases on heating. The metals are good conductors at room temperature but their conductivity decreases on heating.

Chemical properties

The elements are weakly electronegative non-metals or weakly electropositive metals, and in consequence are relatively inactive at ordinary temperatures. Silicon and carbon are powerful reducing agents at high or moderately high temperatures (p. 184). Charcoal and coke are the most reactive varieties of carbon (see below).

1. Air. Carbon, silicon, germanium and tin are unaffected by air at ordinary temperatures, but burn when strongly heated in air or oxygen with the formation of the dioxide in each case. Lead tarnishes in cold air, forming a protective grey film of oxide, which is converted to the hydroxide and then the basic carbonate. Molten lead oxidises to lead(II) oxide which when heated to 470 °C oxidises further to trilead tetroxide (red lead), Pb_3O_4.

2. Water. The first four elements are unaffected by water. Lead is not attacked by pure air-free water but ordinary soft water containing dissolved oxygen reacts with lead to form slightly soluble lead(II) hydroxide $Pb(OH)_2$. Water containing lead hydroxide in solution is dangerously poisonous. Most drinking water is moderately hard. Sulphate and carbonate ions present quickly form a protective layer of lead(II) sulphate and lead(II) carbonate which prevents further action.

Strongly heated carbon, silicon and tin react with steam,

$$C + H_2O \rightarrow CO + H_2 \text{ (water gas)}; \quad Si + 2H_2O \rightarrow SiO_2 + 2H_2;$$
$$Sn + 2H_2O \rightarrow SnO_2 + 2H_2.$$

3. Acids. *Hydrochloric acid.* Non-metals of the Group are unaffected. Tin and lead are little affected by dilute hydrochloric acid. Hot concentrated acid reacts vigorously with tin but very slowly with lead; M^{2+} ions and hydrogen being formed in each case.

Sulphuric acid, when dilute or cold concentrated, has little or no effect on any element in the Group. Hot concentrated sulphuric acid oxidises carbon to carbon dioxide, tin to tin(IV) sulphate, lead to lead(II) sulphate, and is itself reduced to sulphur dioxide; silicon is unaffected.

Nitric acid when dilute does not attack the non-metals of the Group. Action on tin and lead is slow, although with lead it becomes quite vigorous on heating, forming lead(II) nitrate and oxides of nitrogen. Concentrated nitric acid does not affect silicon. Carbon is oxidised to carbon dioxide, the acid being reduced to nitrogen dioxide. Germanium and tin react vigorously and similarly giving hydrated dioxides, $MO_2.nH_2O$ and nitrogen dioxide,

$$M + 4HNO_3 \rightarrow MO_2\downarrow + 4NO_2\uparrow + 2H_2O.$$

Lead reacts vigorously giving lead(II) nitrate and oxides of nitrogen. Fuming nitric acid (100%) has little or no effect on tin or lead.

Miscellaneous. Organic acids attack lead considerably. Hydrofluoric acid is the only acid which reacts with silicon, forming hydrogen and fluorosilicic acid, $\quad Si + 6HF \rightarrow 2H_2\uparrow + H_2SiF_6.$

4. Alkalis. Aqueous alkalis have little or no action on carbon, germanium or lead. Silicon and tin react forming hydrogen and oxo-anions in solution,

$$Si + 4OH^- \rightarrow 2H_2\uparrow + SiO_4^{4-} \quad \text{(orthosilicate ion)},$$
$$Sn + 2OH^- + 4H_2O \rightarrow 2H_2\uparrow + [Sn(OH)_6]^{2-} \quad \text{(hydroxystannate ion)}.$$

Silicon reacts very readily even with very dilute solutions, but tin reacts slowly even with hot concentrated solutions.

5. Combination with non-metals. In general, the temperature required increases as the electronegativity difference between the two reacting elements decreases.

All members of the Group combine readily with fluorine, although carbon needs a high temperature, and all but carbon combine with chlorine when heated, tetrachlorides being formed, except with lead which forms lead(II) chloride. All combine vigorously with oxygen when heated, forming dioxides, except lead which forms lead(II) oxide. All combine with sulphur when heated in its vapour; quadrivalent sulphides being formed with carbon, silicon and germanium, but bivalent sulphides with tin and lead.

Carbon and silicon form binary compounds, carbides and silicides, when heated strongly with metals. When heated together silicon carbide, SiC is formed. They also form alloys when mixed with molten metals.

Tin and lead form alloys with other metals, and with each other, the product in this case being solder.

Uses

Carbon. *Diamond* has a very high refractive index and dispersive power; first quality diamonds are used as jewels because of these properties. Most diamonds are used industrially, because of their great hardness, for drilling and grinding hard material including rock, for cutting glass, and for the bearings of precision instruments.

Graphite is used in the manufacture of 'lead' pencils and oil paints. Colloidal graphite mixed with oil is a valuable lubricant for the cylinders of internal combusion engines. Because of its good electrical conductivity graphite is used as electrodes in electrolysis and as brushes in electric motors and generators. Large quantities are used to slow down neutrons in nuclear reactors.

Charcoal, made by heating wood in the absence of air, is used in drawing and, because of its porous nature and resulting large surface area, as an adsorber of gases in, for example, gas-masks and vacuum tubes.

Animal charcoal, made by heating bones in the absence of air, also has good adsorbing power, used in decolorising liquids such as sugar solution.

Carbon black (*including lampblack and vegetable black*) is made by burning hydrocarbons in a limited supply of air; also as a by-product in the production of town gas made from petroleum. 137 500 tons of carbon black were produced in the U.K. in 1963. About 90 % of the production is used as a reinforcing agent for natural and synthetic rubbers. It is also used in making printer's ink, boot polish and paint.

Coals, the most important carbon-containing minerals, are used in vast quantities, (1) as solid fuels, (2) for conversion to coal-gas and soft coke, and (3) for conversion to *hard coke*, the most important reducing agent in metallurgy, by heating selected coals in special coke-ovens.

(1) *Outline of coal-gas manufacture*. Suitable bituminous coal is fed into the top of large vertical retorts heated to about 1000 °C by producer gas. Coke is removed from the bottom of the retorts and volatile products pass out at the top. The hot gases travel through the water-cooled pipes of condensers at the bottom of which coal-tar and ammoniacal liquor collect.

Complete removal of ammonia is effected in scrubbers where the coal-gas ascends through water descending over rotating paddles. Hydrogen sulphide is removed in the purifiers where the gas passes over moist hydrated iron(III) oxide, bog iron ore,

$$Fe_2O_3 + 3H_2S \rightarrow Fe_2S_3 + 3H_2O.$$

The purified gas is stored in a gas-holder. Coal-gas has an approximate composition by volume of: hydrogen, 50 %; methane, 30 %; carbon monoxide, 10 %; ethylene, carbon dioxide, nitrogen and oxygen together, 10 %.

Some of the coke from the retorts is used to make producer-gas needed to heat the retorts; the remainder is sold as a solid fuel or for the manufacture of producer-gas or water-gas.

The coal-tar is fractionally distilled to give many compounds the most important being benzene, toluene, naphthalene, anthracene, phenol, creosote and pitch. From these a great variety of useful organic compounds is manufactured.

Ammonium sulphate, a valuable fertiliser, is made from the ammoniacal liquor by distilling with lime, absorbing the evolved ammonia in dilute sulphuric acid, evaporating and crystallising.

The spent oxide from the purifiers is used in the manufacture of sulphuric acid (p. 486).

(2) *Manufacture of producer-gas and water-gas.* Producer-gas is made by blowing a controlled supply of air through white-hot coke,

$$C + O_2 + 4N_2 \rightarrow CO_2 + 4N_2; \quad CO_2 + C + 4N_2 \rightarrow 2CO + 4N_2.$$
$$\text{2 vols.} \quad \text{4 vols.}$$

The approximate composition of producer-gas is seen to be one-third carbon monoxide and two-thirds nitrogen by volume. The reaction is exothermic and so the required temperature is maintained.

The manufacture of water-gas is outlined on p. 284.

Note. Coal-gas is now made in Britain in very much smaller quantities than it used to be because of increases in the cost of coal and of the manufacturing processes involved. Town gas is now made more cheaply from oil. Thus in 1960 over 90% of gas was made from coal, but in 1967 barely 40%.

But the most revolutionary factor is that vast quantities of natural gas were discovered under the North Sea a few years ago. Underwater pipelines have been laid from some of the North Sea fields to the east coast, and it is planned to cover most of Britain in the next few years. North Sea gas is methane.

Silicon, germanium, tin and lead. Exceptionally pure silicon and germanium are of great value as semi-conductors in transistors. Silicon, as ferrosilicon, is added to steel as a deoxidiser.

Almost half of the tin produced is used in the manufacture of tin-plate, thin sheet-steel coated with tin. Alloys of tin include bronze (p. 587), solder (50% tin, 50% lead), pewter (75% tin, 25% lead) and type-metal (10% tin, 75% lead, 15% antimony).

Lead is widely used as sheets in roofing, and in lining vessels required to withstand acid corrosion; as water and gas-pipes, and sheathing for cables; in making shot, and accumulator plates; as a shielding material against radiation, including X-rays. Alloys of lead are given under tin.

Compounds in which the elements are quadrivalent

It is convenient to use a general symbol, X, to represent any of the elements in the Group.

The quadrivalent compounds include: hydrides XH_4; chlorides XCl_4 and other halides; oxides XO_2; hydroxides (or oxo-acids) $X(OH)_4$ which may lose molecules of water; silicates; carbides; sulphides XS_2.

Chlorides, XCl₄

All the elements form liquid chlorides of this type. All are covalent.

Preparation. All except lead(IV) chloride can be prepared by the action of chlorine on the element, its sulphide or oxide, sometimes with carbon also present. For example,

$$\text{(i)} \qquad CS_2 + 3Cl_2 \xrightarrow[\text{FeCl}_3,\ 30°]{\text{catalyst}} CCl_4 + S_2Cl_2.$$

Disulphur dichloride (commonly called sulphur monochloride) then reacts with excess carbon disulphide to give more tetrachloride, leaving sulphur

$$CS_2 + 2S_2Cl_2 \xrightarrow[30°]{\text{FeCl}_3} CCl_4 + 6S.$$

$$\text{(ii)} \qquad SiO_2 + 2C + 2Cl_2 \xrightarrow{\text{heat}} SiCl_4 \uparrow + 2CO \uparrow.$$

Lead(IV) chloride, $PbCl_4$, is formed when cold concentrated hydrochloric acid reacts with lead(IV) oxide

$$PbO_2 + 4HCl \rightarrow PbCl_4 + 2H_2O.$$

The yellow solution contains hexachloroplumbic(IV) acid formed as follows,

$$PbCl_4 + 2HCl \rightarrow H_2PbCl_6.$$

Ammonium chloride is added. Ammonium hexachloroplumbate(IV) is formed, the crystals are removed and treated with cold concentrated sulphuric acid. Lead(IV) chloride separates as an oily yellow liquid.

Physical properties. All the quadrivalent chlorides are liquids which are non-electrolytes and therefore covalent. All are colourless except lead(IV) chloride (yellow), and all except carbon tetrachloride (tetrachloromethane) fume in moist air, because of hydrolysis. Their physical properties are summarized in the following table.

	Appearance	Type of bonding	Shape of molecule	C.N.	Density (g cm⁻³)	b.p. (°C)
CCl_4	Colourless liquid	Covalent	Tetrahedral	4	1.58	77
$SiCl_4$	Colourless liquid fuming in moist air	Covalent	Tetrahedral	4	1.48	58
$GeCl_4$	Colourless liquid fuming in moist air	Covalent	Tetrahedral	4	1.89	83
$SnCl_4$	Colourless liquid fuming in moist air	Covalent	Tetrahedral	4	2.27	114
$PbCl_4$	Oily yellow liquid fuming in moist air	Covalent	Tetrahedral	4	3.18	Decomposes

Structure and bonding in the molecules. All the molecules are tetrahedral, the central Group IVB element having a co-ordination number of 4.

Although the bonds are covalent, they have a substantial amount of ionic character, more pronounced in silicon tetrachloride than in the tetrachlorides of carbon or germanium since silicon has a much lower electronegativity than carbon or germanium. Although each bond is polar the molecules as a whole have no dipole moments because of their symmetry.

Fig. 114. Carbon tetrachloride molecule.

Density trends among the tetrachlorides. Two main factors account for these.

(1) Four chlorine atoms are a constant part of the molecules of all five tetrachlorides. Differences in density of the molecules themselves will therefore be caused by differences in atomic density (p. 197) of the atoms of the central elements. These are approximately: carbon (diamond), 10.4; silicon, 6.9; germanium, 15.8; tin (grey), 16.8; lead, 22.5 g cm⁻³. The trends in these figures correspond to the trends in the densities of the liquids.

(2) In the liquids van der Waals' forces of attraction between molecules increase in passing down the Group in step with increase in the total number of electrons in the molecules (ch. 7, p. 101). This of itself would cause closer packing and increased density, but the partial negative charges on the chlorine atoms of silicon tetrachloride are greater than those on the chlorine atoms of carbon tetrachloride because silicon is much less electronegative than carbon. Hence the resulting repulsive forces between the

molecules are greater, and reduce the attractive forces to a value less than for carbon tetrachloride. This causes a decrease in density which reinforces the effect of atomic density.

Boiling point trends. These are similar to those for density: a decrease from carbon tetrachloride to silicon tetrachloride followed by a fairly steady rise thereafter. The explanation is similar to that in part (2) of the explanation for density trends.

It is worth noting that the number of electrons in the germanium atom is the average of the numbers in the silicon and tin atoms and that the density and boiling point of germanium tetrachloride are very nearly the average of those of the tetrachlorides of silicon and tin.

Chemical properties. *Effect of heat.* All except lead(IV) chloride are stable when moderately heated. Lead(IV) chloride decomposes slowly even at room temperature and rapidly when heated, into $PbCl_2$, lead(II) chloride and chlorine. This reaction illustrates the greater stability of the bivalent state in lead.

Action of water, alkalis and acids. Carbon tetrachloride differs greatly from the others in being rather inert chemically at ordinary temperatures. It is unaffected by water, alkalis or acids except at high temperatures, for reasons already given, p. 361. It does, however, react with metals, chlorides of the metals being formed.

Water. The fact that the other tetrachlorides fume in moist air (liberation of hydrogen chloride) shows the ease with which they are hydrolysed, the reason being that the number of electrons in the valency shells of silicon, germanium, tin, and lead can be increased beyond the octet by using the *d* orbitals in their atoms; the central atom in each can act as an acceptor of electrons. Oxygen atoms in water or hydroxyl ions act as donors of

Unstable intermediate product

$$Cl-X-OH \; + \; HCl$$

electrons and therefore form dative covalencies with the central atoms in each case, forming first hydroxides then oxides, hydrogen chloride being eliminated. The reactions are shown in steps in the diagram opposite. A similar reaction takes place three more times, the overall action being,

$$XCl_4 + 4H_2O \rightarrow X(OH)_4 + 4HCl,$$

followed to some extent by

$$X(OH)_4 \rightarrow XO_2 + 2H_2O.$$

The action is very vigorous with silicon tetrachloride* and goes to completion, the compound first formed, $Si(OH)_4$, being ortho-silicic acid H_4SiO_4. With the others the action is less vigorous and is reversible. With them ortho-acids are not formed, but instead hydrated oxides of the type $XO_2 . nH_2O$.

Tin(IV) chloride mixed with a very small quantity of water gives a solution from which crystals of tin(IV) chloride, $SnCl_4 . 5H_2O$, butter of tin, are deposited. This compound is a salt containing the complex ion $[Sn(H_2O)_4]^{4+}$. Tin(IV) chloride reacts with hydrochloric acid forming hexachlorostannic acid,
$$SnCl_4 + 2HCl \rightarrow H_2SnCl_6.$$

The best known salt of this acid is ammonium hexachlorostannate(IV) $(NH_4)_2SnCl_6$, known as 'pink salt', made by adding ammonium chloride to a solution of tin(IV) chloride (cf. $(NH_4)_2PbCl_6$) p. 374.

Uses. Carbon tetrachloride is a valuable solvent (non-inflammable) used in dry-cleaning. It is used also in fire extinguishers, its non-inflammable and very dense vapour blanketing and smothering the flames. It must not be used on burning sodium, since it reacts vigorously with sodium. Another important use is in the manufacture of 'freon', i.e. dichlorodifluoromethane, CCl_2F_2, an excellent refrigerant, non-toxic, non-corrosive, non-inflammable, and of suitable boiling point (30 °C). Silicon tetrachloride is used in making silicones. Tin(IV) chloride is an intermediate in the recovery of tin from scrap tin-plate and in the manufacture of organo-tin compounds. Both butter of tin and pink salt are used as mordants in dyeing.

Hydrides, XH_4

See p. 262 for an account of hydrides in general.

All the elements of Group IV B form covalent tetrahydrides with tetrahedral molecules. Their names are methane, and by analogy, silane,

---

* Silicon tetrachloride is a potential hazard in Schools, because of the danger of the bottle bursting as a result of hydrolysis.

germane, stannane, and plumbane. Plumbane is very difficult to prepare. It is formed in small quantities when a solution of a lead salt is electrolysed using a small lead cathode. Plumbane is so unstable that little is known about it.

Physical properties. All are colourless gases. The boiling points of the liquefied hydrides increase fairly steadily from methane $-161\,°C$, to plumbane, approximately $-13\,°C$. These are much lower than the boiling points of the tetrachlorides, because of the great decrease in the total number of electrons in the molecules, and consequent decrease in intermolecular attraction. Also, the drop in boiling point between carbon tetrachloride and silicon tetrachloride is not found with the hydrides, because the charges on the hydrogen atoms of methane and silane are very similar in size (though opposite in sign), as may be seen from the electronegativities (Si, 1.7; H, 2.1; C, 2.5).

Chemical properties. Methane, a paraffin, is very much more stable than the others for reasons already given.

When heated, they all decompose into their elements with increasing ease down the Group, from methane at $800\,°C$ to plumbane at $0\,°C$. This shows the decrease in strength of the X—H bonds with increasing atomic radius.

Methane does not burn in air below $500\,°C$. Silane, in complete contrast, is spontaneously inflammable in air at room temperature, forming silicon dioxide and water. Germane catches fire at an intermediate temperature. The other two have not been investigated fully.

Methane is unaffected by water, acids, or alkalis. Silane although little affected by pure water is immediately hydrolysed by water containing a trace of alkali,

$$SiH_4 + 2NaOH + H_2O \rightarrow Na_2SiO_3 + 4H_2,$$

or $\qquad SiH_4 + 2OH^- + H_2O \rightarrow SiO_3^{2-} + 4H_2.$

Germane and stannane (unexpectedly) are not hydrolysed by water, dilute alkalis, or dilute acids.

Some other hydrides, and related compounds. Methane is the first of an enormous family of hydrocarbons, the paraffins, general formula C_nH_{2n+2} where n can increase almost without limit.

Silicon (and germanium), but not tin and lead, form a few homologues of silane and germane of general formula X_nH_{2n+2}, but here the value of n is very limited, the highest being found in hexasilane Si_6H_{14} and octo-germane Ge_8H_{18}. All the silanes are spontaneously inflammable in air. A number of other analogous compounds are known; for example, corresponding to chloroform $CHCl_3$ are silico-chloroform, $SiHCl_3$, and germano-chloroform, $GeHCl_3$. These differ markedly from chloroform in chemical properties.

Oxides, XO_2

All the elements form oxides of this type. Carbon dioxide is, however, the only one which consists of molecules, and is a gas at ordinary temperature. The others are crystalline solids of high melting point. These crystals are either giant molecules or ionic crystals, i.e. CO_2 is a molecular formula; SiO_2 is an empirical formula and is more accurately written $(SiO_2)_n$.

Three of the five oxides, those of carbon, silicon, and tin occur naturally in very important quantities (pp. 363–4).

Preparation: as in ch. 16, p. 252. Lead(IV) oxide cannot be made by heating the metal in air or oxygen. It is easily prepared by the action of dilute nitric acid on red lead (Pb_3O_4),

$$2PbO \cdot PbO_2 + 4HNO_3 \rightarrow 2Pb(NO_3)_2 + 2H_2O + PbO_2.$$

The most striking feature in the table on p. 380 is the extraordinary difference between the melting point of carbon dioxide and those of the others. In this property (and many others) carbon differs much more from silicon than silicon and the other members of the Group differ among themselves. (The same is true of the nitrogen and oxygen Groups.)

Why is carbon dioxide a gas while the other oxides are solids of high melting point? The immediate reason is that carbon can form stable, multiple, covalent bonds, as here in the molecule O=C=O, while the other elements of the Group cannot. In this structure all the valency bonds of the carbon atom are linked to *oxygen* atoms. In spite of the apparent 'unsaturation' usually associated with double bonds, the molecule of carbon dioxide is comparatively unreactive (so is the double bond in the carboxyl group—$C\diagup^{O}_{\diagdown OH}$ of carboxylic-acids). Since the molecule is linear it has no overall dipole moment. Partial charges on the individual atoms are small. For these reasons the intermolecular attractions are small and so carbon dioxide is a gas at ordinary temperature. The fact that carbon forms stable, covalent, double bonds with oxygen, while silicon and

Physical properties of dioxides of Group IV B elements

| | Appearance | m.p. (°C) | Density (g cm⁻³) | Allotropy or polymorphism | Crystal | | |
					Structure	C.N.	Predominant type of bonding
CO_2	Colourless gas	−56	Solid, 1.2	—	The molecule is linear O=C=O	2:1	Covalent
SiO_2	White solid	1710	2.6	Trimorphic	Quartz (hexagonal) Cristobalite (cubic)	4:2} 4:2}	Covalent
GeO_2	White solid	1120	4.7	Dimorphic	Quartz (hexagonal) Rutile (tetragonal)	4:2 6:3	Covalent Ionic
SnO_2	White solid	Sublimes, 1800 Melts, 1130	6.7	Trimorphic	Commonest form, rutile (tetragonal)	6:3	Ionic
PbO_2	Dark brown solid	Decomposes at 300	9.0	—	Rutile (tetragonal)	6:3	Ionic

Note:

(1) The ratio of the co-ordination numbers in each oxide is always 2:1, the same as in the formula XO_2.

(2) The bonds in the oxides are always of intermediate type.

germanium do not, is explained in terms of atomic radii. The carbon atom is much smaller than the silicon or germanium atoms (atomic radii: C, 0.77; Si, 1.17; Ge, 1.22 Å), and because of this, the p orbitals needed to form a double bond between a carbon atom and an oxygen atom can approach each other closely enough for the second bond to be formed. This does not happen with Si and the other elements of the Group. Si$=$O bonds do not exist. Because the energy of the Si—O bond (89 kcal mol^{-1}) is much greater than that of the Si—Si bond (42 kcal mol^{-1}), Si—O bonds are always formed in preference to Si—Si bonds, therefore when

silicon is oxidised, the basic unit of structure of the oxide is—$\overset{|}{\underset{|}{\text{Si}}}$—O—.

These groups then link up in three dimensions by means of their free valencies to form giant molecules as shown in simplified form in Fig. 115, p. 382.

Structure and bonding. The co-ordination numbers show a steady increase from carbon dioxide 2:1 to lead(IV) oxide 6:3, and a related change in bond character from covalent to ionic, with germanium dioxide acting as a bridge between the two, one of its allotropes having a co-ordination number of 4:2 and the other 6:3. (Compare the case of the two structures of tin in the table of the properties of the elements, one structure being covalent with co-ordination number 4, the other showing metallic bonding and a co-ordination number of 6.) The first two solids have the quartz structure (among others), while the last three have the rutile structure in common.

In the elements, there is a fivefold increase in density from graphite to lead. The increase in density from solid carbon dioxide (1.2) to lead(IV) oxide (9.0) is about sevenfold. In both cases the reasons are the same: an increase in atomic density of the Group IV elements combined with an increase in closeness of packing shown by the increase in co-ordination number. The higher rate of increase with the oxides results from the very low density of the first member of the series, solid carbon dioxide, a molecular crystal.

The rutile structure has already been described (p. 138). The cristobalite structure shown by one form of silica is not common but is of special interest because of its close relationship to the diamond structure (p. 128). It is merely the diamond structure with an oxygen atom inserted in the middle of each Si—Si bond. Some of the features of this can be shown simply in two dimensions as in Fig. 115, the structure growing out until it reaches the crystal boundaries. Each silicon atom is seen to be surrounded by four oxygen atoms and each oxygen atom bonded to two silicon atoms.

The openness of the packing is also clear. Although the simplified diagram is useful, it is dangerously incorrect since it shows the four bonds of each silicon atom in two dimensions, when in fact the most important thing about them is that they are arranged tetrahedrally in three dimensions.

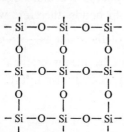

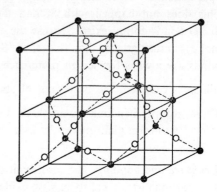

Fig. 115. Simplified diagram showing number of bonds on each atom and 4:2 co-ordination.

Fig. 116. β-Cristobalite structure, cubic unit cell. ●, Si; ○, oxygen.

Figure 116 shows the three-dimensional arrangement of the structure. Only four of the eight small cubes have atoms inside them (see p. 128). The silicon atoms are tetrahedrally disposed to each other. Since the oxygen atoms lie on the lines joining the silicon atoms, the oxygen atoms are also tetrahedrally disposed to each other. Also, and very important, each silicon atom is surrounded tetrahedrally by four oxygen atoms, the basic *group* of the structure being therefore SiO_4; but since each oxygen atom is shared between two groups the empirical formula is again seen to be SiO_2, co-ordination 4:2.

In quartz, the SiO_4 tetrahedra are arranged in a spiral round a vertical axis. The spiral may be left-handed or right-handed. The structures are therefore mirror images, and are optically active, one dextro- and the other laevo-rotatory. There are also two varieties of quartz, α and β, both of which exist in dextro- and laevo-rotatory forms.

Chemical properties (see also ch. 16, p. 249). *General.* In passing down the Group there is, as always in a Main Group, an increase in the basic nature of the oxide, i.e. a decrease in acidic nature. The oxides of carbon and silicon are acidic only (weakly), those of the others are amphoteric (weakly acidic and weakly basic).

Heat. The oxides are all stable to heat, except lead(IV) oxide which decomposes at about 300 °C to lead(II) oxide and oxygen.

Water. Carbon dioxide is fairly soluble in water, some of it reacting to give carbonic acid in solution. The others are *slightly soluble (GeO$_2$)* or insoluble.

Caustic alkalis. All react with hot concentrated solutions of caustic alkalis (CO_2 reacts with cold dilute alkali also) and with fused alkali (SiO_2 reacts with fused Na_2CO_3 also) yielding soluble salts with the Group IV elements in the anions, the ease of the reaction decreasing down the Group, showing diminishing acidity

$$XO_2 + 2OH^- \rightarrow XO_3{}^{2-} + H_2O,$$

where $XO_3{}^{2-}$ represents the carbonate, silicate, germanate, stannate, or plumate ion.

Acids. Carbon dioxide is unaffected by acids, and the next four are little affected, except that silica reacts very readily with hydrofluoric acid forming silicon tetrafluoride, and, with excess acid, fluorosilicic(IV) acid H_2SiF_6. Lead(IV) oxide is not affected by dilute acids, but reacts readily with cold concentrated hydrochloric acid (p. 374). With hot concentrated sulphuric acid lead(IV) oxide gives lead(II) sulphate, water and oxygen. These reactions show lead(IV) oxide to be the most basic oxide of the Group but still a weak base, thus confirming the Group trend.

Lead(IV) oxide differs from the others in being a powerful oxidising agent, e.g. it oxidises sulphur to sulphur dioxide, which then combines with excess lead(IV) oxide PbO_2 to give lead(II) sulphate. This reaction again illustrates the greater stability of the bivalent state in lead.

Uses. About 200,000 tons per annum of carbon dioxide are used in the United Kingdon. The main uses are: (1) In making aerated waters and beers (this accounts for about one third of the total). (2) As a heat-transfer medium in nuclear reactors. (3) In solid form as a refrigerant known as dry ice (because it sublimes and so no liquid is formed). (4) Carbon dioxide is used during welding to shield the metal from oxidation. (5) In the manufacture of sodium carbonate (p. 312), ammonium sulphate (p. 435), white lead (pp. 404–5) and urea (used in making urea-formaldehyde plastics). (6) In fire-extinguishers.

Silica in the form of quartz sand is used in large quantities in the building industry for making mortar, cement, concrete, and silica bricks; in making glass; as fused silica in making scientific apparatus. Because of its low coefficient of thermal expansion, apparatus made from fused silica can withstand sudden changes of temperature without cracking. Finely divided silica is used in large quantities as a white re-inforcing filler for rubber.

Cassiterite, SnO_2, is the chief source of tin. Tin(IV) oxide is used in making enamels and glazes.

Lead(IV) oxide is used in the manufacture of matches and in lead-acid accumulators.

Ortho-acids, $X(OH)_4$ or H_4XO_4

There is no evidence for the existence of any ortho-acids of the Group IV B elements, either in solid form or in aqueous solution, with the exception of orthosilicic acid H_4SiO_4 (in solution). The other substances formerly regarded as ortho-acids are now known to be hydrous oxides, $XO_2.nH_2O$, where n is variable and indefinite. Salts of orthosilicic acid (and also orthogermanic acid) are known, e.g. zinc orthosilicate Zn_2SiO_4 (*willemite*) and zirconium orthosilicate $ZrSiO_4$ (*zircon*).

Meta-acids, $XO(OH)_2$ or H_2XO_3

None of these acids has been isolated, but their salts are well known: the carbonates, metasilicates, metagermanates, stannates and plumbates. Since no orthocarbonates, orthostannates, orthoplumbates are known, it is not necessary to use the prefix meta in describing the XO_3^{2-} salts or acids in these cases.

Carbonic acid and its salts. See chs. 15 and 16.

Silicic acid and the silicates. Orthosilicic acid is formed in solution when silicon tetrachloride reacts with water

$$SiCl_4 + 4H_2O \rightarrow Si(OH)_4 + 4HCl.$$

Here one molecule of silicon tetrachloride gives one molecule of orthosilicic acid. The reaction, however, does not stop there. It is followed by a series of reactions in which the molecules of orthosilicic acid combine together, with the elimination of water. The first step in this series between two molecules of $Si(OH)_4$ may be shown as follows, remembering that the molecule $Si(OH)_4$ has a tetrahedral structure, like the molecule $SiCl_4$, Further similar reactions take place at the hydroxyl groups of the new molecule (2) so that the structure grows in three dimensions in the directions indicated by the dotted lines, till all the $Si(OH)_4$ molecules have reacted, the final product being a giant molecule of silicon dioxide (silica)

$$\underset{\text{(1)}}{\text{HO}-\underset{\overset{|}{\text{OH}}}{\overset{\overset{|}{\text{OH}}}{\text{Si}}}-\text{O}\colon\!\text{H}} \;+\; \underset{\text{(1)}}{\text{HO}\colon\!\underset{\overset{|}{\text{OH}}}{\overset{\overset{|}{\text{OH}}}{\text{Si}}}-\text{OH}} \;\rightarrow\; \underset{\text{(2)}}{--\text{HO}-\underset{\overset{|}{\text{OH}}}{\overset{\overset{|}{\text{OH}}}{\text{Si}}}-\text{O}-\underset{\overset{|}{\text{OH}}}{\overset{\overset{|}{\text{OH}}}{\text{Si}}}-\text{OH}--} \;\; +\text{H}_2\text{O}$$

Hypothetical pyrosilicic acid

with the cristobalite structure shown on p. 382, or a related structure made up of the same units, SiO_4 tetrahedra with each oxygen atom shared between two tetrahedral groups. The final process of removing all the water from the silica is carried out by filtering off the silica precipitate and heating it. The overall reaction is important for three reasons; (1) it serves as a foundation for an understanding of the structure of the silicates, of which most of the earth's crust is composed; (2) a similar reaction is used as a stage in preparing silicones, substances with a great variety of uses; (3) it is an example of a large class of reactions called *polymerisations*, common in organic chemistry. This particular example is a condensation-polymerisation because water is eliminated in the process.

The silicate minerals

The basic structural unit of silica, SiO_2, silicates and alumino-silicates is the SiO_4 tetrahedron.

Three facts of great importance in understanding silicate structures are:

(1) *All structures are built of SiO_4 tetrahedra.*

(2) *Tetrahedra may be joined to each other by corners only, never by edges or faces.* Joining by a corner means that the two silicon atoms at the centres of the joined tetrahedra share the *single* oxygen atom at the junction.

(3) *The anionic charges on the SiO_4 tetrahedra depend on the number of corners shared.*

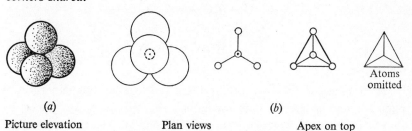

(a)
Picture elevation

(b)
Plan views Apex on top

Atoms omitted

Fig. 117. Diagrams of SiO_4 tetrahedra.

The three-dimensional structure of the SiO_4 tetrahedron may be represented by Fig. 117; the right-hand diagram is most useful because of its simplicity.

Orthosilicates are a convenient starting point for an account of silicate structures. Orthosilicic acid H_4SiO_4 or

$$HO—\underset{\underset{OH}{|}}{\overset{\overset{HO}{|}}{Si}}—OH$$

forms orthosilicates when hydrogen atoms are replaced by metal atoms. The orthosilicate anion, $SiO_4{}^{4-}$, is tetrahedral in shape and has the electronic structure shown in the diagram. The four electrons needed to complete the octets are obtained from metal atoms and give the anion its quadruple negative charge.

$$\left[\ :\overset{\cdot\cdot}{\underset{\cdot\cdot}{O}}:\ \ :O\underset{\cdot\times}{\overset{\times\cdot}{\;Si\;}}O:\ \ :\overset{\cdot\cdot}{\underset{\cdot\cdot}{O}}:\ \right]^{4-}$$

Orthosilicate anion

Two rules essential for systematising silicate structures are:

(1) For each corner shared, the number of oxygen atoms per silicon atom is reduced by half an atom.

(2) For each corner shared, the anionic charge per silicon atom is reduced in size by one unit.

The steps between $SiO_4{}^{4-}$ and $SiO_2{}^0$ can be filled in, giving the five main classes of silicate structure shown in the table, p. 387. The charges on the structures are quickly checked by the oxidation-number method, p. 162.

Notes on the table. (1) The third line in the table can be arrived at by progressive dehydrations of orthosilicic acid thus,

$$2H_4SiO_4 - H_2O \rightarrow H_6Si_2O_7,$$
$$2H_4SiO_4 - 2H_2O \rightarrow 2H_2SiO_3,$$
$$2H_4SiO_4 - 3H_2O \rightarrow H_2Si_2O_5,$$
$$2H_4SiO_4 - 4H_2O \rightarrow 2SiO_2.$$

(2) In *amphiboles* the two chains are joined together by the corners of alternate tetrahedra. In each chain, half the tetrahedra are joined by three corners, half by two. Half the silicon atoms have therefore the equivalent of $2\frac{1}{2}$ oxygen atoms; half have the equivalent of three oxygen

386

The five main classes of silicate structures

	Class A	Class B	Class C	Class D	Class E
Number of corners shared	0	1	2	3	4
Empirical formula per silicon atom	$[SiO_4]^{4-}$	$[SiO_{3\frac{1}{2}}]^{3-}$	$[SiO_3]^{2-}$	$[SiO_{2\frac{1}{2}}]^{1-}$	$[SiO_2]^0$
Empirical formula cleared of fractions	$[SiO_4]^{4-}$	$[Si_2O_7]^{6-}$	$[SiO_3]^{2-}$	$[Si_2O_5]^{2-}$	SiO_2
Anionic or molecular formula	$[SiO_4]^{4-}$	$[Si_2O_7]^{6-}$	$([SiO_3]^{2-})_n$	$([Si_2O_5]^{2-})_n$	$(SiO_2)_n$
Nature of structure	Discrete orthosilicate anions	Discrete pyrosilicate anions	CHAINS One-dimensional giant anions	SHEETS Two-dimensional giant anions	FRAMEWORKS Three-dimensional giant molecules
			Single chain in PYROXENES Double chain in AMPHIBOLES $(Si_4O_{11}^{6-})_n$, p 386		β-cristobalite

In silicate minerals of classes A to D the charges on the anions are neutralized and the structures held together by cations usually one or more from Na^+, K^+, Ca^{2+}, Mg^{2+}, and Fe^{2+}

EXAMPLES	A small class	A very small class	Two large groups:	Two large groups:	Two groups:
	Zircon $Zr(SiO_4)$	Thortveitite $Sc_2(Si_2O_7)$	(1) PYROXENES e.g. *Diopside* $CaMg(SiO_3)_2$	(1) CLAYS. These contain OH^- ions also. e.g. *Talc* $Mg_3(Si_4O_{10})(OH)_2$	(1) $(SiO_2)_n$ e.g. cristobalite
	Forsterite $Mg_2(SiO_4)$ *Olivine* $Fe^{2+}Mg^{2+}(SiO_4)$		(2) AMPHIBOLES These contain OH^- ions also. Both groups are easily split into strands	(2) MICAS (see p 388) These are aluminosilicates which, like clays, contain OH^- ions	(2) ALUMINOSILICATES A large and important group including ZEOLITES. Aluminosilicates consist of three-dimensional giant anions with cations in the interstices, p 388

* This is the most important line to remember; the others follow from it.

atoms. Every two silicon atoms have thus $5\frac{1}{2}$ oxygen atoms, a ratio of 4:11. The formula for this anionic structure is $[(Si_4O_{11})^{6-}]_n$. An important amphibole is tremolite, an asbestos, $Ca_2Mg_5(Si_4O_{11})_2(OH)_2$. The OH^- ions are attached to Mg^{2+} ions. Tremolite can be cleft into strands, which can be separated into thin fibres, which in turn can be woven into cloth.

(3) *Clays*, e.g. talc, cleave easily in directions parallel to the sheets and so are flaky.

(4) *Micas*, like the clays, consist of anionic sheets held together by cations between the sheets. But they show a new feature: the silicon atoms in some of the tetrahedra are replaced by aluminium atoms, which are of similar size. When one of the silicon atoms in the structure $(Si_4O_{10})^{4-}$ is replaced by an aluminium atom, the anionic charge is altered to $5-$, $(AlSi_3O_{10})^{5-}$, because of the difference between Al^{3+} and Si^{4+} (there is a corresponding increase in the number of cationic charges needed to produce overall electric neutrality). The aluminium is here behaving as a non-metal giving an aluminate anion. Minerals containing silicate and aluminate anions are called *aluminosilicates*. Micas, like clays, contain hydroxyl groups. An example of the mica group is *muscovite*

$$KAl_2(OH)_2[AlSi_3O_{10}]^{5-}$$

in which one quarter of the silicon atoms in $[Si_4O_{10}]^{4-}$ has been replaced by an aluminium atom. An interesting feature of muscovite is that some of its aluminium atoms are in the cationic part of the structure along with potassium atoms, and some in the anionic part along with silicon atoms. Micas can be cleft easily in directions parallel to the sheets, into transparent sheets, less than a thousandth of an inch thick. This is because the covalent bonding within the sheets is strong, while the ionic bonding between the sheets is weak.

Class E. Three-dimensional frameworks: silica, *felspars and zeolites all based on* $(SiO_2)_n$. In these, each tetrahedron shares all four corners with its neighbours. Quartz and cristobalite belong to this class. They have been discussed. They differ from other members of the class in consisting of SiO_2 only; they are not silicates. Their formula is $(SiO_2)_n$. A lattice of this formula is neutral overall, and so cannot contain cations; it is a giant molecule, not a giant anion.

All other members of Class E are aluminosilicates, in which some of the silicon atoms in the SiO_4 tetrahedra are replaced by aluminium atoms as in the micas. A most important result of this is that the covalent framework is no longer electrically neutral, but becomes negatively charged, i.e. it becomes a giant anion. Thus when a quarter of the silicon atoms in $4SiO_2$

is replaced by an aluminium atom, an anionic unit of formula $(AlSi_3O_8)^{1-}$ is obtained. (Note that in all aluminosilicates of Class E the sum of the aluminium and silicon atoms in the anion is always half the number of the oxygen atoms; also, each aluminium atom produces a charge of -1 on the anion because of the difference in oxidation number between $Al(+3)$ and Si $(+4)$.) The anionic charge is neutralised by cations as in *orthoclase* $K(AlSi_3O_8)$, the best known member of an important group of minerals in Class E called the *felspars*, which are major constituents of many rocks. All minerals of Class E have a strong covalent tetrahedral framework throughout the whole crystal structure. They are therefore difficult to cleave and are very hard. Orthoclase is not quite as hard as quartz because quartz has no cations in its structure. The cations play no part in holding together the basic anionic structure.

The *zeolites* (Greek = boiling stones) are so called because when heated they froth, water and steam being given off. Zeolites differ from other members of Class E in having *molecules* of water in their composition, not just hydroxyl ions. A common zeolite is *analcite* $Na(AlSi_2O_6)H_2O$, a sodium aluminosilicate, in which a third of the silicon atoms in $(SiO_2)_3$ has been replaced by an aluminium atom. Zeolites have a much more open structure than felspars. Their structure is permeated by channels containing the water molecules. The channels also contain the sodium ions or other cations in the structure, attached by ionic bonds to the negatively charged oxygen ions of the framework. When the zeolite is heated the water passes out of the channels, but the structure of the mineral is not altered. The dehydrated zeolite has the property of absorbing water or water vapour and may therefore be used as a dehydrating agent. Some zeolites have the power of absorbing gases whose molecules are small enough to enter the channels, thus separating these molecules from ones that are too large to pass in. Thus they can be used as molecular sieves. When hard water is passed through a tube packed with pieces of zeolite the Mg^{2+} and Ca^{2+} ions causing the hardness are adsorbed by the zeolite in preference to its own sodium ions, which pass into the water. This method of softening water is called *ion-exchange*. More efficient ion exchangers than zeolites are now made artificially from synthetic resins. A diagram of the simplest of the Class E minerals, cristobalite, has been given on p. 387. It is not possible to draw simple diagrams of the other members of the class. Models are more instructive.

Uses. Among the most important building materials are silicate minerals and their derivatives, in the form of sandstone, granite, gabbro, bricks, cement (made by roasting common clay, an impure aluminium silicate, with limestone), concrete (a mixture of cement, sand, broken silicate rocks, and water), and slates. Kaolin a purer aluminium silicate is used in making china; as a filler in paper, rubber, cotton and other textiles; and in medicine as an absorbent for both internal and external use. Clays are also used in making pottery, glazes, earthenware and tiles.

Ordinary glass is made by fusing together sodium carbonate, limestone and sand, SiO_2; it is therefore a mixture of sodium silicate and calcium silicate (soda-glass). Glass is a super-cooled liquid, i.e. it is non-crystalline. If potassium carbonate is used as well as sodium carbonate a glass of higher melting point is obtained.

Glasses for special purposes include pyrex glass, flint glass and crown glass. These all contain additional compounds:

Pyrex glass contains boron and aluminium oxides which give a glass with a very low coefficient of thermal expansion. This makes the glass less likely to crack when heated or cooled quickly, therefore very suitable for use in the home, the laboratory, and chemical industry.

Flint or crystal glass contains potassium silicate and lead(II) silicate (made by adding lead(II) oxide). The glass has a high refractive index and so is used for making lenses and cut-crystal glassware.

Crown glass contains phosphorus pentoxide. It has a smaller refractive index than flint glass. A mixture of flint and crown glasses can be made to have any required refractive index.

Water-glass, sodium silicate, is made by fusing sand and sodium carbonate; the solution of the melt in water is used for preserving eggs, as an adhesive, and for fire-proofing wood.

Because of its infusibility and fibrous nature, large quantities of asbestos are made into fire-proof cloth for firemen's clothes, and theatre safety curtains; and, mixed with cement, in the manufacture of fire-proof sheets and roofing tiles.

Mica sheets have high flexibility, elasticity, and transparency. These properties, together with the high electrical and thermal resistance of mica, the high value of its dielectric constant, and its great dielectric strength, account for its great importance in the electrical and radio industries, where it is used in condensers, generators, motors and in the heating elements of electric irons, toasters and other forms of heater. It is also used as windows in stoves and furnaces.

The uses of zeolite have been mentioned on p. 389.

The silicones

These are a group of compounds containing—$\overset{|}{\underset{|}{Si}}$—O—$\overset{|}{\underset{|}{Si}}$—chains with organic alkyl and aryl radicals attached. They are of theoretical interest and considerable practical importance. Silicones may be made starting from silicon tetrachloride. This reacts with an ethereal solution of methyl magnesium iodide (a Grignard reagent) as follows:

$$\underset{\overset{|}{Cl}}{\overset{\overset{Cl}{|}}{Cl-Si-Cl}} + 2Mg\underset{I}{\overset{CH_3}{\diagup}} \rightarrow \underset{\overset{|}{CH_3}}{\overset{\overset{CH_3}{|}}{Cl-Si-Cl}} + 2MgICl$$

Dimethyl dichloro silane

The dimethyl dichloro silane is then hydrolysed in the same way as silicon tetrachloride itself,

$$\underset{\overset{|}{CH_3}}{\overset{\overset{CH_3}{|}}{Cl-Si-Cl}} + 2H_2O \rightarrow \underset{\overset{|}{CH_3}}{\overset{\overset{CH_3}{|}}{HO-Si-OH}} + 2HCl$$

The product of hydrolysis then undergoes condensation-polymerisation in a way similar to orthosilicic acid,

$$HO-\underset{\overset{|}{CH_3}}{\overset{\overset{CH_3}{|}}{Si}}-[OH+H]O-\underset{\overset{|}{CH_3}}{\overset{\overset{CH_3}{|}}{Si}}-[OH+H]O-\underset{\overset{|}{CH_3}}{\overset{\overset{CH_3}{|}}{Si}}-OH + \cdots \rightarrow HO-\underset{\overset{|}{CH_3}}{\overset{\overset{CH_3}{|}}{Si}}-O-\underset{\overset{|}{CH_3}}{\overset{\overset{CH_3}{|}}{Si}}-O-\underset{\overset{|}{CH_3}}{\overset{\overset{CH_3}{|}}{Si}}-O-\cdots + nH_2O$$

The product is a chain structure. By varying the conditions of hydrolysis and polymerisation, cross-links between chains can be formed. Different alkyl groups can be introduced by using different Grignard reagents. Many different silicones have been made. They may be regarded as intermediate between organic compounds and silica.

Properties. They all show great resistance to physical and chemical changes produced by heat, cold, oxygen and moisture. They are good electrical insulators. They have low surface tensions and therefore wet surfaces easily and completely. Silicone films are strongly water-repellant.

Uses. These depend on the properties listed above. Silicone oils (with chains of about ten silicon atoms per molecule) do not increase much in viscosity when cooled, and so are used for low temperature lubrication. They may also be heated to fairly high temperatures, 250 °C and above, without decomposing. Greases with similar properties have molecules with longer chains.

Cross-linked silicones form resins which are used for insulation in electric motors and transformers because of their power to withstand fairly high temperatures without decomposition or combustion. For the same reason silicone rubbers are used in electrical insulation.

Silicones are used for water-proofing fabrics, and in polishes for cars, furniture, boots and other leather articles. Water falling on the treated article rolls into balls and runs off instead of penetrating the surface.

Silicones added to paints increase their resistance to weathering and heat. Silicone paints are therefore used for smoke-stacks, ovens, boilers and exhaust silencers.

Because of their power of wetting surfaces easily, they are used as mould release agents, e.g. in the form of lacquers for coating frying pans, tins for bread-baking, and moulds for rubber articles, so that the omelettes, loaves or tyres do not stick. In the laboratory, silicone grease is useful for lubricating glass tubes before pushing them through rubber stoppers (the tubes remain free for long periods); also for lubricating glass taps.

It is seen that the properties of the silicones are a blend of those of silicates and paraffins, both of which are charactersied by a considerable degree of chemical inertness.

Carbides

Classification. Carbon forms binary compounds with most elements. The term 'carbide' is restricted to compounds of carbon with elements of lower electronegativity than itself (excluding hydrogen).

All carbides are solids of high melting point. They fall into three classes according to the type of bonding exhibited, the second class being intermediate in bond-type between (1) and (3):

(1) salt-like carbides (ionic binding): carbides of metals;

(2) alloy-type or interstitial carbides (metallic bonding): carbides of metals;

(3) covalent carbides (giant molecule structure): carbides of non-metals.

Salt-like carbides are formed chiefly by Main Group metals with valencies of three or less, i.e. Groups IA and B, IIA and B and IIIB.

Alloy-type carbides are formed from transition metals, chiefly of Groups IVA to Group VIII. These metals have atoms with incompletely filled *d* orbitals, and use four or more electrons per atom in metallic bonding.

Carbides include compounds of great practical importance, e.g. calcium carbide, and carbides present in steels (p. 565).

All carbides may be made by the action of carbon on the element or its oxide, usually at high temperatures; except those of Group IB and IIB metals, which are made at room temperature by passing acetylene into a solution containing metal ions.

1. Salt-like carbides

These are of two types (a) acetylides and (b) methanides.

(a) **Acetylides.** So called because they give acetylene (C_2H_2) on hydrolysis, and therefore contain the anion $(C{\equiv}C)^{2-}$. The equation for the hydrolysis is:

$$M^{2+}C{\equiv}C^{2-} + 2H—OH \rightarrow M(OH)_2 + H—C{\equiv}C—H,$$

or
$$C_2^{2-} + 2H^+ \rightarrow C_2H_2.$$

Examples of acetylides are: Na_2C_2, MgC_2, CaC_2, SrC_2, BaC_2, commonly called carbides, and Cu_2C_2, Ag_2C_2, ZnC_2, CdC_2, called acetylides.

Manufacture or preparation. (i) For metals of A families: by strongly heating carbon with the metal or its oxide, for example calcium carbide is manufactured by heating strongly a mixture of calcium oxide and coke to a temperature of about 2000 °C in an electric furnace, using Söderberg electrodes (p. 345)
$$CaO + 3C \rightarrow CaC_2 + CO\uparrow.$$

(ii) For metals of B families: by passing acetylene into aqueous ammoniacal solutions of copper(I) chloride or silver nitrate,

$$2AgNO_3 + C_2H_2 \rightarrow Ag_2C_2 + 2HNO_3.$$

Physical properties. When pure all are transparent, crystalline, ionic solids, with fairly high or very high melting points. All are colourless except copper(I) acetylide which is dark reddish-brown. Commercial calcium carbide is grey.

Carbides of the alkaline earth Group all have the calcium carbide structure, which is similar to the sodium chloride structure, each Ca^{2+} ion being surrounded octahedrally by six C_2^{2-} ions, and each C_2^{2-} ion by six Ca^{2+} ions.

Chemical properties. Acetylides of metals of A families are hydrolysed by water, often vigorously,

$$Na_2C_2 + 2H_2O \rightarrow 2NaOH + C_2H_2,$$
$$CaC_2 + 2H_2O \rightarrow Ca(OH)_2 + C_2H_2.$$

Those of metals of B families are not hydrolysed by water alone (except ZnC_2) but require dilute hydrochloric acid,

$$Ag_2C_2 + 2HCl \rightarrow 2AgCl\downarrow + C_2H_2.$$

The A-type are fairly stable towards heat; but two of the B-type, copper(I) acetylide and silver acetylide are dangerously explosive when heated or struck. Calcium carbide reacts with atmospheric nitrogen when heated in air, forming calcium cyanamide and carbon,

$$CaC_2 + N_2 \rightarrow CaCN_2 + C.$$

(b) **The Methanides.** The methanides give methane on hydrolysis with water. This reaction, together with data from investigation of their structure, are evidence that they contain C^{4-} anions. The best known methanides are aluminium carbide, Al_4C_3, and beryllium carbide, Be_2C. The equations for their hydrolysis are:

$$(Al_4)^{12+} \ (C_3)^{12-} \ + \ 12H—OH \ \longrightarrow 4Al(OH)_3 \ + \ 3CH_4\uparrow$$

$$\text{or} \qquad C^{4-} \ + \ 4H^+ \ \longrightarrow CH_4$$

Physical properties. Methanides are harder than acetylides. Aluminium carbide is a pale yellow crystalline solid; beryllium carbide is brick red. Both have high melting points.

Chemical properties. Both carbides are stable to heat. Both are hydrolysed by water alone giving methane (equation as above). The action is quicker with dilute hydrochloric acid.

2. Alloy-type (interstitial) carbides

Almost all metals crystallise in close-packed structures. The two most important holes or interstices in these structures are octahedral holes (p. 125) and tetrahedral holes (p. 123), octahdceral holes being larger. The lattices of some transition metals, e.g. titanium and tungsten, have octahedral holes big enough for small atoms such as carbon to fit neatly into them. The difference in electronegativity between carbon and these metals is not great enough to alter greatly the metallic bonding. For each metal atom in the lattice there is one octahedral hole. When all are filled with carbon atoms, alloys of the composition AB are obtained, e.g. titanium carbide, TiC, and tungsten carbide, WC.

Physical properties. Because the metallic bonding is not much altered by the carbon atoms, the alloys show metallic electrical conductivity. The carbon atoms interfere with the ability of the metal atoms to slide over each other; the alloys are therefore much harder, approaching diamond hardness, and more brittle (less malleable) than the metals. Like the metals, the alloys are opaque. The carbon atoms form some degree of bonding with the metal atoms, and so the alloys have very high melting points; the increased bonding also contributes to the increased hardness.

Chemical properties. The alloys are rather inert chemically except to oxidising agents.

Other important interstitial carbides with more complex structures are the carbides of iron, manganese and nickel: Fe_3C, Mn_3C, Ni_3C. These are present in steels (p. 565).

3. Covalent carbides (giant molecules)

These are carbides of non-metals with electronegativities a little lower than that of carbon. The two chief ones are formed from carbon's neighbours in the Periodic Table: silicon carbide, SiC, and boron carbide, B_4C.

Preparation or manufacture. By the reduction of the oxides with carbon at high temperatures in the electric furnace,

$$SiO_2 + 3C \rightarrow SiC + 2CO \uparrow.$$

Properties. Silicon carbide in one of its forms has the diamond structure. Both carbides are extremely hard solids of high melting point. Silicon carbide is grey. Boron carbide forms black shiny crystals, and has an appreciable electrical conductivity. Both are very resistant to chemical action.

Uses of carbides. Large quantities of calcium carbide are used in making acetylene which is used in the manufacture of many organic compounds and in welding.

Another important use of calcium carbide is in making calcium cyanamide $CaCN_2$. A stream of nitrogen is passed over a mixture of calcium carbide and calcium fluoride (acting as flux and catalyst), heated to 1000° C,

$$CaC_2 + N_2 \rightarrow CaCN_2 + C.$$

The black mixture produced is called *nitrolime* and is used as a fertiliser because, when put into the soil, it is hydrolysed to give ammonia by the action of bacteria,

$$CaCN_2 + 3H_2O \rightarrow CaCO_3 + 2NH_3 \uparrow.$$

Calcium cyanamide is also used as a source of organic chemicals e.g. melamine.

Tungsten carbide is used in making a very hard outer layer on the cutting edges of tools and the point of ball-point pens. Steels are interstitial alloys of iron and carbon. Silicon carbide (carborundum) and boron carbide, because of their almost diamond hardness are used as abrasives in grinding, polishing, drilling and tool-sharpening.

Sulphides, XS_2

All members of the Group except lead form quadrivalent sulphides. All are covalent, although the bonds in tin(IV) sulphide have much more ionic character than those of the others. Carbon disulphide is the only one which consists of discrete molecules; it is a volatile liquid at ordinary temperatures. The others are crystalline solids of moderate to high melting point; they have a giant-molecule structure.

Preparation or manufacture. All may be made by heating a mixture of the two elements concerned, e.g. for carbon disulphide, sulphur vapour is passed over white-hot coke or charcoal, the carbon disulphide vapour formed being removed and condensed,

$$C + 2S \rightleftharpoons CS_2.$$

With silicon disulphide and germanium disulphide the product is purified by sublimation. In the case of tin(IV) sulphide a mixture of tin, sulphur and ammonium chloride is heated. An alternative method of making GeS_2 and SnS_2 is to pass hydrogen sulphide into a solution of the chloride in hydrochloric acid,

$$SnCl_4 + 2H_2S \rightleftharpoons SnS_2 + 4HCl.$$

In a more modern process for making carbon disulphide in large quantities, sulphur vapour and methane are heated together to 600° C, with silica gel as catalyst, $\quad CH_4 + 4S \rightarrow CS_2 + 2H_2S.$

Physical properties. Carbon disulphide and silicon disulphide are colourless, germanium disulphide pale yellow, and tin(IV) sulphide golden yellow. Silicon disulphide forms fibrous crystals which consist of infinite chains of SiS_4 tetrahedra with opposite edges in common and van der Waals' forces between the chains (Fig. 118). Each silicon atom has a half-share in four

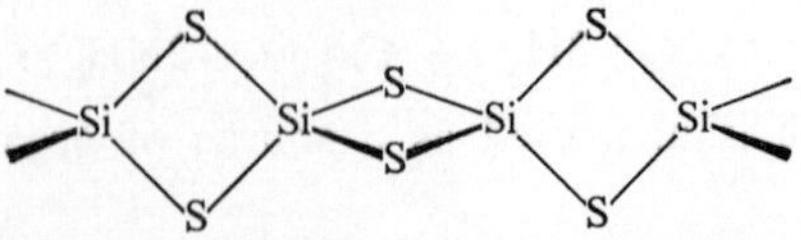

Fig. 118. Structure of silicon disulphide.

sulphur atoms equivalent to full control of two. The molecular formula of the chain is therefore $(SiS_2)_n$, and the structure is a one-dimensional giant molecule.

Tin(IV) sulphide has the cadmium iodide layer structure (p. 140).

Caution. Carbon disulphide is toxic when the vapour is inhaled or the liquid is absorbed through the skin.

Chemical properties. *Effect of water.* All are insoluble in water, but all except tin(IV) sulphide are hydrolysed by water, carbon disulphide at temperatures above 150 °C, silicon disulphide rapidly in the cold, germanium disulphide slowly. The general reaction is

$$XS_2 + 2H_2O \rightarrow XO_2 + 2H_2S.$$

Note. Tin(IV) sulphide is soluble in moderately concentrated hydrochloric acid giving a solution of tin(IV) chloride.

Effect of alkali sulphides. All react with solutions of the alkali sulphides including ammonium sulphide, giving soluble thiosalts with the Group IVB element in the anion, i.e. the sulphides 'dissolve' e.g.

(i) $CS_2 + Na_2S \rightarrow Na_2CS_3$,
　　　　　Sodium thiocarbonate

(ii) $SnS_2 + (NH_4)_2S \rightarrow (NH_4)_2SnS_3$.
　　　　　Ammonium thiostannante

Compare (i) $CO_2 + 2NaOH \rightarrow Na_2CO_3 + H_2O$,
　　　　 (ii) $SnO_2 + 2NaOH \rightarrow Na_2SnO_3 + H_2O$.

The sulphides are therefore 'anhydrosulphides' of thiocarbonic, thiosilicic, thiogermanic, and thiostannic acids, just as the oxides are anhydrides of carbonic $\rightarrow$ stannic acids. It follows that the sulphides are acidic or amphoteric.

Alkalis react with the sulphides giving a mixture of oxo-salts and thiosalts, e.g. carbonate and thiocarbonate.

Uses. Carbon disulphide in large quantities is used in making viscose rayon and cellophane; also in the manufacture of carbon tetrachloride (p. 374). It is a good solvent for sulphur, phosphorus, iodine, bromine, resins and fats.

Tin(IV) sulphide (mosaic gold) is used as a gold paint.

Compounds in which the elements are bivalent

In descending the Group there is an increasing tendency for the pair of *s* electrons in the valency shell to become inert. The bivalent state therefore becomes increasingly stable and reaches its maximum stability in lead when for the first time the bivalent compounds are more stable as a rule than the quadrivalent ones, e.g. $PbCl_2$ and $PbCl_4$. Bivalent compounds are always more ionic than the corresponding quadrivalent ones (Fajans' rules). Carbon appears to be bivalent in carbon monoxide, but the electronic configuration is more complicated (p. 399).

Carbon monoxide

Laboratory preparation. (1) By dehydration of formic acid with concentrated sulphuric acid. Sodium formate may be used instead of formic acid,

$$H.COOH \rightarrow CO\uparrow + H_2O.$$

The gas is collected over water. Concentrated sulphuric acid on oxalic acid or oxalates produces a mixture of carbon monoxide and dioxide.

(2) By passing a slow stream of carbon dioxide over red-hot charcoal,

$$C + O_2 \rightarrow CO_2; \quad CO_2 + C \rightarrow 2CO.$$

Manufacture. Carbon monoxide is not made in a pure state on the large scale but is an important constituent of water-gas, producer-gas, and coal-gas, pp. 372–3.

It is formed also during the incomplete combusiton of carbon or carbon compounds, e.g. in the exhaust gases from internal combustion engines; when a bunsen burner 'burns back'; and in explosions in coal-mines.

Physical properties. It is a colourless, odourless gas, slightly soluble in water, slightly less dense than air (relative density, 14; air, 14.4), difficult to liquefy, and extremely poisonous. Less than 1 % in air is fatal when inhaled, because the haemoglobin of the blood combines with carbon monoxide in preference to oxygen, forming carboxy-haemoglobin, thus preventing the blood from acting as an oxygen carrier, and causing death by oxygen-starvation of the tissues.

Molecular formula. When a mixture of carbon monoxide and oxygen is exploded in a eudiometer it is found that two volumes of carbon monoxide combine with one volume of oxygen to give two volumes of carbon dioxide at the same temperature and pressure. Given the molecular formulae O_2

and CO_2 the molecular formula of carbon monoxide is seen to be CO. This is confirmed by its relative density of 14.

Carbon monoxide + oxygen		→ carbon dioxide
2 vol.	1 vol.	2 vol.
2 mol.	1 mol.	2 mol. (Avogadro)
1 mol.	$\frac{1}{2}$ mol.	1 mol.
CO +	$\frac{1}{2}O_2$ →	CO_2

Structure and bonding. Three equivalent ways of showing the approximate structure of the molecule of carbon monoxide are,

$$\overset{-}{C}\!\!=\!\!\overset{+}{O} \quad C\overset{\leftarrow}{=\!\!=}O \quad \overset{\times}{\underset{\times}{x}}C\overset{\cdot}{\underset{\cdot}{\times}}O\overset{\cdot}{\cdot}$$

These indicate that the molecule has a considerable dipole moment, whereas in fact it has a very small one. More accurately, the molecule is considered to be a resonance hybrid of $C\overset{\leftarrow}{=\!\!=}O$ and $C\!\!=\!\!O$. This accounts for its low dipole moment and its chemical behaviour, in particular its ability to act as an electron donor, but not as an electron acceptor.

Chemical properties. Most important is its great reducing power especially at moderate temperatures. In its reducing actions, carbon monoxide is itself oxidised to the quadricovalent state, an increase in oxidation number from $+2$ to $+4$. Carbon dioxide is its usual oxidation product.

(1) Carbon monoxide does not support combustion, but burns with a pale blue flame to form carbon dioxide.

(2) It may be regarded as the anhydride of formic acid since (*a*) it is formed by dehydration of formic acid, and (*b*) it reacts with hot sodium hydroxide solution under pressure to give sodium formate.

(3) The reducing power of carbon monoxide for oxides *decreases* greatly with temperature; whereas that of carbon in the reaction

$$2C + O_2 \rightarrow 2CO$$

increases greatly (p. 184).

(4) In sunlight or in the presence of activated charcoal as catalyst at 150° C carbon monoxide combines with chlorine to form carbonyl chloride (phosgene), $$CO + Cl_2 \rightarrow COCl_2.$$

Phosgene is a colourless, poisonous, easily liquified gas, used in the manufacture of dyes and plastics.

(5) Carbon monoxide and sulphur vapour combine to form carbon oxosulphide, COS. This reaction is analagous to the burning of carbon monoxide.

399

(6) An ammoniacal or hydrochloric acid solution of copper(I) chloride is used in gas-analysis to absorb carbon monoxide. An addition compound, $CuCl.CO.2H_2O$ is formed.

(7) An important type of reaction shown by carbon monoxide is the formation of volatile addition compounds called carbonyls with many transition metals of Groups VI, VII and VIII. Examples are tetracarbonyl nickel(o), $Ni(CO)_4$ and pentacarbonyliron(o), $Fe(CO)_5$. The structure of tetracarbonylnickel(o) is tetrahedral. In the formation of carbonyls, the carbon atom donates its lone pair of electrons to the central metal *atom* forming co-ordinate bonds as shown. The metal atom in carbonyls is considered to have zero valency since all the electrons in the bonds are supplied by the carbon atoms.

Uses. Carbon monoxide is used in the reduction of ores; in the manufacture of very pure metals, e.g. nickel (p. 576) and iron (p. 566); as a constituent of fuel gases; and in the manufacture of phosgene, sodium formate and methanol (p. 288).

Oxides, MO

Preparation. Both oxides may be prepared by adding sodium hydroxide solution (not in excess) to solutions of salts of the metals in the bivalent state. The hydroxide precipitate (white) is filtered off, washed, and dehydrated at a low temperature (approximately 100 °C) to give the oxide. Tin(II) oxide may be made by heating tin(II) oxalate,

$$SnC_2O_4 = SnO + CO + CO_2.$$

Lead(II) oxide exists in two forms called litharge (Greek = silver stone) and massicot. Litharge may be prepared by heating lead to a temperature well above its melting point; massicot by heating lead(II) carbonate or nitrate to a temperature lower than that at which the lead(II) oxide fuses.

Physical properties. Tin(II) oxide is a blue-black solid, litharge an orange solid, and massicot a yellow solid.

Chemical properties. Tin(II) oxide smoulders in air forming tin(IV) oxide. When lead(II) oxide is heated in air to about 470 °C, red lead, Pb_3O_4, trilead tetroxide, is obtained.

Both monoxides are amphoteric, dissolving in acids to give the corresponding salts, and in solutions of caustic alkalis to give solutions of alkali stannites or plumbites, e.g. Na_2SnO_2 or Na_2PbO_2, salts of stannous acid, H_2SnO_2, or plumbous acid, H_2PbO_2. Lead(II) oxide is more basic than tin(II) oxide. This is shown by the fact that tin(II) oxide dissolves much more readily than lead(II) oxide in sodium hydroxide solution.

Solutions of alkali stannites are very powerful reducing agents while alkali plumbite solutions are not reducing agents. The ease of oxidation of tin(II) oxide, alkali stannite solutions (and tin(II) chloride solutions) shows the greater stability of tin in the quadrivalent state. Lead, by contrast is more stable in the bivalent state. Tin(II) oxide and lead(II) oxide are both reduced by heating with hydrogen, carbon or carbon monoxide; lead(II) oxide more easily (i.e. at a lower temperature) than tin(II) oxide.

Uses. Large quantities of lead(II) oxide are used in making storage battery plates, other lead compounds, flint glass (p. 390) and as a *drier* for paints, where it quickens the setting of the paint, a process of atmospheric oxidation.

Hydroxides, M(OH)$_2$

For preparation see the first stage in the preparation of oxides, p. 400. The hydroxides, like the oxides, are amphoteric, lead(II) hydroxide being more basic than tin(II) hydroxide. Both therefore dissolve in acids and in caustic alkali solutions, the more acidic tin(II) hydroxide dissolving more readily than lead(II) hydroxide. The equations below show the formation of the hydroxy-stannite ion and the hydroxy-plumbite ion by the *addition* of *one* hydroxyl ion to the hydroxide to form the hydroxy-stannite ion and the hydroxy-plumbite ion, thus

$$Sn(OH)_2 + OH^- \rightleftharpoons [Sn(OH)_3]^-,$$
$$Pb(OH)_2 + OH^- \rightleftharpoons [Pb(OH)_3]^-.$$

Uses. Alkaline solutions of tin(II) chloride are used in vat dyeing and dye printing.

Chlorides, MCl$_2$

Preparation. By the usual methods for making chlorides (p. 240).

(1) The action of chlorine on the heated metals gives tin(IV) chloride,

$SnCl_4$, and lead(II) chloride respectively, another example of the greater stability of the bivalent state in lead.

(2) By the action of boiling concentrated hydrochloric acid on the metal (finely divided in the case of lead),

$$M + 2H^+ + 2Cl^- \rightarrow M^{2+} + 2Cl^- + H_2\uparrow.$$

On cooling the solutions (diluted in the case of lead) white crystals of tin(II) chloride dihydrate, $SnCl_2.2H_2O$ (tin salt), and lead(II) chloride, $PbCl_2$, are formed.

(3) For lead(II) chloride: addition of chloride ions to a solution containing lead(II) ions gives a white precipitate of the sparingly soluble lead(II) chloride.

Anhydrous tin(II) chloride may be prepared by passing hydrogen chloride over heated tin, or by dehydrating the dihydrate by heating in an atmosphere of hydrogen chloride to prevent hydrolysis.

Physical properties. Both chlorides are white crystalline solids: $SnCl_2$, melting point 247 °C; $PbCl_2$, melting point 500 °C. $SnCl_2$ is very soluble in water (provided the water is not in excess) and also in organic solvents, e.g. ethanol, ether, acetone. Lead(II) chloride, on the other hand, is but slightly soluble in cold water, more soluble in hot, and almost insoluble in alcohol. $SnCl_2.2H_2O$ (melting point 40 °C) has similar solubilities to $SnCl_2$. The vapour densities of the chlorides show that the vapours consist mainly of discrete single molecules (therefore covalent) $SnCl_2$ and $PbCl_2$. But the aqueous solutions contain Sn^{2+} and Pb^{2+} ions. Molten lead(II) chloride is a fairly good conductor of electricity: molten tin(II) chloride is not so good.

Structure and bonding. (1) *In the crystals.* Tin(II) chloride's rather low melting point, high solubility in ethanol, and ready hydrolysis in aqueous solution indicate a mainly covalent structure. Lead(II) chloride has a structure which is mainly ionic. This is supported by its fairly high melting point and fairly good conductivity of the melt; its very slight solubility in ethanol, and by the fact that it is little hydrolysed in aqueous solution.

(2) *In the vapour phase.* As already said, the vapours of both chlorides consist mainly of discrete molecules, $SnCl_2$, and $PbCl_2$. These are V-shaped, not linear. This is because the metal atom has round it one lone pair as well as two bonding pairs (Fig. 119), which lie all in the same plane. The Cl—M—Cl angle is less than 120° because the repulsion between the lone pair and the pair in each covalent bond is greater than the repulsion of the

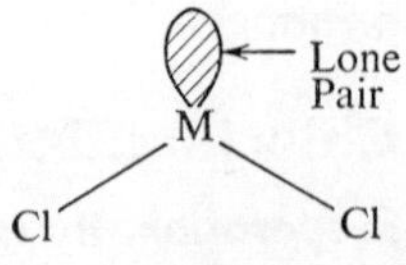

Fig. 119

402

bonding pairs for each other. The existence of V-shaped structures in the vapour state means the existence of covalent bonding, since covalent bonds are rigidly directional.

Chemical properties. *Water.* Tin(II) chloride is considerably hydrolysed in dilute aqueous solution, giving a white precipitate of the basic chloride, tin(II) hydroxychloride,

$$SnCl_2 + H_2O \rightleftharpoons Sn(OH)Cl + HCl.$$

Because tin(II) chloride is a good reducing agent the solution is also slowly oxidised on standing in air, the reaction products being a cream-coloured precipitate of basic tin(II) chloride with some hydrated tin(IV) oxide, $SnO_2.xH_2O$, and a solution containing hydrated tin(IV) ions $[Sn(H_2O)_4]^{4+}$. The hydrolysis does not proceed to completion because, since the action is reversible, it is stopped when the hydrochloric acid reaches a sufficient concentration. (*Note.* A solution for testing reactions of tin(IV) ions in qualitative analysis is made by dissolving the penta-hydrate $SnCl_4.5H_2O$ in dilute hydrochloric acid.)

Lead(II) chloride, in contrast is not oxidised in solution, nor appreciably hydrolysed.

Alkalis. Addition of caustic alkali solutions to solutions containing Sn^{2+} ions or Pb^{2+} ions give white precipitates of hydroxides, soluble in excess of alkali (see hydroxides). When lime water is added to a hot concentrated solution of lead(II) chloride a white precipitate of basic lead(II) chloride, Pb(OH)Cl is formed.

Acids. On addition of concentrated hydrochloric acid to tin(II) chloride or lead(II) chloride, solutions containing complex chlorostannous or chloroplumbous acids of formulae $HMCl_3$ and H_2MCl_4 are obtained, e.g.

$$SnCl_2 + 2HCl \rightarrow H_2SnCl_4 \quad \text{(tetrachlorostannous acid).}$$

Salts containing the ions, $SnCl_4^{2-}$ and $PbCl_4^{2-}$, chlorostannites and chloroplumbites, respectively, may be prepared.

When dilute hydrochloric acid is added to a solution containing Pb^{2+} ions in sufficient concentration a white precipitate of lead(II) chloride is obtained. The solubility of this precipitate in water is decreased by adding an excess of dilute hydrochloric acid (common ion action). If a sufficient quantity of concentrated hydrochloric acid is added the precipitate dissolves completely because of the formation of the soluble chloroplumbous acids.

Reducing action. Tin(II) chloride is a good reducing agent; lead(II) chloride is not a reducing agent. Tin(II) chloride solution reduces solutions of gold salts to gold, silver salts to silver, mercury(II) salts first to mercury(I) salts, then to metallic mercury; iron(III) salts to iron(II) salts; and also many organic compounds, e.g. nitrobenzene to aniline. Equations for mercury salts are given on p. 607. With iron(III) ions the equation is

$$2Fe^{3+} + Sn^{2+} \rightarrow 2Fe^{2+} + Sn^{4+}.$$

Tin(II) chloride solution and lead(II) chloride solution are themselves reduced by zinc which has a greater negative standard electrode potential than either tin or lead M^{2+}/M. When a strip of zinc is suspended in a solution of tin(II) chloride or of lead(II) chloride, tin or lead are deposited on the zinc in the form of tree-like structures. An equivalent weight of zinc passes into solution.

Uses. Tin(II) chloride is a good reducing agent in qualitative and quantitative analysis, and also in the manufacture of organic compounds, e.g. diazonium salts are reduced to hydrazine salts. It is also used as a mordant in dye printing. Basic lead(II) chloride is used as a pigment.

Lead(II) bromide, PbBr₂, and lead(II) iodide, PbI₂. These may be precipitated in a similar way to lead(II) chloride; the bromide is white, the iodide golden yellow. They have a general resemblance to lead(II) chloride but the iodide is more covalent than the others. The solubilities in cold water are small in all three lead(II) halides, but the chloride is more soluble than the bromide, which is much more soluble than the iodide. They are all much more soluble in hot water than in cold (from five to ten times) and crystallise readily when their hot nearly saturated solutions are cooled. Lead(II) iodide crystallises in fine golden spangles, but its aqueous solution is colourless, because in it the compound is completely ionised, and both lead(II) ions and iodide ions are colourless.

Oxo-salts

The only important oxo-salts in Group IVB are those of lead. Most lead(II) salts are insoluble or sparingly soluble except the nitrate and the acetate. Their solubilities are similar to those of the corresponding barium salts, partly because the Pb^{2+} and Ba^{2+} ions are very similar in size.

Lead(II) carbonate, PbCO₃

Normal lead(II) carbonate is formed as a white precipitate, $PbCO_3$, on adding a solution of sodium hydrogen carbonate to a cold solution containing lead(II) ions, usually lead(II) nitrate solution. If sodium carbonate solution is used the white precipitate formed is basic lead(II) carbonate, $Pb(OH)_2 . 2PbCO_3$; this is known as *white lead*. It is a valuable pigment used in making oil paints of high quality; their main disadvantage is that the paint-film gradually darkens because of the formation of black lead(II) sulphide by interaction with hydrogen sulphide in the air. White lead is manufactured mainly by the precipitation process, which gives a very pure product. Granulated lead in lead(II) acetate solution is oxidised with air to give basic lead(II) acetate. Carbon dioxide is then passed in to precipitate white lead. The regenerated lead(II) acetate solution is then re-used.

Lead(II) carbonate has an extremely small solubility in water; but it is readily soluble in those acids which form soluble lead(II) salts, in concentrated solutions of caustic alkalis and in concentrated ammonium acetate solution. When heated, lead(II) carbonate decomposes at a fairly low temperature (approximately 300 °C) into lead(II) oxide and carbon dioxide.

Lead(II) nitrate, $Pb(NO_3)_2$

(Tin(II) nitrate can be isolated in crystalline form but is very unstable. The action of dilute nitric acid on tin gives a solution containing a mixture of tin(II) and tin(IV) nitrates.)

Lead(II) nitrate is prepared (as usual for nitrates) by the action of dilute nitric acid on lead, lead(II) oxide or carbonate. Its crystals are colourless, without water of crystallisation, and readily soluble in water, forming a solution which is not hydrolysed. On heating, the solid decomposes into lead(II) oxide, nitrogen dioxide, and oxygen, a reaction which is used in the preparation of nitrogen dioxide.

Lead(II) sulphate, $PbSO_4$

(Tin(II) sulphate, $SnSO_4$, is a white crystalline solid readily soluble in water.)

Lead(II) sulphate being almost insoluble in water (like barium sulphate) is made by precipitation. It is a white stable solid, insoluble in water and dilute acids, but soluble in concentrated sulphuric acid, in concentrated caustic alkali solutions, and in concentrated ammonium acetate solution because of the formation of weakly dissociated lead(II) acetate and also complex ions. It is stable on heating up to a temperature of about 1000 °C.

Lead(II) chromate, PbCrO₄

When a solution of potassium chromate is added to a solution containing lead(II) ions, a bright yellow precipitate of lead(II) chromate is formed,

$$Pb^{2+} + CrO_4^{2-} = PbCrO_4\downarrow.$$

Lead(II) chromate is extremely insoluble in water, the least soluble of lead(II) salts, insoluble in acetic acid solution, but readily soluble in dilute nitric acid, and fairly soluble in caustic alkali solutions forming a chromate and a plumbite. It melts at 844 °C, but begins to decompose at temperatures not much above this. Lead(II) chromate is used as a pigment 'chrome yellow'.

Lead(II) acetate, Pb(CH₃COO)₂.2H₂O

This is made by dissolving lead(II) oxide in excess acetic acid. It is a white solid, readily soluble in cold water, and much more so in hot. It is very poisonous. Lead(II) acetate is very slightly ionised in aqueous solution and is therefore covalent.

Sulphides, MS

Tin forms a sulphide SnS, as well as SnS₂. Lead forms a sulphide PbS but no PbS₂; this again illustrates the greater stability of lead in the bivalent state.

Occurrence. Tin(II) sulphide is not found native. In sharp contrast, lead(II) sulphide is the most important ore of lead. The mineral galena (lead glance) is mainly lead(II) sulphide, PbS. Its crystals belong to the cubic system and show both cubic and octahedral forms. The crystals are dark grey in colour with a strong metallic lustre, i.e. they are opaque and reflect light like a mirror, hence the name lead *glance*. They show good cleavage parallel to the cube faces.

Preparation. (1) Both sulphides may be synthesised by passing sulphur vapour over the heated metal.

(2) Both may be precipitated by passing hydrogen sulphide into a solution containing the M²⁺ ions.

Physical properties. Both sulphides are insoluble crystalline solids of high melting point. Tin(II) sulphide varies in colour from dark brown to almost black; lead(II) sulphide is grey-black.

Structure and bonding. The bonding in both is mainly covalent with some metallic character, shown by their lustre and electrical conductivity. Lead(II) sulphide has been known for many years to be a semi-conductor, and was widely used as a rectifier in wireless receivers ('crystal' sets). The structures of the two sulphides are, however, quite different. Tin(II) sulphide forms orthorhombic crystals. The lattice is a highly deformed rock-salt lattice with a layer-type structure, which accounts for the flaky nature of the crystals. Lead(II) sulphide has a normal rock-salt structure. This is most unexpected, and does not imply that the bonding is ionic: ionic sulphides form colourless transparent crystals; lead(II) sulphide is very different (see above). The structure is probably formed because of the presence of the inert electron-pair in the lead atom.

Chemical properties. *Water.* Both sulphides are insoluble in water.

Acids. Both are insoluble in very dilute hydrochloric acid (about 0.3 M), but, as the concentration increases, so also does the solubility until both are completely dissolved in moderately concentrated warm hydrochloric acid (about 3 M) forming solutions containing hydrated Sn^{2+} and Pb^{2+} cations and also $[SnCl_4]^{2-}$ and $[PbCl_4]^{2-}$ anions. This reaction shows the basic character of tin and lead (formation of cations) and their amphoteric character, since they also form anions.

Dilute sulphuric acid has little action on the sulphides, but hot dilute nitric acid (about 5 M) dissolves lead(II) sulphide readily, because the liberated hydrogen sulphide is oxidised to sulphur, thus preventing the reverse reaction. Hot dilute nitric acid (about 5 M) converts tin(II) sulphide to an almost white insoluble residue, presumably hydrated tin(IV) oxide.

Caustic alkali solutions (*LiOH, NaOH, KOH*). Tin(II) sulphide dissolves with difficulty in the cold, but is soluble in excess of hot caustic alkali solution, giving a solution containing both stannite and thiostannite anions,

$$2SnS + 4OH^- \rightarrow SnO_2^{2-} + SnS_2^{2-} + 2H_2O,$$

or $$2SnS + 2OH^- \rightarrow [HSnO_2]^- + [HSnS_2]^-.$$

Note. Tin(II) oxide is more acidic than tin(II) sulphide, since the oxide dissolves more readily in caustic alkali solutions than the sulphide.

Lead(II) sulphide is insoluble in caustic alkali solutions, a fact which shows that it is less acidic than tin(II) sulphide. This difference is used in the separation of the two sulphides in qualitative analysis.

Lead(II) oxide is more acidic than lead(II) sulphide since the oxide dissolves in caustic alkali solutions.

Ammonium sulphide solutions. Tin(II) sulphide is insoluble in colourless ammonium sulphide solution $(NH_4)_2S$, but dissolves readily in yellow ammonium sulphide solution $(NH_4)_2S_x$, which first oxidises the tin(II) sulphide to tin(IV) sulphide $(SnS+S \rightarrow SnS_2)$, which then dissolves in ammonium sulphide solution forming a solution of ammonium thio-stannate, $$SnS_2+S^{2-} \rightarrow [SnS_3]^{2-}.$$

Addition of excess dilute hydrochloric acid to this solution precipitates tin(IV) sulphide, $$SnS_3^{2-}+2H^+ \rightarrow SnS_2+H_2S.$$

Lead(II) sulphide is insoluble in ammonium sulphide or polysulphide solution because it cannot be oxidised to PbS_2, which does not exist. This shows that tin(II) sulphide is superior to lead(II) sulphide in reducing power. All other tin(II) salts show the same superiority.

Heat. When lead(II) sulphide is heated in air it is converted into a mixture of lead(II) oxide and lead(II) sulphate.

Trilead tetroxide, Pb₃O₄ (red lead)

Preparation. Massicot (unfused lead(II) oxide) is heated in air at about 470 °C for several hours. The action is reversed at 550 °C and above,

$$6PbO+O_2 \underset{550°}{\overset{470°}{\rightleftharpoons}} 2Pb_3O_4.$$

Physical properties. It is a brilliant scarlet solid insoluble in water. Pb_3O_4 may be regarded as $Pb_2^{II}[Pb^{IV}O_4]$, lead(II) orthoplumbate, a salt of orthoplumbic acid H_4PbO_4 or $Pb(OH)_4$. Just as calcium carbonate may be written as a compound of a basic oxide and an acidic oxide $(CaO.CO_2)$ so lead(II) orthoplumbate, may be written as $2PbO.PbO_2$; PbO is here acting as a basic oxide containing bivalent lead and PbO_2 as an acidic oxide containing quadrivalent lead. Red lead on this formulation would be mainly covalent, being the salt of a weak base and a weak acid. Red lead is best described as a mixed oxide containing Pb^{II}, Pb^{IV}, and O^{2-}.

Chemical properties. Red lead behaves chemically as if it were a loose compound of lead(II) oxide and lead(IV) oxide. It is an oxidising agent easily reduced to the metal.

Action with acids. It reacts with warm dilute nitric acid to give a solution of lead(II) nitrate and a residue of lead(IV) oxide,

$$2PbO.PbO_2+4HNO_3 \rightarrow 2Pb(NO_3)_2+PbO_2\downarrow+2H_2O.$$

With hot concentrated hydrochloric acid, chlorine is liberated and lead(II) chloride formed. With hot concentrated sulphuric acid oxygen is liberated and lead sulphate formed. The last two are redox reactions in which the oxidising agent is lead(IV) oxide.

Uses. Red lead is used as a pigment in oil paints, especially as a first coat for structural steel-work; in the form of a putty with linseed oil for joints in pipes and plates; in making glass and pottery-glazes; in matches.

Similarities between boron and silicon (diagonal)

Although silicon has a much larger atomic radius than boron, their electronegativities are similar because the effective nuclear charge of silicon is greater than that of boron.

Boron and silicon occur naturally as oxo-compounds, borates and silicates. This indicates that the B—O bond has stability comparable to that of the Si—O bond.

The elements are solids of high melting point and low density, hard, brittle, and with low electrical conductivities which increase on heating, i.e. they are semi-conductors. These properties are typical of non-metallic elements with a giant-molecular structure. Chemically the elements are rather inert, and are always covalent but with the power to increase their covalencies by acting as electron acceptors.

Compounds. The oxides are very weakly acidic solids showing no amphoteric tendency. When the molten oxides solidify they form glasses. The molten oxides can dissolve metal oxides to form borate and silicate glasses. Mixed borosilicate glasses, e.g. Pyrex, have good heat-resisting properties because of their low thermal expansion.

Borates and silicates show a great number of structures. Metaborates and pyroxene silicates have similar chain structures.

Hydrides of boron and silicon are volatile, spontaneously inflammable, and readily hydrolysed in a similar way (pp. 350, 378).

Fluorides are also hydrolysed similarly,

$$4BF_3 + 3H_2O \rightarrow 3HBF_4 + B(OH)_3;$$

$$3SiF_4 + 4H_2O \rightarrow 2H_2SiF_6 + Si(OH)_4.$$

Chlorides are hydrolysed to form boric and silicic acids, along with hydrochloric acid.

Exercises

1. Calculate the contents of the unit cell of β-cristobalite, and verify that the result corresponds to the empirical formula of silica.
2. Show the relation between the properties and uses of the elements of Group IV B.

3. Some of Mendeléeff's predictions of the properties of germanium and its compounds are given on p. 15. Use your knowledge of trends in the Periodic Table to explain each of these predictions as fully as possible. Extend the list to other compounds, giving reasons for any statements made.

4. Give a short account of the classification of carbides. Name and give the formula of at least one carbide in each class, and show that its properties and uses depend on its structure and bonding.

5. A student given 1 g of lead dioxide was asked to prepare as pure a specimen of lead carbonate as possible. This was his account: '1 g of the lead dioxide was warmed with nitric acid (50 ml 2M) until dissolved. Aqueous sodium carbonate (20 ml 2M) was added. The mixture was evaporated to dryness and ignited.'

Point out the mistakes in the above account and describe carefully, with suitable explanation, how the preparation should have been carried out. (L)

6. Name an important ore of lead and outline how the metal is obtained from it.

Compare the properties of the dioxide and chlorides of lead with those of the dioxides and chlorides of carbon and silicon. (J.M.B.)

7. Describe carefully how you would obtain from metallic tin (*a*) two different anhydrous chlorides of tin; (*b*) a solution of sodium hexahydroxostannate(IV) (sodium stannate). What explanation can you offer for the following experimental facts?

(i) If hydrogen sulphide is passed through a dilute acidified solution of tin(II) chloride [stannous chloride] a brown precipitate is obtained. The precipitate, after removal and washing, is found to form a clear solution with yellow ammonium sulphide solution. On the addition of dilute hydrochloric acid to the clear solution a yellow precipitate is formed and hydrogen sulphide is given off.

(ii) An acidified solution of tin(II) chloride [stannous chloride] becomes cloudy on dilution with water.   (J.M.B.)

8. Outline the commercial preparation of (*a*) water gas, (*b*) acetylene. How, and under what conditions, do the following pairs of substances react together: (i) carbon monoxide and nickel; (ii) carbon monoxide and sodium hydroxide; (iii) acetylene and water; (iv) acetylene and hydrogen? (C)

9. Compare the properties and reactions of silicon with those of (*a*) carbon, (*b*) boron, showing how far the first comparison illustrates the resemblance between two elements of the same group in the Periodic Table, and how far the second illustrates the so-called 'diagonal relationship'.   (L)

10. Give an account of the chemical properties of the element tin and describe four of its principal compounds.

The element germanium (Mendeléeff's eka-silicon) lies in Group IV of the Periodic Table below carbon and silicon and above tin and lead. What properties would you predict for this element, for its oxide GeO_2 and for its chloride $GeCl_4$?   (O & C)

11. Describe briefly how the chemical characteristics of elements in the same group of the Periodic Table change with increasing atomic number, taking the elements carbon, silicon, germanium, tin and lead as examples. Suggest possible reasons for the gradations in properties.   (O & C)

12. Starting from silica how could you obtain (a) a colloidal dispersion of hydrated silica (silicic acid), (b) silica gel?

Comment upon the following facts:
   (i) scientific instruments which need to be kept dry may have silica gel containing a little anhydrous cobalt chloride placed inside them;
   (ii) if silica is fused with sodium carbonate, carbon dioxide is evolved, but if carbon dioxide is passed through an aqueous solution of sodium silicate, hydrated silica is precipitated.
   (iii) the boiling point of methane is below that of the corresponding hydride of silicon but the boiling point of water is above that of hydrogen sulphide.   (J.M.B.)

13. Give the names and formulae of **three** oxides of lead and outline their preparation in the laboratory, starting from the metal. What action has hydrochloric acid on each of these oxides? Classify these oxides stating briefly the reasons for the classification adopted.

How would you prepare pure samples, starting from lead, of (a) lead nitrate, (b) lead sulphate?   (J.M.B.)

14. Write a concise account of the oxides of the Group IVB elements (C, Si, Ge, Sn, Pb) to illustrate and explain the changes in properties within this group of the Periodic Table.   (O & CS)

24

GROUP VB: THE NITROGEN GROUP

Atomic properties of the Nitrogen Group elements

Element	Symbol	Atomic no.	Atomic weight	Covalent radius (Å)
Nitrogen	N	7	14.01	0.75
Phosphorus	P	15	30.97	1.06
Arsenic	As	33	74.92	1.19
Antimony	Sb	51	121.80	1.38
Bismuth	Bi	83	209.00	1.46

Relationship of the Group to the Periodic Table

Nitrogen and oxygen, which is at the head of Group VI, have certain features in common. Both are colourless, odourless, diatomic gases which comprise the principal constituents of the atmosphere and they differ strikingly from the following element in each of their Groups, i.e. phosphorus and sulphur respectively. Again, however, these latter two elements bear a striking superficial resemblance to one another. They are coloured non-metallic solids which occur in several allotropic modifications, and readily burn in air; white phosphorus particularly so.

Group VA elements, vanadium, niobium and tantalum, have five valence electrons like the Group VB elements, and thus show similar valencies.

General Group features

Nitrogen, like the first member of all *p*-block Groups, differs widely from the other members of the Group. Phosphorus, arsenic, antimony and bismuth form a fairly closely related series of elements. The reasons for the relative uniqueness of nitrogen are similar to those described for carbon, namely: (1) a very small atomic radius, (2) inability to show a greater covalency than four, (3) great stability of the free element.

As usual, the most powerful unifying property amongst these elements is the similarity of their outer electronic configuration of five electrons, i.e. s^2p^3, see the following table.

Electron configurations, electronegativities, and electrode potentials of the Group V elements

Element	Electron configuration						Electro-negativities	Electrode potentials (V)
	K	L	M	N	O	P		
Nitrogen	2	5	—	—	—	—	3.07	—
Phosphorus	2	8	5	—	—	—	2.06	—
Arsenic	2	8	18	5	—	—	2.20	+0.25
Antimony	2	8	18	18	5	—	1.82	+0.21
Bismuth	2	8	18	32	18	5	1.67	+0.23

As they have five valence electrons in their outer shell, Group V elements can acquire stabilised valency states by either of two main processes.

(1) *Electron transfer.* By gaining three extra electrons each atom could reach the highly stabilised noble gas electron structure of eight electrons in the outermost shell. However, as there is no increase in the positive charge on the nucleus there is nothing to counterbalance the strong repulsive forces set up by this relatively large number of extra electrons, and the triply charged negative ion is seldom formed. Small atoms can form highly charged negative ions more readily than large ones, because of the stronger attractive force on the electrons that exists when they are closer to the nucleus. The nitrogen atom is the smallest in Group V, and in combination with very strongly electropositive metals the nitride ion, N^{3-}, is produced, e.g. $Ca_3^{2+}N_2^{3-}$ and $Li_3^+N^{3-}$. It is unstable in aqueous solution, however, and immediately hydrolyses. There is no evidence of the larger phosphorus atom forming discrete phosphide ions, P^{3-}, but in compounds such as sodium phosphide, Na_3P, the binding must have considerable ionic character.

In order to acquire the electron structure of the preceding noble gas five electrons would have to be lost from each atom. The energy required to produce this M^{5+} ion is enormous and the process never occurs. However, amongst the heavier elements the 'inert pair' effect operates, and as the two outermost s electrons form a stabilised duplet loss of the three p electrons leads to a stable M^{3+} ion. This is most stable with bismuth, less stable with antimony, and very unstable with arsenic.

(2) *Electron sharing.* As the five valence electrons are distributed throughout the *s* and *p* orbitals in the outer shell to give three unpaired *p* electrons, these can pair off with unpaired electrons in another atom or atoms to form three covalent bonds. Besides this covalency of 3 all except nitrogen are capable of showing a covalency of 5. This arises when all five valence electrons are unpaired (see below). The energy required to unpair the *s* electrons comes from the reaction, and it is also necessary to have an easily accessible empty orbital to accommodate the displaced electron.

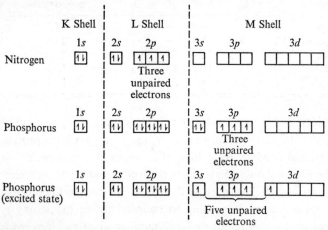

Fig. 120. A pictorial representation of the electronic configurations of nitrogen and of phosphorus. The up and down arrows represent electrons that are spinning in opposite directions.

No such orbital is available in nitrogen, so it is not able to expand its octet and cannot show a covalency of 5.

Because of the inert pair effect the outermost *s* electrons are progressively more difficult to unpair as the Group is descended and this makes the quinquevalent compounds more difficult to produce.

Although the tricovalent nitrogen atom may not accept further electrons it contains a lone pair of electrons which it can use for binding purposes as in the formation of the ammonium radical, e.g.

$$
\begin{array}{c}
\text{H} \\
| \\
\text{H}\!-\!\overset{..}{\text{N}}\!: + \text{H}^+ \rightarrow \\
| \\
\text{H}
\end{array}
\left[
\begin{array}{c}
\text{H} \\
| \\
\text{H}\!-\!\text{N}\!-\!\text{H} \\
| \\
\text{H}
\end{array}
\right]^{+}
$$

In this way nitrogen may show a covalency of 4 which is the covalency maximum for Period 2 elements. Phosphorus is a very much weaker donor of its electron pair when in the tricovalent state. However, owing to the availability of the $3d$ orbitals, in contrast to nitrogen, phosphorus is able to accept further electrons both in the tricovalent and quinquecovalent states to form such compounds as PCl_5 and KPF_6. The latter salt contains the PF_6^- ion in which phosphorus displays the covalency maximum for Period 3.

A summary of the valencies discussed above is given in the table below. In general, the principal valencies of the Group are three and five; the compounds of nitrogen and phosphorus are essentially covalent; arsenic, antimony and bismuth become progressively more metallic.

Summary of the Group V valencies

Element	Simple ions		Covalencies			
	M^{3-}	M^{3+}	3	4	5	6
N	N^{3-}	—			—	—
P	—	—				
As	—	?	(Decreasing		stability)	
Sb	—	Sb^{3+}		↓		↓
Bi	—	Bi^{3+}	↓	—	↓	—

Nitrogen differs from the rest of the Group, but resembles its neighbours carbon and oxygen in the readiness with which it forms multiple bonds. For example, it combines with itself to form a triply bonded diatomic molecule, $:N\equiv N:$, which has a very short internuclear distance (1.09 Å) (see p. 111) and a very high bond strength. Because of the strength of the nitrogen–nitrogen triple bond, a large amount of energy is required to disrupt the molecule (dissociation energy $= 941$ kJ mol^{-1}, i.e. 225 kcal mol^{-1}) which must be split prior to reaction and so it is chemically very inert even though it is the third most electronegative element. Under ordinary conditions, the rest of the Group are not able to form diatomic molecules owing to their greater reluctance to form multiple bonds. Instead, at least in some of the allotropic modifications of phosphorus, arsenic and perhaps antimony, they occur as separate tetratomic, tetrahedral molecules. The tendency to form covalent bonds is much reduced in the denser allotropes, particularly as the Group is descended. Antimony and bismuth are predominantly metallic, but even these are not true metals as they have a co-ordination number of three, which indicates preferred directions of binding. Ideally, metals have a co-ordination number of twelve and each metal atom is equidistant from all its immediate neighbours in a close-packed structure (see p. 123). It is these varied states of aggregation that cause a great many of the acute differences that exist amongst these elements. For instance, phosphorus–phosphorus single bonds are not as strong as nitrogen–nitrogen triple bonds and are consequently more easily broken and phosphorus is more reactive than nitrogen. In fact, it is a very reactive element and combines vigorously with oxygen, the halogens and sulphur. The remaining three elements also combine energetically with these elements and they also form a range of alloys with many metals.

The elements

Occurrence

Seventy-eight per cent by volume of the atmosphere is composed of nitrogen as the diatomic gas N_2. Large deposits of inorganic nitrogen compounds are rare, and the most important is in the desert regions of Northern Chile where Chile saltpetre, $NaNO_3$, is mined. Unlike nitrogen phosphorus is much too reactive to occur native and is chiefly found as phosphates in such ores as apatite, $3Ca_3(PO_4).CaF_2$. Ninety per cent of the phosphate rock mined is used in the production of fertilisers.

Arsenic, antimony, and bismuth are less abundant, and occur chiefly as sulphide ores, e.g. arsenical pyrites, $FeAsS$; stibnite, Sb_2S_3; bismuth glance, Bi_2S_3.

Both nitrogen and phosphorus are essential constituents of all plant and animal tissue; nitrogen in the form of compounds, known as proteins; phosphorus either in complex organic molecules such as adenosine triphosphate or as calcium orthophosphate which is particularly important in bones and teeth.

The nitrogen cycle

Although nitrogen is an essential foodstuff for living material only a few very simple organisms are capable of assimilating the free element and converting it into plant protein. The rest of the plant kingdom relies on being able to absorb nitrogen from the soil as soluble nitrates and to a lesser extent nitrites and ammonium salts. Animals are unable to feed on nitrogen in this form and can develop protein of their own only by digesting the protein of plants or other animals. As a result there is a vital interrelation between plants, animals, the soil, and the nitrogen of the atmosphere, and it is called the nitrogen cycle.

Nitrogen of the atmosphere is brought into the life cycle in two ways.

(1) By bacteria, e.g. *Bacillus radicicola* which is found in colonies in nodules on the roots of leguminous plants such as beans, peas, clover, etc. *Bacillus radicicola* converts atmospheric nitrogen into protein some of which passes to the host plant.

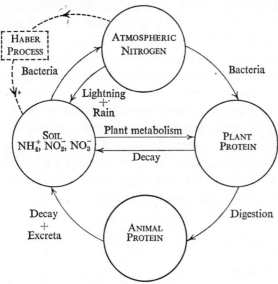

Fig. 121. The nitrogen cycle.

(2) Nitrogen undergoes a certain amount of reaction with oxygen under the influence of electric discharges and the product is washed to the ground by rain water as nitric and nitrous acids which combine with basic materials in the soil to form salts. Not all this combined (sometimes called 'fixed') nitrogen is retained, however, as some bacteria in the soil break the nitrates down into free nitrogen which returns to the atmosphere. At the same time, plants absorb the nitrogen-containing salts out of the soil, and convert them into protein.

When the plant dies, the processes of decay eventually convert the proteins into ammonia which accumulates in the soil as ammonium salts. Bacterial action leads to the conversion of these ammonium salts into nitrites and then nitrates which can be used to regenerate fresh supplies of protein by plant metabolism. Much of the plant protein ingested by animals is excreted mainly as urea, $CO(NH_2)_2$, and if this is returned to the soil it easily hydrolyses to yield carbon dioxide and ammonia:

$$CO(NH_2)_2 + H_2O \rightarrow CO_2 + 2NH_3.$$

417

When dead animals decay, as with plants, most of the nitrogen in their protein decomposes to ammonia, which if it accumulates in the soil replenishes the nutriments essential for plant growth.

Systematic cropping of plants and animals from the land, coupled with the practice of allowing most of the nitrogenous material involved to pass into the sea as waste, rapidly denudes the soil of its reserve of essential minerals. Fortunately, chemical industry is able to make good the balance with artificial fertilisers. Enormous quantities of ammonia and nitric acid are produced annually for conversion into nitrogenous fertilisers. Modern methods of manufacture, such as the Haber process (p. 427) and the catalytic oxidation of ammonia, get their supplies of nitrogen from the atmosphere and in a sense are man-made adjuncts to the nitrogen cycle.

Phosphorus in the form of phosphate is another mineral essential to soil fertility which is being continually extracted by plant cropping. Replenishment of this loss with artificial fertilisers such as superphosphate is at the expense of a limited number of ore deposits and since there are no natural restoring processes as there are with nitrogen this method will only serve as long as reserves last.

Isolation

Industrial Methods

(a) *Nitrogen.* Very large quantities are produced by the fractional distillation of liquid air (p. 467).

(b) *Phosphorus.* A mixture of calcium orthophosphate, e.g. as apatite, coke, and crushed quartz, is heated to about 1500 °C in an electric furnace. At this temperature, phosphorus pentoxide vapour is displaced from the phosphate ore by the more weakly acidic oxide silicon dioxide owing to it being non-volatile under these conditions,

$$2Ca_3(PO_4)_2 + 6SiO_2 \rightarrow 6CaSiO_3 + P_4O_{10}.$$

The hot coke reduces the phosphorus pentoxide liberating phosphorus vapour and carbon monoxide which conveniently maintains an inert atmosphere and so prevents the hot phosphorus inflaming,

$$P_4O_{10} + 10C \rightarrow P_4 + 10CO.$$

The hot gases expand out of the furnace through electrostatic precipitators to remove any dust particles that are blown out with them. Phosphorus vapour then condenses out under water as white phosphorus. Calcium silicate collects at the bottom of the furnace as a molten slag, and is tapped off from time to time. A fresh charge of raw material can be added to the furnace through a hopper when required and so the process is continuous.

Most of the crude phosphorus is then converted into other chemicals, but should it be necessary, purification is achieved by melting it under chromic acid solution to oxidise away the impurities.

(c) *Arsenic, antimony and bismuth.* A method of isolation applicable to each of these elements is the roasting of the sulphide ore to the oxide which is then reduced by carbon, e.g.

$$Sb_2S_3 + 5O_2 \rightarrow Sb_2O_4 + 3SO_2,$$
$$Sb_2O_4 + 4C \rightarrow 2Sb + 4CO,$$
$$As_4O_6 + 6C \rightarrow As_4 + 6CO.$$

Laboratory methods. A number of methods are available for preparing nitrogen.

(1) Nitrogen containing about 1 % of noble gases, i.e. argon, etc., may be obtained from air by eliminating the other constituents. Carbon dioxide is absorbed by bubbling through alkali and if the air is then slowly passed over red-hot copper to remove the oxygen *atmospheric nitrogen* remains and may be collected over water,

$$2Cu + O_2 \rightarrow 2CuO.$$

(2) Nitrogen free from noble gases is evolved in the decomposition of ammonium nitrite. As this is an unstable solid it is common practice to heat a solution containing ammonium and nitrite ions prepared by dissolving together equimolecular amounts of sodium nitrite and ammonium chloride or sulphate. A brisk effervescence occurs and the gas may then be led through acidified potassium dichromate solution to remove traces of oxides of nitrogen also produced,

$$NH_4^+ + NO_2^- \rightarrow 2H_2O + N_2.$$

(3) Ammonium dichromate is a red crystalline solid that decomposes violently on gentle heating. Flashes of light, nitrogen, and steam are evolved, together with a copious deposit of green chromium(III) oxide,

$$(NH_4)_2Cr_2O_7 \rightarrow Cr_2O_3 + 4H_2O + N_2.$$

(4) Other methods include the action of chlorine, bromine, bleaching powder, or sodium hypobromite on concentrated ammonia solution and the decomposition of nitrogen monoxide over heated copper filings,

$$2Cu + 2NO \rightarrow 2CuO + N_2.$$

Physical properties

In general, two main allotropic modifications may be distinguished: (1) an opaque metallic form which predominates as the Group is descended, and (2) a less dense, transparent, white (or yellow) form which becomes increasingly unstable as the Group is descended. This is summarised below.

Element	Metallic form	Non-metallic form
N	Non-existent	↑
P	|	|
As	Increasingly stable	Increasingly stable
Sb	|	|
Bi	↓	Non-existent

Black phosphorus resembles graphite in appearance, properties, and structure. It is an iron-grey coloured solid with a metallic lustre and a crystal lattice in which the phosphorus atoms bind themselves strongly into corrugated double layers and as adjacent double layers bind together only weakly it imparts a flaky effect to the allotrope. The density is 2.7 g cm^{-3}, and it is a fair conductor of heat and electricity. Doubt exists about it being the most stable allotrope of phosphorus, and it is reported to revert slowly to the white allotrope on standing. *Black arsenic* and *black antimony* are unstable allotropes intermediate between the metallic and non-metallic forms of these elements. *Grey arsenic* and *grey antimony* are the common stable metallic allotropes. They are the densest form of the element and, like bismuth, are lustrous, crystalline brittle metals with conducting properties. These metals have layer structures of the same general type as black phosphorus and are therefore not ideally metallic, however, the structure tends to involve greater metallic character as the Group is descended.

The only stable modification of nitrogen under ordinary conditions is the diatomic gas, N_2. As the molecules are perfectly symmetrical and non-polar, they have only weak van der Waals' forces of attraction for each other, and so the melting point and boiling point of the gas are very low. At 20 °C 1.5 cm^3 of the gas dissolve in 100 cm^3 of water, which is about half the solubility of oxygen.

No continuous variation in properties exists between nitrogen and the rest of the Group, owing to the abrupt change in the structure of the elements in passing from nitrogen to phosphorus. It seems likely that the non-metallic modification of phosphorus, arsenic and antimony is composed of tetratomic molecules, i.e. P_4, As_4 and Sb_4, respectively. The binding within each molecule is covalent and as individual molecules have only weak attraction for each other, the allotrope is a typical low-melting covalent solid.

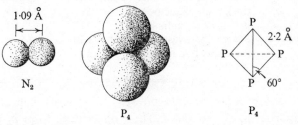

Fig. 122. The figures represent molecules of nitrogen and tetratomic phosphorus. The nitrogen atoms interpenetrate considerably owing to the multiple bonding. Each phosphorus atom is situated at the corner of a regular tetrahedron and each bond angle is thus 60°, the internuclear distance is about double that in the nitrogen molecule.

White phosphorus is a soft waxy translucent mass (transparent when freshly sublimed) freely soluble in carbon disulphide, ether, benzene, and other inert solvents, but it is insoluble in water. Even at ordinary temperatures it is appreciably volatile and the vapour is extremely poisonous. Reaction of this vapour with the atmosphere produces a faint green light visible in the dark (chemiluminescence). White phosphorus is metastable and on prolonged exposure to light undergoes an allotropic change to *red phosphorus*. The change is catalysed by a trace of iodine and can be further accelerated by heating to 250 °C in an inert atmosphere; above this temperature the change is reversed. *Yellow arsenic* and *yellow antimony* closely resemble white phosphorus except that they are increasingly unstable. Yellow arsenic rapidly turns into the grey form on warming or under the influence of light or a catalyst, e.g. bromine or iodine. Yellow antimony turns black even in the dark at −90 °C. Bismuth occurs only in the metallic state.

Red phosphorus is not a pure allotrope and is composed mainly of *violet phosphorus* the structure of which has not yet been established. However, red phosphorus is a stable commonly occurring form. It is a dark red opaque powder insoluble in carbon disulphide, benzene, etc., non-volatile and non-toxic. The density (2.3 g cm⁻³) is intermediate between that of the black (2.7) and white (1.8) forms.

Physical properties of the Group V elements

Element (common allotrope)	Appearance	m.p. (°C)	b.p. (°C)	Density (g cm⁻³)
N	Colourless, odourless gas	−210	−196	0.96
P (white)	White translucent waxy solid	44	280	1.83
P (red)	Dark red opaque powder	597	431 (s)	2.34
As (grey)	Iron-grey crystalline	817	633 (s)	5.73
Sb (grey)	Silvery-white lustrous metal	630	1375	6.69
Bi	Reddish-white lustrous metal	273	1560	9.80

Vapour density measurements on red phosphorus indicate that it initially vaporises as P_2 molecules. These dimerise to form P_4 molecules and on cooling it is white phosphorus which condenses out. White phosphorus vapour consists of P_4 molecules up to 800 °C above which temperature dissociation into P_2 molecules begins to occur. All forms of arsenic vaporise as As_4 molecules and these also begin to dissociate above 800 °C into diatomic molecules, i.e. As_2. Antimony vapour behaves similarly, but bismuth vapour contains only Bi_2 molecules and single Bi atoms, the proportion of which increases at higher temperatures.

Chemical properties

The difference in reactivity between nitrogen and the non-metallic allotropes of the other elements in the Group is again the result of the different elemental structures involved (see p. 421). Whereas the diatomic molecule of nitrogen is a very stable structure, the P—P bonds in the tetrahedral molecule of white phosphorus, for example, are under a certain amount of strain as a result of the small bond angles, and this reduces the stability of the molecule which correspondingly increases its reactivity. The metallic modifications are much more stable and less reactive. Red phosphorus is also much more stable than white phosphorus and this is reflected in its lower reactivity. The difference in chemical energy between the two forms is evolved as heat during the allotropic change, i.e.

$$\text{white } P_4 \rightarrow \text{red } P_4; \quad \Delta H = -61.9 \text{ kJ mol}^{-1}.$$

1. Air. Atmospheric oxygen and nitrogen combine under the influence of an electric discharge to form nitrogen monoxide oxide, NO,

$$N_2 + O_2 \rightarrow 2NO.$$

Oxidation to nitrogen dioxide then follows, and this is absorbed from the atmosphere by rain to give a mixed solution of nitric and nitrous acids. The unstable nitrous acid rapidly converts to nitric acid. In the past this reaction scheme was used commercially to produce nitric acid, but the cost of the electricity required to produce a suitable electric arc made the process uneconomical in comparison with the catalytic oxidation of ammonia.

White phosphorus is slowly attacked by air unless it is finely divided or the temperature is above 50 °C in which case it spontaneously inflames. For this reason white phosphorus is stored under water. It burns with a pale yellow flame, evolving dense white fumes of phosphorus pentoxide,

$$P_4 + 5O_2 \rightarrow P_4O_{10}.$$

Red phosphorus exposed to air gets damp owing to slow oxidation to orthophosphoric acid. It does not inflame in air below 260 °C, and it is not customarily stored under water.

Metallic arsenic, antimony and bismuth are stable in dry air, but inflame on strong heating with the formation of the corresponding trivalent oxide in each case, e.g.

$$As_4 + 3O_2 \rightarrow As_4O_6.$$

2. Water. Has no effect, but phosphorus vapour, antimony and bismuth will reduce steam at high temperature.

3. Non-metals. At elevated temperatures nitrogen is sufficiently reactive to combine directly with hydrogen, especially if a catalyst is used (Haber process, p. 427). Hydrides of the other Group V elements cannot be prepared directly.

Chlorine reacts vigorously with all the elements in the Group apart from nitrogen which is unaffected. White phosphorus inflames spontaneously as do powdered arsenic, antimony and bismuth.

Red phosphorus reacts less energetically, and only burns in chlorine on heating. Ordinarily the trichloride is formed, but with an excess of chlorine the pentachloride is produced, e.g.

$$P_4 + 6Cl_2 \rightarrow 4PCl_3,$$

$$P_4 + 10Cl_2 \rightarrow 4PCl_5.$$

White phosphorus combines vigorously with sulphur. Red phosphorus, arsenic, antimony, and bismuth also combine directly with sulphur on heating.

4. Metals. Lithium combines slowly with nitrogen even at room temperature, and more rapidly on heating to form lithium nitride,

$$6Li + N_2 \rightarrow 2Li_3N.$$

Other metals also combine directly with nitrogen at elevated temperatures, forming nitrides, e.g. Group IIA metals. Phosphides, arsenides, and antimonides are produced similarly, but they become progessively more intermetallic in nature down the Group. Arsenic alloys very readily with heavy metals and is added to lead, making it harder and more fusible. Lead shot is made from this alloy. The principal use of antimony and bismuth is in a number of commercially important alloys. They too are used as hardening elements, and as their alloys expand on solidification they are particularly useful for castings and type-metal. Mostly, however, bismuth is used in producing low-melting alloys to be used as plugs in automatic water-sprinklers and safety valves.

	Bi	Sb	Sn	Pb	Cd	Cu
Bearing metals	—	7–20	90–50	—	—	1–3
Type metal	—	15	3	82	—	—
Wood's metal (71°C)	50	—	12.5	25	12.5	—
Rose's metal (94°C)	50	—	23	27	—	—

5. Acids. Nitrogen is not affected by acids. The remaining elements are all less electropositive than hydrogen and therefore cannot displace it from an acid. They are, however, attacked by the oxidising acids. Both red and white phosphorus dissolve in strong oxidising acids to form orthophosphoric acid, e.g. moderately concentrated nitric acid,

$$P_4 + 10HNO_3 + H_2O \rightarrow 4H_3PO_4 + 5NO + 5NO_2.$$

Arsenic, antimony and bismuth dissolve in concentrated nitric acid with the evolution of oxides of nitrogen to form respectively, a solution of arsenic acid, H_3AsO_4, a white residue of hydrated antimony(v) oxide, and a solution of bismuth(III) nitrate. These reactions illustrate the greater metallic character of the elements as the Group is descended. Moderately concentrated nitric acid converts antimony into the oxide, Sb_4O_6. Hot dilute nitric acid dissolves arsenic as arsenious acid, H_3AsO_3; bismuth as bismuth(III) nitrate but has little action on antimony. Boiling concentrated sulphuric acid dissolves bismuth as bismuth(III) sulphate and sulphur dioxide is given off,

$$6H_2SO_4 + 6e \rightarrow 3SO_4{}^{2-} + 6H_2O + 3SO_2 \quad \text{(reducing process)}$$
$$2Bi - 6e \rightarrow 2Bi^{3+} \quad \text{(oxidising process)}$$
$$\overline{2Bi + 6H_2SO_4 \rightarrow 2Bi^{3+} + 3SO_4{}^{2-} + 6H_2O + 3SO_2}$$

Antimony behaves similarly, but arsenic, which is even less electropositive, acts as a non-metal, and is oxidised to arsenious acid.

6. Alkalis. White phosphorus dissolves readily in a solution of a strong alkali on warming. This reaction does not occur with the red modification. A spontaneously inflammable gaseous mixture of phosphine, hydrogen and diphosphine is given off, and the corresponding hypophosphite remains in solution,
$$P_4 + 3OH^- + 3H_2O \rightarrow 3H_2PO_2{}^- + PH_3.$$

Arsenic is only slightly attacked unless fused alkali is used when it dissolves rapidly to give the arsenite and hydrogen is evolved,

$$As_4 + 12OH^- \rightarrow 4AsO_3{}^{3-} + 6H_2.$$

The remaining elements in the Group are unaffected.

Active nitrogen

Commonly occurring molecular nitrogen gives a misleading impression of the reactivity of the element. Since the atoms are bound together so strongly in the molecule dissociation is difficult, but as nitrogen has a high

A comparison of the properties of red and white phosphorus

White	Red
White translucent waxy solid	Dark red opaque powder
Soluble in carbon disulphide, etc.	Insoluble in organic solvents
Density, 1.8 g cm^{-3}	Density, 2.3 g cm^{-3}
Melting point, 44 °C	Melting point, 597 °C
Detectably volatile at room temperature	Non-volatile
Exhibits chemiluminescence in air	No chemiluminescence
Poisonous	Non-poisonous
Spontaneously ignites in air at about 50 °C	Ignites in air only above 260 °C
Spontaneously ignites in chlorine	Less reactive, heat required
Reacts in alkaline solution	No action

electronegativity and forms strong bonds with other elements when dissociation does occur, the free atoms are very reactive. Free nitrogen atoms are produced by subjecting nitrogen gas under low pressure to electric discharges. The *active nitrogen* so formed is chemically very reactive and will combine in the cold with mercury and sulphur. The dissociation is not permanent, and the atoms gradually recombine. During this period the gas glows with a yellow light.

Compounds: I, Hydrides

Commonly known hydrides of the Group V elements are listed: NH_3, ammonia; PH_3, phosphine; AsH_3, arsine; SbH_3, stibine; BiH_3, bismuthine; N_2H_4, hydrazine; P_2H_4, diphosphine.

Preparation

1. *Direct combination.* Group V elements are generally inert towards hydrogen, but it will combine to some extent with nitrogen on sparking a mixture of the two gases. As ammonia is decomposed on sparking, the reaction is reversible and an equilibrium is reached,

$$N_2 + 3H_2 \rightleftharpoons 2NH_3.$$

2. *Displacement from salts.* Ammonia and phosphine are the only two hydrides sufficiently basic to form salts, e.g. ammonium chloride, NH_4Cl, phosphonium iodide, PH_4I. Treatment of these salts with a strong base displaces the less strongly basic volatile hydride, e.g.

$$\left[\begin{array}{c} H \\ | \\ H-N-H \\ | \\ H \end{array} \right]^{+} + :\ddot{O}-H^{-} \rightarrow H-\ddot{N}: + H-\ddot{O}-H.$$

Ammonia is usually prepared in the laboratory by heating an intimate mixture of equal parts of ammonium chloride and calcium oxide. The gas is dried over calcium oxide and collected by upward delivery.

Phosphonium iodide (p. 436) is the only common stable phosphonium salt, and it evolves pure phosphine when reacted with potassium hydroxide solution,
$$PH_4I + OH^- \rightarrow H_2O + I^- + PH_3.$$

3. *Hydrolysis of binary compounds.* Nitrides, phosphides, arsenides and antimonides are decomposed by water, more rapidly by dilute acids, with the evolution of the corresponding hydride (see p. 264). This method is of no practical importance in preparing ammonia, but can be used to prepare phosphine, e.g. from aluminium phosphide, AlP.

$$AlP + 3H_2O \rightarrow Al(OH)_3 + PH_3.$$

The gas can be freed from any diphosphine by washing with concentrated sulphuric acid and then collected over water. Arsine is most conveniently prepared in a similar way. Stibine is evolved by treating an alloy of two parts of magnesium and one part antimony with dilute hydrochloric acid. After washing and drying, all three gases may be collected pure by condensing them in a U-tube surrounded by liquid air as the coolant.

4. Reductions with nascent hydrogen. A mixture of the corresponding hydride and hydrogen is obtained by generating nascent hydrogen, e.g. with zinc and dilute sulphuric acid, in a solution of an arsenic, antimony, or bismuth compound. Only traces of bismuthine are obtained as it is so thermally unstable. The hydride may be freed from hydrogen by condensing it out as described above, and the hydrogen allowed to escape.

The white allotrope of phosphorus can be reduced directly to phosphine with caustic alkali solution. Diphosphine and hydrogen are also formed (p. 425). Even so, this is a commonly used method of preparing phosphine.

Industrial preparation of ammonia. The principal methods of producing ammonia on the industrial scale are:

(*a*) synthesis (Haber process),

(*b*) from the gas-works liquor.

The ammoniacal liquor obtained from coal-carbonisation processes is largely converted directly into the fertiliser ammonium sulphate. This represents about 25 % of the total annual production in the U.K. which is approximately $1\frac{1}{4}$ million tons.

The Haber process. Direct combination between nitrogen and hydrogen is a very slow exothermic reaction at ordinary temperatures in the absence of a catalyst,

$$N_2 + 3H_2 \rightleftharpoons 2NH_3; \quad \Delta H = -92 \text{ kJ } (-22 \text{ kcal}).$$

Since it is also a reversible reaction it is possible to apply Le Chatelier's principle and it can be seen that at equilibrium the yield of ammonia can be improved by:

(*a*) increasing the pressure, as the forward reaction is accompanied by a diminution from four to two volumes of gas;

(*b*) decreasing the temperature.

Although a reduced temperature improves the equilibrium concentration of ammonia the reaction becomes too slow to be economical and a compromise temperature is chosen which does not decrease the yield too drastically and yet maintains the reaction at a satisfactory rate. Increased pressure is also used and this speeds up the reaction and also improves the yield of ammonia. A catalyst is used to improve still further the rate at which equilibrium is attained.

The hydrogen needed for the process may be obtained from water, natural gas, coal or oil, depending which is the most suitable in the circumstances. In the U.K. the catalytic steam re-forming of natural gas is the most economical process. A mixture of natural gas with an excess of steam pre-heated by passing through heat exchangers is led over a nickel catalyst at 750 °C and the following reaction occurs (see p. 284)

$$CH_4 + H_2O \rightleftharpoons CO + 3H_2; \quad \Delta H = +206 \text{ kJ mol}^{-1}.$$

Air is now added to the equilibrium mixture which is then passed through a second reaction chamber where most of the unreacted methane is oxidised away as this would otherwise adversely affect the ammonia synthesis reaction. By controlling the amount of air introduced a 3:1 hydrogen to nitrogen mixture is obtained.

Compounds of oxygen and of sulphur poison the catalyst in the ammonia synthesis and have to be removed. Most of the carbon dioxide can be absorbed in a hot solution of potassium carbonate under pressure. Carbon monoxide and the remaining traces of carbon dioxide are removed by washing with ammoniacal copper(I) acetate.

The purified nitrogen–hydrogen mixture, compressed to 200–350 atmospheres, is then passed over the catalyst. This is usually finely divided iron promoted with small quantities of aluminium oxide and potassium hydroxide. During the reaction heat is evolved and is used to maintain the catalyst at the optimum working temperature which is about 350–400 °C. The gases leaving the converter contain about 10–20 % of ammonia which is removed either by absorbing in water or condensing under refrigeration. Uncombined nitrogen and hydrogen are recycled.

Uses of ammonia. (a) *Fertilisers*. Most of the ammonia produced nowadays is used in one form or another as fertiliser, e.g. ammonium sulphate.

(b) *Nitric acid*. Nitric acid is almost entirely produced by the catalytic oxidation of ammonia (see p. 448).

(c) *Nylon*. Ammonia is an essential raw material in the manufacture of nylon.

(d) *Metallurgy*. Ammonia is used as an inert or reducing atmosphere in many metallurgical processes, e.g. bright heat-treatment and furnace brazing of steel, nickel and nickel alloys, copper and copper alloys.

(e) *Rubber*. As an aid to the production of good quality rubber.

(f) *Other uses*. Ammonia is also used as a refrigerant, in water purification and as a neutralising agent.

Physical properties

The simple hydrides, MH_3, are all colourless gases under ordinary conditions. Some of their important physical constants are given in the following table.

Physical properties of Group V hydrides

Compound	Odour	m.p. (°C)	b.p. (°C)	Solubility vol./vol. (20 °C)
NH_3	Characteristic pungent	−78	−33	739.00
PH_3*	Decaying fish	−134	−87	0.26
AsH_3*	Garlic-like	−116	−62	0.20
SbH_3*	Disagreeable	−88	−17	0.20
BiH_3	—	—	22	—

* Exceptionally poisonous.

Ammonia is the most soluble of gases. Concentrations of up to 50 % w/w are possible in ice-cold water. Ordinary commercial ammonia solution contains 35 % w/w of ammonia and has a specific gravity of 0.880, i.e. the liquid expands considerably with the dissolved ammonia. On boiling the solution, all the ammonia is expelled and this is often used as a convenient source of ammonia gas. The other hydrides are heavier than air and sparingly soluble. Owing to the instability of bismuthine many of its properties have not yet been determined. The exceptional solubility of ammonia and its relatively high melting point and boiling point compared with those of phosphine are the result of its ability to develop hydrogen bonding. This property is more fully described on p. 107.

Each of these hydrides has a pyramidal molecular structure. The ammonia molecule is illustrated in Fig. 123; see also p. 265.

It follows from the electronegativities of nitrogen (3.07) and hydrogen (2.1) that the N—H bonds will have appreciable ionic character and tend to reinforce the region of high electron density on the nitrogen atom resulting from its lone pair of electrons. Since this is at the apex of the pyramidal molecule and each hydrogen atom has a slight positive charge, the molecule as a whole is strongly dipolar. This sets up an electrostatic attraction for adjacent molecules so that ammonia gas and liquid ammonia are associated and freely dissolve in water. As phosphorus (2.06) has just about the same electronegativity as hydrogen (2.1), there is very little charge separation within the phosphine molecule, and so no strong electrostatic forces are present to produce hydrogen bonding. Consequently the melting point, boiling point and other physical properties of phosphine are compatible with its molecular weight. There is a steady increase in the magnitude of the physical properties with atomic weight for the rest of the hydrides as they also are not associated.

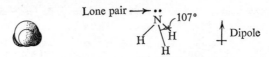

Fig. 123. The ammonia molecule.

Liquid ammonia. The strong intermolecular forces enable ammonia to be liquefied fairly easily either by cooling or pressure (9 atmospheres at 20 °C). Liquid ammonia is neutral to litmus and its physical properties are very closely related to those of water. It has a relatively high dielectric constant ($k = 22$; cf. for H_2O, $k = 80$), and as the strongly dipolar nature of the ammonia molecule leads to the solvation of charged particles, liquid ammonia is a fairly good ionising solvent, readily dissolving, for example, nitrites, nitrates, cyanides, and chlorides. Liquid ammonia has the unique property of dissolving the alkali metals and alkaline earth-metals without reaction. The blue solution obtained is useful as a powerful reducing agent.

Chemical properties

1. Air. Whereas ammonia does not burn in air, *pure* phosphine ignites spontaneously at temperatures above 150 °C. As it is ordinarily prepared, phosphine ignites at room temperature as the result of traces of diphosphine produced at the same time,

$$PH_3 + 2O_2 \rightarrow H_3PO_4.$$

In order to burn ammonia, it is necessary either to use air enriched with oxygen or heat it to its temperature of decomposition when its hydrogen will then burn to form water,

$$4NH_3 + 3O_2 \rightarrow 2N_2 + 6H_2O.$$

To carry the oxidation a stage further and burn ammonia to oxides of nitrogen, a catalyst is required, e.g. heated platinum,

$$4NH_3 + 5O_2 \rightarrow 4NO + 6H_2O.$$

The marked difference in behaviour of ammonia and phosphine towards air results from nitrogen having a greater affinity for hydrogen than for oxygen, the opposite being the case with phosphorus. A similar relationship was noted between carbon and silicon.

Arsine and stibine both burn to the trioxide in an unlimited supply of air, but if the oxygen supply is limited or if the flame is cooled, only the hydrogen burns and the Group V elements deposit on the cold surface. Ease of thermal decomposition increases down the Group, both stibine and bismuthine decompose slowly even at room temperature,

$$4AsH_3 \rightarrow As_4 + 6H_2.$$

The growing instability follows the trend of increasing atomic radius of the central atom of the hydride molecule, and is attributed to the known weakness of the covalent bond between atoms which differ appreciably in size, i.e. Bi, 1.46 Å; H, 0.37 Å.

Marsh's test for arsenic takes advantage of the thermal instability of arsine to detect traces of arsenic. The material under test is placed in a flask with dilute sulphuric acid and pure zinc, when any arsenic present is reduced to arsine. Evolved gases are freed from any hydrogen sulphide produced by passing over lead(II) acetate paper and then dried with anhydrous calcium chloride. They are then led through a hard glass tube heated at one spot to red heat, where the arsine present decomposes and a black mirror of arsenic deposits beyond the heated zone. By adopting a standard procedure the method can give a quantitative estimate of the amount of arsenic in the material by comparing the intensity of the stain with those in standard tubes produced with known amounts of arsenic.

2. Reducing action. As a result of the relative ease with which these hydrides part with their hydrogen, they frequently act as reducing agents. This property becomes more pronounced with the growing instability of the compounds towards the bottom of the Group.

Ammonia gas passed over a heated metal oxide will decompose, and the liberated hydrogen is then able to reduce the oxide, e.g.

$$3CuO + 2NH_3 \rightarrow 3Cu + N_2 + 3H_2O.$$

Chlorine has a strong affinity for hydrogen, and will oxidise an excess of ammonia to nitrogen. The hydrogen chloride formed then combines with more ammonia to give ammonium chloride,

$$2NH_3 + 3Cl_2 \rightarrow N_2 + 6HCl.$$

An excess of chlorine is to be avoided as this leads to substitution of the hydrogen atom and formation of nitrogen trichloride, which is a highly explosive yellow oil,

$$2NH_3 + 6Cl_2 \rightarrow 2NCl_3 + 6HCl.$$

Phosphine ignites spontaneously in chlorine, burning to phosphorus trichloride,

$$PH_3 + 3Cl_2 \rightarrow PCl_3 + 3HCl.$$

Easily reducible metal cations, e.g. Cu^{2+}, Ag^+, are displaced from solution either as the free metal or the corresponding phosphide, arsenide or antimonide. Phosphine displaces a mixture of copper and copper(II) phosphide from copper(II) sulphate solution. Dilute silver nitrate solution is reduced to silver by arsine and silver antimonide by stibine,

$$AsH_3 + 6Ag^+ + 3H_2O \rightarrow H_3AsO_3 + 6Ag + 6H^+,$$

$$SbH_3 + 3Ag^+ \rightarrow Ag_3Sb + 3H^+.$$

3. Addition reactions. In just the same way as water forms a large number of hydrates, ammonia forms numerous ammines, e.g. $[Ag(NH_3)_2]^+$, $[Cu(NH_3)_4]^{2+}$ and $[Co(NH_3)_6]^{3+}$.

The region of high electron density on the nitrogen atom is attracted to the positively charged cation to which the ammonia molecules adhere. The bonding is not entirely electrostatic, and some interpenetration of the electron clouds does occur varying in extent with the nature of the electron acceptor. Besides forming complex ions in this way, ammonia also forms addition compounds with electron acceptors, such as BF_3 (see pp. 90, 349).

Phosphine, arsine, and other hydrides in the Group have much smaller dipole moments than ammonia and there is a corresponding decrease in their ability to form addition compounds and act as electron donors. Amongst the higher homologues the inert pair effect further restricts donation of the lone pair.

4. Basic properties. Particularly important is the addition reaction with the proton, H^+. As described earlier, an ammonia molecule forms a stable dative covalent bond with a proton in the formation of the ammonium radical, NH_4^+. In this way ammonia behaves as a base and will combine directly with an acid to form a salt, e.g.

$$2NH_3 + 2H^+ + SO_4^{2-} \rightarrow 2NH_4^+ + SO_4^{2-}.$$

Ammonia dissolved in water behaves like a solution of a weak base. First, as a result of the hydrogen bonding between them, ammonia and water molecules combine and ammonia hydrate is formed. Secondly, this entity ionises to a slight extent into NH_4^+ and OH^-,

$$\underset{\underset{\displaystyle H}{|}}{\overset{\overset{\displaystyle H}{|}}{H-N:}} + \underset{\underset{\displaystyle H}{|}}{H-O} \rightleftharpoons \underset{\underset{\displaystyle H}{|}}{\overset{\overset{\displaystyle H}{|}}{H-N:}} \cdots \underset{\underset{\displaystyle H}{|}}{H-O} \rightleftharpoons NH_4^+ + OH^-.$$

To be strictly accurate, it is *ammonia hydrate* which is feebly ionised, and it is better to refer to ammonia solutions as being weakly basic rather than use the popular but incorrect phrase, 'ammonium hydroxide is a weak base'.

Phosphine shows only feeble basic character. Its aqueous solution has no alkaline properties, but in the complete absence of moisture it will combine with the hydrogen halides to form phosphonium salts which are analogous to the ammonium salts.

These are described more fully below. As expected, the remaining simple hydrides show no basic properties.

5. Acidic properties. Partial withdrawal of electrons from the hydrogen atom by the nitrogen atom in a molecule of ammonia leaves them with a slight positive charge. However, the proton-donating properties of

A comparison of the properties of ammonia and phosphine

Ammonia	Phosphine
Pungent colourless gas	Colourless gas smelling of decaying fish
Much lighter than air	Slightly heavier than air
Very soluble in water	Sparingly soluble in water
Boiling point, $-33\,°C$	Boiling point, $-87\,°C$
Considerable dipole	Weak dipole
Liquid ammonia is a good ionising solvent	Liquid phosphine is of no use as a solvent
Decomposes at about 500 °C	Decomposes at temperatures above 440 °C
Does not burn in air	Pure phosphine ignites spontaneously at 150 °C
Turns moist red litmus blue	No affect on litmus
Forms stable ammonium salts	Phosphonium salts very easily hydrolysed
Reducing agent	Strong reducing agent
Excess chlorine gives NCl_3	Ignites in chlorine giving PCl_5
Does not reduce copper(II) sulphate solution	Reduces copper(II) sulphate solution
Gives sodamide with heated sodium	No comparable reaction

ammonia are negligible. If ammonia is passed over heated potassium or sodium one hydrogen atom per molecule is replaced by a metal atom and potassamide KNH_2, or sodamide, $NaNH_2$, is formed, but this is the extent to which ammonia resembles acids.

$$2Na + 2NH_3 \rightarrow 2NaNH_2 + H_2.$$

The electronegativities of phosphorus and hydrogen are such as to leave the hydrogen atoms with a slight negative charge and it shows no acidic character.

Ammonium salts

Many stable salts of the ammonium ion NH_4^+ are known. They are white, crystalline, soluble solids. As the ammonium ion has the same charge as the alkali metal ions and its ionic radius is intermediate between that of the potassium ion and rubidium ion it is not surprising that ammonium salts have certain resemblances to the corresponding salts of potassium and rubidium; note $K^+ = 1.33$ Å; $NH_4^+ = 1.43$ Å; $Rb^+ = 1.48$ Å.

Ammonium and potassium salts have similar solubilities and usually crystallise from aqueous solution in the anhydrous condition, this contrasts with the behaviour of sodium salts which are generally hydrated. Although there is a certain amount in common between ammonium and alkali-metal salts the fact that ammonia is a volatile and easily oxidisable gas imparts certain distinctive features to ammonium salts.

(1) Ammonium salts of the strong acids are fully ionised. Their aqueous solutions are acidic owing to a slight degree of hydrolysis;

$$NH_4^+ + H_2O \rightleftharpoons NH_3 \text{ (aq.)} + H_3O^+.$$

Hydrogen bonding stabilises the presence of the small amount of ammonia in the equilibrium mixture but if the ammonia is expelled from the solution by boiling the equilibrium is displaced to the right and the solution becomes distinctly acidic.

(2) As ammonia is so volatile ammonium salts of volatile acids readily dissociate and sublime on heating, e.g. the chloride and the carbonate.

(3) Ammonium salts of strong oxidising acids often decompose on heating with oxidation of the ammonia to nitrogen or dinitrogen oxide, N_2O, or both, e.g. the nitrite, nitrate and dichromate.

Ammonium chloride, NH_4Cl, may be crystallised from solutions obtained by treating ammonia solution or ammonium carbonate with a slight excess of hydrochloric acid, or it may be sublimed from a mixture of sodium chloride and ammonium sulphate,

$$2NaCl + (NH_4)_2SO_4 \rightarrow 2NH_4Cl + Na_2SO_4.$$

On heating, ammonium chloride dissociates into ammonia and hydrogen chloride; as the gases cool they reform as solid ammonium chloride,

$$NH_4Cl \rightleftharpoons NH_3 + HCl.$$

Ammonium carbonate, (NH₄)₂CO₃ (sal volatile), is prepared commercially by subliming it from a mixture of calcium carbonate (chalk) and ammonium sulphate,

$$CaCO_3 + (NH_4)_2SO_4 \rightarrow (NH_4)_2CO_3 + CaSO_4.$$

The solid obtained is a mixture of the carbonate, hydrogen carbonate and ammonium carbamate, $NH_4(NH_2CO_2)$. Replacement of an —OH group in carbonic acid

$$\begin{matrix} H-O \\ \\ H-O \end{matrix} \Big\rangle C=O$$

by —NH₂ gives carbamic acid

$$\begin{matrix} H_2N \\ \\ H-O \end{matrix} \Big\rangle C=O.$$

The solid smells strongly of ammonia, and on heating decomposes into ammonia, carbon dioxide and steam,

$$(NH_4)_2CO_3 \rightarrow 2NH_3 + CO_2 + H_2O.$$

Ammonium sulphate, (NH₄)₂SO₄, is the most widely used artificial nitrogenous fertiliser. It is made either by neutralising sulphuric acid with ammonia or by absorbing ammonia in a suspension of calcium sulphate (anhydrite or gypsum), and then passing in carbon dioxide. Calcium carbonate is precipitated and can be filtered off. Ammonium sulphate crystallises from the filtrate on evaporation,

$$CaSO_4 + 2NH_3 + H_2O + CO_2 \rightarrow 2NH_4^+ + SO_4^{2-} + CaCO_3.$$

It is isomorphous with potassium sulphate. As sulphuric acid is not volatile ammonium sulphate does not sublime as readily as the two previous salts, and on heating it loses ammonia and is converted to the hydrogen sulphate,

$$(NH_4)_2SO_4 \rightarrow NH_4HSO_4 + NH_3.$$

Ammonium nitrite, NH₄NO₂, is very unstable and on heating decomposes with oxidation of the ammonia to nitrogen (see p. 419).

Ammonium nitrate, NH_4NO_3, is another important nitrogenous fertiliser which is prepared in bulk by neutralising nitric acid with ammonia and crystallising the product from solution. Usually it is mixed with powdered calcium carbonate and marketed as *nitro-chalk*. This has the advantage over the pure nitrate in not 'caking' and being less prone to violent detonation which is a distinct risk when the nitrate is stored in bulk.

On heating gently, ammonium nitrate melts and decomposes with brisk effervescence evolving dinitrogen oxide and steam,

$$NH_4NO_3 \rightarrow N_2O + 2H_2O.$$

Stronger heating may cause the decomposing salt to inflame. Several explosives contain ammonium nitrate, e.g. ammonal (aluminium powder/ammonium nitrate); amatol (trinitrotoluene/ammonium nitrate).

Phosphonium salts

As phosphine is a much weaker base than ammonia its salts are much less stable. The most commonly known phosphonium salt is the iodide, PH_4I. It is formed by direct combination of phosphine and hydrogen iodide in anhydrous conditions. The reaction is easily reversed by heating, and the salt is completely dissociated at 60 °C,

$$PH_3 + HI \rightleftharpoons PH_4I.$$

An alternative method of preparation is to dissolve white phosphorus and iodine in carbon disulphide in a flask from which the air has been flushed by an inert gas, e.g. carbon dioxide. On evaporating away the solvent, the phosphorus tri-iodide that remains is hydrolysed by a little water to phosphorous acid and hydrogen iodide,

$$P_4 + 6I_2 \rightarrow 4PI_3 + 12H_2O \rightarrow 12HI + 4H_3PO_3.$$

When this mixture is heated the phosphorous acid disproportionates and the phosphine evolved combines with the hydrogen iodide produced in the hydrolysis and collects as a white sublimate of phosphonium iodide in a cooled receiver,

$$4H_3PO_3 \rightarrow 3H_3PO_4 + PH_3 \xrightarrow{HI} PH_4I.$$

Phosphonium iodide is strongly hydrolysed by water (contrast ammonium halides),
$$PH_4I + H_2O \rightleftharpoons PH_3 + H_3O^+ + I^-.$$

A chloride and bromide are also known, but these are even less stable.

Higher hydrides

Hydrazine, N_2H_4, is a colourless unstable liquid. It dissolves readily in water, and forms a stable hydrate, $N_2H_4 . H_2O$. Hydrazine is a weaker base than ammonia, but is dibasic and can form two series of salts, e.g. $N_2H_5^+Cl^-$ and $N_2H_6^{2+}(Cl^-)_2$; the former salt is stable in aqueous solution, the latter immediately hydrolyses. The reducing action of hydrazine is much greater than that of ammonia.

Disphosphine, P_2H_4, is a colourless spontaneously inflammable liquid. Unlike hydrazine it has no basic properties, but it is a powerful reducing agent.

Compounds: II, Oxides

In general, the most important oxides of the Group are quinquevalent and trivalent, e.g. P_4O_{10} and P_4O_6. Tetroxides are also known, e.g. N_2O_4, the most important oxide of nitrogen. The main oxides of nitrogen, phosphorus, and arsenic are listed in the table below.

Oxidation no. of E	N	P	As	Sb	Bi	Name
+5	N_2O_5	P_4O_{10}	As_2O_5	Sb_2O_5	Bi_2O_5	Pentoxides
+4	N_2O_4	P_4O_8	—	—	—	Tetroxides
+3	N_2O_3	P_4O_6	As_4O_6	Sb_4O_6	Bi_2O_3	Trioxides
+2	NO	—	—	—	—	Nitrogen monoxide
+1	N_2O	—	—	—	—	Dinitrogen oxide

Quinquevalent oxides

Methods of preparation. (1) *Direct combination.* In a plentiful supply of air, white phosphorus burns to phosphorus pentoxide. None of the remaining quinquevalent oxides in the Group can be prepared by this method as they decompose at high temperatures.

(2) *Dehydration of the quinquevalent oxo-acid.* The elements of water are removed from pure concentrated nitric acid with phosphorus pentoxide, and dinitrogen pentoxide can be distilled from the reaction mixture and collected as a white solid in a cooled receiver,

$$4HNO_3 + P_4O_{10} \rightarrow 2N_2O_5 \quad + \quad 4HPO_3.$$
$$\text{Metaphosphoric acid}$$

Oxo-acids of quinquevalent arsenic, antimony and bismuth are progressively less stable and readily lose water. Arsenic and antimonic acids are prepared by oxidising the element with concentrated nitric acid and they dehydrate to the quinquevalent oxide on heating. The quinquevalent oxides become progressively less stable down the Group and decompose on heating. Bismuth(v) oxide is very unstable and has only been prepared in an impure form by treating bismuth(III) oxide with a very powerful oxidising agent.

Physical properties. Dinitrogen pentoxide is a fairly stable, volatile solid (melting point, 30 °C; boiling point, 45–50 °C) which is essentially crystals of nitronium nitrate, $NO_2^+NO_3^-$.

However, the volatility of the solid indicates that it easily changes into a covalent molecular vapour. In anhydrous solvents such as concentrated sulphuric, nitric or orthophosphoric acids ionic dissociation occurs to produce the nitronium ion, e.g.

$$N_2O_5 + 3H_2SO_4 \rightarrow 2NO_2^+ + 3HSO_4^- + H_3O^+.$$

The nitronium ion is isoelectronic with carbon dioxide (i.e. has a similar electron structure) and has a similar linear structure, i.e. $O{=}N^+{=}O$.

Phosphorus pentoxide is a misleading term as vapour density measurements show the true molecular formula to be P_4O_{10}. Like dinitrogen pentoxide it is a white deliquescent solid (melting point, 580 °C), but the crystal structure is very different and it also exhibits polymorphism. The common form consists of discrete covalent P_4O_{10} molecules. Each of the four phosphorus atoms in a molecule is tetrahedrally surrounded by four oxygen atoms. Six of the oxygen atoms in the molecule are bridging atoms between the four phosphorus atoms, as shown in Fig. 125.

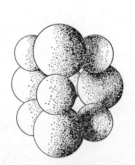

Fig. 124. Molecular structure of
phosphorus trioxide.

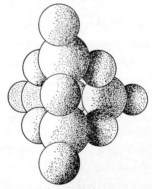

Fig. 125. Molecular structure of
phosphorus pentoxide.

Chemical properties. *Water.* Phosphorus pentoxide is the best known of these compounds, and is particularly important in view of its great affinity for water. So effective is it as a dehydrating agent that it will remove even the elements of water from compounds which are themselves regarded as drying agents, e.g. it dehydrates concentrated sulphuric acid to sulphur trioxide. Practical applications of phosphorus pentoxide include the drying of gases and liquids, and in certain preparations which involve dehydrations, e.g. the conversion of acetamide to methyl cyanide,

$$CH_3-C{\overset{O}{\underset{NH_2}{}}} \xrightarrow[(P_4O_{10})]{-H_2O} CH_3-C{\equiv}N.$$

Phosphorus pentoxide is the anhydride of phosphoric acid, but this can exist in several distinct forms each containing a different proportion of water. Besides orthophosphoric acid which is the common form and referred to simply as phosphoric acid, there are metaphosphoric acid, HPO_3, and pyrophosphoric acid, $H_4P_2O_7$. With water, phosphorus pentoxide gives first metaphosphoric acid which then hydrates further to the pyro- and ortho-acids. The exact nature of the product depends on the quantities used and the conditions; see further below.

Dinitrogen pentoxide also has a powerful affinity for water, and is the anhydride of nitric acid, $N_2O_5+H_2O \rightarrow 2HNO_3$.

Arsenic pentoxide dissolves slowly in water to give a solution of arsenic acid, H_3AsO_4. Antimony(v) oxide is only sparingly soluble in water, but it gives an acidic solution. Impure bismuth(v) oxide is insoluble. It does have acidic properties, however, and a few impure alkaline bismuthates have been isolated, e.g. sodium bismuthate, $NaBiO_3$.

These oxides illustrate an important generalisation that can be applied to all the Groups of the Periodic Table, i.e. the highest oxidation state becomes less stable down the Group.

Trivalent oxides

Methods of preparation. (1) *Direct combination.* In a limited supply of air white phosphorus burns mainly to phosphorus trioxide. Traces of phosphorus pentoxide are also produced. When the mixture is distilled in the absence of air pure phosphorus trioxide passes over as it is the more volatile of the two oxides. Arsenic, antimony and bismuth burn in air to the corresponding trivalent oxide, but in contrast to phosphorus trioxide they are not oxidised to the quinquevalent oxide by oxygen and no special precautions are needed. Antimony has a tendency to burn to antimony(IV) oxide, Sb_4O_8, which may be an impurity in the antimony(III) oxide so formed,

$$Sb_4 + 3O_2 \rightarrow Sb_4O_6.$$

Note. As mentioned earlier, antimony can also be oxidised to antimony (III) oxide with moderately concentrated nitric acid.

(2) *Decomposition* of bismuth(III) nitrate, basic carbonate, or hydroxide by heat leaves bismuth(III) oxide. This method is unique to bismuth as the other elements in the Group do not form hydroxides or stable salts.

Physical properties. Pure dinitrogen trioxide is a pale blue solid which exists only below its melting point $-102\ ^\circ C$.

Phosphorus trioxide like the pentoxide differs strikingly from the nitrogen compound. It is a white solid (melting point, $24\ ^\circ C$) whose true molecular formula is P_4O_6. Four phosphorus atoms and six oxygen atoms are covalently bound into a structure which corresponds to that of phosphorus pentoxide without the four apical oxygen atoms, see Fig. 124. The weak binding between these molecules results in the high volatility of the solid. It is also soluble in organic solvents, e.g. carbon disulphide, ether, benzene, etc., and is a non-conductor.

Vapour density measurements show that arsenic trioxide and antimony(III) oxide have molecular weights which correspond to a molecular formula similar to that of phosphorus trioxide, i.e. As_4O_6 and Sb_4O_6, respectively. They also have the same molecular structure. Both are white solids. Arsenic trioxide easily sublimes below its melting point ($275\ ^\circ C$), dissolves in organic solvents, and is moderately soluble in water. In contrast to the typical covalent molecular lattices of the other Group V trivalent oxides the structure of bismuth(III) oxide is ionic.

Chemical properties. (1) *Heat.* Dinitrogen trioxide is very unstable, and is largely dissociated in the liquid and vapour states,

$$2N_2O_3 \rightleftharpoons 2NO + N_2O_4.$$

On heating in air phosphorus trioxide inflames and oxidises to phosphorus pentoxide. Even on exposure to air under ordinary conditions slow oxidation to the pentoxide occurs. Heated above $210\ ^\circ C$ in the absence of air phosphorus trioxide polymerises to a compound called phosphorus tetroxide whose structure and formula have not yet been established with certainty. Vapour density measurements indicate the molecular formula P_4O_8. It is the mixed anhydride of phosphorous and phosphoric acids. The trivalent oxides of arsenic, antimony and bismuth are stable to heat.

(2) *Water.* Dinitrogen trioxide is the anhydride of nitrous acid and this

is the primary product in the reaction with water, but it is very unstable and rapidly decomposes,

$$N_2O_3 + H_2O \rightarrow 2HNO_2.$$

Cold water slowly hydrolyses phosphorus trioxide to phosphorous acid,

$$P_4O_6 + 6H_2O \rightarrow 4H_3PO_3.$$

A vigorous and complex reaction occurs with hot water. Phosphine and phosphoric acid are amongst the products.

Arsenic trioxide is only moderately soluble in water and solutions have a faintly acidic reaction owing to the formation of a hydrated form called arsenious acid,

$$As_4O_6 + 6H_2O \rightleftharpoons 4As(OH)_3.$$

Antimony(III) and bismuth(III) oxides are insoluble in water.

(3) *Alkalis.* The reaction of nitrogen and phosphorus trioxides with cold dilute alkalis is similar to that with water. A solution of the alkali nitrite or hydrogen phosphite is formed,

$$P_4O_6 + 8OH^- \rightarrow 4HPO_3^{2-} + 2H_2O.$$

Arsenic trioxide and antimony(III) oxide both readily dissolve in alkalis; arsenites and antimonites are formed in solution. As expected for oxides towards the bottom of the Group, they are progressively less acidic. Bismuth(III) oxide has no acidic properties and is unaffected by alkalis. The even greater 'metallic' character of the bismuth(III) oxide is entirely consistent with the fact that of all the elements in the Group bismuth has the largest atomic radius and lowest electronegativity.

(4) *Acids.* As acidic properties decrease down the Group, the basic properties increase. Thus, whereas nitrogen and phosphorus trioxides have no basic properties arsenic trioxide dissolves more readily in hydrochloric acid than it does in water owing to a reversible equilibrium that exists in solution,

$$As_4O_6 + 12HCl \rightleftharpoons 4AsCl_3 + 6H_2O.$$

Antimony(III) oxide also dissolves in hot concentrated sulphuric acid; the sulphate, $Sb_2(SO_4)_3$, crystallises on cooling. Concentrated nitric acid oxidises the trioxides of phosphorus and arsenic to the pentoxides, but with antimony(III) oxide a basic nitrate is formed. Bismuth(III) oxide readily dissolves in acids to form the corresponding bismuth salt.

The general trend of increasing basicity as the Group is descended is well illustrated by these oxides,

N_2O_3	P_4O_6	As_4O_6	Sb_4O_6	Bi_2O_3
Acidic	Acidic	Amphoteric	Amphoteric	Basic

It should be noted, however, that dinitrogen trioxide is only weakly acidic whilst phosphorus trioxide is much more acidic.

Other oxides

The other important oxides in this Group are derived from nitrogen. They are dinitrogen tetroxide, N_2O_4, nitrogen monoxide (nitric oxide), NO, and dinitrogen oxide (nitrous oxide), N_2O. The tetroxide is composed wholly of N_2O_4 molecules in the solid form, but the liquid dissociates and at room temperature the vapours contain brown fumes of nitrogen dioxide, NO_2. All these oxides are covalent, but a detailed description of the binding sets special problems as an example will make clear.

Nitrogen has five electrons in its outer shell, and oxygen has six, so that when these atoms combine, unless there is an even number of nitrogen atoms, the molecule will contain an odd electron. Thus nitrogen monoxide and nitrogen dioxide are paramagnetic (see p. 527). Furthermore, the formula N_2O cannot be accounted for in terms of classical valency, and is depicted as a resonance hybrid of two forms (Fig. 126).

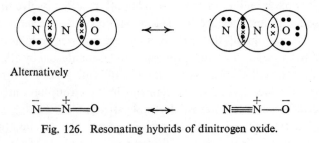

Fig. 126. Resonating hybrids of dinitrogen oxide.

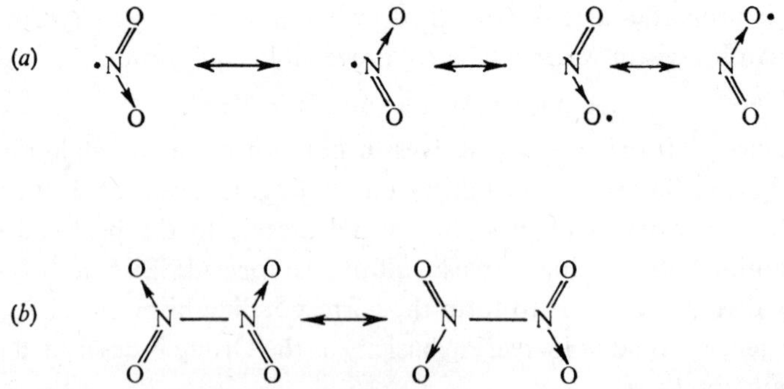

Fig. 127. Resonating hybrids of (*a*) nitrogen dioxide and (*b*) dinitrogen tetroxide.

The structures of nitrogen dioxide and its dimer dinitrogen tetroxide, N_2O_4, are also resonance hybrids (Fig. 127). The odd electron is shared over the whole nitrogen dioxide molecule which is symmetrical.

To represent nitrogen monoxide by formulae of this kind is impossible. Although $:\!\ddot{N}\!\!=\!\!\ddot{O}\!:$ may be written, the single electron is shared over the whole molecule.

Nitrogen is able to form stable multiple bonds with oxygen, whereas phosphorus shows this property only to a slight extent. This leads to wide differences between their oxides, e.g. phosphorus is unable to form lower oxides comparable to those of nitrogen.

Except for the pentoxide all the oxides of nitrogen are endothermic compounds. This is because the energy released in the bonding of nitrogen to oxygen in these oxides is less than that needed to dissociate the nitrogen plus oxygen molecules involved, both of which have high heats of dissociation (see p. 498, Halogens). Another general feature of the oxides of nitrogen is their ability to act as oxidising agents. This is characteristic of the oxides of highly electronegative non-metals (cf. chlorine) and stems from the ease with which they can furnish atomic oxygen: a consequence of the relative ease with which the bond between two atoms of similar electronegativity can be ruptured.

Dinitrogen oxide (nitrous oxide), N_2O. On gentle heating ammonium nitrate decomposes and evolves dinitrogen oxide, which can be collected over water.

$$NH_4NO_3 \rightarrow N_2O + 2H_2O.$$

As a precaution heating is usually discontinued after about two-thirds of the solid has decomposed. Pure dinitrogen oxide is obtained by warming a solution containing equimolecular amounts of hydroxylamine hydrochloride and sodium nitrite.

$$NH_3OH^+ + NO_2^- \rightarrow N_2O + 2H_2O.$$

Dinitrogen oxide is a colourless gas with a faint sweetish smell. It is about one and a half times as dense as air (cf. CO_2) and is slightly soluble in water (0.7 vol. in 1 vol. of water at 20 °C). Very pure dinitrogen oxide mixed with oxygen is administered as an anaesthetic, e.g. by dentists.

The solution of dinitrogen oxide in water is neutral and it is unaffected by acids and alkalis, cf. NO, CO. Chemically dinitrogen oxide is unreactive at ordinary temperature. At about 500 °C it decomposes into its elements. Once decomposition has been started the combustible material will continue to burn in the oxygen liberated. Moreover, it will burn more brightly than in air since dinitrogen oxide contains 33% oxygen by volume as against the 20% in air. Brightly burning sulphur, phosphorus and charcoal burn brilliantly in the gas, and even a glowing splint is rekindled. However,

443   15-2

the odour and behaviour towards nitrogen monoxide enable it to be distinguished from oxygen,

$$P_4 + 10N_2O \rightarrow P_4O_{10} + 10N_2.$$

The molecular formula of dinitrogen oxide has been determined by decomposing the gas in a eudiometer with an electrically heated iron wire. All the oxygen liberated combines with the heated iron and it is found that the volume of the gas remains unaltered. Thus, dinitrogen oxide contains its own volume of nitrogen and by Avogadro's hypothesis the molecular formula is N_2O_x. Vapour density measurements show the molecular weight to be 44 hence $x = 1$ and the formula is N_2O.

Nitrogen monoxide (nitric oxide), NO. Several methods are available for preparing this gas:

(1) *From* 1:1 *nitric acid.* Equal volumes of water and concentrated nitric acid are mixed and poured on to some copper turnings in a flask. A brisk effervescence ensures; nitrogen monoxide is evolved and may be collected over water in which any nitrogen dioxide formed readily dissolves,

$$3Cu + 8HNO_3 = 3Cu(NO_3)_2 + 4H_2O + 2NO.$$

A very effective method of purification is to absorb the nitrogen monoxide in iron(II) sulphate solution. When the dark brown solution obtained is warmed nitrogen monoxide is regenerated free from impurities.

(2) *From a nitrate.* When a solution of potassium nitrate, dilute sulphuric acid, and iron(II) sulphate is warmed nearly pure nitrogen monoxide is evolved, $\quad 3Fe^{2+} + 4H^+ + NO_3^- \rightarrow 3Fe^{3+} + 2H_2O + NO.$

Nitrogen monoxide is a colourless gas, slightly heavier than air and sparingly soluble in water. The odour is unknown as nitrogen monoxide combines instantly with the oxygen of the air and is oxidised to the familiar brown fumes of nitrogen dioxide,

$$2NO + O_2 \rightleftharpoons 2NO_2.$$

Thus reactions of nitrogen monoxide should be carried out in the absence of air.

Like dinitrogen oxide, nitrogen monoxide is unaffected by both acids and alkalis and is another neutral oxide. However, it is the most stable of the nitrogen oxides and does not decompose appreciably into its elements until about 1000 °C. Ordinarily the gas does not support combustion but if the burning material is hot enough to cause decomposition it continues to burn and does so with enhanced brilliance (NO is 50% oxygen by volume). Consequently, burning magnesium and phosphorus continue to burn, but the gas extinguishes burning sulphur, charcoal, or wax taper.

Having a single unpaired electron not only makes nitrogen monoxide paramagnetic but also increases its reactivity and the extent of its chemistry. Nitrogen monoxide also combines readily with chlorine and bromine to give the coloured gases nitrosyl chloride (orange yellow) and nitrosyl bromide (red),

$$2NO + Cl_2 \rightarrow 2NOCl.$$

Loss of the odd electron leaves the *nitrosonium ion, NO^+*. The compound $NO^+HSO_4^-$, nitrosonium hydrogen sulphate, is a well-known intermediate in the lead chamber process for sulphuric acid manufacture. Other salts containing this ion are also known, e.g. nitrosonium perchlorate $NO^+ClO_4^-$. The nitrosonium ion NO^+ is isoelectronic with the carbon monoxide molecule CO and the cyanide ion, CN^-, i.e. two atomic nuclei are imbedded in a cloud of fourteen electrons in each case.

In common with the cyanide ion and carbon monoxide, nitrogen monoxide forms complexes with certain cations by means of electron donation. For example, the hexacyanoferrate(III) ion, $[Fe(CN)_6]^{3-}$, is converted to the pentacyanonitrosylferrate(III) (nitroprusside) ion by replacing a cyanide ion by a nitrogen monoxide molecule, i.e.

$$[Fe(CN)_5NO]^{2-}.$$

Here the nitrogen monoxide molecule transfers its odd electron to the Fe^{3+} ion and then donates a further two electrons so that three electrons are involved in the binding. Similarly, the hydrated iron(II) ion reversibly absorbs nitrogen monoxide and the ion produced, $[Fe(H_2O)_5NO]^{2+}$, is responsible for the brown coloration observed when nitrogen monoxide is bubbled into iron(II) sulphate solution and in comparable situations, i.e. the brown ring test,

$$[Fe(H_2O)_6]^{2+} + NO \rightleftharpoons [Fe(H_2O)_5NO]^{2+} + H_2O.$$
$$\text{Pale green} \qquad\qquad \text{Brown}$$

Formula. When passed over a heated iron wire nitrogen monoxide gives half its volume of nitrogen. From this and vapour density measurements the formula NO is deduced.

Nitrogen tetroxide, N_2O_4, and nitrogen dioxide, NO_2. The dense brown gas nitrogen dioxide is evolved in the vigorous reduction of concentrated nitric acid with copper turnings,

$$Cu + 4HNO_3 \rightarrow Cu(NO_3)_2 + 2NO_2 + 2H_2O.$$

The gas may be collected by downward displacement.

445

Another method of preparation is the thermal decomposition of the nitrate of a weakly electropositive metal, e.g. lead(II) nitrate,

$$2Pb(NO_3)_2 \rightarrow 2PbO + 4NO_2 + O_2.$$

The evolved gas is passed through a U-tube surrounded by an ice/salt freezing mixture. Dinitrogen tetroxide condenses as a yellow liquid.

Below its melting point, -10 °C, dinitrogen tetroxide is a colourless solid. The liquid at its melting point is slightly dissociated into nitrogen dioxide which is strongly coloured. Dissociation increases with rising temperature, and the colour of the vapour darkens accordingly. At 22 °C it is reddish-brown, and boils giving off a brown vapour. The colour of the vapour darkens on further heating, and at 150 °C is almost black. At this temperature dissociation into single molecules is complete. Above 150 °C decomposition of nitrogen dioxide occurs, and at 620 °C this change is complete, and the gas is now colourless,

$$N_2O_4 \quad \rightleftharpoons \quad 2NO_2 \quad \rightleftharpoons \quad 2NO + O_2.$$

| Colourless | Dark brown | Both colourless |

Recombination occurs on cooling. The weak bond between the nitrogen atoms in the dimer, and therefore its ready dissociation, arises from the fact that both atoms have a partial positive charge as the more electronegative oxgyen atoms take a greater share of the bonding electrons.

Nitrogen dioxide reacts with water and behaves as the mixed anhydride of nitric and nitrous acids,

$$2NO_2 + H_2O \rightarrow HNO_3 + HNO_2.$$

Nitrous acid is unstable and decomposes into nitrogen monoxide and nitric acid. With alkalis equivalent quantities of nitrate and nitrite are formed,

$$2NO_2 + 2OH^- \rightarrow NO_2^- + NO_3^- + H_2O.$$

Nitrogen dioxide readily gives up its oxygen, thus phosphorus, sulphur and charcoal burn vigorously in the gas, to yield their oxides and nitrogen. Similar reactions occur with white-hot copper or iron,

$$4Cu + 2NO_2 \rightarrow 4CuO + N_2.$$

The strong oxidising power of nitrogen dioxide finds application in the lead chamber process for the manufacture of sulphuric acid where it is used to oxidise sulphur dioxide to sulphur trioxide at normal temperatures.

Just as the nitrogen monoxide molecule could lose its odd electron to form the nitrosonium ion, NO^+, the nitrogen dioxide molecule also loses its odd electron fairly readily and forms the nitronium ion, NO_2^+, about which more will be said in connection with the reactions of nitric acid.

Compounds: III, Oxo-acids

The principal quinquevalent and trivalent oxo-acids of Group V are listed in the table below:

Oxidation state of E	N	P	As	Sb	Bi
+5	HNO_3, nitric acid	H_3PO_4, phosphoric acid	H_3AsO_4, arsenic acid	$HSb(OH)_6$, antimonic acid	$HBiO_3$, bismuthic acid
+3	HNO_2 nitrous acid	H_3PO_3, phosphorous acid; H_3PO_2, hypophos- phorous acid	$As(OH)_3$, arsenious acid	—	—

No lower oxo-acid of antimony is known, but there is a hydrated oxide, Sb_2O_3(aq.), which shows acidic properties and dissolves in alkalis to give antimonites which are well defined salts, e.g. $NaSbO_2$. Whereas antimony(III) hydroxide is unstable and probably does not exist as a definite compound the greater metallic character of bismuth is shown by its ability to form bismuth(III) hydroxide $Bi(OH)_3$, a compound which shows no acidic properties.

Condensed forms of several of these acids are known, e.g. meta- and pyrophosphoric acids. These are formed by the loss of water molecules between orthophosphoric acid molecules which then link together by means of P—O—P bonds (see later). Numerous other oxo-acids of nitrogen and phosphorus are also known, e.g. hypophosphorous acid, H_3PO_2, is a white crystalline solid, salts of which are usually prepared by boiling white phosphorus with strong alkalis. Not all the acids can be isolated and some are known only by their salts.

Nitric acid, HNO_3

Laboratory preparation. Equal weights of sodium or potassium nitrate and concentrated sulphuric acid are heated together in a glass retort. The nitric acid vapour evolved condenses in the neck of the retort and collects in a flask cooled by tap water placed over the neck of the retort,

$$NO_3^- + H_2SO_4 \rightarrow HSO_4^- + HNO_3.$$

Part of the nitric acid decomposes, especially if there is overheating and the nitrogen dioxide produced dissolves in the acid turning it yellow.

Ammonia oxidation process. Large-scale production of nitric acid is now carried out exclusively by the oxidation of ammonia gas with the oxygen of the air in the presence of a catalyst.

Dry ammonia gas and dust-free air are preheated and passed at a pressure of 8 atmospheres through a platinum-rhodium alloy gauze pad maintained at about 900 °C. The ammonia is converted to nitrogen monoxide and water vapour on the surface of the catalyst, and a large amount of heat is developed. This is sufficient to heat the catalyst and the optimum temperature is maintained by adjusting the rate of flow of the gas,

$$4NH_3 + 5O_2 \rightarrow 4NO + 6H_2O; \quad \Delta H = -905.3 \text{ kJ} \ (-216.4 \text{ kcal}).$$

The hot gases leaving the converter are cooled in heat interchangers and the nitrogen monoxide produced is further oxidised by oxygen of the air to nitrogen dioxide,
$$2NO + O_2 \rightleftharpoons 2NO_2.$$

Nitrogen dioxide dissolves in the condensed water vapour produced in the reaction and dilute nitric acid is formed. The oxidation of nitrogen monoxide is slow and additional air is blown into the nitrous gas which is passed up through a series of baffles against a flow of dilute nitric acid in a large tower in which the oxidation and absorption is completed. Heat is evolved in the absorption of the nitrogen dioxide and water cooling is necessary,

$$3NO_2 + H_2O \rightarrow 2HNO_3 + NO; \quad \Delta H = -115.4 \text{ kJ} \ (-27.6 \text{ kcal}).$$

Air is blown through the acid leaving the absorption tower to remove dissolved oxides of nitrogen. A typical plant works to an overall efficiency of conversion of ammonia to nitric acid of 92%, and the acid produced has a concentration of about 60%.

Nitric acid containing 95–99% HNO_3 can be made either by concentrating the 60% solution or by modifying the oxidation process. In the sulphuric acid concentration process the 60% solution of nitric acid and concentrated sulphuric acid are passed into the top of a tall tower packed with acid resistant rings and heated by steam injected into the bottom of the tower. Nitric acid vapour passes from the top of the tower and is condensed. Strong acid can be made directly by isolating the dinitrogen tetroxide produced in the catalytic oxidation of ammonia and oxidising this under pressure using oxygen instead of air.

Physical properties. Pure nitric acid melts at $-41.6\ °C$, and boils with partial decomposition at 86 °C. The liquid is slightly dissociated,

$$2HNO_3 \rightleftharpoons N_2O_5 + H_2O.$$

Dinitrogen pentoxide decomposes slowly into oxygen and dinitrogen tetroxide, N_2O_4, so the acid soon develops a slight yellow coloration. Nitric acid is miscible with water and if the dilute acid is distilled the boiling point gradually rises to 122 °C when a constant boiling-point mixture containing 68% HNO_3 distils. This is the commonly known concentrated nitric acid of density 1.4 g cm^{-3}. It is usually yellow in colour owing to dissolved oxides of nitrogen and the colour deepens on exposure to sunlight because the acid undergoes photochemical decomposition,

$$4HNO_3 \rightarrow 4NO_2 + 2H_2O + O_2.$$

When heated, i.e. by passing through a heated silica tube, the acid undergoes the same decomposition. By distilling the ordinary commerical concentrated nitric acid from concentrated sulphuric acid fuming nitric acid distils and is yellow in colour.

Nitric acid vapour contains covalent HNO_3 molecules the general shape of which is shown in Fig. 128. The nitric acid molecule is planar. It cannot be adequately represented by a single structural formula as the shorter N—O bonds are identical and have considerable multiple bond character. Two N=O bonds would give nitrogen a covalency of 5 which is forbidden, and the structure is best considered as a resonance hybrid of two forms,

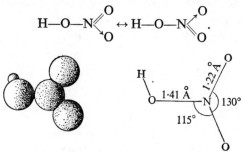

Fig. 128. The molecular structure of nitric acid.

Chemical properties. (1) *Acidic properties.* Pure nitric acid has no action on metals or carbonates and behaves as an ordinary covalent liquid. However, the highly electronegative atoms draw the electrons away from the hydrogen atom and turn it into an incipient proton. In the presence of water proton transfer occurs and the following equilibrium is established,

$$HNO_3 + H_2O \rightleftharpoons H_3O^+ + NO_3^-, \quad K_1 = \text{large value.}$$

449

In 0.1 molar solutions, the acid is about 93% dissociated and its behaviour is that of a strong monobasic acid.

(2) *Oxidising action.* Concentrated nitric acid is a powerful oxidising agent. The action is complex and the nature of the product depends on (*a*) the concentration of the acid, (*b*) the temperature, and (*c*) the reducing agent. During the oxidation the nitric acid is reduced to water and, depending on the conditions, any of the following: nitrogen dioxide, nitrous acid, nitrogen monoxide, dinitrogen oxide, nitrogen, hydroxylamine (NH_2OH) and ammonia (the last two compounds are basic and in acid solution gain a proton and become NH_3OH^+ and NH_4^+ respectively). Frequently the product contains several of the nitrogen-containing species, and as there are several reactions going on at once no single equation can adequately represent the overall process.

Concentrated nitric acid oxidises iron(II) ions to the iron(III) state, and nitrogen monoxide is evolved,

$$3Fe^{2+} + NO_3^- + 4H^+ \rightarrow 3Fe^{3+} + 2H_2O + NO.$$

Many organic compounds are oxidised by nitric acid. Mixed with aniline it has been used as a rocket fuel, burning to water vapour, carbon dioxide, and nitrogen. Less destructive is the oxidation of toluene to benzoic acid,

$$C_6H_5.CH_3 \xrightarrow{\text{HNO}_3} C_6H_5.COOH.$$

Toluene   Benzoic acid

(3) *Non-metals.* As a result of its strong oxidising ability concentrated nitric acid converts a number of non-metallic elements to the corresponding oxide or oxo-acid. For instance, if a piece of glowing charcoal is dropped on to a few cubic centimetres of concentrated nitric acid it burns brilliantly to carbon dioxide and brown fumes of nitrogen dioxide are evolved,

$$C + 4HNO_3 \rightarrow 2H_2O + 4NO_2 + CO_2.$$

Phosphorus is oxidised to phosphoric acid, arsenic to arsenic acid, sulphur to sulphuric acid and iodine to iodic acid,

$$3I_2 + 10HNO_3 \rightarrow 2H_2O + 10NO + 6HIO_3.$$

(4) *Metals.* In addition to its acidic properties nitric acid is also a strong oxidising agent. This is because the nitrate ion, NO_3^-, in the presence of hydrogen ions behaves as an electron acceptor. This is shown in the following half-reaction (see p. 163),

$$NO_3^- + 2H^+ + e \rightarrow NO_2 + H_2O,$$
$$NO_3^- + 4H^+ + 3e \rightarrow NO + 2H_2O,$$
$$NO_3^- + 9H^+ + 8e \rightarrow NH_3 + 3H_2O.$$

Besides the reduction products shown in the above equations, dinitrogen oxide, nitrogen and hydroxylamine may also be formed. The ammonia produced immediately reacts with the acid to form ammonium nitrate. Metals above hydrogen in the E.C.S. are in fact the only ones that are capable of forming ammonia and hydroxylamine.

Nitric acid has no affect on gold or platinum. Aluminium and iron are rendered *passive* by the concentrated acid. It is probable that the passivity of the last two metals is the result of the initial formation of an impervious oxide film which prevents further attack.

Very dilute nitric acid has little oxidising action, and magnesium will displace hydrogen from it (cf. Mn),

$$Mg + 2H^+ \rightarrow Mg^{2+} + H_2.$$

Concentrated nitric acid dissolves tin and antimony with the evolution of oxides of nitrogen and a white residue of the hydrated oxide remains. All other metals dissolve completely to give a solution of the nitrate. During oxidations with nitric acid more than one reaction may be going on at the same time, and the predominant reaction will depend on the condition. Thus, 33 % nitric acid (i.e. 1:1) is chiefly reduced to nitrogen monoxide by copper,

$$3Cu + 8H^+ + 2NO_3^- \rightarrow 3Cu^{2+} + 2NO + 4H_2O,$$

and concentrated nitric acid is chiefly reduced to nitrogen dioxide,

$$Cu + 4H^+ + 2NO_3^- \rightarrow Cu^{2+} + 2NO_2 + 2H_2O.$$

Although neither concentrated nitric nor concentrated hydrochloric acid alone will dissolve gold or platinum, when mixed in the proportion $1HNO_3 : 3HCl$, they have added dissolving power and corrode the noble metals. In consequence, the mixture is called *aqua regia*. The extra solvent power is the result of complex ion formation. For example, it is easier to oxidise gold to the $AuCl_4^-$ ion than to the Au^{3+}, i.e. a complex ion of the cation with chloride ions in the mixed acids is more stable than the simple hydrated cation,

$$Au + 6H^+ + 3NO_3^- + 4Cl^- \rightarrow AuCl_4^- + 3NO_2 + 3H_2O.$$

(5) *Nitrations*. Concentrated nitric acid is an important reagent for preparing organic nitrates and nitro compounds. Cellulose nitrate (popularly known as nitrocellulose or gun-cotton) and glyceryl trinitrate (better known by the misnomer nitroglycerine) are two important organic nitrate esters manufactured on the large scale for use in explosives. The cellulose (i.e. paper or dried cotton) or glycerine is nitrated by adding it to a mixture of concentrated nitric and sulphuric acid (mixed acid), e.g.

$$\begin{array}{ccc}
\text{CH}_2\text{OH} & & \text{CH}_2\text{ONO}_2 \\
| & & | \\
\text{CHOH} + 3\text{HONO}_2 & \rightarrow & \text{CHONO}_2 + 3\text{H}_2\text{O} \quad \text{(absorbed by the H}_2\text{SO}_4\text{).} \\
| & & | \\
\text{CH}_2\text{OH} & & \text{CH}_2\text{ONO}_2 \\
\text{Glycerine} & & \text{Glyceryl trinitrate}
\end{array}$$

Nobel (1867) discovered that the highly explosive and shock-sensitive liquid nitroglycerine could be stabilised by absorbing it on an inert support such as kieselguhr. The solid obtained is called dynamite. Mixtures of nitroglycerine and gun-cotton are used in manufacturing explosives such as gelignite and cordite.

The essential difference between organic nitrates and nitro compounds is that the latter have the nitrogen atom combined directly to a carbon atom, and not an oxygen atom as is the case in the former compounds. Mixed acid is also used for producing nitro compounds, but this time the attacking species is the nitronium ion, NO_2^+. It has been shown that *pure* nitric acid undergoes auto-ionisation thus,

$$2\text{HNO}_3 \rightleftharpoons \text{NO}_2^+ + \text{NO}_3^- + \text{H}_2\text{O}.$$

This accounts for the surprising fact that although pure nitric acid behaves as a neutral covalent liquid, it conducts electricity. A similar ionisation occurs in non-aqueous solvents such as concentrated sulphuric acid,

$$\text{H}_2\text{SO}_4 + \text{HNO}_3 \rightleftharpoons \text{NO}_2^+ + \text{HSO}_4^- + \text{H}_2\text{O}.$$

Thus, the nitration of, for example, benzene, C_6H_6, may be formulated as follows:

$$\underset{\text{Benzene}}{\text{C}_6\text{H}_6} + \text{NO}_2^+ \rightarrow \underset{\text{Nitrobenzene}}{\text{C}_6\text{H}_5\text{NO}_2} + \text{H}^+.$$

Phosphoric acids

Hydrolysis of phosphorus pentoxide might be expected to produce the orthoacid H_5PO_5, i.e. $P(OH)_5$. However, no compound with this formula is known and no derivatives of it have been isolated. Consequently its first dehydration product is termed orthophosphoric acid. The relationship between the different phosphoric acids is illustrated below,

Unknown   Ortho   Meta

A dehydration product intermediate between the ortho and meta phosphoric acids is also known, it is called pyrophosphoric acid,

$$O \leftarrow \overset{\overset{\displaystyle OH}{|}}{\underset{\underset{\displaystyle OH}{|}}{P}} - O - \boxed{H + H - O} - \overset{\overset{\displaystyle OH}{|}}{\underset{\underset{\displaystyle OH}{|}}{P}} \rightarrow O \qquad \xrightarrow{-H_2O} \qquad O \leftarrow \overset{\overset{\displaystyle OH}{|}}{\underset{\underset{\displaystyle OH}{|}}{P}} - O - \overset{\overset{\displaystyle OH}{|}}{\underset{\underset{\displaystyle OH}{|}}{P}} \rightarrow O$$

Two molecules of the ortho acid   Pyrophosphoric acid

Methods of preparation. Pure orthophosphoric acid is prepared in the laboratory by oxidising red phosphorus with warm 33 % nitric acid and then evaporating the clear solution until the acid crystallises out. The temperature must not rise above 180 °C or more pyrophosphoric acid will be formed, $P_4 + 10HNO_3 + H_2O \rightarrow 4H_3PO_4 + 5NO + 5NO_2$.

Orthophosphoric acid is also made by digesting calcium phosphate or bone ash with dilute sulphuric acid. Insoluble calcium sulphate is filtered off and the remaining solution is concentrated. Treatment of phosphate rock with 70 % sulphuric acid converts it to a mixture of calcium sulphate and the soluble calcium dihydrogen orthophosphate, $Ca(H_2PO_4)_2$ which is used as a soil dressing and is sold commercially under the name of *superphosphate*.

Orthophosphoric acid heated to 200–300 °C gradually loses water, and is converted to pyrophosphoric acid. Further heating yields metaphosphoric acid which cannot be dehydrated further and volatilises at red heat.

Physical properties. Ortho- and pyrophosphoric acids are colourless crystalline solids whose melting points are 47 and 62 °C respectively. Metaphosphoric acid is a colourless deliquescent glassy mass. It has the empirical formula HPO_3, but is polymeric and best expressed as $(HPO_3)_n$. Trimetaphosphates and tetrametaphosphates are known and have cyclic structures.

Chemical properties. *Acidic properties.* All three acids are readily soluble in water, and together with their ions they change into one another only slowly. Thus, their solutions and those of their salts have distinctive properties.

Orthophosphoric acid is a moderately strong acid in its first ionisation, but as the charge on the anion increases further ionisation becomes increasingly difficult (see p. 258),

$$H_3PO_4 \rightleftharpoons H^+ + H_2PO_4^- \rightleftharpoons 2H^+ + HPO_4^{2-} \rightleftharpoons 3H^+ + PO_4^{3-}.$$

Being a tribasic acid it can form three series of orthophosphates, e.g. NaH_2PO_4, Na_2HPO_4, Na_3PO_4. The sodium dihydrogen salt is weakly acidic and will turn blue litmus red, but is neutral to methyl orange. Disodium hydrogen orthophosphate is alkaline to methyl orange and neutral to phenolphthalein. Trisodium orthophosphate gives a strongly alkaline solution owing to hydrolysis. If the volume of alkali required to neutralise a given portion of orthophosphoric acid using methyl orange as indicator is doubled and added to the same amount of the acid, the disodium hydrogen salt is obtained. Three times the volume of alkali is needed to produce the trisodium salt.

Pyrophosphoric acid is tetrabasic, but only the normal and dihydrogen salts are commonly known, e.g. $Na_4P_2O_7$ and $Na_2H_2P_2O_7$. Pyrophosphates are readily prepared by heating the monohydrogen orthophosphates, e.g.

$$2Na_2HPO_4 \xrightarrow{250°C} Na_4P_2O_7 + H_2O.$$

Metaphosphoric acid is hydrated to orthophosphoric acid by boiling water and more slowly by cold water. The relationship between the phosphoric acids may be expressed as follows,

$$H_3PO_4 \xrightarrow{\text{Heat}} H_4P_2O_7 \xrightarrow{\text{Heat}} (HPO_3)_n$$

Boiling water

Metaphosphates, e.g. $NaPO_3$, are formed when the dihydrogen ortho-phosphates are heated,

$$NaH_2PO_4 \rightarrow NaPO_3 + H_2O.$$

Distinguishing tests for ortho-, meta- and pyrophosphates

Reagent	Ortho-	Pyro-	Meta-
Neutral $AgNO_3$ solution	Yellow ppt.	White ppt.	White ppt.
Albumen (white of egg)	No action	No action	Coagulates

Quinquevalent oxo-acids of arsenic, antimony and bismuth

As the atomic radius increases down the Group, so a greater number of oxygen atoms can be accommodated around the central atom of the oxo-acid. Nitrogen can surround itself comfortably with only three oxygen atoms, and the oxo-acid is HNO_3; phosphorus and arsenic are able to accommodate four oxygen atoms as in phosphoric acid, H_3PO_4, and arsenic acid, H_3AsO_4. The antimony atom is larger still and can surround itself with six oxygen atoms, e.g. antimonic acid, $HSb(OH)_6$. As previously mentioned, the higher oxidation states becomes less stable towards the bottom of the Group, and it has not proved possible to produce bismuthic acid, but a few impure salts of the acid $HBiO_3$ have been prepared, e.g. sodium bismuthate, $NaBiO_3$.

Arsenic pentoxide dissolves in water to give arsenic acid which is a moderately strong tribasic acid which forms a series of arsenates which resemble the phosphates and are often isomorphous with them, e.g. Na_3AsO_4, Na_2HAsO_4, NaH_2AsO_4. In contrast to the phosphate ion the arsenate ion is an oxidising agent and will oxidise the iodide ion to free iodine,

$$H_2O + \underset{\text{Arsenate ion}}{AsO_4^{3-}} + 2I^- \rightleftharpoons \underset{\text{Arsenite ion}}{AsO_3^{3-}} + I_2 + 2OH^-.$$

The reaction is reversible, but if the iodine is removed by titration with sodium thiosulphate solution, for instance, it goes to completion. On the other hand, a solution of an arsenite in the presence of a sufficient concentration of hydroxyl ions, e.g. from the addition of sodium hydrogen carbonate (note, ordinary alkalis would react with the iodine), is completely oxidised to arsenate by iodine solutions. Arsenic acid also slowly oxidises hydrogen sulphide to sulphur and sulphite to sulphate.

Antimony(v) oxide is insoluble in water, but dissolves in alkalis with the formation of the antimonate ion $[Sb(OH)_6]^-$.

Nitrous acid, HNO_2

Nitrous acid is too unstable to isolate pure, but a solution of it is readily prepared by acidifying a solution of a nitrite. Aqueous solutions of nitrous acid are also unstable and decompose into nitric acid with the evolution of nitrogen monoxide,

$$3HNO_2 \rightarrow H_3O^+ + NO_3^- + 2NO.$$

It is a very weak monobasic acid giving rise to a series of salts called the nitrites (see below). The acid is also an effective oxidising agent as well as behaving as a reducing agent in certain circumstances.

Oxidising action. Nitrous acid immediately liberates iodine from a solution of an iodide (*note*, the action is much slower with nitric acid),

$$4H^+ + 2NO_2^- + 2I^- \rightarrow I_2 + 2NO + 2H_2O.$$

455

It also oxidises the tin(II) ion to the tin(IV) ion, iron(II) salts to iron(III) salts, sulphurous acid to sulphuric acid, and hydrogen sulphide to sulphur.

Reducing action. In the presence of strong oxidising agents, the nitrite ion acts as a reducing agent, and is oxidised to the nitrate ion, e.g. by potassium permanganate,

$$5NO_2^- + 6H^+ + 2MnO_4^- \rightarrow 5NO_3^- + 2Mn^{2+} + 3H_2O.$$

Nitrites. Alkali metal nitrates except lithium decompose on heating to the corresponding nitrite, $\quad 2NO_3^- \rightarrow 2NO_2^- + O_2 \uparrow .$

Sodium nitrite is an important raw material in the dye industry and it is manufactured on the large scale in association with the manufacture of nitric acid. An equimolecular mixture of nitrogen monoxide and nitrogen dioxide obtained from the catalytic oxidation of ammonia is passed into a solution of sodium hydroxide,

$$2OH^- + NO + NO_2 \rightarrow 2NO_2^- + H_2O.$$

Separation from the accompanying nitrate is achieved by fractional crystallisation.

Nitrites are all soluble in water, and are decomposed by acids with the evolution of brown fumes of nitrogen dioxide. The reaction proceeds easily in the cold and serves to distinguish nitrites from nitrates which do not evolve brown fumes in the presence of cold acids.

Phosphorous acid, H_3PO_3

Phosphorus trioxide dissolves in cold water to give a solution of phosphorous acid. Alternatively, it may be crystallised from the solution obtained by hydrolysing phosphorus trichloride,

$$PCl_3 + 3H_2O \rightarrow H_3PO_3 + 3HCl.$$

It is a white crystalline solid and is very soluble in water. When heated in the dry state it melts at 74 °C, and at higher temperatures undergoes disproportionation (i.e. decomposes into a compound of phosphorus in a higher oxidation state and also one in which it is in a lower oxidation state) into phosphine and phosphoric acid (cf. decomposition of nitrous acid),

$$4H_3PO_3 \rightarrow PH_3 + 3H_3PO_4.$$

The structure of the acid is unusual as it is not the simple trihydroxide

$P(OH)_3$, but a dihydroxide with one hydrogen atom attached directly to the phosphorus atom, i.e.

$$\overset{\displaystyle OH}{\underset{\displaystyle OH}{H-P}} = O.$$

As a consequence the acid is only dibasic. It seems probable that the presence of the hydrogen atom joined directly to the phosphorus atom is responsible for the surprising fact that phosphorous acid is stronger than phosphoric acid. Phosphorous acid is also a good reducing agent, and will liberate the free element from easily reducible ions such as those of silver and mercury(II),

$$H_2O + H_3PO_3 + 2Ag^+ \rightarrow 2H^+ + H_3PO_4 + 2Ag.$$

Arsenious acid, As(OH)₃

Arsenic trioxide, As_4O_6, dissolves slightly in water to give a solution which has an acidic reaction to litmus owing to the formation of the very weak arsenious acid. Unlike phosphorous acid, it has never been obtained in the free state, but like nitrous acid it can be both oxidised and reduced.

Oxidising action. Tin(II) chloride in concentrated hydrochloric acid solution will reduce the arsenite ion to arsenic, and nascent hydrogen reduces it still further to arsine.

$$AsO_3^{3-} + 3H^+ + 6[H] \rightarrow AsH_3 + 3H_2O.$$

Reducing action. Strong oxidising agents such as the permanganate or dichromate ion oxidise the arsenite ion to arsenate. As decribed in the section on arsenic acid, iodine in the presence of hydroxyl ions will also oxidise arsenite to arsenate.

Compounds: IV, Chlorides

Tri-chlorides	Penta-chlorides
NCl_3	—
PCl_3	PCl_5
$AsCl_3$	—
$SbCl_3$	$SbCl_5$
$BiCl_3$	—

Because nitrogen is restricted to a maximum of four covalent bonds, it is incapable of forming a pentachloride. Of the three elements, phosphorus, arsenic and antimony, only arsenic does not form a pentachloride, which is probably because it has the highest electronegativity. Bismuth does not form a quinquevalent chloride probably because of the inert-pair effect.

Trichlorides

Methods of preparation. (1) *Direct combination.* Phosphorus, arsenic, antimony and bismuth all combine directly with chlorine and this is the usual method of preparing phosphorus trichloride. Dry chlorine is passed over white phosphorus in a distilling flask which may be gently warmed in a water-bath. An excess of chlorine is avoided to prevent formation of the pentachloride. Phosphorus trichloride distils over and may be purified by redistillation over white phosphorus which reduces any pentachloride which may have been produced.

(2) *From hydrochloric acid.* Bismuth(III) oxide and antimony(III) sulphide both dissolve in concentrated hydrochloric acid and yield a solution of the corresponding chloride. Arsenic trichloride, together with hydrogen chloride, can be distilled from a solution of arsenic trioxide in concentrated hydrochloric acid. A better method of preparing arsenic trichloride is to pass dry hydrogen chloride over arsenic trioxide heated to about 180 °C,

$$As_4O_6 + 12HCl \rightleftharpoons 4AsCl_3 + 6H_2O.$$

Physical properties. Some properties of these compounds are listed below:

Some physical properties of Group V B trichlorides

Compound	Appearance	m.p. (°C)	b.p. (°C)
NCl_3	Yellow explosive oil	—	71
PCl_3	Colourless volatile liquid	-92	76
$AsCl_3$	Colourless liquid	-16	130
$SbCl_3$	Soft, colourless mass	73.2	221
$BiCl_3$	White solid	232	441

Antimony(III) chloride and bismuth(III) chloride are deliquescent. Owing to the readiness with which it is hydrolysed phosphorus trichloride fumes in moist air. All these chlorides are covalent compounds and have a pyramidal molecular structure similar to the one exhibited by their simple hydrides. Increasing electropositivity of the elements towards the bottom

458

of the Group imparts greater ionic character to the binding, and this is reflected in the increases in the melting and boiling points.

Chemical properties. (1) *Hydrolysis.* Nitrogen trichloride undergoes slow decomposition with water to form hypochlorous acid and ammonia. Presumably the inability of a nitrogen atom in a molecule of nitrogen trichloride to accept further electrons restricts its behaviour to that of an electron donor. Co-ordination to a hydrogen atom of a water molecule may occur through the lone pair of electrons of the nitrogen atom,

The hydrolysis of phosphorus trichloride and arsenic trichloride follows a more conventional course in which hydrogen chloride and the appropriate oxo-acid of the Group V element is produced,

$$PCl_3 + 3H_2O \rightarrow 3HCl + H_3PO_3 \quad \text{(phosphorous acid),}$$
$$AsCl_3 + 3H_2O \rightleftharpoons 3HCl + As(OH)_3 \quad \text{(arsenious acid).}$$

Arsenic trichloride is less completely hydrolysed than phosphorus trichloride. Antimony(III) chloride gives a clear solution when dissolved in a limited amount of water, but on dilution antimony oxide chloride, SbOCl, separates as a white precipitate. As the hydrolysis is reversible an increase in the concentration of the hydrochloric acid will redissolve the precipitate, $$SbCl_3 + H_2O \rightleftharpoons SbOCl + 2HCl.$$

Aqueous solutions of bismuth(III) chloride also precipitate the oxide chloride (BiOCl) on dilution and again the precipitate redissolves if hydrochloric acid is added.

(2) *Addition reactions.* With the exception of nitrogen trichloride these compounds have a tendency to act as electron *acceptors* and can take on additional chloride ions to form complex chlorine anions, e.g. $[SbCl_4]^-$, $[BiCl_5]^{2-}$. Addition compounds with other substances such as ammonia, amines, and ethers are also formed, e.g. $PCl_3.6NH_3$, $(CH_3)_2O \rightarrow SbCl_3$. Phosphorus trichloride takes up molecular oxygen, or even oxygen in the combined state provided it can be removed fairly easily, to form phosphorus oxide trichloride, $POCl_3$,

Addition reactions also readily occur with sulphur and chlorine to give thiophosphoryl chloride, $PSCl_3$ and PCl_5, respectively. Arsenic trichloride does not readily form addition compounds. This may seem anomalous since it occupies a position in the Group midway between elements which form addition compounds fairly easily. However, this variation in behaviour follows the order of decreasing electronegativity and it seems reasonable to assume that the greater electron density on the stronger electron attracting arsenic atom will inhibit the acceptance of further electrons more than with other less electronegative Group V atoms.

Quinquevalent chlorides

The non-existence of nitrogen pentachloride is a natural consequence of the inability of the nitrogen atom to expand its octet. Bismuth presumably forms no quinquevalent chloride owing to the influence of the inert pair effect. Arsenic also forms no pentachloride and this can be interpreted in terms of the higher electronegativity of this element compared with either phosphorus or antimony. For As—Cl bonds are less polar and therefore less stable, than either P—Cl or Sb—Cl bonds and as both phosphorus pentachloride and antimony(v) chloride are unstable the non-existence of arsenic pentachloride is not surprising.

Phosphorus pentachloride, PCl_5

Preparation. Direct combination is not a satisfactory method for preparing phosphorus pentachloride and it is usually prepared by the action of excess chlorine on phosphorus trichloride,

$$PCl_3 + Cl_2 \rightleftharpoons PCl_5; \quad \Delta H = -125.5 \text{ kJ } (-30 \text{ kcal}).$$

Phosphorus trichloride is run dropwise into a flask through which is passed a stream of dry chlorine. Excess of chlorine improves the equilibrium concentration of the pentachloride and as the reaction is exothermic, cooling improves the yield still further.

Physical properties. Phosphorus pentachloride is a yellowish white solid which fumes strongly in moist air. It sublimes and then dissociates on heating. Above 300 °C dissociation into PCl_3 and Cl_2 is complete.

There is evidence which suggests that solid phosphorus pentachloride is an ionic lattice composed of PCl_4^+ and PCl_6^- ions. In this latter ion phosphorus exhibits its covalency maximum of 6. Covalent PCl_5 molecules exist in the vapour state, however, together with the products of dissociation. The instability of phosphorus pentachloride makes it an effective chlorinating agent.

Chemical properties. As a general rule phosphorus pentachloride will react with compounds containing the —OH group by replacing it with a chlorine atom and also evolving hydrogen chloride.

(1) With *water* phosphorus oxide trichloride is formed first,

$$PCl_5 + H_2O \rightarrow POCl_3 + 2HCl.$$

But with excess water the reaction proceeds a stage further,

$$3H_2O + POCl_3 \rightarrow H_3PO_4 + 3HCl.$$

(2) *Simple alcohols*, in the same way as water are violently attacked at ordinary temperatures, e.g.

$$C_2H_5OH \quad + PCl_5 \rightarrow \quad C_2H_5Cl \quad + POCl_3 + HCl.$$
Ethanol $\qquad\qquad\qquad$ Chloroethane

(3) *Carboxylic acids* react less vigorously, e.g.

$$CH_3COOH + PCl_5 \rightarrow \quad CH_3COCl \quad + POCl_3 + HCl.$$
Acetic acid $\qquad\qquad$ Acetyl chloride

Convenient laboratory methods of preparing phosphorus oxide trichloride include the distillation of either phosphorus pentachloride with anhydrous oxalic acid or phosphorus trichloride with potassium chlorate,

$$(COOH)_2 + PCl_5 \rightarrow POCl_3 + CO_2 + CO + 2HCl,$$
$$3PCl_3 + KClO_3 \rightarrow 3POCl_3 + KCl.$$

Antimony(v) chloride, SbCl₅

This can also be prepared by the action of chlorine on antimony(III) chloride. It melts at 4 °C and boils at 140 °C with some dissociation into the trivalent chloride and chlorine. Hot water hydrolyses it to hydrated antimony(v) oxide, Sb_2O_6(aq.).

Exercises

1. Discuss the inclusion of nitrogen and phosphorus in the same Group of the Periodic Classification by comparing the physical and chemical properties of (*a*) these two elements, (*b*) their hydrides, and (*c*) their chlorides. (L)

2. Give the names and formulae of the oxides of nitrogen and assign each to its class. Describe and explain what occurs when each of these oxides is treated with water. Describe the laboratory preparation of (*a*) the lowest, and (*b*) the highest of these oxides. (L)

3. Outline the industrial preparation of phosphorus. Compare the properties of its hydrides, oxides and chlorides with those of the corresponding compounds of nitrogen. (L)

4. The hydrolysis of (*a*) trivalent oxides and (*b*) trivalent chlorides of Group V B elements reflects the increasing metallic character of the element as the Group is descended. Discuss this statement.

5. Give an account of the molecular structures of white phosphorus and its principal oxides, showing how they are related.

6. Compare and contrast the structures and properties of: (*a*) ammonia and phosphine, (*b*) water and hydrogen sulphide, (*c*) carbon dioxide and silicon dioxide. (OS)

7. (*a*) Give an account of the manufacture of *either* hydrogen or nitric acid, explaining carefully the reasons for the physical and chemical conditions under which the process is carried out.

Give *two* industrial uses of the substance which you select. (*b*) How and under what conditions does nitric acid react with (i) copper, (ii) iron, (iii) sulphur? (O)

8. Outline the laboratory preparation of a sample of dinitrogen tetroxide. Describe and explain what happens when it is heated from -10 to $600\,^{\circ}\text{C}$.

Suggest electronic structures for dinitrogen tetroxide and the other nitrogen-containing molecules formed from it on heating to $600\,^{\circ}\text{C}$. Point out any unusual structural features. (C)

9. Explain the following facts:

(*a*) a solution of ammonium chloride has a slightly acid reaction.

(*b*) a molar solution of ammonium chloride has an osmotic pressure appreciably less than double that of a molar solution of a non-electrolyte.

(*c*) the vapour density of ammonium chloride is a quarter of its molecular weight.

(*d*) when ammonium hydroxide is added to a solution of zinc chloride a white precipitate appears which gradually redissolves. (L)

10. Illustrate from the chemistry of the element nitrogen, its oxides and chlorides, the anomalous character of the first element in a Periodic Group. (O & C)

11. Describe the preparation of samples of (i) potassium nitrite, (ii) ammonium nitrate, (iii) sodamide, starting from potassium nitrate as the only available compound of nitrogen.

What is the action, if any, of dilute hydrochloric acid on the three prepared salts? (C)

25

GROUP VIB: THE OXYGEN GROUP

Group VIB consists of the elements oxygen, sulphur, selenium, tellurium and polonium. All are non-metals except polonium, although tellurium shows some tendency to semi-metallic character. Enough will be said on the last three to justify their inclusion in the Group.

Relationship of Group VIB to the Periodic Table

Group VIB forms the fourth column of the p-block. In consequence, the last three elements have eighteen electrons in their penultimate shell. Elements in Group VIB are more electronegative than the nitrogen Group elements to their left, but less electronegative than the halogens to their right (Fig. 23, p. 72).

The relationship between the A and B families in Group VI is not very close. Group VIA consists of the metals chromium, molybdenum and tungsten. Only chromium will be treated in this book. Its relationship to Group VIB will be considered under chromium, p. 549.

General Group characteristics

Atomic properties of Group VIB elements

Element	Symbol	Atomic no.	Atomic weight	Electronic configuration K	L	M	N	O	P	Group valency $(8-N)$ or N	Maximum valency shown	Other co-valencies
Oxygen	O	8	16.00	2	6	—	—	—	—	2	4	—
Sulphur	S	16	32.06	2	8	6	—	—	—	2, 6	6	4
Selenium	Se	34	78.96	2	8	18	6	—	—	2, 6	6	4
Tellurium	Te	52	127.6	2	8	18	18	6	—	2, 6	6	4
Polonium	Po	84	210.00	2	8	18	32	18	6	2, 6	6	4

Similarities between the members of the Group

The fundamental similarity is that, being in Group VIB they all have six electrons in their valency shells. The elements in the Group (except polonium) can attain the octet in three ways: (1) By gaining two electrons,

463

thus forming bivalent anions X^{2-}. (2) By forming two covalent bonds, two single or one double, e.g.

$$\begin{matrix} H \\ \ \ \ \ \ \searrow O \\ H \nearrow \end{matrix} \quad \text{or} \quad O{=}C{=}O.$$

The elements (except polonium) are therefore non-metals. Valency shown in these compounds is the lower Group valency. (3) By forming univalent ions XH^-. The X^{2-} ion is stable in solid compounds but cannot exist in aqueous solution, e.g. consider the O^{2-} ion. In aqueous solution it immediately extracts a proton H^+ from a water molecule forming two OH^- ions thus,

$$O^{2-} + HOH \to 2OH^-,$$

or
$$\left[:\ddot{O}:\right]^{2-} + HOH \to 2\left[:\ddot{O}:H\right]^-.$$

The singly charged OH^- ion is much more stable than the doubly charged O^{2-} ion. The hydrogen sulphide anion HS^- is formed in a similar way,

$$S^{2-} + HOH \to HS^- + OH^-,$$

but is much less stable than the OH^- ion because of its greater size. Thus the hydrogen sulphide anion is hydrolysed in boiling water forming hydrogen sulphide

$$HS^- + HOH \to H_2S \uparrow + OH^-.$$

HSe^- and HTe^- ions are very unstable.

Compounds formed in all the above ways make up a considerable part of the chemistry of the Group, including as they do oxides, hydroxides, sulphides, selenides, tellurides and many organic compounds.

Allotropy is shown by all the elements although in the case of tellurium it is not well established.

Oxygen and sulphur show similarity by the fact that many compounds of oxygen have analogous compounds in which sulphur takes the place of oxygen, e.g. H_2O, H_2S; CO_2, COS, CS_2; CuO, CuS; SnO_2, SnS_2; Na_2O, Na_2S; $KCNO$, $KCNS$; C_2H_5OH, C_2H_5SH; $(C_2H_5)_2O$, $(C_2H_5)_2S$. Analogous reactions take place,

$$CO_2 + 2NaOH \to H_2O + Na_2CO_3 \quad \text{(sodium carbonate)},$$
$$CS_2 + 2NaSH \to H_2S + Na_2CS_3 \quad \text{(sodium thiocarbonate)}.$$

Differences within the Group

These follow closely the established trends for B families in the Main Groups (pp. 76–7).

Further atomic properties of Group VIB elements

Element	Covalent atomic radius (Å)	Ionic radius of X^{2-} (Å)	Electro-negativity (Allred–Rochow)
Oxygen	0.74	1.40	3.50
Sulphur	1.04	1.84	2.44
Selenium	1.17	1.98	2.48
Tellurium	1.37	2.21	2.01
Polonium	1.52	—	1.76

In passing down the Group there is a change in the nature of the elements in conformity with the general decrease in electronegativity. Oxygen and sulphur are non-metals, selenium and tellurium show semi-metallic character, especially the latter which is a solid with fine silvery metallic lustre, and which has an ionic dioxide, TeO_2, containing Te^{4+} ion (inert pair effect). Polonium is a radioactive metal, half-life 138 days, which resembles lead in being soft, dense and of low melting point. It shows the inert-pair effect to a greater extent than tellurium.

Oxygen stands apart from sulphur and the other members of the Group, which show a fairly strong resemblance to each other, with a gradual trend from sulphur to polonium.

Differences between oxygen and sulphur

(1) The most important is that almost the only covalency shown by oxygen is 2 (although its maximum is 4) whereas sulphur often shows covalencies of 4 and 6 (its maximum), by using some of the d orbitals in its M shell. As a result, a large part of the chemistry of sulphur has no parallel in that of oxygen, i.e. whenever sulphur has valencies of 4 or 6.

(2) Oxygen has a much smaller atomic radius than sulphur and therefore a much higher electronegativity, one result being the ability of oxygen to form hydrogen bonds (p. 107–8). The most important example is water, which is a unique compound of vast importance in all branches of chemistry including biochemistry (p. 291). Sulphur does not form hydrogen bonds.

The effect of the electronegativity difference between oxygen and sulphur on the properties of corresponding compounds will be considered later.

(3) Oxygen forms stable double or multiple covalent bonds with itself and other elements more readily than sulphur; e.g. compare the molecules O_2 and S_8 (pp. 468–9).

(4) Related to (3) is the fact that sulphur has a much stronger tendency than oxygen to form chains of atoms with itself, e.g. in its molecule, in plastic sulphur, and in polysulphides and thionic acids. The longest oxygen chain contains two atoms —O—O— as in H_2O_2 but is unstable. The immediate reason for this is that the —O—O— bond energy, 138 kJ mol^{-1} is much less than that of —S—S—, 251 kJ mol^{-1}, and so an —S—S— bond is more likely to be formed than an —O—O— one, and to be more stable when formed. This difference is opposite to that in Group IVB whose first member, carbon, has an extraordinary capacity for forming chains, while the second, silicon, has it in a very small degree.

(5) When oxygen has formed two covalent bonds as in water (and many organic compounds) it may donate one of its lone pairs to an electron-acceptor atom or ion. The most important case of this is the formation of the hydroxonium ion H_3O^+ thus,

Oxygen has a covalency of 3 in this ion. Maximum covalency of 4 is very rare. One example is in basic beryllium acetate.

(6) All cations in aqueous solution, and in hydrated crystals, are hydrated because the oxygen atom in the water molecule is sufficiently negatively charged to form a stable link with cations.

Note. Four important related chemical species mentioned above are,

$$O^{2-}, \quad OH^-, \quad H_2O, \quad H_3O^+.$$

The elements

Occurrence

Oxygen accounts for about 50 % of the combined weight of the lithosphere, hydrosphere and atmosphere. It is the most widely distributed and by far the most abundant of the elements. It occurs free in the atmosphere (23 % by weight, 21 % by volume); and, in the hydrosphere and lithosphere, combined as oxides, mainly water, silica, alumina, iron oxides and titanium(IV) oxide; oxo-salts, silicates, aluminosilicates, carbonates and sulphates of sodium, potassium, calcium, iron, magnesium and barium.

Sulphur (0.05 % of the lithosphere) occurs free, and in combination mainly as sulphides and sulphates. The sulphides iron pyrites FeS_2, zinc blende ZnS, galena PbS, copper pyrites $CuFeS_2$, are of great economic importance, the first for its sulphur (p. 485), the others as the most important ores of zinc, lead and copper. Sulphates include *barytes*, $BaSO_4$, gypsum,

$$CaSO_4 \cdot 2H_2O,$$

anhydrite, $CaSO_4$, and the soluble sulphate Epsom salt, $MgSO_4 \cdot 7H_2O$.

Isolation

Oxygen is made on the large scale in enormous quantities by the fractional distillation of liquid air. The nitrogen boils out of the liquid at a lower temperature than oxygen. The liquid remaining in the still is almost pure oxygen. It is stored as a liquid in insulated tanks, or gasified and compressed into steel cylinders.

In the laboratory, oxygen is usually prepared by heating a mixture of potassium chlorate with manganese(IV) oxide as a catalyst.

Other methods include electrolysis of water; action of water on sodium peroxide; action of hydrogen peroxide on manganese(IV) oxide or acidified potassium permanganate solution; and one of great historical interest in connection with Davy's work on chlorine, the displacement of oxygen by chlorine, by heating calcium oxide to redness in chlorine,

$$2CaO + 2Cl_2 \rightarrow 2CaCl_2 + O_2.$$

This reaction is explained by the fact that the free energy (p. 184) of $CaCl_2$ is more negative than that of CaO at 700 °C and below.

Sulphur in the free state is found in large quantities underground in Louisiana and Texas. Its extraction is therefore a mining operation; but ordinary mining is not practicable because of a layer of quicksands between the sulphur and the surface. The Frasch method used is somewhat similar to that used for oil: a hole about 1 ft in diameter is drilled down to the sulphur, and lengths of piping consisting of three concentric pipes are lowered down the drill-hole. Superheated water, 155 °C, is forced down the outer annular space in the piping, compressed air forced down the inner pipe, and a frothy mixture of molten sulphur and air, with some water, is forced up to the surface through the middle annular space. The froth is much less dense than liquid sulphur, hence easier to push up to the surface. This is the most important source of sulphur, producing about 70 % of the world's needs. Free sulphur is also found in Sicily. The sulphur-bearing rock contains about 15–20 % free sulphur. The rock is stacked in brick kilns, and ignited at the top. The heat produced melts the sulphur lower down, which runs into troughs.

Large quantities of sulphur are produced from the natural gas found at Lacq in the south of France. The gas, a mixture mainly of methane and ethane, also contains about 15 % of hydrogen sulphide which is removed and oxidised to sulphur.

Further large quantities of sulphur are recovered from Town gas (made from oil or coal) in the same way as above. Spent oxide from gas works has already been mentioned; so also has iron pyrites (p. 467).

Physical properties of oxygen and sulphur

A striking difference is that oxygen is a gas at ordinary temperatures (melting point of solid oxygen is -219 °C), sulphur a solid (melting point 113 °C). This is because their molecules have very different structures O_2 and S_8 (see pp. 130–1). Oxygen and sulphur are very slightly soluble in water but readily soluble in organic solvents.

Allotropy

Oxygen has two allotropes, oxygen itself and ozone, both of which are gases at ordinary temperatures. The allotropy of sulphur is complex.

Allotropy of oxygen. (1) *Oxygen* is paramagnetic (p. 527), i.e. when liquid it is attracted quite strongly by a magnet. Oxygen must therefore have unpaired electrons in its molecule, since paramagnetism is always associated with this kind of electronic structure. Its structure cannot be $\overset{\times}{\underset{\times}{\times}}\!O\!\overset{\times}{\underset{\times}{\times}}\!:\!\overset{\bullet\bullet}{\underset{\bullet\bullet}{O}}\!:$ since all the electrons are paired. Using the valency bond method, its formula is shown as a resonance hybrid (p. 96) between the two forms $:\!\overset{\bullet\bullet}{\underset{\bullet\bullet}{O}}\!:\!\overset{\times\times}{O}\!\overset{\times}{}$ and $:\!\overset{\bullet\bullet}{O}\!:\!\overset{\bullet\bullet}{\underset{\times\times}{O}}\!\overset{\times}{}$. The result may be written as $:\!O\!\overset{\times\times}{\underset{\times}{\vdots}}\!O\!\overset{\times}{}$ showing the molecule to be held together by one normal covalent bond plus two 3-electron bonds, the strength of the bonding being roughly equivalent to an ordinary double bond. The molecular orbital method (p. 110) gives a neater solution.

(2) *Ozone* has a relative density of 24 (Dumas's method). Its molecular formula is therefore O_3. The molecule is V-shaped, with an inter-bond angle of about 117°. Its structure is a resonance hybrid mainly of two forms

and

The central oxygen atom is tricovalent.

One double bond, one single, and one lone pair, make up three sets of electrons. The molecule is therefore planar, the bond angle being slightly less than 120° because of the stronger repulsion of the lone pair.

Preparation of ozone. Oxygen is converted into ozone by passing a silent electrical discharge through a slow stream of oxygen in the apparatus shown in Fig. 129. The electrical energy causes dissociation of some oxygen molecules into atoms, $O_2 \rightarrow 2O$; some of the atoms then combine with oxygen molecules to form ozone $O + O_2 \rightarrow O_3$. The overall action is

$$3O_2 \rightleftharpoons 2O_3; \Delta H \text{ positive.}$$

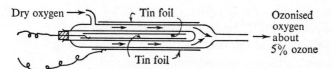

Fig. 129. Ozoniser.

Allotropy of sulphur. In the solid phase there are four main polymorphs (solid allotropes) of sulphur, three crystalline, one amorphous.

Crystalline. Orthorhombic sulphur, consisting of S_8 molecules; monoclinic sulphur consisting of S_8 molecules; purple sulphur consisting of S_2 molecules.

Amorphous. Plastic, fibrous or amorphous sulphur, a super-cooled liquid, containing long chains of sulphur atoms which are not arranged in a regular manner with respect to each other.

(1) *Orthorhombic sulphur.* Stable at room temperature and up to 96 °C, and consists of S_8 molecules in which eight sulphur atoms are covalently bound into puckered, saw-tooth rings, Fig. 131. The molecules, being

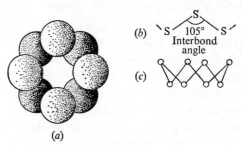

Fig. 130. Crystal of orthorhombic sulphur.

Fig. 131. Sulphur molecule S_8. (*a*) Plan view, atoms to scale; (*b*) side elevation; (*c*) picture view S_8 framework (coronet shaped).

469

non-polar, are packed together by weak intermolecular forces (van der Waals'). Orthorhombic sulphur melts therefore at a low temperature, 113 °C, and, because the molecules are large as well as non-polar, is insoluble in water and readily soluble in organic solvents, e.g. carbon disulphide and toluene. The S_8 ring has an interbond angle of 105° which is close to the tetrahedral angle ($109\frac{1}{2}°$), the reduction being caused by the repulsion of two lone pairs in each atom (Fig. 75, p. 131).

A similarly shaped molecule with a saw-tooth ring is cyclo-octane, C_8H_{16}.

(2) *Monoclinic (prismatic) sulphur*. Stable from 96 °C to its melting point at 119° C. The crystals (molecular), like those of the orthorhombic form consist of S_8 molecules, but their arrangement in the crystal is not known. Their solubility is very similar to that of orthorhombic sulphur.

Fig. 132. Crystal of monoclinic sulphur.

Crystals of orthorhombic sulphur are made by dissolving powdered roll-sulphur in carbon disulphide, filtering, and allowing the solution to evaporate slowly (see Fig. 130). Monoclinic crystals are made by melting roll sulphur, cooling, piercing the crust and pouring out the remaining liquid. When the crust is cut out, needle-shaped crystals (Fig. 132) are found on the underside and in the basin. Monoclinic sulphur reverts to orthorhombic below 96 °C.

$$\text{orthorhombic} \overset{96°}{\rightleftharpoons} \text{monoclinic.}$$

This type of allotropy is called *enantiotropy*, because the changes are reversed by change of temperature.

(3) *Purple sulphur*. When sulphur vapour at 500 °C and 1 *mmHg pressure*, consisting mainly of S_2 molecules, is chilled suddenly to the temperature of liquid nitrogen (-195 °C) there is formed a purple, solid paramagnetic allotrope consisting of S_2 molecules and therefore analogous to O_2 molecules. It is very unstable at higher temperatures, changing to a mixture of crystalline and amorphous forms.

(4) *Plastic sulphur* is made by melting roll sulphur, heating the liquid to a temperature near to its boiling point, then pouring it into cold water. The resulting solid, plastic sulphur, is transparent and of a colour varying from amber to rich brown. The solid has little elasticity, but can be kneaded like putty, and pulled into very long thin fibres in a way similar to glass softened by strong heating. Also like glass it is a highly viscous supercooled liquid which has been shown to consist of long chains each containing thousands of sulphur atoms arranged in spirals, with eight

atoms per turn. Insoluble in all liquids including carbon disulphide, it reverts gradually to orthorhombic sulphur.

Dynamic equilibrium in liquid sulphur. Sulphur melts between 113 and 119 °C (depending on the rate of heating) to form an amber-coloured mobile liquid. On further heating, the colour darkens and viscosity increases until, at about 190 °C, the liquid is dark red-brown, then quite suddenly becomes so viscous that it will not pour. The colour deepens with further heating but the viscosity decreases until at 445 °C the liquid boils giving a bromine-coloured vapour, which condenses on the cooler upper parts of the vessel to a powdery pale yellow solid called *flowers of sulphur*.

There is no agreed explanation of all these changes, but the simplest hypothesis and the one most likely to be correct is that a dynamic equilibrium exists between S_8 molecules, formed when the liquid melts, and spiral chains of sulphur atoms of many different lengths,

$$S_8 \rightleftharpoons (S)_n.$$

At the melting point, the liquid consists mainly of S_8 molecules. The liquid is mobile because spheroidal S_8 molecules can easily roll past each other. As vibrational energy of the atoms in the molecule increases with rise in temperature, S_8 rings break forming very chemically active, free radicals, which combine to form long-chain *high polymers*. At 190 °C the liquid is thought to consist mainly of very long chains which become tangled and therefore find greater difficulty in moving past each other, hence the great increase in viscosity. When this liquid is cooled suddenly, the equilibrium is fixed and plastic sulphur formed. At higher temperatures, the chains split up and gradually reform S_8 molecules until at boiling point, the liquid again consists mainly of S_8 molecules which then break away into the vapour phase.

Dynamic equilibrium in the vapour phase. As the temperature of the vapour is increased, the S_8 molecules split up into S_2 molecules. This change is complete at about 1000 °C and is accompanied by a deepening of the colour to dark red. As heating continues, the S_2 molecules begin to dissociate into sulphur atoms and the colour lightens to yellow. Dissociation is complete at about 2000 °C. The processes take place in reverse order on cooling,

$$\underset{\text{Gas}}{S_8} \underset{\text{Cool}}{\overset{\text{Heat}}{\rightleftharpoons}} 4S_2 \underset{\text{Cool}}{\overset{\text{Heat}}{\rightleftharpoons}} 8S \quad \text{(simplified)}.$$

The liquid and vapour-phase changes are examples of *dynamic allotropy*.

Note. Orthorhombic, monoclinic and molten sulphur up to 150 °C, and sulphur vapour at boiling point all consist of S_8 ring molecules.

Chemical properties of oxygen and sulphur

Note. The chemical properties of orthorhombic and monoclinic sulphur are essentially the same. It is inconvenient to use the formula S_8 for sulphur except on special occasions.

1. General. Both elements are fairly reactive. The apparent lack of action of oxygen at room temperature on metals other than those of Groups I A and II A is not complete. Some immediate reaction does take place but is stopped or greatly slowed down by the formation of a very thin film of the oxide of the metal. For substantial action heat is required to supply the activation energy needed to break or loosen the bonds of the oxygen molecule. The same is true for sulphur. Oxygen and sulphur are less reactive than the halogens, which have relatively small activation energies.

2. Air. Sulphur does not react at ordinary temperatures, but when heated in air it burns with a fine blue flame to form sulphur dioxide, heat being liberated. Traces of sulphur trioxide are formed.

3. Water, dilute acids. Neither element reacts with water or dilute acids.

4. Concentrated sulphuric acid and concentrated nitric acid. No reaction with oxygen. Both acids oxidise sulphur thus,

$$S + 6HNO_3 \rightarrow H_2SO_4 + 6NO_2 + 2H_2O,$$
$$S + 2H_2SO_4 \rightarrow 2H_2O + 3SO_2.$$

5. Alkalis. No action with oxygen. Sulphur forms a mixture of sulphide, sulphite, polysulphide, and thiosulphate (p. 226).

6. Action with other elements. Oxygen and sulphur combine readily with most elements, on gentle or moderate heating, to form oxides and sulphides respectively. When the action has been started no further heating is needed; the reaction proceeding with increased speed because of the heat evolved. Many elements burn brilliantly in oxygen. Phosphorus reacts with oxygen in the cold. Nitrogen combines with oxygen in the electric arc forming nitrogen monoxide.

7. Action with compounds. Many compounds burn when heated in oxygen. Nitrogen monoxide is oxidised by oxygen in the cold to give nitrogen dioxide.

Combustion of either elements or compounds in air or oxygen is one of the most important of all chemical reactions, i.e. oxygen is a very powerful oxidising agent. The reactions associated with rusting and respiration are slow forms of combustion of universal importance. The drying and hardening of paints involve oxidation of the linseed oil in them. Alkaline pyrogallol reacts with oxygen in the cold, and is used in gas analysis to remove oxygen from gaseous mixtures. The usual test for oxygen is its power to relight a glowing wooden splint; dinitrogen oxide behaves similarly.

Uses of oxygen and sulphur

Oxygen. (1) In oxy-acetylene and oxy-hydrogen blow-pipe flames for cutting and welding steel.

(2) By mountaineers, divers, airmen, firemen and in the treatment of diseases such as pneumonia and the resuscitation of persons apparently drowned or asphyxiated.

(3) Liquid oxygen is used in rocket fuels.

(4) In the high-pressure gasification of coal.

(5) Oxygen is used in enormous quantities in steel-making (p. 562).

Sulphur. Its chief use is in the manufacture of sulphuric acid. Other uses are in the manufacture of sulphur dioxide, carbon disulphide, sodium thiosulphate, sulphites for bleaching wood-pulp and removing lignum from it, gunpowder, matches, ointments, insecticides, plant sprays, and in vulcanising rubber.

Properties and uses of ozone. Ozone is a very pale blue gas with a characteristic smell. It liquefies at −112 °C giving a dark blue liquid (dangerous since it explodes readily with great violence). Ozone is about fifteen times as soluble in water as oxygen.

Its chemical properties are very different from those of oxygen, mainly because it is an endothermic compound, therefore unstable except at high temperatures and one of the most powerful oxidising agents known. It decomposes slowly at room temperature but rapidly when warmed and by the action of a catalyst. As a rule substantial reaction of oxygen with elements and compounds takes place at moderately high temperatures. Ozone, on the other hand, reacts to completion or nearly so with many substances at ordinary temperature. Ozone oxidises lead(II) sulphide to lead sulphate, hydrogen sulphide to sulphuric acid, aqueous potassium iodide solution to iodine, and most metals to their oxides. In these reactions only one atom of the ozone molecule is used for oxidation. Oxygen is therefore liberated,

$$O_3 + 2I^- + H_2O \rightarrow I_2 + 2OH^- + O_2 \quad \text{(quantitative: used for}$$
$$\text{determination of ozone).}$$

In some cases the whole molecule is used and no oxygen liberated, e.g. sulphur dioxide oxidised to sulphur trioxide, and many organic compounds containing a double bond, such as ethylene which forms an ozonide, turpentine which absorbs ozone quantitatively and rubber which deteriorates badly in the process. Ozone also bleaches many dyes by oxidation. Common tests for ozone are its smell, and the facts that it turns starch/potassium iodide blue, blackens silver and causes mercury to 'tail' because of the formation of oxide on its surface. Ozone oxidises hydrogen peroxide,

$$H_2O_2 + O_3 \rightarrow H_2O + 2O_2 \uparrow.$$

In this reaction the O_2^{2-} ion has been oxidised to O_2 by loss of electrons.

Ozone is used as a bleaching agent for oils and paper pulp. It kills micro-organisms and is therefore used for purifying and deodorising air and for sterilising drinking water.

Compounds of oxygen and sulphur

Oxygen has a valency of 2 in almost all its compounds. The Group relationship between oxygen and sulphur (selenium and tellurium) can therefore be shown only for this valency state.

Hydrides

Both water and hydrogen sulphide are covalent compounds. The most surprising thing about them is that water (molecular weight 18) is a liquid at room temperature while hydrogen sulphide (molecular weight 34) is a gas. This is because of hydrogen bonding in water (p. 267). A comparison of the two is given there.

Occurrence. Water is widespread. Hydrogen sulphide occurs in volcanic gases and in some mineral springs. It is produced during the putrefaction or organic matter containing sulphur.

Preparation. By the general methods for making hydrides,

(1) $$H_2 + S \xrightarrow{\text{Heat}} H_2S,$$

(2) $$FeS + 2HCl \rightarrow FeCl_2 + H_2S.$$

When reaction (2) is used, hydrogen from the action of acid on iron in the iron(II) sulphide is always present. Pure hydrogen sulphide is made by passing hydrogen and sulphur vapour over finely divided nickel at 450 °C.

Physical properties. Hydrogen sulphide has a characteristic smell of bad eggs and is very poisonous. For structure and bonding, see p. 266.

Chemical properties. The single-bond energies of water and hydrogen sulphide are 460 and 339 kJ mol^{-1} respectively. As a result water is very stable and hydrogen sulphide unstable. (When passed through a red-hot tube it is decomposed into its elements.) Water does not burn, being already oxidised to a stable state. Hydrogen sulphide burns readily (low ignition temperature) with a flame the colour of burning sulphur. In excess air the products are water and sulphur dioxide. Sulphur is deposited in a limited supply of air.

Acidity. Water is neutral but amphoteric; hydrogen sulphide in aqueous solution is a weak dibasic acid,

$$H_2O + H_2O \rightleftharpoons H_3O^+ + OH^-, \quad K_1 = 10^{-15};$$
$$H_2O + H_2S \rightleftharpoons H_3O^+ + HS^-, \quad K_1 = 10^{-7},$$

For the complete ionisation of hydrogen sulphide,

$$H_2O + HS^- \rightleftharpoons H_3O^+ + S^{2-}, \quad K_2 = 10^{-14}.$$

It is at first sight surprising that acidity increases from water to hydrogen sulphide. This trend is continued down the whole Group. For explanation, see pp. 269–70.

Hydrogen sulphide reacts with aqueous alkalis to form sulphides and hydrogen sulphides, e.g. Na_2S, $NaHS$,

$$H_2S + 2OH^- \rightleftharpoons S^{2-} + 2H_2O; \quad H_2S + OH^- \to HS^- + H_2O.$$

Oxidation and reduction. Water can act as an oxidising agent by taking electrons, i.e. it oxidises other substances and in the process the water is itself reduced, the product being hydrogen,

$$H^+ \text{ (from water)} + e \xrightarrow{\text{reduction}} \tfrac{1}{2}H_2,$$

or

$$H_2O + e \xrightarrow{\text{reduction}} \tfrac{1}{2}H_2 + OH^-.$$

The half-reaction equations and redox potentials (p. 157) are,

in neutral solution, non-standard electrode potentials,

(a) $H^+(10^{-7}M) + e \underset{\text{oxidation}}{\overset{\text{reduction}}{\rightleftharpoons}} \tfrac{1}{2}H_2,$ $\qquad E = -0.41$ V,

or (b) $H_2O + e \rightleftharpoons \tfrac{1}{2}H_2 + OH^- (10^{-7}M),$ $\qquad E = -0.41$ V.

The forward action is reduction of the oxidising agent. Water will oxidise any reducing agent with a greater negative redox potential than its own, e.g.

$$Na \xrightarrow{\text{oxidation}} Na^+ + e, \qquad E^\ominus = -2.71 \text{ V}$$

$$H^+(10^{-7}\text{M}) + e \xrightarrow{\text{reduction}} \tfrac{1}{2}H_2, \qquad E = -0.41 \text{ V}$$

adding $\qquad Na + H^+ \xrightarrow{\text{redox}} Na^+ + \tfrac{1}{2}H_2.$

As H^+ ions are removed from the water, an equivalent quantity of OH^- ions is produced. This is shown in equation (*b*), p. 475.

Water can act as a reducing agent by giving electrons, the product being oxygen. The half-reaction equation and redox potential in neutral solution are

$$H_2O \xrightarrow{\text{oxidation}} \tfrac{1}{2}O_2 + 2H^+(10^{-7}\text{M}) + 2e, \qquad E = +0.81 \text{ V}.$$

Because of this high positive value for water, strong oxidising agents are needed to oxidise water to oxygen.

Hydrogen sulphide is a much stronger reducing agent than water. This agrees with its lower bond energy and lower thermal stability (p. 475). In acid solution

$$H_2S \xrightarrow{\text{oxidation}} S + 2H^+(\text{M}) + 2e, \quad E = +0.14 \text{ V}$$

$$\tfrac{1}{2}O_2 + 2H^+(\text{M}) + 2e \xrightarrow{\text{reduction}} H_2O, \qquad E = +1.23 \text{ V}$$

$$H_2S + \tfrac{1}{2}O_2 \xrightarrow{\text{redox}} H_2O + S.$$

Hydrogen sulphide in aqueous solution is slowly oxidised by oxygen from the air to give a milky precipitate of sulphur, which is its usual oxidation product, although with powerful oxidising agents, sulphuric acid is formed,

$$H_2S + 2O_2 \rightarrow H_2SO_4.$$

Common reactions of hydrogen sulphide as a reducing agent are,

Substance reduced	
Moist sulphur dioxide	$SO_2 + 2H_2S \rightarrow 2H_2O + 3S \downarrow$
Halogens in aqueous solution	$Cl_2 + H_2S \rightarrow 2HCl + S \downarrow$
Nitric acid	$2HNO_3 + H_2S \rightarrow 2H_2O + 2NO_2 + S \downarrow$
Concentrated sulphuric acid	$H_2SO_4 + H_2S \rightarrow SO_2 + 2H_2O + S \downarrow$
Hydrogen peroxide solution	$H_2O_2 + H_2S \rightarrow 2H_2O + S \downarrow$
Iron(III) chloride solution	$2Fe^{3+} + H_2S \rightarrow 2Fe^{2+} + 2H^+ + S \downarrow$
Dichromate in acid solution	$Cr_2O_7{}^{2-} + 8H^+ + 3H_2S \rightarrow 2Cr^{3+} + 7H_2O + 3S \downarrow$
	Orange $\qquad\qquad$ Green
Permanganates in acid solution	$2MnO_4{}^- + 6H^+ + 5H_2S \rightarrow 2Mn^{2+} + 8H_2O + 5S \downarrow$
	Purple $\qquad\qquad$ Colourless

The best way to build up balanced ionic equations is by using half-reactions as shown on p. 163.

Gaseous hydrogen sulphide reacts slowly at room temperature with many metals, e.g. silver and copper, forming a film of sulphide which stops the reaction.

When hydrogen sulphide is passed into aqueous solutions of salts, characteristic precipitates of sulphides of the metals are often produced (pp. 240–3).

Test for hydrogen sulphide. (1) Smell, (2) it turns moist lead(II) acetate paper to silvery black (PbS).

Molecular formula of hydrogen sulphide. Its vapour density is 17, hence molecular weight 34. Since the atomic weight of sulphur is 32 its formula must be H_2S. This is confirmed by the fact that when one volume of hydrogen sulphide is heated with metallic copper, the sulphur is removed as copper(I) sulphide and one volume of hydrogen remains.

Oxides and sulphides. These are derivatives of water and hydrogen sulphide. Sulphides and hydrogen sulphides of the metals are salts of hydrogen sulphide gas, hydrosulphuric acid. In a limited sense, oxides and hydroxides of the metals are salts of water. (For oxides, see pp. 249–53; for sulphides, pp. 240–6).

Hydrogen peroxide and hydrogen persulphide. For hydrogen peroxide, see p. 295. Hydrogen persulphide, H_2S_2, is analogous to hydrogen peroxide. Its molecule H_2S_2 is the same shape as H_2O_2. The persulphide ion $\left[:\ddot{S}{-}\ddot{S}: \right]^{2-}$ or $S_2{}^{2-}$ is analogous to the peroxide ion in $O_2{}^{2-}$. Iron pyrites FeS_2 is iron(II) persulphide.

Halides

Some of the halides of oxygen are treated in Group VIIB as oxides of the halogens. Their properties are very different from those of the halides of sulphur.

Sulphur hexafluoride, SF_6, prepared by direct combination of the elements, is a colourless gas, chemically inert (unaffected by fused KOH), because in it the maximum covalency of sulphur is reached, the molecule then being fully saturated. The molecule is octahedral.

Disulphur dichloride, S_2Cl_2 (sulphur monochloride), is prepared by passing dry chlorine over molten sulphur in a retort, S_2Cl_2 being collected in a cooled receiver. It is an amber, unpleasant smelling liquid, slowly hydrolysed by water,

$$2S_2Cl_2 + 3H_2O \rightarrow 4HCl + H_2SO_3 + 3S \downarrow ,$$

similar in structure to H_2O_2 (p. 296). Disulphur dichloride is used in vulcanising rubber.

Oxides and oxo-acids of sulphur

Sulphur forms six oxides, two of which are very important, namely, sulphur dioxide and sulphur trioxide.

Sulphur dioxide, SO_2

Sulphur dioxide occurs in volcanic gases and in the products of combustion of coal or coke.

Preparation. (1) By burning sulphur in air or oxygen. Some sulphur trioxide is also formed.

(2) By reducing hot concentrated sulphuric acid with a metal. Many metals bring this about but copper is usually used,

$$Cu + 2H_2SO_4 \rightarrow CuSO_4 + 2H_2O + SO_2 \uparrow .$$

The reaction is more complex than this: the black residue contains copper(I) and copper(II) sulphides as well as anhydrous copper(II) sulphate.

(3) By heating a sulphite (usually sodium sulphite crystals) or hydrogen sulphite with dilute hydrochloric or dilute sulphuric acid.

For its production on an industrial scale see p. 485–6.

Physical properties. It is a colourless poisonous gas with the acrid choking smell of burning sulphur; more than twice as dense as air, it is collected by upward displacement of air. Because it is easily liquefied (-10 °C) it is conveniently stored under pressure (3 atmospheres) in canisters; sulphur dioxide is very soluble in water (see below).

Molecular formula. Sulphur burns in oxygen to produce an equal volume of sulphur dioxide. Its formula is therefore S_xO_2. Vapour density is found to be 32, therefore molecular weight is 64. Since atomic weight of sulphur is 32, the molecular formula is SO_2.

Structure of the molecule. By experiment the molecule is found to be V-shaped, with a bond angle of 120°, which explains why the molecule has a dipole moment. The structure indicates sp^2 hybridisation (p. 142) of the sulphur atom with two hybrid orbitals used to form bonds with the oxygen atoms, and the third orbital occupied by a lone pair. This state is shown below at (*a*) and accounts for four electrons of the S atom.

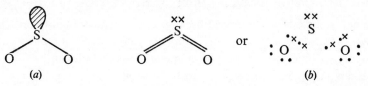

(*a*)   (*b*)

Experiment shows also that the S—O bond lengths are identical and considerably shorter than S—O single bonds. They are in fact double bonds. The final structure is shown on the right of diagram (*a*). The second bond in each double bond is a π bond. The four electrons in the two π bonds (two from S and one from each O are delocalised (see shapes of covalent molecules, p. 142)) forming electron clouds above and below the three atoms of the molecule. The sulphur atom has ten electrons in its outer shell; each oxygen atom has eight (diagram (*b*)). It is possible that the lone pairs on the oxygen atoms form π bonds to some extent with the sulphur atom, being accommodated in the vacant $3d$ orbitals of the sulphur atom. The SO_2 molecule exists in the gaseous phase and also in solid sulphur dioxide (molecular crystals).

Further evidence of the double bonds in SO_2 is shown in that it forms addition compounds quite readily as in the following reactions, the first of which is of great importance as it is the basis for the contact process for the manufacture of sulphuric acid (pp. 486–7),

$$2SO_2 + O_2 \rightleftharpoons 2SO_3,$$
$$SO_2 + Cl_2 \rightarrow SO_2Cl_2 \quad \text{(sulphuryl chloride)},$$
$$SO_2 + PbO_2 \rightarrow PbSO_4,$$
$$SO_2 + Na_2O_2 \rightarrow Na_2SO_4.$$

In each of these reactions the sulphur dioxide is acting as a reducing agent (oxidation number of sulphur increasing from 4 to 6).

Further chemical properties. (1) Sulphur dioxide does not burn nor support combustion except of burning metals, e.g. sodium and magnesium

$$2Mg + SO_2 \rightarrow 2MgO + S.$$

(2) It is very soluble in water but much less so than ammonia and hydrogen chloride. The solution contains sulphurous acid, H_2SO_3 (p. 480) which is oxidised very slowly by atmospheric oxygen to H_2SO_4. Sulphur dioxide is absorbed by aqueous alkalis, reacting to form sulphites and

hydrogen sulphites. Sulphur dioxide turns lime water milky; with excess SO_2 the liquid goes clear again (cf. CO_2),

$$Ca(OH)_2 + SO_2 \rightarrow CaSO_3 \downarrow + H_2O; \quad CaSO_3 + H_2SO_3 \rightarrow Ca(HSO_3)_2.$$

The milky stage is easily missed because of the great solubility of SO_2 in water and also because calcium sulphite is sufficiently soluble to show a tendency to supersaturation. The course of the reaction can be followed by adding a piece of litmus paper to the lime water.

(3) Moist sulphur dioxide (i.e. sulphurous acid) is a strong reducing agent and bleaching agent (see p. 481–2). It also acts as an oxidising agent with more powerful reducing agents, e.g. burning magnesium (see above) and with moist hydrogen sulphide,

$$2H_2S + SO_2 \rightarrow 2H_2O + 3S \downarrow .$$

Tests for sulphur dioxide. (1) Smell; (2) it decolorises moist potassium permanganate paper; (3) it turns moist potassium dichromate paper from orange to green.

Uses. Large quantities are used in the manufacture of sulphuric acid, sulphurous acid and sulphites, e.g. when passed in excess into a suspension of calcium hydroxide in water a solution of calcium hydrogen sulphite is formed, which is used in the manufacture of paper from wood pulp. The solution dissolves the lignin in the wood, leaving cellulose which is made into paper. Sulphur dioxide is a bleaching agent for straw, wool, silk, flour and sugar (materials for which chlorine is unsuitable) bleaching by reduction. It kills fungi and bacteria and so is used in preserving fruits. It is used as a refrigerant.

Sulphurous acid, H_2SO_3

Preparation. It is formed when sulphur dioxide dissolves in water. Like carbonic acid, it exists only in aqueous solution. Attempts to isolate it by removal of water from the solution result in complete decomposition of the acid with evolution of sulphur dioxide. It is a fairly weak dibasic acid (p. 259),

$$H_2SO_3 \rightleftharpoons H^+ + HSO_3^-, \quad K_1 = 1.5 \times 10^{-2};$$
$$HSO_3^- \rightleftharpoons H^+ + SO_3^{2-}, \quad K_2 = 1 \times 10^{-7}.$$

These dissociation constants show that the hydrogen ions are produced almost entirely by the first ionic dissociation and that the concentration of HSO_3^- ions in the equilibrium mixture is very much greater than that of SO_3^{2-} ions.

Structure of sulphurous acid and the sulphite ion, $SO_3{}^{2-}$. H_2SO_3 is usually shown as in the diagram, (a) where it is pyramidal; but some evidence supports the tetrahedral structure in (b). In (a) the sulphur atom has a lone pair of electrons and a total of ten electrons in its external shell; in (b) it has no lone pair, but has twelve electrons in its external shell (its maximum covalency). It is often useful to write H_2SO_3 as $SO(OH)_2$, a simplification of formula (a).

$$(a) \qquad\qquad (b)$$

The sulphite ion has a pyramidal structure (very similar to the (a) structure of H_2SO_3), in which all the S—O bonds are of equal length and all are intermediate in character between single and double bonds, but nearer to double bonds. A first approximation to the structure is given in the diagram below. The ion contains twenty-six electrons in the valency

shells: six from each of the atoms, plus two taken from the hydrogen atoms when the H^+ ions split off. The pyramidal structure (with a tetrahedral disposition of each of its four parts) results from sp^3 hybridisation of the S atom: three σ bonds are formed with the oxygen atoms, the fourth orbital being occupied by a lone pair. So far five of the sulphur atom's valency electrons have been accounted for. The sixth forms a delocalised π bond (broken line) with an electron from an oxygen atom. The electron left behind on the other two oxygen atoms by the hydrogen atoms are shown as giving each of the atoms a single negative charge. The electron of the π bond should be thought of as distributed over the whole ion, and the two negative ionic charges as distributed over all the oxygen atoms and to a lesser extent the sulphur atom, not localised as the diagram shows.

Chemical properties. The following reactions show the sulphite ion or sulphurous acid, acting as a reducing agent. In these the sulphite ion is oxidised to the sulphate ion,

$$SO_3{}^{2-} + H_2O \rightarrow SO_4{}^{2-} + 2H^+ + 2e.$$

Substance reduced

Halogens $\qquad$ $Cl_2 + H_2O + SO_3^{2-} \rightarrow 2Cl^- + 2H^+ + SO_4^{2-}$

Hydrogen peroxide solution $\qquad$ $H_2O_2 + SO_3^{2-} \rightarrow H_2O + SO_4^{2-}$

Iron(III) chloride solution $\qquad$ $2Fe^{3+} + H_2O + SO_3^{2-} \rightarrow 2Fe^{2+} + 2H^+ + SO_4^{2-}$

Dichromate in acid solution $\quad Cr_2O_7^{2-} + 8H^+ + 3SO_3^{2-} \rightarrow 2Cr^{3+} + 3SO_4^{2-} + 4H_2O$

Permanganate in acid $\qquad 2MnO_4^- + 6H^+ + 5SO_3^{2-} \rightarrow 2Mn^{2+} + 5SO_4^{2-} + 3H_2O$
solution

Derivates of sulphurous acid

Sulphites and hydrogen sulphites (pp. 240–5).

Thionyl chloride, SOCl₂, is the acid chloride of sulphurous acid (p. 260).

Preparation. (1) By passing sulphur dioxide over phosphorus penta-chloride,

$$PCl_5 + SO_2 \rightarrow POCl_3 + SOCl_2.$$

(2) By heating a mixture of phosphorus pentachloride and a sulphite,

$$2PCl_5 + Na_2SO_3 \rightarrow 2NaCl + 2POCl_3 + SOCl_2.$$

In both methods the thionyl chloride (boiling point 78 °C) is separated from the phosphorus oxychloride (boiling point 107 °C) by fractional distillation.

Structure. The SOCl₂ molecule has a pyramidal structure.

Properties. Thionyl chloride is a colourless liquid which fumes in moist air because of hydrolysis to hydrogen chloride (and sulphur dioxide). It is rapidly hydrolysed by water in the same way,

$$SOCl_2 + H_2O \rightarrow 2HCl + SO_2.$$

It is used in organic chemistry to replace hydroxyl groups by chlorine atoms, e.g. the preparation of alkyl chlorides and acid chlorides,

$$C_2H_5OH + SOCl_2 \rightarrow C_2H_5Cl + SO_2 \uparrow + HCl \uparrow,$$
$$CH_3 . COOH + SOCl_2 \rightarrow CH_3 . COCl + SO_2 \uparrow + HCl \uparrow.$$

The required product is easily purified because the other products are evolved as gases. It is also used in the preparation of anhydrous metal chlorides from the hydrated chlorides because it reacts with and removes the water of crystallisation according to the equation given above.

Sulphur trioxide, SO_3

Preparation. (1) Direct combination of sulphur dioxide and oxygen by passing a mixture of the dried gases over heated platinised asbestos (as catalyst). Air may be used instead of oxygen,

$$2SO_2 + O_2 \rightleftharpoons 2SO_3.$$

This very important reaction is used as a stage in the manufacture of sulphuric acid (p. 486).

(2) Heating some sulphates or hydrogen sulphates,

$$Fe_2(SO_4)_3 \rightarrow Fe_2O_3 + 3SO_3,$$

$$\left\{ \begin{array}{l} 2NaHSO_4 \rightarrow H_2O + Na_2S_2O_7 \quad \text{(sodium pyrosulphate),} \\ Na_2S_2O_7 \;\; \rightarrow Na_2SO_4 + SO_3 \uparrow . \end{array} \right\}$$

(3) Dehydrating concentrated sulphur acid with phosphorus pentoxide,

$$2H_2SO_4 + P_4O_{10} \rightarrow 4HPO_3 + 2SO_3.$$

The sulphur trioxide is collected as a white crystalline solid in a receiver cooled in a mixture of ice and salt.

Physical properties. Sulphur trioxide at room temperature is a white volatile crystalline solid which exists in two allotropic modifications, melting points 17 °C and 40 °C.

Molecular formula. Sulphur trioxide vapour heated to 1000 °C decomposes completely into sulphur dioxide and oxygen. The volume relationships are,

$$\text{Sulphur trioxide} \xrightarrow{\;1000°\;} \text{Sulphur dioxide} + \text{oxygen,}$$

2 vol.	2 vol.	1 vol.
2 mol.	2 mol.	1 mol. (Avogadro)
$2S_xO_y$ $\longrightarrow$	$2SO_2$ +	O_2.
	(already established)	(already established)

Hence $x = 1$, $y = 3$ and molecular formula is SO_3. The vapour therefore consists of single SO_3 molecules, i.e. it is monomeric. (This result is confirmed by a value of 40 for its relative density.)

Structure. *Vapour.* The SO_3 molecule has zero dipole moment, which indicates that it is planar and symmetrical, all the O—S—O bond angles being 120°. The S—O bond lengths are all equal and shorter than single S—O bonds, showing a partly double bond character (as in SO_2 whose bonds are the same length as in SO_3). The simplest formulation of the structure is as shown below; although it should be remembered that the π bonding is not complete.

Solid sulphur trioxide. All three forms are polymers, this polymerisation showing the instability of the S=O double bonds. One form has ice-like crystals (melting point 17 °C). It consists of S_3O_9 molecules (i.e. it is trimeric) which have ring-like structures. This form is unstable, and on standing at ordinary temperature in the presence of traces of water, slowly changes into one of the stable forms. These consist of fibrous, needle-shaped crystals, resembling asbestos, whose structure shows infinite chains of SO_4 tetrahedra linked together by sharing the oxygen atoms at two of their corners (cf. asbestos structure, pp. 386–7).

$$\begin{array}{ccccccc} & O & & O & & O & \\ & \| & & \| & & \| & \\ -S & -O & -S & -O & -S & -O- \\ & \| & & \| & & \| & \\ & O & & O & & O & \end{array}$$

Note the *single* bonds forming the links in the chain. The difference between the two stable forms is thought to be that one has more cross-linking between the chains than the other.

Chemical properties. The presence of double bonds in the SO_3 molecule and the relative instability of the π bond in the double bond, are confirmed by the readiness of sulphur trioxide to form *addition* compounds, with itself as in its solid allotrope, or with other molecules, as in most of its reactions, examples of which follow.

Solid sulphur trioxide fumes strongly in moist air. It combines vigorously with water with the evolution of much heat and the formation of sulphuric acid. It is therefore sulphuric anhydride. In this reaction one of the double bonds in SO_3 has been converted to a single bond. It also combines readily with concentrated sulphuric acid forming fuming sulphuric acid (oleum). When the ratio of molecules is one to one, the product is disulphuric acid $H_2S_2O_7$ (pyrosulphuric acid). Continued addition of SO_3 produces a series of polysulphuric acids.

Sulphur trioxide combines vigorously with basic oxides forming sulphates. So much heat is evolved that the mass becomes white hot,

$$Ba^{2+}O^{2-} + SO_3 \rightarrow Ba^{2+}SO_4^{2-}; \quad \Delta H \text{ negative.}$$

Sulphur trioxide combines with hydrogen chloride to form chlorosulphonic acid.

One or both double bonds have been converted to single bonds in these reactions.

Sulphur trioxide may act as an oxidising agent.

Sulphuric acid, H_2SO_4

This is probably the most important of all manufactured chemicals. It is so widely used that its consumption is closely related to the industrial prosperity of a country. If supplies of sulphuric acid were cut off from an industrial country, its economy would suffer a crippling blow, more serious than would result from the cutting off of any other raw material.

World production of sulphuric acid is about 30 million tons a year (Britain, 3 million).

Manufacture. There are two processes, the *contact process*, and the *lead-chamber process*. In Britain about five-sixths of the total is made by the former. Both processes have three main stages:
  (1) production of sulphur dioxide;
  (2) oxidation of sulphur dioxide to sulphur trioxide;
  (3) combination of sulphuric trioxide with water to form sulphuric acid.
In the lead-chamber process, stages (2) and (3) take place simultaneously.

Production of sulphur dioxide. Methods are the same for both processes
  (1) By burning native sulphur in air.
  (2) By burning iron pyrites FeS_2 in air (other sulphide ores, especially ZnS are also used),

$$4FeS_2 + 11O_2 \rightarrow 2Fe_2O_3 + 8SO_2.$$

485

(3) By burning spent oxide from the purifiers of coal-gas works (spent oxide is a mixture containing 50% iron(III) oxide and 50% sulphur).

(4) From anhydrite $CaSO_4$ (anhydrous calcium sulphate). Because of the unlimited supply of this source of sulphur in Britain large quantities are used in the manufacture of sulphuric acid.

Anhydrous calcium sulphate is very stable. The forward reaction in the following equation takes place to a slight extent only, even at 1400 °C. At this temperature sulphur trioxide is decomposed into sulphur dioxide and oxygen,

$$CaSO_4 \rightleftharpoons CaO + SO_3; \ \Delta H \text{ positive}; \ SO_3 \rightleftharpoons SO_2 + \tfrac{1}{2}O_2; \ \Delta H \text{ positive}.$$

Removal of oxygen and sulphur dioxide by draught favours the forward reaction, so does the removal of calcium oxide by combination with the acid oxides silica and alumina (Al_2O_3). Calcium sulphate can be reduced to calcium sulphide by reduction with carbon. The calcium sulphide then reacts with excess calcium sulphate. These reactions are the basis of the process as follows.

Anhydrite process. A powdered mixture of anhydrite, coke, sand and furnace ashes containing alumina is heated strongly in a rotary cylindrical kiln 11 ft wide and 100 yd long. The following reactions take place,

$$CaSO_4 + 2C \rightarrow CaS + 2CO_2,$$
$$3CaSO_4 + CaS \rightleftharpoons 4CaO + 4SO_2,$$
$$CaO + SiO_2 \rightarrow CaSiO_3,$$
$$CaO + Al_2O_3 \rightarrow Ca(AlO_2)_2 \quad \text{(calcium aluminate)}.$$

The gases issuing from the kiln contain about 9% sulphur dioxide, along with nitrogen, carbon dioxide and a little oxygen. The solid passing out of the kiln is ground up finely giving the valuable by-product Portland cement.

From now on the contact process and lead-chamber process will be described separately.

Contact process. Sulphur dioxide is oxidised to sulphur trioxide,

$$2SO_2 + O_2 \rightleftharpoons 2SO_3; \ \Delta H \text{ negative}$$

$$\underbrace{\text{2 vol.} \quad \text{1 vol.}}$$

$$\text{3 vol.} \qquad \text{2 vol.}$$

It follows from Le Chatelier's principle that the forward reaction is favoured by

(1) increase in pressure because the forward reaction results in reduction of pressure;

(2) low temperatures because it results in an increase in temperature;

(3) excess of air (the cheapest reagent);

(4) removal of sulphur trioxide from the reaction vessel.

It is found in practice that (*a*) increasing the pressure does not justify the extra cost involved, and (*b*) at low temperatures the rate of reaction (rate of attainment of equilibrium) is too slow. To overcome this difficulty and keep the temperature as low as possible a catalyst is used. The required conditions are found to be normal pressure, a temperature of 450 °C in presence of a catalyst, and excess air. The process takes its name from the fact that the reaction takes place by contact of the gaseous mixture with the surface of the solid catalyst.

Procedure in outline is as follows. The sulphur dioxide must be dry and free from impurities especially dust particles containing arsenic compounds which poison the catalyst. Dust is removed by passing the gas at high speed round a cyclonic dust separator, in which the dust is thrown to the sides. The gas is then cooled and water washed, the sulphur dioxide dissolving in the water being removed from solution by passing air through it. The moisture particles in the gas are precipitated electrostatically, then the gas is dried by scrubbing with concentrated sulphuric acid.

The dried air-and-gas mixture, heated to about 450 °C, is passed through layers of catalyst consisting of a silica-gel carrier impregnated with vanadium(v) oxide, V_2O_5. Sulphur dioxide is converted to the trioxide. The reaction is exothermic but the temperature is not allowed to rise above 600 °C. The gases are then cooled and passed up a tower, down which runs concentrated sulphuric acid, which absorbs the sulphur trioxide. The resulting acid is then diluted with water to give 98 % sulphuric acid. The acid produced by the contact process is pure.

Note. Sulphur trioxide vapour is not absorbed efficiently by water alone, through which much of it passes as a mist.

The lead-chamber process. The essential difference between this and the contact process is that the catalyst is a gas, nitrogen monoxide, and that most of the reactions take place in the gaseous phase (homogeneous catalysis). The overall reactions of the process are,

$$(1) \qquad NO + \tfrac{1}{2}O_2 \rightarrow NO_2,$$
from the air
$$(2) \qquad SO_2 + NO_2 \rightarrow SO_3 + NO,$$
$$(3) \qquad H_2O + SO_3 \rightarrow H_2SO_4.$$

NO produced in (2) is then re-oxidised to NO_2. Other reactions than the three given take place, but their relative importance has not been established. Only one intermediate product will be mentioned, nitrosyl hydrogen sulphate.

Procedure. Hot gases from the burners contain sulphur dioxide and excess air. A mixture of oxides of nitrogen (NO and NO_2) made by the catalytic oxidation of ammonia (p. 448) is added and the gases then freed from dust by passage through electrostatic precipitators. If this is not done the dust contaminates the final sulphuric acid.

The gases then pass through five vessels in series: Tower 1 (Glover tower); three lead-lined acid-resistant chambers each of which may be as big as a school hall; and Tower 2 (Gay-Lussac tower).

Tower 1 is packed with flints. The gases enter the foot of the tower, down which trickles a mixture of weak sulphuric acid from the chambers and more concentrated nitrated sulphuric acid from the bottom of Tower 2. The nitrated acid contains nitrosyl hydrogen sulphate $[NO]^+[HSO_4]^-$, i.e. sulphuric acid in which one atom of hydrogen has been replaced by the nitrosyl ion (or nitrosonium ion), $[NO]^+$. Tower 1 carries out four operations:

(1) cools the gases from the burners;

(2) concentrates the acid by evaporating water;

(3) produces a further quantity of sulphuric acid by the reaction,

$$2[NO]^+[HSO_4]^- + 2H_2O + SO_2 \rightarrow 3H_2SO_4 + 2NO;$$

(4) nitrogen monoxide formed in the last reaction joins the stream of gases passing up the tower.

Acid leaving the bottom of the tower is therefore purer and more concentrated (80 % H_2SO_4). Some is sold as Tower or Glover acid. The remainder is pumped to the top of Tower 2.

Lead chambers. The gases leaving the top of Tower 1 pass into the first of the three lead-lined chambers. Here additional water as a very fine mist is sprayed into the gases from the roof. Sulphuric acid, formed according to the equations already given, condenses on the sides and collects on the floor. The two other chambers complete the reactions. Most of the chamber acid (70 % H_2SO_4) is sold as such, but some is pumped to the top of Tower 1.

The gases leaving the last chamber consist of excess oxygen, nitrogen, some water vapour and a considerable quantity of oxides of nitrogen which must be recovered. This is the purpose of Tower 2.

Tower 2. The gases enter the foot of the tower, which is packed with coke down which trickles 80 % cold sulphuric acid from Tower 1. The oxides of nitrogen ($NO + NO_2$) react with the acid, producing nitrosyl hydrogen sulphate acid (about 2 % of the total) thus,

$$2H_2SO_4 + N_2O_3 \rightarrow 2[NO]^+[HSO_4]^- + H_2O.$$

The nitrated acid from the bottom of the tower is pumped to the top of Tower 1. The gases from the top of Tower 2 consist mainly of nitrogen and excess oxygen. They pass up a chimney into the atmosphere.

Acid from the chamber process is not usually concentrated beyond about 78 to 80 %. If purer and more concentrated acid is required it is got from the contact process.

Uses. These are, in order of quantity used in Britain: (1) Manufacture of superphosphate (calcium dihydrogen phosphate + calcium sulphate) as a fertiliser. (2) Manufacture of white paint-pigments e.g. barium sulphate, titanium(IV) oxide; also extraction of lanthanides. (3) Manufacture of rayon. (4) Manufacture of detergents from oils; also manufacture of soaps. (5) Manufacture of ammonium sulphate as a fertiliser, the ammonia coming from either (*a*) gas-works, as a by-product, or (*b*) synthesis of ammonia (Haber process). (6) Pickling of iron or steel sheet or wire to remove oxide film before tinning, galvanising, plating or enamelling. (7) In the dyestuffs industry. (8) Manufacture of sulphates of metals. (9) Manufacture of plastics. (10) In the refining of petroleum oils. (11) Manufacture of hydrochloric acid and sodium sulphate from common salt. (12) Manufacture of explosives, especially nitro-glycerine, guncotton, trinitrotoluene (TNT), trinitrophenol (picric acid). (13) In accumulators.

Physical properties. Ordinary concentrated sulphuric acid (98 % H_2SO_4, 2 % H_2O), *oil of vitriol*, is a colourless, odourless, viscous liquid, density 1.84 at 16 °C; it forms a constant boiling mixture, distilling over at 330 °C, unchanged in composition but with some dissociation. At 450 °C the vapour is completely dissociated into SO_3 and steam. 100 % H_2SO_4 freezes at 10 °C.

Structure. (1) The molecular formulae of water and sulphur trioxide (both in the gaseous state) are H_2O (formula weight 18) and SO_3 (formula weight 80). When 18 g of water and 80 g of sulphur trioxide react, the product is 98 g of a liquid which, by its properties is shown to be concentrated sulphuric acid. The empirical formula of the acid is therefore H_2SO_4.

(2) Sulphuric acid forms only two series of salts, therefore its molecule contains two atoms of hydrogen replaceable by a metal.

489

(3) Concentrated sulphuric acid reacts with phosphorus pentachloride forming sulphuryl chloride, a volatile liquid with a vapour density of 67.5 and so a molecular weight of 135. Analysis of sulphuryl chloride shows it to have an empirical formula of SO_2Cl_2. Its molecular formula is therefore also SO_2Cl_2. Phosphorus pentachloride attacks substances containing the hydroxyl group, which is replaced by an atom of chlorine. It follows that sulphuric acid has the formula $SO_2(OH)_2$.

(4) X-ray analysis of sulphates confirms the fact that they contain SO_4 groups and shows that the groups are tetrahedral in shape. The molecule of sulphuric acid is therefore tetrahedral. It may be represented thus:

$$\begin{array}{cc} HO & O \\ \diagdown & \diagup\!\!\!\diagup \\ & S \\ \diagup & \diagdown\!\!\!\diagdown \\ HO & O \end{array}$$

Structure of $SO_4{}^{2-}$. This contains four σ bonds giving a tetrahedral structure, and two non-localised π bonds. The S—O bond lengths are all equal (1.49 Å), i.e. intermediate between single and double in character. Note, maximum covalency of sulphur is 6.

$$\begin{array}{ccc} & \ddot{O}{\cdot} & \\ & \| & \\ {}^{-}\!:\!\ddot{O}\!\!- & \!\!S\!\!- & \!\!\ddot{O}\!: {}^{-} \\ & \| & \\ & \underset{\cdot\cdot}{.O.} & \end{array}$$

Composition of concentrated sulphuric acid. The high boiling point and viscosity indicate association of molecules by hydrogen bonding (cf. water) thus:

$$\begin{array}{cccc} {-}{-}H{-}O & O{-}{-}H{-}O & O{-}{-}H{-}O & O{-}{-} \\ \diagdown\;\;\diagup\!\!\!\diagup & \diagdown\;\;\diagup\!\!\!\diagup & \diagdown\;\;\diagup\!\!\!\diagup & \\ S & S & S & \\ \diagup\;\;\diagdown\!\!\!\diagdown & \diagup\;\;\diagdown\!\!\!\diagdown & \diagup\;\;\diagdown\!\!\!\diagdown & \\ {-}{-}H{-}O & O{-}{-}H{-}O & O{-}{-}H{-}O & O{-}{-} \end{array}$$

In the presence of water, sulphuric acid ionises, mainly thus:

$$H_2SO_4 + H_2O \rightleftharpoons H_3O^+ + HSO_4^-,$$

forming a solution of high specific conductivity. As the concentration of the acid is increased its specific conductivity decreases till it reaches a minimum (almost zero) at 96% H_2SO_4. On addition of SO_3 to this, the specific conductivity rises until with 100% H_2SO_4 the value indicates a fair degree of ionisation. Self ionisation, analogous to that of water is known to take place,

$$2H_2SO_4 \rightleftharpoons H_3SO_4^+ + HSO_4^-.$$

Another important equilibrium in 100% H_2SO_4 is one which produces SO_3,

$$2H_2SO_4 \rightleftharpoons SO_3 + H_3O^+ + HSO_4^-.$$

The fact that 100% H_2SO_4 fumes in air is evidence of the forward reaction. SO_3 produced in this reaction is the chief agent in the important organic reaction of sulphonation (p. 492).

Chemical properties. Sulphuric acid is very corrosive. It can behave in four ways: (1) as a strong dibasic acid, (2) as a dehydrating agent, (3) as an oxidising agent, (4) as a sulphonating agent.

(1) *Acidic properties.* When dilute it shows the usual acid properties: sour taste, effect on litmus, action on metals, bases, carbonates, and hydrogen carbonates. Sulphuric acid is dibasic, forming sulphates and hydrogen sulphates. In aqueous solution it ionises according to the equation,

$$H_2SO_4 + H_2O \rightleftharpoons H_3O^+ + HSO_4^-, \quad K_1 \simeq 10^{-3};$$
$$HSO_4^- + H_2O \rightleftharpoons H_3O^+ + SO_4^{2-}, \quad K_2 = 1.2 \times 10^{-2}.$$

These reactions again show the great affinity of water molecules for protons. The values of K_1 and K_2 show that the concentration of HSO_4^- ions greatly exceeds that of SO_4^{2-} ions.

For action on salts, see p. 245.

(2) *Dehydration action.* Sulphuric acid especially when concentrated, reacts vigorously with water with the liberation of much heat. The reaction is dangerous, therefore when diluting sulphuric acid care must be taken always to add the *acid* slowly *to* the *water*. Concentrated sulphuric acid is a powerful dehydrating agent: it removes the elements of water from many compounds, e.g. hydrated copper(II) sulphate and most forms of organic matter such as wood, paper, cloth, animal and vegetable tissue, oxalic acid, formic acid, sugar, ethanol. It is a useful drying agent for gases which do not react with it, oxygen, nitrogen, sulphur dioxide and chlorine. It is used in desiccators and in a number of reversible reactions where water is one of the products: the removal of this by sulphuric acid favours the forward reaction, e.g. esterification and nitration (p. 451–2).

(3) *Oxidising action.* (*a*) The action of dilute sulphuric acid on metals which are above hydrogen in the electrochemical series is a redox reaction, in which hydrogen ions from the acid take electrons from the atoms of the metal (pp. 152–5). (*b*) Concentrated sulphuric acid reacts as an oxidising agent with (i) metals, (ii) non-metals, (iii) some compounds.

(i) Metals. Cold concentrated sulphuric has little or no action on most metals, but sodium, potassium, and magnesium liberate hydrogen from it.

Hot concentrated acid reacts with most metals, including copper, mercury and silver but not platinum or gold, forming the sulphate of the metal, water and sulphur dioxide by reduction of the acid. Action is slow with magnesium, aluminium, and iron. With lead a high temperature is needed and reaction may be very rapid if the lead is impure. A typical reaction simplified is

$$\text{(1)} \quad Cu \rightarrow Cu^{2+} + 2e, \qquad \text{Oxidation of Cu}$$

$$\text{(2)} \; 2H_2SO_4 + 2e \rightarrow SO_4^{2-} + SO_2 + 2H_2O,$$

$$\text{Reduction of } H_2SO_4$$

$$\text{(1)} + \text{(2)} \qquad \overline{Cu + 2H_2SO_4 \rightarrow Cu^{2+}SO_4^{2-} + SO_2 + 2H_2O.}$$

(ii) Non-metals. Cold concentrated acid has little effect on carbon or sulphur; when hot it oxidises them to carbon dioxide and sulphur dioxide respectively, being itself reduced to sulphur dioxide.

(iii) Compounds, see p. 512.

(4) *Sulphonation.* When benzene is refluxed with 100% sulphuric acid, benzene sulphonic acid is formed,

$$C_6H_6 + SO_3 \rightleftharpoons C_6H_5SO_3H.$$

SO_3 is produced by the reaction

$$2H_2SO_4 \rightleftharpoons SO_3 + H_3O^+ + HSO_4^-.$$

Derivatives of sulphuric acid. Sulphates and hydrogen sulphates (pp. 240–7).

Sulphuryl chloride, SO_2Cl_2. This is the acid chloride of sulphuric acid, also called dichlorosulphonic acid.

Preparation. (1) By the prolonged action of phosphorus pentachloride on sulphuric acid.

$$\text{HO}\!\!>\!\!S\!\!<\!\!^{O}_{O} \;\; + \;\; 2PCl_5 \longrightarrow \text{Cl}\!\!>\!\!S\!\!<\!\!^{O}_{O} \; + 2POCl_3 + 2HCl$$

(2) By combination of sulphur dioxide and chlorine in sunlight or in the presence of charcoal or camphor as catalyst,

$$SO_2 + Cl_2 \rightleftharpoons SO_2Cl_2.$$

A colourless liquid (boiling point, 69 °C), it is hydrolysed slowly by water,

$$SO_2Cl_2 + 2H_2O \rightleftharpoons H_2SO_4 + 2HCl.$$

The molecule is tetrahedral.

Chlorosulphonic acid, HOSO$_2$Cl. This acid is the mono-acid chloride of sulphuric acid, prepared by the action of dry hydrogen chloride on fuming sulphuric acid:

$$Cl \longrightarrow \boxed{H + HO} \underset{HO}{\overset{O}{\diagdown}} S \underset{O}{\overset{O}{\diagup}} \longrightarrow \underset{HO}{\overset{Cl}{\diagdown}} S \underset{O}{\overset{O}{\diagup}} + \ \ H_2O$$

$$\text{(absorbed by H}_2\text{SO}_4\text{)}$$

It is a colourless fuming liquid, (boiling point 151 °C) which is hydrolysed violently by water,

$$HOSO_2Cl + H_2O \rightleftharpoons H_2SO_4 + HCl.$$

Its molecule is tetrahedral.

Other oxygen acids of sulphur

Thiosulphuric acid, H$_2$S$_2$O$_3$, and thiosulphates (Greek: theion-sulphur). The formula for the acid and its anion is got by replacing an oxygen atom in H$_2$SO$_4$ or SO$_4{}^{2-}$ by a sulphur atom. Thiosulphuric acid has the structure

$$\underset{H-O}{\overset{H-O}{\diagdown}} S \underset{O}{\overset{S}{\diagup}}$$

The acid has not been isolated but its salts are well known, especially sodium thiosulphate pentahydrate, Na$_2$S$_2$O$_3$.5H$_2$O, which forms colourless monoclinic crystals, very soluble in water. It is prepared by boiling sodium sulphite solution with flowers of sulphur, filtering and crystallising,

$$SO_3{}^{2-} + S \rightarrow S_2O_3{}^{2-}.$$

Properties. When sodium thiosulphate solution is acidified with dilute hydrochloric or sulphuric acid, a pale yellow precipitate of sulphur gradually forms, in a solution of sulphurous acid,

$$S_2O_3{}^{2-} + 2H^+ \rightarrow S\downarrow + SO_2\uparrow + H_2O.$$

This reaction shows the instability of thiosulphuric acid (cf. action of acids on sulphites).

Sodium thiosulphate crystals, when heated gently, dissolve in their water of crystallisation, which is then driven off leaving the solid anhydrous salt. On further heating it melts, darkens in colour and gives a yellow sublimate of sulphur. The residue when cold is yellow and is a mixture of sodium sulphate, sulphide and pentasulphide,

$$4Na_2S_2O_3 \rightarrow 3Na_2SO_4 + Na_2S_5,$$

$$Na_2S_5 \rightarrow Na_2S + 4S.$$

Iodine solution oxidises thiosulphate ion to tetrathionate ion,

$$2(S_2O_3)^{2-} + I_2 \rightarrow (S_4O_6)^{2-} + 2I^-.$$

In this reaction the oxidation number of sulphur has been increased from $+2$ to $+2\frac{1}{2}$. A different reaction takes place with chlorine, although it is also an oxidation,

$$S_2O_3{}^{2-} + 4Cl_2 + 5H_2O \rightarrow 10H^+ + 2SO_4{}^{2-} + 8Cl^-.$$

The reaction with bromine is similar. A small amount of tetrathionate is also formed in both cases.

The above reactions show that two characteristic reactions of thio-sulphate are (1) its reducing action in which it is oxidised to tetrathionate, and (2) its decomposition into sulphide and sulphate.

Uses. (1) As a standard solution in the determination of iodine, or any oxidising reagent which liberates iodine from potassium iodide solution. (2) As an antichlor after bleaching (see action with chlorine). (3) In 'fixing' photographic negatives or prints. This process involves the removal from the photographic emulsion of unaffected silver bromide as a soluble complex salt. The simplest of those formed in the process is $Na[Ag(S_2O_3)]$.

Polythionic acids and polythionates. These acids have the general formula $H_2S_nO_6$, in which $n = 2$ to 6. They are named according to the value of n, dithionic, trithionic, etc., and have the general structure:

$$\overset{\displaystyle O}{\underset{\displaystyle O}{\overset{\|}{\underset{\|}{HO-S}}}}-S \cdots -\overset{\displaystyle O}{\underset{\displaystyle O}{\overset{\|}{\underset{\|}{S}}}}-OH$$

These acids illustrate the chain-forming capacity of sulphur atoms. Sodium tetrathionate is formed in the reaction between iodine and sodium thiosulphate solution.

Dithionous acid should be mentioned because its salt, sodium dithionite, $Na_2S_2O_4$ is a very powerful reducing agent, used in the dye industry and in analytical and preparative chemistry.

Peroxosulphuric acid. The substitution of the perioxde group —O—O— (or $O_2{}^{2-}$) for a single oxygen atom in the formula of an oxygen acid gives a peroxo acid. Thus from sulphuric acid is derived H_2SO_5, peroxomono-sulphuric acid; and from disulphuric acid, $H_2S_2O_7$, is derived $H_2S_2O_8$, peroxodisulphuric acid.

The sulphur atom in sulphuric acid is in its maximum oxidation state of

494

+6. Oxidation of sulphuric acid by (1) hydrogen peroxide or (2) anodic oxidation, therefore takes place by the oxidation of oxygen from oxidation number -2 to oxidation number -1 (in O_2^{2-}).

Peroxodisulphuric acid, $H_2S_2O_8$. *Preparation.* (1) By the action of 1 mole of H_2O_2 on 2 moles of chlorosulphonic acid $ClSO_2OH$,

$$HO-\underset{\underset{O}{\|}}{\overset{\overset{O}{\|}}{S}}-\boxed{Cl+H}-O-O-\boxed{H+Cl}-\underset{\underset{O}{\|}}{\overset{\overset{O}{\|}}{S}}-OH \rightarrow$$

$$HO-\underset{\underset{O}{\|}}{\overset{\overset{O}{\|}}{S}}-O-O-\underset{\underset{O}{\|}}{\overset{\overset{O}{\|}}{S}}-OH+2HCl.$$

(2) Electrolysis of moderately concentrated sulphuric acid (60%) at $0\,°C$ with a high current density and platinum anode. Hydrogen is liberated at the cathode and peroxodisulphuric acid formed in solution at the anode,

cathode reaction: $\quad 2H^+ + 2e \rightarrow H_2\uparrow$,

anode reaction: $\quad 2HSO_4^- \rightarrow H_2S_2O_8 + 2e$.

If ammonium (or potassium) hydrogen sulphate solution is used instead of sulphuric acid, ammonium (or potassium) peroxodisulphate crystallises out at the anode.

Properties. The acid is a colourless crystalline solid (melting point $60\,°C$). It is a strong dibasic acid. The acid and its salts are good oxidising agents, liberating iodine slowly from potassium iodide solutions, oxidising iron(II) ions to iron(III), sulphite to sulphate, and Mn^{2+} to MnO_4^- in the presence of Ag^+ ions as catalyst. A solution of the acid may be hydrolysed in two stages: (1) on gentle heating,

$$H_2S_2O_8 + H_2O \rightarrow H_2SO_4 + H_2SO_5 \quad \text{(peroxomonosulphuric acid)}.$$

(2) On further heating,

$$H_2SO_5 + H_2O \rightarrow H_2SO_4 + H_2O_2.$$

Hydrogen peroxide is manufactured by a process using these reactions.

Peroxomonosulphuric acid, H_2SO_5, is prepared by the action of 1 mole of H_2O_2 on (1) 1 mole of chlorosulphonic acid,

$$HO-\underset{\underset{O}{\|}}{\overset{\overset{O}{\|}}{S}}-\boxed{Cl+H}-O-O-H \rightarrow HO-\underset{\underset{O}{\|}}{\overset{\overset{O}{\|}}{S}}-O-O-H+HCl,$$

or (2) 1 mole of sulphuric acid (moderately concentrated),

$$H_2SO_4 + H_2O_2 \rightarrow H_2SO_5 + H_2O.$$

It is also made by the hydrolysis of peroxodisulphuric acid (as above).

Properties. Peroxomonosulphuric acid is a colourless crystalline solid (melting point 45 °C). It is a good oxidising agent, like $H_2S_2O_8$, but differs from it in liberating iodine immediately from potassium iodide solution.

The twelve oxygen acids of sulphur described above, all contain two atoms of hydrogen per molecule and all are dibasic except H_2SO_5.

Additional note on oxygen and sulphur

Oxygen is the most electronegative element, except for fluorine. All binary compounds of oxygen are therefore oxides except oxygen difluoride. Almost all elements form oxides, and many form sulphides; but compounds of oxygen with sulphur are oxides, not sulphides. Oxides are of great importance in inorganic chemistry because basic oxides and acidic oxides react with water (another oxide) directly or indirectly to form hydroxides and oxo-acids. Oxo-acids in turn form oxo-salts, a very large, varied, and important group of compounds.

Exercises

1. Compare the oxides and corresponding sulphides of a number of typical elements with respect to structure, and related physical and chemical properties. Give explanations where possible.
2. Sulphur has valencies of 2, 4 and 6. Oxygen in almost all its compounds is restricted to a valency of 2. This difference might be expected to result in the existence of many more compounds of sulphur than of oxygen. Is this expectation fulfilled?
3. Give a concise account of the allotropy of sulphur.
4. Give the names and structural formulae of twelve oxygen acids of sulphur, and show how these acids are related to each other.
5. Describe **one** method by which sulphur is obtained from a natural source. Describe how you would prepare from sulphur, crystals of (*a*) sodium sulphite, (*b*) sodium thiosulphate. How, and under what conditions, does sulphuric acid react with (i) formic acid, (ii) sulphur, (iii) sodium bromide? (C)
6. Describe how you would prepare (using sulphur as the only source of that element) specimens of (*a*) disulphur dichloride, S_2Cl_2; (*b*) sodium thiosulphate. How, and under what conditions, does sulphuric acid react with (i) benzene, (ii) sulphur, (iii) iron? (C)

7. Mention **two** large-scale methods (other than the burning of sulphur) by which sulphur dioxide is produced.

Outline the conversion of sulphur dioxide to concentrated sulphuric acid by the contact process, paying particular attention to the physico-chemical principles involved.

Describe and explain one method in each case by which it can be shown that sulphuric acid is (*a*) dibasic, (*b*) a dehydrating agent. Under what conditions does sulphuric acid react with (i) magnesium, (ii) copper? State the nature of the reaction in each case and explain it in terms of electron transfer. (J.M.B.)

8. Describe concisely **two** methods used for the manufacture of sulphuric acid.

Describe with experimental details how you would prepare a crystalline sample of ferrous ammonium sulphate from 100 ml of 4N sulphuric acid, iron wire and concentrated ammonium hydroxide solution (O & C).

9. For the reaction

$$2SO_2 + O_2 \rightleftharpoons 2SO_3; \qquad \Delta H_{298} = -22 \cdot 6 \text{ kcal mole}^{-1}$$

describe, with reasons, the effect on the position of equilibrium of (*a*) temperature, (*b*) pressure, (*c*) a platinum catalyst, (*d*) excess oxygen.

Calculate values of the equilibrium constant at 1000 °C from the two sets of data given below.

	Partial pressures (atm)		
	P_{SO_2}	P_{O_2}	P_{SO_3}
(1)	0·27	0·41	0·32
(2)	0·46	0·18	0·36	(O & C)

10. Explain the meanings of the terms *peroxide* and *neutral oxide*.

Compare and contrast the oxides, X_2O_3, of phosphorus, arsenic and bismuth, by reference to their reactions with

  (i) sodium hydroxide solution,

  (ii) concentrated hydrochloric acid,

  (iii) iodine solution. (C)

26

GROUP VIIB: THE HALOGENS

The non-metallic elements fluorine, chlorine, bromine, iodine, and the short-lived radioactive element astatine, comprise the seventh Main Group of the Periodic Classification and are known collectively as *the halogens*. This term was coined by the early experimentalists from Greek words which when translated mean *salt-producer*, as they were impressed by the ability of these elements to combine directly with metals to form salts.

Relationship of Group VII B to the Periodic Table

Like the alkali metals, the halogens form a very closely related Group of elements. They are the last chemically active elements in each of the Periods 2–6 in the Periodic Table. As discussed elsewhere (p. 282), there are arguments for placing hydrogen, the active element in Period 1, at the head of Group VIIB, but even though it shows one or two superficial similarities to these elements (e.g. diatomic gas, H_2, formation of singly charged anion, H^-), it is not a halogen. Immediately following each halogen and completing each Period there is a noble gas element. In most forms of the Periodic Table the relative positions of the halogens and the alkali metals are shown at the opposite ends of a series of horizontal rows, and this clearly emphasises the diametrically opposed chemical behaviour of these two Groups of elements. But it must not be forgotten that there are no artificial breaks in the order of elements from lightest to heaviest, and the atomic number increases stepwise from halogen to noble gas to alkali metal so that the halogens are separated from the alkali metals by only one Group and not by five or fifteen elements depending on the Period.

In some ways the properties of fluorine resemble those of oxygen more closely than they do those of chlorine, e.g. (1) the hydrides HF and H_2O are strongly associated whereas hydrogen chloride is not; (2) the solubility, melting point and boiling point of fluorides are generally closer in magnitude to the corresponding oxides than they are to the chlorides; and (3) both oxygen and fluorine combine directly with carbon whereas the other halogens do not.

General Group features

Atomic properties of the halogens

Element	Symbol	Atomic no.	Atomic weight	Covalent radius (Å)	Ionic radius M⁻ (Å)	Electro-negativity
Fluorine	F	9	19.00	0.72	1.36	4.10
Chlorine	Cl	17	35.45	0.99	1.81	2.83
Bromine	Br	35	79.90	1.14	1.95	2.74
Iodine	I	53	126.90	1.33	2.16	2.21
Astatine	At	85	(210.00)	—	—	—

The trends amongst the elements of Group VII B are similar to those already described during the discussion on the previous Groups. As usual for the first member of a *p*-block Group fluorine stands apart from the other halogens. All the halogens form diatomic molecules in the gaseous state. The two atoms in each molecule are joined by a single covalent bond. As the Group is descended there is a progressive increase in the size of the molecule (Fig. 133). The electrons in the outer shell only are shown, and the distance between the nuclei, i.e. the covalent bond length, is given below each molecule.

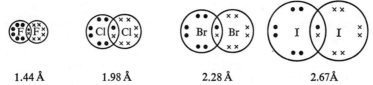

| 1.44 Å | 1.98 Å | 2.28 Å | 2.67Å |

Fig. 133. Bond lengths and electronic structures of the halogen molecules.

Two of the main factors contributing to the outstanding reactivity of these elements are (1) the comparative ease with which the molecule can be dissociated into atoms, and (2) the high electron affinity of the individual atoms. Values for the energy required to dissociate the diatomic molecules of a few common gaseous elements are given below:

	N_2	O_2	H_2	F_2	Cl_2	Br_2	I_2
kJ mol⁻¹	941	495.0	432.5	157.7	239.3	190.0	148.5
kcal mol⁻¹	225	118.3	103.4	37.7	57.2	45.4	35.5

Dissociation energies ($X_2 \rightarrow 2X$) for some common diatomic molecules.

Except in cases where the halogen molecule adds on to another particle, for instance in the formation of polyhalides, e.g.

$$I^- + I_2 \rightarrow [I-I-I]^-,$$

the molecule must be disrupted before the element can react. The figures above emphasise how much more difficult it is for elements such as nitrogen, oxygen and hydrogen to *enter* into a reaction than it is for the halogens. Relative to its position in the Group it will be noticed that the dissociation energy of fluorine is abnormally low; this is another way of saying that the strength of the covalent bond joining the two fluorine atoms is weaker than might have been expected from the trend shown by the other halogens. Two possible reasons have been suggested for this:

(1) A stronger repulsion between the non-bonding electrons in the fluorine molecule owing to the short bond length and therefore closer approach of the electrons than in the other halogens. This tends to force the atoms apart and assist in dissociating the molecule.

(2) A strengthening of the bond in the other halogens owing to partial multiple bond formation, a process denied to fluorine as it is unable to expand its octet.

Owing to the small size of the fluoride ion (*note*, F^-, 1.33 Å; Cl^-, 1.81 Å), its hydration energy and the lattice energy of its compounds are appreciably greater than those of other halides. Together with the ease with which the fluorine molecule is dissociated these properties establish it as the most reactive halogen.

Ion	Hydration energies kJ mol^{-1}	Lattice energies kJ mol^{-1}	
		K^+	Ca^{2+}
F^-	-457	-787	-2579
Cl^-	-384	-703	-2246
Br^-	-351	-657	—
I^-	-307	-644	—

The reactivity of the halogens diminishes down the Group, but although iodine is much less reactive than chlorine or bromine, it is still a very reactive element and combines directly with such elements as sulphur, phosphorus, iron, and mercury.

The radius of the halide ions increases progressively from fluoride to iodide, and the tendency towards covalency as expressed by Fajans' rules (see p. 110) increases in the same order. Thus the fluoride of a particular metal is its most ionic compound and the other halides are progressively less ionic as the Group is descended, with the highest degree of covalency being shown by the iodide. Whilst it is not always obvious whether the halides of weakly electropositive elements are essentially ionic or essentially covalent, the properties of the non-metallic halides are typically covalent. At room temperature they are gases, liquids, or solids of low melting point, they are non-conductors of electricity and are generally hydrolysed by water. In all these compounds the halogen atom is bound to the non-metal by a single covalent bond.

Electropositive character of iodine. According to the trends established in the preceding Groups the heaviest element iodine would be expected to show the most 'metallic' character amongst these elements.

Note. Astatine should be the most metallic and the evidence so far suggests that this is the case. There is no direct physical evidence of metallic binding in iodine, save perhaps a few slight hints:

(1) just above its melting point iodine has a perceptible conductivity which in typical 'metallic' fashion *diminishes* with rising temperature;

(2) the lustre of the crystals.

However, there is definite chemical evidence of iodine showing electropositive character:

(1) Iodine cations exist in solution. Neutral complex-forming compounds such as pyridine (py) stabilise the I^+ ion and crystalline derivatives have been separated out, e.g. dipyridine iodine nitrate $[pyIpy]^+NO_3^-$. Electrolysis of this salt in anhydrous trichloromethane yields iodine at the *cathode* only. As chlorine and bromine form no comparable compounds this emphasises the greater relative *tendency* of iodine towards electropositive character.

(2) Hypoiodous acid is amphoteric. As it is largely basic it can be regarded as iodine hydroxide, and such compounds as ICl and ICN may be considered as salts of this base. ICl conducts electricity when fused, and appears to furnish I^+ and ICl_2^- ions in non-aqueous solvents. Both the molecules have a high proportion of ionic character in the sense I^+Cl^-, I^+CN^-—which is not surprising as both $-Cl$ and $-CN$ are more electronegative than iodine.

Special features of fluorine.

(1) Fluorine is invariably unicovalent, whereas the other halogens all show covalencies of 3 and 5, and chlorine and iodine also show a covalency of 7.

(2) Other elements show their highest covalence in combination with fluorine, e.g. OsF_8, IF_7 and SF_6. In this respect, fluorine resembles oxygen more than chlorine as oxygen is also notable for stabilising higher oxidation states, e.g. SO_3 exists but SCl_6 does not.

(3) Hydrofluoric acid is a weak acid in contrast to hydrochloric, hydrobromic, and hydriodic acids, which are all very strong acids. Also it is unique in forming *acid salts* containing the hydrogen difluoride anion $[HF_2]^-$.

(4) Hydrogen fluoride is strongly hydrogen-bonded and, like water, has an abnormally high boiling point and melting point as well as being an excellent ionising solvent. Here again there is more in common between oxygen and fluorine than fluorine and chlorine.

(5) The solubility of fluorides often differ markedly from the solubilities of other halides of the same metal, e.g. the alkaline earth-metal halides are all very soluble in water except the fluorides which are insoluble; conversely silver fluoride is the only soluble silver halide.

(6) Metals show their highest degree of ionic character when in combination with fluorine thus AlF_3 and SnF_4 are ionic, but the corresponding chlorine compounds are covalent.

(7) As fluorine is the only halogen more electronegative than oxygen it often behaves differently to the other halogens in reactions with oxygen-containing compounds, e.g. water,

$$2H_2O + 2F_2 \rightarrow 4H^+ + 4F^- + O_2,$$

contrast $\qquad H_2O + Cl_2 \rightarrow H^+ + Cl^- + HOCl.$

Hydrogen peroxide, oxygen difluoride, and sometimes ozone are also formed in the reaction between fluorine and water.

(8) Fluorine and chlorine also differ in their behaviour towards alkalis. With cold dilute aqueous alkalis fluorine gives a fluoride and oxygen difluoride,

$$2F_2 + 2OH^- \rightarrow 2F^- + OF_2 + H_2O,$$

contrast $\qquad Cl_2 + 2OH^- \rightarrow Cl^- + OCl^- + H_2O.$

If the alkali is hot and concentrated oxygen is evolved,

$$2F_2 + 4OH^- \rightarrow 4F^- + O_2 + 2H_2O,$$

contrast $\qquad 3Cl_2 + 6OH^- \rightarrow 5Cl^- + ClO_3^- + 3H_2O.$

(9) Fluorine is like oxygen in that it combines directly with carbon and this contrasts with the behaviour of the other halogens which are without effect on it. These properties show that there is more disparity between fluorine and chlorine than there is amongst the other elements in the Group.

The elements
Occurrence

The elements are too reactive to occur in the free state, but their compounds are widely distributed. Owing to their solubility in water, halides are finally washed into the sea, except perhaps with fluorides where precipitation, e.g. as calcium fluoride, occurs. Compounds of chlorine make up about 0.14% of the composition of the earth's crust, and they are by far the most abundant halides. Sodium chloride is the most important of these compounds, and it occurs principally either dissolved in sea water or as deposits of *rock salt*.

Bromine is much less abundant than chlorine with which it generally occurs. Iodine is even less abundant than bromine. Sodium iodate, $NaIO_3$, from the *Chile saltpetre* beds and the ashes of certain seaweeds are the principal sources of iodine. Two important minerals containing fluorine are *fluorspar*, CaF_2, and *cryolite*, Na_3AlF_6.

Isolation

These are all electronegative elements, and in order to liberate them from their simple compounds, it is usually necessary to reverse their general tendency to acquire electrons. This can be done either by means of oxidising agents or electrolytically,

$$2X^- \rightarrow X_2 + 2e.$$

Iodine is the least electronegative halogen, and forms stable compounds with oxygen which are fairly easily reduced to iodine.

Fluorine. The affinity of fluorine for electrons is so strong that the fluoride ion can be discharged only by electrolytic means. Considerable quantities of fluorine are now obtained in this way by electrolysing a molten mixture of potassium fluoride dissolved in anhydrous hydrofluoric acid. It is essential to exclude all traces of water since it is attacked vigorously by fluorine liberating oxygen which, in turn, leads to disintegration of the graphite anodes. The electrolysis cell must also be made of materials resistant to attack by fluorine and so designed as to keep the fluorine separated from the hydrogen liberated at the cathode to prevent an explosive recombination. The electrode processes in such a cell are

at the anode: $F^- \rightarrow \frac{1}{2}F_2 + e,$

at the cathode: $H^+ + e \rightarrow \frac{1}{2}H_2.$

Chlorine. The commercial demand for chlorine is very great. Industrially it is obtained as a by-product in the manufacture of sodium hydroxide from sodium chloride solution and in the electrolysis of fused sodium chloride, fused magnesium chloride and fused calcium chloride for their respective metals (see pp. 308, 302, 322).

Laboratory methods. (1) Chlorine is most commonly prepared by gently heating concentrated hydrochloric acid with manganese(IV) oxide,

$$MnO_2 + 4HCl \rightarrow MnCl_2 + Cl_2 + 2H_2O.$$

It seems probable that the manganese(IV) oxide dissolves initially as manganese(IV) chloride, $MnCl_4$. The dark brown solution formed in the cold from which only a little chlorine is evolved possibly contains manganese(III) chloride, $MnCl_3$, as well. On heating, the higher chlorides decompose to the chloride, $MnCl_2$, with the evolution of chlorine,

$$MnO_2 + 4HCl \rightarrow MnCl_4 + 2H_2O,$$
$$MnCl_4 \rightarrow MnCl_2 + Cl_2.$$

The gas may be conveniently collected over saturated sodium chloride solution in which it is much less soluble than it is in cold water. Otherwise it may be freed from hydrogen chloride fumes by bubbling through a little water, then dried by bubbling it through concentrated sulphuric acid, and collected by downward delivery as it is about two and a half times as heavy as air.

(2) Concentrated hydrochloric acid may also be oxidised to chlorine with potassium permanganate. The reaction proceeds rapidly in the cold, and by controlling the rate at which the acid is added to the crystals an easily regulated stream of chlorine is obtained,

$$2KMnO_4 + 16HCl \rightarrow 2KCl + 2MnCl_2 + 5Cl_2 + 8H_2O.$$

(3) Chlorine may also be conveniently obtained from bleaching powder by the action of dilute acids,

$$CaOCl_2 + 2HCl \rightarrow CaCl_2 + Cl_2 + H_2O,$$
$$CaOCl_2 + H_2SO_4 \rightarrow CaSO_4 + Cl_2 + H_2O.$$

Bromine. Sea water, liquors obtained from the Dead Sea or from the Stassfurt salt beds, all contain bromides. On the industrial scale, the free element is obtained by oxidising the bromide, ion Br^-, with chlorine,

$$2Br^- + Cl_2 \rightarrow Br_2 + 2Cl^-.$$

The volatile bromine is expelled from the reaction mixture and condensed prior to purification by redistillation.

Owing to the high dilution of the bromine set free in sea water a considerable amount of hydrolysis to bromide and hypobromite occurs unless a sufficient proportion of hydrogen ions is added to displace the equilibrium well to the left,

$$Br_2 + H_2O \rightleftharpoons Br^- + HOBr + H^+.$$

Acidification to a pH of about 3.5 reduces the hydrolysis to under 1%. A current of air is then used to carry the bromine from the dilute solution to a tower where it is reduced to hydrogen bromide by an excess of sulphur dioxide and water vapour,

$$SO_2 + Br_2 + 2H_2O \rightarrow 2HBr + H_2SO_4.$$

As the hydrogen bromide is absorbed by the acid liquors this leads to a considerably enriched bromide solution from which the bromine is finally liberated once more with chlorine. The residual mixed acid (HCl and H_2SO_4) is used to acidify fresh supplies of sea water, and so add to the economy of the process.

In the laboratory, bromine may be prepared by distilling a mixture of potassium bromide, manganese(IV) oxide, and moderately concentrated sulphuric acid in a retort, and collecting the bromine that distils over in a water-cooled receiver,

$$2Br^- + MnO_2 + 3H_2SO_4 \rightarrow Br_2 + 2HSO_4^- + Mn^{2+} + SO_4^{2-} + 2H_2O.$$

Iodine. The iodides present in the ash of burnt seaweed may be oxidised to free iodine by distilling with manganese(IV) oxide and sulphuric acid,

$$2I^- + MnO_2 + 3H_2SO_4 \rightarrow I_2 + 2HSO_4^- + Mn^{2+} + SO_4^{2-} + 2H_2O.$$

Principally, however, iodine is obtained from the mother liquors of Chile saltpetre in which it is present as sodium iodate, $NaIO_3$. Sodium hydrogen sulphite is used to reduce the iodate to iodine,

$$2IO_3^- + 5HSO_3^- \rightarrow I_2 + 3HSO_4^- + 2SO_4^{2-} + H_2O.$$

Alternatively, by treating the iodate with sodium hydrogen sulphite and copper(II) sulphate solution, a precipitate of copper(I) iodide is obtained from which iodine is liberated by heating with sulphuric acid and iron(III) oxide or pyrolusite, MnO_2.

Crude iodine is purified by subliming it from a mixture with potassium iodide. This removes any chlorine or bromine which may be present as iodine monochloride, ICl, or iodine monobromide, IBr,

$$I^- + ICl \rightarrow I_2 + Cl^-.$$

Physical properties

Partly because they are both volatile and soluble these are the only elements with any appreciable odour. Fluorine and chlorine are both pungent gases; bromine has a biting disagreeable smell and iodine, which is perceptibly volatile even at room temperature, has a distinct characteristic smell.

Some physical properties of the halogens

Element	Appearance	m.p. (°C)	b.p. (°C)	Density (g cm^{-3})	Solubility (g/100 g at 20 °C)
Fluorine	Pale yellow gas	− 219.6	− 187.9	1.11*	Decomposes water
Chlorine	Greenish yellow gas	− 102.4	− 34.0	1.57*	0.59
Bromine	Dark red heavy liquid	− 7.2	+ 58.2	3.14	3.6
Iodine	Grey-black lustrous flakes	+ 113.6	+ 184.5	4.94	0.018

* For liquid fluorine and chlorine at their boiling point.

A fairly regular change in properties occurs with increasing atomic number. Colour deepens down the Group, and there is a change of state from gas to solid. Melting points, boiling points and density also increase progressively down the Group. This is because the elements retain the diatomic molecular condition in the gas, liquid and solid states. With increasing atomic size the molecules are more readily polarisable and inter-molecular attractions are stronger. Thus, under ordinary conditions iodine is a crystalline solid with a slight 'metallic' lustre; however, the lattice energy is small and iodine readily sublimes.

The halogens are dissolved in water to some extent, and impart their colour to the solution. The solubility in organic solvents such as carbon disulphide, tetrachloromethane, trichloromethane and benzene is quite appreciable. Solutions of iodine in carbon disulphide and tetrachloro-methane are violet, the same colour as the vapour.

Chemical properties

1. Metals. A striking feature of these elements is their reactivity towards metals and the typically salt-like character of the compounds formed with the more electropositive metals, e.g.

$$2K + F_2 \rightarrow 2K^+F^-, \quad \text{ignites spontaneously;}$$
$$Mg + Cl_2 \rightarrow Mg^{2+}Cl_2^-, \quad \text{burns brightly;}$$
$$2Al + 3Br_2 \rightarrow 2AlBr_3, \quad \text{vigorous attack;}$$
$$Hg + I_2 \rightarrow HgI_2, \quad \text{combines energetically on warming.}$$

Only a few metals, such as gold, platinum, and a few others in the platinum family tend to be unaffected by the halogens, but even these elements may be corroded by one or other of the halogens, e.g. bromine easily corrodes gold, but does not attack platinum. While the reactivity of the halogens towards a particular element diminishes as the Group is descended, the reactions of bromine and iodine appear more energetic in comparison with chlorine than would be expected on this basis, e.g. potassium combines explosively with iodine, this is a consequence of their being a liquid and a solid respectively, and therefore more concentrated reagents than the gaseous chlorine.

2. Non-metals. None of the halogens combines directly with oxygen, nitrogen or carbon (except that fluorine attacks carbon), but the other non-metals are all attacked, often with considerable vigour, e.g. chlorine combines explosively with hydrogen and inflames with phosphorus. As with metals, the reactivity of the halogens towards a particular non-metal diminishes as the Group is descended, and the application of heat is often needed for combination to occur. This is well illustrated in their behaviour towards hydrogen described on p. 510. The principal difference from the combination with metals is that non-metals produce compounds which are essentially covalent and are gases, liquids, or low-melting solids, e.g.

PF_3	PCl_3	PBr_3	PI_3
Colourless gas	Colourless liquid	Colourless liquid	Red solid
b.p. $-95\,°C$	b.p. $75.9\,°C$	b.p. $176\,°C$	m.p. $61\,°C$

A property of the halogens is the ability to combine directly amongst themselves to form binary interhalogen compounds. These are listed in the following table. Here again, the ability of the more electronegative halogen—most marked in the case of fluorine—to stabilise higher oxidation states is clearly demonstrated.

Interhalogen compounds

	Chlorine	Bromine	Iodine
F	ClF_3 (g)	BrF_5 (l)	IF_7 (g)
	ClF (g)	BrF_3 (l)	IF_5 (l)
	—	BrF (l)	—
Cl	—	$BrCl$ (g)	ICl (s)
	—	—	ICl_3 (s)
Br	—	—	IBr (s)

The interhalogens have the general formula AB_n where $n = 1, 3, 5$ or 7. They are all volatile covalent substances and most of them are rather unstable, but none is explosive.

3. Water. Bromine is moderately soluble in water, chlorine is less soluble, and iodine is only sparingly soluble. Some of the dissolved halogen reacts with the water, and a reversible equilibrium is rapidly established with the hypohalous acid (i.e., HOCl, HOBr or HOI), and the hydrohalic acid (i.e. HCl, HBr, HI, acids largely dissociated in aqueous solution) which are produced,

$$X_2 + 2H_2O \rightleftharpoons HOX + H_3O^+ + X^-.$$

In saturated aqueous solutions of the halogens at 25 °C about one-third of the total dissolved chlorine is present as hypochlorous acid and hydrochloric acid, only about 1 % of dissolved bromine is hydrolysed, and there is a negligible amount of hypoiodous acid in a saturated solution of iodine.

Both chlorine water and bromine water evolve oxygen when exposed to sunlight owing to the decomposition of the hypohalous acid,

$$2HOCl \rightarrow 2HCl + O_2,$$

$$4HOBr \rightarrow 2H_2O + 2Br_2 + O_2.$$

The apparent difference in the decompositions follows from the equilibrium given above in which the back reaction is more important for hydrobromic acid than it is for hydrochloric acid. The halic acid (i.e. $HClO_3$, $HBrO_3$ and HIO_3) is another possible decomposition product, in the aqueous solution of a halogen,

$$3HOCl \rightarrow HClO_3 + 2HCl,$$

$$5HOX \rightarrow HXO_3 + 2H_2O + 2X_2 \quad (X = Br \text{ or } I \text{ only}).$$

508

4. Alkalis. In the first instance chlorine, bromine and iodine react with cold aqueous alkalis to give a solution containing the hypohalite and halide ions,

$$X_2 + 2OH^- \rightarrow X^- + OX^- + H_2O.$$

However, at room temperature and above both the hypobromous ion OBr^- and hypoiodous ion OI^- rapidly disproportionate, e.g.

$$3OI^- \rightarrow 2I^- + IO_3^-.$$

As the hypobromite or hypoiodite is completely converted to the bromate or iodate respectively the reaction of alkalis with bromine or iodine is therefore best represented by the equation,

$$3X_2 + 6OH^- \rightarrow 5X^- + XO_3^- + 3H_2O.$$

The hypochlorite ion is more stable and good yields of chlorate are obtained only by passing chlorine into a hot concentrated solution of an alkali.

5. Oxidising action. Because chlorine has such a great affinity for hydrogen it often rapidly oxidises compounds containing this element. For example, in direct sunlight a mixture of methane and chlorine reacts explosively,

$$CH_4 + 2Cl_2 \rightarrow C + 4HCl.$$

In diffused sunlight the hydrogen atoms of methane are successively substituted by chlorine atoms,

$$CH_4 + Cl_2 \rightarrow HCl + CH_3Cl \quad \text{(chloromethane)},$$
$$CH_3Cl + Cl_2 \rightarrow HCl + CH_2Cl_2 \quad \text{(dichloromethane)},$$
$$CH_2Cl_2 + Cl_2 \rightarrow HCl + CHCl_3 \quad \text{(trichloromethane)},$$
$$CHCl_3 + Cl_2 \rightarrow HCl + CCl_4 \quad \text{(tetrachloromethane)}.$$

Warm turpentine inflames in chlorine,

$$C_{10}H_{16} + 8Cl_2 \rightarrow 10C + 16HCl.$$

Hydrocarbons in general react similarly.

Chlorine also oxidises ammonia to nitrogen (see p. 431) and hydrogen sulphide to sulphur,

$$8NH_3 + 3Cl_2 \rightarrow 6NH_4Cl + N_2,$$
$$H_2S + Cl_2 \rightarrow 2HCl + S.$$

In solution chlorine will oxidise sulphurous acid to sulphuric acid, bromides to bromine and iodides to iodine,

$$H_2SO_3 + Cl_2 + H_2O \rightarrow H_2SO_4 + 2HCl,$$
$$2Br^- + Cl_2 \rightarrow 2Cl^- + Br_2,$$
$$2I^- + Cl_2 \rightarrow 2Cl^- + I_2.$$

Bromine behaves similarly but less vigorously. Iodine is a much weaker oxidising agent and it is often easier to oxidise the iodide ion I^- to iodine. However, it quantitatively oxidises the thiosulphate ion to tetrathionate: an important reaction in volumetric analysis,

$$2S_2O_3^{2-} + I_2 \rightarrow S_4O_6^{2-} + 2I^-.$$

Uses

Large quantities of chlorine are used in the manufacture of non-inflammable industrial solvents such as trichloroethylene, $CHCl.CCl_2$, and tetrachloromethane. It is also used in the manufacture of hydrochloric acid and bromine, in the preparation of polyvinyl chloride and other plastics, and in bleaching. In this latter respect chlorine may either be used directly with water, or after conversion into bleaching fluid, i.e. sodium hypochlorite solution or bleaching powder (see p. 516). Chlorine has a strong germicidal action and is used in the sterilisation of drinking water.

Bromine is used commercially in the production of 1,2-dibromoethane, $C_2H_4Br_2$. This is added to the lead tetraethyl used in *anti-knock* petrols to prevent any accumulation of lead in petrol engines. Bromine is also used medicinally, e.g. as potassium bromide and in photography, i.e. as silver bromide.

Iodine is most commonly used in medicine as a result of its powerful germicidal action. Smaller amounts are used in the production of dyes and in the photographic industry.

Compounds

Hydrides, HX

Preparation. There are three main processes in which hydrogen halides are formed:

(1) *Direct combination.* This, in principle, is the simplest method, and is applied commerically in the manufacture of hydrochloric acid. The affinity of the halogens for hydrogen diminishes rapidly as the Group is descended and this is clearly illustrated by the Heats of Formation ($\Delta H_f^\ominus$), and the ease with which the hydrogen halide dissociates on heating.

Fluorine combines with extreme violence even at very low temperatures; at $-253\,°C$ solid fluorine and liquid hydrogen explode to hydrogen fluoride, $\quad H_2 + F_2 \rightarrow 2HF; \quad \Delta H_f^\ominus = -270$ kJ per mol HF.

No thermal dissociation even at 1000 °C.

Chlorine will not combine with hydrogen in the dark at room temperature, but the mixture explodes on heating or exposure to sunlight,

$$H_2 + Cl_2 \rightarrow 2HCl; \quad \Delta H_f^{\ominus} = -96 \text{ kJ per mol HCl.}$$

Negligible dissociation at 1000 °C.

Bromine reacts with hydrogen only in direct sunlight or at elevated temperatures (above 500 °C). The combination proceeds smoothly at 300 °C in the presence of a catalyst,

$$H_2 + Br_2 \rightarrow 2HBr; \quad \Delta H_f^{\ominus} = -34 \text{ kJ per mol HBr.}$$

0.5 % dissociation at 1000 °C.

Iodine combines incompletely with hydrogen on heating

$$H_2 + I_2 \rightleftharpoons 2HI; \quad \Delta H_f^{\ominus} = +25 \text{ kJ per mol HI.}$$

33 % dissociation at 1000 °C.

The principal method of manufacturing hydrochloric acid nowadays is by burning together the hydrogen and chlorine evolved in the preparation of sodium hydroxide by the electrolysis of sodium chloride solution (see p. 308), and then dissolving the hydrogen chloride produced in distilled water. The commercial concentrated acid has a density of 1.19 and contains 38 % of hydrogen chloride.

(2) *Displacement from salts.* Generally metallic fluorides, chlorides, bromides and iodides froth energetically in the cold with concentrated sulphuric acid, and the corresponding hydrogen halide is evolved in all cases. The method is used commercially in the manufacture of hydrofluoric acid from fluorspar, CaF_2, and it is the usual method of preparing hydrogen chloride in the laboratory. Rock salt is used, as the lumps prevent the excessive frothing and 'caking' experienced with the fine crystals,

$$CaF_2 + H_2SO_4 \rightarrow 2HF + CaSO_4,$$
$$NaCl + H_2SO_4 \rightarrow NaHSO_4 + HCl.$$

Hydrochloric acid was formerly manufactured on a large scale by this method as part of the *Leblanc soda process.* In this the hydrogen sulphate is heated to red heat when a further quantity of hydrogen chloride is evolved and sodium sulphate remains,

$$NaCl + NaHSO_4 \rightarrow Na_2SO_4 + HCl.$$

The process is still used to a limited extent to meet the demand of the glass industry for sodium sulphate.

The action with bromides and iodides is complicated by secondary reactions. These arise as hydrogen bromide and hydrogen iodide, are progressively stronger reducing agents than hydrogen chloride and are fairly easily oxidised by the concentrated sulphuric acid,

$$2HBr + H_2SO_4 \rightarrow SO_2 + 2H_2O + Br_2,$$
$$6HI + H_2SO_4 \rightarrow S + 4H_2O + 3I_2,$$
$$8HI + H_2SO_4 \rightarrow H_2S + 4H_2O + 4I_2.$$

Syrupy orthophosphoric is another acid which is less volatile than the hydrogen halides, and has the advantage over concentrated sulphuric acid in that it is a non-oxidising agent, and no secondary reactions develop so that it can be used to prepare hydrogen bromide and hydrogen iodide.

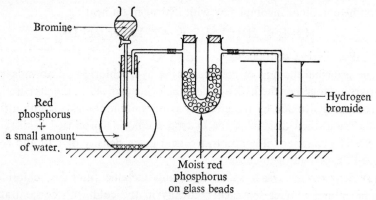

Fig. 134. Preparation of hydrogen bromide.

(3) *Hydrolysis of covalent halides.* Hydrogen bromide and hydrogen iodide are best prepared by this method. The most convenient procedure is to hydrolyse phosphorus tribromide or phosphorus tri-iodide prepared *in situ*. The technique is illustrated in Fig. 134. As iodine is a solid it is necessary to transpose the positioning of the halogen, and the water shown in the diagram when preparing hydrogen iodide,

$$PX_3 + 3H_2O \rightarrow H_3PO_3 + 3HX.$$

As the gases are heavier than air and soluble in water they are collected by downward delivery. Hydrogen iodide can be dried with anhydrous calcium iodide.

Physical properties. Hydrogen halides are colourless pungent smelling gases which fume in moist air. Their principal physical properties are given below. Apart from hydrogen fluoride there is a regular gradation in properties as the Group is descended. The anomalous properties of hydrogen fluoride are the result of its strong tendency to associate (see p. 267).

Physical properties of the hydrogen halides

Compound	m.p. (°C)	b.p. (°C)	Solubility (g/100 g at 10 °C)	Composition of constant boiling-point mixture
HF	−83.1	+19.9	Miscible	35 % HF at 120 °C
HCl	−114.2	−85.0	51.1	20 % HCl at 110 °C
HBr	−86.9	−66.7	120.0	48 % HBr at 125 °C
HI	−50.8	−35.4	153.6	57 % HI at 127 °C

Pure hydrogen halides are covalent compounds, as a result they do not conduct electricity. Their solubility in non-ionising solvents, such as benzene and trichloromethane, in which the molecules of the hydrogen halide are undissociated, is only slight. Water is an extremely effective solvent for the hydrogen halides, e.g. 770 g of HCl dissolve in one litre of water at 20 °C. Because of its strong affinity for water, gaseous hydrogen chloride is sometimes used as a dehydrating agent, e.g. in esterification. Aqueous solutions of hydrogen halides are good electrolytes.

If a dilute aqueous hydrohalic acid is distilled it loses water faster than it loses hydrogen halide, and the concentration of the residual acid increases up to a certain composition when it distils unchanged. Similarly, if a concentrated solution is boiled it loses hydrogen halide faster than it does water and the concentration of the residual acid falls once again to that of the *constant boiling-point mixture* when it distils over unchanged at a fixed temperature.

Chemical properties. In the absence of water, the hydrogen halides tend to be unreactive and in general their chemical properties are the properties of the aqueous solutions.

(1) *Acid character.* The reaction between the hydrogen halides and water is strongly exothermic, thus hydrogen chloride, bromide, and iodide are practically completely dissociated in solution. Expressing this simply,

$$H_2O + HX \rightarrow H_3O^+ + X^-.$$

Because the highly electronegative halogen atom attracts the electrons away from the hydrogen atom in the HX molecule it becomes an incipient proton (see p. 269). As it approaches a lone pair of electrons on a water molecule the halogen atom gains full control of the bonding pair and the water molecule captures the proton,

$$\overset{..}{H-O:}+\overset{\delta+\ \ \delta-}{H-Cl} \rightleftharpoons H-\overset{..}{O}\cdots H-Cl \rightleftharpoons H_3O^+ + Cl^-.$$

Therefore aqueous solutions of these hydrogen halides are in effect solutions of hydroxonium ions H_3O^+ and halide ions, X^-. Since the hydroxonium ion is responsible for acidic properties their solutions are all strong acids, and their strength increases down the Group for the reasons given on p. 269. In contrast, hydrofluoric acid is a weak acid because the hydrogen fluoride dissociates to a considerably smaller extent and also the F^- ions produced tend to combine with undissociated hydrogen fluoride molecules, especially in concentrated solutions,

$$HF \rightarrow H^+ + F^-,$$
$$F^- + HF \rightarrow [HF_2]^-.$$

Aqua regia, a mixture of three parts of concentrated hydrochloric acid and one part of concentrated nitric acid, dissolves such metals as gold and platinum which are ordinarily unattacked by the separate acids. It readily liberates chlorine and nitrosyl chloride, NOCl,

$$3HCl + HNO_3 \rightarrow Cl_2 + 2H_2O + NOCl.$$

Aqua regia is a very powerful oxidising agent and is often used to clean glassware which has become greasy, e.g. burettes.

(2) *Reducing action.* There is a steady strengthening of the reducing action of the aqueous solutions as the Group is descended,

	HF	No reducing action
	HCl	Strong oxidising agents liberate free chlorine, e.g. sodium peroxide, lead(IV) oxide, $KMnO_4$, $K_2Cr_2O_7$, etc.
Diminishing affinity for hydrogen	HBr	Fairly readily oxidised. Hydrogen peroxide, concentrated sulphuric acid liberate bromine, but neither attacks HCl
	HI	An effective reducing agent. All ordinary oxidising agents will liberate iodine, e.g. oxygen, nitric acid, potassium permanganate, chlorine, bromine, iron(III) salts, concentrated sulphuric acid even in the cold, etc.

Aqueous solutions of hydriodic acid are stable in the absence of oxygen but turn brown in air as iodine is set free. The action is hastened by sunlight,

$$O_2 + 4H^+ + 4I^- \rightarrow 2H_2O + 2I_2.$$

The reducing action of concentrated hydriodic acid finds application in organic chemistry in converting alkyl iodides and alcohols to saturated hydrocarbons,

$$C_2H_5OH + 2HI \xrightarrow{250°} C_2H_6 + H_2O + I_2.$$

A little red phosphorus added to the reaction mixture combines with the free iodine which is then hydrolysed back to hydriodic acid and so the strength of the acid is maintained.

Oxides

After fluorine, oxygen is the most electronegative element; then follow the other halogens. Thus in combination with oxygen, fluorine is in a different category from the other halogens. Chlorine, bromine and iodine tend to assume positive oxidation states with oxygen, this is the opposite of their more usual tendency to acquire the negative oxidation state, X^-. Bromine has a much less extensive chemistry with oxygen than either chlorine or iodine, and there is little regularity to be found amongst their oxides. All the oxides of chlorine are explosive gases or liquids. The most stable halogen oxide is iodine pentoxide, I_2O_5.

Iodine pentoxide is the anhydride of iodic acid, HIO_3. It is a white solid prepared by heating iodic acid to 200 °C,

$$2HIO_3 \rightleftharpoons I_2O_5 + H_2O.$$

Oxo-acids

Fluorine forms no oxo-acids. Otherwise, four main categories of oxo-acid may be recognised:

Hypohalous   HOX, e.g. HOCl, HOBr, HOI. Exist in solution only
Halous HXO_2, e.g. $HClO_2$. Unstable, though salts are also known
Halic HXO_3, e.g. $HClO_3$, $HBrO_3$, HIO_3. Comparatively stable
Perhalic HXO_4, e.g. $HClO_4$, HIO_4. Perchloric is the strongest acid.

Besides showing acid properties, the halogen oxo-acids are also oxidising agents.

Hypohalous acids, HOX

The reaction of halogens with water does not constitute a practical method of preparing an aqueous solution because of unfavourable equilibria mentioned earlier. However, the H_3O^+ and X^- ions may be removed by shaking with mercury(II) oxide, this drives the reaction forward, e.g.

$$Cl_2 + 2H_2O \rightleftharpoons H_3O^+ + Cl^- + HOCl,$$
$$2H_3O^+ + 2Cl^- + HgO \rightarrow 3H_2O + HgCl_2.$$

Mercury(II) chloride, unlike most salts, is only slightly ionised.

All of the hypohalous acids are rather unstable, and are progressively less stable down the Group. None can be obtained in the pure state.

They are weak acids; weaker even than carbonic acid, but are good oxidising agents, and give chlorine water and bromine water their bleaching property.

Hypochlorites. By far the most important of these is sodium hypochlorite. In solution this is used commerically as a disinfectant and a bleaching agent. It is made on a large scale by electrolysing cold sodium chloride solution in such a way that the chlorine evolved at the anode mixes with the alkaline solution at the cathode,

$$2OH^- + Cl_2 \rightarrow Cl^- + OCl^- + H_2O.$$

For most purposes the chloride content of the solution does not matter.

(1) Sodium hypochlorite is strongly hydrolysed,

$$OCl^- + H_2O \rightarrow OH^- + HOCl.$$

Hypochlorous acid decomposes in either of two possible ways,

$$2HOCl \rightarrow 2HCl + O_2,$$
$$3HOCl \rightarrow 2HCl + HClO_3.$$

Sunlight or salts of cobalt, iron or nickel catalyse the first reaction. On warming, sodium hypochlorite evolves oxygen and decomposes into a solution of sodium chloride and sodium chlorate.

(2) Dilute acids liberate chlorine from sodium hypochlorite solution,

$$HOCl + Cl^- + H^+ \rightarrow H_2O + Cl_2.$$

(3) Owing to the readiness with which it relinquishes its oxygen hypochlorous acid and its salts are strong oxidising agents. Thus in acid solution hypochlorites liberate iodine from potassium iodide solution and oxidise iron(II) ions to the iron(III) state,

$$HOCl + 2I^- + H^+ \rightarrow H_2O + Cl^- + I_2,$$
$$HOCl + 2Fe^{2+} + H^+ \rightarrow H_2O + Cl^- + 2Fe^{3+}.$$

The bleaching action of hypochlorites is also an oxidising reaction as it is the hypochlorous acid set free which reacts with the colouring matter,

$$HOCl + \quad dye \quad \rightarrow HCl + (dye + O).$$
$$\text{Coloured} \qquad \text{Colourless}$$

Bleaching powder

Industrial preparation. Bleaching powder is produced on a large scale by passing chlorine through a counter current of slaked lime (calcium hydroxide) which is being continuously agitated. The nature of the product is complex and best considered as a mixture of calcium hypochlorite, $Ca(OCl)_2$ and basic calcium chloride, $CaCl_2 . Ca(OH)_2 . H_2O$.

Physical properties. Bleaching powder is a white powdery solid. It is only very slightly soluble in water and is non-deliquescent, in contrast to calcium chloride. It also smells of chlorine.

Reactions. Bleaching powder behaves essentially as a source of hypochlorous acid and its reactions can be considered to be those of a hypochlorite (i.e. calcium hypochlorite) and are similar to those described for sodium hypochlorite.

(1) *Oxygen releasing reactions.* If an aqueous suspension of bleaching powder is shaken with a solution of a cobalt salt there is a rapid evolution of oxygen. Oxygen is also evolved if bleaching powder is heated.

(2) *Chlorine releasing reactions.* Acids liberate chlorine from bleaching powder,
$$HOCl + Cl^- + H^+ \rightarrow H_2O + Cl_2.$$

The chloride ion may come from the bleaching powder or from hydrochloric acid if this is added.

On standing in air bleaching powder absorbs carbon dioxide. This liberates hypochlorous acid which decomposes and evolves chlorine.

(3) *Oxidising reactions.* Bleaching powder shows the same oxidising properties as sodium hypochlorite.

It is used to bleach fabrics and paper pulp, and as a disinfectant.

Halic acids, HXO₃

Solutions of both chloric acid and bromic acid may be prepared by adding dilute sulphuric acid to either barium chlorate or barium bromate respectively,
$$Ba(ClO_3)_2 + H_2SO_4 \rightarrow 2HClO_3 + BaSO_4 \downarrow.$$

Iodic acid is prepared by oxidising iodine with warm concentrated nitric acid,
$$3I_2 + 10HNO_3 \rightarrow 6HIO_3 + 10NO + 2H_2O.$$

When cool, white crystals of iodic acid may be filtered off and recrystallised from the minimum quantity of hot water. A solution of iodic acid behaves as a strong acid and it is also an oxidising agent.

Chlorates. A mixture of chlorate and chloride is formed by passing chlorine into a hot concentrated solution of caustic alkali,
$$3Cl_2 + 6OH^- \rightarrow ClO_3^- + 5Cl^- + 3H_2O.$$

As only five-sixths of the alkali are converted to chlorate this is not a very efficient method. Both sodium and potassium chlorate are manufactured on the large scale by the electrolysis of the corresponding chloride at a temperature of 60–70 °C in such a way that the products at the anode and

517

the cathode mix freely. Under these conditions the chlorate is formed in solution and the hydrogen discharged at the cathode is liberated. As sodium chlorate is very soluble, evaporation of the solution first deposits crystals of sodium chloride which can be filtered off. As the solubility of sodium chloride changes only slightly with temperature, cooling produces crystals of sodium chlorate. On the other hand, potassium chlorate is only sparingly soluble in cold water and so crystallises out of solution before the unchanged potassium chloride.

Potassium chlorate melts at about 400 °C and then begins to solidify owing to the decomposition into a mixture of potassium perchlorate and potassium chloride, $4KClO_3 \rightarrow 3KClO_4 + KCl.$

At higher temperatures it decomposes with effervescence into potassium chloride and oxygen. In the solid state it is used as an oxidising agent, e.g. in matches and fireworks.

Bromates. Potassium bromate is similar to potassium chlorate but does not form a perbromate when heated.

Iodates. If iodine is stirred into a hot concentrated solution of potassium hydroxide until only a small excess of the alkali remains, white crystals of the sparingly soluble potassium iodate separate out on cooling.

On strong heating it behaves like the chlorate and bromate and decomposes into the iodide and oxygen. Potassium iodate is an oxidising agent and because it can be obtained in a high degree of purity it is a useful standard substance in volumetric analysis for standardising sodium thiosulphate solution. This is because in the presence of an excess of iodide ions and an excess of acid it will quantitatively oxidise the iodide to free iodine, $IO_3^- + 5I^- + 6H^+ \rightarrow 3I_2 + 3H_2O.$

Exercises

1. How and under what conditions does iodine react with (a) nitric acid, (b) phosphorus, (c) hydrogen, (d) chlorine, (e) potassium chlorate, (f) mercury?
2. From the standpoint of the Periodic Law compare (a) the methods of preparation, (b) the physical and chemical properties of the halogen hydracids.
3. Chlorine, bromine and iodine form a family of elements remarkable for their general similarity of chemical behaviour and for the graduation of their physical properties. Discuss and illustrate this statement.

(L)

4. Give an account of the industrial preparation and uses of chlorine.

Compare and contrast the properties of chlorine with those of fluorine.

5. Outline the commercial production of chlorine and give two large-scale uses for the element.

Starting from chlorine, how would you prepare a pure sample of potassium perchlorate? Outline, with the aid of a diagram, the electronic structure of the perchlorate anion. How would you demonstrate the presence of chlorine in a sample of acetyl chloride? (C)

6. Explain the following observations:

(i) Hydrogen fluoride is both less volatile and a weaker acid than hydrogen chloride.

(ii) Silver chloride dissolves in ammonia solution; silver iodide does not.

(iii) Chlorine and methane react rapidly when exposed to strong sunlight.

(iv) Pure hydrogen bromide is not readily obtained by the action of concentrated sulphuric acid on sodium bromide.

(v) Sulphuric acid and hydrochloric acid are equally strong, yet hydrogen chloride is evolved by the action of concentrated sulphuric acid on sodium chloride. (C)

7. What do you know of the discovery, manufacture, properties, and uses of fluorine? Discuss the chemical differences between fluorine and chlorine. (LS)

8. By reference to the properties of the halogens and of their compounds with hydrogen, explain the features you would expect to find in a Group in the Periodic Table. (O & C)

9. Suggest a scheme for classifying, according to their structure and properties, compounds of the general formula AaXx, where A is any element and X a halogen. Indicate, with reasons, how the following would fit into your scheme:

$$HF, \ AgBr, \ ICl, \ HgCl_2, \ KI_3,$$
$$BF_3, \ AuCl_3, \ NCl_3, \ SnCl_4, \ PCl_5, \ SF_6. \quad (CS)$$

10. Give ionic equations for **three** redox reactions which are used in volumetric analysis and state clearly which substances are oxidized and which are reduced.

The reaction between bromine and thiosulphate ion is said to be represented by the equation:

$$4Br_2 + S_2O_3{}^{2-} + 5H_2O = 8Br^- + 2HSO_4{}^- + 8H^+.$$

How would you confirm the stoichiometry of the reaction by means of volumetric analysis? (O & C)

PART IV
TRANSITION ELEMENTS

27

AN INTRODUCTION TO TRANSITION ELEMENTS

What is a transition element?

Mendeléeff originally used the term *transitional* to describe the elements in Group VIII because he visualised them as forming a transition between the A and B Groups. With only a few exceptions the elements of Group VIII and the other transition Groups in the long form of the Periodic Table possess certain characteristics which not only distinguish them from the Main Group elements but also show that they are related to one another. As a consequence of this and also for another more fundamental reason discussed further below, all the elements in the *transition Groups* are referred to as *transition elements*.

The transition elements

					Transition Groups					
Period	IIIA	IVA	VA	VIA	VIIA		VIII		IB	IIB
4	Sc	Ti	V	Cr	Mn	Fe	Co	Ni	Cu	Zn
5	Y	Zr	Nb	Mo	Tc	Ru	Rh	Pd	Ag	Cd
6	La*	Hf	Ta	W	Re	Os	Ir	Pt	Au	Hg
7	Ac†	—	—	—	—	—	—	—	—	—

* Fourteen lanthanide elements. † Fourteen actinide elements.

Transition elements and electron structure

Whereas Main Group elements correspond to the building up of s and p electron sub-shells in the outer shell of an atom the transition elements, whose symbols are shown above, correspond to the different electron structures which arise from the filling of the d sub-shell which lies just below the outer shell. Because of this these elements are sometimes referred to as the *d-block elements*. As the elements collectively described as *lanthanides* and *actinides* are two series of elements in which the $4f$ and

523

$5f$ sub-levels respectively are being filled and as they also exhibit special chemical features it is convenient to omit them from the following discussion. A full account of the relationship between the position of an element in the Periodic Table and its electron configuration is given in ch. 5 and the reader is advised to re-read the section referring to Period 4 (p. 58) at this stage. The outer electronic configuration of the first transition series is summarised below:

Sc	Ti	V	Cr	Mn	Fe	Co	Ni	Cu	Zn
$3d^14s^2$	$3d^24s^2$	$3d^34s^2$	$3d^54s^1$	$3d^54s^2$	$3d^64s^2$	$3d^74s^2$	$3d^84s^2$	$3d^{10}4s^1$	$3d^{10}4s^2$

As the characteristic properties of transition elements referred to above are the result of partly filled d sub-shells, transition elements have been defined as those which, as elements, have partly filled d sub-shells. But Group IB elements have complete d sub-shells and yet exhibit typical transition properties (i.e. variable valency, coloured ions, complex ion formation, paramagnetism, catalytic ability, pronounced *metallic* properties). However, these elements do use d electrons in compound formation. So by extending the definition to include *elements with partly filled d sub-shells in any of their commonly occurring oxidation states as well as the atomic state*, Group IB elements are included.

Group IIB elements (Zn, Cd and Hg) never have a partly filled d sub-shell either as elements or in the combined state. Neither do they show typical transition properties to any appreciable extent (except complex ion formation). Group IIIA (Sc, Y and La) is another Group of elements which do not show many of the properties associated with typical transition elements. They are transition elements by definition as there is one d electron in the partly filled d sub-shell of each atom. But in compounds they mostly occur as the tripositive ion, and as this has no d electrons (the atom having lost its only one) they do not exhibit transition properties and behave like Main Group elements. In order to maintain a rational classification, the elements of Group IIIA and Group IIB are referred to as *non-typical transition elements* and the elements in the remaining transition Groups are *typical transition elements*.

General features

There are 59 transition elements. They are all metals and thus constitute the bulk of the metallic elements (75). Among them are to be found some of the most important and widely used technological materials, e.g. Fe, Cu, Cr, W, Mn, Ni, Ti and Zn. This is usually a consequence of the exceptional mechanical properties displayed by these metals, which in turn reflects the strong metallic binding so characteristic of typical transition elements. Other characteristic properties of typical transition elements have already been mentioned. Certain of these properties vary progressively across the series and in some cases (e.g. paramagnetism), it is possible to correlate the variation in bulk properties with the changing electron structure as the atomic number increases.

Among the Main Group elements attention was focused on the vertical relationships that exist amongst the elements. Trends may also be distinguished amongst the transition Groups. Note that the melting points, boiling points and densities of typical transition metals and also of Group IIIA elements, increase down the Group. Melting points and boiling points decrease down Group IIB. As a general rule there is a closer relationship between the elements in Periods 5 and 6 than there is between the elements in Periods 4 and 5. This is less apparent towards the end of the series and in fact cadmium is more closely similar to zinc than it is to mercury. More important, however, are the horizontal relationships that exist among consecutive members across each transition series, especially about the middle of the series.

Atomic radii

The variation in atomic radii across each transition series is shown in Fig. 135.

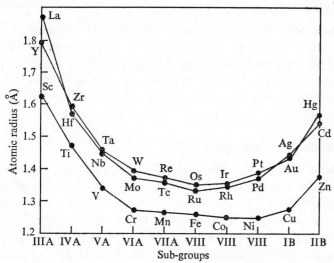

Fig. 135. Atomic radii across the transition series.

As the nuclear charge increases with increasing atomic number across the Periods it strengthens the electric field attracting the electrons towards the nucleus and this leads to the diminution in the radius across the Periods. Opposing this effect are the forces of repulsion between the electrons, and as a shell approaches completion these forces reach a maximum and even exceed the attractive force from the increased nuclear change so that the electron cloud expands. All this follows the pattern of events described for the elements in the short Periods (see p. 66). Where the *d*-block elements differ is that electrons enter an inner *d* shell and thereby add to the primary screening effect. Consequently as the nuclear charge increases so does the screening effect and as a result the effective nuclear charge increases only slightly and there is little change in atomic radius. This is particularly noticeable in the region of Group VIII. When the 18-electron shell is completely filled the screening effect is more noticeably enhanced and this is reflected in the increase in size of the following element, i.e. Group I B and then Group II B. The close resemblances which occur between horizontal neighbours amongst the *d*-block elements is partly explained by the similarity of their outer electron configuration since it is this inner *d* shell which is being filled. This feature is accentuated by the similarity in their atomic radii. The very close similarity between the radii of the elements in Periods 5 and 6 results from a *lanthanide contraction* similar in origin to the *d*-block contraction.

Reactivity

Electrode potentials shown in the graph on p. 154 illustrate the wide range in electropositive character amongst these elements, some of which comprise the most unreactive of metals (e.g. Au and Pt) whilst others are quite highly electropositive (e.g. Ti). Generally reactivity diminishes down the Group, and transition elements as a class are much less reactive than the metals of Groups I A and II A.

Characteristic properties

1. *Variable valency*. The relationship between electronic structure and position in the Periodic Table is brought out by considering the maximum Group valency, which is equal to the Group number. Stable valencies for the first transition series are summarised on the opposite page. If osmium is included in the summary, a valency of 8 for Group VIII is also included. The greater number of valency states shown by elements near the centre of the series is dependent on the maximum valency state, since there is a strong tendency to show all states from two up to the maximum. However, the non-typical transition elements of Group IIIA and Group IIB show a constant valency of 3 and 2 respectively. Several Main Group elements have more than one principal valency but these differ from each other by 2, e.g. Sn and Pb, 2 and 4; P, As, Sb and Bi, 3 and 5.

Group no. ...	IIIA	IVA	VA	VIA	VIIA	VIII			IB	IIB
Element	Sc	Ti	V	Cr	Mn	Fe	Co	Ni	Cu	Zn
Maximum valency	3	4	5	6	7	6	4	4	2	2
	—	3	4	3	6	3	3	2	1	—
Other valencies		2	3	2	4	2	2			
			2		3					
					2					

The trends in the variability and numerical magnitude of valency states across the Period closely follows the increasing number of ($3d$ and $4s$) electrons which total 3 for Group IIIA and 8 for iron (and osmium) in Group VIII. After iron the number and magnitude of the valency states diminish as the d sub-shell fills up and fewer unpaired electrons become available for bond formation.

With the exception of scandium all the elements show a valency of 2. This can be correlated with the loss of the two outer s electrons from the neutral atom. By losing all three valence electrons an atom of scandium gains the very stable electron configuration of argon and this accounts for its readiness to form the Sc^{3+} ion. Similarly, loss of the $4s$ electrons from a zinc atom exposes the fairly stable 18-electron structure and this limits further ionisation. As the neutral copper atom has only one $4s$ electron to lose before exposing this same 18-electron structure the possibility of forming copper(I) compounds can be appreciated. Generally it is because of the similarity in the energies of the $3d$ and $4s$ orbitals in the neutral atoms of the transition elements that they are able to form such a wide variety of stable valency states. However, as the exact conditions determining the relative stabilities of these various valencies are both numerous and complex the matter will not be pursued further at this stage.

2. Paramagnetism. Most substances are weakly repelled from a strong magnetic field whilst others are weakly attracted to it; these substances are termed *diamagnetic* and *paramagnetic* respectively. In some cases the force of attraction is so large they constitute a special class of substances called ferromagnetics, e.g. iron, cobalt and nickel. Paramagnetic measurements on ions are made either on substances in bulk (i.e. salts) or on their aqueous solutions. All but a few typical transition metal ions are paramagnetic. Non-typical transition metals do not form paramagnetic ions.

The magnitude of the paramagnetic effect varies according to the ion, this is illustrated in Fig. 136 for some ions from the first transition series. The attraction of a magnetic field is strongest for the Fe^{3+} and Mn^{2+} ions and then diminishes to Sc^{3+} and Zn^{2+} at the beginning and end of the series respectively, both of these ions being diamagnetic.

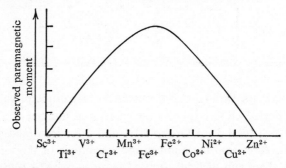

Fig. 136. Variation in the paramagnetic effect shown by selected ions across the first transition series.

The magnetic properties of materials in bulk are the result of the number and arrangement of their constituent electrons, neutrons and protons. As the magnetic effects produced by electrons are some thousand-fold stronger than those produced by the nucleus they are of primary importance. It seems certain that paramagnetic behaviour is caused by unpaired electrons (see p. 50) in the atom, molecule, or ion, and that the intensity of the effect is related to the number of these unpaired electrons. The outer electronic configuration of the ions used in the previous graph are given on the page opposite showing the number of unpaired electrons present. It will be seen that the paramagnetic effect of the various ions rises to a maximum in step with the increasing number of unpaired electrons.

Theoretical calculations based on the number of unpaired electrons in an ion give values for the paramagnetic moments in fairly good agreement with those observed experimentally. As the electron structures above assume the correctness of Hund's rule of maximum multiplicity (i.e. orbitals are occupied singly before pairing occurs, see p. 50) this result is evidence for the validity of the rule.

Ion	3d orbital electron structure					No. of unpaired electrons
Sc^{3+}						0
Ti^{3+}	1					1
V^{3+}	1	1				2
Cr^{3+}	1	1	1			3
Mn^{3+}	1	1	1	1		4
Mn^{2+}, Fe^{3+}	1	1	1	1	1	5
Fe^{2+}	2	1	1	1	1	4
Co^{2+}	2	2	1	1	1	3
Ni^{2+}	2	2	2	1	1	2
Cu^{2+}	2	2	2	2	1	1
Zn^{2+}	2	2	2	2	2	0

3. Metallic properties. Transition metals show the physical properties common to all metals (see p. 190). By referring to the graphs given on pp. 196 and 202, it will be seen that the densities and melting points of the elements rise to a maximum amongst the transition elements of Periods 4, 5 and 6. Densities reach a maximum near Group VIII; melting points and boiling points near Group VIA. In each case it is the metals of the transition series which constitute the pronounced peaks in the curves and this demonstrates how much higher the values of these properties are for typical transition metals than for Main Group elements.

Typical transition metals generally show good mechanical properties, i.e. they are tough, malleable and ductile. Together with the high melting points and boiling points the toughness of these metals indicates strong metallic binding. Much stronger in fact than can be accounted for in terms of the s electrons in the outermost shell. Undoubtedly electrons in the underlying d sub-shell also participate in the binding. It is suggested that the unpaired d electrons contribute to the binding possibly by forming covalent bonds with unpaired electrons in neighbouring atoms. In moving across the transition series from left to right the number of unpaired electrons rises to a maximum of five in the chromium Group VIA after which pairing commences and their number decreases to zero at zinc. This has the effect of strengthening the metallic lattice up to the chromium Group whereafter it would progressively weaken. The variation in the observed melting points and boiling points is in fairly good agreement with the pattern of behaviour one would expect on this basis. Changes in metallic structure amongst the metals cause some to have values which appear anomalous, e.g. manganese. Metals in Group VIII and Group IB tend to be softer and more ductile than those at the beginning of the transition series. Possibly this reflects the weaker metallic binding in these Groups coupled with the fact that most of them crystallise with face-centred cubic structures and therefore have more glide-planes (see p. 194) than the remaining metals which generally crystallise with body-centred cubic and hexagonal close-packed structures. It is because of their close-packed structures and the compactness of their atoms that these transition elements have such high densities. It can be seen from the graph on p. 525 that the atomic radius of the metals in the long Periods reaches a minimum amongst the Group VIII elements and this can be correlated with the exceptionally high density of these elements (see p. 198).

4. Coloured ions. One of the most characteristic properties of typical transition metals is the fact that they all give coloured ions in aqueous solution and most of their compounds are coloured. The colours shown in aqueous solution by some hydrated ions from the first transition series are given below. Besides the colourless ions formed by the non-typical transition elements some are also formed by certain typical transition elements (i.e. those towards the ends of the series), e.g. Cu^+, Ag^+ and Ti^{4+}. All these ions have a completely filled or completely empty sub-shell of d electrons whereas the coloured ions all have an incomplete d sub-shell.

Those transition metal ions which exhibit colour absorb certain of the radiations from the white light falling upon them and as a consequence the

Ion	Colour	No. of unpaired electrons
Sc^{3+}	Colourless	0
Ti^{3+}	Purple	1
V^{3+}	Green	2
Cr^{3+}	Violet	3
Mn^{3+}	Violet	4
Fe^{3+}	Yellow	5
Mn^{2+}	Pink	5
Fe^{2+}	Green	4
Co^{2+}	Pink	3
Ni^{2+}	Green	2
Cu^{2+}	Blue	1
Zn^{2+}	Colourless	0

transmitted light is coloured. It is argued that these ions are capable of absorbing radiations from the visible spectrum, since the differences in energy between the d orbitals within a particular ion are of the same order of magnitude as the energies of the radiations constituting white light. If a light photon of a particular wavelength has the same energy as that existing between two d orbitals an electron in the orbital of lower energy can absorb the photon and in so doing will move into the orbital of higher energy—provided this orbital has a vacancy. Consequently the ion filters out this particular wavelength and so appears coloured. As the energy levels of the d orbitals vary from ion to ion they absorb different wavelengths and therefore often have different colours.

The differences in energy between the orbitals in the ions of the Main Group elements are too large for an electron to be raised to a higher level by absorbing a photon from the visible spectrum. However, more highly energetic radiations in the ultra violet are absorbed (see p. 45).

Until now the discussion has been about ions in aqueous solution but it must be stressed that the environment of the ion is critical in determining its colour. Thus in aqueous solution the ions are always hydrated and the surrounding water molecules have a profound effect on the energies of the d orbitals. For example the $[Cu(H_2O)_4]^{2+}$ ion is blue as in copper(II) sulphate solution but the simple Cu^{2+} ion is white as in anhydrous copper sulphate. Furthermore, the tetrammine copper(II) ion $[Cu(NH_3)_4]^{2+}$ formed in ammonia solution is deep blue.

5. Complex ions. Although complex ion formation is not an exclusive property of transition metals it does reach a maximum among these elements. Not only does the small size and comparatively high charge of transition metal ions favour the acceptance of a lone pair of electrons from the ligand molecule or ion (see p. 236), but the special electronic configuration of these ions furnishes the necessary orbitals of appropriate energy to accommodate them. Even though there is a wide variation in complexing ability amongst the various transition metal ions certain general trends may be distinguished. When a transition metal is able to form more than one ion the one with the highest charge forms complexes of greater stability—presumably a reflection of its greater attraction for electrons. For example the Co^{2+} ion does not form a stable complex with ammonia whereas the Co^{3+} ion does, i.e. $[Co(NH_3)_6]^{3+}$. It is generally the case that the stablest complexes are formed when the donor atom of the ligand is nitrogen or oxygen as in hydrates or ammines, for example. Furthermore, it has been found that the bivalent ion of the elements in the latter half of the first transition series form complexes with a particular ligand which progressively increase in stability from Mn^{2+} to Cu^{2+} and then become less stable in passing to Zn^{2+}.

6. Catalytic ability. Most of the common catalysts are to be found amongst the transition elements, e.g. platinum, nickel, iron, chromium, manganese, etc. Catalysis is believed to operate through a mechanism involving reactions on the surface of the catalyst. The large number of valence electrons and available d orbitals in atoms of the transition elements possibly facilitate electron redistributions amongst reacting particles in close proximity on the surface of the catalyst and this would accelerate the reaction.

7. Interstitial compounds. Small atoms, in particular hydrogen, boron, carbon and nitrogen, are able to fit into the interstices in the transition metal lattice, forming materials which are chemically similar to the metals themselves but frequently differ greatly in physical properties especially hardness. The composition of these 'metals' is variable and cannot be expressed by a simple chemical formula, i.e. they are *non-stoichiometric*.

Related to the interstitial compounds are the *alloys*. *Interstitial alloys* and *substitutional alloys* are of major importance in metallurgy and formed with great facility by the transition metals. In the former, small non-metal atoms (e.g. H, B, C, N) enter some of the interstices in the transition metal lattice and impart to the alloy useful features which neither of the individual elements exhibits, e.g. enhanced hardness. Owing to the similarity in their size some transitional metal atoms are able to replace one another in the metallic lattice and form *substitutional alloys* amongst themselves. Alloy steels are an important example of this type of material, in which iron atoms are substituted by chromium, manganese or nickel atoms, etc., to give the steel more useful and widely applicable properties. Other examples include the brasses (p. 588) and coinage alloys, cupro-nickel, cupro-gold and platinum-iridium.

Relationships between Transition Groups and Main Groups

These relationships are discussed more fully in the appropriate chapters.

Resemblances between the elements of a particular transition Group and their counterparts in the corresponding Main Group are closest for the two 'bridging' Groups, i.e. IIIA and IIB. These two Groups start and finish the transition series respectively. They comprise the non-typical transition elements whose properties are often more typical of Main Group elements. Moving from the ends of the transition series towards Group VIII similarities between Main Group and transition Group diminish and almost vanish at Group VIII whose counterpart is found in the noble gases; note, *noble* metals, *noble* gases. Within any particular Main Group in general it is the element in Period 3 which shows the closest similarity to the elements in the corresponding transition Group.

Exercises

1. What is a transition element? Give an account of the properties of transition elements which distinguish them from Main Group elements.
2. Write explanatory notes on the following: (*a*) interstitial compound, (*b*) paramagnetic ions, (*c*) coloured ions, (*d*) variable valency.
3. Discuss the trends in atomic radius and electron structure that exist between the elements in the first transition series. To what extent do these two *atomic properties* account for the trends in bulk properties amongst these elements.
4. Give an account of the vertical trends among the elements in the transition Groups. Indicate any similarities or differences to the vertical trends amongst the Main Group elements.
5. Explain concisely what is meant by the Periodic Classification of the elements, indicating with one example of each, the significance of the terms 'group', 'short period', and 'transition element'.

   How is the electronic structure of an element related to (*a*) its position in the Periodic Classification, (*b*) its valency?

   Give the electronic structures of the following atoms: argon, carbon, chlorine, sodium.

   How is it that iron (atomic number 26) can have two valencies?   (J.M.B.)
6. What justification is there for classifying zinc as a transition element?
7. The following elements form part of the first transition series.

Element	Outer electronic structure
Ti	$3d^2\ 4s^2$
V	$3d^3\ 4s^2$
Cr	$3d^5\ 4s^1$
Mn	$3d^5\ 4s^2$
Fe	$3d^6\ 4s^2$
Co	$3d^7\ 4s^2$
Ni	$3d^8\ 4s^2$
Cu	$3d^{10}\ 4s^1$

Select any **three** elements and give examples from their chemistry to illustrate (*a*) typical properties of transition metal compounds and (*b*) the changing behaviour of elements along the series. Explain briefly the causes of the properties which you describe.   (O & CS)

28

SOME TRANSITION ELEMENTS OF PERIOD 4: TITANIUM, VANADIUM, CHROMIUM, MANGANESE, IRON, COBALT AND NICKEL

Horizontal relationships are very much closer with transition elements than with Main Group elements. Most of the well-known and important transition metals are in the first transition series in Period 4 which includes those listed above and also copper and zinc. Period relationships are more important although general Group relationships exist. Reference will be made occasionally to potassium and calcium to show that Period 4 trends continue without a break.

Atomic properties. For electronic configurations, see p. 612. Because most of the transition elements under discussion have two electrons in their external shells, they are metals, and all show a positive electrovalency of two, except scandium which is always trivalent.

Elements from scandium to manganese inclusive have a maximum valency which is the upper Group valency (equal to the Group number). Other valencies are shown by all members of the series except zinc, which always has a valency of 2, and scandium. Valencies higher than four are covalencies.

Titanium

Titanium is in Group IV A, and has the electronic configuration 2, 8, (8+2), 2. Its valencies in order of stability are 4, 3 and 2. When quadrivalent it uses all four electrons in excess of the 2, 8, 8 (argon) configuration.

Occurrence

Titanium (0.6 % of earth's crust) ranks seventh in order of abundance of metals. It is widely dispersed in small quantities in all types of rock. The two most important ores are *ilmenite*, $FeTiO_3$ or $FeO.TiO_2$ (iron(II) titanate), and *rutile*, TiO_2.

Isolation

The chief problem in its large-scale manufacture is that its great affinity for oxygen, nitrogen, carbon and hydrogen at high temperatures prevents the formation of sufficiently pure metal. Even small quantities of impurity make the metal brittle and useless. For these reasons pure *intermediates* must first be made. In all commercial processes, highly purified titanium(IV) chloride is reduced with magnesium or sodium under a protective atmosphere of argon or helium.

Preparation of titanium(IV) chloride. Chlorine is passed over a heated mixture of rutile and carbon. Titanium(IV) chloride vapour (boiling point 136 °C) is condensed and purified by fractional distillation (to remove $FeCl_3$, etc.),

$$TiO_2 + 2C + 2Cl_2 \rightarrow TiCl_4 + 2CO.$$

Reduction of titanium(IV) chloride. Magnesium or sodium is melted in a steel vessel in an atmosphere of argon or helium. Liquid titanium(IV) chloride is fed in and the vapour formed is reduced to the metal,

$$TiCl_4 + 2Mg \rightarrow Ti + 2MgCl_2.$$

The reaction is highly exothermic and the temperature is allowed to rise to about 850 °C. Metallic titanium separates as a spongy solid, since the temperature is well below its melting point. Molten magnesium chloride is tapped from the bottom; the titanium sponge remaining stuck to the sides of the vessel and bridging across. Magnesium chloride and magnesium trapped in the sponge are volatilised *in vacuo*. The sponge is then melted by an electric arc in an atmosphere of argon and the metal cast into ingots.

Physical properties

Titanium is a metal with a silvery lustre, with low density, 4.5 g cm^{-3}, and high melting point 1700 °C. When pure it is ductile, hard and strong (like steel).

Chemical properties

At ordinary and moderately high temperatures titanium shows great resistance to corrosion because of the formation of a thin protective film of oxide, TiO_2. Thus it is stable in air at ordinary temperatures and is not attacked by water, even sea water, in which respect it is superior to stainless steel. It decomposes steam on strong heating,

$$Ti + 2H_2O \rightarrow TiO_2 + 2H_2 \uparrow.$$

Cold hydrofluoric acid and cold dilute sulphuric acid dissolve titanium,

$$Ti + 3H^+ \rightarrow Ti^{3+} + 1\tfrac{1}{2}H_2.$$

Cold hydrochloric acid or nitric acid of any concentration have no effect on titanium; hot concentrated hydrochloric acid dissolves it to give a violet solution of titanium(III) chloride, $TiCl_3$; and in hot concentrated nitric acid it is oxidised, giving a white precipitate, $TiO_2 . xH_2O$, an action very similar to that for tin (p. 371). Aqueous sodium hydroxide, cold or hot, has no action on titanium. Titanium combines with chlorine at 300 °C forming titanium(IV) chloride $TiCl_4$. At red heat it burns in oxygen forming titanium(IV) oxide. At 800 °C it burns in nitrogen forming the nitride, TiN. When it burns in air a mixture of oxide and nitride is formed. Heated strongly with carbon it forms the carbide, TiC.

Uses

Because of its high strength-to-weight ratio and resistance to corrosion up to 500 °C it is used in the construction of aircraft skins and jet engines. Other uses depend on its great power for combining with oxygen and nitrogen, e.g. (1) in the form of its alloy with iron (ferrotitanium) it is added to molten steel to remove combined oxygen and nitrogen, which are harmful in steel; (2) in the production of high vacua by removing the last traces of air; (3) in making jewellery.

Compounds of titanium

Titanium forms Ti^{2+} ions by loss of its two $4s$ electrons, Ti^{3+} ions by loss of its two $4s$ electrons and one of its $3d$ electrons, and shows a covalency or ionic valency of 4 by using its two $4s$ electrons and its two $3d$ electrons. The quadrivalent titanium(IV) compounds are the most stable Trivalent titanium(III) compounds are powerful reducing agents. The bivalent compounds are of less importance.

Titanium(IV) oxide, TiO_2. Occurs naturally as the mineral rutile which has the ionic structure shown on p. 138, a structure also found in three oxides of Group IVB: GeO_2, SnO_2 and PbO_2. Pure titanium(IV) oxide is obtained from rutile by dissolving it in concentrated sulphuric acid. On dilution $Ti(OH)_4$ is precipitated by hydrolysis, filtered off, washed and ignited. Titanium(IV) oxide is a white, very stable solid, insoluble in water. Amphoteric, it dissolves slowly in concentrated sulphuric acid to give titanyl sulphate, $[TiO][SO_4]$ and reacts with fused sodium hydroxide forming sodium titanate, Na_2TiO_3 (analogous to Na_2SiO_3).

Uses. Large quantities are used as a white pigment in paint manufacture, perhaps the best white pigment because of its great covering power and its property of being unaffected by hydrogen sulphide in the air (which darkens white lead paints by forming black lead(II) sulphide). Titanium(IV) oxide is also used in making India paper, a thin tough printing paper made opaque by the titanium(IV) oxide filler.

Titanium(IV) chloride, TiCl$_4$. This is an intermediate in the manufacture of titanium, where its preparation is outlined. It is a colourless, covalent liquid (boiling point 136 °C), fuming strongly in moist air. It is hydrolysed rapidly by water to give titanium(IV) oxide (hydrated),

$$TiCl_4 + 2H_2O \rightarrow TiO_2 + 4HCl.$$

Titanium(IV) chloride dissolves in concentrated hydrochloric acid forming chlorotitanic acid, H_2TiCl_6. When sprayed into the air, it gives a voluminous white smoke and is therefore used to make smoke-screens. Another of its uses is as a catalyst in the manufacture of polyethylene.

Titanium(III) chloride, TiCl$_3$. A violet solution of titanium(III) chloride can be made by dissolving titanium in hot concentrated hydrochloric acid. This solution is a powerful reducing agent used in volumetric analysis. It is kept in an atmosphere of hydrogen to prevent oxidation.

An interesting reaction of solutions of titanium salts is the formation of a bright golden yellow colour on the addition of hydrogen peroxide solution. The colour is caused by peroxotitanic acid, H_4TiO_5, and is used as a test for titanium, and for hydrogen peroxide.

Titanium carbide, TiC. See p. 394.

Relationship between A and B families of Group IV

The fundamental relationships is shown by the identity in the number of valency electrons. For example:

tin	2,	8,	18,	18, **4**
titanium	2,	8,	8+**2**, **2**	

i.e. both elements show the Group valency of 4.

The relationship is almost as close as in Group III and is found chiefly in the quadrivalent state, i.e. when the elements show the Group valency. The resemblances between compounds of titanium and those of tin are often considerable, mainly because of similarity in ionic radii: Ti^{4+}, 0.68 Å; Sn^{4+}, 0.71 Å.

(1) Action of concentrated nitric acid on titanium is very similar to that on tin.

(2) Titanium(IV) oxide has the same structure as the quadrivalent oxides of germanium, tin and lead and like them is amphoteric. TiO_2, like SnO_2, is white when cold, yellow when hot.

(3) The quadrivalent chlorides of titanium, silicon, germanium and tin are all colourless, covalent, volatile liquids consisting of tetrahedral molecules. They all fume in moist air because of the same type of hydrolysis. Titanium(IV) chloride and tin(IV) chloride give addition compounds with organic electron donor molecules, e.g. ethers.

Vanadium

Vanadium is in Group VA, and has the electronic configuration 2, 8, (8+3), 2. The maximum oxidation state of vanadium is +5 and these compounds are oxidising agents. The oxidation state +4 is the most stable. Oxidation states of +3 and +2 also exist and are ionic. The V^{3+} and V^{2+} ions are both reducing agents.

Occurrence

Although the element is widely distributed (0.02 % of the earth's crust) deposits of economic value are rare. *Vanadinite*, $3Pb_3(VO_4)_2.PbCl_2$ and *carnotite*, $2K(UO_2)VO_4.3H_2O$ are the principal ores.

Isolation

Vanadium has a great affinity for oxygen, carbon, and nitrogen at elevated temperatures (cf. Ti) and this makes the isolation of the pure metal a difficult process. However, the greatest commercial demand for vanadium is in the form of an iron alloy called *ferrovanadium*. This can be produced by reducing a mixture of iron(III) oxide and vanadium(V) oxide with carbon in an electric furnace.

Physical properties

Metallic properties become progressively more pronounced in passing along the Period from titanium to vanadium. Thus vanadium is a hard, lustrous, high-melting, dense metal.

Chemical properties

Characteristically for a *d*-block element vanadium is relatively inert *under normal conditions* and like its neighbours titanium and chromium is corrosion resistant. On heating in air it combines with oxygen to form mainly vanadium(v) oxide but vanadium(iv) oxide and vanadium(iii) oxide are also formed. It also combines directly with chlorine to give vanadium(iv) chloride, and with carbon and nitrogen to give interstitial carbides and nitrides respectively. These latter compounds again illustrate the *d*-block character of vanadium.

Vanadium is unaffected by non-oxidising acids but dissolves in nitric acid and concentrated sulphuric acid. It is also unaffected by alkalis.

Uses

Vanadium is used principally as an alloying addition for the production of steels of exceptional toughness. Compounds of vanadium are used as drying accelerators in paint and in the manufacture of glass.

Compounds of Vanadium

The range of oxidation states and the coloured ions (but not in the $+5$ oxidation state as there are no unpaired *d*-electrons) illustrate yet again the characteristic *d*-block properties of vanadium.

Vanadium(v) compounds

Ammonium metavanadate is a white solid obtained directly from vanadium ores and is the starting point for most of the chemistry of vanadium. It decomposes on heating to vanadium(v) oxide,

$$2NH_4VO_3 \rightarrow V_2O_5 + 2NH_3 + H_2O.$$

Vanadium(v) oxide is an orange powder (N.B. an incomplete *d* sub-shell is not the only cause of colour, cf. Pb_3O_4, AgI, etc.). It dissolves very slightly in water to give a pale yellow acidic solution which reddens blue litmus. Strongly alkaline solutions readily dissolve it and form simple ortho-vanadate(v) ions, VO_4^{3-}. Less strongly alkaline solutions produce a range of complex polyvanadate(v) ions.

Vanadium(v) oxide also displays feeble basic properties and is thus amphoteric. In very strong acids it dissolves mainly as the pale yellow

18-2

VO_2^+ ion. But with hydrochloric acid it liberates chlorine thus illustrating the oxidising nature of vanadium(v) compounds,

$$V_2O_5 + 6H^+ + 2Cl^- \rightarrow 2VO^{2+} + Cl_2 + 3H_2O.$$

Vanadium(v) oxide is a versatile catalyst, e.g. for accelerating the oxidation of sulphur dioxide to sulphur trioxide in the contact process.

Vanadium(ɪv) compounds

Fairly mild reducing agents will reduce vanadium(v) to vanadium(ɪv),

e.g.
$$VO_3^- + Fe^{2+} + 4H^+ \rightarrow VO^{2+} + Fe^{3+} + 2H_2O,$$
$$2VO_3^- + 2I^- + 8H^+ \rightarrow 2VO^{2+} + I_2 + 4H_2O.$$

Sulphur dioxide effects a similar result. The vanadyl(ɪv) ion, VO^{2+}, is bright blue in acid solution.

Vanadium(ɪv) oxide is a dark blue amphoteric solid significantly more basic than vanadium(v) oxide.

Vanadium(ɪɪɪ) compounds

Magnesium or tin will reduce an acidified solution of VO^{2+} ions to V^{3+} ions. Alternatively, vanadium(v) may be reduced to vanadium(ɪɪɪ) with copper powder, i.e.

$$VO_3^- + Cu + 6H^+ \rightarrow V^{3+} + Cu^{2+} + 3H_2O.$$

The hydrated V^{3+} ion is green. It is fairly easily oxidised back to the more stable vanadium(ɪv) oxidation state,

$$2V^{3+} + I_2 + 2H_2O \rightarrow 2VO^{2+} + 2I^- + 4H^+.$$

It is also slowly oxidised by air.

Vanadium(ɪɪɪ) oxide is basic.

Vanadium(ɪɪ) compounds

Zinc amalgam will reduce vanadium(v) in acid solution to vanadium(ɪɪ). The hydrated V^{2+} ion, i.e. $V(H_2O)_6^{2+}$, is violet coloured. It is a powerful reducing agent and is rapidly oxidised in air to the hydrated V^{3+} ion. It also reduces copper(ɪɪ) sulphate solution to copper, vanadium(v) to vanadium(ɪv) and will liberate hydrogen from water.

$$Cu^{2+} + 2V^{2+} \rightarrow 2V^{3+} + Cu,$$
$$2VO_3^- + V^{2+} + 6H^+ \rightarrow 3VO^{2+} + 3H_2O.$$

Chromium

Chromium is in Group VI A. Its electronic configuration is, 2, 8, (8 + 5), 1. Chief valencies are 2 (ionic), 3 (ionic) and 6, the Group valency, (covalent). In the last of these it uses all its electrons in excess of the 2, 8, 8, (argon) electronic configuration. Other valencies are 4 (e.g. CrF_4 and CrO_2) and 5 (e.g. CrF_5).

Occurrence

Chromium (0.02 % of lithosphere) is the twenty-first in order of abundance of the elements and does not occur free in nature. *Chromite*, iron(II) chromite, $FeCr_2O_4 = FeO . Cr_2O_3$, its chief ore, is the source of chromium and all its important compounds.

Most compounds of chromium and the pure metal itself are made from sodium dichromate which is manufactured from chromite as follows:

Sodium dichromate, $Na_2Cr_2O_7 . 2H_2O$

Powdered chromite mixed with anhydrous sodium carbonate and quicklime is roasted in a reverberatory furnace with excess of air. Chromite is oxidised to chromate by oxygen from the air, and iron(II) oxide to iron(III) oxide. The quicklime keeps the mixture porous and allows free access of air,

$$4FeCr_2O_4 + 8Na_2CO_3 + 7O_2 \rightarrow 8Na_2CrO_4 + 2Fe_2O_3 + 8CO_2 \uparrow .$$

Soluble sodium chromate is extracted with water, and concentrated sulphuric acid added forming sodium dichromate in solution,

$$2Na_2CrO_4 + H_2SO_4 \rightarrow Na_2SO_4 + Na_2Cr_2O_7 + H_2O.$$

When cooled, sodium sulphate decahydrate separates and is removed. When the remaining solution is concentrated, sodium dichromate dihydrate crystallises. It is an orange-red deliquescent solid, readily soluble in water and a good oxidising agent.

Isolation

(1) Industrially, starting from chromite, chromium is made in the form of ferrochrome, an alloy of chromium and iron containing about 60% chromium. Chromite is heated with carbon in a furnace,

$$FeCr_2O_4 + 4C \rightarrow Fe + 2Cr + 4CO \uparrow .$$

The ferrochrome produced contains carbon as chromium carbide, Cr_3C_2. More chromite is therefore added to the impure molten ferrochrome to oxidise the carbon to carbon monoxide which is evolved. Removal of carbon is necessary because ferrochrome is used mainly in the manufacture of stainless steels and other alloy steels containing chromium. Steel to which the ferrochrome is later added has already the exact percentage of carbon required (p. 562).

(2) Chromium metal free from iron is made from sodium dichromate thus:

Sodium dichromate is first reduced to chromium(III) oxide, Cr_2O_3, by heating with charcoal or sawdust,

$$Na_2Cr_2O_7 + 2C \rightarrow Cr_2O_3 + Na_2CO_3 + CO \uparrow.$$

Chromium(III) oxide is then reduced to chromium with aluminium powder (thermite process, p. 185),

$$Cr_2O_3 + 2Al \rightarrow Al_2O_3 + 2Cr.$$

(3) Much chromium is produced by electrolysis as a protective plating on steel articles. The electrolyte used is an aqueous solution of chromic acid and sulphuric acid.

Physical properties

Chromium is a metal with a bright cold slightly bluish lustre having a higher density (7.2 g cm^{-3}) and melting point ($1890\ °C$) than titanium. Even when pure it is very hard and rather brittle.

Chemical properties

Chromium is very resistant to corrosion because of a thin film of oxide (Cr_2O_3) which makes the metal passive to some extent. Chromium does not tarnish in air at ordinary temperatures and even when warmed the tarnish is superficial. It is unaffected by cold or hot water, or sea water, but reacts at red heat with steam forming chromium(III) oxide and hydrogen, $\qquad 2Cr + 3H_2O \rightarrow Cr_2O_3 + 3H_2.$

Non-oxidising acids, hydrochloric acid and dilute sulphuric acid react with chromium slowly in the cold, rapidly with increase in temperature and concentration, giving hydrogen and sky blue chromium(II) ions Cr^{2+}(aq.), which are rapidly oxidised in air to green chromium(III) ions Cr^{3+}(aq.). With hot concentrated sulphuric acid sulphur dioxide is evolved and chromium(III) sulphate formed. Cold nitric acid, dilute or concentrated, has no action on chromium beyond rendering it passive because of the formation of a thicker and tougher film of chromium(III) oxide. With boiling dilute nitric acid there is a slow action which ceases when heating stopped. Passive chromium is not affected by hydrochloric or sulphuric acid. Chromium, when not made passive, displaces copper, tin and nickel from solutions of their salts as would be expected from its electrode potential.

Chromium combines directly and vigorously, when heated, with chlorine, oxygen, sulphur, nitrogen and carbon forming chromium(III) chloride, oxide, sulphide, nitride and carbide respectively, the temperature required increasing in passing from chloride to carbide.

Aqueous sodium hydroxide attacks chromium slowly forming sodium chromite in solution and liberating hydrogen,

$$2Cr + 2OH^- + 6H_2O \rightarrow 2Cr(OH)_4^- + 3H_2 \uparrow .$$

Uses

Already mentioned are: in making alloy steels and in electroplating (p. 542). *Nichrome*, an alloy containing 60% nickel, 25% iron, 15% chromium is used as wire or ribbon for electric heating elements because of its high electrical resistance, melting point and resistance to atmospheric corrosion at high temperatures.

Compounds of chromium

Relationships among chromium's chief compounds are shown in the table on p. 544. Increase in acidic character with increase in proportion of oxygen, i.e. increase in oxidation number, is seen clearly (see p. 253). Stabilities of oxidation states given, apply to all compounds of chromium.

Chromium(II) compounds (chromous)

Anhydrous chromium(II) chloride, CrCl_2, is made by passing hydrogen chloride over heated chromium. It forms colourless deliquescent crystals. A solution of chromium(II) chloride is made (1) by dissolving the metal in hot concentrated hydrochloric acid, or (2) by reducing a solution containing sexivalent chromium, e.g. sodium dichromate, with zinc and hydrochloric acid. The orange colour of $Cr_2O_7^{2-}$ ion gradually gives place to the rich green of the Cr^{3+}(aq.) ion and finally to the sky blue of the Cr^{2+}(aq.) ion. The experiment may be done in a test-tube with a stopper carrying a bunsen valve.

Chromium(II) sulphate solution is made in a similar way.

Chromium(II) salts are powerful reducing agents, rapidly oxidised on contact with air.

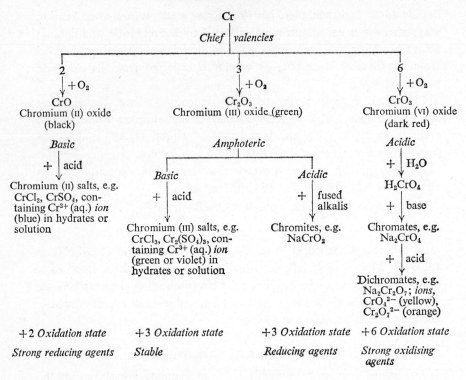

Cr

Chief | valencies

2	3	6
$\downarrow +O_2$	$\downarrow +O_2$	$\downarrow +O_2$
CrO	Cr_2O_3	CrO_3
Chromium (II) oxide (black)	Chromium (III) oxide (green)	Chromium (VI) oxide (dark red)

Basic — *Amphoteric* — *Acidic*

Basic (left, +2): $+$ | acid → Chromium (II) salts, e.g. $CrCl_2$, $CrSO_4$, containing Cr^{2+} (aq.) *ion* (blue) in hydrates or solution

Amphoteric — Basic: $+$ | acid → Chromium (III) salts, e.g. $CrCl_3$, $Cr_2(SO_4)_3$, containing Cr^{3+} (aq.) *ion* (green or violet) in hydrates or solution

Amphoteric — Acidic: $+$ | fused alkalis → Chromites, e.g. $NaCrO_2$

Acidic (right, +6): $+$ | H_2O → H_2CrO_4

$+$ | base → Chromates, e.g. Na_2CrO_4

$+$ | acid → Dichromates, e.g. $Na_2Cr_2O_7$; *ions*, CrO_4^{2-} (yellow), $Cr_2O_7^{2-}$ (orange)

$+2$ *Oxidation state* $+3$ *Oxidation state* $+3$ *Oxidation state* $+6$ *Oxidation state*

Strong reducing agents   *Stable*   *Reducing agents*   *Strong oxidising agents*

Chromium(III) compounds (chromic)

Chromium(III) oxide, Cr_2O_3. Its preparation by reduction of sodium dichromate with carbon has been given (p. 542). Other methods are: (1) burning the metal in oxygen; (2) heating chromium(III) hydroxide $Cr(OH)_3$; and (3) heating a mixture of sodium dichromate and ammonium chloride, or ammonium dichromate alone,

$$(NH_4)_2Cr_2O_7 \xrightarrow{\text{heat}} Cr_2O_3 + N_2\uparrow + 4H_2O.$$

Chromium(III) oxide is a green, amphoteric solid, insoluble in water but dissolving with difficulty in acids (e.g. hot concentrated HCl) to form chromium(III) salts, and reacting with fused caustic alkalis to form chromites, $$Cr_2O_3 + 2OH^- \rightarrow 2CrO_2^- + H_2O.$$

Chromium(III) hydroxide, $Cr(OH)_3$, is formed as a grey-green gelatinous precipitate when ammonia solution or sodium hydroxide solution is added to a solution of a chromium(III) salt,

$$Cr^{3+} + 3OH^- \rightarrow Cr(OH)_3\downarrow .$$

Chromium(III) hydroxide like chromium(III) oxide is amphoteric and dissolves slowly in excess of sodium hydroxide solution (but not in excess of ammonia solution), and also in dilute acids giving the same products as chromium(III) oxide. It is oxidised to chromate by heating with sodium hydroxide solution and hydrogen peroxide solution.

Chromium(III) chloride, $CrCl_3$. The anhydrous salt is made by passing chlorine over heated chromium, and sublimes in the stream of chlorine if the temperature is raised to about 600 °C. Pink-violet crystals are formed, almost insoluble in water, unless a trace of reducing agent such as $CrCl_2$ or $SnCl_2$ is present, when it dissolves readily giving a green solution from which the dark green deliquescent hexahydrate $CrCl_3.6H_2O$ can be crystallised. The hexahydrate shows isomerism and exists in three forms which can be made under different conditions. The table on p. 546 gives their properties and formulae.

Chromium(III) sulphate, $Cr_2(SO_4)_3.xH_2O$. A number of different soluble hydrated chromium(III) sulphates are known. In one of these all the sulphate groups can be precipitated as barium sulphate by addition of barium chloride solution to a solution of the sulphate. Another sulphate, on similar treatment gives no precipitate. Facts like these are interpreted in the same way as shown opposite for the chlorides.

Chrome alums. See p. 356.

Chromium(VI) compounds

Chromium(VI) oxide, CrO_3 (chromic anydride) and chromic acids. Chromium(VI) oxide crystallises as deep red needle-shaped crystals on cooling a solution made by adding concentrated sulphuric acid to a cold saturated solution of potassium dichromate,

$$Cr_2O_7^{2-} + 2H_2SO_4 \rightarrow 2HSO_4^- + H_2O + 2CrO_3 \downarrow.$$

The crystals may be separated by decantation, or by filtering through asbestos or a sintered glass plate. Paper is not used because chromium(VI) oxide is a very powerful oxidising agent and chars it. After being washed with concentrated nitric acid the crystals are dried in warm air. Chromium(VI) oxide melts at 196 °C and decomposes on further heating,

$$4CrO_3 \rightarrow 2Cr_2O_3 + 3O_2.$$

Chromium(VI) oxide is deliquescent and very soluble in water, forming an orange red, strongly acid solution which contains chromic acid,

$$H_2CrO_4(H_2O.CrO_3)$$

Isomerism of chromium(III) chloride hexahydrate

Colour	No. of Cl⁻ ions removed as AgCl by AgNO₃ solution	Effect of drying in desiccator over conc. H_2SO_4	Formula	Name
Dark green	One Cl removed, therefore two Cl in complex cation	Two H_2O removed, therefore four in complex cation	$[Cr(H_2O)_4Cl_2]^+Cl^- . 2H_2O$	Dichlorotetraquochromium(III) chloride dihydrate
Pale green	Two Cl removed, therefore one Cl in complex cation	One H_2O removed, therefore five in complex cation	$[Cr(H_2O)_5Cl]^{2+}(Cl^-)_2 . H_2O$	Chloropentaquochromium(III) chloride monohydrate
Grey-blue (blue-violet solution)	All Cl removed, therefore no Cl in complex cation	No water removed, therefore six in complex cation	$[Cr(H_2O)_6]Cl_3$	Hexaquochromium(III) chloride

Note that the co-ordination number of chromium in these complex ions is 6, the usual number for complexes of Cr^{3+}.

546

and dichromic acid ($H_2O.2CrO_3$), and may also contain the polychromic acids, e.g. trichromic acid $H_2Cr_3O_{10}(H_2O.3CrO_3)$, and tetrachromic acid, $H_2Cr_4O_{13}(H_2O.4CrO_3)$. None of these has been isolated but salts of all are known.

Chromates and dichromates

Sodium dichromate, $Na_2Cr_2O_7.2H_2O$. An outline of its manufacture and properties has been given on p. 541.

Potassium dichromate, $K_2Cr_2O_7$. This salt which is much less soluble than sodium dichromate, is made by mixing hot concentrated solutions of sodium dichromate and potassium chloride. Sodium chloride is precipitated and removed. When the remaining solution is cooled, orange-red crystals of potassium dichromate separate. Potassium dichromate has no water of crystallisation and keeps better than the sodium salt because it is not deliquescent. It melts at 400 °C without decomposition, is moderately soluble in cold water, much more so in hot, therefore easily purified by recrystallisation. Because of these properties and its oxidising powers, it is a very useful oxidising agent in volumetric analysis in solutions acidified with dilute sulphuric acid or dilute hydrochloric acid (which it does not oxidise, cf. $KMnO_4$),

$$Cr_2O_7{}^{2-}+14H^++6e \rightarrow 2Cr^{3+}+7H_2O.$$

Ammonium dichromate, $(NH_4)_2Cr_2O_7$ is made by adding ammonia solution *not in excess*, to chromic acid solution,

$$2H_2CrO_4+2NH_3 \rightarrow (NH_4)_2Cr_2O_7+H_2O.$$

Relation between chromate and dichromate. Addition of alkali to a solution containing dichromate ions (orange-red) converts them to chromate ions (yellow),
$$Cr_2O_7{}^{2-}+2OH^- \rightarrow 2CrO_4{}^{2-}+H_2O.$$

The process is reversed by addition of acid,

$$2CrO_4{}^{2-}+2H^+ \rightarrow Cr_2O_7{}^{2-}+H_2O.$$

These are acid-base reactions (proton transfer) not redox reactions (electron transfer) because the oxidation number of chromium ($+6$) remains unchanged.

Potassium chromate, K_2CrO_4, may be made by adding a solution of potassium hydroxide to one of potassium dichromate (see above).

Lemon yellow crystals, isomorphous with potassium sulphate, are formed. Potassium chromate is very soluble in water, a good oxidising agent in acid solution, and very stable to heat.

Chromates of lead, barium and silver. These insoluble salts are met with in analysis: in qualitative analysis, precipitation of lead(II) chromate (bright yellow) and barium chromate (pale yellow) is used to identify Pb^{2+} and Ba^{2+}; while precipitation of silver chromate (red-brown) shows the end-point in the titration of Cl^- or Br^- in neutral solution with silver nitrate using potassium chromate as indicator.

Chromyl chloride, (CrO_2Cl_2). This is the acid-chloride of chromic acid (cf. SO_2Cl_2) and is prepared by warming a dry mixture of potassium dichromate and sodium chloride with excess concentrated sulphuric acid. Chromyl chloride distils over, condensing as a dark red liquid (resembling bromine). Sulphuric acid liberates hydrochloric acid from sodium chloride. The second stage may be formulated as the action of hydrochloric acid on chromic acid, the forward reaction going to completion because of removal of water by sulphuric acid. Chromyl chloride is a covalent volatile liquid (boiling point 117 °C) soluble without decomposition in organic solvents (e.g. ether) but completely hydrolysed by water. Hydrolysis with sodium hydroxide solution gives a yellow solution of sodium chromate and sodium chloride.

Bromides and iodides do not give compounds corresponding to chromyl chloride so its formation is a specific test for chlorides.

Test for chromium as chromate (or for hydrogen peroxide). When hydrogen peroxide solution is added to acidified dichromate solution a deep blue solution is formed containing the unstable chromium peroxide, CrO_5, which is stabilised by dissolving in ether.

Complexes. Chromium, especially in its trivalent state, forms a very large number and variety of complex ions. In them the co-ordination number is almost always 6. Examples already given include $[Cr(H_2O)_6]^{3+}$, $[Cr(H_2O)_5Cl]^{2+}$, $[Cr(H_2O)_4Cl_2]^+$. Similar complex ions with NH_3 instead of H_2O are well known. Others contain both NH_3 and H_2O, e.g.
$$[Cr(NH_3)_3(H_2O)_3]^{3+}.$$

Uses of chromium compounds

Sodium dichromate is the most important of all chromium compounds because it is used in the manufacture of chromium metal (p. 542) and in making most other chromium compounds. It is used in tanning leather (chrome leather); in making lead chromate (chrome yellow) and chromium(III) oxide (chrome green) which are valuable pigments in paints, plastics and rubber; as an oxidising agent in industry and laboratories; and as a mordant in dyeing.

Chromite (p. 541) is chemically neutral and very refractory and so is used in lining steel furnaces.

Potassium chromate is used to make potassium chrome alum (p. 356). Ammonium dichromate is used in fireworks and as a mordant in dyeing.

Chromic acid is used in chromium plating and in anodising aluminium to improve its resistance to corrosion. Chromium(III) oxide is used as a catalyst in making polythene and other organic compounds.

Relationship between A and B families of Group VI

Chromium and sulphur are clearly very different but both show the Group valency of 6 and their sexivalent compounds show many resemblances, physical and chemical. Some corresponding compounds are given below:

SO_3, CrO_3; H_2SO_4, H_2CrO_4; $H_2S_2O_7$, $H_2Cr_2O_7$; SO_2Cl_2, CrO_2Cl_2; $ClSO_2OK$, $ClCrO_2OK$; $Na_2SO_4 . 10H_2O$, $Na_2CrO_4 . 10H_2O$; K_2SO_4, K_2CrO_4; $BaSO_4$, $BaCrO_4$; $PbSO_4$, $PbCrO_4$.

The obvious difference between each pair is that all the sulphur compounds are colourless, all the chromium compounds coloured. Similarities in properties are often close, e.g. sulphates and chromates are often isomorphous, and often have roughly similar solubilities and trends in solubilities, with chromates generally more soluble than sulphates. See p. 338 for solubilities of Group II A sulphates and chromates.

Manganese

Manganese, in Group VII A, has electronic configuration 2, 8 (8 + 5), 2, and shows all valencies from 1 to 7 inclusive. In the last of these, the Group valency, all its electrons in excess of the 2, 8, 8 electronic configuration are used. Valencies of 2, 4, 6 and 7 are important. Of these the most stable is 2. Valency 2 is always ionic, 4 may be ionic or covalent, 6 and 7 are covalent.

Occurrence

Manganese, 0.09 % of lithosphere, fourteenth in order of abundance of the elements (eighth among metals) does not occur free in nature. Its chief ore is pyrolusite, MnO_2 (the name comes from Greek *pyr-*, fire, + *luo*,

'I wash', and refers to the use, known to the ancient Egyptians and Romans, of manganese(IV) oxide in decolorising glass made green by iron from the silica used. The manganese(IV) oxide oxidises iron(II) silicate to iron(III) (yellow) and this colour is neutralised by the pale purple of manganese(II) silicate).

Isolation

(1) The most important use of the metal is to improve the quality of steel (p. 565). For this purpose it is made as an alloy of manganese, iron and carbon, called ferromanganese, by the reduction of a mixture of pyrolusite and oxides of iron with carbon in a blast furnace. Ferromanganese contains about 80 % manganese; an alloy with 20 % or less manganese is called *spiegeleisen* (German *spiegel*, 'mirror', +*eisen*, 'iron').

(2) Pure manganese is made by the thermite process (p. 185). Because the reaction between manganese(IV) oxide and aluminium is too violent, the oxide is first strongly heated to convert it into red trimanganese tetroxide, Mn_3O_4. Distillation *in vacuo* is used to obtain a high degree of purity.

Physical properties

Manganese when pure has a silvery-white lustre, but is usually a very pale pink tinge. Its density, 7.2 g cm^{-3}, is a little higher than that of chromium but melting point 1240 °C and boiling point 2100 °C are much lower. This may be attributed to the half-filled d sub-shell of the manganese atom, which has additional stability, the electrons being therefore less available for metallic bonding. Another effect of this is the difference in structure between manganese and all the other transitional metals. Like chromium, manganese is hard and brittle.

Chemical properties

Manganese has a greater negative standard electrode potential than chromium (p. 154). This is a reversal of the trend along the Period and in part accounts for the fact that manganese, in general, is the most reactive of the transition metals of Period 4. Manganese is stable in air at ordinary temperatures; liberates hydrogen slowly from water (p. 216) and from steam at red heat; reacts readily with hydrochloric acid and dilute sulphuric acid giving Mn^{2+} ions in solution and liberating hydrogen. With cold, very dilute nitric acid it also gives hydrogen, but with more concentrated acid, oxides of nitrogen. With hot concentrated sulphuric acid it gives sulphur dioxide. Aqueous alkalis have little or no effect on manganese.

Uses

Very large quantities of ferromanganese are used in steel making (p. 560). Other alloys are manganese bronze or brass (Cu, Zn and some Mn) and *manganin* (Cu, 85%; Mn, 12%; Ni, 4%) used for standard resistance coils because of its very low temperature coefficient of resistance. *Duralumin* (p. 348) contains $\frac{1}{2}$% Mn.

Compounds of manganese

The table on p. 552 shows the increase in acidic character of oxides with increasing proportion of oxygen, i.e. with increase in oxidation state. The stabilities of the different oxidation states indicated in the table apply to all compounds of manganese.

Bivalent, i.e. manganese(II) compounds (manganous)

Manganese(II) oxide, MnO, a green insoluble solid, is made by reducing MnO_2 by heating it in a stream of hydrogen, or by heating the carbonate or hydroxide in a stream of nitrogen. It dissolves in dilute acids to give manganese(II) salts, and is a reducing agent, easily oxidised in air to Mn_2O_3.

Manganese(II) hydroxide, Mn(OH)$_2$, is formed as a white precipitate by adding sodium hydroxide solution to a manganese(II) salt solution. The precipitate is insoluble in excess sodium hydroxide and is a moderately strong base having a slight solubility in water and forming a normal carbonate. Like the oxide, manganese(II) hydroxide is a reducing agent, forming brown hydrated manganese(IV) oxide in air.

Manganese(II) salts. Two common soluble salts, the chloride $MnCl_2.4H_2O$ and sulphate $MnSO_4.5H_2O$ (isomorphous with $CuSO_4.5H_2O$) are made in the usual ways (below 8 °C the sulphate crystallises as $MnSO_4.7H_2O$ isomorphous with $FeSO_4.7H_2O$). These salts owe their colour to the pale pink $[Mn(H_2O)_6]^{2+}$ ion. The same salts are produced by the action of hydrochloric or sulphuric acid on manganese(IV) oxide. Manganese(II) sulphate is one of the most stable compounds of manganese.

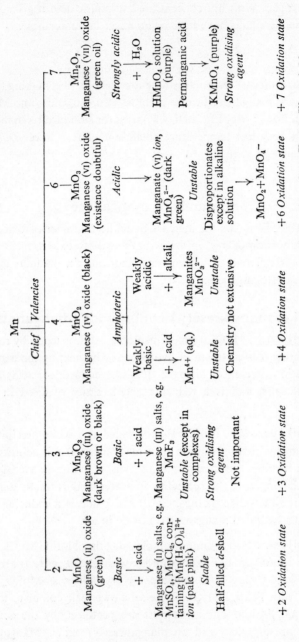

Mn

Chief | Valencies

2

MnO
Manganese (II) oxide (green)

Basic

+ | acid
↓

Manganese (II) salts, e.g. MnSO₄, MnCl₂, containing [Mn(H₂O)₆]²⁺ *ion* (pale pink)

Stable

Half-filled *d*-shell

+ 2 Oxidation state

3

Mn₂O₃ oxide
Manganese (III) oxide (dark brown or black)

Basic

+ | acid
↓

Manganese (III) salts, e.g. MnF₃

Unstable (except in complexes)

Strong oxidising agent

Not important

+ 3 Oxidation state

4

MnO₂ oxide
Manganese (IV) oxide (black)

Amphoteric

Weakly basic   *Weakly acidic*

+ | acid   + | alkali
↓   ↓

Mn⁴⁺ (aq.)   Manganites MnO₃²⁻

Unstable   *Unstable*

Chemistry not extensive

+ 4 Oxidation state

6

MnO₃
Manganese (VI) oxide (existence doubtful)

Acidic

↓

Manganate (VI) *ion*, MnO₄²⁻ (dark green)

Unstable

Disproportionates except in alkaline solution
↓

MnO₂ + MnO₄⁻

+ 6 Oxidation state

7

Mn₂O₇
Manganese (VII) oxide (green oil)

Strongly acidic

+ | H₂O
↓

HMnO₄ solution (purple)

Permanganic acid
↓

KMnO₄ (purple)

Strong oxidising agent

+ 7 Oxidation state

Trimanganese tetroxide, Mn₃O₄ (p. 550) may be regarded as a mixed oxide of Mn(III), Mn(IV), and O²⁻.

Two common insoluble salts, the carbonate, white, and sulphide, pale pink are prepared by precipitation (p. 242),

$$Mn^{2+} + 2HCO_3^- \rightarrow MnCO_3 \downarrow + H_2O + CO_2 \uparrow \quad \text{(in presence of excess } CO_2\text{)},$$
$$Mn^{2+} + S^{2-} \rightarrow MnS \downarrow \quad \text{(in alkaline solution).}$$

Manganese(II) carbonate and manganese(II) sulphide turn brown by atmospheric oxidation.

Trivalent, i.e. manganese(III) compounds

These compounds are not important.

Manganese(III) oxide, Mn$_2$O$_3$, is made as a black or dark brown powder by heating manganese dixoide in air at 700 °C for a long time. It dissolves in cold, moderately concentrated sulphuric acid, from which solution unstable green crystals of manganese(III) sulphate, $Mn_2(SO_4)_3$, separate.

Quadrivalent, i.e. manganese(IV) compounds

The only important compound in this class (and the most important compound of manganese) is manganese(IV) oxide, MnO_2. A few stable complex compounds containing $Mn^{(IV)}$ are known.

Manganese(IV) oxide, MnO$_2$, occurs native as pyrolusite, which has the rutile structure (p. 138) and therefore contains Mn^{4+} ions. A black solid, insoluble in water, dilute acids and dilute alkalis, it is converted, when heated to 700 °C, into Mn_2O_3 and at higher temperatures to Mn_3O_4, oxygen being given off in both actions. Manganese(II) nitrate when heated gives manganese(IV) oxide,

$$Mn(NO_3)_2 \rightarrow MnO_2 + 2NO_2 \uparrow.$$

In hydrated form, it is obtained by oxidation of the Mn^{2+} ion or reduction (in alkaline solution) of MnO_4^- ion.

Manganese(IV) oxide is amphoteric and an oxidising agent. The following reactions show its weakly basic character. For action with concentrated hydrochloric acid, see p. 504. With cold concentrated sulphuric acid manganese(IV) oxide has no action, but manganese(III) sulphate is formed on warming and oxygen evolved. Stronger heating converts manganese(III) sulphate to the stable manganese(II) sulphate plus oxygen. Manganese(IV) oxide does not give hydrogen peroxide with acids. It is therefore not a peroxide. Weakly acidic properties are shown by the reaction of manganese(IV) oxide with fused caustic alkalis or alkaline earth oxides forming manganites, e.g. calcium manganite(IV), a salt of hypothetical manganous(IV) acid, H_2MnO_3. Manganites are unstable and of little importance.

Manganese(IV) oxide behaves as an oxidising agent towards hydrochloric acid and also when heated with dilute sulphuric and oxalic acid,

$$MnO_2 + C_2O_4^{2-} + 4H^+ \rightarrow Mn^{2+} + 2H_2O + 2CO_2;$$

similarly when it oxidises cold iron(II) sulphate solution plus dilute sulphuric acid to iron(III) sulphate and when it oxidises hydrogen peroxide in the presence of dilute sulphuric acid,

$$MnO_2 + 4H^+ + 2e \rightarrow Mn^{2+} + 2H_2O$$

$$\overset{(2+)(2-)}{H_2O_2} \rightarrow 2H^+ + O_2 + 2e$$

$$\overline{MnO_2 + H_2O_2 + 2H^+ \rightarrow Mn^{2+} + 2H_2O + O_2 \uparrow}.$$

Manganese(IV) oxide acts as a catalyst in the decomposition of potassium chlorate (p. 467) and hydrogen peroxide (p. 296).

Sexivalent, i.e. manganese(VI) compounds

In these the manganese atom is always covalent; Mn^{6+} could not exist. The existence of manganese(VI) oxide MnO_3 has not been established but the corresponding manganate(VI) anion MnO_4^{2-} is well known, although manganic(VI) acid, H_2MnO_4, has not been isolated.

Potassium manganate(VI), **K_2MnO_4**, is prepared by fusing manganese(IV) oxide with potassium hydroxide and an oxidising agent (KNO_3 or $KClO_3$ or plenty of air),

$$2MnO_2 + 4KOH + O_2 \rightarrow 2K_2MnO_4 + 2H_2O.$$

Very dark green crystals of the very soluble K_2MnO_4 (isomorphous with K_2CrO_4 and K_2SO_4) are obtained from the concentrated aqueous extract of the melt. The manganate(VI) ion is stable only in strongly alkaline solutions. In weakly basic, neutral or weakly acidic solution it *disproportionates* (undergoes self-oxidation and reduction) into permangante ion, MnO_4^-, and MnO_2, manganese(IV) oxide,

$$3MnO_4^{2-} + 2H_2O \rightleftharpoons 2MnO_4^- + MnO_2 \downarrow + 4OH^-.$$

Passage of CO_2 favours the forward reaction by converting OH^- to HCO_3^-.

Septivalent, i.e. manganese(VII) compounds

Potassium permanganate, $KMnO_4$, is the most important.

Manganese(VII) oxide, **Mn_2O_7**, permanganic anhydride, is formed by the action of cold concentrated sulphuric acid on potassium permanganate (*caution*: *do not attempt this because of explosion danger*). It separates as a heavy green oil.

Potassium permanganate, KMnO$_4$, is manufactured by the electrolytic oxidation (anodic) of alkaline potassium manganate(VI) solution (p. 554),

$$MnO_4^{2-} - e \rightarrow MnO_4^-.$$

Another method is to oxidise MnO_4^{2-} with chlorine,

$$MnO_4^{2-} + \tfrac{1}{2}Cl_2 \rightarrow MnO_4^- + Cl^-.$$

In chemical analysis, qualitative or quantitative, Mn^{2+} ions (pale pink) are oxidised to MnO_4^- ions (dark purple) by the action of (1) sodium bismuthate, $NaBiO_3$, or (2) ammonium peroxodisulphate (p. 495) in presence of Ag^+ ions as catalyst.

Potassium permanganate forms dark purple crystals isomorphous with potassium perchlorate, $KClO_4$. It is fairly soluble in water (a saturated solution at 20 °C is about 2M). On gentle heating, 250 °C, it decomposes into manganate(VI), manganese(IV) oxide and oxygen,

$$2KMnO_4 \rightarrow K_2MnO_4 + MnO_2 + O_2.$$

At higher temperatures it decomposes into potassium manganite(IV) K_2MnO_3 and oxygen. The permanganate ion is a powerful oxidising agent. In the presence of dilute sulphuric acid and a reducing agent, MnO_4^- ion, containing Mn in the $+7$ oxidation state, is reduced to Mn^{2+}, often at room temperature,

$$MnO_4^- + 8H^+ + 5e \rightarrow Mn^{2+} + 4H_2O.$$

If insufficient acid is present the half-reaction is

$$MnO_4^- + 4H^+ + 3e \rightarrow MnO_2 \downarrow + 2H_2O.$$

Neither hydrochloric nor nitric acid reacts in this way. The former reduces potassium permanganate and the latter is itself an oxidising agent.

In neutral or weakly alkaline solution the half-reaction is

$$MnO_4^- + 2H_2O + 3e \rightarrow MnO_2 \downarrow + 4OH^-.$$

Potassium permanganate oxidises concentrated hydrochloric acid to chlorine at room temperature (a method of preparing chlorine).

Potassium permanganate does not react with hydrogen unless the hydrogen is generated in situ in acid solution, when slow reduction to a colourless solution containing manganese(II) ions takes place.

Potassium permanganate is widely used as an oxidising agent in volumetric analysis where the reactions are carried out in acid solution (dilute H_2SO_4) with permanganate solution in the burette. Examples of such oxidations are, Fe^{2+} to Fe^{3+}, NO_2^- to NO_3^-, SO_3^{2-} to SO_4^{2-}, I^- to iodine (all at room temperature), oxalic acid and oxalates to CO_2 and H_2O (at $80\,°C$); also at room temperature and in the presence of dilute sulphuric acid, it oxidises hydrogen peroxide to oxygen,

$$2MnO_4^- + 16H^+ + 10e \rightarrow 2Mn^{2+} + 8H_2O$$
$$5H_2O_2 \rightarrow 10H^+ + 5O_2 + 10e$$

$$\overline{2MnO_4^- + 16H^+ + 5H_2O_2 \rightarrow 2Mn^{2+} + 8H_2O + 5O_2 \uparrow}.$$

In alkaline solution, potassium permanganate oxidises potassium iodide to potassium iodate,

$$2MnO_4^- + 4H_2O + 6e \rightarrow 2MnO_2 + 8OH^-$$
$$I^- + 3H_2O \rightarrow IO_3^- + 6H^+ + 6e$$

$$\overline{2MnO_4^- + I^- + H_2O \rightarrow 2MnO_2 \downarrow + IO_3^- + 2OH^-}.$$

Complex ions of bivalent Mn: $[Mn(H_2O)_6]^{2+}$, $[Mn(CN)_6]^{4-}$; of trivalent Mn: $[Mn(CN)_6]^{3-}$; of quadrivalent Mn: unstable $[MnCl_6]^{2-}$, stable $[MnF_6]^{2-}$ hexafluoromanganate(IV) ion; of sexivalent Mn: $[MnO_4]^{2-}$; of septavalent Mn: $[MnO_4]^-$.

Uses of compounds of manganese

Pyrolusite, MnO_2, is used chiefly to make ferromanganese (pp. 550, 560) and compounds of manganese. Other uses are: to decolorise glass (p. 550); to form brown glazes on pottery; as an oxidising agent (depolariser) in Leclanché cells, wet or dry; as a 'drier' for linseed oil paints (it hastens the oxidation which converts the oil to a tough solid) and as an oxidising agent in the manufacture of organic compounds.

Potassium permanganate is widely used as an oxidising agent and germicide.

Relationship between A and B families of Group VII

The fundamental relationship is shown by the identity in number of valency electrons. For example:

Chlorine   2, 8, **7**
Manganese 2, 8, 8+**5**, **2**

The elements manganese and chlorine are very different, but as usual for members of the same Group, they show the Group valency of 7, and resemblances are confined to this valency. They are not so close as in Group VI. Septivalent oxides of manganese and chlorine are unstable oily covalent liquids which decompose violently on heating. Both are powerful oxidising agents. They react with water forming corresponding per-acids $HMnO_4$ and $HClO_4$, the latter being the more stable. Both acids are strong, but perchloric acid in aqueous solution is not an oxidising agent. The salts are often isomorphous, e.g. $KMnO_4$ and $KClO_4$, both soluble in water, the former much more so (cf. K_2CrO_4 and K_2SO_4). The chlorine compounds are colourless, those of manganese highly coloured, as expected.

Iron

Iron is in Group VIII (A-type), the first of the triad iron, cobalt, nickel. Its electronic configuration is 2, 8, $(8+6)$, 2. All valency states from 1 to 6 are known, but iron does not show a valency of 8, the Group valency, using all electrons above 2, 8, 8, although osmium, the first member of the Period 6 triad does. The sexivalent state for iron is rare. These facts show the decreasing tendency of transition metals to use d electrons when the d level is more than half-filled. Bivalent and trivalent are the most common and important states; both give rise to simple cations, Fe^{3+} being the more stable.

Occurrence

Iron (4.5% of lithosphere) is the second most common metal in nature. Some occurs free in meteorites. Chief ores are haematite, Fe_2O_3 (Greek *haima*, 'blood', a reference to its colour); magnetite (lodestone), Fe_3O_4; limonite, $Fe_2O_3.3H_2O$; siderite, $FeCO_3$ (Greek *sideros*, 'iron'); and iron pyrites FeS_2 (Latin *pyrites*, 'firestone', perhaps because it burns), used in the manufacture of sulphuric acid, not iron, because sulphur has a very harmful effect on steel. Iron pyrites is iron(II) persulphide (p. 477).

Isolation

Iron is by far the most important of all the metals in everyday use. Small amounts of pure iron are made (p. 566) but almost all iron is used in the form of *steel, cast iron* or *wrought iron,* all of which contain other elements, some beneficial, e.g. carbon, up to a point, and manganese, some harmful, e.g. sulphur and phosphorus.

The first main stage, smelting, in the production of iron from its ore is reduction of iron oxides with carbon. The product is a very impure iron called pig iron or cast iron.

Smelting of iron ore. This is carried out in a blast furnace, a steel-clad, firebrick structure about 100 ft high and 20 ft maximum internal diameter (Fig. 137). The largest in Europe, 250 ft high, is at Margam, South Wales.

Oxide ores are broken into pieces about the size of a fist, but siderite is first roasted outside the furnace to convert it to iron(III) oxide. Iron oxides mixed with coke and limestone are fed into the furnace via the cup-and-cone charger. Figure 137 shows the main reactions in the furnace and the zones in which they take place. Most important is the forward reaction of equation (1). By Le Chatelier's principle this is favoured by (*a*) low

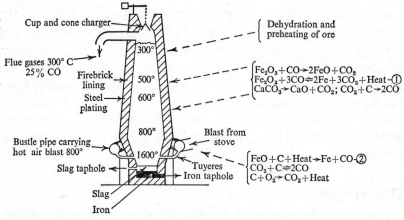

Fig. 137. Blast furnace (elevation).

temperature and (*b*) excess carbon monoxide; and therefore takes place in the middle of the furnace, forming spongy iron. Reaction (2) is favoured by high temperatures and therefore takes place near the bottom. As the iron passes down the furnace it absorbs carbon partly as iron carbide, Fe_3C; phosphorus from reduction of phosphates in the ore as iron phosphide, Fe_3P; sulphur from the coke as iron(II) sulphide; and silicon, from reduction of silica, as ferrosilicon. This impure iron melts at about 1200 °C and collects at the bottom. The purpose of limestone is to form calcium oxide, which combines with and removes acidic oxides, especially silica, present as gangue in the iron ore, forming an easily fusible slag mainly calcium silicate, $CaSiO_3$. This slag collects on top of the iron, protecting it from oxidation by the hot blast. The air blast is heated by passing it through a stove almost as big as the furnace filled with white-hot chequered brick-work previously heated by the combustion of the flue gases from the furnace top. When enough iron has collected, slag is tapped from the upper taphole and the iron through the lower from which it runs into channels in sand where it solidifies and is then broken up into lengths of about 2 ft called *pigs*. Sometimes it is run into a huge ladle and taken immediately to steel furnaces. Tapping takes place every 4 or 5 h. The furnace runs continuously, day and night, for many months, being shut down when the lining needs renewing. The charge of the furnace is converted either into gases removed at the top, or slag and iron removed at the bottom. Daily output is about 1000 tons of pig iron for a large furnace.

Properties and uses of pig iron (cast iron). This is a very impure iron of variable composition, but containing about 93 % iron, and impurities whose maximum amounts are approximately C $3\frac{1}{2}$%, Mn 1 %, P 2 %, S 0.1 %, Si 1 %, which reduce the melting point to 1200 °C and make the metal very brittle (small pieces are easily broken with a hammer, or even when dropped). Pig iron cannot be worked by hammering, cold or hot, because it melts sharply without softening, but can be cast. By far its most important use is in the manufacture of steel and wrought iron, although some is used (as cast iron) for articles which need not stand up to shocks and shears, e.g. stove,, fancy cast-iron work, railings, guttering, piping, bedstead, radiators, lamp-posts, and cylinder blocks.

Manufacture of steel from pig iron. Pure iron is soft and malleable, with properties greatly altered by small quantities of other elements, especially carbon. Cast iron having 3–4 % carbon is too brittle and hard. Wrought iron (0.1 % carbon) is malleable, but too soft for most purposes. Steel, an alloy of iron and 0.1–1.5 % carbon, can be made with the precise carbon content needed to give it the mechanical properties desired. Two impurities very harmful to steel are sulphur and phosphorus even in very small quantities. These are not tolerated in excess of 0.05 %, because sulphur makes steel brittle at red-heat (red-short), while phosphorus makes it brittle at ordinary temperatures (cold-short). Two main processes, (1) the open-hearth process, (2) the Bessemer process, are used in steel manufacture to reduce the carbon content of pig iron to between 0.1 and 1.5 % and the sulphur and phosphorus to 0.05 % or less.

The Siemens–Martin open-hearth process with a basic furnace lining is used in Britain for about 55 % of its steel output. Most British pig iron has a high phosphorus content derived from native ores high in phosphorus. Furnaces able to remove phosphorus from pig iron must have basic linings.

A reverberatory furnace is used, i.e. one in which the flame is deflected down on the charge (Fig. 138) ('reverberate', to beat back). Pre-heated producer gas with excess pre-heated air is fed into the furnace and ignited. Outgoing hot flue gases are used to heat incoming gas and air as in the blast furnace. The shallow hearth is lined with dolomite. A mixture of pig iron, steel scrap and quicklime is charged into the furnace. At about 1600 °C most of the impurities in the molten metal are burned out in the order silicon, manganese, carbon, the necessary oxygen coming from the excess air,

$$Si + O_2 \rightarrow SiO_2; \quad Mn + \tfrac{1}{2}O_2 \rightarrow MnO; \quad C + \tfrac{1}{2}O_2 \rightarrow CO.$$

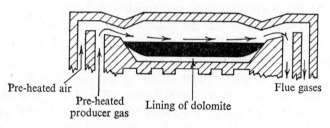

Pre-heated air

Pre-heated producer gas

Lining of dolomite

Flue gases

Fig. 138. Open-hearth furnace (elevation).

Carbon monoxide escapes in the flue gases, but silica combines with the oxides of calcium, manganese and iron(II) to form a molten silicate slag ($MSiO_3$) on the surface of the metal. The remaining silicon, phosphorus and sulphur, and some of the carbon are now removed by adding oxidisers, mainly iron ore and mill-scale (the oxidised skin of a steel ingot which is broken off while it is going through a rolling mill), together with more lime. Silicon dioxide, phosphorus pentoxide, and sulphur trioxide, all acidic, combine with calcium oxide (basic) forming calcium silicate, phosphate and sulphate which pass into the slag. Samples are taken at intervals and the percentage carbon in the steel determined. When this is reduced to about 0.1 %, the calculated weight of ferromanganese (Fe, Mn, C) is added. Manganese deoxidises and desulphurises the steel. Carbon raises the carbon content to the required value. After time for mixing, the furnace is tapped into a ladle, a little more ferromanganese added, and the steel run into moulds where it solidifies to ingots. The whole process up to tapping takes about 10 hours. About 100 tons of steel are produced in one operation. The slag produced contains calcium phosphate. It is ground to powder and sold as a fertiliser (basic slag).

Note. Oil firing is now being used in the open-hearth process.

The Bessemer process, with basic lining, is used in Britain for about 5%
of its steel output. Most steel produced on the continent is Bessemer.

The Bessemer converter is a pear-shaped vessel made of steel plates lined
with dolomite, and mounted on trunnions so that it may be turned into
a horizontal position by a rack-and-pinion. Calcium oxide is first charged
as a slag-former, then about 25 tons of molten pig iron from nearby blast
furnaces are run into the horizontal converter which is then brought
upright, and a compressed-air blast passed in through holes in the bottom
thence up through the molten metal. The chemistry of the process is the

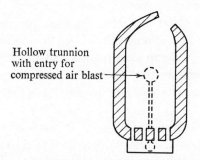

Hollow trunnion
with entry for
compressed air blast

Fig. 139. Bessemer converter (elevation).

same as in the open-hearth. Heat liberated in burning out the impurities
maintains the temperature required to keep the metal liquid (*no fuel costs*).
During the blow, flames of burning carbon monoxide shoot out of the
converter-mouth. When the flames die down all the carbon has been
burnt out. But the blast is kept on to burn out the phosphorus, and the
flame is replaced by a dense brown smoke. This afterblow lasts 2 or 3 min.
The metal at this stage has no carbon, but contains oxides and gases from
the blow. The converter is then tilted and the steel poured into a ladle to
which the calculated weight of ferromanganese is added as a deoxidiser,
and to raise the carbon content to the required value. Twenty minutes is
sufficient for the whole process. The slag produced is sold as a fertiliser.

Bessemer steel is cheaper than open-hearth steel, but its quality is less
good because the rapidity of the process makes it less easily controllable;
also because nitrogen is absorbed by the steel, making it somewhat brittle.
Another great advantage of the *open-hearth* process is its ability to use steel
scrap. Also it produces much more steel at each operation. Its main disadvantages are that the operation is much slower, and fuel costs are high.

The processes so far described are unsuitable for making special high-quality hard steels (alloy steels) because control of temperature and other conditions are not accurate enough. These disadvantages are overcome by using electric furnaces.

Electric process. Basic lined arc furnaces are chiefly used for the main production of electric steel, about 16 % of the total in Britain.

The use of electric heating excludes all oxidising gases and allows oxidation and reduction to be controlled by varying the composition of the slag. Addition of alloys to the steel can be made without loss to the slag. The furnace charge usually consists mainly of selected steel scrap, so the process as at present used is really a secondary one starting off with simple carbon steel made by other processes. The usual practice has three stages:

(1) Lime and ore or mill-scale are charged first, to form the foundation for an oxidising slag. Scrap steel follows and the arcs are then struck. After about $1\frac{1}{2}$ hours, melting is complete, and silicon, manganese, and phosphorus have been removed into the slag, while the carbon content will be almost correct.

(2) The slag is raked off and replaced by a reducing slag composed of lime, fluorspar, carbon and *ferrosilicon*, added to the metal bath. Sulphur and oxygen are removed from the steel into the slag.

(3) Alloy additions are made to give steel of the desired composition, and after checking by analysis of samples in the laboratory the steel is tapped.

Use of oxygen in steel-making. The use of pure oxygen has revolutionised steel-making, and also the pre-refining of pig iron in the ladle. A water-cooled tube, called a lance, is put into the open-hearth furnace or through the top of a converter with a solid bottom to a point near the surface of the metal. Oxygen is blown through the lance at supersonic speed to penetrate through the slag to the metal. Rate of oxidation of impurities is greatly increased, time reduced, and absorption of nitrogen by the steel prevented. Fuel costs in the open-hearth are lower. Steel scrap can be used in Bessemer-type converters because of the greater heat available. The result in all cases is to produce a better and cheaper steel.

Oxygen is now being used in enormous quantities, usually made (by the fractional distillation of liquid air) at the steel works. The first tonnage oxygen plant for steel-making in Britain was erected at Margam in 1956 for open-hearth furnaces. The British steel industry is now using about 5000 tons of oxygen a day.

Pure oxygen is used in all types of steel-making processes: open-hearth

562

furnaces, modified Bessemer converters, and electric furnaces. The biggest changes have been made using converters. Two very important new developments in this sphere are the L.D. process (so called because it was developed at two Austrian steel towns, Linz and Donawitz) and the Kaldo process, which uses an inclined rotating converter blown with oxygen from the top. Figure 140 gives a simple diagram of the L.D. converter in the upright position. The oxygen travelling at supersonic speed penetrates the slag and oxidises impurities in the metal as already described.

The L.D. process accounts for about 21 % of the steel made in Britain, the Kaldo process for about $2\frac{1}{2}$ %.

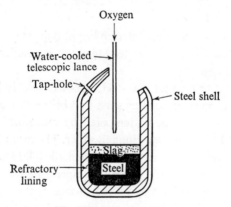

Fig. 140. L.D. converter.

To remove phosphorus from high phosphorus pig iron, lime is included in the initial charge, and after a first blow with pure oxygen alone, a second follows in which lime is injected in the gas stream through the lance. The furnace lining must be basic. Acid linings made of silica may be used in dealing with pig irons low in phosphorus.

Britain produces about 25 million tons of steel per year.

Properties and uses of steel. Classification of steel is based in the first instance on the percentage of carbon in the steel.

Mild steel (0.1–0.2% C) is fairly soft, malleable and ductile; can be forged (shaped by hammering and pressing while hot) but cannot be hardened by heat treatment (see below); used in making boiler plates, girders, bars, tubes, rivets, nuts and bolts.

Medium carbon steel (0.2–0.7% C) is malleable and ductile but harder than mild steel; can be forged, welded, hardened and tempered; used in making rails, girders, axles, tyres, castings.

High-carbon steel (0.7–1.5 % C). Up to 1.0 % C, the steel can be forged; it is hard but can be toughened and made malleable by tempering. From 1.0 % C upwards, the steel cannot be forged, but can be hardened and tempered. Innumerable articles are made from it: hammers, taps, dies, punches, cutting tools of all sorts, machine tools, hard-steel parts of machinery and engines of all sorts.

The properties of steels depend not only on percentage of carbon but on the heat treatment to which they have been subjected, and on the presence of other alloying metals (see below).

Heat treatment of medium and high-carbon steels. Annealing, hardening and tempering.

Annealing. When the steel is heated to bright redness (950 °C), held there to 'soak' for some time, then cooled slowly, it is comparatively soft and can be machined easily.

Hardening. If, after heating, the steel is cooled quickly by quenching in oil or water, it becomes as hard as glass and brittle instead of tough.

Tempering. Hard steel can be tempered by reheating to a lower temperature (200–310 °C) then quenching in water. The result is to make it less hard but much tougher, stronger and more malleable. Different temperatures produce different qualities of steel. Temperature can be judged by the colour of the oxide layer forming on the surface of the steel: a pale straw colour (210 °C) is suitable for razor blades (very hard); a dark blue for springs and hack-saw blades (less hard and less brittle). The lower the reheat temperature, the more hard the resulting steel, because less change takes place.

Explanation of the changes caused by heat treatment. Iron exists in three allotropic forms, stable over different temperature ranges, and having different powers of dissolving carbon.

		910°		1400°		1535°	
Allotrope	α-iron	$\rightleftharpoons$	γ-iron	$\rightleftharpoons$	δ-iron	$\rightleftharpoons$	Molten iron
Structure	B.C.C.		F.C.C.		B.C.C.		
Maximum weight of dissolved carbon	0.1 %		1.7 %		0.1 %		5 %

Carbon in a steel at a temperature somewhat above 910 °C is present as a solid solution in γ-iron, atoms of carbon occupying the octahedral holes in the F.C.C. lattice. If steel is cooled quickly, carbon has no time to crystallise (as graphite) from the α-iron formed and in which it is insoluble.

It remains as a kind of supersaturated or colloidal solid-solution in α-iron. This solid solution, called *martensite* is very hard and brittle, and so therefore is the quenched steel. This steel remains hard unless it is reheated, because although martensite is meta-stable, its rate of conversion at ordinary temperatures is negligible. However, when hardened steel is tempered by mild reheating, the martensite is converted into a mixture of minute parallel plates of α-iron, *ferrite*, and a hard iron carbide, Fe_3C, called *cementite*. This mixture is called *pearlite*; the tempered steel composed of it is hard because of the cementite but tough and malleable because of the ferrite.

It is believed that α- and δ-iron are varieties of the same allotrope, rather than two distinct allotropes.

Another important process in steel-making is *case-hardening*. The surface or 'case' of medium carbon and alloy steels is converted into a hard, high-carbon steel by heating it in contact with carbon or sodium cyanide, followed by heat treatment. Alloy steels may also be case-hardened by heating in an atmosphere of dry ammonia, a very hard skin of metal nitrides being formed. Case-hardened steels are used where there is need of a hard bearing surface with a tough malleable core, e.g. in ball bearings, gudgeon pins, armour plates for warships and armour-piercing shells (see Alloy steels below).

Alloy steels (special steels). All steels contain small amounts of manganese and silicon. Many contain substantial amounts of manganese, nickel, chromium, vanadium, tungsten and other transition metals.

Manganese steel (12 % Mn) is very hard and tough; used for points and crossings in railways, for jaws of crushing and grinding machinery and for safes.

Stainless steels, various types (Cr, a corrosion resisting element, 13–18 %; Ni, 0–6 %), are used for cutlery, razor blades, kitchen sinks, pots, pans, oven-ware, tea-pots, trays, watch-cases, garden tools, car parts, chemical plant, tubes, etc. Stainless steel is not ferromagnetic. For this reason it is used for making weights for use with analytical balances.

Nickel, chromium, vanadium steels (0.15 V) are widely used for armour plate, cutting tools and machine parts.

High-speed tool steels contain chromium, vanadium and 15 % tungsten, a metal of great hardness and the highest melting point of all metals. They retain their hardness, temper and edge even at red-heat.

Invar (36 % Ni) has a very low coefficient of thermal expansion; it is used for clock pendulums and measuring instruments.

Alnico (Fe, Ni, Co, Al, Cu) makes very powerful permanent magnets for magnetos and loudspeakers.

Silicon steels (1 % Si) are used for springs; (5 % Si) for cores of electromagnets because of their low magnetic retentivity and high permeability.

Wrought iron (less than 0.1 % C) is made by melting pig iron with Fe_2O_3 which oxidises the impurities, the process being hastened by stirring. As the metal becomes purer it gradually becomes pasty. Lumps are removed and the slag squeezed out under steam hammers. Wrought iron is rather soft, but tough, malleable and ductile, never becoming brittle and always showing great resistance to fatigue; it resists corrosion better than steel; can be easily forged and welded (e.g. by blacksmiths). Wrought iron was widely used, but is now largely superceded by mild steel. However, because of its special properties and the fact that when overstrained it stretches but does not snap, as steel usually does, it is still used, for example, in making chains, railway couplings, and crane-hooks.

Pure iron may be made by the reduction of pure iron(II) oxide (made by heating iron(II) oxalate) with hydrogen, or by thermal decomposition of pentacarbonyliron(O), $Fe(CO)_5$, a pale viscous liquid, made by passing carbon monoxide over finely divided iron at 120° C. Pure iron loses its magnetism immediately the applied field is removed; it is therefore used for cores of electric motors and transformers. The m.p. of pure iron is 1535 °C whereas that of pig iron is 1200 °C (p. 559).

Properties of iron (pure or almost pure)

Physical. Iron is a silvery metal, density 7.9 g cm^{-3}, i.e. higher than manganese or chromium; melting point 1535 °C, i.e. intermediate between manganese and chromium.

Allotropy (p. 564), mechanical properties (p. 566) and ferromagnetism (p. 528) have been considered. Note that at 768 °C iron ceases to be ferromagnetic and becomes paramagnetic (p. 527); this change is reversible.

Chemical. Iron, as expected, has a higher electronegativity and a less negative standard electrode potential (p. 211) than the preceding elements in its Period. A moderately reactive element, stable in dry air at ordinary temperatures (although finely divided iron is pyrophoric, i.e. ignites spontaneously in air) it rusts rapidly in moist air (p. 210). For action on water, see p. 567. At red-heat iron liberates hydrogen from steam forming Fe_3O_4; the action is reversible. Hydrochloric and dilute sulphuric acids react readily with iron. With cold concentrated sulphuric acid there is little or no reaction (the acid can be stored or transported in mild steel vessels as also can 75% H_2SO_4). Hot concentrated sulphuric acid reacts with iron giving sulphur dioxide and iron(II) sulphate. With cold dilute nitric acid, iron(II) nitrate solution is formed while the acid is reduced to oxides of nitrogen and some ammonia, which then forms ammonium nitrate. Warm dilute nitric acid gives iron(III) nitrate solution. Concentrated nitric acid, cold or hot and other oxidising agents, e.g. chromic acid, hydrogen peroxide, render iron passive because of formation of tri-iron tetroxide as a protective film. Hot concentrated sodium hydroxide attacks iron quite considerably even in the absence of air, forming $[Fe(OH)_4]^{2-}$ ions in solution.

Iron when heated combines with chlorine, oxygen, sulphur and carbon forming iron(III) chloride, tri-iron tetroxide, iron(II) sulphide, iron carbide (Fe_3C), respectively, the less electronegative the non-metal, the higher the temperature required. Iron appears not to form a nitride when heated in nitrogen, but if heated to 500 °C in dry ammonia it readily forms one, Fe_2N. Water has little effect on di-iron nitride.

The rusting of iron. This is the most important example of metallic corrosion, a spontaneous process which is electrochemical in nature (p. 211), i.e. rusting involves the transfer of electrons along the surface of the metal under the influence of a potential difference (P.D.). The end-product of the process, rust, is hydrated iron(III) oxide $Fe_2O_3.xH_2O$. Rusting of iron requires (1) oxygen, (2) water, and (3) carbon dioxide or some other compound, acid or salt, which in solution in the water forms the electrolyte. During rusting, impurities in the iron, e.g. carbon, cause local potential differences on the metal surface; and, very important, differences in oxygen concentration in the electrolyte at different parts of the metal surface cause potential differences.

Consider a drop of water, containing carbon dioxide in solution, resting on an iron surface (Fig. 141). The drop (circular) is thinner at the circumference than at the centre. The oxygen concentration at the iron is greater at the circumference. Oxygen readily consumes electrons and in approximately neutral solution the main cathodic reaction is

$$\tfrac{1}{2}O_2 + H_2O + 2e \rightarrow 2OH^-. \tag{1}$$

Thus the part of the iron under the circumference of the drop is cathodic and the part under the centre of the drop anodic. Electrons required for reaction (1) are pulled out of iron atoms near the centre of the plate: Fe^{2+} ions are therefore formed and pass into solution,

$$Fe \rightarrow Fe^{2+} + 2e. \tag{2}$$

Thus there is an electron flow through the metal from centre to circumference as shown. In the electrolyte, the Fe^{2+} cations move to the cathode and the OH^- anions to the anode. They meet at some intermediate zone where iron(II) hydroxide is precipitated, away from both electrodes so that no blocking of the electrodes by insoluble films takes place, and corrosion continues. Iron(II) hydroxide is eventually oxidised to $Fe_2O_3 . xH_2O$ (rust). There may be intermediate reactions involving formation of iron(II) carbonate and hydrogen carbonate.

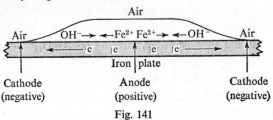

Fig. 141

It is seen that pitting of the iron surface, the result of localised anodic corrosion, occurs at the *centre* of the water-drop, i.e. rusting is greatest in those areas away from the air.

Compounds of iron

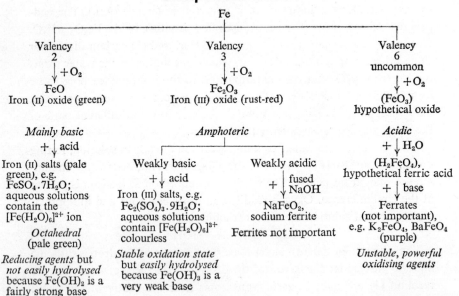

The greater stability of iron (III) compounds is attributed to the half-filled $3d$ sub-shell in Fe^{3+}, thus 2, 8, (8+5).

568

Oxides

There are three oxides of iron: FeO, Fe_3O_4, Fe_2O_3.

Iron(II) oxide, FeO, is made by heating iron(II) oxalate in an inert atmosphere, $$FeC_2O_4 \rightarrow FeO + CO\uparrow + CO_2\uparrow.$$

It is a pyrophoric solid. Some other properties are indicated in the above chart. In addition iron(II) oxide is non-stoichiometric, its usual composition being $Fe_{0.95}O$.

Iron(III) oxide, Fe$_2$O$_3$, a rust-red solid, occurs naturally as haematite, and may be prepared by heating an iron(II) oxo-salt whose anion is an oxidising agent, e.g. $FeSO_4$, or almost any iron salt with free access of air.

Tri-iron tetroxide, Fe$_3$O$_4$ (black), occurs naturally as magnetite; may be prepared by heating iron in oxygen or steam; very strongly ferromagnetic, not active chemically; reacts with acids as a mixed oxide $FeO.Fe_2O_3$, giving a mixture of iron(II) and iron(III) salts in solution,
$$Fe_3O_4 + 8H^+ \rightarrow Fe^{2+} + 2Fe^{3+} + 4H_2O.$$

Bivalent, i.e. iron(II) compounds (ferrous)

Iron(II) hydroxide, Fe(OH)$_2$, insoluble, is obtained as a dirty green gelatinous precipitate by addition of a solution containing hydroxyl ions to one containing iron(II) ions (p. 254). When pure it is white but is rapidly oxidised by dissolved oxygen to iron(II, III) hydroxide $Fe_3(OH)_8$. It is amphoteric, being a fairly strong base, and also weakly acidic (see chart, p. 568).

Anhydrous iron(II) chloride, FeCl$_2$ (white), is made by heating iron filings in a stream of hydrogen chloride. A number of hydrates are known, the one stable at room temperature being $FeCl_2.4H_2O$.

Iron(II) sulphate, FeSO$_4$.7H$_2$O, soluble, is made conveniently by the action of dilute sulphuric acid on iron (p. 218). It forms pale blue-green crystals which on gentle heating decompose leaving the white anhydrous salt. On stronger heating this decomposes into iron(III) oxide, sulphur dioxide and sulphur trioxide. Like other iron(II) salts it forms a dark greenish brown addition compound with nitrogen monoxide,
$$[Fe(NO)(H_2O)_5]^{2+}SO_4^{2-},$$
in which one molecule of water in the hydrated iron(II) ion has been replaced by NO (brown ring test, p. 445).

Ammonium iron(II) sulphate, $FeSO_4(NH_4)_2SO_4.6H_2O$, the best known of a series of double sulphates with the general formula $M^{II}SO_4, M_2^ISO_4.6H_2O$, where M^I is alkali metal ion or ammonium, is prepared by crystallising a solution containing iron(II) sulphate and ammonium sulphate in roughly equimolar proportions. It is pale green. The other members of the series are made similarly. Ammonium iron(II) sulphate is less easily oxidised than iron(II) sulphate and is therefore a better standard in volumetric analysis.

Iron(II) carbonate, $FeCO_3$, insoluble, is the only iron(II) compound occurring naturally (as siderite). Precipitated as a white solid when air-free solutions of sodium carbonate and an iron(II) salt are mixed, the precipitate rapidly turns brown by atmospheric oxidation. When carbon dioxide is passed into an aqueous suspension of iron(II) carbonate it dissolves giving a solution of iron(II) hydrogen carbonate, $Fe(HCO_3)_2$.

Iron(II) sulphide, **FeS,** insoluble, is made by direct synthesis or by precipitation using colourless ammonium sulphide solution. It is a black metallic looking solid which readily dissolves in dilute acids evolving hydrogen sulphide (the usual method of preparation of this gas). A more correct formulation is $Fe_{0.86}S$ showing that iron(II) sulphide, like the oxide, is non-stoichiometric.

Trivalent or iron(III) compounds (ferric)

Iron(III) hydroxide, $Fe(OH)_3$, or more correctly $Fe_2O_3.xH_2O$, insoluble, is formed as a rust-red gelatinous precipitate by adding a solution containing hydroxide ions to one containing iron(III) ions. It is amphoteric: weakly basic and weakly acidic. Iron(III) carbonate does not exist because the hydroxide is too weak a base.

Iron(III) chloride, $FeCl_3$ (soluble). The anhydrous salt is made by synthesis and is covalent, subliming when heated and condensing as very deep red crystals. The vapour is dimeric, containing Fe_2Cl_6 molecules (like Al_2Cl_6) but dissociates at higher temperatures first into the monomer, then into iron(II) chloride and chlorine (like $CuCl_2$). Various hydrates are known, $FeCl_3.6H_2O$ (yellow) the best known, being stable at room temperature. The aqueous solution is also yellow, the colour in both cases being that of the $[Fe(Cl)(H_2O)_5]^{2+}$ ion. On warming and diluting, the solution becomes darker because of hydrolysis, giving eventually a deep red-brown colloidal solution of iron(III) hydroxide, $Fe(OH)_3(H_2O)_3$ (pp. 244–5).

Iron(III) sulphate, $Fe_2(SO_4)_3.9H_2O,$ soluble, is prepared by boiling iron(II) sulphate solution with dilute sulphuric acid and an oxidising agent, e.g. nitric acid or hydrogen peroxide. On concentrating and cooling, colourless crystals separate. The salt is very soluble in cold water and much hydrolysed.

The anhydrous salt, cream coloured, is got by heating the hydrate gently. With stronger heating iron(III) sulphate decomposes easily into iron(III) oxide and sulphur trioxide, again showing the weakly basic nature of iron(III) oxide. Anhydrous iron(III) sulphate appears to be very slightly soluble in cold water, and slightly soluble in hot when the ratio of salt to water is very small. But if say 0.5 g solid is put into a small volume of water, about 2 cm³, and boiled for one minute, the solubility is very much greater (tested roughly by the bulk of precipitate got on adding sodium hydroxide solution).

Iron(III) sulphate forms alums (p. 356) with sulphates of alkali metals and ammonium, the most important being ammonium iron(III) sulphate, $(NH_4)_2SO_4.Fe_2(SO_4)_3.24H_2O$ (pale pinkish violet), known as 'ferric alum'.

Iron(III) sulphide, $Fe_2S_3,$ insoluble, can be made by passing H_2S over warm $Fe_2O_3.xH_2O$ as in the manufacture of coal-gas (p. 372).

Complex compounds of iron

Apart from the hydrated iron(II) and iron(III) ions and pentacarbonyliron(0) already mentioned (p. 566), the commonest complex salts are potassium hexacyanoferrate(II) and hexacyanoferrate(III).

Potassium hexacyanoferrate(II) (potassium ferrocyanide)

$$K_4[Fe(CN)_6].3H_2O,$$

is manufactured from the spent oxide from gas-works' purifiers, which contains Prussian blue formed by absorption of hydrogen cyanide, HCN, in the gas. The spent oxide is heated with slaked lime, and the soluble $Ca_2[Fe(CN)_6]$ formed, extracted with water and converted to $K_4Fe(CN)_6$ by treatment with potassium carbonate, K_2CO_3. Potassium hexacyanoferrate(II) may be prepared by adding excess potassium cyanide solution to iron(II) sulphate solution,

$$Fe^{2+} + 6CN^- \rightarrow [Fe(CN)_6]^{4-},$$

filtering, concentrating and crystallising. It is a yellow solid.

Potassium hexacyanoferrate(III) (potassium ferricyanide), $K_3[Fe(CN)_6]$,

is made by oxidising potassium hexacyanoferrate(II) solution with chlorine,

$$[Fe(CN)_6]^{4-} + \tfrac{1}{2}Cl_2 \to [Fe(CN)_6]^{3-} + Cl^-.$$

It forms dark red crystals which have no water of crystallisation.

Sodium nitroprusside, $Na_2[Fe(CN)_5NO].2H_2O$, disodium pentacyano-nitrosyl ferrate(II) is prepared by adding powdered potassium hexacyano-ferrate(II) to nitric acid (1 vol. conc. acid + 1 vol. water), boiling for some time, cooling, then neutralising with sodium hydroxide solution. On evaporation, ruby red crystals of sodium nitroprusside separate. The hexacyanoferrate(II) is first oxidised to hexacyanoferrate(III) which then reacts with nitrogen monoxide formed by reduction of HNO_3,

$$Na_3[Fe(CN)_6] + NO \to NaCN + Na_2[Fe(CN)_5(NO)].$$

The salt is not very stable in aqueous solution. Its solution is used as a test for alkali sulphide (not H_2S) in solution. When the solutions are mixed a fine purple colour is formed.

Interconversion of Fe^{2+} and Fe^{3+}

$$Fe^{2+} \underset{\text{reduction}}{\overset{\text{oxidation}}{\rightleftharpoons}} Fe^{3+} + e.$$

The oxidation is brought about by the usual oxidising agents, e.g. potassium permanganate plus dilute sulphuric acid, hot dilute nitric acid, potassium dichromate plus dilute sulphuric acid, manganese(IV) oxide plus dilute sulphuric acid, chlorine.

Reduction is brought about by the usual reducing agents: hydrogen sulphide, sulphurous acid, zinc plus dilute hydrochloric acid.

Distinction between Fe^{2+} and Fe^{3+}

Reagent in solution	Fe^{2+} in solution	Fe^{3+} in solution
NH_4OH	Dirty green gelatinous ppt. insoluble in excess	Rust-brown gelatinous ppt. insoluble in excess
$K_4Fe(CN)_6$	White ppt. turning blue	Ppt. of Prussian blue
$K_3Fe(CN)_6$	Ppt. of Turnbull's blue	Brown colour. No ppt.
KCNS, potassium thiocyanate	No coloration	Intense deep red colour

Note. (1) It has been shown that Prussian blue and Turnbull's blue are identical, having the composition $KFe^{III}[Fe^{II}(CN)_6]$. The reactions are:

Prussian blue: $\quad K^+ + Fe^{3+} + [Fe^{II}(CN)_6]^{4-} \rightarrow KFe^{III}[Fe^{II}(CN)_6]^{4-}$;

Turnbull's blue: the first reaction is oxidation of Fe^{2+} ions by hexacyanoferrate(III) ions thus: $\quad Fe^{2+} + [Fe^{III}(CN)_6]^{3-} \rightarrow Fe^{3+} + [Fe^{II}(CN)_6]^{4-}$,

followed by the reaction for Prussian blue.

(2) The red colour formed with iron(III) ions and thiocyanate ions is mainly $Fe(CNS)_3$, thiocyanatoiron(III).

Uses of iron compounds

Most important of all is the use of the ores in making iron and steels. Others are: in chemical analysis; iron(III) oxide is used as a pigment, venetian red, as a polish (rouge) and as a catalyst; iron pyrites is used in the manufacture of sulphuric acid; iron(II) sulphate in the manufacture of ink, weed killer and Prussian blue, itself used as a pigment.

Cobalt

Cobalt is the second member of the first Group VIII triad and has electronic configuration 2, 8, (8 + 7), 2. The decreasing tendency to form high oxidation states in passing along the transition series from manganese is very marked with cobalt (and nickel). Cobalt shows no important valency higher than 4, its most important being an electrovalency of 2 in the cobalt(II) ion Co^{2+}. The simple cobalt(III) ion Co^{3+} is very unstable, so is the hydrated ion $[Co(H_2O)_6]^{3+}$, but cobalt forms numerous stable complexes in which it has a covalency (or oxidation state) of $+3$.

Occurrence

Cobalt (0.004 % of lithosphere) always occurs associated with nickel and is found free in meteorites with iron and nickel. The most important ores of cobalt are *smaltite*, $CoAs_2$, and *cobaltite*, $CoAsS$.

Isolation

Various methods are used. In one of these the ore is roasted in air, first with sodium carbonate then with silica. The cobalt is thus converted to tricobalt tetroxide, and impurities, mainly iron and arsenic, removed as slag. Tricobalt tetroxide is then reduced by heating with carbon, water-gas, or aluminium.

Physical properties

Cobalt is a silvery-white metal with a pinkish tinge, tougher, stronger and harder than pure iron; density 8.9 g cm^{-3}, melting point 1495 °C. It has two structures, H.C.P. and F.C.C., and is ferromagnetic.

Chemical properties

With standard electrode potential of -0.28 V, it is less reactive than iron, is stable in air at ordinary temperature, but slowly oxidises to cobalt(II) oxide on heating. While not reacting with water, red-hot cobalt decomposes steam giving cobalt(II) oxide and hydrogen. Cobalt displaces hydrogen slowly from hydrochloric and dilute sulphuric acids forming hydrated cobalt(II) ions $[Co(H_2O)_6]^{2+}$ (pink). Dilute nitric acid reacts with cobalt, oxides of nitrogen and $[Co(H_2O)_6]^{2+}$ ions being formed. It is made passive by concentrated nitric acid. Aqueous alkalis have little or no action on cobalt. When heated, cobalt combines with chlorine, oxygen, sulphur and carbon, but not with nitrogen.

Uses

Cobalt is used to make alloy-steels (p. 566) and non-ferrous alloys for making high-speed cutting tools, e.g. *stellite* (50 % Co, 25 % Cr, 15 % W, 5 % Mo plus a little C and Fe) and *widia metal* (tungsten carbide bonded with 10 % Co).

Compounds of cobalt

Simple Co(II) compounds containing Co^{2+} ions or $[Co(H_2O)_6]^{2+}$ ions are much more stable than the corresponding compounds of Co(III). Indeed Co^{3+} or Co^{3+}(aq.) salts are such powerful oxidising agents that they oxidise water to oxygen and are themselves reduced to the Co(II) state. They are of little importance.

On the other hand, Co(III) complexes in which the complexing agent is other than water, are much more stable than the corresponding Co(II) complexes, e.g. potassium pentacyanocobaltate(II), $K_3[Co(CN)_5]$, is such a powerful reducing agent, i.e. the Co(II) atom so readily loses an electron to form Co(III), that it reduces water to hydrogen,

$$H^+ + OH^- + e \rightarrow \tfrac{1}{2}H_2 + OH^-,$$

and is itself oxidised to potassium hexacyanocobaltate(III), $K_3[Co(CN)_6]$.

The hydrated cobalt cobalt(II) ion in solution is pink and in hydrated salts it has varying shades of pink or red. Anhydrous salts are blue.

Common soluble cobalt(II) salts are the chloride, $CoCl_2.6H_2O$, nitrate $Co(NO_3)_2.6H_2O$, and sulphate, $CoSO_4.7H_2O$. They are made by the general methods. When a solution of the chloride is concentrated or when the salt is heated, the colour changes from pink to blue. The change is reversible, hence the use of cobalt(II) chloride solution as invisible ink and of cobalt(II) chloride paper (dried) as a test for water. The colour change is caused partly by loss of water, but mainly by the formation of a new complex ion,

$$[Co(H_2O)_6]^{2+}+4Cl^- \rightleftharpoons [CoCl_4]^{2-}+6H_2O.$$
$$\text{Red} \qquad\qquad\qquad \text{Blue}$$

The sulphate forms a pink double sulphate with ammonium sulphate, isomorphous with the corresponding iron(II) compound (p. 570).

Common insoluble cobalt(II) compounds are the oxide, CoO (brown); hydroxide, $Co(OH)_2$ (greenish blue); carbonate, $CoCO_3$ (pink); and sulphide, CoS (black) which is precipitated by adding an alkali sulphide to a solution containing Co^{2+} ions.

Important stable soluble complexes of Co(III) are potassium hexacyano-cobaltate(III) (potassium cobalticyanide), many cobalt-ammines, e.g. $[Co(NH_3)_6]^{3+}Cl_3$ and sodium hexanitrocobaltate(III) (sodium cobaltinitrite) $Na_3[Co(NO_2)_6]$ which is used as a test for K^+ ions: when solid sodium hexanitrocobaltate(III) is added to a solution containing K^+ ions, a yellow precipitate of slightly soluble potassium hexanitrocobaltate(III),

$$K_3[Co(NO_2)_6]$$

is formed, insoluble in dilute acetic acid. Cobalt(III) sulphate,

$$Co_2(SO_4)_3.18H_2O$$

is a blue salt immediately decomposed by water.

Uses of cobalt compounds

Cobalt salts of organic fatty acids are used as driers in oil paint, that is, in small amounts, they speed up the hardening of paint films by atmospheric oxidation. They act also as catalysts in the manufacture of some organic compounds. Cobalt oxide is added to glass and enamels to give them a blue colour.

Nickel

Nickel is the last member of the triad iron, cobalt, nickel. Its electronic configuration is 2, 8, (8+8), 2. Nickel continues the trend towards fewer high oxidation states and greater stability in the lower states. The only common and stable valency of nickel is 2, although Ni(III) and Ni(IV) occur in a few complexes and oxides.

Occurrence

Nickel (0.01 % lithosphere) is found free in meteorites with iron and cobalt. Its most important ores are *pentlandite* FeS with about 4 % Ni as NiS, and *garnierite*, a magnesium-nickel silicate.

Isolation (from pentlandite)

The ore is crushed, concentrated by flotation, then roasted in air with silica which removes the iron as iron silicate slag. The residue, mainly nickel(II) oxide, is reduced by heating in water gas at 350 °C leaving impure metal. Carbon monoxide is passed over this at 60 °C forming tetracarbonyl nickel(o) $Ni(CO)_4$, a gas which is carried over with excess carbon monoxide into a vessel containing nickel pellets at 200 °C. At this temperature the tetracarbonylnickel(o) decomposes, depositing pure nickel on the pellets. The carbon monoxide is recirculated,

$$Ni + 4CO \underset{200°}{\overset{60°}{\rightleftharpoons}} Ni(CO)_4.$$

Isolation from garnierite differs from that from pentlandite only in the early stages of the process.

Properties

Nickel and cobalt are very similar in physical and chemical properties. A well-known example of this is the precipitation of nickel as black nickel(II) sulphide in the same qualitative analysis group as cobalt(II) sulphide, also black.

Physical. Almost the same as cobalt. Melting point a little lower (Ni, 1455 °C; Co, 1495 °C).

Chemical. Almost the same as cobalt; standard electrode potential a little less negative (Ni, -0.25 V; Co, -0.28 V). The only obvious difference so far is that the colour of the hydrated nickel(II) ion $[Ni(H_2O)_6]^{2+}$ is green, that of $[Co(H_2O)_6]^{2+}$ is pink.

Uses

The most important use of nickel is in making alloys, ferrous and non-ferrous. For ferrous alloys (alloy steels), see p. 565; for *nichrome*, p. 543. Non-ferrous alloys of nickel include: *monel metal* (70% Ni, 30% Cu) which is strong, malleable and resistant to corrosion, therefore widely used in chemical industry; *cupro-nickel* (75% Cu, 25% Ni) used for making British silver coins; *German silver* (80% Cu, 10% Zn, 10% Ni) for silver-plated table-ware and ornaments; and *manganin* (p. 551). Pure nickel is used in electroplating and for crucibles and spatulas in the laboratory; also as an important catalyst in organic hydrogenations, e.g. the manufacture of margarine from oils.

Compounds of nickel

All well-known nickel compounds, except oxides and hydroxides, contain nickel in the bivalent state only.

Common insoluble nickel compounds. Nickel(II) oxide, NiO (green), is a basic oxide. Nickel(II) hydroxide, $Ni(OH)_2$, is formed as a gelatinous green precipitate by adding ammonia solution to aqueous Ni^{2+}. It is soluble in excess of ammonia giving a blue solution containing the hexamminenickel(II) ion $[Ni(NH_3)_6]^{2+}$. Nickel(II) carbonate, $NiCO_3$ (pale green), is precipitated by sodium hydrogen carbonate solution from aqueous Ni^{2+}; nickel(II) sulphide, NiS, by alkali sulphide solution ; nickel(II) cyanide, $Ni(CN)_2$ (green), by CN^- ions—it is soluble in excess of CN^- giving tetracyanonickelate(II) ion $[Ni(CN)_4]^{2+}$ which is unstable.

Common soluble nickel salts are made by the methods given on p. 240. Nickel(II) sulphate, $NiSO_4.7H_2O$ is green, the anhydrous salt yellow. It forms a green double sulphate with $(NH_4)_2SO_4$, ammonium nickel(II) sulphate $(NH_4)_2SO_4.NiSO_4.6H_2O$, used in ammoniacal solution as the electrolyte in nickel plating. Ammonium nickel(II) sulphate is isomorphous with the corresponding iron(II) and cobalt(II) double sulphates. Nickel(II) chloride, $NiCl_2.6H_2O$, is green, the anhydrous salt yellow. Nickel sulphate and chloride are used in very large quantities in electroplating. The oxide is added to enamels and glass to give a brown colour. Nickel hydroxide forms the positive plate in nickel–iron and nickel–cadmium alkaline storage batteries, widely used in industry.

577

Differences between cobalt and nickel

Test	Cobalt	Nickel
Colour of compounds	Various shades of pink or red	Green
Colour of borax bead	Blue	Brown
Dimethyl glyoxime solution + aqueous M^{2+} ions + excess ammonia solution	No ppt. from dilute solution	Bulky red ppt.
M^{2+} ions in dil. HCl + pentan-1-ol + solid KCNS. Shake	Blue colour in alcohol layer (top) because of complex ion $[Co(CNS)_4]^{2-}$	No colour
Metal heated with CO at 60 °C and ord. pressure	Carbonyl not formed in these conditions	Gaseous $Ni(CO)_4$ formed

Relation between Group VIII A and Group 0 (or VIII B)

The fundamental relationship is shown by the identity in number of valency electrons. For example:

$$\text{xenon} \quad 2, \quad 8, \quad 18, \quad 18, \quad \mathbf{8}$$
$$\text{osmium} \quad 2, \quad 8, \quad 18, \quad 32, \quad 8+\mathbf{6}, \quad \mathbf{2}$$

No close relationship is to be expected. However, there are some resemblances. The Group valency of 8 is shown by some of the metals of the A family (e.g. osmium) and by some of the noble gases (e.g. xenon, p. 279). The substantial relative inertness of the gases of the B family justifies the term noble gases. The relative inertness of some of the metals of the A families, e.g. iridium, platinum, palladium and to a less extent nickel, justifies the term noble metals. A much greater measure of inertness exists in the B family than in the A.

Exercises

1. (*a*) Account for the growing industrial importance of titanium metal.
   (*b*) Outline its manufacture from rutile, stating the difficulties involved and describing how they were overcome.
2. Describe (*a*) the manufacture of sodium dichromate from chromite, and (*b*) the preparation of potassium manganate(VI) and its conversion into potassium permanganate.
3. Explain the changes caused by the heat treatment of steel.
4. Give a comparative account of (*a*) the oxides, and (*b*) the chlorides of iron.

5. Suggest how reasonably pure samples of the following may be obtained: (a) potassium hexacyanoferrate(II) from iron(III) chloride; (b) potassium permanganate from manganese(IV) oxide; (c) potassium dichromate from chromium(III) oxide. (C)

6. Explain the chemistry of the production of steel from cast iron. For each of the following processes give one experimental method: (a) the oxidation of iron(II) ions to iron(III) ions, (b) the reduction of iron(III) ions to iron(II) ions, (c) the preparation of a sample of iron(III) oxide starting from iron.
    In (a) and (b) describe how you could demonstrate the success of each process. (J.M.B.)

7. What is an alum? Describe the preparation of **either** potash alum from alumium, **or** iron alum from iron(II) sulphate and ammonium sulphate. Give a concise account of **one** method of determining the percentage of iron in iron alum. (O)

8. Describe how a specimen of metallic chromium may be prepared in the laboratory from chromium(III) oxide (Cr_2O_3). What do you know of the uses of chromium?
    Given a mixture of potassium chloride and potassium dichromate, indicate how you would (a) prepare a specimen of chromium(III) oxide, (b) identify the potassium and chloride radicals. (O)

9. Compare the chemistry of corresponding compounds of iron and either chromium or manganese. Discuss the chemistry and constitution of complex compounds containing iron. (OS)

10. A crystalline salt, readily soluble in water, may contain one or more of the following metal ions: Cu^{2+}, Fe^{2+}, Cr^{3+}, Zn^{2+}. You have available common laboratory reagents but no means of precipitating sulphides. Devise a scheme of separation by which you could identify the metal ions present in the salt. (L)

11. State and explain, with one example of each, **three** characteristics of a transition metal. (O & C)

12. Explain the meaning of the terms *transition metal* and *complex ion*, illustrating your answers by reference to **one** of the following elements: chromium. manganese, iron or copper. (O & C)

13. Describe the characteristic electronic structures of the transition elements and show how they are related to their position in the Periodic Table. What are the characteristic properties of these elements and their compounds? Give one example of each of the properties you mention.

(J.M.B.S)

14. Describe briefly the extraction of titanium from its ores. Why is the process which you describe used in preference to other methods of extraction? Give two important uses of titanium and/or its compounds. (O & C)

29

GROUP IB: COPPER, SILVER AND GOLD

Atomic properties of copper, silver and gold

Element	Symbol	Atomic no.	Atomic weight	Atomic radius (Å)	Ionic radius M+ (Å)
Copper	Cu	29	63.5	1.17	0.96
Silver	Ag	47	107.9	1.34	1.26
Gold	Au	79	197.0	1.34	1.37

Copper, silver and gold comprise the last but one Group in the transition series and are known collectively as the *coinage metals*. They are amongst the earliest known of the metals: copper in the form of bronze dates from prehistoric times (the Bronze Age); silver and gold were known and valued over 6000 years ago.

Relationships of Group IB to the Periodic Table

Elements in the last half of the three transition series

Group ...	VIII			IB	IIB
Outer electronic configuration ...	d^6s^2	d^7s^2	d^8s^2	$d^{10}s^1$	$d^{10}s^2$
Period 4	Fe	Co	Ni	Cu	Zn
Period 5	Ru	Rh	Pd	Ag	Cd
Period 6	Os	Ir	Pt	Au	Hg

The properties of copper, silver and gold resemble the properties of the preceding elements in Group VIII more closely than they do the properties of the elements in the Zinc Group. One reason for this is that apart from their ability to form complexes, e.g. $[M(NH_3)_4]^{2+}$, $[MCl_4]^{2-}$, $[M(CN)_4]^{2-}$, zinc, cadmium and mercury do not show the characteristic transition properties of the coinage metals and the Group VIII elements. Thus the bivalent salts of iron, cobalt, nickel and copper are coloured and isomorphous, whereas although there are some close resemblances between copper(II) and zinc salts the latter are all white (unless the anion is coloured). Also, zinc and cadmium are reactive elements which readily liberate hydrogen from acids in sharp contrast to the unreactive coinage metals which are amongst the least electropositive of the metals and are unable to discharge hydrogen ions from solution. Nickel, palladium and platinum are also unreactive. The inertness of platinum is such that like gold it is unaffected by all acids save aqua regia. Palladium resembles silver.

Mercury, at the bottom of Group II B, in contrast to zinc and cadmium, is less electropositive than hydrogen. As a consequence its behaviour towards, air, water, non-metals and acids closely resembles that of copper and of silver. Similarities between mercury and the coinage metals also exist amongst their compounds, thus the oxides of mercury, silver and gold are thermally unstable and the univalent chlorides of copper, silver and mercury are all white insoluble solids.

The relationship of Group IB to Group IA

As mentioned on p. 532 the resemblances between the properties of the elements in the A Groups and those in the B Groups are a minimum in Group I and in Group VII. However, Group IA and Group IB have a vitally important feature in common: one electron in the outer shell of the neutral atom. Because of this the elements of both Groups show a valency of 1 and therefore take the same Group number. Copper, silver and gold are unreactive heavy metals and their physical and chemical properties are very different from the highly reactive, light, easily fusible metals of Group IA (i.e. sodium, etc.). Apart from a few isolated resemblances,

*Number of electrons in the occupied shells of
the elements of Groups IA and IB*

Group IA			Group IB		
Element	Atomic no.	Electronic configuration	Element	Atomic no.	Electronic configuration
Lithium	3	2, 1			
Sodium	11	2, 8, 1			
Potassium	19	2, 8, 8, 1	Copper	29	2, 8, 18, 1
Rubidium	37	2, 8, 18, 8, 1	Silver	47	2, 8, 18, 18, 1
Caesium	55	2, 8, 18, 18, 8, 1	Gold	79	2, 8, 18, 32, 18, 1

e.g. the nitrates and sulphates of silver and sodium are white isomorphous solids, the valency is their only comparable property. The differences between the two Groups arise from their different atomic radius and inner electron structure. The coinage metal has a smaller atomic radius than the comparable alkali metal (e.g. Cu, 1.17 Å; K, 2.03 Å) and the outermost electron is preceded by a shell of 18 electrons and not eight as in the alkali metal atoms.

General Group features

Although the 18-electron shell is stabilised relative to one containing incomplete sub-shells it is much less stable than the eight-electron shell. This is revealed by comparing those elements which precede the alkali metals and those which precede the coinage metals. The former elements are noble gases and the latter are themselves metals from which it is possible to withdraw electrons and form ions in chemical reactions. As expected copper, silver and gold all form compounds in which they are univalent. Compounds in which the element has a higher valency are also formed. Copper forms a series of bivalent compounds and this is its most stable valency. Trivalent copper compounds have also been formed, e.g. K_3CuF_6. A number of bivalent silver compounds have been made, e.g. AgF_2 and AgO, but they are much less stable than the univalent silver compounds. Gold shows a valency of either 1 or 3 but is covalently bound or complexed in all of these latter compounds, e.g. $AuCl_3$, $[AuCl_4]^-$. To produce the ions of the higher valency states it is necessary to unpair a d electron, consequently these ions show transition properties, e.g. the hydrated Cu^{2+} ion is coloured blue.

Principal valencies, electronegativities and electrode potentials of the coinage metals

Element	Principal valencies	Electro-negativity	Standard electrode potential M^+/M (V)
Cu	I, **II**	1.75	+0.52
Ag	**I**, II	1.42	+0.80
Au	**I**, **III**	1.42	+1.68

The most stable valency is written in heavy type. This does not mean that univalent copper and gold compounds are unstable, in fact, under anhydrous conditions they are perfectly stable. But as the chemistry of a compound is in general the chemistry of its aqueous solution it is the stability under these conditions that is most important. The ionisation energies of Cu^+ and Cu^{2+} are 744 and 2700 kJ mol^{-1} respectively (i.e. 178 and 645 kcal mol^{-1} respectively). Therefore *in vacuo* the Cu^+ ion is 1954 kJ mol^{-1} (i.e. 467 kcal mol^{-1}) more stable than the simple Cu^{2+} ion. In aqueous solution, however, the hydration energies of the Cu^+ and Cu^{2+} ions are 481 (approximately) and 2300 kJ mol^{-1} respectively (i.e. 115 and 550 kcal mol^{-1} respectively), and under these conditions the very much larger hydration energy of the more highly charged and probably smaller copper(II) ion gives it greater stability. In aqueous solution therefore there is rapid disproportionation of compounds,

$$2Cu^+(aq.) \rightarrow Cu + Cu^{2+}(aq.).$$

The elements
Occurrence

All three elements occur in the metallic state and this is the principal mode of occurrence for gold. The most important ores of copper and of silver are both sulphides; chalcopyrite, $CuFeS_2$, and silver glance, Ag_2S, respectively. Copper also occurs as basic carbonates, i.e. malachite, $CuCO_3.Cu(OH)_2$, and azurite, $2CuCO_3.Cu(OH)_2$. Copper ores in use nowadays seldom contain more than 4 or 5 per cent of copper.

Extraction of copper from copper pyrites

Since most of the world's copper is obtained from chalcopyrite this is the only process which will be described in detail. Five main steps in the process may be distinguished.

(1) *Concentration.* The crushed ore is freed from clay, sand and other earthy materials by agitating it with a mixture of water and oil so that a froth collects on the surface. This carries with it the particles of ore and the impurities sink to the bottom. The froth is skimmed off and filtered.

(2) *Roasting.* Excess sulphur and impurities such as arsenic and antimony are driven out of the concentrated ore, largely in the form of oxides, by roasting. At the same time the iron is converted mainly to iron(II) oxide as it is more readily oxidised than copper,

$$2CuFeS_2 + 4O_2 \rightarrow Cu_2S + 2FeO + 3SO_2.$$

(3) *Smelting.* The iron(II) oxide produced during the roasting is removed by heating the ore in a reverberatory furnace with silica. Iron(II) silicate is

formed as a slag which floats on top of the fused *matte* of copper(I) sulphide and residual iron(II) sulphide,

$$FeO + SiO_2 \rightarrow FeSiO_3.$$

(4) *Reduction*. The fused matte is run into a converter. Silica is added and air is blown through the mixture. This oxidises the iron(II) sulphide to iron(II) oxide which combines with the silica and is removed as a slag of iron(II) silicate. Sulphur burns away as sulphur dioxide. Oxidation of the copper(I) sulphide follows. The copper(I) oxide produced then reacts with the remaining copper(I) sulphide until all the copper compounds are reduced to the metal,

$$2Cu_2S + 3O_2 \rightarrow 2Cu_2O + 2SO_2,$$
$$Cu_2S + 2Cu_2O \rightarrow 6Cu + SO_2.$$

The molten copper is run out of the converter into moulds. As it solidifies the copper emits sulphur dioxide and this gives it a blistered appearance.

(5) *Refining*. The blocks of *blister* copper are made the anodes of an electrolysis cell. Thin sheets of pure copper are made the cathode and the electrolyte is acidified copper(II) sulphate solution. When the current is passing copper dissolves from the anode and deposits on the cathode. Impurities are either left behind on the anode (e.g. Ag and Au) or pass into solution as ions, and copper of 99.9 % purity is obtained. World production of new copper is about six million tons annually.

Extraction of silver and of gold

In the cyanide process the silver- or gold-bearing rock is crushed and then agitated with an alkali cyanide solution through which a current of air is blown. The metal passes into solution as a complex ion, i.e.

$$[Ag(CN)_2]^-, \quad [Au(CN)_2]^-,$$
$$4Ag + 8CN^- + O_2 + 2H_2O \rightarrow 4[Ag(CN)_2]^- + 4OH^-.$$

The free metal can be precipitated from this solution by treatment with zinc in the presence of alkali,

$$2[Ag(CN)_2]^- + Zn + 4OH^- \rightarrow 2Ag + [Zn(OH)_4]^{2-} + 4CN^-.$$

Both silver and gold may be purified by electrolysis.

Physical properties

The density, melting point, and boiling point of copper, silver and gold are given below, together with the corresponding values for nickel, palladium and platinum as well as zinc, cadmium and mercury for comparison. The diminishing values of the physical properties towards the end of each transition series, e.g. Ni–Cu–Zn, is indicative of a progressive weakening of the metallic bonding.

Variation in physical properties in the end of each transition series

Element	Period 4			Period 5			Period 6		
	Ni	Cu	Zn	Pd	Ag	Cd	Pt	Au	Hg
Density	8.9	8.92	7.13	12.03	10.5	8.64	21.45	19.3	13.6
m.p. (°C)	1455	1083	419	1150	960	321	1769	1063	−38.9
b.p. (°C)	2840	2582	906	3127	2177	765	3827	2707	357
		Decrease			Decrease			Decrease	
		→			→			→	

The d level orbitals of the elements in the Copper Group are all filled and as there are no unpaired d electrons it seems reasonable to assume that there will be a pronounced weakening of the metallic bonding in passing from nickel to copper, for example, and that the physical properties of copper should be similar to those of zinc which also has no unpaired d electrons. However, it will be noticed that the physical properties of the element in the Copper Group are more similar to those of the preceding element in the Nickel Group than they are to those of the following element in the Zinc Group. This means that although the d level is filled it is not completely inert and these d electrons are still able to participate in the metallic bonding and so impart transition metal characteristics to the element, even though it is to a less marked degree than found amongst those metals in the middle of the transition series.

Copper is a tough, soft, reddish metal; silver is white; gold is yellow. All three take a high polish and are notable for their malleability and ductility; gold can be beaten into foil 10^{-5} cm thick. The electrical and thermal conductivities of these metals are higher than those of all the other elements and silver is the best conductor of all. The exceptional conducting efficiency of these metals is thought to be another manifestation of the effect on the metallic bonding of the supposedly inert shell of eighteen electrons. It is suggested that a d electron in this shell is 'promoted' to the outermost shell where it would be particularly mobile and give greater conductivity to the electron flux.

Chemical properties

1. *Air.* Copper, silver and gold come below hydrogen in the electro-chemical series, therefore they are resistant to air. Gold is renowned for its unreactivity and is totally unaffected by air.

None of the metals burn in air but at red-heat a copper surface becomes coated with a salmon-pink inner layer of copper(I) oxide, Cu_2O, and an outer layer of black copper(II) oxide, CuO. Although it appears unaffected by dry air, after prolonged exposure to the ordinary atmosphere copper eventually develops a thin green surface film of the basic sulphate, $CuSO_4.3Cu(OH)_2$. In coastal regions a basic chloride $CuCl_2.3Cu(OH)_2$ may also develop. Silver tarnishes in air contaminated with sulphur compounds, e.g. hydrogen sulphide, owing to the formation of a thin black film of silver sulphide, Ag_2S, on the surface of the metal. It is because of their weak reactivity and stability towards air that these metals have proved so useful in the making of coins.

2. *Water.* The metals are not affected by water either at ordinary conditions or at red-heat.

3. *Non-metals.* The direct combination of copper with oxygen is appreciable only at elevated temperatures and the surface film of oxide produced tends to restrict further action. Copper is readily attacked by the halogens and also by sulphur.

Silver has a strong affinity for sulphur and gold will dissolve in an aqueous solution of a halogen or in solutions which generate them, e.g. aqua regia (see p. 514), otherwise both these metals are less reactive than copper.

4. *Acids.* Copper has a greater positive electrode potential than that of hydrogen and is unable to discharge hydrogen ions to any appreciable extent. The equilibrium given below lies almost completely to the left and only imperceptible quantities of copper(I) ion and dissolved hydrogen are present in solution, $Cu + H^+ \rightleftharpoons Cu^+ + \frac{1}{2}H_2$.

As described on p. 218 boiling concentrated hydrochloric acid dissolves copper *with the evolution of hydrogen* since the copper(I) ions are complexed as $[CuCl_2]^-$ by the halide ions and this removal of metal ions from the reaction mixture together with the high concentration of hydrogen ions displaces the equilibrium to the right,

$$2Cu + 2H^+ + 4Cl^- \rightarrow 2[CuCl_2]^- + H_2.$$

If the acid is also an oxidising agent, e.g. nitric acid or hot concentrated sulphuric acid, or if the acid and metal are in contact under oxidising conditions such as in the presence of air or of an added oxidising agent, e.g. potassium chlorate, corrosion of the metal occurs but hydrogen is not evolved. Hot concentrated sulphuric acid probably oxidises the copper directly and sulphur dioxide is evolved. The action is generally summarised by the simple equation,

$$Cu + 2H_2SO_4 \rightarrow CuSO_4 + 2H_2O + SO_2.$$

But as copper(I) and copper(II) sulphides also occur amongst the products the reaction is clearly more complex (see p. 478).

Dilute nitric acid (1:1) dissolves copper with the evolution of nitrogen monoxide together with small amounts of other oxides of nitrogen,

$$3Cu + 8HNO_3 \rightarrow 3Cu(NO_3)_2 + 4H_2O + 2NO.$$

Concentrated nitric acid attacks copper very vigorously and copious brown vapours of nitrogen dioxide are evolved,

$$Cu + 4HNO_3 \rightarrow Cu(NO_3)_2 + 2H_2O + 2NO_2.$$

Silver is more resistant to attack by acids than copper but in general reacts similarly. Gold is unaffected by all acids except aqua regia (see p. 514).

5. Alkalis. Strong alkalis are without action on copper, silver and gold.

6. Catalytic ability. Another instance of the transition metal character of copper is displayed by its ability to act as a catalyst in numerous reactions. Thus in the presence of heated copper, methanol vapour is oxidised to formaldehyde by the oxygen of the air

$$CH_3OH + \tfrac{1}{2}O_2 \rightarrow CH_2O + H_2O.$$

In the Deacon process copper compounds (e.g. copper(II) chloride, copper(I) chloride, copper(II) chromite, etc.) catalyse the aerial oxidation of hydrogen chloride to chlorine,

$$4HCl + O_2 \rightarrow 2Cl_2 + 2H_2O.$$

7. Alloys. Copper readily alloys with other metals. The bronzes and the brasses are two alloys of great technical importance. The principal constituents of bronze are copper (90 %) and tin (10 %) but minor quantities of other metals may be added to give the bronze special qualities, e.g. small amounts of zinc and lead make machining easier (gun metal). Bronzes are tougher and more resistant to wear than copper and as they give good castings they are widely used for sculptures and machine parts.

Copper coins contain tin (4%) and zinc (1%). Brass is essentially an alloy of copper and zinc with a zinc content generally between 18 and 30%. Brass is softer than bronze and more easily worked but it is harder and more resistant to corrosion than pure copper.

Devarda's alloy (Cu, 50%; Al, 45%; Zn, 5%) is very brittle and easily powdered. This powder is useful in the laboratory as it readily liberates nascent hydrogen from caustic alkalis and this produces a powerful reducing medium. Under these conditions the nitrate ion is reduced to ammonia which is evolved and so provides a test for a nitrate which can be used when interfering anions make the brown ring test inapplicable.

Silver is usually alloyed with a little copper to harden it and as pure gold is too soft for most purposes it is also hardened by alloying with a little copper or silver. The gold content of an alloy is measured in carats. Pure gold is defined as 24 carat. Thus 18 carat gold contains 18 parts by weight of gold in 24 parts.

Uses

Copper is one of the most important technical metals. Owing to its exceptional ability to conduct electricity copper is extensively used in electrical circuits and applicances. Copper is also a very good conductor of heat and is therefore widely used in the construction of steam pipes and boilers.

Considerable amounts of copper are converted into alloys such as the brasses, bronzes and coinage metal.

Silver and gold are popular precious metals and are used in the making of jewellery, and articles of artistic value. Large quantities of silver are converted into silver nitrate for use in the photographic industry.

Compounds of copper

All copper(I) compounds, except the highly insoluble ones such as copper(I) chloride, CuCl, and copper(I) cyanide, CuCN, are hydrolysed by water to the corresponding copper(II) compound and copper. This does not mean that copper(II) compounds are always the most stable. The relative stabilities of the Cu^+ and Cu^{2+} ions depends very largely on the anion with which they are associated and whether or not the compound is soluble or insoluble in water. Thus, in the presence of iodide ions the Cu^{2+} ion precipitates out as insoluble white copper(I) iodide,

$$2Cu^{2+} + 4I^- \rightarrow 2CuI + I_2.$$

Similarly, with cyanide ions,

$$2Cu^{2+} + 4CN^- \rightarrow 2CuCN + (CN)_2.$$

It is clear that such reactions can occur only with feebly electronegative anions which readily lose an electron.

A copper atom is converted into a copper(II) ion by the loss of *two* electrons. This necessitates the removal of an electron from the *d* shell as there is only one electron in the outermost shell of the copper atom. Consequently the copper(II) ion exhibits transition properties, i.e. colour, ability to form complexes readily and paramagnetism. The *d* shell of the copper(I) ion is filled and so this ion does not show transition properties.

Oxides

Copper(I) oxide, Cu$_2$O. If copper(II) sulphate solution is added to a solution of sodium hydroxide in the presence of sodium potassium tartrate (Rochelle salt) a deep blue solution is formed (*Fehlings solution*). The tartrate ions form a complex ion with the Cu^{2+} ions and so prevent the precipitation of copper(II) hydroxide. In this condition the copper(II) ion is converted into a reddish brown precipitate of copper(I) oxide by warming with glucose which behaves as a mild reducing agent.

Copper(I) oxide dissolves in dilute nitric acid and in dilute sulphuric acid with simultaneous disproportionation into copper and the copper(II) ion. In the case of nitric acid, oxides of nitrogen are also evolved as it attacks the copper produced,

$$Cu_2O + 2H_3O^+ \rightarrow Cu^{2+} + Cu + 3H_2O.$$

Concentrated hydrochloric acid also dissolves copper(I) oxide but in this case disproportionation does not occur as the Cu^+ ion is held in solution as the complex ion, $[CuCl_2]^-$.

Copper(II) oxide, CuO. Black copper(II) oxide is a typical basic oxide prepared by any of the general methods.

Copper(II) hydroxide, Cu(OH)$_2$. Sodium hydroxide solution added to a solution of a copper(II) salt gives a light blue precipitate of copper(II) hydroxide. With ammonium hydroxide the light blue precipitate dissolves in excess of the reagent to give a deep blue solution. This is due to the formation of the tetrammine copper(II) ion, $[Cu(NH_3)_4]^{2+}$.

589

Chlorides

Copper(I) chloride, CuCl. By dissolving copper(II) chloride, copper(II) oxide or copper(II) carbonate in an excess of concentrated hydrochloric acid and boiling the mixture with copper turnings the copper(II) ions are reduced to the copper(I) state. Complex ion formation with the chloride ions keeps the copper(I) chloride in solution as $[CuCl_2]^-$. However, if this solution is poured into a large excess of cold boiled water an immediate white precipitate of copper(I) chloride is formed. Rapid filtration and drying is necessary to prevent oxidation to the copper(II) compound.

Copper(I) chloride is dimeric, Cu_2Cl_2, in the vapour state, and is covalent in the solid state. It dissolves in concentrated hydrochloric acid and in ammonia solution owing to the formation of soluble complex ions, e.g. $[CuCl_2]^-$, $[CuCl_4]^{3-}$ and $Cu(NH_3)Cl$. Both these solutions are able to dissolve carbon monoxide and are used for this purpose in gas analysis,

$$CuCl + CO + H_2O \rightarrow CuCl.CO.H_2O.$$

Copper(II) chloride, CuCl₂. Direct combination of chlorine and copper occurs quite readily on gentle heating to give the brownish yellow anhydrous salt. When prepared from solution by any of the general methods (not acid + metal) green crystals of the dihydrate, $CuCl_2.2H_2O$, separate out.

Dilute solutions of copper(II) chloride are blue. More concentrated solutions are greenish yellow. In the presence of an excess of chloride ions the solution is brown. These changes follow the conversion of blue hydrated copper(II) ions, $[Cu(H_2O)_6]^{2+}$ (see p. 237), present in dilute solutions into the brown complex copper(II) chloride ions formed when the chloride ion concentration is increased, e.g. $[CuCl_4]^{2-}$. Intermediate between these two extremes are solutions containing varying amounts of both ions which produce a greenish yellow colour.

If the dry solid is strongly heated it dissociates into copper(I) chloride and chlorine, $\qquad 2CuCl_2 \rightleftharpoons 2CuCl + Cl_2.$

Oxo-salts

Only the copper(II) salts are important. They are usually blue or green in colour and in dilute aqueous solution show the characteristic blue colour of the hydrated copper(II) ion.

Copper(II) sulphate, CuSO₄.5H₂O. This well-known salt may be prepared by dissolving either copper(II) oxide or carbonate in dilute sulphuric acid.

It is manufactured on the large scale by blowing air through a heated mixture of copper and dilute sulphuric acid until a sufficient concentration of the sulphate is obtained.

On heating to about 100 °C the pentahydrate, $CuSO_4.5H_2O$, loses four molecules of water of crystallisation and the monohydrate, $CuSO_4.H_2O$, remains. This last molecule of water of crystallisation can only be driven off by heating the salt to about 250 °C. Investigation of the crystal structure of the pentahydrate with X-rays has revealed that one of the molecules of water of crystallisation is bound differently from the other four. This is described more fully on p. 239 and accounts for the stepwise dehydration of $CuSO_4.5H_2O$. Anhydrous copper(II) sulphate is white and is used as a test for water which rapidly restores the blue colour of the pentahydrate.

Copper(II) sulphate is used for copper plating by electrolysis, in dyeing and in calico printing. It also finds use in agriculture as a fungicide, e.g. *Bordeaux mixture* (copper(II) sulphate, lime and water) for spraying potatoes and vines. It is also used as a wood preservative.

Copper(II) nitrate, $Cu(NO_3)_2.3H_2O$. Prepared by any of the general methods it is a dark blue crystalline salt and is very deliquescent. It decomposes on heating,

$$2Cu(NO_3)_2 \rightarrow 2CuO + 4NO_2 + O_2.$$

Copper(II) carbonate. Only basic carbonates are known. These occur naturally as malachite, $CuCO_3.Cu(OH)_2$, which is a green solid, and azurite, $2CuCO_3.Cu(OH)_2$, a blue solid. Addition of sodium carbonate or sodium hydrogen carbonate solution to a solution of a copper(II) salt gives a green precipitate of a basic carbonate similar in composition to malachite.

Compounds of silver

The only common compounds of silver are those in which it has an oxidation number of $+1$.

Silver oxide, Ag_2O. A brown precipitate of silver oxide is obtained by adding a solution containing hydroxyl ions to a solution of a silver salt,

$$2Ag^+ + 2OH^- \rightarrow Ag_2O\downarrow + H_2O.$$

Ammonia solution used in excess redissolves the precipitated oxide owing to the formation of a complex silver cation with the NH_3 molecules, i.e. $[Ag(NH_3)_2]^+$. On standing this ammoniacal silver nitrate solution slowly deposits an explosive black powder which is probably silver nitride, Ag_3N.

Ammoniacal silver nitrate is a mild oxidising agent as the $[Ag(NH_3)_2]^+$ ion is readily reduced to silver. Thus, on warming with acetaldehyde a silver mirror is deposited on the sides of the test-tube.

Silver oxide is almost insoluble in water. However, it is quite a strong base and moist silver oxide turns red litmus blue, indicating the presence of hydroxyl ions. If refluxed with an alkyl halide moist silver oxide will hydrolyse it to the corresponding alcohol and is useful in this respect whenever the stronger alkalis would react too vigorously,

$$2C_2H_5I + Ag_2O + H_2O \rightarrow 2C_2H_5OH + 2AgI\downarrow.$$

If dry silver oxide is used the alkyl halide reacts to form an ether,

$$2C_2H_5I + Ag_2O \rightarrow C_2H_5{-}O{-}C_2H_5 + 2AgI\downarrow.$$

Silver oxide is thermally less stable than the oxides of copper and decomposes at 300 °C $\quad 2Ag_2O \rightleftharpoons 4Ag + O_2.$

Silver halides. All except the fluoride are insoluble in water and may be prepared by precipitation. The colour of the precipitate increases in intensity down the Group: silver chloride, $AgCl$, is white, silver bromide, $AgBr$, is pale yellow, and silver iodide, AgI, is a deeper shade of yellow.

Solutions of ammonia, sodium thiosulphate and potassium cyanide all dissolve silver chloride quite readily owing to complex ion formation, i.e. $[Ag(NH_3)_2]^+$, $[Ag_2(S_2O_3)_3]^{4-}$ and $[Ag(CN)_2]^-$. Silver bromide is only sparingly soluble in ammonia solution and silver iodide is almost insoluble.

Both silver chloride and silver bromide are sensitive to light and darken appreciably on exposure to sunlight. Because of this silver bromide is used in the light-sensitive emulsion on photographic plates or films.

Silver nitrate, $AgNO_3$. This is the most common soluble salt of silver and is usually prepared by crystallisation from a solution of the metal in nitric acid. It separates as colourless crystals. Silver nitrate is very soluble in water. It melts at a relatively low temperature (217 °C). On stronger heating it decomposes into the metal, nitrogen dioxide, and oxygen,

$$2AgNO_3 \rightarrow 2Ag + 2NO_2 + O_2.$$

Silver carbonate, Ag_2CO_3. On adding an alkali carbonate solution to silver nitrate solution a pale yellow precipitate of silver carbonate separates. This salt is also decomposed on heating and owing to the thermal instability of the oxide metallic silver is left while oxygen and carbon dioxide are evolved,

$$2Ag_2CO_3 \rightarrow 4Ag + 2CO_2 + O_2.$$

Silver sulphate, Ag$_2$SO$_4$. As it is only slightly soluble in water silver sulphate may be precipitated by adding a concentrated solution of a sulphate to a concentrated solution of silver nitrate,

$$2Ag^+ + SO_4^{2-} \rightarrow Ag_2SO_4.$$

Silver sulphide, Ag$_2$S. A black precipitate of silver sulphide is obtained by bubbling hydrogen sulphide into a solution of a silver salt.

Exercises

1. Starting with copper how would you prepare samples of the following: (*a*) copper(II) oxide, (*b*) tetrammine copper(II) sulphate monohydrate, (*c*) copper(I) oxide, (*d*) copper(II) sulphide, (*e*) copper(I) iodide.
2. To what extent does copper and its compounds display characteristic transition metal properties?
3. Describe and explain the changes that occur when: (*a*) copper(II) sulphate crystals are heated; (*b*) ammonia solution is added dropwise to copper(II) sulphate solution; (*c*) silver nitrate is heated.
4. Compare and contrast the physical and chemical properties of copper and zinc.
5. What properties justify the inclusion of copper, silver and gold in the same Group of the Periodic Table?
6. The Standard electrode potentials, E°, between the metals and their unipositive ions are listed below for the elements of Groups IA and IB.

Group IA ELEMENT		Group IB ELEMENT	
Li	−3.02	Cu	+0.52
Na	−2.71	Ag	+0.80
K	−2.92	Au	+1.42
Rb	−2.99		
Cs	−3.02		

How do you account for:
   (*a*) the large differences in the values of E° between the two groups.
   (*b*) the anomalously large negative value for Li?
   Explain briefly how the chemical behaviour of these elements is related to their positions in the electrochemical series. (O & C)
7. A double salt of copper(II) sulphate and ammonium sulphate was found to contain 27.03 % of water of crystallisation and to yield, on analysis, 19.39 % of its own weight as copper(II) oxide. Calculate the empirical formula of the double salt.
   Describe how you would obtain from it specimens of (*a*) copper(I) oxide, (*b*) copper(I) chloride. (C)
8. Describe, without giving details of the manufacture, how pure copper may be obtained from a copper sulphide ore. State the colour, solubility in water

and behaviour on heating in air, of the following compounds: copper(I) oxide, copper(II) carbonate, hydrated copper(II) nitrate, hydrated copper(II) sulphate. (O & C)

9. Molar solutions of copper(II) sulphate (solution A) and potassium sulphate (solution B) were mixed in the proportions shown below. The mixed solutions were then allowed to evaporate to dryness and the residues examined.

   (a) 10 cm³ of A and 5 cm³ of B gave a mixture of light blue and darker blue crystals.

   (b) 10 cm³ of A and 10 cm³ of B gave light blue crystals only.

   (c) 5 cm³ of A and 10 cm³ of B gave a mixture of light blue and colourless crystals.

   The light blue crystals were found to contain 24.4 per cent of water of crystallisation.

   Interpret these results as fully as you can and suggest a formula for the light blue crystalline substance. What ions would you expect to be present in its aqueous solution? Give one test for the identification of each ion. (C)

30

GROUP IIB:
ZINC, CADMIUM AND MERCURY

Relationship of Group IIB to the Periodic Table

Group IIB comes at the end of the d block of the Period Table. The horizontal relationships that exist in the transition series do not extend beyond Group IIB, and there are no noteworthy points of similarity between zinc, cadmium, and mercury, and the corresponding elements of Group IIIB (Ga, In, Tl). Immediately preceding zinc, cadmium and mercury are the Group IB metals copper, silver, and gold respectively. The characteristic properties of typical transition elements which lead to the close resemblances between the coinage metals and the preceding elements in the middle of the transition series are not developed in the Zinc Group elements, save in their ability to form complex ions, e.g. with ammonia, halide ions and cyanide ions. Therefore, as they do not exhibit variable valency, coloured ions, paramagnetism, high melting point, high boiling point and catalytic ability, Group IIB metals are not typical transition elements, and there is a change of chemical type in passing from Group IB to Group IIB. Even though fundamental differences exist between the two Groups, as mentioned in the last chapter, there are certain resemblances between the salts of zinc and those of bivalent copper, also many notable similarities exist between the properties of copper and silver in Group IB, and mercury in Group IIB. Thus, mercury is a *noble* metal, and its electrode potential is closer in magnitude to those of the coinage metals than it is to the elements of its own Group. Consequently, mercury resembles more closely the behaviour of copper and silver towards air, water, acids, oxygen, halogens, sulphur, etc., than it does that of zinc and cadmium.

Relationships between Group IIA and Group IIB

Each element in Group IIA and Group IIB shows a positive valency of 2. This follows from the similarity of their electronic configurations. The following table shows that each atom has two valence electrons in the outermost shell and all the previous sub-levels are completely filled.

*Number of electrons in the occupied shells of
the elements in Groups II A and II B*

Group II A			Group II B		
Element	Atomic no.	Electronic configuration	Element	Atomic no.	Electronic configuration
Beryllium	4	2, 2			
Magnesium	12	2, 8, 2			
Calcium	20	2, 8, 8, 2	Zinc	30	2, 8, 18, 2
Strontium	38	2, 8, 18, 8, 2	Cadmium	48	2, 8, 18, 18, 2
Barium	56	2, 8, 18, 18, 8, 2	Mercury	80	2, 8, 18, 32, 18, 2

Similarities between the A and B families of this Group are not extensive, but they are more numerous than exist between the A and B families of Group I. Most notable are the resemblances between zinc and magnesium, e.g. both form sulphates, $MSO_4.7H_2O$ and double sulphates,

$$K_2SO_4.MSO_4.6H_2O,$$

which are isomorphous, their chlorides are deliquescent and hydrolysed to a similar extent and they both precipitate basic carbonates with sodium carbonate solution in contrast to calcium which precipitates a normal carbonate. Magnesium, zinc, cadmium and mercury form organo-metallic compounds fairly readily, e.g. $M(CH_3)_2$, etc.

General Group characteristics

Atomic properties of zinc, cadmium and mercury

Element	Symbol	Atomic no.	Atomic weight	Atomic radius (Å)	Ionic radius M^{2+} (Å)
Zinc	Zn	30	65.4	1.25	0.74
Cadmium	Cd	48	112.4	1.41	0.97
Mercury	Hg	80	200.6	1.44	1.10

The metallic binding is much weaker in these elements than in the coinage metals, and they are notably low melting and volatile. Mercury is the only metal liquid at room temperature. It is suggested that the two outer electrons in the mercury atom show the inert-pair effect (see p. 94). Accepting this as a fact, it follows that all the electrons in the mercury atom are in stabilised states, and the pronounced weakness of the metallic binding and general inertness of the element are readily understandable.

Besides showing the Group valency of 2, mercury also appears univalent in a number of compounds. In mercury(I) compounds the mercury atoms are always joined in pairs by a single covalent bond, e.g. mercury(I) chloride, Cl—Hg—Hg—Cl. Similarly the mercury(I) ion is Hg^+—Hg^+, or Hg_2^{2+}. As a single positive charge is associated with each mercury atom the mercury(I) ion appears unipositive in the electrochemical sense, but in effect each atom is bivalent, i.e. an electrovalency of 1 plus a covalency of 1.

Ionisation energies, electrode potentials, and electronegativities
of Group II B metals

Element	Standard electrode potentials M^{2+}/M (V)	Electro-negativity	Ionisation energy of M^{2+} (kJ mol^{-1})
Zinc	-0.76	1.66	2635
Cadmium	-0.40	1.46	2498
Mercury	$+0.85$	1.44	2811

There is a considerable difference in the values of the electrode potentials of these elements. Thus while zinc and cadmium readily discharge hydrogen ions from acid solutions (provided the metals are not too pure), mercury has a greater positive electrode potential than hydrogen, and therefore cannot displace it from acids.

Amongst the bivalent compounds those of cadmium are the most ionic. Zinc compounds are partly covalent and mercury(II) compounds are essentially covalent. This shows in their properties. Many mercury(II) compounds are fairly volatile, and easily sublime, e.g. $HgCl_2$. They also dissolve readily in organic solvents. The large number of stable compounds containing mercury linked to carbon or to nitrogen, e.g. mercury dimethyl,

$$H_3C—Hg—CH_3,$$

or mercury(II) amidochloride,

$$H_2N—Hg—Cl,$$

is further evidence of the tendency of mercury to form strong covalent bonds. Oxides of these metals show basic properties, but they weaken rapidly in the order of increasing electronegativity of the metal. Cadmium oxide also shows very feeble acidic properties, and dissolves in fused potassium hydroxide. Zinc oxide is more noticeably amphoteric and readily dissolves in strong alkali solutions. Similarly, zinc hydroxide dissolves in an excess of alkali, whereas cadmium hydroxide remains undissolved. It is surprising that such an electropositive metal as zinc (-0.76 V) should show acidic properties to the extent that it does. It is believed that zinc hydroxide, $Zn(OH)_2$ readily co-ordinates with hydroxyl ions and forms a soluble complex ion, i.e. $[Zn(OH)_4]^{2-}$, and therefore dissolves in strong alkalis (cf. Al, p. 225).

Zinc compounds are all white. Cadmium and mercury(I) and mercury(II) sulphides are coloured so are the iodides of mercury. Except for the oxides, hydroxides, carbonates and sulphides, the more commonly encountered bivalent compounds are soluble in water. In contrast, mercury(I) salts, like the corresponding silver and copper(I) salts, are mainly insoluble in water.

An exceptional feature of the simple bivalent ions is their strong tendency to form complexes. There is a progressive increase in the stability of the complex ions as the Group is descended which is the reverse of the trend amongst the Main Groups. A few of their commoner complex ions is given below:

$$[Zn(CN)_4]^{2-}, \qquad [Cd(CN)_4]^{2-}, \qquad [Hg(CN)_4]^{2-},$$
$$[Zn(NH_3)_4]^{2+}, \qquad [Cd(NH_3)_4]^{2+}, \qquad [Hg(NH_3)_4]^{2+},$$
$$[CdCl_3]^{-}, \qquad [HgI_4]^{2-},$$
$$[CdCl_4]^{2-}, \qquad [HgCl_4]^{2-}.$$

The elements

Occurrence

All three elements have a relatively low percentage composition in the earth's crust. Zinc is more abundant than the two heavier elements. It is generally regarded as being commonly occurring as its ores are highly concentrated in a few easily accessible deposits. Zinc blende, ZnS, is the principal ore of zinc and is found at Broken Hill, Australia, and in North America. There is no economically important ore of cadmium. It is obtained from zinc ores in which it is one of the main impurities (1–5%). As with zinc the chief ore of mercury is the sulphide, cinnabar, HgS. This ore has been mined at Almaden in Spain since Roman times, and is still the main source of mercury in the Western world. Small amounts of free mercury occur as droplets distributed throughout the ore. Calamine, $ZnCO_3$, is a less important ore of zinc.

Isolation

Most methods of isolation take advantage of the high volatility of these metals, and arrange for them to distil from the furnace, and then condense prior to purification. The oxides are fairly readily reduced by coke, and even this is unnecessary in the isolation of mercury as it distils directly from the sulphide ore during roasting provided the temperature is kept above the boiling point of mercury.

$$HgS + O_2 \rightarrow Hg + SO_2.$$

Very pure mercury is obtained by distillation under vacuum.

In each of the five methods of isolating zinc the naturally occurring sulphide ore is first oxidised by roasting in air. The oxidised ore is then either reduced with carbon or dissolved in acid for electrolytic recovery. The electrolytic process is not carried out in the U.K. but accounts for about half the total world production of zinc (4–4.5 million tons annually). The chief methods for isolating zinc are given below.

1. *Imperial smelting process.* The sulphide ore is roasted in air to the oxide,
$$2ZnS + 3O_2 \rightarrow 2ZnO + 2SO_2.$$

The sulphur dioxide is collected and converted to sulphuric acid. About 2 tons of sulphuric acid are obtained for every ton of zinc. The oxide is then mixed with coke and lime and fed into the top of a blast furnace. Preheated air is blown in at the bottom. At the temperature of the furnace (1000 °C) the coke burns to carbon monoxide and this reduces the oxide to zinc which vaporises out of the furnace,

$$ZnO(s) + CO(g) \rightarrow Zn(g) + CO_2(g).$$

Lead(II) sulphide is a common impurity in the zinc ore and is similarly roasted to the oxide and then reduced to the metal in the blast furnace. Being much less volatile than zinc the lead is liquid at the temperature of the furnace and trickles to the bottom where it is tapped off from time to time. Impurities form a molten slag with the lime and this collects in a layer above the lead and is also run off periodically.

The zinc vapour in the hot gases (1000 °C) leaving the furnace must be shock chilled to prevent re-oxidation to zinc oxide (N.B. the oxide of carbon is only more stable than the oxide of zinc at temperatures above the boiling point of zinc, see p. 184). This is achieved by passing the hot gases into a condenser filled with an intense spray of lead droplets initially at 450 °C. The molten lead leaving the condenser is at about 560 °C and

599

saturated with zinc. The lead is cooled prior to re-cycling and the layer of molten zinc that collects on the surface is skimmed off. Impurities in the zinc are lead, cadmium, iron and copper. Purification is effected by redistilling the zinc.

2. Electrolytic process. This method of preparing zinc can use lower grade ores than the distillation process, and also allows easy recovery of other metals in the ore. The sulphide ore is roasted in air under controlled conditions which give a maximum yield of zinc sulphate,

$$ZnS + 2O_2 \rightarrow ZnSO_4.$$

The mixture of oxide and sulphate produced is digested with dilute sulphuric acid and the solution of zinc sulphate obtained is treated with a suspension of calcium hydroxide which neutralises the acid and precipitates hydroxides of iron and aluminium which are removed. Other impurities in the solution which are less electropositive than zinc, such as cadmium and copper(II) ions, are precipitated as the free metal by the addition of zinc dust. Prior to electrolysis the purified zinc sulphate solution is acidified. A high current density is required and very pure zinc is deposited at the aluminium cathode.

Removal from solution of those metal ions less electropositive than zinc is essential to the success of the method. Zinc is well above hydrogen in the electrochemical potential series, and the only reason the hydrogen does not discharge preferentially to the zinc is that a pure zinc cathode has a very high hydrogen over-potential (see p. 220). If ions of metals less electropositive than zinc are present in solution, e.g. Cd^{2+}, Cu^{2+}, Ag^+, they will be deposited on the cathode and as these metals have a lower over-potential towards hydrogen it will discharge at these impurities in preference to the discharge of zinc ions and the efficiency of the electrolysis is diminished. Besides this, the impure zinc produced would be very susceptible to corrosion owing to local couples set up by the impurities.

Physical properties

All three are white lustrous metals, but zinc and cadmium rapidly become dulled in air. Their common physical properties have much lower values than those of copper, silver, and gold respectively. In fact, their relatively low melting points and ease of vaporisation are striking features of these metals. Particularly is this true of mercury, and as mercury vapour is highly toxic indiscriminate dispersal of the metal around the laboratory should be avoided. Like almost all metals their vapours are monatomic.

Physical properties of the Zinc Group metals

Element	Density (g cm^{-3})	m.p. (°C)	b.p. (°C)
Zn	7.1	419	910
Cd	8.6	321	778
Hg	13.6	−39	357

The densities of zinc, cadmium and mercury are about average (i.e. about 7.0) or above average for metals (contrast this with the light metals in Group IIA, e.g. Mg, 1.7). Mercury has relatively low thermal and electrical conductivities in contrast to zinc and cadmium which are both good conductors. This is another manifestation of the feeble *metallic* nature of mercury brought about by the inert-pair effect. Cadmium is soft and ductile. Zinc tends to be brittle at room temperature, but between 100–150 °C it is quite ductile; above 200 °C it becomes brittle again.

Zinc and cadmium, like magnesium, have metallic structures which deviate slightly from the perfect hexagonal close-packing of true metals in which each atom is equidistant from twelve other atoms—six in its own plane, three above and three below (see p. 123). Thus the three atoms in each of the upper and lower layers are at a greater distance from the central atom than the six atoms in its own plane. This suggests that there is some covalent character in the binding of these metals, i.e. a hint of non-metallic properties.

Chemical properties

1. Air. Zinc and cadmium are oxidised by air and form protective films (p. 209). Pure mercury in dry air does not tarnish, but impurities in the metal, or the atmosphere in a laboratory, lead to the formation of an oxide film which causes the mercury to *tail*. Zinc burns with a vivid blue-green flame forming a white residue of zinc oxide. Cadmium burns with a red flame and the residue is brown. Mercury has a very weak affinity for oxygen and even at its boiling point the two elements combine slowly to form the red oxide, HgO. At about 400 °C and above the process is reversed, and the oxide rapidly decomposes into its elements again.

2. Water. The metals are not affected by water under ordinary conditions, but red-hot zinc liberates hydrogen from steam.

3. Non-metals. Zinc, cadmium and mercury combine directly with the halogens and with sulphur, but in contrast to the alkaline earth-metals they do not combine directly with either nitrogen or hydrogen. Mercury and iodine combine when rubbed together in a mortar with a little alcohol as solvent. Olive-green mercury(I) iodide, Hg_2I_2, is formed if excess mercury is used, and if excess iodine is used scarlet mercury(II) iodide, HgI_2, if formed,

$$2Hg + I_2 \rightarrow Hg_2I_2,$$
$$Hg + I_2 \rightarrow HgI_2.$$

4. Acids. Very pure zinc and cadmium have such high hydrogen overpotentials (see p. 220) they are almost unaffected by non-oxidising acids. However, if the metal is impure or if a little copper is deposited on its surface by adding a few drops of copper(II) sulphate solution to the acid, reaction is rapid,

$$2H^+ + Zn \rightarrow Zn^{2+} + H_2.$$

Mercury has a lower electrode potential than hydrogen and will not displace it from acids and is therefore unaffected by non-oxidising acids. All three readily dissolve in dilute nitric acid, but oxides of nitrogen are evolved and not hydrogen. This follows since any hydrogen produced would be in the powerfully reducing nascent condition and instantly enter into secondary reactions with the nitric acid as it is an oxidising agent. Concentrated nitric acid behaves similarly, but the reaction is more vigorous. Zinc, cadmium and mercury also dissolve in hot concentrated sulphuric acid with the evolution of sulphur dioxide,

$$2H_2SO_4 + Hg \rightarrow Hg^{2+} + SO_4^{2-} + 2H_2O + SO_2.$$

5. Alkalis. Zinc dissolves in hot strong alkali solution and hydrogen is evolved; cadmium and mercury are unaffected by alkalis. Zincate ions pass into solution. These are often written as ZnO_2^{2-} but are better represented by $[Zn(OH)_4]^{2-}$,

$$Zn + 2OH^- + 2H_2O \rightarrow Zn(OH)_4^{2-} + H_2.$$

6. Alloys and amalgams. A common feature of the coinage metals and the metals of the Zinc Group is their ability to form a wide range of technically important and widely used alloys. The principal alloys of zinc are the brasses in which it is alloyed with copper (see p. 587). Cadmium is used in low-melting alloys such as Wood's metal (Bi—Pb—Sn—Cd). Amalgams (i.e. alloys of mercury) can often be prepared simply by pushing small lumps of the metal into the mercury. Amalgams may be solid or liquid depending on the composition and temperature. Alloys are generally simple mixtures of the metals they contain, but materials of definite composition may be formed, e.g. $CaZn_4$, melting point 680 °C; NaHg, melting point 212 °C.

7. Organo-metallic compounds. Compounds containing metallic atoms and organic fragments have been known for many years. Frankland in 1849 produced the first *organo-metallic compound*, when he reacted zinc with methyl iodide and formed methyl zinc iodide,

$$Zn + CH_3I \rightarrow CH_3ZnI.$$

When this is heated it yields zinc dimethyl, $Zn(CH_3)_2$, which is an unstable, evil-smelling liquid. The alkyl derivatives of cadmium are similar. Mercury reacts readily with organic compounds, and the products are much more stable than the corresponding zinc and cadmium compounds. The organo-metallic chemistry of mercury is already extensive.

Uses

Large quantities of zinc are used to produce a corrosion-resistant coating on iron. In the *galvanising process* sheet iron is cleaned in dilute sulphuric acid then dipped in molten zinc. After passing between rollers a thin film of zinc is left on the surface of the iron. In the closely allied *sherardising process* the iron article is heated with zinc dust. The layer of zinc can also be produced on the surface of the iron by electrolysis. The iron article is made the cathode the anode is made of zinc and the electrolyte is zinc sulphate solution.

Zinc is used in the production of alloys, e.g. brass. It is also used as the container for 'dry' batteries which serves as the anode as well.

Mercury metal is used in the construction of a wide range of scientific equipment, e.g. thermometers, barometers, high vacuum pumps, as well as for other laboratory purposes. Mercury compounds are used mostly as fungicides, and to some extent herbicides, as well as in the production of pharmaceuticals and anti-fouling paints.

Compounds

As the mercury(I) compounds are so very differerent in their properties from the other compounds of the elements in the Group they are treated separately in a following section. Mercury(II) compounds are included in a general treatment of the bivalent compounds of zinc and cadmium.

Oxides, MO

Zinc, cadmium, and mercury(II) oxides are solids which may be prepared by any of the general methods (p. 252) when applicable; note, mercury(II) carbonate and mercury(II) hydroxide do not exist. Under ordinary conditions colour deepens down the Group. Zinc oxide is white, cadmium oxide is brown and mercury(II) oxide is red. A yellow form of mercury(II) oxide which differs from the red form in particle size only is precipitated from a solution of a mercury(II) salt by excess strong alkali solution,

$$Hg^{2+} + 2OH^- \rightarrow HgO + H_2O.$$

On heating, zinc oxide turns yellow and mercury(II) oxide turns black; both revert to their original colour on cooling. Mercury(II) oxide is the only one which is thermally unstable and decomposes into its elements on further heating,
$$2HgO \rightarrow 2Hg + O_2.$$

Reduction of cadmium oxide is more difficult and zinc oxide is the stablest oxide in the Group.

All three oxides are insoluble in water, but dissolve in acids to give the corresponding salt and water. Mercury(II) oxide is only feebly basic. Zinc oxide also has acidic properties and is amphoteric; dissolving readily in alkalis as well as in acids, e.g.

$$ZnO + H_2SO_4 \rightarrow ZnSO_4 + H_2O,$$
$$ZnO + 2OH^- + H_2O \rightarrow [Zn(OH)_4]^{2-}.$$
$$\text{Zincate ion}$$

Solid zincates have been crystallised from solution, but they are unstable and strongly hydrolysed. Neither cadmium nor mercury(II) oxides has any appreciable acidic character. Presumably this is because the complex ions $[Cd(OH)_4]^{2-}$ and $[Hg(OH)_4]^{2-}$ are unstable.

Cadmium oxide resembles the alkaline earth oxides, but differs markedly from the oxides of zinc and mercury as it is a three-dimensional ionic aggregate like sodium chloride, whereas the other two are essentially co-valent structures with a diamond-type lattice (i.e. Wurtzite and zinc blende respectively, see p. 139).

Uses. Zinc oxide is used as a white pigment in paints which have the advantage over lead-based paints in that they do not blacken when exposed to air polluted with hydrogen sulphide. Zinc oxide has a certain therapeutic value, and is used in ointments, dusting powders, and is a constituent of calamine lotion (as is zinc carbonate). Zinc oxide is also used in cosmetic powders and creams.

Hydroxides, M(OH)$_2$

Both zinc hydroxide and cadmium hydroxide are obtained as white gelatinous precipitates by adding alkali to a solution of one of their salts. An excess of strong alkali dissolves the zinc hydroxide precipitate as it is amphoteric. However, both hydroxides behave similarly towards an excess of ammonia solution and dissolve owing to the formation of the complex tetrammine ion, e.g. $[Zn(NH_3)_4]^{2+}$. The colourless solutions so obtained contrast with the coloured solutions formed by the complex ions of typical transition metals, e.g. the deep blue solution of tetrammine copper(II) ion $[Cu(NH_3)_4]^{2+}$. Group II B hydroxides dissolve in acids in the usual way and are decomposed to the oxide on heating. No hydroxide of mercury has been obtained and when an alkali is added to a solution of a mercury(II) salt the oxide is precipitated. A similar reaction occurs with solutions of silver salts.

Chlorides, MCl$_2$

Mercury(II) chloride sublimes from a dry mixture of sodium chloride and mercury(II) sulphate under the action of heat,

$$2NaCl + HgSO_4 \rightarrow Na_2SO_4 + HgCl_2.$$

It may also be obtained by heating the metal with chlorine; the anhydrous chlorides of zinc and cadmium can also be prepared by this method. Solutions of the chlorides are formed by dissolving the oxide in dilute hydrochloric acid. The metal carbonates and hydroxide of zinc and cadmium also dissolve in hydrochloric acid to form the chloride in the usual way. Zinc and cadmium chlorides crystallise out as hydrates, e.g. $ZnCl_2 . 2H_2O$, but mercury(II) chloride crystals are not hydrated. Zinc chloride cannot be dehydrated by heating as it hydrolyses to a basic chloride in a similar manner to magnesium chloride,

$$ZnCl_2 + H_2O \rightarrow Zn(OH)Cl + HCl.$$

In contrast to the coloured salts of the typical transition metals the chlorides of zinc, cadmium and mercury are all white. Some of their more important physical properties are summarised below. Zinc and cadmium chlorides have a fundamentally different structure from mercury(II) chloride as they both crystallise in essentially ionic aggregates, whereas mercury(II) chloride is covalent and crystallises as a molecular lattice of loosely bound neutral molecules. As described on p. 143 these molecules are linear owing to the electrostatic repulsion between the two bonding pairs of electrons.

Physical properties of the Zinc Group chlorides

Chloride	m.p. (°C)	b.p. (°C)	Solubility in water (g/100 g at 25 °C)	Solubility in ethanol (g/100 g at 25 °C)
$ZnCl_2$	318	730	420	10
$CdCl_2$	568	964	120	1.5
$HgCl_2$	280	303	7	50.5

Zinc chloride is extremely deliquescent and is one of the most soluble substances known. Anhydrous zinc chloride is soluble in ethanol, as well as in other organic solvents. It also has a relatively low melting point and boiling point. These properties illustrate the partially covalent character of this compound. The higher values of the melting point and boiling point and the smaller solubility in organic solvents of cadmium chloride agree well with the general tendency of cadmium salts to be more ionic than the corresponding zinc compounds. The small solubility of mercury(II) chloride in water and its ready solubility in organic solvents follow from its covalent nature as do the low melting point and boiling point.

Mercury(II) chloride is not hydrolysed by water, and its aqueous solution has a very low conductivity as it is only ionised to a very small extent (approximately 1 %). Zinc chloride dissociates in water into hydrated zinc ions and chloride ions. As the hydrated cation is slightly hydrolysed the solution is acidic, i.e.

$$[Zn(H_2O)_6]^{2+} + H_2O \rightleftharpoons [Zn(H_2O)_5OH]^+ + H_3O^+.$$

Surprisingly cadmium chloride solution is a weak electrolyte. The effect is complex, but is probably the result of imperfect dissociation, i.e. formation of $CdCl^+$ as well as Cd^{2+} and Cl^-, and of complex ion formation, i.e.

$$[CdCl_3]^-, \quad [CdCl_4]^{2-}.$$

Zinc chloride and mercury(II) chloride both combine directly with ammonia gas to form ammines, e.g. $[Zn(NH_3)_4]Cl_2$ and $[Hg(NH_3)_2]Cl_2$, cf. $[Ca(NH_3)_8]Cl_2$ (p. 333). The mercury(II) ammine $[Hg(NH_3)_2]Cl_2$ is obtained as a white precipitate by adding mercury(II) chloride solution to a boiling solution of ammonia and ammonium chloride. The precipitate melts without decomposition. If ammonia solution is added to mercury(II) chloride solution the white precipitate obtained does not melt on heating, but decomposes into mercury(II) chloride, ammonia, and nitrogen,

$$2NH_3 + HgCl_2 \rightarrow HgNH_2Cl\downarrow + NH_4^+ + Cl^-.$$

Mercury(II) chloride is a mild oxidising agent, and its reduction by tin(II) chloride solution immediately produces a white precipitate of mercury(I) chloride. This is then gradually reduced to mercury and the precipitate slowly turns black,

$$2HgCl_2 + Sn^{2+} \rightarrow Sn^{4+} + 2Cl^- + Hg_2Cl_2\downarrow,$$
$$Hg_2Cl_2 + Sn^{2+} \rightarrow Sn^{4+} + 2Cl^- + 2Hg\downarrow.$$

Zinc chloride dissolves zinc oxide, and the liquid obtained sets to a hard insoluble white solid which is sometimes used as a cement in dentistry. The ability of zinc chlorides to dissolve oxides makes it a useful flux for soldering as it dissolves away any oxide formed on the surface of the hot metal which would stop the solder *biting*. The double salt with ammonium chloride $2NH_4Cl.ZnCl_2$ is used as *soldering salt*.

Mercury(II) ioidide, HgI₂, is precipitated from mercury(II) chloride solution by a little alkali-metal iodide solution. Initially the precipitate is yellow, but very rapidly turns red. Like the oxide and sulphide it is dimorphous,

$$Hg^{2+} + 2I^- \rightarrow HgI_2\downarrow.$$

The yellow form is stable above 126 °C. When the iodide is sublimed it is the yellow form which condenses. The gradual change to the red form can be accelerated by mechanical pressure, e.g. scratching with a glass rod. The initial precipitate of mercury(II) iodide will dissolve if an excess of the alkali-metal iodide solution is added, owing to complex ion formation, i.e.

$$2I^- + HgI_2 \rightarrow [HgI_4]^{2-}.$$

Salts of this complex ion are known, e.g. $K_2[HgI_4].2H_2O$. A solution of this compound made alkaline with potassium hydroxide solution is *Nessler's Reagent*, and is used as a sensitive test for ammonia with which it gives an orange coloration. The insoluble copper(I) and silver compounds $Cu_2[HgI_4]$ and $Ag_2[HgI_4]$ are used in heat-sensitive paints which give warning of overheating, e.g. $Cu_2[HgI_4]$ is dimorphous, and the transition temperature is 70 °C when it changes colour from red to black.

Sulphides, MS

Zinc, cadmium and mercury(II) sulphides are all naturally occurring, and they constitute the principal ores of zinc and of mercury. In the laboratory they are usually prepared by precipitation methods, e.g. with hydrogen sulphide,

$$Hg^{2+} + S^{2-} \rightarrow HgS\downarrow.$$

Colour deepens with increasing atomic weight; zinc sulphide is white, cadmium sulphide is yellow, and precipitated mercury(II) sulphide is black. These solids have a diamond-type lattice in which the cation has a co-ordination number of 4 and is tetrahedrally surrounded by sulphide ions. Like the oxide, mercury(II) sulphide exists in two differently coloured modifications, and a red form, which occurs naturally as cinnabar, may be prepared by subliming the black form. Mercury has a co-ordination number of 6 in the red form which has a distorted sodium chloride lattice.

The insolubility of these solids in water and in acids increases as the Group is descended and mercury(II) sulphide is very insoluble in water and non-oxidising acids, but it dissolves in oxidising acid mixtures, e.g. *aqua regia*, concentrated hydrochloric acid + bromine water. Zinc sulphide readily dissolves in very dilute acids and hydrogen sulphide is evolved. Cadmium sulphide is less soluble in acids, but if the acid strength exceeds 2 molar it will not precipitate from solution. Most schemes of qualitative analysis take advantage of the varying solubility in acids of these and other sulphides to separate and identify the parent element, e.g. hydrogen sulphide in slightly acidic solution precipitates HgS, PbS, Bi_2S_3, CuS, CdS, SnS, SnS_2 and Sb_2S_3 (i.e. Group II), but not ZnS, MnS, NiS or CoS (i.e. Group IV in the qualitative analysis table) which are precipitated in alkaline solution.

Zinc sulphide and cadmium sulphide are used in making fluorescent paints for coating cathode-ray tube screens, etc.

All three sulphides are used as pigments. Cadmium yellow, CdS, and vermilion, HgS, are expensive, but greatly valued by artists for their brilliance and permanence of colour. *Lithopone* is a mixture of zinc sulphide and barium sulphate prepared by double decomposition between zinc sulphate and barium sulphide which finds use in paints and as a filler in linoleums,

$$Zn^{2+} + SO_4^{2-} + Ba^{2+} + S^{2-} \rightarrow ZnS\downarrow + BaSO_4\downarrow.$$

Oxo-salts

The carbonates, sulphates and nitrates of zinc and cadmium may be prepared by any of the general methods given in ch. 15. Alkali metal hydrogen carbonate solutions are used to precipitate the simple carbonates as solutions of alkali metal carbonates precipitate basic carbonates. Basic mercury(II) carbonate is precipitated from mercury(II) salt solutions irrespective of the precipitating agent. Mercury(II) sulphate and nitrate may be crystallised from solutions obtained by dissolving the metal in the appropriate hot concentrated acid.

These salts are all white solids. The sulphates and nitrates are ionic and readily dissolve in water to give conducting solutions. Mercury(II) sulphate and nitrate are considerably hydrolysed in dilute aqueous solution (i.e. salts of a weak base) and basic salts precipitate, e.g. $HgSO_4.2HgO$ and $Hg(NO_3)_2.2HgO$.

The sulphates and nitrates all crystallise from solution as hydrates. Those hydrates which separate out at room temperature are summarised in the table below. Note the trend.

Number of molecules of water per formula of the common hydrate

Element	Sulphate	Nitrate
Zn	7	6
Cd	$\frac{8}{3}$	4
Hg	1	1

The nitrates are deliquescent. Zinc sulphate, $ZnSO_4.7H_2O$, is iso-morphous with magnesium sulphate and forms a similar series of double salts of the type $M_2^ISO_4.M^{II}SO_4.6H_2O$ where $M^I = Na^+, K^+, NH_4^+$, etc., and $M^{II} = Zn^{2+}, Mg^{2+}, Cd^{2+}$ or Hg^{2+}.

The salts are all decomposed by heat and those of mercury are exceptional and behave like the corresponding compounds of silver and gold as they decompose to the metal and not the oxide, e.g.

$$Hg(NO_3)_2 \rightarrow Hg + 2NO_2 + O_2,$$

$$CdCO_3 \rightarrow CdO + CO_2,$$

$$ZnSO_4.7H_2O \xrightarrow{100°} ZnSO_4.H_2O \xrightarrow{240°} ZnSO_4 \xrightarrow[\text{ignition}]{\text{strong}} ZnO + SO_3.$$

Mercury(I) compounds

The diatomic ion Hg_2^{2+} is a feature peculiar to mercury and is another instance of the exceptional nature of this interesting element. X-ray investigation of several mercury(I) salts has confirmed the existence of Hg_2^{2+} ions in the solid state. Equilibrium constant measurements have proved that solutions of mercury(I) salts contain Hg_2^{2+} ions and not Hg^+ ions. Also, as this latter ion has an unpaired electron it would be para-magnetic whereas mercury(I) compounds are diamagnetic both as solids and in solution.

Mercury(I) salts are ionic and highly ionised in solution which contrasts with the very low dissociation of many mercury(II) compounds. A certain amount of hydrolysis occurs and the solutions react acid. In general, however, mercury(I) compounds are less soluble than the corresponding mercury(II) compound. Mercury(I) sulphate and chloride are both sparingly soluble, but the nitrate readily dissolves in water. A similar solubility relationship exists between copper(II) and copper(I) compounds. There is also a similarity between the solubility of mercury(I) salts and silver salts (AgCl and Hg_2Cl_2 precipitate in Group I of the qualitative analysis tables).

The disproportionation represented by the equilibrium,

$$Hg_2^{2+} \rightleftharpoons Hg + Hg^{2+},$$

lies well to the left provided that the mercury(II) ion is not removed from the equilibrium, e.g. by precipitation or by complexing. Thus no hydroxide, oxide or sulphide of Hg_2^{2+} can be precipitated from aqueous solution by the addition of the appropriate anion, nor have these compounds been prepared by other means. The reactions that occur are,

$$Hg_2^{2+} + 2OH^- \rightarrow Hg + HgO + H_2O,$$

$$Hg_2^{2+} + S^{2-} \rightarrow Hg + HgS.$$

On the other hand, mercury readily reduces the mercury(II) ion Hg^{2+} to the mercury(I) ion Hg_2^{2+}.

The mercury(I) ion differs from mercury(II) as it forms very few complexes, and attempts to prepare complexes with ammonia or the halogens lead to the formation of the mercury(II) complex with simultaneous separation of free mercury.

Mercury(I) chloride, Hg_2Cl_2. This salt may be sublimed as a white crystalline mass by heating either a mixture of mercury(II) chloride and mercury or a mixture of mercury(II) sulphate, mercury, and sodium chloride,
$$HgCl_2 + Hg \rightarrow Hg_2Cl_2,$$

$$HgSO_4 + Hg + 2NaCl \rightarrow Hg_2Cl_2 + Na_2SO_4.$$

It may also be precipitated from mercury(I) nitrate solution, e.g. by the addition of dilute hydrochloric acid,

$$Hg_2^{2+} + 2Cl^- \rightarrow Hg_2Cl_2.$$

Besides being sparingly soluble in water it also differs from the covalent mercury(II) chloride as it is insoluble in organic solvents. Mercury(I) chloride sublimes without melting at 383 °C.

Mercury(I) chloride blackens when treated with aqueous ammonia, and this test is used as means of identification in qualitative analysis. The blackening is caused by the separation of free mercury from the disproportionation of the Hg_2^{2+} ion. The dark residue also contains the insoluble $HgNH_2Cl$,

$$Hg_2Cl_2 + 2NH_3 \rightarrow Hg + HgNH_2Cl + NH_4^+ + Cl^-.$$

Exercises

1. Compare and contrast the oxides and chlorides of copper and mercury.
2. What are the principal similarities between zinc and magnesium?
3. To what extent do the atomic structure and the physical and chemical properties of mercury correspond to its position in the Periodic Table?
4. Give an account of the isolation of pure zinc on the industrial scale.
   How may the following be obtained from zinc: (a) zinc oxide, (b) anhydrous zinc chloride, (c) zinc sulphide. What are the uses of these compounds?
5. Describe, with essential experimental details, the preparation from zinc of (a) zinc chloride, (b) zinc sulphide, (c) zinc carbonate, (d) zinc hydroxide. Give *two* industrial uses of zinc. (C)
6. Describe the characteristic features of the chemistry of mercury. How far do the chemical properties of mercury justify its inclusion in the same group of the Periodic Table as zinc? (C)
7. Describe simple experiments you would make to place the metals zinc, magnesium, calcium and copper in their correct order in the electrochemical series.
   Often the more electropositive elements have the more basic oxides. Discuss this statement in connection with the above four metals. (C)
8. How does zinc occur in nature? Give an account of the electrolytic extraction of zinc.
   Outline important uses of zinc that depend on (a) its resistance to oxidation and (b) its solubility in acids or in ammonium chloride. (L)
9. Calcium and zinc both have two electrons in the outermost (4s) orbitals of their atoms. Some data for these elements are listed below. Comment on the values given and indicate the relationship between them and the chemical properties of the two elements.

Element (M)	Calcium	Zinc
Outer electronic structure	$3d^0 4s^2$	$3d^{10} 4s^2$
1st ionization energy (kcal mole^{-1})	140	216
2nd ionization energy (kcal mole^{-1})	270	420
3rd ionization energy (kcal mole^{-1})	1180	930
Ionic radius of M^{2+} (Å)	0·94	0·69
Standard electrode potential $M^{2+}_{(aq)}M$ (V)	−2·87	−0·76
Heat of formation of MO (kcal mole^{-1})	190	110

(O & CS)

The electronic configurations of the ground states of the elements

The configurations for some of the lanthanide and actinide elements are uncertain.

Period, element and atomic number			K	L		M			N				O				P			Q
			1s	2s	2p	3s	3p	3d	4s	4p	4d	4f	5s	5p	5d	5f	6s	6p	6d	7s
1	H	1	1																	
	He	2	2																	
2	Li	3	2	1																
	Be	4	2	2																
	B	5	2	2	1															
	C	6	2	2	2															
	N	7	2	2	3															
	O	8	2	2	4															
	F	9	2	2	5															
	Ne	10	2	2	6															
3	Na	11	2	2	6	1														
	Mg	12	2	2	6	2														
	Al	13	2	2	6	2	1													
	Si	14	2	2	6	2	2													
	P	15	2	2	6	2	3													
	S	16	2	2	6	2	4													
	Cl	17	2	2	6	2	5													
	Ar	18	2	2	6	2	6													
4	K	19	2	2	6	2	6		1											
	Ca	20	2	2	6	2	6		2											
	Sc	21*	2	2	6	2	6	1	2											
	Ti	22*	2	2	6	2	6	2	2											
	V	23*	2	2	6	2	6	3	2											
	Cr	24*	2	2	6	2	6	5	1											
	Mn	25*	2	2	6	2	6	5	2											
	Fe	26*	2	2	6	2	6	6	2											
	Co	27*	2	2	6	2	6	7	2											
	Ni	28*	2	2	6	2	6	8	2											
	Cu	29*	2	2	6	2	6	10	1											
	Zn	30*	2	2	6	2	6	10	2											
	Ga	31	2	2	6	2	6	10	2	1										
	Ge	32	2	2	6	2	6	10	2	2										
	As	33	2	2	6	2	6	10	2	3										
	Se	34	2	2	6	2	6	10	2	4										
	Br	35	2	2	6	2	6	10	2	5										
	Kr	36	2	2	6	2	6	10	2	6										
5	Rb	37	2	2	6	2	6	10	2	6			1							
	Sr	38	2	2	6	2	6	10	2	6			2							
	Y	39*	2	2	6	2	6	10	2	6	1		2							
	Zr	40*	2	2	6	2	6	10	2	6	2		2							
	Nb	41*	2	2	6	2	6	10	2	6	4		1							
	Mo	42*	2	2	6	2	6	10	2	6	5		1							
	Tc	43*	2	2	6	2	6	10	2	6	6		1							
	Ru	44*	2	2	6	2	6	10	2	6	7		1							
	Rh	45*	2	2	6	2	6	10	2	6	8		1							
	Pd	46*	2	2	6	2	6	10	2	6	10									
	Ag	47*	2	2	6	2	6	10	2	6	10		1							
	Cd	48*	2	2	6	2	6	10	2	6	10		2							

* Transition elements.

Period, element and atomic number	K	L		M			N				O				P			Q
	1s	2s	2p	3s	3p	3d	4s	4p	4d	4f	5s	5p	5d	5f	6s	6p	6d	7s
5 In 49	2	2	6	2	6	10	2	6	10		2	1						
Sn 50	2	2	6	2	6	10	2	6	10		2	2						
Sb 51	2	2	6	2	6	10	2	6	10		2	3						
Te 52	2	2	6	2	6	10	2	6	10		2	4						
I 53	2	2	6	2	6	10	2	6	10		2	5						
Xe 54	2	2	6	2	6	10	2	6	10		2	6						
6 Cs 55	2	2	6	2	6	10	2	6	10		2	6			1			
Ba 56	2	2	6	2	6	10	2	6	10		2	6			2			
La 57*	2	2	6	2	6	10	2	6	10		2	6	1		2			
Ce 58†	2	2	6	2	6	10	2	6	10	2	2	6			2			
Pr 59†	2	2	6	2	6	10	2	6	10	3	2	6			2			
Nd 60†	2	2	6	2	6	10	2	6	10	4	2	6			2			
Pm 61†	2	2	6	2	6	10	2	6	10	5	2	6			2			
Sm 62†	2	2	6	2	6	10	2	6	10	6	2	6			2			
Eu 63†	2	2	6	2	6	10	2	6	10	7	2	6			2			
Gd 64†	2	2	6	2	6	10	2	6	10	7	2	6	1		2			
Tb 65†	2	2	6	2	6	10	2	6	10	9	2	6			2			
Dy 66†	2	2	6	2	6	10	2	6	10	10	2	6			2			
Ho 67†	2	2	6	2	6	10	2	6	10	11	2	6			2			
Er 68†	2	2	6	2	6	10	2	6	10	12	2	6			2			
Tm 69†	2	2	6	2	6	10	2	6	10	13	2	6			2			
Yb 70†	2	2	6	2	6	10	2	6	10	14	2	6			2			
Lu 71†	2	2	6	2	6	10	2	6	10	14	2	6	1		2			
Hf 72*	2	2	6	2	6	10	2	6	10	14	2	6	2		2			
Ta 73*	2	2	6	2	6	10	2	6	10	14	2	6	3		2			
W 74*	2	2	6	2	6	10	2	6	10	14	2	6	4		2			
Re 75*	2	2	6	2	6	10	2	6	10	14	2	6	5		2			
Os 76*	2	2	6	2	6	10	2	6	10	14	2	6	6		2			
Ir 77*	2	2	6	2	6	10	2	6	10	14	2	6	9					
Pt 78*	2	2	6	2	6	10	2	6	10	14	2	6	9		1			
Au 79*	2	2	6	2	6	10	2	6	10	14	2	6	10		1			
Hg 80*	2	2	6	2	6	10	2	6	10	14	2	6	10		2			
Tl 81	2	2	6	2	6	10	2	6	10	14	2	6	10		2	1		
Pb 82	2	2	6	2	6	10	2	6	10	14	2	6	10		2	2		
Bi 83	2	2	6	2	6	10	2	6	10	14	2	6	10		2	3		
Po 84	2	2	6	2	6	10	2	6	10	14	2	6	10		2	4		
At 85	2	2	6	2	6	10	2	6	10	14	2	6	10		2	5		
Rn 86	2	2	6	2	6	10	2	6	10	14	2	6	10		2	6		
7 Fr 87	2	2	6	2	6	10	2	6	10	14	2	6	10		2	6		1
Ra 88	2	2	6	2	6	10	2	6	10	14	2	6	10		2	6		2
Ac 89*	2	2	6	2	6	10	2	6	10	14	2	6	10		2	6	1	2
Th 90†	2	2	6	2	6	10	2	6	10	14	2	6	10	1	2	6	1	2
Pa 91†	2	2	6	2	6	10	2	6	10	14	2	6	10	2	2	6	1	2
U 92†	2	2	6	2	6	10	2	6	10	14	2	6	10	3	2	6	1	2
Np 93†	2	2	6	2	6	10	2	6	10	14	2	6	10	4	2	6	1	2
Pu 94†	2	2	6	2	6	10	2	6	10	14	2	6	10	5	2	6	1	2
Am 95†	2	2	6	2	6	10	2	6	10	14	2	6	10	7	2	6		2
Cm 96†	2	2	6	2	6	10	2	6	10	14	2	6	10	7	2	6	1	2
Bk 97†	2	2	6	2	6	10	2	6	10	14	2	6	10	8	2	6	1	2
Cf 98†	2	2	6	2	6	10	2	6	10	14	2	6	10	10	2	6		2
Es 99†	2	2	6	2	6	10	2	6	10	16	2	6	10	11	2	6		2
Fm 100†	2	2	6	2	6	10	2	6	10	14	2	6	10	12	2	6		2
Mv 101†	2	2	6	2	6	10	2	6	10	14	2	6	10	13	2	6		2
No 102†	2	2	6	2	6	10	2	6	10	14	2	6	10	14	2	6		2

* Transition elements.
† Lanthanide and actinide elements.

Atomic radii and electronegativities in Transition Groups

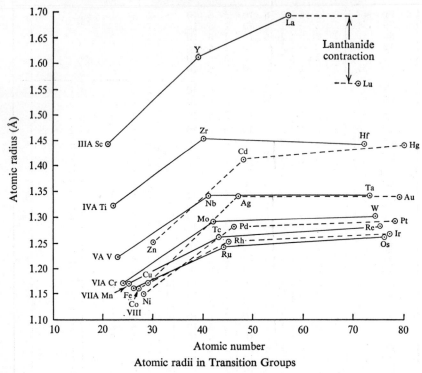

Atomic radii in Transition Groups

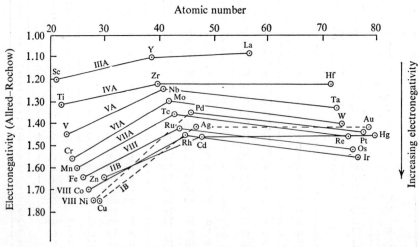

Electronegativities in Transition Groups

BIBLIOGRAPHY

Addison, W. E. *Structural Principles in Inorganic Compounds*. Longmans, 1961.

Aynsley, E. E. and Dodd, R. E. *General and Inorganic Chemistry*. Hutchinson Educational, 1963.

Bell, C. F. and Lott, K. A. K. *Modern Approach to Inorganic Chemistry*. Butterworths, 1963.

British Iron and Steel Federation. *Technical Developments in the Steel Industry*, 1963.

Brown, G. I. *A Simple Guide to Modern Valency Theory*. Longmans, 1953.

Chilton, J. P. *Principles of Metallic Corrosion*. Royal Institute of Chemistry, Monographs for Teachers no. 4, 1961.

Cotton, F. A. and Wilkinson, G. *Advanced Inorganic Chemistry*. Interscience, 1963.

Evans, R. C. *An Introduction to Crystal Chemistry*. Cambridge University Press, 1964.

Fowles, G. W. A. *A Structural Basis for Teaching Inorganic Chemistry*. The School Science Review 1958, xxxix, 234.

Gillespie, R. J. and Nyholm, R. S. *Inorganic Stereochemistry*. Quarterly Reviews of the Chemical Society, 1957, xi, 339.

Glasstone, S. *Textbook of Physical Chemistry*. Macmillan, 1951.

Heslop, R. B. and Robinson, P. L. *Inorganic Chemistry*. Elsevier, 1960.

Ives, D. J. G. *Principles of the Extraction of Metals*. Royal Institute of Chemistry, Monographs for Teachers no. 3, 1960.

Jones, H. R. *The Classification of Oxides*. The School Science Review, 1962, xliv, 95.

McGlashan, M. L. *Physico-chemical Quantities and Units*. Royal Institute of Chemistry, Monographs for Teachers no. 15, 1968.

Moeller, T. *Inorganic Chemistry*. John Wiley, 1952.

Palmer, W. G. *Experimental Inorganic Chemistry*. Cambridge University Press, 1954.

Parkes, G. D. *Mellor's Modern Inorganic Chemistry*. Longmans, 1961.

Pauling, L. *General Chemistry*. Freeman, 1959.

Phillips, F. C. *An Introduction to Crystallography*. Longmans, 1960.

Remy, H. *Treatise on Inorganic Chemistry*. Elsevier, 1956.

Samuel, D. M. *Industrial Chemistry—Inorganic*, Royal Institute of Chemistry, Monographs for Teachers no. 10, 1966.

Sanderson, R. T. *Chemical Periodicity*. Reinhold, 1960.

Sharpe, A. G. *Principles of Oxidation and Reduction*. Royal Institute of Chemistry, Monographs for Teachers no. 2, 1960.

Sidgwick, N. V. *The Chemical Elements and their Compounds*. Oxford University Press, 1950.

Sisler, H. H. *Electronic Structure, Properties, and the Periodic Law*. Reinhold, 1963.

Stark, J. G. and Wallace, H. G. *Chemistry Data Book*. John Murray, 1969.

Wells, A. F. *Structural Inorganic Chemistry*. Oxford University Press, 1962.

Wood, C. W. and Holliday, A. K. *Inorganic Chemistry*. Butterworths, 1964.

INDEX